W9-CTS-084

Patagonia Connection S.A.

AT SEA LEVEL, THE BEST LEVEL!

Join us on our adventure... to the South of Silence. We have the perfect combination: Daylight sailing through the patagonian channels aboard the catamaran PATAGONIA EXPRESS, coupled with lodging on shore at TERMAS DE PUYUHUAPI Hotsprings Hotel and SPA.

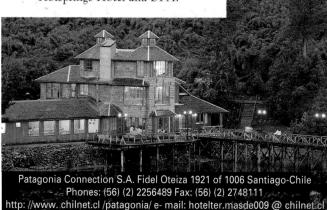

You won't find a country with more contrasts than Chile.

You won't find an airline with more flights to Latin America than the Iberia Group.

From the most elegant Spanish colonial architecture to the most modern city skyscrapers, from sun-drenched beaches, deserts and salt flats to awesome glaciers and ski resorts, few countries have more to offer the explorer than Chile.

And of course, with our Circular Fares which give you the freedom to travel throughout Latin America as you please, no one proves a better travelling companion than the Iberia Group.

To book, call Iberia Group Reservations on **0171-830 0011** or contact your specialist travel agent.

Leading the way to Latin America.

Chile Handbook

South American Handbook, the longest running
guidebook in the English language, has provided
generations of travellers with comprehensive coverage
of the entire continent. This Handbook is in
Footprint's series of new guides to the individual
countries of Latin America. The first to be published
are Handbooks to Peru, Chile and Ecuador &
Galápagos. These will be followed by guides to Brazil,
Colombia, Bolivia, Argentina, Venezuela and Cuba.

Chile
Handbook

Charlie Nurse

Latin America series editor: Ben Box

Footprint Handbooks

Those who travel heedlessly from place to place,
observing only their distance from each other, and
attending only to their accommodation at the inn at
night, set out fools, and will certainly return so.

Lord Chesterfield, Letter to his Son, 30 October 1747

Footprint Handbooks

6 Riverside Court, Lower Bristol Road
Bath BA2 3DZ England
T 01225 469141 F 01225 469461
E mail handbooks@footprint.cix.co.uk
www.fooprint-handbooks.co.uk

ISBN 0 900751 85 1 ISSN 1363-741x
CIP DATA: A catalogue record for this book is
available from the British Library

In North America, published by

PASSPORT BOOKS

a division of *NTC/Contemporary Publishing Company*
Lincolnwood, Illinois USA

4255 West Touhy Avenue, Lincolnwood
(Chicago), Illinois 60646-1975, USA
T 847 679 5500 F 847 679 24941
E mail NTCPUB2@AOL.COM

ISBN 0-8442-4917-3
Library of Congress Catalog Card
Number: 96-72522
Passport Books and colophon are registered
trademarks of NTC Publishing group

©Footprint Handbooks Limited
1st Edition
March 1997

**Every effort has been made to ensure that
the facts in this Handbook are accurate.
However travellers should still obtain
advice from consulates, airlines etc about
current travel and visa requirements and
conditions before travelling. The authors
and publishers cannot accept responsibility
for any loss, injury or inconvenience,
however caused.**

Cover design by Newell and Sorrell; cover
photography by Edward Parker; Sue
Mann/South American Pictures; and Life
File/Andrew Ward

Production: Design by Mytton Williams;
Typesetting by Jo Morgan, Ann Griffiths and
Melanie Mason-Fayon; Maps by Sebastian
Ballard, Aldous George and Kevin Feeney;
Charts by Angus Dawson and Ann Griffiths;
Original line drawings by Andrew Newton;
Proofread by Rod Gray and David Cotterell.

Printed and bound in Great Britain by
Clays Ltd., Bungay, Suffolk

Contents

The Editors

Ben Box

A doctorate in medieval Spanish and Portugese studies provided very few job prospects for Ben Box, but a fascination for all things Latin. While studying for his degree, Ben travelled extensively in Spain and Portugal. He turned his attention to contemporary Iberian and Latin American affairs in 1980, beginning a career as a freelance writer at that time. He contributed regularly to national newspapers and learned tomes, and after increasing involvement with the *South American Handbook*, became its editor in 1989. Although he has travelled from the US/Mexico border to southern Chile (not all in one go) and in the Caribbean, Ben recognizes that there are always more places to explore. He also edits the *Mexico and Central American Handbook* and jointly edits the *Caribbean Islands Handbook* with Sarah Cameron. To seek diversion from a household immersed in Latin America, he plays village cricket in summer and cycles the lanes of Suffolk.

Charlie Nurse

Charlie Nurse is a Latin American aficionado through and through. Following his degree in history and politics he did 6 months research in Ecuador and travelled throughout Central America. After this he taught for a year in Spain during the fascinating period at the end of the Franco era. A year working and travelling in Nicaragua and Mexico was the next adventure. Six years ago Charlie turned his attention to Chile and has been responsible for the Chile section of the *South American Handbook*. He has travelled the length and 'breadth' of Chile over the past few years and was the obvious choice to develop and write the new *Chile Handbook*.

Specialist contributors

Peter Pollard for Geology and Climate sections; Dr Nigel Dunstone (University of Durham) for Flora and Fauna; Huw Clough for Archaeology and Prehistory; Dr Valerie Fraser (University of Essex) for Fine Art and Sculpture; Ben Box for Literature; Nigel Gallop for Music and Dance; Jaime Baez for Food; Simon Harvey and Mark Duffy for Adventure Tourism; Josselyn van der Pol and Leandro Yáñez Sarmiento for Skiing; Robert and Caroline Ely for Yachting and Sailing; Sarah Cameron for the Economics section; and David Snashall for Health.

Introduction and hints

IN NOVEMBER 1996 the Chilean city of Puerto Varas played host to the World Congress on Adventure Travel and Ecotourism, highlighting the way in which this small Andean country is rapidly becoming an important travel destination for visitors from all over the world. Most countries, of course, claim to have something for visitors of all ages throughout the year: in the case of Chile this is closer to the truth than normal. Chile's unique shape, strung along the edge of the Pacific for over 4,000 km and wedged between the Ocean and the Andes, give it a range of climates and geographical features exceeded by few other countries and mean that there are alternatives available for travellers all year round. From the deserts of the far north where it never rains to the glaciers of the Torres del Paine National Park, Chile has everything in between: lakes, forests, volcanoes, rushing rivers, Mediterranean style countryside with vineyards and orchards.

Though Chile's geographical and climatic variety is regularly noted by journalists and other observers, the character of the Chilean people is seldom the subject of comment. Often seen as slightly more reserved than most European stereotypes of the inhabitants of South America, Chileans are as hospitable, welcoming and helpful as any people on earth, and more so than most. For the traveller who makes the effort, the people are perhaps Chile's unsung tourist attraction.

Isolated behind the natural barriers of the Andes and the

Atacama desert, Chile was for centuries a remote destination for the traveller. As the European or North American shopper will appreciate especially in winter, Chile is no longer remote nor her people inward-looking. Just as Chilean wines and fruit make their claim for a place on our tables, Chileans are responding imaginatively and with their customary courtesy to the increases in the number of visitors from countries far afield. This first edition of the *Chile Handbook* attempts to unveil the variety of types of travel available in Chile. In common with the *South American Handbook* on which it is modelled, new editions will appear regularly; though whereas the *South American Handbook* will continue to be updated annually, the next edition of this volume will appear in 2 years time. As always we welcome comments and suggestions from travellers and other correspondents to make the 1999 edition a more complete volume.

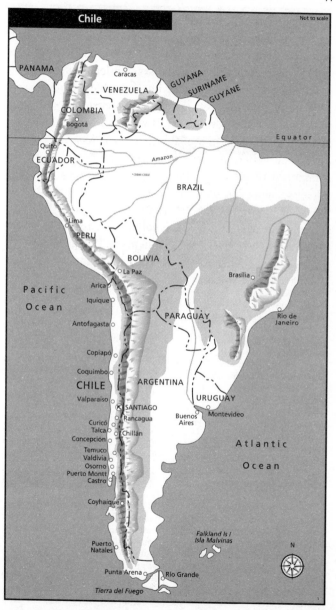

Chile

Not to scale

PANAMA

Caracas

VENEZUELA

GUYANA

SURINAME

GUYANE

COLOMBIA

Bogotá

Equator

Quito

ECUADOR

Amazon

CHDM CHILE

BRAZIL

Lima

PERU

BOLIVIA

La Paz

Brasília

Pacific

Ocean

Arica

Iquique

Antofagasta

PARAGUAY

Río de
Janeiro

Copiapó

Coquimbo

CHILE

ARGENTINA

Valparaiso

SANTIAGO

URUGUAY

Rancagua

Buenos
Aires

Montevideo

Curicó

Talca

Chillán

Concepción

Atlantic

Temuco

Valdivia

Osorno

Ocean

Puerto Montt

Castro

Coyhaique

Falkland Is /
Isla Malvinas

N

Puerto
Natales

Punta Arena

Río Grande

Tierra del Fuego

Where to go

In common with the practice established by the *South American Handbook* this volume makes no attempt to be prescriptive. Tastes in travel vary as in everything else. This is particularly important in light of the great variety of attractions available in Chile. There are, however, a number of places which stand out as the most popular destinations for travellers.

Any list of such destinations would have to include Chilean Patagonia, notably the Torres del Paine National Park, one of the great parks of the world. Almost as popular, and at the other end of the country, is the small oasis town of San Pedro del Atacama, a centre for excursions to geysers, saltflats and mountains. Lying between the two, and easily accessible, is the island of Chiloé; though often likened to Ireland, it is more evocative of a bygone age, before the advent of modern commercial agriculture. The Lake District, just N of Chiloé, is a major attraction for both Chileans and foreign travellers: lakes, volcanoes, forests, rivers and waterfalls offer some of the most picturesque scenery in the country.

Chile is, however, much richer for the tourist than this list of highlights suggests. Less visited, but still popular options exist: the northern city of La Serena is one of the most attractive in the country; the main port, Valparaíso, has a special feel and is close to beaches which, if popular at weekends in summer, are deserted at other times; the

Lauca National Park, situated in the far N, offers volcanoes, saltflats and a richly varied birdlife all at high altitude; Santiago, the capital, though hardly among the most beautiful cities in the world, has one of the most varied cultural scenes in South America and is close to ski resorts, beaches and fine walking country; the northern cities of Arica and Iquique are centres for excursions into the Atacama desert.

Alternative attractions abound: Lake Lanalhue and the Sierra de Nahuelbuta, S of Concepción, receive far fewer visitors than the lakes further S and offer varied scenery, good facilities and a range of activities; the Carretera Austral, best travelled by mountain-bike, is sparsely inhabited but rapidly opening up to tourism and the lakes round Coyhaique are a good alternative to those of the Lake District; some of the coastal resorts W of the Central Valley have miles of sand and few visitors. A final suggestion is Easter Island with its unique archaeology but easily reached from Santiago by plane.

The two main factors which determine possible itineraries in Chile are 1) the time at your disposal; 2) how and where you enter the country. It is obvious to say that the more time you have, the more you can see and those with the luxury of unlimited time can travel the length of the country at leisure. Distances between the cities and tourist centres are never forbidding and lateral excursions, to coast or mountains, are easily made. Those on a shorter timescale have to make decisions, though, because this long ribbon of a country does not lend itself to circular routes. Should you go N, or S? To do both requires some backtracking, but no matter because a little imagination can guarantee that retracing your steps can be done without repetition.

If you enter Chile by air, you arrive in Santiago. Where you go from there depends on your interest and the time of year. In high summer the only limitations may be that the popular resorts (eg beaches like Viña del Mar and surroundings, lakeside resorts like Pucón) may be full and travel may be booked in. In mid-winter, the further S you go, the colder it gets and the greater the chance that transport will either be disrupted, or not running at all.

Travellers who enter from neighbouring Argentina and Bolivia often do so by one of the following five routes, all of which can be recommended: 1) by road to Santiago from Mendoza; 2) by bus and boat to Puerto Montt from Bariloche; 3) the Patagonian road route from El Calafate to Puerto Natales, or the road and ferry crossings from Tierra del Fuego to Punta Arenas; and 5) the two train journeys from Bolivia to Arica and Calama. A sixth option is the land route from Tacna, Peru, to Arica. Entering in the S means that the only way is 'up', likewise, entering in the N means that you have to head S. In either direction, how far you go is a matter of choice and time.

The following suggestions are merely intended to give a rough idea of how long you could spend in a particular region. They do not allow for the detailed exploration to which the first encounter may lead.

1. **Santiago**: from a few days to a few weeks. Much depends on whether you are using the capital as a base for visiting nearby areas, which include: Valparaíso,

Viña del Mar and the coast; the vineyards of the Central Valley; the Andean foothills; the ski resorts.

2. **Valparaíso and Viña del Mar**: again, from a couple of days to however long you wish to spend on the beach. Valparaíso can be seen in 1-2 days, more if you include Viña as well.

3. **La Serena and the Elqui Valley**: no more than a week, for the seaside, the pisco-producing valley and Gabriela Mistral's homeland. Careful timing will be required if you wish to visit the astronomical observatories.

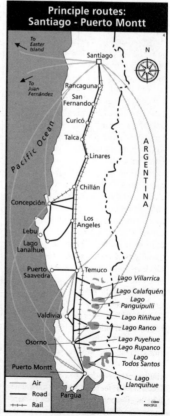

Principle routes: North of Santiago

Not to scale

PERU
To Tacna
Visviri
To La Paz
Putre
Arica
BOLIVIA
Mamiña
Iquique
Pica
To Oruro
Ollagüe
Tocopilla
Calama
San Pedro de Atacama
Antofagasta
To Salta
Pacific Ocean
Taltal
El Salvador
To Paso de San Francisco
Chañaral
Caldera
Copiapó
Huasco
Vallenar
ARGENTINA
Vicuña
La Serena
Pisco Elqui
Paso del Agua Negra
Ovalle
Illapel
La Ligua
To Mendoza
Los Andes
Viña del Mar
Valparaíso
SANTIAGO

--- Air
—— Road
+++ Rail

4. **Between La Serena and Antofagasta**: look out for the flowering of the desert if the area is lucky enough to have spring rain.

5. **San Pedro de Atacama**: growing in importance as a tourist centre. To see the lunar landscapes, the geysers, the life at high altitudes, a week should suffice, with additional time to visit the copper mine at Chuquicamata and the city of Antofagasta.

6. **The Far North**: a minimum of a week here would allow time to explore the Lauca National Park, the cities of Arica and Iquique with their historical associations and the region's mining past. Note that from Santiago to Arica by bus takes 28 hrs, compared with about 3½ by plane.

7. **Heading S through the Central Valley** towards the Lake District: suggesting lengths of stay begins to get a bit more difficult here. The options for making detours off the longitudinal highway grow in number, especially into the National Parks on the way up to the Andes. Any of the following deserve more than a passing glimpse: Rancagua, Curicó, Talca and Vilches, Chillán and Ñuble province, Concepción and the coast S of Concepción including Lago Lanalhue; Parque Nacional Nahuelbuta. It's really a question of taking your pick.

8. If the **Lake District** proper is your goal, then this is an area of almost unlimited choice. Some lakes are more developed than others, but on almost any you can find quiet corners. Temuco, the city at the northern end of the region, is worth a day or two; Puerto Montt at the southern end demands a little longer (from Santiago by bus 15 hrs; by train 19 hrs; by plane 1 hr 40 mins). In between, apart from the lakes, there are many protected areas of great beauty. The lakes with the largest number of tourist facilities are: Villarrica and Llanquihue, followed by Calafquén, Panguipulli,

**Principle Routes:
South of Puerto Montt**

Coyhaique is the main town. 4-7 days can be added with a cruise to the Laguna San Rafael.

11. For anyone going to **Chilean Patagonia**, whether flying, crossing from Argentina, or taking the 4-day sea journey from Puerto Montt, a visit to the Parque Nacional Torres del Paine is a must. This requires at least an overnight stay, but to make the most of the hiking possibilities in this stunning region, allow 5-6 days. With the added attractions around Punta Arenas and Puerto Natales, plus Tierra del Fuego, a further 4-5 days could be added here.

12. Lastly, the **Pacific Islands**: Juan Fernández is served by plane from Santiago, which is the only option if short of time. By boat a visit is very time-consuming. Easter Island, also reached by plane, has a lot to see, so if making the effort to get there, do not dash in and out.

TOURISM IN CHILE

Chile's geographical and climatic variety mean that most tourist activities are possible somewhere in the country. Most outdoor activities and adventure tourism are covered in detail below. Travellers interested in the arts will find Santiago offers one of the most varied and active arts programmes in South America. Lovers of the poetry and prose will want to visit the three museums associated with the life of the poet, Pablo Neruda (see **Literature**, below): in Santiago, Valparaíso and Isla Negra. For wine-lovers there are visits to vineyards and *bodegas*, several of the most famous of which are near Santiago. Those interested in geology and wildlife will be attracted by Chile's network of National Parks.

Although Chile is no longer a cheap country, many of the above types of tourism can be enjoyed by budget travellers especially if they avoid the most popular destinations and travel off season.

Puyehue and Todos Los Santos on the way to Argentina. You may choose to spend a week in one place, or use the time to move from lake to lake, interspersing the water's edge with trekking, climbing, hot springs and a visit, for instance, to Valdivia, with the colonial forts at the nearby river's mouth.

9. The island of **Chiloé** is worth several days of exploring, but it might be an idea to take rain gear.

10. The **Carretera Austral**: although a bit of a dead end in the sense that once you have reached the end you have to turn round and come back, the road is worth several days (longer if going by bike). The scenery is magnificent and the atmosphere still feels pioneering.

ADVENTURE TOURISM

Chile might have been designed for adventure tourism. The main population centres are not more than a few hours' drive away from the *Cordillera*: its great length provides an extremely diverse terrain and enables visitors and Chileans alike to practice a wide range of adventure activities throughout the year. In the high summer month of Jan, for instance, when Parinacota volcano in the N is shrouded in cloud, the Torres del Paine in Patagonia enjoy their main season and the ski slopes in the centre of the country are ideal for mountain biking.

The infrastructure for what might be termed 'soft' adventure tourism, such as a half-day's rafting on a Grade 3 river (quite a thrill), or a day spent climbing a volcano and returning to your nearby hotel, is quite good. Agencies in centres such as Pucón, Puerto Varas and Puerto Montt organize combinations of activities, many for one day but some for longer durations. Santiago is also well-placed for short trips, especially to the ski resorts nearby. Some of the world's top rafting and fishing is also easily accessible.

'Tougher' adventure tourism, such as camping at high altitudes, in the unforgiving Atacama Desert, on the inhospitable Patagonian Ice Cap, or even off the recently built Carretera Austral, are also possible, though it is often difficult to obtain information, particularly on high grade mountaineering. Chile offers boundless opportunities for well-equipped independent adventure: the best way to see the Atacama Desert is in your own (or rented) 4WD vehicle and a mountain bike is still the best form of transport on the Carretera Austral. It is important to check the experience of agencies offering expeditions to remote areas.

Among the organizations involved in adventure tourism several deserve special mention:

● CATA (Consejo de Autoregulación de Aventura), Arzobispo Casanova 3, Providencia, Santiago, T 735-8034, F 777-2375 is a new organization formed by the more reputable agencies to try (with mixed success) to regulate adventure tourism to ensure safety and exclude 'cowboy' operators. It works closely with Conaf.

● Conaf (Corporación Nacional Forestal) regulates adventure activities within the National Parks, following CATA's written guidelines on matters such as the experience required of guides, types of activity provided, size of groups and safety requirements.

● Sernatur has a separate section specializing in providing information on adventure tourism and ecotourism located within its head office in Santiago.

● **Further reading** *Una Aventura Navegando Los Canales del Sur de Chile* by Alberto Mantellero is a guide to sailing the southern coast, with maps; also available is *Regata*, a monthly sailing magazine. Climbers will find *Cumbres de Chile*, a book and tapes on 20 peaks, of interest. The first part of a 5-year project to cover 100 peaks, it has also appeared in parts in *El Mercurio. The High Andes*, by John Biggar (Castle Douglas, Kirkudbrightshire: Andes, 1996), contains three chapters with information on Chilean peaks. Conaf (see Santiago, **Tourist offices**, page 100) has published *Guía de Parques Nacionales y Otras Áreas Silvestres Protegidas de Chile*, US$12, a very useful guide to the main parks containing information on access, camping sites, flora and fauna; *Chile Forestal* is a monthly magazine published by Conaf with articles on the parks and ecological issues. On the Carretera Austral, see *Cuentos de la Carretera Austral* by René Peri Fagerstrom.

CLIMBING

There are four distinct terrains for climbing in Chile: each poses different problems.

Rock climbing is not organized on a national basis, though *ENAM* (Escuela Nacional de Montaña de Santiago) runs courses in rock climbing as well as ice climbing. Adventure tourism agencies are just beginning to offer rock climbing activities. The three granite towers in the **Parque Nacional Torres del Paine** are the best known and most difficult climbs, but they are in such demand that a climbing fee is levied (the only place where this occurs in Chile). On the shores of **Lago Todos Los Santos** there are very high cliffs (800m) at the eastern end and at Cerro Picada (800m) on the NW shore.

Chile has high mountains such as **Tupungato** and **Ojos del Salado** which rival the Argentine peak of Aconcagua for climbing. Like the latter they pose few technical difficulties but the weather can be vicious and the altitude should be taken very seriously. Moreover, Ojos del Salado is not easily accessible.

By contrast some of the most important high altitude ice climbs are easily reached from Santiago: the **Loma Larga** and **Plomo** massifs are 2-3 hrs' drive from the capital. The *Federación de Andinismo* can advise on the better known and more difficult climbs such as El Plomo, El Altar and El Morado, though it is less useful for information of mountains further afield and its offices are often closed.

Volcanoes provide the fourth type of climbing. There are hundreds to choose from, ranging from the high altitude **Parinacota** in the far N and remote **Licancábur** on the Bolivian frontier to the chain of much lower cones in the Lake District and along the Carretera Austral. Some of these, such as **Puntiagudo** and **Corcovado** with their distinctive plugs are difficult climbs. The easiest and most popular are **Villarrica** and **Osorno**, though Conaf rightly controls access to these because the crevasses are hazardous. Osorno, with its seracs and ice caves is a more attractive climb, but Villarrica has the dubious advantage of being more active and hiring guides is much cheaper.

Permission must be obtained from the *Dirección de Fronteras y Límites*, p 5, Ministerio de Relaciones Exteriores, Bandera 52, Santiago, T 671-4210, F 697-1909, to climb some mountains in frontier areas, notably Ojos del Salado and Parinacota. Preferably apply 3 months in advance (Chilean embassies abroad can help).

Mountain rescue services are provided by the *Cuerpo de Socorro Andino*, based in Santiago but with rescue groups in popular climbing areas: if organizing a climb register with them, often at the entry control to the mountain and with the local *carabineros*. Away from the popular areas you are on your own, which can also be one of Chile's main attractions.

● **Information** *Federación de Andinismo de Chile*, Almte Simpson 77A, Santiago, T 222-0888, F 222-6285, in theory open daily but frequently closed especially in Jan/Feb (high season), has a small museum (1100-1330, 1700-2000, free) and library (weekdays except Wed 1930-2100). The shop in the foyer sells climbing guides and equipment and is often open when the office is closed; *Escuela Nacional de Montaña (ENAM)*, at same address, T 222-0799, holds seminars and conferences on climbing, runs rock and ice climbing courses and qualification courses for guides in Santiago and elsewhere. Also administers the *Carnet de La Federación de Chile*, a climbing card which is often required to climb mountains especially where Conaf control access. The *carnet* can be renewed through Conaf offices.

TREKKING

Chile offers limitless possibilities for both short and long treks in vastly differing landscapes: a one-day hike to the **Valle de la Luna** near San Pedro de Atacama is half a continent away from the famous circuit of the **Parque Nacional Torres del Paine**. Over 1,000 km of new hiking opportunities have been opened up by the building of the Carretera Austral, though the heavy rainfall in this area can be a drawback.

Within the national parks there are often short 2-3 hr signposted nature trails, starting from a visitor's centre, where, in season, there are sometimes lectures (usually only in Spanish) on flora and fauna and other highlights of the park.

SKIING

Chile's major international ski resorts lie in the Andes near Santiago and are described in the text.

Most skiing elsewhere is on volcanoes to the S of Santiago, although backcountry ski-mountaineering is quite possible on the volcanoes of the northern *altiplano* (guide essential, expertise required). The larger resorts in the S are Termas de Chillán, Villarrica/Pucón and Antillanca, 400 km, 750 km and 900 km from Santiago respectively, all of which have accommodation on or near the slopes. There are, however, alternatives to these: many suitable volcanoes close to towns have a small base lodge and a lift which functions at weekends or peak periods. Here prices tend to be very reasonable and basic equipment rental is usually possible in the nearest town. Hitching is often the only form of transport though determined questioning in the nearest town may put you in touch with the local *Club Andino* through whom it is sometimes possible to arrange transport. After all the effort to reach the snow, the atmosphere is happy-go-lucky and the outback skiing is great. Examples of these tiny resorts are Antuco, Llaima and Lonquimay, but don't be limited to these: ask locally.

In the southern resorts skiing is for the laid-back and adventurous only. Snow conditions tend to become more spring-like and slushy the further S you go. Lift systems are not the most modern, fast or well maintained, piste preparation is mediocre and the weather is often more rainy than snowy. Despite all these disadvantages skiing on top of an active volcano looking down onto five huge lakes, as is the case at Villarrica/Pucón, is truly a memory which will last a lifetime.

MOUNTAIN BIKING

Cheap mountain bikes, of variable quality, are manufactured in Chile. Mountain biking is a popular activity, particularly on descents from the Continental Divide and from *refugios* on volcanoes such as Antillanca and Osorno. Touring the length of the Carretera Austral by mountain bike is also popular.

PARAPENTING AND HANG GLIDING

Aerial sports are usually organized in Santiago, although there is a parapenting centre at the Antillanca ski resort.

CANYONING

The southern bank of the Río Petrohué offers many fantastic canyons for climbing. Nearby *Aquamotion* have fixed rope ladders in the canyon of the Río Leon, 30 mins by boat from Petrohué on the southern shore of Lago Todos Los Santos.

RAFTING AND KAYAKING

Over 20 rivers between Santiago and Tierra del Fuego are excellent for white water rafting. Apart from the Maipo, which is the most easily accessible from Santiago, the main ones are the Cachapoal, Teno, Claro, Maule and Biobío (see Section 7); the Trancura, Fuy, Bueno, Rahue and Petrohué (see Section 8); the Yelcho, Futaleufú, Corcovado, Palena and Baker (see Section 10); and the Serrano and Tyndall (see Section 11).

Some of these rivers run through spectacular mountain scenery: one of the most beautiful is the Río Petrohué, which flows between the Osorno and Calbuco volcanoes and has lush temperate rainforest along its banks. The Río Biobío, Chile's most famous river for rafting is in decline: one dam has already been built and the completion of a second, due in 1997, will mark the end of a great rafting river. Some expert rafters have long maintained that the Biobío was, in any case, inferior to the Río Futaleufú. This river, E of Chaitén, will inevitably become known as one of the great Grade 5 rafting rivers in the world.

Rafting is generally well organized and equipment usually of high quality. Access to the headwaters of most rivers is easy. Many agencies, particularly in Santiago, Pucón and Puerto Varas, offer half-day trips to Grade 3 rivers for beginners, US$40-69 pp. Rafts should ideally carry 6 people and certainly no more than 7 plus guide.

The most attractive waters for sea kayaking are around the islands off eastern Chiloé or around Hornopirén, just off the northernmost section of the Carretera Austral in the fjords of the sheltered Gulf of Ancud. The highlight for lake kayaking is the annual open competition on Lago Llanquihue, involving five stages totalling 310 km around the lake shore. Kayaks can be hired from *Oceanic*, Santiago (F 2325539) and *Kayak Equipment*, San Vicente de Paul 5831, La Reina, Santiago (T/F 277-5288) and *Canoas Tours*, Rosario 1305, Puerto Varas (T 233587). Courses are available at the *Chiloé Sea Kayaking Centre* near Dalcahue and are bookable through *Altué Expeditions* in Santiago.

There are regattas on Llago Llanquihue every Sat, racing lasers, vagabonds and catamarans, organized by a group of local sailors known as the Northwest fleet. Other water sports, such as diving and surfing, are generally practised in northern Chile.

SAILING AND YACHTING

Sailing, both wind and motor powered, is becoming increasingly popular as the Chilean economy continues to expand. Protected harbours, yacht clubs and racing fleets can be found at most sizable coastal towns from Arica southwards. Lagos Villarrica and Llanquihue are particularly popular for sports sailing and windsurfing: there are weekly regattas on both lakes and more important annual regattas. The biggest regatta is the biennial event in Jan (even years) from Puerto Montt around the coast of Chiloé.

The best ocean sailing is in the relatively sheltered waters from Puerto Montt S via the Archipiélago de los Chonos to Cape Horn. You should allow at least a week to begin to do justice to Chiloé and the islands off its eastern shore. Three weeks or more are required to reach the glaciers of Laguna San Rafael.

Chartering A variety of sail and power boats can be chartered from *MDS Charters* in Puerto Montt (address under Puerto Montt). Most charters are skippered: unusually good sailing credentials are required for a bareboat charter. For the really adventurous a dozen or more sailing yachts are based in Ushuaia/Puerto Williams: these are blue water sailing yachts doing charters to Cape Horn and Antarctica. They advertise in sailing magazines and are often booked a year in advance.

Yacht Facilities There are three travel lifts in Valdivia, among them a 35-ton lift and complete yacht repair facility at the modern Awolplast boatyard. The Valdivia yacht club often has slips available. At Puerto Montt Marina del Sur is a brand new marina with 65 slips, showers and laundry: a new hydraulic lift was scheduled for operation by early 1997 and a tidal grid (with 25 ft tides) is also available. Budget minded sailors can pick up a mooring at the Club Náutico. South of Puerto Montt there are no marina facilities. Complete re-provisioning can be carried out in Puerto Montt, Castro, Puerto Aisén, Puerto Natales and Ushuaia; odds and ends can be obtained at Melinka and Puerto Aguirre, but fuel and other supplies are virtually unobtainable between Puerto Aguirre and Puerto Natales.

Navigation The yachting season runs

Sailing through the southern channels

The real Mecca for cruising boats is along the coast from Puerto Montt to Cape Horn via Chiloé, among the islands of the Archipiélago de los Chonos and further S through the channels of Patagonia. There is probably no better way to see this stunningly spectacular and remote part of South America than by yacht during the summer months. It is largely undiscovered as a cruising ground: during the 1995/1996 cruising season only about 17 foreign yachts passed through the channels.

These archipelagoes provide some of the finest and most challenging sailing in the world. In general the navigation and the weather conditions become more difficult as you go S. At the very tip of this 1,600 km long stretch of islands and glacier-backed fjords is, of course, the sailor's supreme challenge, western Tierra del Fuego and Cape Horn. Anyone who can take their boat this far S is already among a hardy but slowly growing band of experts, some of whom now cross the formidable Drake Straits S of the Cape, normally in Jan or Feb, to cruise to Antarctica.

For lesser mortals a much friendlier region lies just S of Puerto Montt, at approximately 42S, a region dotted with populated islands which, with their hedged patchworks of pasture, wheat and potato fields, look like Western England or Maine a century ago. The sailing, especially in Jan-March, is tough but sporty rather than dangerous. These waters, shown on charts as the Gulf of Ancud and the Gulf of Corcovado, are completely protected by Chiloé from the giant swells of the southern Pacific. The weather is at best unsettled and even the fishermen and farmers frequently get it wrong. Strong winds can suddenly die to a flat calm, burning sun may be wiped out by squalls of rain and even hail. That's summer. Winter is Scottish.

Tides of 6-8m mean strong rips; shoals are frequent, but usually well marked on charts, 'usually' meaning that special care is needed around the smallest islands, especially on the mainland side. It's rare to be out of sight of land and you mostly know where you are to within 100m or so even without electronics.

The best harbours are, from N to S, Quemchi, Mechuque, Quehui, Castro, Queilén and Quellón. Fuel for outboard motors is usually available at Quemchi, Castro, Chonchi and Queilén. Water generally has to be brought aboard in jerry cans filled from a friendly householder's kitchen tap. Connections to shore electricity do not exist and, indeed, the smaller islands only have power themselves for an hour or two at night. The larger islands have at least a couple of general stores but much better to stock up in Puerto Montt or Castro. The same applies for recharging batteries. Robert and Caroline Ely of the Yacht *Elyxir* (Seattle, USA).

PLM_BX01

from Nov to March in these southern waters. South of 45S the weather is significantly worse than at corresponding latitudes in Europe and North America. Weather forecasts are provided by the Chilean Navy and are updated twice daily: they are broadcast over HF radio by voice and weatherfax map. Their accuracy is quite good considering the massive unstable low pressure systems which regularly roll in off the Southern Ocean. Complete chart portfolios are stocked at the Navy administration offices in Puerto Montt and Puerto Williams. Individual charts cost US$23 each and are generally superior to the US charts. A high quality colour chart atlas containing 28 cm x 43 cm reductions of the entire Chile chart portfolio was due to be released in early 1997. Charts can be ordered from the Chilean Navy.

FISHING

The lakes and rivers of Regions IX (Araucanía), X (Los Lagos) and XI (Aisén) offer great opportunities for fishing, especially trout (Rainbow, Brown and Fario) and salmon (Coho and Chinook). The season runs from 15 Nov to the first Sun in May except on Lago Llanquihue where it starts on 15 September. A licence is required whether for 1 day or a longer period: licences are usually obtained from the local *Municipalidad*. There are so many waters that overfishing is generally not a problem though probably the most exciting possibilities lie along the Carretera Austral. Organized fly fishing with a guide can be expensive: trolling and spinning are the more widely practised methods.

Sea fishing is popular between Puerto Saavedra in the IX Region (Auracanía) and Maullín in the X Region (Los Lagos: the main centres are Mehuín, the Valdivia coast from Niebla to Curiñanco, Maicolpue, Llico and Maullín itself where salmon may be caught in the sea.

The Lake District is popular for trout fishing. Both Rainbow and Fario trout are found in all the major lakes; the largest fish are found in Lago Llanquihue, while Lago Todos Los Santos, on which very few boats are permitted, is noted for quantity. Salmon fishing is particularly popular with visitors from Europe and North America. Apart from the main lakes, Lago Maihue and Lagunas El Toro, El Encanto and Paraíso (all in the Parque Nacional Puyehue) have been recommended. In the southern Lake District the main rivers for salmon fishing include the Ríos Pescado, Petrohué, Puelo, Maullín and, on Chiloé, the Chepu and Pudeto.

The greatest fishing area in Chile lies along the Carretera Austral: Lago Yelcho and the Ríos Futaleufú and Palena are important areas for fly fishing, while further S the rivers and lakes around Coyhaique offer some of the best fishing in the world.

Santiago and Valparaíso residents fish at the mountain resort of Río Blanco.

● **Fishing equipment** *Pesca Mundo Caza*, Benavente y M Rodríguez, Puerto Montt; *Winkler Deportes*, Antonio Varas 841, Puerto Montt; *Lagollan*, San José 315, Puerto Varas.

● **Useful information** For details on licences and local conditions, contact the Asociación de Pesca y Caza, or Sernap, San Antonio 427, p 8, Santiago, open Mon-Fri 0900-1400. Check with Sernatur on closed seasons. Outside Chile, all information can be obtained from Sport Elite Ltd, Woodwalls House, Corscombe, Dorchester, Dorset, UK, DT2 0NT, T 093589-1477, F 093589-1797 (Major J A Valdes-Scott).

HORSERIDING

Mountain horse treks are organized in Santiago. South of Concepción there is more of an equine culture than further N. One of the best places for hiring and riding horses is along the W coast of Chiloé. Expect to pay US$3 per hour.

COMPETITION CALENDAR

Jan: *Chiloé/Puerto Montt Regatta* (every 2 years, next 1998); *International Rally of Kayaking*, Lago Llanquihue, 310 km, 5 stages; *Regatta*, Lago Villarrica; *Pentathlon*, Lago Todos Los Santos/Petrohué.

Jan/Feb: *International Triathlon*, Pucón.

Feb: *International windsurfing contest* (slalom and speed categories), Lago Llanquihue, incorporating a rafting, canoeing and kayaking competition on Río Petrohué; *Rafting Open*, Pucón, beginners and experts categories.

April: *International Mountain Bike Competition*, Antillanca.

Sept: Horseracing on beach in Parque National Chiloé (Chepu sector) and kayaking and canoeing races on Río Chepu.

Oct: *International Surfing Competition*, Pichilemu.

How to go

GETTING AROUND

Very few nationalities need consular visas to visit Chile. Those that do are New Zealand, Guyana, Haiti, Kuwait, Cuba and some African and ex-Communist countries. The normal length of stay permitted for tourists is 90 days.

International air services to Chile are good and visitors should experience no problems in finding a convenient flight from Europe, North or South America. London, Paris, Madrid, Amsterdam, Frankfurt and Rome all have flights to Santiago, while from the USA, Miami, New York and Los Angeles are the main hubs for direct flights or connections. All the South American capitals, plus Mexico City and San José (Costa Rica) are served direct. There are also flights to the Falkland Islands/Islas Malvinas.

Overland connections by road are generally good, although some of the high Andean passes will be closed by snow in winter. Passenger train services connect Chile with Bolivia and Peru.

Domestic air services are good and frequent. All parts of the country are served by three major airlines and, in the S, a number of smaller companies fly to Patagonian destinations. The highways are well-paved, with buses run by many competing firms providing generally first-class service. Motorists will encounter no problems on Chilean roads and hiring a vehicle is easy, but not cheap. Passenger trains in the N run only cross-border services. South out of Santiago passengers are carried as far as Puerto Montt, but the extent of the service varies with the domestic tourist season.

Beyond Puerto Montt, shipping is a vital link between communities (eg on the northern stretch of the Carretera Austral, to/from Chiloé, Puerto Montt-Puerto Natales) and in the high season reservations are essential.

PRACTICALITIES

Tourist information is provided by the Secretaría Nacional de Turismo, Sernatur, which has an extensive network of offices the length of the country. Leaflets and maps are readily available. Outside Chile, prospective visitors are advised to contact the commercial departments at embassies.

The unit of currency is the peso. Changing dollars into pesos is straightforward, with dollars cash and travellers' cheques acceptable in banks and exchange houses. ATMs are also to be found in all major towns and cities. The further from the capital you go, the worse the exchange rates tend to be, but not by huge amounts. There is no point in taking your spending money in any currency other than dollars.

Good hotels are easy to find throughout the price range and as Chileans travel a lot within their own country, there is no shortage of places to stay outside the cities and resorts. In some places you may find a preponderance of accommodation catering for families (eg at the beach, or at some lakes). On the other hand, in the S especially, many family homes offer rooms in which the standard can range from the simple to the very comfortable. There is a good network of youth hostels, and campsites, though generally expensive, are widespread.

Chile's speciality is seafood, both fish and shellfish, and excellent local dishes can be enjoyed everywhere. There are also plenty of meat dishes, with *empanadas* (turn-overs filled with a variety of ingredients – every recipe is slightly different) are very popular.

Chilean wine is now renowned worldwide, so part of the enjoyment can be in seeking out brands and visiting *bodegas* whose products you may not find at home. *Pisco*, a grape spirit, is also distilled; the most common way to drink it is in a *pisco sour*. Of course there are a great many other foods and drinks and since the Central Valley is so fruitful, the visitor should have no difficulty in eating and drinking well, whatever his or her taste.

Spanish is the official language, but the speed with which it is spoken and its pronunciation can leave some foreigners floundering. The ear may take a bit of time to get accustomed. German is spoken in the southern areas where immigration has been heaviest. It is best not to rely on English when travelling around.

Postal services are efficient. The telephone service has been opened up to competition and eight carriers are operating. This may be a source of confusion, but it does mean that phone rates are not excessively high and making international calls is uncomplicated.

WHEN TO GO

Ideal visiting times vary according to geographical location: the Lake District and far S are best visited between Dec and Mar; for the N June to Sept will be cooler, unless visiting the Lauca National

Park. Santiago and the Central Valley are best in spring (Sept-Nov) or autumn (Mar-April). Further details are given in the climate sections below.

HEALTH

For anyone travelling overseas health is a key consideration. With sensible precautions the visitor to Chile should remain as healthy as at home. There are general rules to follow which should keep you in good health when travelling in Latin America. These are dealt with in detail in the full health section on page 423.

KEEPING HEALTHY IN CHILE

Before you travel make sure the medical insurance you take out is adequate. Have a check up with your doctor, if necessary, and arrange your immunizations well in advance. Try ringing a specialist travel clinic if your own doctor is unfamiliar with health in Latin America. There are actually no vaccinations demanded by immigration officials in Chile, but you would do well to be protected by vaccination against typhoid, polio, tetanus and hepatitis A, if you are living rough or spending time in rural areas. There is no malaria in Chile.

WHILE YOU ARE TRAVELLING

Despite the fact that there is no tropical disease in Chile and hygienic standards are higher than in, for example, the Andean countries, the commonest affliction of visitors to Chile will still be travellers diarrhoea. Shellfish are always a risk, but particularly delicious in Chile – they should be safe in well run hygienic establishments. Occasionally the sale of shellfish is restricted in Chile due to so-called 'red tides' which render the fish poisonous at certain times of the year. Fruit is plentiful and excellent, but ensure it is washed or peel it yourself. Avoid raw food, undercooked food (including eggs) and reheated food. Food that is cooked in front of you and offered hot all through is generally safe.

Tap water in Chile is generally unsafe to drink. The better hotels have their own water purification systems and in many restaurants you can get boiled water, water that has been filtered or more popular, commercially bottled water. In the major cities water tends to be overchlorinated for safety, which may make it taste unpleasant. There are excellent doctors and very good hospitals in Santiago and some of the other major cities, but don't expect good facilities away from the major centres.

ALTITUDE AND CLIMATE

In Chile you can travel within a few hours by road or rail from sea level to over 3,000m – enough to give you 'soroche' if you have travelled directly from the coast. If you are climbing higher, respect the altitude and follow the advice in the main health section. There are various local remedies such as mate de coca – particularly popular in the Highlands, helpful and perfectly legal.

Parts of Chile are extremely hot and dry, mainly in the N. Keep up your fluid intake. It can also be extremely cold and wet the further S you go, so take appropriate clothing. In the S and at high altitude the ultra-violet rays of the sun are particularly strong, so do not forget your hat and sun protection cream.

RETURNING HOME

Report any symptoms to your doctor and say exactly where you have been.

Writing to the editor

Many people write to us - with corrections, new information, or simply comments. If you want to let us know something, we would be delighted to hear from you. Please give us as precise information as possible, quoting the edition and page number of the Handbook you are using and send as early in the year as you can. Your help will be greatly appreciated, especially by other travellers. In return we will send you details about our special guidebook offer.

For hotels and restaurants, please let us know:

- each establishment's name, address, phone and fax number
- number of rooms, whether a/c or air-cooled, attached (clean?) bathroom
- location - how far from the station or bus stand, or distance (walking time) from a prominent landmark
- if it's not already on one of our maps, can you place it?
- your comments - either good or bad - as to why it is distinctive
- tariff cards
- local transport used

For places of interest:

- location
- entry, camera charge
- access - by whatever means of transport is most appropriate, eg time of main buses or trains to and from the site, journey time, fare
- facilities - nearby drinks stalls, restaurants, for the disabled
- any problems, eg steep climb, wildlife, unofficial guides
- opening hours
- site guides

Horizons

GEOLOGY AND LANDSCAPE

Chile is smaller than all other South American republics save Ecuador, Paraguay, Uruguay and the Guianas. Its territory is a ribbon of land lying between the Andes and the Pacific, 4,329 km long and, on average, no more than 180 km wide. Its range of climates and scenery, matched by few, if any other countries, poses great problems for surface communication and administration. Because of hostile environments the far N and extreme S are sparsely populated.

In the N Chile has a short 150 km E-W frontier with Peru. In the far N its eastern frontier is with Bolivia – 750 km long – but from San Pedro de Atacama S to Patagonia and Tierra del Fuego it shares over 3,500 km of frontier with Argentina. In the main this frontier follows the crest of the Andes, but this is by no means the case throughout and there have been frequent frontier disputes with Argentina since independence. Chile has a short Atlantic coastline at the eastern end of the Straits of Magellan. Its sovereignty over the islands S of Tierra del Fuego gives it control over Isla Navarino, the site of the most southerly permanent settlement in the world, Puerto Williams. Various island archipelagos in the Pacific, including Easter Island/Rapa Nui and the Juan Fernández group, are under Chilean jurisdiction.

Structure

Although there are surface remnants of older rock formations, notably in the Coastal Ranges between 30°S and 60°S, most have disappeared with the dramatic creation of the Andes which started around 80,000 years ago in the late Cretaceous period and continues to this day. The South American Plate, moving westwards, meets the Nasca and Antarctic Plates which are moving eastwards and sinking below the continent. These two plates run more or less parallel between 26°S and 33°S and the friction between them creates a geologically unstable zone, marked by frequent earthquakes and volcanic activity. The area of Concepción has been particularly susceptible to both land and undersea quakes and the city was destroyed twice in the 18th century by tidal waves before being moved to its present site. The Quaternary Period was marked by the advance and retreat of the Antarctic Ice Sheet which at its maximum extent covered all of the Chilean Andes and the entire coastline S of Puerto Montt.

All of the Chilean Pacific islands were formed by underwater volcanoes associated with fracture zones between the Nasca and Antarctic Plates, Easter Island gaining its characteristic triangular shape from the joining together of three lava flows.

The Northern Desert

Northern Chile has a similar form to Peru immediately to the N; the coastal range rises to 1,000-1,500m; inland are basins

known as *bolsones*, E of which lie the
Andes. The Atacama Desert is, by most
measures, the driest area on earth and
some meteorological stations near the
coast have never reported precipitation.
This dry climate is brought about by the
interaction of the high pressure belt over
the Western Pacific and the cold Humboldt Current flowing N along the coast
which create a mass of stable, cool air.
Under these conditions only condensation mists can be formed along the coastal
range and these are soon dispersed by
inland radiation to leave clear skies.

Water is therefore at a premium for
those who inhabit the region between
the Peruvian border and Copiapó, an
area of great economic activity based
upon mining. Water is piped in from the
E and in the Andean foothills streams
flow into alluvial fans on the eastern side
of the inland basins which can act as
reservoirs and may be tapped by drilling
wells. One river, the Río Loa, flows cir-
cuitously from the Andes to Calama and
then through the coastal range to the
coast, but for most of its length it is
deeply entrenched and unsuitable for
agriculture and there is no port at its
mouth. East of Calama and high in the
Andes are the geysers of El Tatio, more
evidence of volcanic activity, which are
fed by the summer rains which fall in
this part of the Andes.

In the past, notably as the ice sheets
retreated, there were many lakes in the
depressions between the Coastal Range
and the Andes. These dried out leaving
one of the greatest concentrations of
salts in the world, rich in mineral deposits especially nitrates, aided by the extreme aridity and the lack of sand at high
altitudes and giving rise to extensive
mining activity since the late 19th century.

Central Chile

South of Copiapó the transition begins
between the deserts of northern Chile
and zone of heavy rainfall in the S. At first
the desert turns to scrub and some seasonal surface water appears. Eventually
rivers fed by winter rains follow deep
trenches to reach the sea, allowing valley
bottoms inland to be irrigated for agriculture.

Further S, near Santiago, the Central
Valley between the Coastal Range and
the Andes reappears, though most of the
rivers flow westwards across it to reach
the Pacific. With its heavier rainfall, forests, National Parks and hot springs, this
is one of the most attractive areas of the
country.

South of Temuco lies the scenic Lake
District, one of the most popular Chilean tourist destinations, with its lakes
formed by glaciation and volcanic activity, its attractive mountain scenery, its
rich volcanic soils and fertile agricultural land.

Southern Chile

South of Valdivia the Coastal Range becomes more broken until near Puerto
Montt it becomes a line of islands as part
of a 'drowned coastline' which extends all
the way S to Cape Horn. The effects of
glaciation can be seen in the U-shaped
valleys and the long deep fjords stretching inland. There are few roads and many
smaller settlements can only be reached
by sea or air. This is a land of dense forests
with luxuriant undergrowth which is virtually impenetrable and difficult to clear
owing to the high water content. Further
S towards Chilean Patagonia, coniferous
forests are limited in expanse because
glaciers have stripped the upper slopes of
soil. Some of the remaining glaciers reach
sea level, notably the San Rafael, which
breaks off the giant icefields of the *Campo
de Hielo Norte*.

The Andes

The whole of Chile is dominated by this
massive mountain range which reaches
its highest elevations in Chile and the
Argentine frontier regions. In the N, near
the Peruvian border the ranges which
make up the Andes are 500 km wide, but

the western ranges which mark the Chilean frontier, are the highest. Sajama, the highest peak in Bolivia, lies only 20 km E of the border, along which are strung volcanoes such as Parinacota (6,330m) and Pomerape (6,240m). Further S, to the SE of San Pedro de Atacama, lies the highest section of the Andes, which includes the peaks of Llullaillaco (6,739m) and Ojos del Salado (altitude from 6,864m to 6,879m to 6,908m depending on your source). Still further S, to the NE of Santiago and just inside Argentina, lies Aconcagua (6,960m).

South of 42°S the Andes become more and more inhospitable, and lower temperatures bring the permanent snowline down from 1,500m at Volcán Osorno near Puerto Montt to 700m on Tierra del Fuego. At the southern end of the Andes are Mount Fitzroy (3,406m) just over the border in Argentina and the remarkable peaks of Paine.

CLIMATE

As the above sections indicate, annual rainfall varies widely: from zero in northern Chile to over 4,000mm on the offshore islands S of Puerto Montt. Throughout the country rainfall is heavier in the winter months (May-Aug).

Temperature variations are lower than might be expected, especially along the coast. In the Atacama temperatures are kept down by the Humboldt Current along the coast and inland daytime temperatures are moderated by altitude, although night-time temperatures below 0°C are common. The Central Valley S of Santiago enjoys the most pleasant climate with short winters and long dry summers. Even in the far S the proximity of the Pacific prevents extremes of cold, although this area is subject to strong westerly winds. Detailed temperature and rainfall patterns are given in the text.

Chilean National Parks

Chile has an extensive system of protected natural areas, covering 7 mn ha in all. These areas (87 in total, excluding the Pacific Islands) are divided into national parks, forest reserves, natural monuments and natural sanctuaries, but these distinctions are of little importance for the visitor. Most of these areas have public access and details of the majority are given in the text. Camping areas are usually clearly designated, especially in the major natural areas, and 'wild' camping is discouraged and frequently banned.

The first forest reserve was the Reserva Forestal Malleco, created in 1907, and the first national park was the Parque Nacional Vicente Pérez Rosales, founded in 1926. The expansion of the system has been based not just on the preservation of national resources which may be under threat, but also on giving access for the public to areas of outstanding beauty.

All of these protected areas are managed by Conaf (the Corporación Nacional Forestal), a dependency of the Ministry of Agriculture which also has responsibility for forestry development. The address of Conaf's head office is given under Santiago, **Tourist offices**. It maintains an office in each of the regions of the country and kiosks in some natural areas and other locations. It publishes an illustrated guide to the parks and maps of the major protected areas which can be obtained from its head office and from some regional offices, the addresses of which are given in the text. As well as the book mentioned in **Adventure Tourism** above, Conaf publishes a useful little book on native trees, *Arboles nativos de Chile, Guía de Reconocimiento*, by Claudio Donoso Zegers (1983).

FLORA AND FAUNA

Chile is an extremely complex country, lying between the western slopes of the Andes and the Pacific Ocean. With a length of 4,345 km and spanning a latitudinal range from 18°S to 56°S, Chile is a land of extremes extending almost from the tropics to the sub-Antarctic. It is effectively isolated from the rest of South America by the high Andes. It is a very narrow country and, since there is relatively little land, it is not surprising that the vast cold oceans and the proximity of Antarctica dominate the climate and hence the flora and fauna. This is in marked contrast to the rest of South America where the fauna and flora are to a large extent determined by the influence of the great rivers, particularly the Amazon and Orinoco.

corporación nacional forestal

As in the rest of South America the dominating topographical feature remains the Andes running N-S with a series of plateaux and snow-capped peaks leaving only a narrow strip of coastal lowlands on the Pacific side. This mountain range vastly influences rainfall; and between 27° and 10° S of the equator it produces an arid strip of land that in northern Chile is known as the Atacama desert.

This arid region is partly caused by the cold Humboldt current flowing N along the coast. Warm moisture laden air over the tropical oceans moves eastward towards the coast where it condenses when in contact with the colder temperatures above the Humboldt current. The resultant fog-bank moves inland where it is heated and eventually vaporizes, only condensing again as it rises over the Andes. Thus the area between the coast and the mountains receives little or no rain accounting for the paucity of plant and animal life here.

The geography of Chile is responsible for the absence of humid tropical forests – tropical Chile is arid or of snowy high altitude, and hence the colourful birds characteristic elsewhere in tropical South America are absent here. Nevertheless there are some 450 species of bird including 12 endemics. The flora of southern South America is referred to as the Chile Patagonia region. Northern Chile is described as arid to Mediterranean vegetation type. Steppe type habitats are also found where growth is restricted by lack of rainfall, comprising xerophytes especially adapted to arid conditions. In central Chile dense belts of temperate forest clothe the westerly slopes consisting of beech and monkey puzzle trees – the conifers *Araucaria*, *Podocarpus* and southern beech *Nothofagus* are characteristic trees of this region which includes the Valdivian forest. These are related to species in South Africa and New Zealand, a consequence of continental drift. The matorral of Chile, maquis or garigue of France and Spain and fynbos of South Africa are of similar composition. Southern Chile may be termed sub-Antarctica in climate. Chilean Antarctic Territory is beyond the scope of this account. Even farther S, between 30° and 25°, the western slopes are characterized by schlerophyll forest which grades into temperate forest. The distribution of vegetation is similar on the eastern slopes of the Andes although there is a rain shadow effect since most of the precipitation will have been dropped on the western slopes.

The cold, nutrient rich Humboldt current provides sustenance for an abundance of sea creatures and the seabirds and marine mammals that depend on them. Along the coast the *Humboldt current zone* is typified by an area of up-dwellings leading to great marine productivity. It is one of the richest fisheries in the world. This zone is home to storm petrels, Humboldt penguins, Peruvian booby and the Inca Tern. The Humboldt penguin can even range into tropical waters on the food provided by this current. The coast is also home for the sea cat *Lutra felina*, a rare coastal living otter which subsists largely on shellfish in the intertidal zone.

Inland from the coast in the N of the country there is an extensive *Desert zone* within which two sub-zones can be distinguished, the virtually lifeless deserts of the Tarapacá, Antofagasta and Atacama regions provide a formidable landscape which is a barrier to most species. Whilst no Chilean birds migrate to North America, a variety of North American species migrate S for the austral summer including plovers, sandpipers, curlews, godwits, phalaropes, gulls and terns, osprey, peregrine falcon and Barn swallow. Only the Gray gull *Laurus modestus* nests here and even it commutes daily some 50 miles to the coast to feed. The *Arid-tropical sub-zone* occurs in several lowland valleys and receives some rain but the remaining parts of this desert are covered with cacti, scrub and huarango (*Prosopis*) trees and these are the characteristic home of the Chilean woodstar, groove-billed ani and the vermillion flycatcher. There are occasional small lush oases in the extreme N which harbour scarce birds.

In central Chile, from La Serena through to Linares, the ocean produces an ameliorating effect on the climate to form a so-called *Mediterranean* zone which is similar in many respects to California. With a wide range of vegetation from arid scrub to grassy plains and lush forest near Coquimbo. There is considerable agricultural and viniculture development interspersed with dense temperate forests and monkey puzzle groves. Characteristic birds include Chilean pigeon and mocking bird, moustached turca and the rufous-tailed plantcutter.

Cooling affects the western slopes of the Andes producing some precipitation and low shrubs and grasses dominate at elevations above 1,000m. In the plateaux zone above 1,700m the characteristic habitat is puna – high elevation steppe or pampas more typical of southern Argentina comprising temperate grasslands, makes up the *Patagonian zone* where crested caracara and ruddy-headed goose are found. On the rolling grasslands the two species of rhea occupy a similar niche to that of the ostriche in Africa; living in small flocks, their anti-predator strategy is to outrun the hunters.

Inland, the *Puna Zone*, a narrow strip situated between the tree line and the snow line, is an inhospitable high altitude habitat, but home to three species of flamingo (Chilean, Andean and the very rare James's), Giant coot and various species of ground tyrants and Andean Condor also live here.

On the Pacific side from 30°S the abundant rainfall transforms the desert landscape into Mediterranean type terrain giving way farther S to beech forests. This forest zone has a distinctive fauna, including hummingbirds and the Magellan conure – the most southerly living member of the parrot family. The *Fuegian zone* comprises fjords and channels, glaciers and extends S to the Straits of Magellan. This sub-Antarctic wet forest is characterized by sphagmum moss, lichens and trees festooned with bromeliads. Mountainous Tierra del Fuego experiences the harshest climate of Chile. Birds found here include the steamer ducks, Magellanic penguin and the Imperial cormorant.

The camels of South America

The llama, alpaca, guanaco and vicuña are all camelids, or South American camels, adapted for the mountainous terrain by having narrower feet than the desert forms. There are estimated to be some 7.7 million camelids, over half of them in Peru. All four species can be seen in Chile, though three of these are only found in the N. The relationships between camelids is very confused: fertile offspring arise from matings between all of them. There is a long-held view that both the llama and the alpaca are descended from wild guanaco.

Guanaco (*lama guanicae*), coffee coloured with a darker head and tail and weighing up to 55 kg, were once found throughout Chile except in rainforest areas. Both a grazer and browser, it lives in deserts, shrub lands, savannah and occasionally on forest fringes. In many areas hunted to extinction, an estimated 20,000 now survive in the far N, especially in the Parque Nacional Lauca, in coastal areas between Antofagasta and Lago Rapel and in the far S including the Parque Nacional Torres del Paine.

Vicuña (*lama vicugna*), weighing up to 20 kg, are like half-sized guanaco, though with a yellower coat and coffee coloured head and tail. Hunted almost to extinction, there were only around 400 in Chile in 1970. Protection has increased their numbers to around 12,000, mainly in the far N and at altitudes of 3,700-4,800m.

Alpaca (*lama paco*) are domesticated animals, weighing 20-30 kg, but appearing much larger because of their wool. Colours vary between black, coffee coloured, mahogany, grey and white. An estimated 20,000 can be found in drier parts of the northern *altiplano*.

Llama (*lama glama*) are also domesticated and are usually found with alpacas. Larger than alpacas and weighing up to 55 kg, their wool varies in colour but is shorter than that of alpacas. They are found only in the area of their domestication which occurred around Lake Titicaca some 4,000-5,000 years ago. Used as pack animals, males can carry loads of up to 40 kg. There are some 40,000 in the Tarapacá and Antofagasta regions of Chile.

As far as the mammal fauna is concerned, it is notable that species richness declines rapidly as one proceeds S of the tropics zone. The most typical inhabitants of the South American savannahs are the rodents which begin to dominate the fauna in the temperate zone. Formerly the jaguar and puma roamed over these plains taking the once abundant pampas and marsh deer, but these predators have been heavily persecuted by man. The puma is the major predator on the guanaco in southern Chile. The characteristic predators of the open spaces are relatively small, and prey on small and medium sized rodents, for example – Geoffroys cat, kod-kod and pampas cat. More widely distributed are the canid predators, including grey fox, crab-eating fox and the maned wolf a stilt-legged predator which, despite its size, concentrates on small mammals and fruit. Smaller predators include the grison and the Patagonian weasel.

Enormous stretches of this grassland have always been almost entirely treeless. The characteristic mammalian fauna are a few deer species, the mara or Patagonian hare and the viscacha which is related to the chinchilla (now extremely rare as a consequence of over-exploitation) and the various members of the llama family. The llama, alpaca, guanaco and vicuna are all lamoids, that is South American camels, which are adapted for the mountainous terrain by having narrower feet than the desert living forms. The vicuna is an alpine puna grazer at altitudes of 3,700-4,800m. The guanaco which is twice as large is both a grazer and a browser occupying deserts, shrub-lands, savannahs and occasionally fringing forests. The relationships between the lamoids is very confused. Fertile offspring arise from matings between all of them. It was a long-held view that the llama and alpaca descended from wild guanaco. None of the former exist outside the centre of domestication which occurred around Lake Titicaca some 4,000-5,000 years ago. There are estimated to be some 7.7 million lameloids, over half in Peru.

The very southern end as exemplified by the Falkland Islands and the coast of the mainland are dominated by marine mammals with 14 species of cetaceans being recorded from this area and only eight species of terrestrial mainland mammals.

History

ARCHAEOLOGY AND PREHISTORY

Earliest origins

Some 50,000 years ago the very first peoples crossed the temporary land bridge spanning Asia and America at the Bering Straits, and began a long migration southwards. They were hunters and foragers, following in the path of huge herds of now extinct animals, such as mammoth, giant ground sloth, and descendants of the camel and horse. The first signs that these people had reached South America dated from around 10,000 BC, if not earlier.

As sources of game in forested valleys dried up, some groups settled along the coasts, particularly drawn by the abundance of marine life provided by the warm Humboldt current in the Pacific. Some of the earliest evidence of humans in Chile have been found in the N, on the coast and in the parched Atacama desert. The coastal people lived on shellfish gathered by the shore, and on fish and sealions speared from boats.

One such group, the Las Conchas people, migrated from the inland valleys to the coast near Antofagasta around 7,500 BC. They were one of the first peoples in South America to take hallucinogenic drugs. Many graves excavated in this region contained mortars, which may have been used to grind up seeds also found nearby. These seeds contained an alkaloid similar to that found in the ayahuasca plant, which is also used for its hallucinogenic effects by modern peoples elsewhere on the sub-continent. Grave artefacts included bags, trays, and tubes that were used for inhaling the drug in the form of snuff, a method employed in curing and adivination practices in the Andean region and coastal Brazil today. Some of the trays and tubes found were decorated with images of supernatural beings and anthropomorphic figures, such as bird-headed angels, styles that are also common in the Andean regions of present-day Peru and Bolivia.

The beginnings of agriculture

Gradually the nomadic lifestyle gave way to more settled occupation of a fixed site, with agricultural subsistence taking over from hunting. Remains of slingshot stones and what seem to be bolas (weights attached to cords used to bring down prey by entangling their legs) have been found alongside bones of mastodons in Monte Verde, near Puerto Montt. Other remains found nearby included agricultural tools and medicinal plants, hearths and house foundations, indications that the site was inhabited for some time by one community and not just a hunters' temporary camp. Crop seeds were also found, including those of potatoes, evidence of very early contact with cultures from as far afield as the Central Andes. Some of these remains were found in a remarkable condition, owing to being buried in a peat bog; mastodon bones even had traces of meat on them. Lower levels at Monte Verde have been controversially dated from 34,000 years ago, but it is widely agreed that the site was settled as early as 10,000 years ago.

By about 2,500 BC agriculture was practised throughout much of Chile, as it was across the rest of the continent. Maize, beans, and squash were found in northern Chile, from as early as 5,000 BC, when they would have been cultivated to supplement hunting and gathering food supplies. The extremely dry climate here is a great preservative,

allowing archaeologists to build up a detailed picture of early life. The people lived in solidly-built adobe houses, arranged in complexes around inner courtyards and corridors, such as the village of Tulor in the San Pedro de Atacama oasis.

The link with Tiahuanaco

These northern people had contacts with neighbouring highland communities (in present-day Bolivia, Argentina, and Peru), shown by the presence of plants and other goods found only in the adjacent regions. The important altiplano culture of Tiahuanaco in present-day Bolivia is thought to have had particularly close links with the N of Chile, helping to stimulate the growth of settlements such as at San Pedro de Atacama. Trade with Tiahuanaco, through llama caravans bringing highland goods and produce, boosted the wealth and cultural development of the desert peoples. Some very fine textiles in particular, were found in this area, showing distinct design similarities with Tiahuanaco. The textiles were hand-spun and coloured with vegetable and cochineal dyes. Clothing and jewellery adornments containing feathers suggested contact even with tropical regions, although they may have obtained these through their altiplano intermediaries. Local ceramics were mostly plain and highly polished, but some items decorated with elaborate dragon-like figures had probably been traded with Tiahuanaco.

By about AD 500-900 the association between San Pedro de Atacama and Tiahuanaco had become even stronger. In return for trading their agricultural produce and other goods, it is thought that the Tiahuanaco people sought the copper, semi-precious stones, and use of grazing lands in northern Chile. Some graves from this period contained bodies with more elaborate clothing, jewellery, imported ceramics and other valuables, suggesting the existence of a wealthy elite, which was also common in central Andean cultures.

Following the demise of Tiahuanaco in about 1,100 AD, a number of cultures arose in the adjacent area bordering southern Bolivia, northern Chile and Argentina, practising derivative agriculture, with terraces and irrigation, and producing ceramics in similar styles. In the Quebrada de Humahuaca several small defensive towns were built, with fortified walls and stone houses. Grave remains have revealed that metallurgy was well developed here; some bodies were adorned with pectorals, bracelets, masks, and bells made of copper, silver and gold. Bone tools were also found, and obsidian projectile points. Shells from the Pacific and ceramics from present-day Bolivian cultures, such as the Huruquilla, showed the existence of widespread trade links.

Mummification was practised from as early as 2,500 BC by coastal peoples, as was also common further N in present-day Peru. The Chinchorro people buried their dead stretched out straight, different from the foetal position used by other Chilean and Peruvian cultures. Internal organs and the brain were removed and the body stuffed with a variety of materials to preserve it. Sticks were attached to the limbs to keep them straight. A mask was placed over the face and a wig of real human hair attached to the head. The body was then coated in a layer of clay and wrapped in animal skins or mats. According to the person's status, they were often buried with their personal possessions, such as clothing, jewellery, musical instruments, and copper items.

By the beginning of the present era most people in Chile, as throughout South America, were leading settled lives in structured communities, farming, and to a greater or lesser degree producing ceramics, textiles, and worked metal objects (mostly in copper and silver; all the evidence shows that it was for personal use – not for tools or weapons – until the Inca era). People in the S of Chile turned to agriculture at a much later date. In Araucania, a region around Temuco long noted for its foraging cultures, horticulture was not practised until around 500 AD. These people also had unusual burial practices; placing the body in an urn inside a funerary canoe, perhaps reflecting the local dependence on fishing for their livelihood. Elaborate artefacts found in some graves, with stone and copper jewellery as well as ceramic offerings, suggest a stratified society of both rich and poor.

Inca expansion

At the peak of its growth in the 16th century, the Inca empire stretched deep into Chile, as far S as the Aconagua valley. The advancing armies of Inca Topa Yupanqui suppressed resistance in the valleys of the Central region, and replaced local structures with their own military administration. They were finally stopped by hostile forest tribes at the Río Maule. This was the southernmost limit of the Inca Empire, some 2,400 miles S of the equator, and the deepest that any imperial movement had penetrated into the southern hemisphere.

One major group, which survived the Inca incursion and resisted conquest by the Europeans right up until the 19th century AD, was the Mapuche (of the Araucanian peoples). They were concentrated in the central valley S and E of the Cordillera de Nahuelbuta. The Mapuche were primarily farmers, but also hunted and fished, both inland and along the coasts and lake shores. Their large cemeteries contained a variety of graves, some in canoes or stone chambers, and some in simple earthen graves, suggesting a social hierarchy. Grave goods were plentiful, with elaborate ceramics, wooden and stone artefacts, and jewellery made of copper and semi-precious stones.

The Far South

Southernmost Patagonia and Tierra del Fuego, straddling present-day Chile and Argentina, are covered with dense forested hillsides and flat pampas grasslands. The climate here is harsh, with extremely cold winters and heavy rainfall all year round. Despite the apparently inhospitable conditions these regions were home to a sizeable population of hunting, fishing and gathering peoples from very early times continuously up to the 19th century AD. Bones of horses and extinct giant sloths have been found near to stone arrow heads, in sites such as Fells's Cave and Palli Aike Cave on the Magellan Straits, dating from approximately 8,000 BC, as evidence of the earliest hunters.

Four distinct cultures developed here: the Haush, Ona, Yahgan, and Alacaluf. The oldest of these was the **Haush**, nomadic hunters of the guanaco mainly confined to the farthest southeastern tip of Tierra del Fuego, in present day Argentina. The Haush hunted with bows and arrows, using guanaco skins for clothing and sometimes for covering their stick-framed houses. They also gathered shellfish and caught fish by the shore, using spears and harpoons.

The **Ona** people also hunted guanaco, ranging on foot across most of the Isla Grande of Tierra del Fuego in family groups. They were strong runners and tall people, some of them 6 ft tall (in fact, all these hunters and gatherers are thought to have been the tallest of the first South American peoples). They wore guanaco skin robes, fur side out, and also guanaco fur moccasins, 'jamni'. They made open-topped shelters out of guanaco skins, made weather-proof with a coating of mud and saliva, and sometimes painted red. The Ona did not use harpoons or spears and only collected shellfish from beaches at low tide.

The **Yahgans** were nomadic coastal hunters, travelling in canoes up and down the coasts of the Beagle Channel and around the islands southwards to Cape Horn. They caught otters, fish, and seals, using spears and harpoons, and used slings and snares to catch birds. The Yahgans' houses were simple, made of sticks and grass, and they wore little clothing, perhaps a small seal skin and skin moccasins in winter.

Similar to the Yahgans, the **Alacalufes** were also nomadic coastal peoples, roaming from Puerto Edén in the Chilean channels, to Yendegaia, in the Beagle Channel. There was some contact with the Yahgan, with whom they would sometimes exchange goods and intermarry. The Alacalufes had similar lifestyles to the Yahgans, but developed various additions, such as raising a sail on their canoes, and using a bow and arrow in addition to the sling when hunting birds or guanaco.

COLONIAL HISTORY

Throughout the colonial period Chile, lacking important resources of precious minerals, inhabited by the warlike Mapuche and never less than 4 months' journey from Europe, was of relatively little importance to Spain except as a frontier zone. The first Spanish expeditions to Chile were led by Diego de Almagro and Pedro de Valdivia both of whom followed the Inca road from Peru to Salta and then W across the Andes. Almagro's expedition of 1535-7, which included 100 Spaniards and some thousands of Indians, many of whom perished, reached the heartland, but, bitterly disappointed at not finding gold, returned to Peru almost immediately. Valdivia's expedition carried out what initially appeared to be a swift and successful conquest, founding Santiago in Feb 1541 and a series of other settlements in the following years. In the 1550s these Spanish settlements were shaken by a Mapuche rebellion which resulted in the death of Valdivia.

War against the Mapuche was to

occupy the Spanish governors who succeeded Valdivia. Known by the Spanish as Araucanians, the Mapuche were fearsome opponents; they soon mastered the use of horses and were effective guerrilla fighters. In 1598 they began a general offensive which destroyed all of the Spanish settlements S of the Río Biobío, revealing the weakness of a colony whose Spanish population was under 8,000. Pushed back into the northern part of the Central Valley, the Spanish were forced to build a string of forts along the Biobío, guarded by a frontier army of 2,000 men, the only force of its type in Spanish America, financed by a special subsidy from the vice-regal capital of Lima. However, Chile was not important enough to warrant a full scale Spanish assault on the Mapuche and for the rest of the colonial period the Spanish presence S of the river would be limited to the island of Chiloé and to the coastal city of Valdivia.

Situated between the Biobío frontier to the S and the deserts to the N, colonial Chile developed as a compact society; most of its population inhabited the Central Valley, most trade was through Valparaíso. In this small isolated society racial intermixing was common; by the end of the 17th century there were few Indians, most having died, intermixed or escaped S of the Biobío. Most of the population was *mestizo* (mixed race), though the society was dominated by a small white élite.

Chile was governed as part of the Viceroyalty of Peru, with its capital in Lima; until the 18th century all trade with Spain had to pass via Lima and trade with other countries was forbidden. This led to uncontrolled smuggling and by 1715 there were 40 French vessels

Pedro de Valdivia

Although Pedro de Valdivia joined the Spanish army as a young man in 1521, serving in Flanders and Italy, little else is known of his early life. In 1535 he was sent to Venezuela, where he joined an expedition sent to Peru to reinforce Francisco Pizarro. In 1537 he became aide de

camp to Pizarro and sided with him in the war between the latter and Diego de Almagro, receiving an award of land and Indians in return. Shortly after he sold his property to finance an expedition southwards to Chile; setting off in 1540 accompanied by 12 white men, one white woman (Inés de Suárez), 1,000 Indians and a few black slaves. Travelling across the arid Atacama Desert, he reached the Copiapó Valley and then moved S to the Mapocho Valley, where he founded Santiago. Receiving further supplies and reinforcements from Peru, he travelled N again, founding La Serena. After a brief expedition to Peru in 1547 where he helped in the defeat of Gonzalo Pizarro by troops sent from Spain, he returned to Chile in 1549, founding the cities of Concepción, Valdivia and Villarrica, before being killed in battle with the Mapuche at Fort Tucapel.

Although Valdivia's military career was as bloody and brutal as those of most of the *conquistadores*, he is seen by many historians as driven more by the spirit of adventure and the excitement of exploring unknown lands than by the desire to acquire gold and silver which motivated many including the Pizarro brothers with whom he was so closely associated.

Town planning in the 16th century

👣 Perhaps the most obvious influence of Spanish settlement for the traveller is the characteristic street plan of towns and cities. Colonial cities were founded by means of an official ceremony which included the tracing of the central square and the holding of a mass. A series of Royal Ordinances issued in Madrid in 1573 laid down the rules of town planning. The four corners of the main *plaza* were to face the four points of the compass "because thus the streets diverging from the plaza will not be directly exposed to the four principal winds, which would cause much inconvenience." The *plaza* and the main streets were to have arcades which were seen as "a great convenience for those who resort thither for trade." Away from the *plaza* the streets were to be traced out "by means of measuring by cord and ruler" in the now-familiar grid-pattern. Once this was done building lots were to be distributed, those near the *plaza* being allocated by "lottery to those of the settlers who are entitled to build around the main plaza".

The Ordinances specified the principles underlying the distribution of the major public buildings: "In inland towns the church is not to be in the centre of the plaza but at a distance from it in a situation where it can stand by itself, separate from other buildings so that it can be seen from all sides. It can thus be made more beautiful and it will inspire more respect. It should be built on high ground so that in order to reach its entrance people will have to ascend a flight of steps. Nearby the *cabildo* and the customs house are to be erected in order to increase its impressiveness but without instructing it in any way. The hospital of the poor who are ill with non-contagious diseases shall be built facing the N and so planned that it will enjoy a southern exposure."

The Ordinances also advised settlers on how to deal with hostility from the indigenous population: "If the natives should wish to oppose the establishment of a settlement they are to be given to understand that the settlers desire to build a town there not in order to deprive them of their property but for the purpose of being on friendly terms with them; of teaching them to live in a civilized way; of teaching them to know God and His Law ... While the new town is being built the settlers ... shall try to avoid communication and intercourse with the Indians. Nor are the Indians to enter the circuit of the settlement until the latter is complete and in condition for defence and the houses built, so that when the Indians see them they will be filled with wonder and will realize that the Spaniards are settling there permanently and not temporarily."

"Royal Ordinances Governing the Laying Out of New Towns" by Zelia Nuttall, *Hispanic American Historical Review*, May 1922, pages 249-254.

trading illegally along the coast. In 1740 direct trade with Spain was permitted and in 1750 Chile was permitted to mint her own currency.

THE WAR OF INDEPENDENCE

Independence came to Spanish America as a result of Napoleon's invasion of Spain in 1808. As Spanish guerrilla forces fought to drive the French out, the colonial élites debated where their loyalties lay: to Napoleon's brother Joseph, now officially King? to the overthrown king, Ferdinand VII, now in a French prison? to the Spanish resistance parliament in Cadiz?

In 1810 a group of leading Santiago citizens appointed a Junta to govern until Ferdinand returned to the throne. Though they protested loyalty to Ferdinand, their move was seen as a challenge

The Hacienda

During the colonial period the *hacienda*, or landed estate was the most important feature of rural society in the Central Valley. In the 17th century Chilean agriculture expanded to meet demands for wheat, tallow, salted beef and cattle hides from Peru while hides were also sent to Potosí and mules to the great fair in Salta. These exports and the need to feed the frontier army led to the development of large scale agriculture. As the *haciendas* grew, small farmers and tenants were gradually forced to become *inquilinos*, a class of peasants tied to the land. The *inquilino* is regarded as the ancestor of the *huaso*, the Chilean cowboy, a figure seen as resourceful, astute, cunning and typically Chilean.

Although *haciendas* grew in response to food shortages, they were very self-contained; *haciendas* had their own supplies of food and clothing, their own vineyards, forges and workshops. Ownership of a *hacienda* was one of the clearest marks of upper class status although many were the property of religious orders. The *hacienda* remained at the centre of rural life in this area and social relations between landowners and *inquilinos* changed little until the Agrarian Reforms of the 1960s. Although no colonial *haciendas* remain, a few dating from the 19th century can be visited, notably Villa Huilquilemu, near Talca.

by the Viceregal government in Lima, which sent an army to Concepción. War broke out between the Chilean 'Patriots' and these 'Royalist' troops supporting Lima. The defeat of the Patriot army at Rancagua in Oct 1814 led to a restoration of colonial rule, but the turning point came in 1817 with the invasion of Chile from Mendoza by San Martín's Army of the Andes, a force of 4,000 men which defeated the Royalists at Chacabuco (12 February 1817). A Royalist counter-attack was defeated at Maipó, just S of Santiago on 5 May 1818, putting an end to Royalist power in the Central Valley. The victory of the small Patriot navy led by Lord Cochrane (see box, page 118) at Valdivia (Jan 1820) helped clear the Pacific coast of Royalist vessels and paved the way for San Martín to launch his seaborne invasion of Peru.

THE 19TH CENTURY

In most of former Spanish America independence was followed by a period of political turmoil, marked by civil wars and dictatorship, which in some cases lasted until the 1860s. In Chile the overthrow of O'Higgins was followed by a brief period of instability but in 1830 conservative forces led by Diego Portales restored order and introduced the Constitution of 1833, which created a strong government under a powerful president. Portales, a Valparaíso merchant who never became president explained his actions thus: "If one day I took up a stick and gave tranquility to the country it was only so that the bastards and whores of Santiago would let me get on with my work in peace". Chile became famous in Latin America as the great example of political stability: the army was reduced to 3,000 men and kept out of politics; after 1831 four successive presidents served the two successive 5-year terms permitted. However, this stability had its other side: civil liberties were frequently suspended, elections rigged, opponents exiled and power lay in the hands of a small landowning elite. Neither was the stability perfect: there were short civil wars in 1851, 1859 and 1891.

After 1879 Chilean territory was enlarged both northwards and southwards. Victory in the War of the Pacific gave her control over the nitrate-rich expanses of the Atacama desert. Although coloniza-

Bernardo O'Higgins

Born in 1778 in Chillán and brought up as Bernardo Riquelme, O'Higgins was the illegitimate son of Ambrose O'Higgins, an Irishman who rose in the Spanish colonial service to become Governor of Chile and Viceroy of Peru and his Chilean mistress, Isabel Riquelme. At the age of 17 Bernardo was sent to study in London where he met Francisco de Miranda and other South American exiles who were plotting to overthrow Spanish colonial rule. Returning to Chile in 1802 after Ambrose's death, he inherited his father's estate and adopted his surname. After the collapse of Spanish rule, O'Higgins was elected to the first National Congress (1811). When war broke out between the Chilean Patriots and Royalist forces, O'Higgins recruited his own troops, distinguishing himself in a number of battles and being wounded at El Roble in Oct 1813. In 1814 he was appointed Commander-in-Chief of the Patriot armies, but defeat a few months later at the Battle of Rancagua (Oct 1814) forced him to retreat with 2,000 men across the Andes to Mendoza. Here he met José de San Martín who was preparing an army to cross the Andes and free Chile from Spanish control as a first step to invading the Spanish stronghold of Peru. Returning to Chile with San Martín, O'Higgins led a risky and unauthorized cavalry charge at the Battle of Chacabuco (12 February 1817) which assured victory. Four days later an assembly of leading Chilean Patriots appointed O'Higgins to the post of Supreme Director, San Martín, having earlier declined the post so that he could invade Peru.

Facing a renewed threat from a Royalist army moving N from Talcahuano, O'Higgins proclaimed Chilean independence in Feb 1818, but in the following month his troops were defeated near Talca and the Supreme Director himself was badly wounded. A few weeks later, O'Higgins, still wounded, galloped onto the battlefield at Maipó, at the head of reinforcements and embraced San Martín crying "Glory to the Saviour of Chile". San Martín replied "Chile will never forget the name of the illustrious invalid who, today, presented himself on the battle-field." This episode, known as "The Embrace of Maipó", is one of the most famous in Chilean history.

As the head of the first Chilean government, O'Higgins remained personally popular, although many of the actions of his government were not. His government abolished aristocratic titles and he personally sketched the plans for a wide boulevard which was to run along a sheep-track on the outskirts of Santiago and which is now the Avenida Bernardo O'Higgins. Although members of the Creole élite disliked measures such as the prohibition of burial inside churches and the approval of a Protestant cemetery, opposition to his government was also partly the result of family rivalries within the élite. O'Higgins' constitution of 1822, which allowed for him to remain in office for a further 10 years, provoked further opposition. When Gen Ramón Freire launched a rebellion in Concepción, this marked the beginning of the end. O'Higgins was forced to resign on 23 January 1823. Six months later a British warship took him to Peru where he accompanied Simon Bolívar on the final campaign against Spanish forces in what was to become Bolivia. His final years were lived out on his estate in the Cañete valley, S of Lima. His support for a military insurrection in Chile in 1826 led to the Chilean government stripping him of all his honours but these were restored to him in 1842 shortly before his death in Oct of that year. He was buried in Lima and in 1869 his remains were returned to Chile.

The War of the Pacific, 1879-1883

One of the few major international wars in Latin America since independence, this conflict had its roots in a border dispute between Chile and Bolivia, the frontier between the two in the Atacama desert being ill-defined at the time of independence. There had already been one conflict: in 1836-1839, when Chile defeated Peru and Bolivia, putting an end to a confederation of the two states. Relations were complicated by the discovery of nitrates in the Atacama in the 1860s: in the Bolivian Atacama province of Antofagasta nitrates were exploited by Anglo-Chilean companies.

CHILE · TRADICIÓN NAVAL

The *Esmeralda* shown on a 35 peso postage stamp

In 1878 the Bolivian government, short of revenue, attempted to tax the Chilean-owned Antofagasta Railroad and Nitrate Company. When the company refused to pay, the Bolivians seized the company's assets. The Chilean government claimed that the Bolivian action broke an 1874 agreement between the two states. When Peru announced that it would honour a secret alliance with Bolivia by supporting her, the Chilean president, Aníbal Pinto, declared war on both states.

None of the three states was prepared; they lacked skilled officers and adequate weapons. Control of the sea was vital and the few ironclad ships far superior to wooden vessels. The Chileans blockaded the Peruvian nitrate port of Iquique with two wooden ships, the *Esmeralda* and the *Covadonga,* Peru sent her two best ironclads, the *Huáscar* and the *Independencia,* to Iquique; in the Battle of Iquique, 21 May 1879, the *Esmeralda* was sunk; but in the course of the battle the *Independencia* ran aground and was captured, thus altering the balance of forces between the two navies. Later, in Oct 1879 off Angamos near Antofagasta, the two Chilean ironclads, *Blanco Encalada* and *Cochrane,* cornered the *Huáscar* and captured her (the *Huáscar* can be visited in the harbour of Talcahuano).

Rather than attack the Peruvian heartland as they had done in the 1836-1839 war, the Chileans invaded the southern Peruvian province of Tarapacá and then landed troops N of Tacna, seizing the town in May 1880 before capturing Arica, further S. In Jan 1881 fresh Chilean armies seized control of Lima. Despite these defeats and the loss of their capital, Peru did not sue for peace, although Bolivia had already signed a ceasefire, giving up her coastal province. Under the 1883 peace settlement Peru gave up Tapapacá to Chile. Although the provinces of Tacna and Arica were to be occupied by Chile for 10 years, it was not until 1929 that an agreement was reached under which Tacna was returned to Peru, while Chile kept Arica.

Apart from souring relations between Chile and her two northern neighbours to this day, the War gave Chile a monopoly over the world's supply of nitrates and enabled her to dominate the southern Pacific coast. The number of streets and squares named after the heroes of the war, especially Arturo Prat and Aníbal Pinto, and after the vessels *Esmeralda* and *Blanco Encalada* gives an impression of the importance of the War in official Chilean history.

The war of the Pacific 1879-1883 & the expansion of Chile's northern frontier

PERU

Tacna
○ Arica
ARICA

BOLIVIA

○ Pisagua
○ Iquique

TARAPACÁ

N

○ Antofagasta

ARGENTINA

CHILE

○ Copiapó

1a

▨ Peruvian province of Tacna, occupied by Chile 1883-1929, restored to Peru 1929.

▤ Provinces of Arica & Tarapacá, Peruvian until 1883, now part of Chile

▨ Bolivian province of Antofagasta, before 1879, southern portion of which was claimed by Chile.

– · – · Present-day Frontiers.

– – – – Peru-Bolivia Frontier before 1879.

— · — · Original frontier between Chile & Bolivia

tion schemes were begun in the Lake District in the 1850s, it was not until victory over Peru in the War of the Pacific was assured that the much enlarged army was sent to put an end to Mapuche independence and thus secure continuous Chilean control over the Pacific coastline S of Arica.

Since the 1860s conflict between President and Congress had become a constant feature of political life. Although the War of the Pacific brought the Chilean government a new source of income, the tax levied on nitrate exports, it also increased the rivalry for control of this income. When, in 1890 Congress rejected the budget, President Balmaceda announced he would use the 1890 budget for 1891. Congressional leaders denounced this as illegal and fled to Iquique, where they recruited an army which defeated Balmaceda's forces and seized the capital. Balmaceda took refuge in the Argentine embassy where he committed suicide. His defeat was important: between 1891 and 1924 Chilean presidents were weak figures and real power lay in Congress, dominated by the élite.

THE 20TH CENTURY

In the years before WW1 the income from nitrates helped build a large railway network, roads and ports and the best education system on the continent. The collapse of the nitrate industry during WW1 led to worker and student unrest which brought down the constitutional system, the military intervening in 1924. A new constitution restored the strong presidency, but the Great Depression brought further economic stress which resulted in a series of short-lived governments including a military-led 100-day Socialist Republic in 1932.

As economic conditions recovered in the 1930s, Chile became once again a model of political stability. Between 1932 and 1970 Chile developed a complex multiparty system: two left wing parties, the Socialists representing the urban workers and miners; the Conservative and Liberal parties, dating from the 19th century, representing the landowners; the Radicals, a centre party representing the middle classes. The Radicals became the key to power, winning the presidency in 1938, 1942 and 1946. One major group remained excluded from political life: the peasants whose votes, controlled by their landlords, gave the Liberals and Conservatives their representation in Congress and enabled the landlords to block rural reform.

The 1958 election, in which the Socialist **Salvador Allende** narrowly failed to defeat the Conservative Jorge Alessandri, shook the right-wing parties and, in the aftermath of the Cuban Revolution, the United States government. In 1964 the US and the Chilean right-wing threw their weight behind **Eduardo Frei**, a Christian Democrat who promised reforms in a 'revolution in freedom'. Frei's achievements in office were impressive: state ownership of 51% of the copper industry; minimum wage and unionization rights for agricultural workers; the 1967 agrarian reform which began replacing the *haciendas* with family farms. These measures raised hopes it could not satisfy especially in the

Salvador Allende Gossens

Born in 1908 into an upper middle class Valparaíso family, Salvador Allende's childhood ambition was to be a doctor, like his grandfather Ramón Allende Padín, a respected Radical politician who became Serene Grand Master of the Chilean Freemasons. While studying medicine he discovered firsthand the appalling living conditions of the poor and the links between poverty and disease. Even before he qualified as a doctor he became active in politics and was briefly imprisoned during the Ibáñez dictatorship. He was a founder member of the Chilean Socialist party in 1933; at about the same time he became an active freemason.

Elected to Congress for Valparaíso at the age of 29, he served as Minister of Health in Aguirre Cerda's Popular Front government of 1939-1942. Elected to the Senate in 1945, he became Senate president in 1965. Allende was a candidate in four presidential elections. In 1952 he gained only 5.45 of the votes, but in 1958 as candidate of the Front for Popular Action, an alliance between the Socialists and Communists, he lost narrowly to the right-wing candidate, Jorge Alessandri. Easily defeated in 1964 by the Christian Democrat, Eduardo Frei, he finally won the presidency in 1970: in a three cornered race he gained 36% of the vote. Lacking a majority in Congress, heading a broad but divided coalition of 8 parties and facing the hostility of much of the Chilean population and of Washington, Allende had increasingly little room for manoeuvre.

When news of the military revolt came through in the early hours of 11 September 1973, Allende went to the Moneda Palace and spoke twice on the

 radio before communications were cut. Though offered a flight out of the country in return for his resignation Allende refused and the Palace was bombed by three Hawker Hunter jets. Most accounts now accept that Allende committed suicide. He was buried in an unmarked grave in Viña del Mar. In Sept 1990 following the return to civilian rule his body was exhumed and transported to Santiago for a state funeral, thousands of people lining the route from the coast.

countryside where workers now enjoyed rights to push for faster land reform. Hostility from the landowners was reflected in Congress where the National party, formed in 1966 by the merger of the Conservatives and Liberals, denounced the government. The president's party was divided between

General Augusto Pinochet Ugarte

Born in Valparaíso in 1915, the son of a customs officer who traced his ancestry to Breton immigrants, Pinochet entered the Escuela Militar (Military Academy) at the age of 17, graduating near the bottom of his class in 1936. His subsequent career included a posting to the Ecuadorean national military academy from 1956 to 1959. In 1964 he became deputy director of the Escuela Militar; among his publications were a history of the War of the Pacific and a textbook on geopolitics. By 1969 he had risen to the rank of Brigadier General and the following year he became commander of the Santiago garrison, one of the most sensitive and influential postings in the Chilean army. When the Army Commander in Chief, Gen Carlos Prats González, became Minister of the Interior in the Allende government in 1972, Pinochet took over as acting Commander-in-Chief. He took over this post again in Aug 1973 on the resignation of Prats. Although Pinochet was a relatively unknown figure and was apparently a late convert to the coup plot against Allende, his position as head of the Army made him an automatic choice to become President of the military junta which took over. In 1974 he became President of Chile, having increased his hold on power by his control over the regime's secret police, the DINA which was headed by a close colleague, Gral Manuel Contreras. Following his election in 1980 as the only candidate in the first elections held under the new constitution, he began a fresh 8-year term (1981-1989) during which he became the longest ever serving Chilean President. In 1986 he narrowly escaped an assassination attempt, escaping the bomb attack with minor bruises. Following his defeat in the 1988 referendum, he did not stand as a candidate in the Dec 1989 elections and handed over the presidency in Mar 1990.

Despite his advancing years and heart surgery in 1992 Pinochet insisted on remaining Commander-in-Chief of the Army until Mar 1998 as specified in the 1980 Constitution. He made it clear that he would oppose any moves to bring members of the armed forces to trial for human rights abuses committed during the dictatorship. In Dec 1990 questions in Congress and in the press about financial scandals involving army officers and his own son-in-law, led him to order all troops to report to barracks. In May 1993 he surrounded the Ministry of Defence with soldiers and ordered generals to wear battle dress to work for a day and in Sept 1996 he suggested that the armed forces should be prepared to carry out another coup if ever that became necessary. With his stern features enhanced by dark glasses Pinochet became the stereotype of the 1970s South American dictator. Often seen as a bluff no-nonsense character, he is also noted for his astuteness, his suspicious mind, his ruthlessness and his hatred of democracy and political parties. Furious after his defeat in the 1988 referendum, Pinochet observed that another plebiscite long ago had elected Barrabas. Although Pinochet himself said in 1981 'not a leaf stirs in Chile without me moving it', it would be wrong to see his dominance as merely the result of repression and fear. To many Chileans who had hated Allende and feared his policies, Pinochet became a popular figure, the human rights abuses and destruction of democracy seen as a price worth paying.

supporters and opponents of reform.

The 1970 election was narrowly won by Salvador Allende, heading a left wing alliance called Unidad Popular. Allende's government launched an ambitious programme of reforms: banking, insurance, communications, textiles and other industries were taken over in the first year and the nationalization of copper was completed. After that the government ran into major problems: the nationalizations had depleted Chile's currency reserves; hostility by domestic business groups and the United States led to capital flight and a US led boycott on international credit; an alliance between the Christian Democrat and National parties in Congress impeached several ministers; a series of anti-government strikes by truck drivers and professional groups brought the country to halt in Oct 1972 and again in Aug 1973; annual inflation rose to over 300% in 1973.

The coup of 11 September 1973, led by **Gen Augusto Pinochet** was widely expected, the armed forces having received open encouragement from Allende's opponents in Congress and outside, but the brutality shocked many accustomed to Chile's peaceful traditions. Left-wing activists (and innocent people mistakenly identified) were arrested; thousands were executed; torture was widespread; at least 7,000 people were held in the national football stadium; by 1978 there were 30,000 Chilean exiles in Western Europe alone. With political parties and labour unions banned, the government adopted free market economic policies under the influence of Milton Friedman and the 'Chicago Boys'.

Under a new constitution, adopted in 1980, Chile became a 'protected democracy' based on the exclusion of political parties and the 'guardianship' of the armed forces who would put forward a single candidate for an 8-year presidential term in 1981. To no one's surprise the candidate was Pinochet, but his bid for a further 8-year term in a plebiscite in 1988 was unsuccessful.

As a result, presidential and congressional elections were held in 1989. A Christian Democrat, **Patricio Aylwin Azócar**, the candidate of the Coalition of Parties for Democracy (CPD, or Concertación), was elected President and took office in Mar 1990 in a peaceful transfer of power. Gen Pinochet remained as Army Commander although other armed forces chiefs were replaced. The new Congress set about revising many of the military's laws on civil liberties and the economy. In 1991 the National Commission for Truth and Reconciliation published a report with details of those who were killed under the military regime, but opposition by the armed forces prevented mass human rights trials.

The presidential and congressional elections of Dec 1993 produced few surprises. The candidate of the governing

1993 Presidential Election

Eduardo Frei	Concertación	58.01%
Arturo Alessandri	Unión por el Progreso	24.39%
José Piñera	Independent	6.18%
Others		11.41%

Congressional Election

	Chamber of Deputies	Senate
Concertación	70	21
Unión por el Progreso	46	14
Independent	4	3
Non Elected		8

Chilean Political Parties

Since 1990 the dominant party in Chile has been the Christian Democrats. A centre party which grew rapidly after its foundation in 1957, the Christian Democrats welcomed the overthrow of Allende, but later became the focus of opposition to the dictatorship. Not strong enough on their own, since 1990 they have contested elections in an alliance known as the Concertación. The other members are the Socialists, a centre-left party traditionally split between different factions, the Radicals and the Partido Por La Democracia, a new centre-left grouping led by ex-socialists. The main opposition to the Concertación has come from the right wing, which is divided into two main parties: Renovación Nacional and the Unión Democrática Independiente: for the 1993 elections they formed an alliance called the Unión por el Progreso. The Chilean Communist Party, which in the 1960s was the largest communist party in Latin America, lost support during the Pinochet years and is now of little importance.

Concertación coalition, the Christian Democrat **Eduardo Frei**, son of the earlier president, was widely expected to win the presidency. More interest focussed on the congressional elections held at the same time: the Concertación failed to achieve the required two-thirds majority in Congress to reform the constitution, replace heads of the armed forces and end the system of non-elected senators.

In Aug 1995, Frei presented bills to make the necessary constitutional reforms to these non-elected powers. He also proposed that investigations continue into the disappearance of some 500 political prisoners in the 1970s. On both issues the military and their political allies appeared to have sufficient support to prevent government success, contrary to public opinion and despite some opposition members favouring reform. In municipal elections in Oct 1996, the Concertación candidates gained 56% of the vote nationwide while the Unión por el Progreso candidates won 33%. Although the status quo was maintained, variations in voting patterns were seen as indicators as to the outcome of the 1997 congressional elections.

People

There is less racial diversity in Chile than in most Latin American countries. Over 90% of the population is *mestizo*. There has been much less immigration than in Argentina and Brazil. The German, French, Italian and Swiss immigrants came mostly after 1846 as small farmers in the forest zone S of the Biobío. Between 1880 and 1900 gold-seeking Serbs and Croats settled in the far S, and the British took up sheep farming and commerce in the same region. The influence throughout Chile of the immigrants is out of proportion to their numbers: their signature on the land is seen, for instance, in the German appearance of Valdivia, Puerto Montt, Puerto Varas, Frutillar and Osorno.

There is disagreement over the number of indigenous people in Chile. The **Mapuche** nation (also called Mapudungun), 95% of whom live in the forest land around Temuco, between the Biobío and Toltén rivers, is put at 1 million by Survival International, but much less by other, including official, statistics (for further details see under Temuco). There are also 15,000-20,000 **Aymara** in the northern Chilean Andes and 2,000 **Rapa Nui** on Easter Island. A political party, the Party for Land and Identity, unites many Indian groupings, and legislation is proposed to restore indigenous people's rights.

The population is far from evenly distributed: Middle Chile (from Copiapó to Concepción), 18% of the country's area, contains 77% of the total population. The Metropolitan Region of Santiago contains, on its own, about 39% of the whole population. Population density in 1992 ranged from 334 per sq km in the Metropolitan Region to 0.8 per square km in Región XI (Aisén).

The rate of population growth per annum is similar to those of Argentina and Uruguay, but lower than most of the rest of Latin America. The cities have higher birth and death rates than the rural areas but infant mortality is higher in the rural areas.

Since the 1960s heavy migration from the land has led to rapid urbanization. By 1992 83.5% of the population lived in urban areas; the most urbanized regions were the Metropolitan Region (96.5% urban) and Región V (90.2% urban). Housing in the cities has not kept pace with this increased population; many Chileans live in slum areas called *callampas* (mushrooms) especially on the outskirts of Santiago.

RELIGION

According to the 1992 Census the population is 76.7% Catholic and 13.2% Protestant. Membership of Evangelical Protestant churches has grown rapidly in recent years, from 6% in the 1970 Census, especially in the Santiago and in Región XI where 22% of the population were members of Protestant Churches in 1992. The largest of these churches is the Pentecostal Methodist Church.

EDUCATION

Chilean literacy rates are lower than those of most other South American states. Census returns in 1992 indicated that among the over-25 age population 8% had completed higher education, 42% had completed secondary education, and 44% had only completed primary education. Higher education provision doubled in the 1980s through the creation of private universities.

Culture

ARTS AND CRAFTS

Chile's traditional crafts are in the main specific to particular places and all have a long history. Present-day handicrafts represent either the transformation of utilitarian objects into works of art, or the continued manufacture of pieces which retain symbolic value. A number of factors threaten these traditions: the loss of types of wood and plant fibres through the destruction of forests; the mechanization of farm labour, reducing the use of the horse; other agricultural changes which have, among other things, led to reductions in sheep farming and wheat growing; migration from the countryside to the city. On the other hand, city dwellers and tourists have created a demand for traditional crafts so their future is to some degree assured.

The Mapuche

From the Mapuche heartland, S of the Río Biobío, comes silverware. Traditional women's jewellery includes earrings, headbands, necklaces, brooches and *tupus* (pins for fastening the *manta*, or shawl). Each item has a Mapuche name (eg *chawai* for earrings). Nowadays, the most common item to be found for sale is earrings, but smaller and in simpler shapes than those worn by Mapuche women. It is a matter of debate whether Mapuche silversmiths had perfected their skills before the arrival of the Spaniards, but the circulation of silver coins in the 18th century gave great impetus to this form of metalwork. (The Universidad Católica in Temuco is in charge of a

project to ensure the continuance of the art.)

The Mapuche are also weavers of sheep's wool, making ponchos, *mantas*, sashes (*fajas*), reversible rugs (*lamas*) with geometric designs, and bedspreads (*pontros*). The colours come from natural dyes. The main producing areas are around Lago Lanalhue, Chol Chol, Nueva Imperial and others (see pages 228 and 239).

Mapuche basketry is made for domestic, agricultural and fishing uses (Lago Lanalhue and the Cautín region). They also make musical instruments: the *trutruca*, a horn 1.5-4m long, *pifilca* (or *pifüllka*), a wooden whistle, the *kultrún* drum, *cascahuilla*, a string of bells, and *trompe*, similar to a Jew's harp. Another craft from this region is the carving of horn or antler (*asta*) in Temuco, to make animals, birds, cups, spoons, etc.

Chiloé

The island is famous for its woollen goods, hand-knitted and coloured with natural dyes. Clothing (such as sweaters, knitted caps, *mantas*, socks), rugs, blankets and patch dolls are sold locally and in Puerto Montt. The main knitting centres are Quinchao, Chonchi and Quellón. Other crafts of Chiloé are model boat building, and basketware from Quinchao and Quellón, not only baskets, but also mats and figurines such as birds and fish (see Section 9).

Cowboy equipment and clothing

Items can be found in any part of the country where there are *huasos*: San Fernando, Chillán, Curicó, Colchagua, Doñihue and also in Santiago. Saddles of leather, wood and iron, wooden stirrups, leather reins, spurs, and hats of straw or other materials is the types of equipment you will see. The clothing comprises ponchos (long, simple in colour and design, used to keep out the rain and wind), *mantas* (shorter, divided into four with a great variety of colour), *chamantos* (luxurious *mantas*, double-sided, deco-

clay figurines and model buildings of Pilén de Cauquenes-Maule (Región VII) and the scented pottery of the nuns of the Comunidad de Santa Clara (Convento de Monjas Claras in Santiago and Los Angeles). These highly-decorated pieces have been made since colonial times, when they achieved great fame.

Basketry

Apart from the areas already mentioned, centres of basket making are Ninhue-Hualte in Ñuble (Región VIII), Hualqui, 24 km S of Concepción, and San Juan de la Costa (from the coast of Osorno, Región X).

Wood

The people of the Atacama region edge trays and make little churches out of cactus wood; they also use cactus for drums and bamboo for flutes of various sizes. Different types of wood are used in the construction of guitars, *guitarrones*, harps and *rabeles* (fiddles), mainly in the Metropolitan Region. Villarrica (see page 245) is a major producer of wooden items: plates, kitchen utensils, but especially decorative objects like animals and birds, jointed snakes and *picarones* (small figures which, when picked up, reveal their genitals). Another craft in wood is the ship in a bottle, made in Coronel (see page 226).

Rari

This village, near the Termas de Panimávida, some 25 km NE of Linares (Región VII), specializes in beautiful, delicate items made from dyed horsehair: bangles and brooches in the shape of butterflies, little hats, flowers, etc.

Lapis lazuli

Mined in the Cordillera de Ovalle, this blue stone (only found otherwise in Afghanistan) is set in silver to make earrings, necklaces and bracelets. Many shops in Santiago (see **Shopping**, page 97) sell the gemstone and objects that incorporate it.

Wooden stirrup

rated with fine patterns of vines, leaves, flowers, small birds, etc) and sashes/*fajas* (either single or tri-coloured, made to combine with *mantas* or *chamantos*).

Other textile-producing areas

Isluga (see page 189): both men and women weave sheep or camelid wool, but each sex makes different items. Men and women also weave in the villages in the vicinity of the Salar de Atacama (eg Tulor, see page 172), not only items of clothing, bags, etc, but also wall-hangings. In the Elqui Valley (see page 142) is Chapilca, which specializes in vegetable-dyed woollen *mantas*, rugs, covers, etc. Another centre for weaving is Quinamávida (see page 213) where natural colours in browns and ochres are used for blankets, rugs and *mantas*.

Ceramics

The two most famous places for ceramics are 1) Quinchamalí (see page 216) near Chillán, where the traditional black ware is incised with patterns in white. Among the unique designs of object are three-legged pigs and turkeys, musical instruments (including as handles on pots), horsemen and the popular *guitarrera* (a woman playing the guitar). 2) Pomaire (see page 105), W of Santiago, is renowned for its terracotta household items which are used in most Chilean homes. Less well-known is the pottery of the Atacama zone, the clay figures of Lihueimo (Región VI), the household items,

Ceramic horse and rider from Quinchamalí
Luis Guzmán Molina "Visión estética
de la cerámica de Quinchamalí",
Atenea, No 458, 1988.

● **Sources** for this section are: *Artesanía tradicional de Chile*, Serie El Patrimonio Cultural Chileno, Ministerio de Educación, 1978; 'Visión estética de la cerámica de Quinchamalí', by Luis Guzmán Molina, *Atenea*, No 458 (Universidad de Concepción, 1988), pages 47-60; *Mapudungun, lengua y costumbres Mapuches*, by Orietta Appelt Martín (Temuco: Magin, 1995); *Arts and Crafts of South America*, by Lucy Davies and Mo Fini (Bath: Tumi, 1994). *Tumi*,the Latin American Craft Centre, specializes in Mexican and Andean products and produces cultural and educational videos for schools: at 23/2A Chalk Farm Road, London NW1 8AG (F 0171-485 4152), 8/9 New Bond Street Place, Bath BA1 1BH (T 01225 462367, F 01225 444870), 1/2 Little Clarendon St, Oxford OX1 2HJ (T/F 01865-512307), 82 Park St, Bristol BS1 5LA (T/F 0117 929 0391). Tumi (Music) Ltd specializes in different rhythms of Latin America.

LITERATURE

From colonial times to independence

The long struggle of the Spaniards to conquer the lands S of their Peruvian stronghold inspired one of the great epics of early Spanish American literature, *La Araucana* by **Alonso de Ercilla y Zúñiga** (1533-1594). Published in three parts (1569, 1578 and 1589), the poem tells of the victories and defeats of the Spaniards (for example Pedro de Valdivia) and the Araucanian Indians during Spain's efforts to push the empire's boundaries southwards. Like a subsequent work, *Arauco domado* (1596), by the criollo Pedro de Oña (1570-1643), the point of view is that of the conquering invader, not a celebration of Chilean, or American identity, although Ercilla does show that the people who resisted the Spaniards were noble and courageous. After Ercilla, literature written in what was to become Chile concentrated on chronicling either the physical or the spiritual conquest of the local inhabitants, which at times incorporated descriptions of the environment and the customs of the region, the first recognition of an identity different from imperial Spain.

Writing in the 18th and early 19th centuries tended to mirror the colonial desire to consolidate the territory which was in Spanish, rather than Mapuche hands. Post-independence, the move was towards the establishment of the new republic. To this end, the Venezuelan **Andrés Bello** (1781-1865) was invited to Santiago from London in 1829 to oversee the education of the new élite. Already famous for his literary journals and strong views on Romantic poetry, Bello made major contributions to Chilean scholarship and law. His main work was *Gramática de la lengua castellana destinada al uso de los americanos* (1847). As Jean Franco says (see bibliographical note at the end of this section), "He was one of the first of many writers to see that a general literary Spanish could act as an important cohesive factor, a spiritual tie of the Hispanic peoples" (page 30).

A cultural haven

Chile's relative political stability in the 19th century helped Santiago to become a cultural centre which attracted many foreign intellectuals (eg the Argentine Diego Sarmiento and the Nicaraguan Rubén Darío). At this time, Chilean writers were establishing a national literary framework to replace the texts of the colonial era. This involved the spreading of 'buenas costumbres', a republican education for the middle classes and the founding of a national identity. Realist fiction captured the public interest. **José Victorino Lastarria** (1817-1888) wrote *costumbrista* stories, portraying national scenes and characters. **Alberto Blest Gana** (1829-1904) enjoyed two periods of success as a novelist, heavily influenced by Balzac. His most popular novel was *Martín Rivas* (1862), the love story of a young man who wins a wife of a higher class. For some, Blest Gana's presentation of Santiago and its class structure is a worthy imitator of the French *comédie humaine*; for others his realism fails either to unite his themes to his sketches of Chilean life, or to rise above a pedestrian style.

20th century prose writing

Well into the 20th century, realism was the dominant mode of fiction, but in several guises. **Baldomero Lillo** (1867-1923) wrote socialist realist stories about the coal miners of Lebu: *Sub terra* (1904) and *Sub sole* (1907). Lillo and other regionalist writers shifted the emphasis away from the city to the countryside and the miserable conditions endured by many Chileans. Other novelists concentrated on the crisis of aristocratic values and the gulf between the wealthy and the deprived: eg **Luis Orrego Luco** (1866-1948), and **Joaquín Edwards Bello** (born 1887).

Another strand was *criollismo*, championed especially by short story writers like **Mariano Latorre** (1886-1955), whose main interest was the Chilean landscape which he described almost to the point of overwhelming his characters. A different emphasis was given to regionalism and *criollismo* by **Augusto d'Halmar** (Augusto Goeminne Thomson, 1882-1950), whose stories in *La lámpara en el molino* (1914) were given exotic settings and were labelled *imaginismo*. D'Halmar's followers, the Grupo Letras

(1920s and 1930s), became openly antagonistic towards the disciples of Latorre, eg **Luis Durand** whose books of the 1920s-40s described in detail *campesino* life. Another branch of realism was the exploration of character through psychology in the books of **Eduardo Barrios** (1884-1963), eg *El niño que enloqueció de amor* (1915), *El hermano asno* (1922) and *Los hombres del hombre* (1950).

The decline of *criollismo*

The anti-fascist views of a group of writers known as the Generation of 1938 (eg Nicomedes Guzmán, 1914-65, Juan Godoy, Carlos Droguett, born 1915, and others) added a politically-committed dimension with support for the working class which coincided with the rise to power of the Frente Popular. At the same time, *Mandrágora*, a journal principally dedicated to poetry, introduced many European literary ideas, notably those of the surrealists. Its influence, combined with a global decline in Marxist writing after WW2 and the defeat of the Frente Popular, contributed to a new generation in the 1950s whose main drive was the rejection of all the *ismos* that had preceded it. The novelists, short-story writers and dramatists were characterized by existential individualism and political and social scepticism. Many writers started publishing in the 1950s, among them **Volodia Teitelboim** (born 1916), a communist exiled to the USSR after 1973, whose novels *Hijo del salitre* (1952) and *La semilla en la arena* (1957) were portrayals of the struggles of the Chilean masses (in 1979 he published *La guerra interna* a mixture of real and imaginary characters in post-coup Chile). Others of the Generation of 1950 were Enrique Lafourcade (born 1927), Claudio Giaconi (born 1927) and José María Vergara (born 1929).

Manuel Rojas (1896-1972) was brought up in Argentina, but his family moved to Chile in 1923. His first short stories, such as *Hombres del sur* (1926),

Travesía (1934) and the novel *Lanchas en la bahía* (1932) were undoubtedly *criollista* in outlook, but he devoted a greater importance to human concerns than his *criollista* contemporaries. By 1951, Rojas' style had changed dramatically, without deserting realism. *Hijo de ladrón* (1951) was perhaps the most influential 20th-century Chilean novel up to that time. It describes the adventures of Aniceto Hevía, the son of a Buenos Aires jewel thief, who crosses the Andes to Valparaíso, ending up, after continually moving on, as a beachcomber. Nothing in his life is planned, or motivated by anything other than the basic necessities. Happiness and intimacy are only brief moments in an unharmonious, disordered life. Aniceto's adventures are continued in *Mejor que el vino* (1958), *Sombras contra el muro* (1963) and *La obscura vida radiante* (1971). To describe the essential isolation of man from the inside, Rojas relaxes the temporal structure of the novel, bringing in memory, interior monologue and techniques to multiply the levels of reality (to use Fernando Alegría's phrase).

The demise of *criollismo* (put by some at 1959) coincided with the influence of the US Beat Generation and the culture epitomized by James Dean, followed in the 1960s by the protest movements in favour of peace, blacks' and women's rights. The Cuban Revolution inspired Latin American intellectuals of the left and the novel-writing 'boom' gained momentum. At the same time, the national political process which led ultimately to Salvador Allende's victory in 1973 was bolstered by writers, folk singers and painters who questioned everything to do with the Chilean bourgeoisie.

To the 1973 coup and beyond

José Donoso (1924-1996) began publishing stories in 1955 (*Veraneo y otros cuentos*), followed 2 years later by his first novel, *Coronación*. The book describes the chaos caused by the arrival of a new maid into an aristocratic Santiago household and introduces many of Donoso's recurring themes: the closed worlds of old age and childhood, madness, multiple levels of reality, the inauthenticity of the upper classes and the subversion of patriarchal society. The stories in *Charleston* (1960), *El lugar sin límites* (1966), about a transvestite and his daughter who live in a brothel near Talca, and *Este domingo* (1966) mark the progression from *Coronación* to *El obsceno pájaro de la noche* (1970), a labyrinthine novel (Donoso's own term) narrated by a schizophrenic, throwing together reality, dreams and fantasy, darkness and light. Donoso achieved the same status as García Márquez, Cortázar and Vargas Llosa with this, his most experimental novel. Between 1967 and 1981 he lived in Spain; in the 1970s he published several novels, including *Casa de campo* (1978), which relates the disintegration of a family estate when the children try to take it over. Back in Chile, he published, among others, *El jardín de al lado* (1981), which chronicles the decline of a middle-aged couple in exile in Spain, *Cuatro para Delfina* (1982), *La desesperanza* (1986) about the return of a left-wing singer from Paris to the daily horrors of Pinochet's regime, and was working on *El mocho* (about coal miners) at his death.

Another writer who describes the bad faith of the aristocracy is **Jorge Edwards** (born 1931). His books include *El patio* (1952), *Los convidados de piedra* (1978), *El museo de cera* (1980), *La mujer imaginaria* (1985) and *Fantasmas de carne y hueso* (1993). His book *Persona non grata* (1973) describes his experiences as a diplomat, including his expulsion from Cuba. **Fernando Alegría** (born 1918) spans all the movements since 1938. His work includes essays, highly respected literary criticism, poetry and novels. He was closely associated with Salvador Allende and was his cultural attaché in Washington in 1970-73. *Recabarren* was published in 1938, after which followed many books, among them *Lautaro, joven libertador del Arauco* (1943), *Caballo de copas* (1957), *Mañana los guerreros* (1964), *El paso de los gansos* (1975), about a young photographer's experiences in the 1973 coup, *Coral de guerra* (1979), also about brutality under military dictatorship, *Una especie de memoria* (1983), Alegría's own memoir of 1938 to 1973, and *Allende: A Novel* (1992). Having been so close to Allende, Alegría could not write a biography, he had to fictionalize it, he said. But the rise and fall of Allende becomes a realization that history and fiction are intimately related, particularly in that Chilean epoch.

The death of Salvador Allende in 1973 and with it the collapse of the left's struggle to gain power by democratic means was a traumatic event for Chilean writers. Those who had built their careers in the 1960s/early 1970s were for the most part exiled (forcibly or voluntarily) and thus were condemned to face the left's own responsibility in Allende's failure. René Jara (see bibliography below, page 58) says that before 1970 writers had not managed to achieve mass communication for their ideas and 1970-73 was too short a time to correct that. Once Pinochet was in power, the task became how to find a language capable of expressing the usurping of democracy without simplifying reality. Those in exile still felt part of Chile, a country temporarily wiped from the map, where their thought was prohibited. Jara is here quoting **Ariel Dorfman** (born 1942), who is most famous for his play *Death and the Maiden* (*La muerte y la doncella* – filmed by Roman Polanski). In an afterword to the English edition, Dorfman says "What we feel when we watch and whisper and ache with these faraway people from faraway Chile could well be that strange trembling state of humanity we call recognition, a bridge across our divided globe." (London, 1990, page 61; new edition, Nick Hern, 1996). Among Dorfman's many

other works are *Muerte en la costa* (1973), *Cría ojos* (1979), *Viudas* (1981) and *La última canción de Manuel Sendero* (1982).

There are many other contemporary male novelists who deserve mention, but this survey will confine itself to **Antonio Skármeta** (born 1940), another exile, in Germany, until 1980, who writes short stories, novels and directs in the theatre and cinema. His short story collections include *El entusiasmo* (1967), *Desnudo en el tejado* (1969), *Tiro libre* (1973) and his novels *Soñé que la nieve ardía* (1975), *No pasó nada* (1980), *Ardiente paciencia* (1985) and *Match-ball* (1989). *Ardiente paciencia*, retitled *El cartero de Neruda* after its successful filming as *Il postino*, is a good example of Skármeta's concern for the enthusiasms and emotions of ordinary people, skillfully weaving the love life of a postman and a bar owner's daughter into the much bigger picture of the death of Pablo Neruda and the fall of Allende.

Women novelists

La casa de los espíritus (1982) by **Isabel Allende** (born 1942) was a phenomenally successful novel worldwide. Allende, a relative of Salvador Allende, was born in Peru and went into exile in Venezuela after the 1973 coup. *The House of the Spirits*, with its tale of the dynasty of Esteban Trueba, which ends with a thinly disguised description of 1973, was followed in 1984 by *De amor y de sombra*, set during the Pinochet regime. The main motivation behind these novels is the necessity to preserve historical reality (see the brief prologue to *Of Love and Shadows*, "Here, write it, or it will be erased by the wind"). The same thing applies in *Paula* (1994), Allende's letter to her daughter in a coma: a possible salvation from the devastation of not being able to contact Paula is through the 'meticulous exercise of writing'. She has also written *Eva Luna* (1987) and *Los cuentos de Eva Luna* (1990), about a fictional Venezuelan storyteller and her stories themselves, and *El plan infinito* (1991).

Isabel Allende is a major voice in Chilean (and Latin American) literature, but she is by no means the first. From the 1920s on, a significant development away from *criollismo* was the rise of the female voice. The first such novelist to achieve major recognition was **Marta Brunet** (1901-67), who brought a unique perspective to the rural themes she handled (including the need to value women), but who has also been described as a writer of the senses (by Nicomedes Guzmán). Her books include *Montaña adentro* (1923), *Aguas abajo* (1943), *Humo hacia el sur* (1946) and *María Nadie* (1957). Also born in 1901, **María Flora Yáñez** wrote about the alienation of women, too, with great emphasis on the imagination as an escape for her female protagonists from their routine, unfulfilled lives (*El abrazo de la tierra*, 1934; *Espejo sin imágen*, 1936; *Las cenizas*, 1942). **María Luisa Bombal** (1910-80) took the theme of alienated women even further (*La última niebla*, 1935; *La amortajada*, 1938, and various short stories): her narrative and her characters' worlds spring from the subconscious realm of female experience and are expressed through dreams, fantasies and journeys loaded with symbolic meaning.

Like her predecessors, Allende employs the marvellous and the imaginary to propose alternatives to the masculine view of social and sexual relations. The same is true of **Lucía Guerra** (born 1942), who published *Más allá de las máscaras* in exile in 1984. Another element in Chilean women's writing (again noted by Jara, page 236) is the flight from domestic space and the discovery of the body as a centre of experience. **Damiela Eltit** (born 1949, novelist, performance and video artist), did not leave Chile after 1973 and was actively involved in resistance movements. Her provocative, intense fiction confronts issues of exploitation, violence, the oppression of

women and volatile mental states. In *Vaca sagrada* (1991) at least, the protagonist's body becomes the expression of her vulnerability, through her blood, her two lovers' effects upon it, the brutality inflicted upon it and her obsession with her heartbeat. The main characters live out their obsessions and fears in a city in which there are no jobs, no warmth. They wander from one end of it to another in a kind of perversion of the hallucinatory wanderings of María Luisa Bombal's unnamed heroine in *La última niebla*. But whereas the latter is drawn along by her dream of her lover, Eltit's heroine, alone, in the dark and the traffic, is followed by an unknown man. "There are no words for the terror I felt, and images were unleashed of death and blindness" (translated by Amanda Hopkinson, *Sacred Cow*, London: Serpent's Tail, 1995, page 69). Three earlier novels, *Lumpérica* (1983), *Por la patria* (1986) and *El cuarto mundo* (1988) maintain the same experimental, challenging approach to contemporary Chilean society.

20th century poetry

In the first half of the 20th century, four figures dominated Chilean poetry, Gabriela Mistral, Vicente Huidobro, Pablo Neruda and Pablo de Rokha. The three men were all socialists, but in their politics and the expression of their views, each followed a different trajectory. Neruda overshadows all other Chilean poets on an international level (and for this reason he is discussed in the accompanying box), but this should not hide the fact that Chile has had a very strong poetic tradition.

Gabriela Mistral (Lucila Godoy Alcayaga, 1889-1957; Nobel Prize 1945) wrote a poetry which rejected elaboration in favour of a simple style with traditional metre and verse forms. Her poetry derives from a limited number of personal roots: she fell in love with Romelio Ureta who, for a variety of reasons, blew his brains out in 1909. This inspired the *Sonetos de la muerte* (1914), which were not published at the time. She never lost the grief of this tragic love, which was coupled with her love of God and her 'immense martyrdom at not being a mother'. Frustrated motherhood did not deprive her of tenderness, nor of a deep love for children. The other main theme was her appreciation of nature and landscape, not just Chile, but also other parts of the world which she visited when her teaching career led to her representing Chile in North and South America and Europe. Her three principal collections are *Desolación* (1923, but re-edited and amplified frequently), *Tala* (1938) and *Lagar* (1954). She also wrote many poems for children.

If Gabriela Mistral relied on the traditions and her verse alone to present her unique view of a lone woman trying to find a place in a male-oriented world, **Vicente Huidobro** (1893-1948) wanted to break with all certainties and he made grand claims for the poet's role in this. His was nothing short of a quest for the infinite and for the language to liberate it (see David Guss' introduction to *The Selected Poetry of Vicente Huidobro*, New York: New Directions, 1981). From Santiago he moved to Buenos Aires, then Paris, where he joined the Cubists, collaborated with Apollinaire and others, began to write in French and got involved in radical politics. Between the 1920s and 1940s he moved from Europe to the USA to Chile, back to Spain during the Civil War, before retiring to Llolleo to confront time and death in his last poems, *Ultimos poemas*, 1948. Huidobro considered himself at the forefront of the avant-garde, formulating *creacionismo*, which basically says that the poet is not bound by the real world, but is free to create and invent new worlds through the complete freedom of the word (see *Manifestes*, 1925). Nevertheless, all the experimentation and imagery which 'unglued the moon' (*Tout à coup*, 1925, No 10), was insufficient to achieve the language of revelation. So in 1931 he composed *Alta-*

zor, a seven-canto poem which describes simultaneously the poet's route to creation and the ultimate frustration imposed by time and the human condition.

Pablo de Rokha (Carlos Díaz Loyola, 1894-1968) was deeply concerned for the destiny of the Chilean people and the advance of international socialism. His output was an uncompromising, epic search for Chilean identity and through it, for all its political commitment, there runs a deep sense of tragedy and inner solitude (especially true in *Fuego negro*, 1951, written after the death of his wife). *Los gemidos* was his first major book (1922); others included *Escritura de Raimundo Contreras* (1929), a song of the Chilean peasant, *Jesucristo* (1933) and *La morfología del espanto* (1942).

These poets, and Neruda especially, furthered the Chilean poetic tradition, but those who came after Neruda in the 1950s were not necessarily keen to emulate his style or his politics. The new generation of poets was still critical of society but, taking their cue from Nicanor Parra, they did not elevate the writer's role in denouncing inhumanity, alienation and the depersonalization of modern life. Instead writer and reader are placed on the same level; rhetoric and exuberant language are replaced by a conversational, ironic tone. **Parra** (born 1914; see box on Violeta Parra and the Parra Family of Chillán, page 218), a scientist and teacher, called this attempt to overcome the influence of Neruda *antipoesía* (antipoetry). In the poem 'Advertencia al lector' in *Poemas y antipoemas* (1954), he writes:

"According to the doctors of the law this book should not be published:
The word rainbow does not appear in it,
Let alone the word grief,
·Chairs and tables, yes, there are aplenty,
Coffins! Writing utensils!
Which fills me with pride
Because, as I see it, the sky is falling to bits."

Pablo Neruda

Pablo Neruda was born in Parral, central Chile, on 12 June 1904. His real name was Ricardo Neftalí Reyes. Two months after his birth his mother died. His father and stepmother soon moved to Temuco and Neruda's childhood memories were dominated by nature and, above all, rain, "my only unforgettable companion", as he described it in *Confieso que he vivido*. Among his teachers in Temuco was Gabriela Mistral. In 1921 he went to study in Santiago, but already he had decided on a literary career. His first book of poems, *Crepusculario* (1923), was published under the pseudonym Neruda, borrowed from a Czech writer; it was postmodernist in style but did not yet reveal the poet's own voice. His next volume, *Veinte poemas de amor y una canción desesperada* (1924) catapulted him into the forefront of Latin American poetry. The freedom of the style and the natural, elemental imagery invoking the poet's two love affairs, with a girl from Temuco and another from the capital, made the collection an immediate success. Three books followed in 1926 before Neruda was sent to Rangoon as Chilean consul in 1927. His experiences in the Orient, including his first marriage, did not alleviate an intense period of solitude and anguish. This inspired one of his finest collections, *Residencia en la tierra* (covering the years 1925-35). The inherent sadness of the *Veinte poemas* becomes despair at the passage of time and human frailty. Reinforcing this overriding theme is a kaleidoscope of images, all seemingly jumbled together and yet deliberately placed to show the chaos and fragmentary nature of man's passage towards death (see particularly "Arte poética").

In the 1930s, Neruda moved to Spain, where he edited the review *Caballo verde para la poesía* and kept company with many poets. The Civil War, especially the death of Federico García Lorca, affected him deeply and his poetic vision changed radically, away from the subjectivity of his earlier work to a more direct poetry, with a strong political orientation. See "Explico algunas cosas" in *Tercera residencia* (1947, which included *España en mi corazón* of 1938), which explains the move towards militancy.

Between 1938 and the election of Gabriel González Videla to the Chilean presidency he worked with the Frente Popular, was consul general in Mexico and maintained his membership of the Communist Party. He also composed at this time his epic poem of Latin American and Chilean history, from a Marxist stance, *Canto general* (1950). It contains 15 cantos, chronicling the natural and human life of the Americas, the oppression of its peoples, from the conquered precolumbian inhabitants to the 20th century labourers. It celebrates Chile and its *campesinos*, its anonymous workers in the copper, coal and salt mines and ends with his own testament, "Yo soy". One of its most famous sections is "Alturas de Machu Picchu" which mirrors the tone of the whole and his own poetic development: from the universal to the "miniscule life", from his own introspection to his new-found role as the voice of the oppressed. Everything now revolves not around futility, but hope and struggle.

Canto general defined Neruda's subsequent enormous output. The political commitment remained, but did not submerge his respect for, and evocation of nature: eg *Odas elementales* (1954), *Nuevas odas elementales* (1957) and *Tercer libro de odas* (1959), which begins with "El hombre invisible":

"for my life, give me all lives,
give me all the sorrow
of all the world
and I will transform it
into hope ...
give me
the daily
struggle,
because these things are my song
the song of the invisible man
who sings with all men."

(Translated by Margaret Sayers Peden, London: Libris 1991, pages 16-18).

Neruda remarried twice and never tired of writing lyric verse, eg *Los versos del capitán* (1950), *Cien sonetos de amor* (1959). He also wrote memoirs such as *Memorial de Isla Negra* (1964), *Confieso que he vivido* (1974).

Extravagaria (1958), whose title suggests extravagance, wandering, variety, vagaries, is full of memory, acceptance and a kind of world-weary joy; see "Aquellos días". Also compare "Walking around", the most pessimistic poem in *Residencia en la tierra* ("It happens that I am tired of being a man" ...) with "A certain weariness":

"I don't want to be tired alone,
I want you to be tired with me ..." I am tired of the hard sea and the mysterious
earth, of the chickens (we never know what they are thinking) ... of getting up ...
of going to bed without glory ... of statues, of remembering.
"I want you to grow tired with me
of everything that is well done.
Of everything that makes us grow old.
Of all that lies in wait to wear out other people
Let us tire of what kills
and of what does not want to die."

(Extravagaria has been translated by Alastair Reid, New York: Farrar, Straus and Giroux, 1974.)

Neruda, who was awarded the Nobel Prize in 1971, died of cancer on 23 September 1973, his death hastened by the Pinochet coup and the military's heartless treatment of him when they removed him from Isla Negra to Santiago. The poet's three properties (see pages 88, 118 and 126) were either ransacked or shut up by the dictatorship, but many of the thousands of Chileans to whom and for whom the poet spoke visited Isla Negra to leave their messsages of respect, love and hope until democracy returned. (See Ariel Dorfman's Afterword in *The House in the Sand*, translation of *Una casa en la arena* by Dennis Maloney and Clark M Zlotchew, Minneapolis: Milkweed, 1990.) For a bilingual anthology, see *Selected Poems of Pablo Neruda*, translated and edited by Ben Belitt (New York: Grove Press, 1961); there are many other translations of individual volumes.

Obra gruesa anthologizes his work to 1969, followed by *Emergency Poems* (1972, bilingual edition, New York), which contain a darker humour, found poems, satire, but remain compassionate, socially committed (see 'Manifiesto'), *Artefactos* (1972) and *Artefactos II* (1982), *Sermones y prédicas del Cristo de Elqui* (1979) and *Poesía política* (1983).

The adherents of *antipoesía* continually sought new means of expression, so that the genre never became institutionalized. There are too many poets to list here, but Gonzalo Rojas (born 1917), Enrique Lihn (1929-88), Armando Uribe (born 1933) and Miguel Arteche (born 1926) are perhaps the best known. Another poetic development of the 1950s onwards was *poesía lárica*, or *de lares*, poetry of one's place of origin (literally, of the gods of the hearth). Its founder and promoter was **Jorge Teillier** (born 1935), whose poems describe a precarious rural existence, wooden houses, fencing, orchards, distant fires, beneath changing skies and rain. The city-dweller is an exile in space and time who returns every-so-often to the place of origin. See especially "Notas sobre el último viaje del autor a su pueblo natal", which evokes the lost frontier of his youth, the changed countryside and his city life. As for the future, "if only it could be as beautiful as my mother spreading the sheets on my bed", but it is only an unpaid bill; "I wish the UFOs would arrive". In his later poems, the violence of the city and the dictatorship invade the *lares*. Among Teillier's books are *Para angeles y gorriones* (1956), *Para un pueblo fantasma* (1978), *Cartas para reinas de otras primaveras* (1985) and *Los dominios perdidos* (1992). Another *poeta lárico*, but also an *antipoeta*, is Floridor Pérez (born 1937). A variation on this type of poetry comes from **Clemente Riedemann** (born 1953), whose *Karra Maw'n* deals with the Mapuche lands and the German immigration in the area.

Many poets left Chile after 1973 (eg Oscar Hahn, Federico Schopf, Waldo Rojas, Gonzalo Millán), but others stayed to attack the dictatorship from within through provocative, experimental works. Several of these writers were members of the Grupo Experimental de Artaud: Damiela Eltit (see above), Raúl Zurita, Eugenia Brito, Rodrigo Cánovas. Zurita's verse is a union of mathematics and poetry, logical, structured and psychological. *Purgatorio* (1979) had an immediate impact and was followed by *Anteparaíso* (1982), *El paraíso está vacío* (1984), *Canto a su amor desaparecido* (1986) and *El amor de Chile* (1987). 'Pastoral de Chile' in *Anteparaíso* reveals most of Zurita's obsessions: Chilean landscapes, love, Chile's distress, sin and religious terminology (perhaps not as overt in other poems). *La Tirana* (1985) by Diego Maquieira is a complex, multireferential work, dealing with a Mapuche virgin, surrounded by a culture which oppresses her and with which she disguises herself. It is irreverent, a 'black mass', threatening to the régime. Carmen Berenguer's *Bobby Sands desfallece en el muro* (1983) is a homage to the IRA prisoner and thus to all political prisoners. She also wrote *Huellas del siglo* (1986) and *A media asta* (1988). Carla Grandi published *Contraproyecto* in 1985, an example of feminine resistance to the coup.

● **Bibliographical note** A great many sources have been consulted in the preparation of this section. Apart from those already mentioned, reference is made to: Cedomil Goic, *La novela chilena. Los mitos degradados* (Santiago: Universitaria, 1991); Kenneth Fleak, *The Chilean Short Story. Writers from the Generation of 1950* (New York: Peter Lang, 1989); René Jara, *El revés de la arpillera, perfil literario de Chile* (Madrid: Hiperión, 1988); Jean Franco, *Spanish American Literature since Independence* (London: Ernest Benn, 1973); Eugenia Brito, *Campos minados. Literatura post-golpe en Chile* (Santiago: Mujeres Cuarto Propio, 1990); *Poesía chilena de hoy. De Parra a nuestros días*, selected by Erwin Díaz (Santiago: Ediciones Documentas, 1989); Lautaro Silva, *Vida y obra de Gabriela Mistral* (Buenos Aires: Andina, 1967); Gordon Brotherston, *The Emergence of the Latin American Novel* (1977) and *Latin American Poetry. Origins and Presence* (Cambridge University Press, 1975); Darío Villanueva y José María Viña Liste, *Trayectoria de la novela hispanoamericano actual* (Madrid: Austral, 1991); Jason Wilson, *Traveller's Literary Companion: South and Central America* (Brighton: In Print, 1993); Gerald Martin, *Journeys through the Labyrinth* (London: Verso, 1989).

FINE ART AND SCULPTURE

The colonial period

There was little home-grown art during the colonial period in Chile, in cultural terms a peripheral territory of the vast Viceroyalty of Peru, but trade with other regions was extensive and Santiago in particular has good collections of non-Chilean colonial art. Perhaps inevitably, during the Spanish colonial era the Catholic church dominated the production of paintings and sculptures. The many new religious foundations needed images of Christ and the saints to reassure the Christian settlers and also to instruct the new converts, and without a strong local school Chile had to meet this demand from elsewhere. The importation of works from Spain was very costly because for taxation purposes all trade with the southern part of the Viceroyalty was required to pass first through Lima, so most patrons relied instead on the major colonial artistic centres of Cusco, Potosí and Quito to supply their requirements.

The churches and monasteries of Santiago give a vivid sense of the thriving art market in colonial Spanish America: sculptures shipped down the coast from Lima and from Quito via Guayaquil, canvases carried across the Andes on mule trains from Cusco and Potosí, and occasionally an itinerant Spanish-trained artist passing through in search of lucrative commissions. Extensive cycles of the lives of Christ, the Virgin and selected saints were particularly popular: a cycle of 40 or 50 large canvases representing the exploits of, say, St Francis provided instant cover for large expanses of bare plaster, a good clear narrative and an exemplary life to follow. Such cycles would have been easy to commission because most Chilean examples are based either on engravings or on other painted cycles and they would also have been relatively easy to hang in the correct sequence, not least because each canvas usually includes a cartouche with a helpful textual summary. So, for example, San Francisco in Santiago has a cycle of 53 paintings of the life of St Francis painted in Cusco in the later 17th century. These are based on a similar cycle in the Franciscan monastery in Cusco by the Indian artist Basilio de Santa Cruz Pumacallao which is in turn derived from a series of European engravings. One of the Santiago paintings, the Funeral of St Francis of 1684, is signed by Juan Zapaca Inca, also, as his name suggests, an Indian and follower of Santa Cruz, and the whole series was probably produced under Zapaca's guidance. Wherever possible the artist has introduced bright-coloured tapestries and rich fabrics embellished with lace and gold embroidery, a mark of the continuing importance of textiles in Andean culture. This is a typical pattern for colonial art: a set of European engravings forms the basis for a large painted cycle which in turn becomes the source for further copies and derivatives. The narrative content and general composition remain constant while the setting, attendant figures, costume and decorative detail are often translated into an Andean indiom.

There are, of course, many different categories of colonial art. The big painted cycles were produced more for the educated inhabitants of the monastic establishments than for a lay audience, and were intended for edification rather than devotion. Popular devotion tends to create increasingly decorated and hieratic images. A good example is that of the so-called Cristo de Mayo. Early in the 17th century Pedro de Figueroa, a friar of the Augustinian monastery in Santiago, carved a figure of the crucified Christ which still hangs in the church of San Agustín. This passionate, unusually defiant image was credited with miraculous powers after it survived a serious earthquake in Santiago in May 1647 (hence the popular name *de Mayo*). The only damage was that the crown of thorns slipped from Christ's head and lodged around his neck. A cult quickly grew up around the image, creating a demand for painted copies which are identifiable by the upward gaze, the distinctive necklace of thorns, and the evenly-distributed lash marks across the body. The Carmelite convent of San José has a locally-produced 18th century example of the Cristo de Mayo which includes attendant saints and garlands of bright flowers, the latter like pious offerings. The Jesuits, always adept at exploiting popular religious fervour, established an interesting local school of sculpture on the island of Chiloé where up until the late 19th century native craftsmen continued to produce boldly expressive Christian images.

After independence

Chile was one of the first countries in America to achieve independence from Spain and in the 19th century its distance from the old colonial centre of Viceregal power worked to its advantage in the field of art. The Lima-born artist José Gil de Castro (died 1841), known as El Mulato Gil, accompanied Bernardo O'Higgins on the campaign for Chilean independence from 1814, working both as an engineer and map-maker and as a portrait painter. His portrait of O'Higgins of 1820 in the Museo Histórico Nacional in Santiago represents him as a towering

giant of a man, immovable as the rocky mountains behind him, while in a painting in the Municipalidad of La Serena of 1818 San Martín is shown standing beside a writing desk, his hand inside his jacket in a distinctively Napoleonic pose, thoughtful and determined. The 19th century also brought European traveller-artists to Chile who helped to confirm the Chilean landscape, peoples and customs as legitimate subjects for paintings, including the German Johann Moritz Rugendas who lived in Chile from 1833 to 1845, and the Englishman Charles Wood (in Chile from 1819 to 1852). Examples of both artists' work can be seen in the Museo Nacional de Bellas Artes. The Frenchman Raymond Monvoisin also spent several years in Chile, from 1843 to 1857. His perceptive portraits of members of the government and the literary élite are interesting for the way in which they link the Chilean tradition of Gil de Castro with European sources, and after his return to France he produced the first major painting dedicated to an event from colonial history, the Mapuche hero Caupolicán taken prisoner by the Spaniards (1859, Museo O'Higginiano, Talca). Caupolicán was celebrated in Chile 10 years later in a bronze statue by Nicanor Plaza (1844-1914) erected on the Cerro Santa Lucía in Santiago, and although it originated as an entry for a competition organized by the US government for a statue to commemorate the Last of the Mohicans, it represents the incorporation of the Indian into national mythology.

The Chilean Academy of Painting was founded in 1849 and although its first presidents were mediocre European artists they too helped to make Chilean subject matter respectable, while the Academy acted as a focus for aspiring young artists. Antonio Smith (1832-1877) rebelled against the rigidity of the academic system, working as a political cartoonist as well as a painter, but his dramatic landscapes grow out of the gradual awakening of interest in Chilean scenery. He transforms the picturesque view into a heroic vision of mountains and valleys, full of air and space and potential. Cosme San Martín (1850-1906), Pedro León Carmona (1853-1899), Pedro Lira (1845-1912), Alfredo Valenzuela Puelma (1856-1909) and English-born Thomas Somerscales (1842-1927) extended the range of possible national subjects in the fields of landscape, portraiture, history and genre. The late 19th century saw a number of important commissions for nationalistic public statuary including the peasant soldier 'El Roto Chileno' in Santiago's Plaza Yungay by Nicanor Plaza's pupil Virginio Arias (1855-1941), and several monumental works by Rebecca Matte (1875-1929).

The 20th century

From the later 19th century until well into the 20th century, Chilean painting was dominated by refracted versions of Impressionism. Artists such as Juan Francisco González (1853-1933) and Alfredo Helsby (1862-1933) introduced a looser technique and more luminous palette to create landscapes full of strong contrasts of sunlight and shadows, a tradition continued by, for example, Pablo Burchard (1873-1964), Agustín Abarca (1882-1953), Arturo Gordon (1883-1944) and Camilo Mori (1896-1973).

The Chilean avant-garde has been dominated by artists who have lived and worked for long periods abroad, many as political exiles. After studying with Le Corbusier in Switzerland and encountering the Surrealists in Paris, Roberto Matt (born 1911) moved to New York in 1939 and began painting uniquely unsettling space-age monsters and machines which circulate in a multi-dimensional chaos. Nemesio Antúnez (1918-1993) developed more earth-bound abstractions of reality: volcanic landscapes viewed through flames and falling rocks, or milling crowds, faceless and powerless. The younger generation includes Eugenio Dittborn (born 1943) who sends 'Airmail Paintings' around the world in an exploration of ideas of transition and dislocation and, because many contain photographs of victims of political violence, of anonymity and loss. Alfredo Jaar (born 1956) creates installations using maps and photographs to document the destructive exploitation of the world's resources, both human and natural. In recent years many exiles have returned home and Santiago is now a cultural centre of growing importance, with women particularly well-represented (for example Carmen Valbuena, born 1955, and Bernarda Zegers, born 1951). Chile is the home of an interesting on-going project called 'Cuerpos Pintados', Painted Bodies, whereby artists from Chile and other Latin American countries are invited to Santiago to paint nude models in the colours and designs of their choice. Watch out for exhibitions of the stunning photographs which are the project's permanent outcome.

MUSIC AND DANCE

At the very heart of Chilean music is the Cueca, a courting dance for couples, both of whom make great play with a handkerchief waved aloft in the right hand. The man's knees are slightly bent and his body arches back. It is lively and vigorous, seen to best advantage when performed by a Huaso wearing spurs. Guitar and harp are the accompanying instruments, while handclapping and shouts of encouragement add to the atmosphere. The dance has a common origin with the Argentine Zamba and Peruvian Marinera via the early 19th century Zamacueca, in turn descended from the Spanish Fandango. For singing only is the Tonada, with its variants the Glosa, Parabienes, Romance, Villancico (Christmas carol) and Esquinazo (serenade) and the Canto a lo Poeta, which can be in the form of a Contrapunto or Controversia, a musical duel.

PROGRAMA

"XI FESTIVAL NACIONAL DE CUECA Y TONADA INEDITA
VALPARAISO 1996"

26 · 27 Y 28 DE ENERO DE 1996

VELODROMO DE PLAYA ANCHA
VALPARAISO

Among the most celebrated groups are Los Huasos Quincheros, Silvia Infante with Los Condores and the Conjunto Millaray. Famous folk singers in this genre are the Parra Family from Chillán, Hector Pávez and Margot Loyola. In the N of the country the music is Amerindian and closely related to that of Bolivia. Groups called 'Bailes' dance the Huayño, Taquirari, Cachimbo or Rueda at carnival and other festivities and precolumbian rites like the Cauzulor and Talatur. Instruments are largely wind and percussion, including *zampoñas* (pan pipes), *lichiguayos*, *pututos* (conch shells) and *clarines*. There are some notable religious festivals that attract large crowds of pilgrims and include numerous groups of costumed dancers. The most outstanding of these festivals are those of the Virgen de La Tirana near Iquique, San Pedro de Atacama, the Virgen de la Candelaria of Copiapó and the Virgen de Andacollo.

In the S the Mapuche nation, the once greatly feared and admired 'Araucanos', who kept the Spaniards and Republicans at bay for 400 years, have their own songs, dance-songs and magic and collective dances, accompanied by wind instruments like the great long *trutruca* horn, the shorter *pifilka* and the *kultrun* drum. Further S still, the island of Chiloé, which remained in the hands of pro-Spanish loyalists after the rest of the country had become independent, has its own unique musical expression. Wakes and other religious social occasions include collective singing, while the recreational dances, all of Spanish origin, such as the Vals, Pavo, Pericona and Nave have a heavier and less syncopated beat than in central Chile. Accompanying instruments here are the *rabel* (fiddle), guitar and accordion.

FOOD

All the necessary ingredients for good cuisine can be found in Chile. The long coastline provides abundant supplies of high quality fish and shellfish. The benign Mediterranean climate of the central regions is perfect for growing a wide variety of fruit and vegetables. The semitropical climate of northern Chile supplies mangos, papayas, *lucumas* and *chirimoyas*, delicious tropical fruits used extensively in local dishes and drinks. The lush grasslands of the S are ideal for dairy and beef farming as well as for growing apples, plums and cherries. Local markets in most parts of the country are full of beautiful fruit and vegetables at very reasonable prices.

Although Chilean cuisine is mostly rooted in the Spanish tradition, it has also been influenced by the German, Italian and other immigrant groups who have settled in the country. Each new wave of immigrants introduced new ideas and combinations of ingredients and flavours. The pastry making skills of the Germans have produced 'onces Alemanas', a kind of high tea with kuchen, fruit tars and gateaux. The original 'pan de Pascua', a traditional Christmas fruit loaf also derives from Germany.

Of all the quality ingredients available, perhaps the most outstanding is the seafood, usually eaten at fish restaurants on the coast. Although there are good fish restaurants in Santiago, the fish restaurants in the popular coastal resorts in the Bay of Valparaíso, are popular with families from the capital, especially in summer when the heat of the interior can be intense. There are some excellent seafood restaurants along the 35 km coastline of the Bay, stretching from Playa Ancha to Concón.

Most of these seafood restaurants receive their supplies of fish and shellfish from local fishing boats which land their catch every morning in the *caletas* or fishing ports. If you have the courage to bargain you may be able to pick up some delicious, fresh fish from the boats or from the stalls along the harbour at good prices. The most popular fish are *merluza* (hake), better known in Viña del Mar as *pescado*, *congrio* (conger), *corvina*, *lenguado* (sole) and *albacora* (sword fish). *Merluza*, which is usually fried, is an inexpensive fish, found in ordinary restaurants. *Congrio* is a very popular quality fish, particularly delicious served as *caldillo de congrio*, a soup containing a large *congrio* steak. *Albacora* is a delicious fish, available mainly in quality restaurants. *Ceviche*, raw fish marinated in lemon juice, is usually made with *corvina*.

A wide selection of shellfish is also available especially around Valparaíso. Look out for *choros* (mussels), *ostiones* (scallops), *ostras* (oysters) and *erizos* (sea-urchins). However the most characteristic products of this area are the delicious *machas, picorocos* and *locos* which are only found in these seas. *Machas a la parmesana* are *machas* prepared in their shells with a parmesan cheese sauce, grilled and served as a starter, or as a canapé with *pisco sour*. *Picorocos*, which are normally boiled or steamed in white wine, are grotesque but have a very intense taste: it may be very disconcerting to be presented with a plate containing a rock with feathery fins but it is well worth taking up the challenge of eating it. *Locos* are the most popular Chilean mollusc, but because of overexploitation its fishing is frequently banned (*en veda*): the ban is lifted periodically, but only for a few days at a time. This situation has led to an extensive illegal trade, both nationally and internationally, with *locos* being exported illegally to parts of Asia where they are eaten as a substitute for a local mollusc. The main crustacean shellfish are *jaiva* (crab), *langosta* (lobster) and the local *centolla*, an exquisite shellfish from the waters of the S.

Packages of dried seaweed, particularly *cochayuyo* which looks like a leathery thong, can be seen for sale along coastal roads. Both *cochayuyo* and *luche*, are made into a cheap, nutricious stew with vegetables and eaten with potatoes or rice. Salmon, until recently only available in the S where the rivers and lakes are full of wild salmon, is now farmed extensively in the S and can be found on menus in many parts of the country.

Among the many snacks sold in Chile, the most famous are *empanadas*, traditionally made with meat and onions. The quality of *empanadas* on sale varies: many are full of onions rather than meat and many places offer *empanadas* filled with seafood or cheese which may be better value. Sandwiches are fairly substantial: typical examples are the *chacarero* which contains salad; *barros luco*, with steak and grilled cheese; and *barros jarpa* with grilled cheese and ham. *Completos*, one of the most popular snacks, betray the German influence on everyday food: though very similar to hot dogs, they are ideally served with plenty of extras, mustard, avocado, choukrut, tomatoes and mayonnaise or any combination of these.

The *South American Handbook* adds: a very typical Chilean dish is *cazuela de ave*, a nutritious stew containing large pieces of chicken, potatoes, rice, and

Empanadas de Pino

Although other fillings are used nowadays for *empanadas*, the traditional filling is *pino*, a mixture of meat, onions, and spices. Most Chilean families have their own recipes: this one was kindly supplied by Manuel and Ximena Fernández.

Ingredients (to make 20 *empanadas*)
Pastry: 1 kg flour; 125g margarine, butter or lard; 1 level spoonful salt; cold water.
Filling: 600g meat, chopped into small pieces (or lean minced meat); 2 large onions; 4 or 5 teaspoons cooking oil; teaspoon each of cumin, black pepper and chilli powder; 1 teaspoon paprika; 3 cloves garlic, finely chopped; salt to taste; 4 hard-boiled eggs; 1 teaspoon flour; 20 black olives; 40 raisins.

Methods
Pastry: in a bowl mix the flour and margarine, add salt (dissolved in half a cup water), gradually add more water to make soft but consistent pastry and leave it for at least 1 hr, then knead it for 10 mins, before replacing it in the bowl and leaving it covered with a clean cloth.

Filling: heat the cooking oil in a large frying pan or pot, then add the onion and fry for about 8 mins. Add spices and salt, then fry for 2 mins. Add meat and fry for 15 mins, stirring continuously, until the onions are crystal-like and softly cooked. Add the flour, lower the heat and simmer for 5 mins. Leave the mixture overnight. Shell the eggs and cut each lengthwise into 5 pieces.

Making the *empanadas*:
Divide the pastry into 20 pieces, then roll each piece into a thin round shape. On one "hemisphere" of each piece of pastry place the following: 1 piece of egg; one heaped teaspoon of the filling; 2 raisins and 1 olive. Carefully paint the rim of each piece of pastry with water, then fold the empty "hemisphere" over to enclose the filling; press the rim down. You should now have a semicircular turnover: paint the outer rim again with water and fold it again towards the centre of the *empanada*.

Bake the *empanadas* in a preheated oven (200°C). After about 5 mins reduce the heat to 150°C and bake for a further 14 mins until the *empanadas* are nicely browned. To improve their appearance paint the *empanadas* with a thin coat of cold water as soon as you remove them from the oven.

Serve hot with Chilean red wine.

---

maybe onions, and green peppers; best if served on the second day. *Valdiviano* is another stew, common in the S, consisting of beef, onion, sliced potatoes and eggs. *Pastel de choclo* is a casserole of meat and onions with olives, topped with a maize-meal mash, baked in an earthenware bowl. *Humitas* are mashed sweetcorn mixed with butter and spices and baked in sweetcorn leaves. *Prieta* is a blood sausage stuffed with cabbage leaves. A normal *parrillada* or *asado* is a giant mixed grill served from a charcoal brazier. The *pichanga* is similar but smaller and without the brazier. *Bistek a lo pobre* (a poor man's steak) can be just the opposite: it is a steak topped by a fried egg, mashed potatoes, onions and salad. A *paila* can take many forms (the *paila* is simply a kind of dish), but the commonest are made of eggs or seafood. *Paila Chonchi* is a kind of bouillabaisse, but has more flavour, more body, more ingredients.

WINE

Chile is a major producer and exporter of fine wines. The wine producing area stretches from the valley of the Río Aconcagua in the N to the Biobío valley in the S. Grapes are produced outside this area, notably around Ovalle and in the Elqui valley near La Serena, which is the main production centre for *pisco*, a clear distilled spirit commonly drunk with lemon as *pisco sour*.

Legislation in 1979 and 1985 established the current system of denominated regions and subregions. There are five denominated wine-growing regions, based around the valleys of the Ríos Aconcagua, Maipo, Rapel, Maule and Biobío. The heartland of Chilean wine production is the Maipo valley, just S of Santiago, which is home to many of the most prestigeous names in Chilean wine. Although the Maipo produces far less wine than the regions to the S, it is considered by many experts to produce the best wines in Chile as a result of the lime content of its soils. For visits to vineyards in this area see below under Santiago.

Pisco Sour

Most Chileans have their own recipe for this famous drink: this one was kindly supplied by Jaime Baez.

Ingredients for 450 ml of *pisco sour*: 200 ml refrigerated 30° *pisco*; 150 ml lemon juice; 2 teaspoons granulated sugar; 1/2 teaspoon egg white.

Method: Put all the ingredients in liquidizer and mix for a few seconds, until the sugar is will dissolved, then place in refrigerator until cold.

NB What is important in making *pisco sour* is the balance between the ingredients; once the mixing is done you can add extra sugar, *pisco* or lemon to taste. The egg white is purely for presentation.

Chile: Demarcated Wine Regions

Wine Regions:
1. Aconcagua
2. Maipo
3. Rapel
4. Maule
5. Bíobío

ERRAZURIZ

MERLOT

1996

EL DESCANSO ESTATE
CURICO VALLEY

Product of Chile

13.0% vol.   PRODUCED AND BOTTLED BY
VIÑA ERRAZURIZ S.A.   75cl e

Chilean wine: an aristocratic tradition

The cultivation of grapes in Chile dates back almost to the Spanish conquest, the first recorded vineyard being established in 1551 in La Serena by Francisco de Aguirre. One of the major motives for early vine-growing was to supply wine for the celebration of mass. In the 18th century the efforts of Madrid to restrict the planting of new vines in order to prevent competition with Spanish wines were largely ignored and vineyards became common on *haciendas* and villages throughout the central valley as far S as the Biobío valley.

Some of the most famous Chilean wines are closely associated with major names in the Chilean elite of the 19th century among them the Errázuriz, Cousiño, Subercaseux and Undurraga families. With the introduction of direct steamship services to Europe, the heads of many of these families travelled to France and returned with French and German grape varieties. New cultivation techniques were also introduced from France. French experts were employed to design the cellars, some of which, with their double walls designed to prevent temperature fluctuations, can be visited today. Some of the largest and most famous of these vineyards were situated just S of Santiago in the floodplains of the Ríos Pirque and Maipo, which were adapted for commercial agriculture by the building of a network of canals. Defended by natural frontiers, the Pacific, the Andes and the Atacama Desert, Chile also benefitted by being one of the very few wine-growing areas in the world not to suffer the devastation of the phylloxera louse which destroyed the vineyards of Europe after 1863.

The main harvest period runs from late Feb to early April, though there are regional variations. Harvest celebrations are often accompanied by two drinks: *chicha*, a partly fermented grape juice and *vino pipeño*, an unfiltered young wine which contains residue from the grapes and dried yeast.

Large scale investment, much of it from the United States and Europe has led to increases in wine production and exports in the last two decades. In 1992

152 million litres of wine were produced of which 73 million were exported. Four large companies now account for 80% of all the wine sold inside Chile: Concha y Toro, Santa Rita, San Pedro and Santa Carolina. A few others, among them Errázuriz/Caliterra, Undurraga, Cánepa and Manquehue, supply most of the rest of the domestic market. Many of the smaller wineries, however, specialize in exports.

Among the interesting names given to wines, two stand out: '120' commemorates the 120 Patriot soldiers under O'Higgins who hid in the Santa Rita cellars in 1814 after their defeat at Rancagua. *Casillero del Diablo*, one of the best known red wines from Concha y Toro, was one of the favourite wines of the founder Don Melchor de Santiago Concha who kept intruders away by spreading the rumour that the corner of the cellar where he kept it was haunted by the devil.

Economy

Structure of production

Chile is endowed with a diversified environment, allowing the production of all temperate and Mediterranean products. Traditional crops, such as cereals, pulse, potatoes and industrial crops (sugarbeet, sunflowerseed and rapeseed) account for about a third of the value added of agriculture, and vegetables for a quarter. Fruit growing has grown rapidly and fresh fruit now accounts for over US$1bn in exports a year, making fruit the second most important earner after copper. Another area of expansion is forestry; timber and wood products make up the third place in exports. More than 80% of the 1.6 million ha of cultivated forest is planted with insignis radiata pine, a species which in Chile grows faster than in other countries. However, native forest has been declining rapidly, partly because of demand by wood chippers. Chile is the most important fishing nation in Latin America and the largest producer of fishmeal in the world. Industrial consumption absorbs about 93% of the fish catch; fresh fish and fish products contribute about 10% of merchandise exports. Salmon farming is being expanded.

The dominant sector of the economy is mining. Chile has been the world's largest producer of copper since 1982 and also produces molybdenum, iron ore, manganese, lead, gold, silver, zinc, sulphur and nitrates. Chile has a quarter of the world's known molybdenum ore reserves and is believed to have around 40% of the world's lithium reserves.

Chile : Fact File

Geographic

Land area	756,626 sq km
forested	22.0%
pastures	18.2%
cultivated	5.7%

Demographic

Population (1995)	14,210,000
annual growth rate (1989-94)	1.6%
urban	85.5%
rural	14.5%
density	18.8 per sq km
Religious affiliation	
Roman Catholic	76.7%
Birth rate per 1,000 (1992)	21.6
	(world av 25.0)

Education and Health

Life expectancy at birth,	
male	70.4 years
female	76.0 years
Infant mortality rate	
per 1,000 live births (1992)	14.3
Physicians (1992)	1 per 889 persons
Hospital beds	1 per 312 persons
Calorie intake as %	
of FAO requirement	106%
Population age 25 and over	
with no formal schooling	5.7%
Literate males (over 15)	81.3%
Literate females (over 15)	80.9%

Economic

GNP (1993 market prices)	US$42,454mn
GNP per capita	US$3,070
Public external debt (1993)	US$16,031mn
Tourism receipts (1993)	US$824mn
Inflation	
(annual av 1989-94)	17.5%
Radio	1 per 3.2 persons
Television	1 per 7.0 persons
Telephone	1 per 9.1 persons

Employment

Population economically active (1993)	5,219,300
Unemployment rate	4.6%
% of labour force in	
agriculture	15.8
mining	1.8
manufacturing	16.0
construction	7.7
Military forces	93,000

Source *Encyclopaedia Britannica*

Mineral ores, most of which is copper, account for half of total export revenue. Fluctuations in world prices for minerals can have a great impact on the balance of payments. Foreign investment is the driving force in mining, which has averaged almost US$900mn a year in the 1990s in exploration and mine development. By 2000 output of copper will be 4 million tonnes a year, over 40% of world production, of which 1.4 million tonnes will be produced by the state company, Codelco, from its five mines, Chuquicamata, El Teniente, Salvador, Andina and Radomiro Tomic (to come on stream in 1998). Privately owned, high-tech mines or joint ventures are responsible for most of the expected growth.

Chile is fortunate in possessing reserves of oil, natural gas and coal, and abundant hydroelectricity potential. Almost all the country's hydrocarbon reserves are in the extreme S, on Tierra del Fuego, in the Strait of Magellan and the province of Magallanes. Natural gas is likely to be piped across the Andes from Argentina from 1997. Two pipelines are planned and up to six new gas-fired power plants may be built in 1998-2002, reducing electricity costs and pollution around Santiago if coal-fired plants are closed.

Manufacturing activity is mostly food processing, metalworking, textiles, footwear and fish processing. The sector has been vulnerable to changes in economic policy: nationalization during the Allende administration in the early 1970s; recession brought about by anti-inflation policies in the mid-1970s; increased competition resulting from trade liberalization in the early 1980s and greater exports together with import substitution in the mid-1980s. The contribution of manufacturing to total gdp fell from 25% in 1970 to 20% in 1994, but its share of exports rose and the sector grew by over 6% a year in the 1990s.

Recent trends

The policies used to bring inflation down from over 500% at the end of 1973 to less than 10% by end-1981 resulted in fiscal balance but an overvalued currency. Freeing the exchange rate in 1982 caused renewed inflation; this was restricted by

Mercosur

In June 1996 Chile signed up to become an associate member of Mercosur, the Southern Cone Common Market. Founded in 1991 by Argentina, Brazil, Paraguay and Uruguay, Mercosur is the world's fourth largest integrated international market. Except in aspiration it is not, however, yet a common market. Most goods are tariff-free inside Mercosur, but there is, as yet, no common external tariff, though in Dec 1995 the four full member states agreed a 5-year programme to establish one. Since, however, there is no freedom of movement for workers, a full common market remains a distant aspiration.

As a result of associate membership, Chile and the full members were due to reduce tariffs on trade by 30% with further reductions by the year 2005 eliminating them altogether. A small group of Chilean food and agricultural imports from Mercosur will not be covered by this: tariffs on most of these will be cut between 2006 and 2011, though wheat, flour and sugar will retain their existing tariffs until at least 2014. Within Chile the main opposition to associate membership came from farmers fearing competition from the large-scale meat and grain producers of Mercosur states: to placate their hostility the government offered US$500mn of support for agriculture over the next 5 years as the Mercosur bill passed through Congress.

tight monetary control and a lower public sector borrowing requirement which caused a severe recession and contraction in gdp. IMF help was sought following a sharp fall in international commercial lending in 1982 and a decline in Chile's terms of trade. In the 1980s Chile negotiated several debt refinancing packages and reduced its foreign debt through schemes which converted debt into equity in Chilean companies. Renewed growth in debt in the 1990s was offset by rising gdp and exports which meant that the debt: gdp ratio fell from 94% in 1985 to an estimated 40% in 1995, while the debt service ratio declined from 48% to about 15% in the same period.

The Government follows anti-inflationary policies, accompanied by structural adjustment and reform. Privatization has been widespread, although certain key companies such as Codelco remain in state hands. Privatizing the pension system and corporate savings have doubled domestic savings to 27% of gdp. Pension funds now manage assets of US$25bn, about 40% of gdp. Rising investor confidence has brought economic growth every year since the mid-1980s and the Chile model has been held up as an example for other debtor countries to adapt to their own needs. Unemployment has fallen and progress is being made in reducing poverty with increased public spending on health and education. Infant mortality has dropped; the literacy rate has risen and the percentage of malnourished children fell from 8.8% in 1982 to 5.3% in 1993.

CONSTITUTION AND GOVERNMENT

Chile is governed under the 1980 Constitution, introduced by the Pinochet military government and approved in a plebiscite on 11 September 1980, although important amendments were made during the transition to civilian

Chile: Regions

Arica
Iquique
BOLIVIA
Antofagasta
Copiapó
La Serena
ARGENTINA
Valparaíso
Santiago — Región Metropolitana de Santiago
Rancagua
Curicó
Talca
Concepción
Chillán
Temuco
Valdivia
Osorno
Puerto Montt
Castro
Coyhaique
Punta Arena
Río Grande
ARGENTINA

Regions:
I. Tarapagá
II. Antofagasta
III. Atacama
IV. Coquimbo
V. Valparaíso
VI. Libertador General Bernardo O'Higgins
VII. Maule
VIII. Bio Bio
IX. Araucanía
X. Los Lagos
XI. Aisén del General Carlos Ibañez del Campo
XII. Magallanes y Antártica Chilena

rule in 1989-1990. The new constitution provided for an 8-year non-renewable term for the President of the Republic (although the first elected president was to serve only 4 years), a bicameral Congress and an independent judiciary and central bank. Although Pinochet was not mentioned by name, only one candidate, nominated by the military was to contest the 1981 and 1988 elections. Only after the rejection of Pinochet in the 1988 vote did most of the provisions come into operation. In Feb 1994, the Congress cut the presidential term of office from 8 years to 6.

Congress is composed of a 120-seat Chamber of Deputies and a 47-seat Senate, eight of whose members are nominated rather than elected. Among the nominated senators are one former head of each of the armed forces and the abolition of nominated senators has been a

major aim of civilian governments since 1990.

Chile is divided into 13 regions, often referred to by Roman numerals although they also have names. The government of each region is headed by an Intendent who is appointed by the President. Although this system was introduced in 1974 to replace the old system of provinces, the 25 provinces still exist though their power has been reduced.

Responsible Tourism

Much has been written about the adverse impacts of tourism on the environment and local communities. It is usually assumed that this only applies to the more excessive end of the travel industry such as the Spanish Costas and Bali. However it now seems that travellers can have an impact at almost any density and this is especially true in areas 'off the beaten track' where local people may not be used to western conventions and lifestyles, and natural environments may be very sensitive.

Of course, tourism can have a beneficial impact and this is something to which every traveller can contribute. Many National Parks are part funded by receipts from people who travel to see exotic plants and animals, the Galápagos (Ecuador) and Manu (Peru) National Parks are good examples of such sites. Similarly, travellers can promote patronage and protection of valuable archaeological sites and heritages through their interest and entrance fees.

However, where visitor pressure is high and/or poorly regulated, damage can occur. It is also unfortunately true that many of the most popular destinations are in ecologically sensitive areas easily disturbed by extra human pressures. This is particularly significant because the desire to visit sites and communities that are off the beaten track is a driving force for many travellers. Eventually the very features that tourists travel so far to see may become degraded and so we seek out new sites, discarding the old, and leaving someone else to deal with the plight of local communities and the damaged environment.

Fortunately, there are signs of a new awareness of the responsibilities that the travel industry and its clients need to endorse. For example, some tour operators fund local conservation projects and travellers are now more aware of the impact they may have on host cultures and environments. We can all contribute to the success of what is variously described as responsible, green or alternative tourism. All that is required is a little forethought and consideration.

It would be impossible to identify all the possible impacts that might need to be addressed by travellers, but it is worthwhile noting the major areas in which we can all take a more responsible attitude in the countries we visit. These include, changes to natural ecosystems (air, water, land, ecology and wildlife), cultural values (beliefs and behaviour) and the built environment (sites of antiquity and archaeological significance). At an individual level, travellers can reduce their impact if greater consideration is given to their activities. Canoe trips up the headwaters of obscure rivers make for great stories, but how do local communities cope with the sudden invasive interest in their lives? Will the availability of easy tourist money and gauche behaviour affect them for the worse, possibly diluting and trivialising the significance of culture and customs? Similarly, have the environmental implications of increased visitor pressure been considered? Where does the fresh fish that feeds the trip come from? Hand caught by line is fine, but is dynamite fishing really necessary, given the scale of damage and waste that results?

Some of these impacts are caused by factors beyond the direct control of travellers, such as the management and operation of a hotel chain. However, even here it is possible to voice concern about damaging activities and an increasing number of hotels and travel operators are taking 'green concerns' seriously, even if it is only to protect their share of the market.

Environmental Legislation Legislation is increasingly being enacted to control damage to the environment, and in some cases this can have a bearing on travellers. The establishment of National Parks may involve rules and guidelines for visitors and these should always be followed. In addition there may be local or national laws controlling behaviour and use of natural resources (especially wildlife) that are being increasingly enforced. If in doubt, ask. Finally, international legislation, principally the Convention on International Trade in Endangered Species of Wild Fauna and Flora (CITES), may affect travellers.

CITES aims to control the trade in live specimens of endangered plants and animals and also 'recognizable parts or derivatives' of protected species. Sale of Black Coral, Turtle shells, protected Orchids and other wildlife is strictly controlled by signatories of the convention. The full list of protected wildlife varies, so if you feel the need to purchase souvenirs and trinkets derived from wildlife, it would be prudent to check whether they are protected. Every country included in this Handbook is a signatory of CITES. In addition, most European countries, the USA and Canada are all signatories. Importation of CITES protected species into these countries can lead to heavy fines, confiscation of goods and even imprisonment. Information on the status of legislation and protective measures can be obtained from Traffic International, UK office T (01223) 277427, e-mail traffic@wcmc.org.uk.

Green Travel Companies and Information The increasing awareness of the environmental impact of travel and tourism has led to a range of advice and information services as well as spawning specialist travel companies who claim to provide 'responsible travel' for clients. This is an expanding field and the veracity of claims needs to be substantiated in some cases. The following organizations and publications can provide useful information for those with an interest in pursuing responsible travel opportunities.

Organizations Green Flag International Aims to work with travel industry and conservation bodies to improve environments at travel destinations and also to promote conservation programmes at resort destinations. Provides a travellers' guide for 'green' tourism as well as advice on destinations, T (UK 01223) 890250. **Tourism Concern** Aims to promote a greater understanding of the impact of tourism on host communities and environments; Stapleton House, 277-281 Holloway Road, London N7 8HN, T (UK 0171) 753-3330, F 753-3331, e-mail tourconcern@gn.apc.org. **Centre for Responsible Tourism** CRT coordinates a North American network and advises on N American sources of information on responsible tourism. CRT, PO Box 827, San Anselmo, California 94979, USA. **Centre for the Advancement of Responsive Travel** CART has a range of publications available as well as information on alternative holiday destinations. T (UK – 01732) 352757.

Publications The Good Tourist by Katie Wood and Syd House (1991) published by Mandarin Paperbacks; addresses issues surrounding environmental impacts of tourism, suggests ways in which damage can be minimized, suggests a range of environmentally sensitive holidays and projects.

Will you help us?

Our authors explore and research tirelessly to bring you
the most complete and up-to-date package of information
possible. Yet the contributions we receive from our readers
are also **vital** to the success of our Handbooks. There are
many thousands of you out there making delightful
(and sometimes alarming!) discoveries every day.

So important is this resource that we make a special offer
to every reader who contacts us with information on
places, experiences, people, hotels, restaurants, well-
informed warnings or any other features which could
enhance the enjoyment of our travellers everywhere.
When writing to us, please give the edition and page
number of the Handbook you are using.

So please take a few minutes to get in touch with us -
we can benefit, you can benefit and all our other readers
can benefit too!

Please write to us at:

Footprint Handbooks,
6 Riverside Court, Lower Bristol Road, Bath BA2 3DZ England
Fax: +44 (0)1225 469461 E Mail travellers@footprint.cix.co.uk

The Santiago Region

THE CAPITAL and its surroundings, from north of the Río Aconcagua to the Río Maipo; within easy reach are several vineyards and Andean ski resorts.

THE LAND

GEOGRAPHY

This area can be divided into three regions; to the E are the peaks of the Andes; to the W is the Coastal Range and between is the Central Valley, much of which is between 600 and 1,000m above sea level. On the E edge of the Central Valley lies the city of Santiago, its suburbs spreading E into the foothills of the Andes.

Over 40% of the people of Chile live in this comparatively small area. The population density of the area around Santiago is over 300 per sq km, though much lower in the valleys around Los Andes.

MOUNTAINS

Much of the E part of this area is taken up by the Andes, which are formidably high in the northern sector; over the border in Argentina, Aconcagua, the highest mountain in the Americas, rises to 6,964m. Chilean peaks above 6,000m in this area include Marmolejo (6,108m), Juncal (6,060m), Nevado El Plomo (6,050m) and Tupungato (6,570m). There is a mantle of snow on the mountains: at Aconcagua it begins at 4,300m. The lower slopes are covered with dense forests. Between the forest and the snowline there are alpine pastures; during the summer cattle are driven up to these pastures to graze. The Coastal Range, over 2,130m high, is lower here than in the northern desert.

RIVERS

Three river systems flow W from the Andes across the Central Valley, cutting their way through the Coastal Range through narrow gorges. In the N the Aconcagua, which rises in Argentina, flows into the sea N of Valparaíso. Further S the Maipo flows S of Santiago, reaching the Pacific near San Antonio; its most important tributary is the Mapocho, the river on which Santiago is situated.

The Santiago Region

Climate

The Santiago area enjoys a "Mediterranean climate" with long dry summers and daytime temperatures rising to over 30°C. Rainfall is heaviest in autumn and winter: long spells of rain are uncommon, storms being heavy and brief. Snowfall is rare, though frost is not uncommon. There is usually less wind in spring and autumn, making smog a more serious problem over the city (forecast levels of smog are published in the daily papers). Smog is usually at its worst in July, exacerbated by the lack of wind, and by the wet and cold. It is lightest in February.

SANTIAGO

(*Pop* almost 5 million; *Alt* 600m; *Phone code* 02) Attractively situated in the Central Valley, Santiago has grown to become the fifth largest city in South America. It is a bustling modern city, the political, economic and financial capital of Chile.

Over 50% of the country's manufacturing industry is located here. It is a major communications centre, home to the country's major newspapers and television stations, as well as the site of three universities. With the country's main international airport nearby at

Founding Santiago
Taken from the back of a 500 peso note

Pudahuel, it is a major entry point for visitors to Chile.

The city is crossed from E to W by the Río Mapocho, which passes through an artificial stone channel, 40m wide, spanned by several bridges. The magnificent chain of the Andes, with its snow-capped heights, is in full view for much of the year, rain and pollution permitting; there are peaks of 6,000m

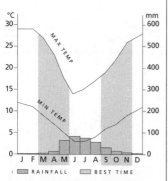

Climate: Santiago

about 100 km away.

As in most cities of its size traffic is a major problem: driving in the city is restricted according to license plate numbers (prohibited registration numbers are published in the press each day).

HISTORY

Santiago was founded by Pedro de Valdivia in 1541 on the site of a small indigenous settlement between the southern bank of the Río Mapocho and the Santa Lucía hill. During the colonial period it was only one of several Spanish administrative and cultural centres; also important were Concepción to the S and La Serena in the North. Nevertheless by 1647 there were 12 churches in the city, but of these only San Francisco (1618) survived the earthquake of that year. A further earthquake destroyed most of the city in 1730.

Following independence the city became more important; in the 1870s under the *Intendente* Benjamín Vicuña MacKenna, an urban plan was drafted, the Santa Lucía hill was made into a public park and the first trams were introduced. As the city grew at the end of the 19th century the Chilean elite, wealthy from mining and shipping, built their mansions W of the centre, around Calle Dieciocho. Expansion E towards Providencia began in 1895. In the 20th century, like most capital cities, Santiago has spread rapidly, especially since the 1950s, with the more affluent moving E into new neighbourhhods in the foothills of the Andes and with new poorer neighbourhoods being established to the W of the centre.

PLACES OF INTEREST

The centre of the old city lies between the Mapocho and the Av O'Higgins, which is usually known as the **Alameda**. From the **Plaza Baquedano** (**Plaza Italia**), in the E of the city's central area, the Mapocho flows to the NW and the Av O'Higgins runs to the SW. From Plaza Baquedano the C Merced runs due W to the **Plaza de Armas**, the heart of the city; it lies 5 blocks S of the Mapocho.

Around the Plaza de Armas

On the eastern and southern sides of the Plaza de Armas there are arcades with shops; on the northern side is the Post Office and the Municipalidad; and on the western side the Cathedral and the archbishop's palace. The **Cathedral**, much rebuilt, contains a recumbent statue in wood of San Francisco Javier, and the chandelier which lit the first meetings of Congress after independence; it also houses an interesting museum of religious art and historical pieces. In the **Palacio de la Real Audiencia** on the Plaza de Armas is the Museo Histórico Nacional (see **Museums**, below). A block W of the Cathedral is the **former Congress** building now occupied by the Ministry of Foreign Affairs (the new Congress building is in Valparaíso). Nearby are the law courts. At C Merced 864, close to the Plaza de Armas, is the **Casa Colorada**, built in 1769, the home of the Governor in colonial days and then of Mateo de Toro, first President of Chile. It is now the Museum of the History of Santiago. From the Plaza de Armas Paseo Ahumada, a pedestrianized street lined with cafés runs S to the Alameda 4 blocks away, crossing Huérfanos, which is also pedestrianized.

Four blocks N of the Plaza de Armas is the interesting **Mercado Central**, at 21 de Mayo y San Pablo. The building faces the Parque Venezuela, on which is the Cal y Canto metro station, the northern terminus of Line 2, and, at its western end, the former **Mapocho Railway Station**, now a cultural centre. If you head E from Mapocho station, along the river, you pass through the Parque Forestal (see below), before coming back to Plaza Baquedano.

Paris, Madrid and Seville?

✍ "Santiago, 'most noble and most loyal,' is a mixture of Paris, Madrid and Seville. It is far ahead of Spanish towns in its electric tramways, broad avenues and brisk movement. But the larger houses are all characteristically Spanish. They are built round a central court or patio, which is usually open to the sky above and full of flowers and graceful shrubs. Very often there are sparkling fountains and statuary also. In fact, through the great gateway of a large Santiago house the most delicious little views of water, flowers and greenery can be gathered in passing. This gateway has heavy wooden doors, carefully locked at night; the windows opening on the street are usually heavily barred, which is by no means a useless precaution". "Chile", by Scott Eliot, quoted in GR Knock, *Spanish America*, London 1925.

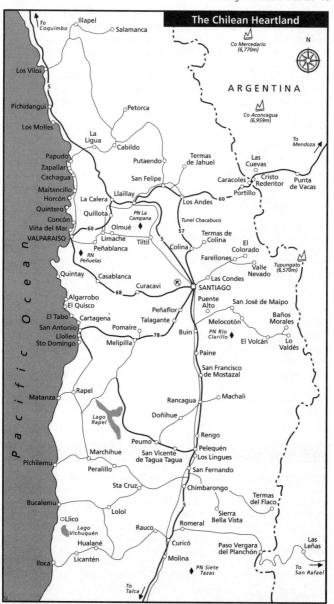

The Chilean Heartland

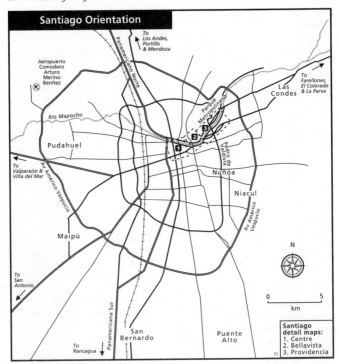

Santiago Orientation

(map labels)
To Los Andes, Portillo & Mendoza
Panamericana Norte
Aeropuerto Comodoro Arturo Merino Benítez
To Farellones, El Colorado & La Parva
Las Condes
Parque Metropolitano
Río Mapocho
Pudahuel
Pedro de Valdivia
To Valparaíso & Viña del Mar
Av Américo Vespucio
Ñuñoa
Niacul
Maipú
Av Américo Vespucio
N
To San Antonio
0   5
km
Panamericana Sur
San Bernardo
Puente Alto
To Rancagua

Santiago detail maps:
1. Centre
2. Bellavista
3. Providencia

Along The Alameda

The Av O'Higgins runs through the heart of the city for over 3 km. It is 100m wide, and ornamented with gardens and statuary: the most notable are the equestrian statues of Generals O'Higgins and San Martín; the statue of the Chilean historian Benjamín Vicuña MacKenna who, as mayor of Santiago, beautified Cerro Santa Lucía (see **Parks and Gardens** below); and the great monument in honour of the battle of Concepción in 1879.

From the Plaza Baquedano, where there is a statue of Gen Baquedano and the Tomb of the Unknown Soldier, the Alameda skirts, on the right, Cerro Santa Lucía, and on the left, the Catholic University. Beyond the hill the Alameda goes past the neo-classical **Biblioteca Na-** cional on the right, which also contains the national archives. Beyond, on the left, between C San Francisco and C Londres, is the oldest church in Santiago: the red-walled church and monastery of **San Francisco**. Inside is the small statue of the Virgin which Valdivia carried on his saddlebow when he rode from Peru to Chile. Near the church cloisters is the Museo de Arte Colonial. South of San Francisco is the Barrio París-Londres, built in 1923-1929, now restored and pedestrianized. Two blocks N of the Alameda on C Agustinas is the **Teatro Municipal**. A little further W along the Alameda, is the **Universidad de Chile**; the **Club de la Unión**, an exclusive social club founded in 1864, is almost opposite (the current building dates from 1925).

Nearby, on C Nueva York is the **Bolsa de Comercio**.

One block further W is the Plaza de la Libertad. To the N of the Plaza, hemmed in by the skyscrapers of the Centro Cívico, is the **Palacio de la Moneda** (1805), the Presidential Palace containing historic relics, paintings and sculpture, and the elaborate 'Salón Rojo' used for official receptions (guided visits only with written permission from the Dirección Administrativa – 3 weeks notice required). Although the Moneda was damaged by air attacks during the military coup of 11 September 1973 it has been fully restored. In front of the Palace is the statue of former President Arturo Alessandri Palma. (Ceremonial changing of the guard every other day, 1000, never on Sun; Sun ceremony is performed Mon.)

The Alameda continues westwards to the **Planetarium** (Av O'Higgins 3349, T 776-2624, US$2.50) and, opposite it on the southern side, the railway station (Estación Central or Alameda). On Av Matucana, running N from here, is the very popular **Parque Quinta Normal** (see below). About 7 blocks W of the Estación Central are the major bus terminals.

Lastarria and Bellavista

Between the Parque Forestal, Plaza Baquedano and the Alameda is the **Lastarria** neighbourhood (Universidad Católica metro). For those interested in antique furniture, objets d'art and old books, the area is worth a visit, especially the **Plaza Mulato Gil de Castro** (C José V Lastarria 305). Occasional shows are put on in the square, on which are the Museo Arqueológico de Santiago in a restored house, a bookshop (*Librería Latinoamericana*), handicraft and antique shops, an art gallery, the Instituto de Arte Contemporáneo and the *Pergola de la Plaza* restaurant. Nearby, on Lastarria, are the **Jardín Lastarria**, a cul-de-sac of craft and antique shops (No 293), *Guten-*

berg, Lafourcade y Cía, an antiquarian bookseller (No 307), the Ciné Biógrafo (No 131) and, at the corner with Merced, the Instituto Chileno-Francés (see below).

The **Bellavista** district, on the N bank of the Mapocho from Plaza Baquedano at the foot of Cerro San Cristóbal (see below), is the main focus of nightlife in the old city. Around C Pío Nono are restaurants and cafés, theatres, entertainments, art galleries and craft shops (especially those selling lapis lazuli).

Providencia

East of Plaza Baquedano, the main E-W axis of the city becomes **Avenida Providencia** which heads out towards the residential areas, such as Las Condes, at the eastern and upper levels of the city. It passes through the neighbourhood of Providencia, a modern area of shops, offices and restaurants around Pedro de Valdivia and Los Leones metro stations, which also contains the offices of Sernatur, the national tourist board. At Metro Tobalaba it becomes Avenida Apoquindo.

PARKS AND GARDENS

Cerro Santa Lucía

Near the heart of the city, bounded by C Merced to the N, Av O'Higgins to the S, Calles Santa Lucía and Subercaseaux, this is a cone of rock rising steeply to a height of 70m. It can be scaled from the Caupolicán esplanade, on which, high on a rock, stands a statue of that Mapuche leader, but the ascent from the northern side of the hill, where there is an equestrian statue of Diego de Almagro, is easier. There are striking views of the city from the top (reached by a series of stairs), where there is a fortress, the Batería Hidalgo (the platform of which is its only colonial survival – the building is closed). Even on smoggy days, the view of the sunset is good; the Cerro closes at 2100. It is best to descend the eastern side, to

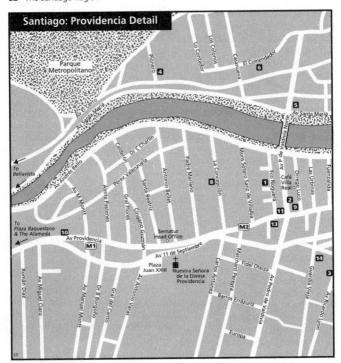

Santiago: Providencia Detail

see the small Plaza Pedro Valdivia with its waterfalls and statue of Valdivia. The area is famous, at night, for its gay community.

Parque O'Higgins

This lies about 10 blocks S of Av O'Higgins. It has a small lake, playing fields, tennis courts, swimming pool (open from 5 Dec), an open-air stage for local songs and dances, a discothèque, the racecourse of the Club Hípico, an amusement park, *Fantasilandia* (admission US$7, unlimited rides, open at weekends only in winter, and not when raining), kite-fighting contests on Sun, and a group of about 20 good 'typical' restaurants, some craft shops, the Museo del Huaso, an aquarium and a small insect and shellfish museum at El Pueblito. Cars are not allowed in the Parque.

● **Access Metro** Line 2 to Parque O'Higgins station. **Bus** from Parque Baquedano via Avs MacKenna and Matta.

Parque Quinta Normal

Situated N of the Estación Central on Av Matucana y D Portales, the Quinta Normal was founded as a botanical garden in 1830. It contains four museums, details of which are given below.

Parque Forestal

This lies due N of Santa Lucía hill and immediately S of the Mapocho. The Museo Nacional de Bellas Artes is in the wooded grounds and is an extraordinary example of neo-classical architecture (details below).

Parque Balmaceda

(Parque Gran Bretaña), E of Plaza

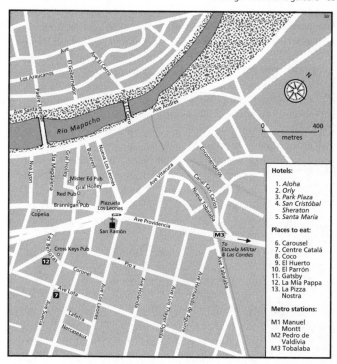

Baquedano, is perhaps the most beautiful in Santiago (the Museo de los Tajamares is here).

Parque Metropolitano

The sharp, conical hill of **San Cristóbal**, forming the Parque Metropolitano, to the NE of the city, is the largest and most interesting of the city's parks. There are two entrances: from Pío Nono in Bellavista and further E from Pedro de Valdivia Norte. On the summit (300m) stands a colossal statue of the Virgin, which is floodlit at night; beside it is the astronomical observatory of the Catholic University which can be visited on application to the observatory's director. Near the Bellavista entrance is a zoo, which has an excellent collection of animals which are well-cared for (open 1000-

1300, 1500-1800 Tues-Fri, 1000-1800 Sat, Sun and holidays).

Further E in the Tupahue sector there are terraces, gardens, and paths; in one building there is a good, expensive restaurant (*Camino Real*, T 232-1758) with a splendid view from the terrace, especially at night, and an Enoteca, or exhibition of Chilean wines from a select range of vineyards. (You can taste one of the three 'wines of the day', and buy if you like, though prices are higher than in shops.) Nearby is the Casa de la Cultura which has art exhibitions and free concerts at midday on Sun. There are two good swimming pools: one at Tupahue; the other, Antilen, can be reached from the road that starts below the Enoteca. East of Tupahue are the Botani-

Santiago: Detail of Bellavista

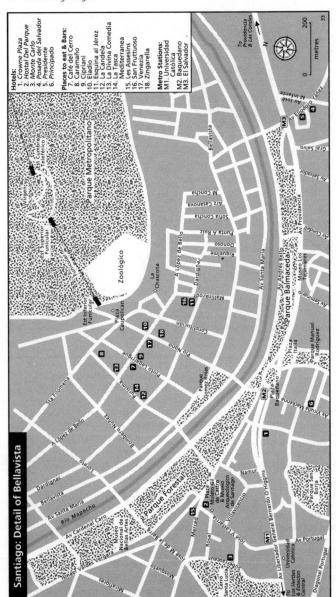

Hotels:
1. Crowne Plaza
2. Hostal Del Parque
3. Monte Carlo
4. Posada del Salvador
5. Presidente
6. Principado

Places to eat & Bars:
7. Café del Cerro
8. Cipriani
9. Eladio
10. Esquina al Jérez
11. La Candela
12. La Divina Comedia
13. La Tasca
14. Mediterranea
15. Les Assesins
16. San Fruttuoso
17. Venezia
18. Zingarella

Metro Stations:
M1. Universidad Católica
M2. Baquedano
M3. El Salvador

33

Stamp showing a Santiago funicular

cal Gardens, with a collection of Chilean native plants, guided tours available.

● **Access By funicular**: every few minutes from Plaza Caupolicán at the northern end of C Pío Nono, stopping on its way at the Jardín Zoológico, US$2 in week, US$2.25 weekends 1000-1900 Mon-Fri, 1000-2000 Sat and Sun (closed for lunch 1330-1430). Fares: from Plaza to zoo US$2.40 (easily walked); from zoo to San Cristobal US$3.20. **By teleférico** from Estación Oasis, Av Pedro de Valdivia Norte via Tupahue to San Cristóbal near the funicular's upper station, 1030-1900 at weekends, 1500-1830 weekdays except Tues (in summer only), US$2.80. A combined funicular/teleférico ticket is US$6. An open bus operated by the *teleférico* company runs to San Cristóbal and Tupahue from the Bellavista entrance with the same schedule as the *teleférico* itself. To get to Tupahue at other times you must take the funicular or a taxi (or walk to/from Pedro de Valdivia metro station, about 1 km). **By taxi** either from the Bellavista entrance (much cheaper from inside the park as taxis entering the park have to pay entrance fee), or from metro Pedro de Valdivia.

MUSEUMS

NB Almost all museums are closed on Mon and on 1 November.

In The Centre

Museo Histórico Nacional, Plaza de Armas 951, in the former Palacio de la Real Audiencia, covers the period from the Conquest until 1925; Tues-Sun, 1000-1730, US$1.

Museo de Santiago, Casa Colorada, Merced 860, history of Santiago from the Conquest to modern times, excellent displays and models, guided tours; Tues-Sat, 1000-1800 (US$1.50), Sun and holidays, 1000-1300.

Museo Chileno de Arte Precolombino, Bandera 361, in the former Real Aduana, representative exhibition of objects from the precolombian cultures of Central America and the Andean region, highly rec; Tues-Sun 1000-1800, US$1.25, Booklet, US$0.35.

Museo Iglesia de la Merced, MacIver 341, colonial religious art and archaeological collection from Easter Island; Tues-Fri 1000-1300, 1500-1800, Sat 1000-1300, US$1.

Museo de Arte Sagrado, in the Cathedral, Mon and Fri only, 0930-1230, 1530-1830, free.

Museo de Arte Colonial, Londres 4, beside Iglesia San Francisco, religious art, includes one room with 54 paintings of the life of St Francis; in the cloisters is a room containing Gabriela Mistral's Nobel medal; also a collection of locks; Tues-Sat 1000-1800, Sun 1000-1400, US$1.

The Palacio de la Alhambra, Compañía 1340 corner of Amunátegui, is a national monument sponsored by the Society of Arts; it stages exhibitions of paintings as well as having a permanent display; Mon-Fri 1100-1300, 1700-1900, T 80875.

Biblioteca Nacional, Moneda 650, temporary exhibitions of books, book illustrations, documents, posters, etc.

Palacio Cousiño, C Dieciocho 438, 5 blocks S of the Alameda, a large mansion in French rococo style with a superb Italian marble staircase. The upper storey was damaged by fire in 1968. Note the family monogram on the curtains, mirrors and doors. Owned by the Municipalidad, it is used for official receptions but is open as a museum; Tues-Fri 0930-1330, 1430-1700, Sat, Sun and holidays 0930-1330, US$3. Guided tours only, in Spanish, English and Portuguese, visitors have to wear cloth bootees to protect the floors.

In the Parque Quinta Normal

Museo Nacional de Historia Natural, which has exhibitions on zoology, botany, mineralogy, anthropology, ethnography and archaeology; Tues-Sun 1000-1745, US$0.80.

Museo Ferroviario containing 13 steam engines built between 1884 and 1953 including a rare surviving Kitson-Meyer (Tues-Fri, 1000-1215, 1400-1700, Sat, Sun and holidays, 1100-1330, 1500-1830, US$1, free to those over 60, photography permit, US$2.50).

Museo Ciencia y Tecnología, US$1, same hours as **Ferroviario**.

Museo Artequín, nearby on Av Portales in the Chilean pavilion built for the 1889 Paris International Exhibition, containing prints of famous paintings and activities and explanations of the techniques of the great masters, rec, daily 1000-1800, US$1.25.

From coal to wine: The Cousiño Dynasty

👣 A small group of families have dominated much of Chilean history since independence, their surnames often recurring as politicians, writers and entrepreneurs. One of the most important was the Cousiño family with its interests ranging from mining to vineyards. Matías Cousiño (1810-1863), the founder of the family's fortunes, began his working life in Copiapó where he helped build the Caldera to Copiapó railway (1848) and became chief assistant to the silver magnate, Carlos Goyenechea. After the deaths of his first wife and Goyenechea, Matías Cousiño married Goyenechea's widow, becoming one of the wealthiest men in Chile. The family fortune was secured when Luis, Matías Cousiño's only son by his first marriage, later married the only daughter of Goyenechea, Isidora.

Matías Cousiño later played an active role in politics and was elected to Congress, but it is as the founder of the first major coal mine in Chile at Lota in 1852 that he is best remembered. Lota became the biggest coal mine in Chile and, until the entry of US capital in the copper industry, the Compañia Minera de Lota was the largest company in the country, largely due to the efforts of four generations of the family. After Matías's death, Luis and Isadora extended the family's fortunes and founded the country's leading newspaper, *El Mercurio*. Luis's son, Carlos, founded the first cement company in Chile and built the first hydroelectric plant. In the 1880s the family pioneered plantation forestry and modern porcelain and glass manufacture.

Mindful of the need to announce their wealth to the world, Luis and Isadora hired a French architect to design the Palacio Cousiño in Santiago. Luis died of tuberculosis in 1873 (aged 38) leaving Isadora, a widow at the age of 37, to oversee its completion. Furnished with tapestries, antiques and pictures imported from France, the palace startled Santiago society with its great luxury and its advanced technology, including its own electricity generators and the first lifts in the country. Isadora's other great project was the famous park in Lota: here overlooking the mine and the town whose workers had contributed so much to the family fortunes, she oversaw the cultivation of plants from all over the world.

One of Luis's other achievements was the transformation of the family's vineyards, Cousiño Macul, on the eastern outskirts of Santiago and among the oldest in the country, which had been purchased by Matías in 1856. Luis imported cuttings from France and engaged French architects to design cellars to the best contemporary standards. It is, however, said that Isadora never permitted the serving of any but French wine in the Palacio Cousiño. It was perhaps fitting that her death, in 1899, occurred in Paris.

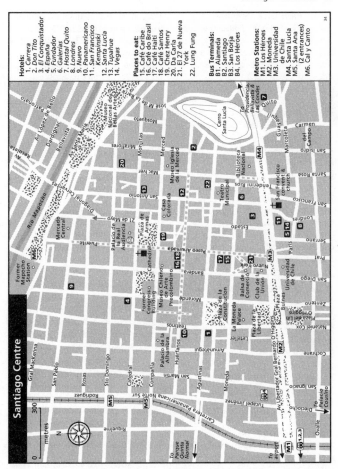

Hotels:
1. Carrera
2. Don Tito
3. El Conquistador
4. España
5. Fundador
6. Galerías
7. Hostal Quito
8. Londres
9. Nuevo
10. Panamericano
11. San Francisco Kempinski
12. Santa Lucía
13. Tupahue
14. Vegas

Places to eat:
15. Café Caribe
16. Café do Brasil
17. Café Haiti
18. Café Santos
19. Chez Henry
20. Da Carla
21. El 27 de Nueva York
22. Lung Fung

Bus Terminals:
B1. Alameda
B2. Santiago
B3. San Borja
B4. Los Héroes

Metro Stations:
M1. Los Héroes
M2. Moneda
M3. Universidad de Chile
M4. Santa Lucía
M5. Santa Ana (2 entrances)
M6. Cal y Canto

Santiago Centre

In Lastarria and Bellavista

Museo Arqueológico de Santiago, in Plaza Mulato Gil de Castro, Lastarria 307, temporary exhibitions of Chilean archaeology, anthropology and precolombian art; Mon-Fri 1030-1400, 1530-1900, Sat, 1030-1400, free.

Museo Nacional de Bellas Artes, in the Parque Forestal, has a large display of Chilean and foreign painting and sculpture; contemporary art exhibitions are held several times a year (Tues-Sat 1000-1800, Sun and holidays 1100-1800, US$0.70). In the W wing of the building is the **Museo de Arte Popular Americano**, a collection of N and S American folk art (this wing is awaiting renovation, so only a small part of the exhibition is on display). Similarly, the **Museo de Arte Contemporáneo** is on limited view as it is normally housed in the W wing.

La Chascona, F Márquez de la Plata 0192, T 777-8741, the house of the poet Pablo Neruda and now headquarters of the Fundación Pablo Neruda. This is really three houses, built on a steep hillside and separated by gardens. Open daily except Mon, 1000-1300, 1500-1800, US$2 guided visits only, English guides can be booked (see page 127).

Museo Tajamares del Mapocho, Parque Balmaceda, Av Providencia 222, an exhibition of the 17th and 18th century walls built to protect the city from flooding by the river, and of the subsequent canalization; Tues-Sat 1000-1800, Sun 1000-1330.

Museo Benjamín Vicuña MacKenna, Av V MacKenna 94, recording the life and works of the 19th century Chilean historian and biographer; occasional exhibitions.

In the Parque O'Higgins

Museo del Huaso, a small, interesting collection of criollo clothing and tools; Tues-Fri 1000-1300, 1430-1715, Sat, Sun and holidays 1000-1800, free.

Acuario Municipal at Local 9, Tues-Fri 1000-2000 (till 2100 Sat, Sun, holidays – small charge).

Museo de Insectos y Caracoles, Local 12, a collection of indigenous items, same hours as the aquarium but open till 2200 at weekends and holidays.

Other Museums

Museo de la Escuela Militar, Los Militares 4500, Las Condes, with displays on O'Higgins, the Conquest, the Pacific War and a room devoted to the medals of Gen Pinochet (not on general display so ask), Mon-Fri 1000-1130, 1530-1830, Sat 0930-1430, Sun 1430-1800, free.

Museo Ralli, Sotomayor 4110, Vitacura, collection of works by modern European and Latin American artists, including Dali, Chagall, Bacon and Miró; Tues-Sun 1100-1700, free.

Museo de Artes Decorativos, Casas Lo Matta, Av Pdte Kennedy 9350, Vitacura, a beautiful museum containing Don Hernán Garcés Silva's bequest to the nation: antique silverplate from South America and Europe, 16th-18th century Spanish colonial and European furniture, 15th century Books of Hours, housed in an 18th century country mansion. Guided tours available; by bus, take Intercomunal No 4 from Mapocho station, or take a taxi; in either case ask to be let out at 'Casas lo Matta'.

Museo Aeronáutico, Camino a Melipilla 5100, Cerrillos Airport, Tues-Sun 1000-1700, displays on space exploration, worth a visit.

EXCURSIONS

To **Maipú**, a suburb 10 km SW of Santiago where a monument marks the site of the Battle of the Maipú, 5 April 1818, which resulted in the final defeat of the Spanish royalist forces in mainland Chile. Nearby is the **National Votive Temple of Maipú**, of fine modern architecture and stained glass; interesting (open daily 0800-2100, also daily mass at 1830, 1730 Sat, 1000-1400, 1600-2000 Sun and religious holidays), and so is the attached **Museo del Carmen** of carriages, furniture, clothing and other colonial and later items, Sat 1600-2000, Sun and holidays, 1100-1400, 1600-2000. Bus from Teatinos y O'Higgins, 45 mins.

LOCAL FESTIVALS

During Nov there is a free art fair in the Parque Forestal on the banks of the Río Mapocho, lasting a fortnight. In Oct or Nov there are a sumptuous flower show and an annual agricultural and industrial show (known as Fisa) in Parque Cerrillos. Religious festivals and ceremonies continue throughout Holy Week, when a priest ritually washes the feet of 12 men. The image of the Virgen del Carmen (patron of the Armed Forces) is carried through the streets by cadets on 16 July.

LOCAL INFORMATION

● **Accommodation**
Check if breakfast and 18% tax is included in the price quoted (if foreigners pay in US$ cash or with US$ TCs, the 18% IVA/VAT should not be charged; if you pay by credit card, there is usually a 10% surcharge).

Hotel prices

L1	over US$200	**L2**	US$151-200
L3	US$101-150	**A1**	US$81-100
A2	US$61-80	**A3**	US$46-60
B	US$31-45	**C**	US$21-30
D	US$12-20	**F**	US$7-11
F	US$4-6	**G**	up to US$3

Expensive hotels In the Providencia area: **L1** *San Cristóbal Sheraton*, Santa María 1742, T 233-5000, F 223-6656, best in town, good restaurant, good buffet lunch, and all facilities, also *Sheraton Towers*, slightly cheaper; **L1** *Park Plaza*, Ricardo Lyon 207, T 233-6363, F 233-6668, good; **A1** *Aloha*, Francisco Noguera 146, T 233-2230/7, F 233-2494, helpful, good restaurant; **A1** *Santa María*, Santa María 2050, T 232-6614, F 231-6287, excellent, friendly, small, good breakfast, other meals good value, highly rec; <u>A1 *Orly*</u>, Pedro de Valdivia 27, metro Pedro de Valdivia, T 232-8225, but has smaller, cheaper rooms with less comfort, small, comfortable, has apartments for rent on Juana de Arco, good, US$70 a day (reductions may be possible); **A1** *Torremayor*, Ricardo Lyon 322, T 234-2000, F 234-3779, clean, modern, good service, good location; **A2** *Posada del Salvador*, Eliodoro Yáñez 893, T 235-9450, F 251-8697, metro Salvador, with bath; **A2** *Presidente*, Eliodoro Yáñez 867, T 235-8015, F 235-9148, almost at Providencia, good value and good location.

In Las Condes: **L1** *Hyatt Regency Santiago*, Av Kennedy N 4601, T 218-1234, F 218-2279, superb, beautifully decorated, highly rec; **A1** *Montebianco*, Isidora Goyenechea 2911, T 233-0427, F 233-0420, small, smart motel; **A2** *Manquehue*, Esteban Dell'Orto 6615, T/F 2128862, very good with new wing and new pool; **A1** *Parinacota*, Av Apoquindo 5142, T 246-6109, F 220-5386, 4-star, small, all services, no pool.

In the central area: **L1** *Carrera*, Teatinos 180, T 698-2011, F 672-1083, enormous rooms, pool, rooftop restaurant (good buffet lunch); **L1** *El Conquistador*, Miguel Cruchaga 920,

T/F 696-5599, and **L1** *Galerías*, San Antonio 65, T 638-4011, F 639-5240, excellent, welcoming; **L1** *San Francisco Kempinski*, O'Higgins 816, T 639-3832, F 639-7826, Lufthansa affiliated, 5-star, good; **L2** *Fundador*, Paseo Serrano 34, T/F 632-2566, helpful, good value; **L2** *Holiday Inn Crowne Plaza*, O'Higgins 136, T 638-1042, F 633-6015, all facilities, also good, spacious, a/c (book through travel agent for better rates); **L3** *Hostal del Parque*, Merced 294, opp Parque Forestal, T 639-2694, F 639-2754, comfortable, quiet, friendly, rec.

A1 *Tupahue*, San Antonio 477, T 638-3810, F 639-5240, comfortable; **A2** *Ducado*, Agustinas 1990, T 696-9384/672-6739, F 695-1271, with breakfast, clean, quiet at back, rec, secure parking; **A2** *Gran Palace*, Huérfanos 1178, T 671-2551, F 695-1095, overpriced, clean, good restaurant; **A2** *Panamericano*, Teatinos 320 y Huérfanos, T 672-3060, F 696-4992, comfortable, serves popular business lunch between 1230 and 1530; **A3** *City*, Compañía 1063, T 695-4526, F 695-6775, old-fashioned, clean, rec; **A3** *Conde Ansúrez*, Av República 25, T 699-6368, F 671-8376, metro República, convenient for central station and bus terminals, clean, helpful, safe, luggage stored; **A3** *Don Tito*, Huérfanos 578, T 639-1987, good service, excellent breakfast, English spoken; **A3** *Libertador*, O'Higgins 853, T 639-4212, F 633-7128, helpful, rec, stores luggage, good restaurant, bar, roof-top pool; **A3** *Majestic*, Santo Domingo 1526, T 695-8366, F 697-4051, with breakfast, pool, English spoken, rec; **A3** *Monte Carlo*, Subercaseaux 209, T 633-9905, F 633-5577, at foot of Santa Lucía, modern, restaurant, with heating, stores luggage; **A3** *Santa Lucía*, San Antonio 327 y Huérfanos, p 4, T 639-8201, garage 2 blocks away, clean, comfortable, good, small, quiet restaurant.

Mid-price hotels In the centre: **B** *Imperio*, O'Higgins 2879, T 689-7774, F 689-2916, nr central station, with bath, good restaurant, parking, clean; **B** *Principado*, Arturo Burhle 015, just off Vicuña MacKenna 1 block S of Plaza Baquedano, T 635-3879, F 222-6065, convenient location, very nice; **B** *Lira*, Lira 314, T 222-2492, F 634-3637, excellent; **B** *Turismo Japón*, Almte Barroso 160, T 698-4500, convenient location, intermittent hot water, helpful, friendly, clean, good breakfast, manager speaks English, best rooms at top, rec; **B** *Res Alicia Adasme*, Moneda 2055, T 696-

0787, hot water, friendly, with breakfast; **B** *Santa Victoria*, Vicuña MacKenna 435, T 634-5753, quiet, small, safe, family run, rec; **B** *Vegas*, Londres 49, T 632-2514, F 632-5084, clean, large comfortable rooms, friendly, good breakfast; **B** *Hostal Quito*, Quito 36, T 639-9918, F 639-7470, without breakfast, central, clean, also appartments; **B** *Hostal Vía Real*, Marín 066, T 635-4676, F 635-4678, charming, friendly, helpful, small, with bath, TV, laundry, rec; **C** *Res Alemana*, República 220 (no sign), T 671-2388, Metro República, hot water, clean, pleasant patio, central, heating on request, good cheap meals available, rec; **C-D** *Res Londres*, Londres 54, T/F 638-2215, nr San Francisco Church, former mansion, large old-fashioned rooms and furniture, few singles, no heating, English spoken, very popular, rec repeatedly (often full by 0900); **C-D** *París*, C París 813, T 639-4037, with bath, no singles, quiet, clean, good meeting place, good value, luggage store, also short-stay.

In Providencia: C *Hostal Parada*, Grau Flores 168, T 460-6640, spacious, clean.

Cheaper hotels In the Centre: D *Hostal Aula Magna*, Vergara 541, T 698-0729, laundry facilities, Metro Toesca; **C** *España*, Morandé 510, T696-6066, with bath, hot water, clean, run down; **D** *Res del Norte*, Catedral 2207, T 696-9251, inc breakfast, friendly, safe, clean, large rooms, convenient, credit cards accepted; **D** pp *San Patricio*, Catedral 2235, T 695-4800, with bath, **E** pp without, with breakfast, clean, safe, friendly, good value; **D** *Maury*, Tarapacá 1112, T 672-5889, F 697-0786, clean, friendly, safe, meals, English and French spoken; **D** *Santo Domingo*, Santo Domingo 735, with bath, E without, cleanish, basic, gloomy; **E** *Indiana*, Rosas 1339, T 714-251, convenient for buses to centre, very basic; **E** pp *Nuevo*, Morandé y San Pablo, T 671-5698, simple but OK, central, erratic hot water, safe, basic, poor beds, use of kitchen (no utensils), cable TV, popular, good meeting place; **E** pp *Olicar*, San Pablo 1265, quiet, clean, rec.

Convenient for bus terminals and Estación Central: near Metro República are: **D** *Res Mery*, Pasaje República 36, off 0-100 block of República, T 696-8883, big green building down an alley, hot showers, quiet, rec; **E** *Alojamiento Diario*, Sanfuentes 2258 (no sign), T 699-2938, shared rooms, clean, safe, kitchen facilities; **E** pp Sazie 2107, T 672-2269, basic. Elsewhere: **C** *Elisa*, Manuel Rodríguez 140,

T 695-6464, with bath, clean, quiet; **C** *Res Los Andes Midi*, Unión Americana 134, huge rooms with ancient furniture, basic, clean, hot water, laundry facilities, noisy; **E** *Res Sur*, Ruiz Tagle 55, meals available. On N side of Alameda opp bus terminals: **F** pp Federico Scotto 130, T 779-9364, use of phone and fax, good meals, cooking facilities, hot water, clean, often full; **E** pp Federico Scotto 079, T 7766484, with breakfast, helpful, luggage stored; **E** pp Huérfanos 2842, T 681-4537, kitchen, laundry, dormitory accommodation.

North of the Plaza de Armas near Mapocho Station: **D** ppRes *Miraflores*, Riquelme 555, T 696-3961, with breakfast, clean, friendly, safe, meals available, rec; **D** *Res Amunátegui*, Amunátegui 652, clean, friendly. Several on Gral MacKenna 1200 block, all very basic inc **D** *San Felipe*, No 1248, T 713816, secure, cheap laundry service, kitchen, noisy (second floor quieter), luggage stored; **E** *Ovallino*, Gral MacKenna 1477 y San Martín, clean, hot water, secure; **E** pp *Casa Andina*, Recoleta 895, T 737-2831, clean, cheap, across the river from Cal y Canto Metro. **NB** Morandé, Gen MacKenna, San Martín and San Pablo are in the red light district.

As the above list shows there is little good accommodation under US$20 a night.

Family accommodation: travellers can find good accommodation in comfortable family guesthouses through *Amigos de Todo el Mundo*, Av Pdte Bulnes, Paseo, 285, dept 201, Casilla 52861 Correo Central, T 672-6525, F 698-1474, Sr Arturo Navarrete, prices from US$16 with breakfast, other meals extra, monthly rates available, also transport to/from airport, rec; **E** pp *Alberto and Paola Peirario*, Chapultepec 5657, T 218-2101, F 204-4652, offer family accommodation, minimum 5 days, Spanish classes; also **E** pp *Sra Marta*, same address depto 401, T 779-7592, similar; **E** pp *Sra Lucía*, Catedral 1029, p 10, dept 1001, T 696-3832, central, friendly, safe, cooking facilities, basic; **E** pp *Sra Fidela*, San Isidro 261, Apt H, T 222-1246, shared bathroom, breakfast, rec; **D** *Casa Paxi*, Llico 968, T 522-9947, F 521-6328, 1 block from Metro Departamental, washing machine, gardens, quiet; **D** *Sra Marta*, Amengual 035, Alameda Alt 4.400, T 779-7592, lado Norte (metro Ecuador), good, hospitable, kitchen facilities, motorcycle parking; **E** *Sra Eliana Zuvic*, Almte Latorre 617, T 696-8700, Metro Toesca, hot water, nice atmosphere, highly rec; **D** pp *Alicia*

Bravo, Artemio Gutiérrez 1328, T 556-6620, with breakfast, helpful, friendly, clean, not very central, rec.

Longer stay accommodation: see the classified ads in *El Mercurio*, flats, homes and family *pensiones* are listed by district, or in *El Rastro* (weekly), or try the notice board at the tourist office. In furnished apartments, if you want a phone you may have to provide an *aval*, or guarantor, to prove you will pay the bill, or else a huge deposit will be asked for. Estate agents handle apartments, but often charge ⅓ of the first month's rent as commission, while a month's rent in advance and 1 month's deposit are required. Rec apartments are *Edificio San Rafael*, Miraflores 264, T 633-0289, F 222-5629 US$29 a day single, US$46 a day double, minimum 3 days, US$600 a month, very central. Staying with a family is an economical and interesting option for a few months. Providencia and Las Condes are residential districts, but the latter is some way from the centre; the area W of Plaza Baquedano, E of Cerro Santa Lucía and S of Parque Forestal is good and central; or you could try Bellavista, but not C Pío Nono where the nightlife goes on until 0300.

Youth hostels: information from Youth Hostal office, Av Providencia 2594, oficina 420, metro Tobalaba, T 233-3226 (worth getting a list of YH addresses around the country as these change). Supplies student cards (2 photos required and proof of student status, though tourist card accepted), US$11. Hostels in the capital inc **E** pp Cienfuegos 151, T 671-8532 (5 mins from metro Los Héroes), modern, clean, satellite TV, no cooking facilities, cafeteria, laundry facilities, parking, highly rec; **E** pp *Res Gloria*, Almte Latorre 447, T 698-8315, Metro Toesca, clean, popular, meals, difficult to use kitchen.

Camping: on the Farellones road near the river; or S of Santiago nr Puente Alto (take Av J Pedro Alessandri S to Las Vizcachas and La Obra where there is a small park on left side of road). At Km 25 S of city on Panamericana, Esso garage offers only a vacant lot near highway. Excellent facilities about 70 km from Santiago at Laguna de Aculeo, called *Club Camping Maki*: inc electricity, cold water, swimming pool, boat mooring, restaurant, but only available to members of certain organizations. An alternative site is *El Castaño* camping (with casino), 1 km away, on edge of lake; very friendly, café sells fruit, eggs, milk, bread and

kerosene; good fishing; no showers, water from handpump.

● **Places to eat**

In The Centre: many places in the centre close early in the evening: after 2200 it is better to try Bellavista or Providencia. In addition to those at the main hotels and those in Parque O'Higgins:

Mainly local food: *Chez Henry*, on Plaza de Armas, expensive restaurant and delicatessen at Alameda 847, which is highly rec; also in Plaza de Armas, *Faison d'Or*, good *pastel de choclo*, pleasant place to have a drink and watch the world go by; *Torres*, O'Higgins 1570, traditional bar/restaurant, good atmosphere, live music at weekends; *Fuente de Soda Orion*, O'Higgins y Manuel Rodríguez, cheap, good pizzas; *Silvestre*, Huérfanos 956, open 0800-2400, good buffet-style; *Mermoz*, Huérfanos 1048, good for lunches; *Bar Nacional No 1*, Huérfanos 1151 and *Bar Nacional No 2*, Bandera 317, good restaurants, popular, local specialities; *Guima*, Huérfanos y Teatinos, good, reasonable prices, good value *almuerzo*; *Café Dante*, Merced 801 y San Antonio, for *pastel de choclo*, lunchtime only; *Bar Central*, San Pablo 1063, typical food, rec; *Fra Diavolo*, París 836 (nr *Res Londres*), lunches only, local and Italian, excellent food and service, popular; *Verdijo*, Morandé 526, noisy, cheap and popular; *Bar-restaurant Inés de Suárez*, Morandé 558, cheap; *El Lugar de Don Quijote*, café, and *Parrilladas de Don Quijote*, restaurant, good, Morandé y Catedral; two doors away is *Congreso*, popular at lunchtime. *Círculo de Periodistas*, Amunátegui 31, p 2, unwelcoming entrance, good value lunches, rec; *Los Adobes de Argomedo*, Argomedo 411 y Lira, hacienda-style, good Chilean food and floor show inc cueca dancing, salsa and folk, Mon-Sat, only place in winter which has this type of entertainment on a Mon.

Seafood: *El 27 de Nueva York*, Nueva York 27, central, pricey, good; *Savory Tres*, Ahumada 327, good but limited choice and closed evenings. Some of the best seafood restaurants are to be found in the Mercado Central (by Cal y Canto metro; lunches only), or at the Vega Central market on the opp bank of the Mapocho.

Oriental: *Guo Fung*, Moneda 1549, rec; *Lung Fung*, Agustinas 715, delicious food, pricey, excellent fixed price lunch, large cage in the centre with noisy parrots; *Pai Fu*, Santa

Rosa 101, good; *Kam Thu*, Santo Domingo 771, nr San Antonio, good, large helpings; all Chinese. *Izakaya Yoko*, Merced 456, good, Japanese, rec.

Others: *Nuria*, MacIver 208, wide selection, US$20 plus; *Da Carla*, MacIver 577, Italian food, good, expensive; and *San Marco*, 2 doors away, better still; *Casa Suiza*, Huérfanos 648, good Swiss food; *Les Assassins*, Merced 297, French, very good, highly rec; *La Omelette*, Agustinas nr Amex, clean and good, closes 2100. *Gran Parrillada la Brasileña*, San Diego, huge portions, rec.

In Lastarria and Bellavista: many, inc *La Pergola de la Plaza* in Plaza Mulato Gil de Castro; better and close by are *Quiche Lorraine* in the Instituto Chileno-Francés, Lastarria 345, highly rec for food, drink and ambience; *Gatopardo*, Lastarria 192, good value and *R*, highly rec. *Café Universitario*, Alameda 395 y Subercaseaux (nr Sta Lucía), good, cheap almuerzos. Many restaurants/bars on Pío Nono inc: *Venezia*, huge servings, good value; *Eladio*, good steaks; *Zingarrella*, Italian, good; *La Puña*, *Los Ladrillos*, popular, lively, and *La Maviola*, speciality pizzas. On Pinto Lagarrigue: *Café del Cerro*, No 192, T 778-308, with live music (check *El Mercurio* for programme), door charge, highly rec; *Cipriani*, No 195, pasta, elegant atmosphere, US$25-30, top class; *Picoroco*, No 123, good seafood. On López de Bello: *Al Mazzat*, No 82, Arab dishes, good; *El Otro Sitio*, No 53, excellent food, elegant not cheap. On Purísima: *Caramaño*, No 257, good seafood, reasonably priced, ring doorbell, rec; *Les Copains*, No 65, French, good food; *La Tasca Mediterránea*, No 153, good food, rec; *La Divina Comida*, No 215, Italian with 3 rooms – Heaven, Hell and Purgatory, highly rec. On Mallinkrodt: *La Esquina al Jérez*, No 102, excellent Spanish; *San Fruttuoso*, No 180, Italian, rec.

In Providencia: on Av Providencia: *El Parrón*, No 1188, *parrilladas*, rec, the local dice game of 'dudo' is played in the bar; *Lomit's*, No 1980, good; *Gatsby*, No 1984, American food, as-much-as-you-can-eat buffet and lunch/dinner, snack bar open till 2400, tables outside in warm weather, good.

Italian: *La Pizza Nostra*, Av Las Condes 6757, pizzas and good Italian food, real coffee, pricey, also at Av Providencia 1975 and Luis Thayer Ojeda 019; *da Renato*, Mardoqueo Fernández 138 (metro Los Leones), good. *La Mía Pappa*, Las Bellotas 267, very popular lunches.

Others: *Olé Olé*, Guardia Vieja 136, Spanish, good food, wide selection; *Coco*, La Concepción 236, good seafood, expensive, rec, reservation advised; *Centre Catalá*, Av Suecia 428 nr Lota, good, reasonably-priced; *Carrousel*, Los Conquistadores 1972, French, very good, nice garden, over US$20.

In Las Condes: many first-class restaurants, inc grills, Chilean cuisine (often with music), French cuisine and Chinese. This area tends to be more expensive than central restaurants. *Seriatutix*, Av Colón 5137, restaurant and disco, live music, café, great atmosphere; *La Tasca de Altamar*, Noruega y Linneo, good seafood, reasonably priced. On Vitacura: *Delmónico*, No 3379, excellent, reasonably priced; *El Madroñal*, No 2911, T 233-6312, excellent, booking essential; *Praga*, No 3917, Czech. On Isadora Goyenechea: *Pinpilinpausha*, No 2900, good; *Martín Carrera*, No 3471, good nouvelle cuisine; *Taj Mahal*, No 3215 (Metro El Golf), T 232-3606, only Indian in Santiago, expensive but excellent. On El Bosque Norte: *München*, German, No 204, rec; *El Club*, No 280 (approx), popular, good value (US$15-20); *Coco Loco*, opp at No 215, good, US$20-30. On Av Las Condes: *La Estancia*, No 13810 (US$20-25), *La Querencia*, No 14980, a bit cheaper, both good; *Santa Fe*, No 10690, excellent Mexican.

Eating on a budget: it is difficult to eat cheaply in the evening apart from fast food, so budget travellers should make the *almuerzo* their main meal. In the centre place lunches from several *fuentes de soda* along Av Santa Rosa between the Alameda and C París. Also: *Casino La Blanquita*, San Martín 75, popular with locals. *Food Garden*, in *galería* at Estado/Ahumada and Huérfanos/Agustinas, p 2, is collection of fast food kiosks, good resting place.

Vegetarian restaurants: *El Huerto*, Orrego Luco 054, Providencia, T 233-2690, rec, open daily, live music Fri and Sat evenings, varied menu, very good but not cheap, popular; *Rincón Vegetariano*, Monjitas 558, cheap fixed price lunches, good, juices, rec, closes 1800.

● **Cafés & bars**

For good coffee try *Café Haití*, *Café Brasil* and *Café Caribe*, all on Paseo Ahumada and elsewhere in centre and Providencia. Note that almost all hotel bars are closed on Sun.

In the centre: *Bucaneros*, Morandé 564,

good value lunches and snacks; *Café Paula*, several branches, eg Estado at entrance to Galería España, excellent coffee and cake, good breakfast, also on San Antonio opp the Teatro Municipal. *Café Colonia*, MacIver 133, rec; *Café Santos*, Huérfanos 830, popular for 'onces' (afternoon tea); *La E*, San Pablo 1310, good coffee; *Bon Bon Oriental*, Merced 345, superb Turkish cakes; *Cafetería Berri*, Rosal 321, live music at weekends; *Tip-Top Galetas* rec for freshly baked biscuits, branches throughout the city, eg Merced 867.

In Bellavista and Lastarrria: *Café de la Dulcería Las Palmas*, López de Bello 190, good pastries and lunches; several on Purísima 100-200, inc *La Candela*. *El Biógrafo*, Villavicencio 398, bohemian style, rec.

In Providencia: *Geo Pub*, Encomenderos 83, owner Francisco Valle speaks English, pub and expensive restaurant with travel films once a week in winter, popular with travellers, rec; *Villa Real*, Pedro de Valdivia 079, rec. Many on Av Providencia inc: *Phone Box Pub*, No 1670, T 496627; *El Café del Patio*, next door, student hang-out; *Salón de Té Tavelli*, Drugstore precinct, No 2124, rec. *Golden Bell Inn*, Hernando Aguirre 27, popular with expatriates; *Cross Keys Pub*, Las Bellotas 270 local 5 (opp *La Mía Pappa*), nr Los Leones metro, with darts, pints, etc, good value. Many other good bars nearby on Av Suecia inc *Mr Ed*, No 1552; *Brannigan Pub*, No 35, good beer, live jazz; *Red Pub*, No 29.

In Las Condes: *El Vikingo*, Rotunda Atena, good atmosphere, cheap; *Café Iguana*, Av Vitacura y La Tranquera; *El Metro* and *Country Village*, Av Las Condes y Estoril; further E on Av Las Condes at Paseo San Damián are several popular bar-restaurants inc *Tequila* and *Mississippi*.

For snacks and ice cream: several good places on Av Providencia inc *Coppellia*, No 2211, *Bravissimo*, No 1406, and *El Toldo Azul*, No 1936.

● **Airline offices**

LanChile, sales office: Agustinas 640, Torre Interamericana, T 699-0505; reservations T 632-3211; **Ladeco**, Huérfanos 1157, T 698-2233 and Pedro de Valdivia 0210, T 251-7204; **National Airlines**, Huérfanos 725, p 3, B, T 633-9288/632-2698; **Aerovías DAP**, Luis Thayer Ojeda 0180, of 1304, Providencia, T 334-9672, F 334-5843; **Alta**, Las Urbinas 30, T/F 244-1777; **British Airways**, Isidora

Goyenechea 2934, Oficina 302, T 601-8614, 232-9560 (for confirmation); **Aerolíneas Argentinas**, and **Viasa**, Moneda 756; **Varig**, Miraflores, between Agustinas and Moneda, T 639-5976; **Aero Perú**, Fidel Oteiza 1953, p 5, T 274-3434; **Ecuatoriana**, T 671-2334; **Lacsa**, Av Providencia 2083, Oficina 22, T 233-6400; **Iberia**, Bandera 206, T 698-1716; **KLM**, San Sebastián 2839, Oficina 202, T 233-0011; **Aeroflot**, Agustinas 640, Local 5, T 632-3914; **South African Airlines**, Moneda 970, p 18, next to Lufthansa (T 698-6490); **LAP**, Agustinas 1141, p 2, T 671-4404; **Swiss Air**, Estado 10, p 10.

● **Banks & money changers**

Banks, open from 0900 to 1400, but closed on Sat. Official daily exchange rates are published in *El Mercurio* and *La Epoca*. **Banco Central de Chile**, Ahumada entre Huérfanos y Agustinas, demands the minimum of formalities, but may charge commission. **Banco O'Higgins**, Bandera 201, changes TCs into dollars with commission on transactions between US$100-1,000. **Citibank**, Ahumada 40.

Casas de Cambio (exchange houses) in the centre are mainly situated on Agustinas and Huérfanos. **Exprinter**, Agustinas 1074, good rates, low commission; **Inter**, Moneda 940, upstairs office at Ahumada 131 (oficina 103); **Cambios Andino**, Ahumada 1062; **Teletour**, Guardia Vieja 55; **Afex**, Moneda 1160, good rates for TCs; **Intermundi**, Moneda 896; **JM Cambios**, Agustinas 1046; **Sr Fernando Sáez** (travel agent), M Cousiño 150, Oficina 322, T 638-2885, good rates. In Providencia several around Av Pedro de Valdivia, eg at Gral Holley 66, good rates; **Casa de Cambio Blancas**, opp *Hotel Orly* on Pedro de Valdivia, and **Mojakar**, Pedro de Valdivia 072. All major currencies can be bought or sold. Some *casas de cambio* in the centre open Sat am (but check first). Normally there is no commission on TCs though rates may be lower. Shop around as terms vary.

American Express, Agustinas 1360 (Turismo Cocha, Av El Bosque Norte 0430, Providencia, for travel information and mail collection), no commission, poor rates (better to change TCs into dollars – no limit – and then into pesos elsewhere). Mastercard at **Fincard**, Alameda 1427, T 698-4260, 2465/7, 3855, 7229, offers its full range of services (even lost or stolen cards are replaced in a couple of days); open 24 hrs. Thomas Cook/Mastercard agent, *Turismo Tajamar*, Orrego Luco 23, T 231-5112. For Cirrus ATMs go to Banco Santander and Banco de Santiago and other banks with Redbank sign. Visa at **Banco Concepción**, Huérfanos y Bandera, but beware hidden costs in 'conversion rate', and **Banco Osorno**, Av Providencia y Pedro de Valdivia, no commission. For stolen or lost Visa cards go to **Transbank**, Huérfanos 777, p 3.

Unless you are feeling adventurous avoid street money changers (particularly common on Ahumada and Agustinas): they will usually ask you to accompany them to a *Casa de Cambio* or somewhere more obscure. Rates for such transactions are no better and the passing of forged notes and mugging are reported.

● **Cultural centres**
Instituto Chileno Británico de Cultura, Santa Lucía 124, T 638-2156, 0930-1900, except 1330-1900 Mon, and 0930-1600 Fri, has English papers in library (also in Providencia, Darío Urzúa 1933, and Las Condes, Renato Sánchez 4369), runs language courses; **British Chamber of Commerce**, Av Suecia 155-c, Providencia, Casilla 536, T 231-4366; **British Council**, Av Eliodoro Yáñez 832, nr Providencia, T 223-4622. The British community maintains the **British Commonwealth Society** (old people's home etc), Av Alessandri 557, T 223-8807, and the interdenominational Santiago Community Church, at Av Holanda 151 (Metro Tobalaba), Providencia, which holds services every Sun at 1045.

Instituto Chileno Francés de Cultura, Merced 298, T 639-8433, in a beautiful house; **Instituto Chileno Alemán de Cultura**, Goethe-Institut, Esmeralda 650, T 638-3185; **German Chamber of Commerce**, Ahumada 131. **Instituto Chileno de Cultura Hispánica**, Providencia 927; **Instituto Chileno Italiano de Cultura**, Triana 843; **Instituto Chileno Israeli de Cultura**, Moneda 812, oficina 613; **Instituto Chileno Japonés de Cultura**, Providencia 2653, oficina 1902.

Instituto Chileno Norteamericano de Cultura, Moneda 1467, T 696-3215, good for US periodicals, cheap films on Fri; also runs language courses and free Spanish/English language exchange hours (known as Happy Hours) which are a good way of meeting people. (Ask also about Mundo Club which organizes excursions and social events.)

Instituto Cultural del Banco del Estado de Chile, Alameda 123, regular exhibitions of paintings, concerts, theatrical performances; **Instituto Cultural de Providencia**, Av 11 de Septiembre 1995 (Metro Pedro de Valdivia), art

exhibitions, concerts, theatre; **Instituto Cultural Las Condes**, Av Apoquindo 6570, nr beginning of Av Las Condes, also with art exhibitions, concerts, lectures, etc.

● **Embassies and consulates**
Argentine Embassy, Miraflores 285, T 633-1076; Consulate Vicuña MacKenna 41, T 222-6853, Australians need letter from their embassy to get visa here, open 0900-1400 (visa US$25, free for US citizens), if you need a visa for Argentina, get it here or in the consulates in Concepción, Puerto Montt or Punta Arenas, there are no facilities at the borders; **Bolivian Embassy**, Av Santa María 2796, T 232-8180 (Metro Los Leones), open 0930-1400; **Brazilian Embassy**, Alonso Ovalle 1665, T 698-2347, p 15, visas issued by Consulate, MacIver 225, p 15, Mon-Fri 1000-1300, US$10 (visa takes 2 days); take: passport, 2 photos, ticket into and out of Brazil, photocopy of first 2 pages of passport, tickets, credit card and Chilean tourist card; **Panamanian Embassy**, Del Inca 5901, T 220-8286 (open 1000-1330); **Paraguayan Consulate**, Huérfanos 886, Oficina 514, T 639-4640, open 0900-1300 (2 photos and copy of first page of passport required for visa); **Peruvian Embassy**, Av Andrés Bello 1751, T 232-6275 (Metro Pedro de Valdivia).

US Embassy, Av Andrés Bello 2800, T 232-2600, F 330-3710; **US Consulate**, T 710133, Merced 230 (visa obtainable here); **Canadian Embassy**, Ahumada 11, p 10, T 696-2256 (prints a good information book).

Australian Embassy, Gertrudis Echeñique 420, T 228-5065, 0900-1200; **Israeli Embassy**, San Sebastian 2812, T 246-1570; **Japanese Embassy**, Av Providencia 2653, p 19; **New Zealand Embassy**, Av Isadora Goyenechea 3516, Las Condes, T 231-4204; **South African Embassy**, Av 11 de Septiembre 2353, Edif San Román, p 16, T 231-2862.

Austrian Embassy, Barros Errázuriz 1968, p 3; **Belgian Embassy**, Av Providencia 2653, depto 1104, T 232-1071; **British Embassy and Consulate**, El Bosque Norte 0125 (Metro Tobalaba), Casilla 72-D, T 231-3737, F 231-9771, will hold letters, open 0900-1200; **Danish Embassy**, Av Santa María 0182, T 737-6056; **Finnish Embassy**, Sótero Sanz de Villalba 55, Oficina 71, T 232-0456; **French Embassy**, Condell 65, T 225-1030; **German Embassy**, Agustinas 785, p 7 y 8, T 633-5031; **Italian Embassy**, Clemente Fabres 1050, T 223-2467; **Netherlands Embassy**, C Las

Violetas 2368, T 223-6825, open 0900-1200; **Norwegian Embassy**, Av Vespucio Norte 548, T 228-1024; **Spanish Consulate**, Av Providencia 329, p 4, T 40239; **Swedish Embassy**, 11 de Septiembre 2353, Torre San Ramón, p 4, Providencia, T 231-2733, F 232-4188; **Swiss Embassy**, Av Providencia 2653, Oficina 1602, T 232-2693, open 1000-1200 (metro Tobalaba).

● **Entertainment**
Cinemas: 'Ciné Arte' (quality foreign films) is very popular and a number of cinemas specialize in this type of film: *El Biógrafo*, Lastarria 181; *Alameda Cultural Centre*, Av Providencia 927, *Casa de Extensión Universidad Católica*, Av B O'Higgins 390, T 222-1157; *Espaciocal*, Goyenechea y Vitacura; *Tobalaba*, Av Providencia 2563, and others, full details are given in the press. Try also Goethe Institut, and Instituto Chileno-Francés (addresses above). Other cinemas tend to show 'sex, violence and war'. Seats cost US$3-5 with reductions on Wed (elsewhere in the country the day varies).

Discotheques: *Gente*, Av Apoquindo 4900, also *Baltas*, Av Las Condes 10690, both expensive, but good. *El Baile*, López de Bello, Bellavista. *Maestra Vida*, Pío Nono 380. Many more, mainly in the Providencia and Las Condes areas.

Nightclubs: some of the restaurants and cafés which have shows are given above. Listings are given in *El Mercurio*, or *La Epoca*. Clubs in Bellavista are cheaper and more down market generally than those in Providencia. *La Cucaracha*, Bombero Núñez 159 (Bellavista), is very popular, floorshow at 2330, US$3.50 cover charge, orchestras, dancing. *Varadero*, on Pío Nono, good. Several tango clubs inc *Club Troilo*, Cumming 795, cheap, unpretentious (tango classes 1800-2000, Fri and Sun). *El Tucano Salsateca*, Pedro de Valdivia 1783, p 4, Wed-Sun 2200-0600, fashionable. *Peña Nano Parra*, San Isidro 57, good folk club, cheap.

Theatres: *Teatro Municipal*, Agustinas y San Antonio, stages international opera, concerts by the Orquesta Filarmónica de Santiago, and the Ballet de Santiago, throughout the year; on Tues at 2100 there are free operatic concerts in the Salón Claudio Arrau; tickets range from US$5.60 for a very large choral group with a symphony orchestra, and US$7 for the cheapest seats at the ballet, to US$80 for the most expensive opera seats. Some cheap seats are often sold on the day of concerts. *Teatro*

Universidad de Chile, Plaza Baquedano, is the home of the Orquesta y Coro Sinfónica de Chile and the Ballet Nacional de Chile; prices from US$1.25-3.50 for concerts to US$1.25-13.50 for ballet.

Free classical concerts are sometimes given in San Francisco church in summer; arrive early for a seat.

There are a great number of theatres which stage plays in Spanish, either in the original language or translations, eg *La Comedia*, Merced 349, *Abril*, Huérfanos 786, *Camilo Henríquez*, Amunátegui 31, *Centro Arrayán*, Las Condes 14891, *El Galpón de los Leones*, Av Los Leones 238, *El Conventillo*, Bellavista 173. Four others, the *Opera*, Huérfanos, *California*, Irarrázaval 1546, *Humoresque*, San Ignacio 1249 and *Picaresque*, Recoleta 345, show mostly Folies Bergères-type revues. *Santiago Stage* is an English-speaking amateur drama group. Outdoor rock concerts are held at the *Estadio Nacional*, Av Unión Latino Americana (metro of same name), and the Teatro Teletón, Rosas 325 (excellent sound system), and elsewhere. Events are listed in *El Mercurio* and *La Epoca*. The most comprehensive listings appear in *El Mercurio's Wikén* magazine on Fri.

● **Hospitals & medical services**
Emergency Pharmacy: Portugal 155, T 382439.

Hospitals: emergency hospital at Marcoleta 377 costs US$60. If you need to get to a hospital, it is better to take a taxi than wait for an ambulance. For yellow fever vaccination and others (but not cholera), *Hospital San Salvador*, J M Infante 551, T 225-6441, Mon-Thur 0800-1300, 1330-1645; Fri 0800-1300, 1330-1545. Also *Vaccinatoria Internacional*, Hospital Luis Calvo, MacKenna, Antonio Varas 360. *Clinica Central*, San Isidro 231, T 222-1953, open 24 hrs, German spoken. *Clinica Alemana*, Vitacura 5951, Las Condes, German and English spoken (bus 344 from centre). Physician: Dr Sergio Maylis, T 232-0853 (1430-1900). Dentist: Antonio Yazigi, Vitacura 3082, Apto 33, T 487962, English spoken, rec. Dr Torres, Av Providencia 2330, Depto 23, excellent, speaks English.

● **Language schools**
Centro de Idiomas Bellavista, Dominica 25, T 777-5933/227-7137, offers Spanish in groups or individually and organizes accommodation. *Escuela de Idiomas Violeta Parra*, Ernesto Pinto Lagarrigue 362A, Recoleta-Barrio Bellavista, T/F 229-8246, courses aimed at

English language teaching: no longer a gold mine

An increasing number of private language institutes offer English language classes. Many of the difficulties involved are highlighted by Russell Trounce, a teacher in Santiago:

"Most of these Institutes are small and new but they have no classes for teachers. If they do have classes they pay woeful salaries, and you can easily be replaced because there are so many teachers seeking work. If you arrive in Santiago these days expecting to pick up easy work teaching English, then you may easily be disappointed. In addition, the Institutes are becoming more fussy and require native speakers with experience, teachers who are clean-cut and well-dressed, and teachers who have residency, or are at least prepared to stay 6 months. The major Institutes won't even look at foreigners who are illegal. Beware of some Institutes who take 20% income tax off your wages (10% is normal). The pay is poor: if you wish to be paid between US\$2.50 and US\$3 after tax per hour then go for it. Santiago is now an expensive city to live in and US\$3 won't buy you a decent meal. I would warn travellers not to come here with too many illusions about teaching English: it takes time to establish yourself as a foreigner and you have to be extremely patient."

Work permits can only be obtained by teachers themselves, not by the Institutes. We have also received reports of more unscrupulous Institutes employing teachers with 90-day tourist visas and 'discovering' as this expires that the teacher is not entitled to work, at which point it is difficult to obtain unpaid wages. English language teachers seeking work should apply in mid-Feb/early Mar with a full curriculum vitae and photo.

budget travellers, information programme on social issues, arranges accommodation and visits to local organizations and national parks; *AmeriSpan Unlimited* has an affiliated school in Santiago, details from PO Box 40513, Philadelphia, PA 19106, USA, T 215-985-4522/800-879-6640, F 215-985-4524, E-mail info@amerispan.com. Many private teachers, inc Carolina Carvajal, T 623-8405, highly rec, and Patricia Vargas Vives, Monitor Araucano 0680, Depto 25AC, Providencia, T 777-0595, qualified and experienced (US\$12.50/hr). Lucía Araya Arévalo, Puerto Chico 8062, Villa Los Puertos, Pudahuel, T 236-0531, speaks German and English. Patricio Ríos, Tobalaba 7505, La Reina, T 226-6926, speaks English, rec.

● **Laundry**

Wet-wash places in the centre: at Agustinas 1532, also *Nataly*, another at Bandera 572, at Catedral y Amunátegui and *Lava Fácil*, Huérfanos 1750, Mon-Sat 0900-2000, US\$4/load. There are plenty of dry-cleaners, eg Merced 494. Nearby, just S of Metro Universidad Católica there are several, inc *American Washer*, Portugal 71, Torre 7, local 4, US\$3, open 0900-2100 inc Sun, can leave washing

and collect it later, also at Monjitas 650. Wet wash laundries in Providencia inc *Marva*, Carlos Antúñez 1823 (Metro Pedro de Valdivia), wash and dry US\$8; Av Providencia 1039, full load, wet wash, US\$5, 3 hrs; *Laverap*, Av Providencia 1600 block; Manuel Montt 67. At the corner of Providencia and Dr Luis Middleton there are several self-service dry cleaners (Metro Pedro de Valdivia, 11 de Septiembre exit).

● **Places of worship**

American Presbyterian Church, Iglesia San Marcos, Av Manquehue Norte 1320, Los Hualtatas, service in English Sun 0915; **Anglican Church**, Holanda 151 (service 1030); **Synagogues**, Tarapacá 870, T 393872, and Las Hortensias 9322, T 233-8868.

● **Post & telecommunications**

Telephones: Compañía de Teléfonos de Chile, Moneda 1151, closed Sun. International phone calls also from: Entel, Huérfanos 1133, Mon-Fri 0830-2200, Sat 0900-2030, Sun 0900-1400, calls cheaper 1400-2200; Fax upstairs. Fax also available at CTC offices, eg Mall Panorámico, 11 de Septiembre, 3rd level (phone booths are on level 1). There are also

CTC phone offices at some metro stations, La Moneda, Escuela Militar, Tobalaba, Universidad de Chile and Pedro de Valdivia for local, long-distance and international calls. There are also phone boxes in the street from which overseas calls can be made. International telex service, Bandera 168. Local calls 50 pesos, only 50 peso coins accepted.

Post Office: Plaza de Armas (0800-1900), poste restante well organized (though only kept for 30 days), US$0.20, passport essential, list of letters and parcels received in the hall of central Post Office (one list for men, another for women, indicate Sr or Sra/Srita on envelope); also has philatelic section, 0900-1630, and small stamp museum (ask to see it). Another office at Moneda 1155. If sending a parcel, the contents must first be checked at the Post Office; paper, tape etc on sale; open Mon-Fri 0800-1900, Sat 0800-1400.

● **Security**

Like all large cities, Santiago has problems of theft. Pickpockets and bagsnatchers, who are often well-dressed, operate especially on the Metro and around the Plaza de Armas. The Cerro Santa Lucía area is reported to be dangerous even in daytime.

● **Shopping**

El Almacén Campesino, Purísima 303, Bellavista, is a cooperative association in an attractive colonial building, selling handicrafts from all over Chile, inc attractive Mapuche weavings, wood carvings, pottery (best bought in Pomaire, 50 km away, see page 105) and beautiful wrought copper and bronze. Prices are similar to those in similar shops in Temuco. Ask about shipping. The gemstone lapis lazuli can be found in a few expensive shops in Bellavista but is cheaper in the arcades on S side of the Plaza de Armas and in the *Centro Artesanal Santa Lucía* (Santa Lucía metro, S exit) which also has a wide variety of woollen goods, jewellery, etc. *Amitié*, Av Ricardo León y Av Providencia (Metro Los Leones). *Dauvin Artesanía Fina*, Providencia 2169, Local 69 (Metro Los Leones) have also been rec. *H Stern* jewellery shops are located at the *San Cristóbal Sheraton, Hyatt Regency* and *Carrera* hotels, and at the International Airport. *Cema-Chile* (Centro de Madres), Portugal 351 and at Universidad de Chile metro stop, *Manos Chilensis*, Portugal 373, *Artesanías de Chile*, Varas 475, *Artesanía Popular Chilena*, Av Providencia 2322 (nr Los Leones metro), and *Artesanía Chilena*, Estado 337, have a good

selection of handicrafts. *Talleres Solidarios*, de la Barra 456, small selection. Antique stores in Plaza Mulato Gil de Castro and elsewhere on Lastarria (Merced end).

Beside and behind the Iglesia de los Dominicos, on Av Nueva Apoquindo 9085, is *Los Graneros del Alba*, or *El Pueblo de Artesanos*, open daily except Mon, 1130-1900; all types of ware on sale, classes given in some shops, interesting. *Restaurant El Granero* is here. To get there, take a No 326 or 327 bus from Av Providencia, marked 'Camino del Alba'; get out at the children's playground at the junction of Apoquindo y Camino del Alba, at the foot of the hill leading up to the church, and walk up.

Mercado Central, between Puente y 21 de Mayo by the Río Mapocho (Cal y Canto metro) is excellent but quite expensive; there is a cheaper market, the *Vega Central*, on the opp bank of the river. There are other craft markets in an alleyway, 1 block S of Av B O'Higgins between A Prat and San Diego, on the 600 to 800 blocks of Santo Domingo (inc pieces from neighbouring countries) and at Pío Nono y Av Santa María, Bellavista. The shopping arcade at the Central Station is good value, likewise the street market outside. Cheap clothes shops in the city, eg on Bandera esp 600 block, are good for winter clothes for travellers who need them (look for sign Ropa Europea). There is a flea market at Franklin y Santa Rosa on Sun am and a good outside fruit market at Puente 815, by *Frutería Martínez*. There is an antique fair on Sun (1000-1400) in the summer and a Fiesta de Quasimodo on the first Sun after Easter at Lo Barnechea, 30 min by bus from Santiago. Parque Arauco is a large modern shopping mall in Las Condes on Av Kennedy, N of Metro Escuela Militar.

Bookshops: book prices tend to be high compared with Europe. *Librería Albers*, Vitacura 5648, Las Condes, T 218-5371, F 218-1458, and 11 de Septiembre 2671, Providencia, T 232-7499 (Spanish, English and German – good selection, cheaper than most, helpful, also German and Swiss newspapers); *Librería Catalonia*, Huérfanos 669; *Feria Chilena del Libro*, Huérfanos nr McIver, and in Drugstore precinct, Providencia 2124; *Librería Inglesa*, Huérfanos 669, local 11, and Pedro de Valdivia 47, Providencia, T 231-9970, good selection of English books, sells *South American Handbook*. *South American Way*, Av Apoquindo 6856, Las Condes, T 211-8078, sells books in English. There are many bookshops in the

Pedro de Valdivia area on Av Providencia. Second-hand English books from *Librería El Patio*, Av Providencia 1652, nearest Metro stop Pedro de Valdivia; exchange for best deal. Also, from Henry at Metro station, Los Leones, and *Books*, next to *Phone Box Pub*, in the courtyard at Av Providencia 1670 (the artist's shop in same precinct sells attractive cards). *Librairie Française*, books and newspapers, C del Estado 337. As well as the antiquarian bookshop mentioned above in the Lastarria district, there are other good antiquarian bookshops on Merced around the corner from Lastarria, eg *América del Sur Librería Editorial*, No 306, *Libros Antiguos El Cid*, No 344. Many stalls on Paseo Ahumada/Huérfanos sell foreign newspapers and journals.

Camera repairs and film: *Harry Müller*, Ahumada 312, Oficina 402, not cheap but good and fairly quick, rec; speaks German and English. For Minolta and Canon repairs, *TecFo*, Nueva York 52, p 2, T 695-2969, rec. Many developers on Ahumada offer 24-hr service of varying quality (some develop, but do not mount, slides, slow service). *Tecnofoto*, Ahumada 131, p 7, Oficina 719, T 672-5004 rec as quick and efficient. *Prontofoto*, Ahumada 264, T 672-1981 good quality and cheap;*Moretto*, Merced 753, rec as cheap and good. *Black Box*, Gral Flores 229 (Metro Mannel Montt), highly rec. For camera batteries and other spares try *Fotocenter*, Ahumada y Huérfanos.

Camping equipment: standard camping gas cartridges can be bought at *Fabri Gas*, Bandera y Santo Domingo, or *Unispot*, Av Providencia 2503. Other equipment for camper-vans from *Bertonati Hnos*, Manuel Montt 2385. Tent repairs: *Juan Soto*, Silva Vildosola 890, Paradero 1, Gran Avenida, San Miguel, Santiago, T 555-8329. *Reinaldo Lippi*, Grenado 566 (nr Santa Lucía hill), T 639-1180, F 639-9169, makes tents, sleeping bags, back packs, etc, sells secondhand kit, and does repairs, most helpful. Camping goods from *Club Andino* and *Federación de Andinismo* (see page 98 below): expensive because these articles are imported. *Lomas*, Santa Rosa y 10 de Julio, good selection of sleeping bags, helpful. Good sleeping bags from *Fuc*, Rengo 1670 (off M Montt), T 225-8862. For packs also try Sr Espinosa, San Martín 835. Repair of camping stoves at *Casa Italiana*, Tarapacá 1120. For second hand equipment try Luz Emperatriz Sanhuela Quiroz, Portal de León, Loc 14, Providencia 2198 (Metro Los Leones).

● **Sports**

Bicycles: for parts and repairs *Importadora Caupolicán*, San Diego 863, T 697-2765, F 696-1937, wide range, helpful. Ask for Nelson Díaz 'a walking encyclopaedia' on bikes.

Clubs: Ñuñoa (T 223 7846), with swimming pool, tennis courts and school; Chess Club, Alameda O'Higgins 898, Mon-Sat 1800, lively.

Football: main teams inc Colo Colo who play at the Estadio Monumental (reached by any bus to Puente Alto; tickets from Cienfuegos 41), Universidad de Chile (Estadio Nacional, Av Grecia 2001, T 239-2212) and Universidad Católica who play at San Carlos de Apoquindo, reached by bus from Metro Escuela Militar.

Other sports: **Running**: the Hash House Harriers hold runs every other week; information through the British Embassy and Consulate. **Tennis**: Santiago Tennis Club; also, Club de Tenís Jaime Fillol, Rancho Melnichi, Par 4. **Bowling**: Bowling Center, Av Apoquindo 5012. **Gymnasium**: Gimnasio Alicia Franché, Moneda 1481, T 696-1681, aerobics and fitness classes (women only); another at Huérfanos 1313, T 671-1562. **Tai Chi** and other martial arts: Raul Tou-Tin, Irarrázaval 1971, T 204-8082. **Cricket**: Sat in summer at Club Príncipe de Gales, Las Arañas 1901 (bus from Tobalaba metro).

Racecourses: Club Hípico, racing every Sun and every other Wed afternoon (at Viña del Mar, Jan-Mar); Hipódromo Chile every Sat afternoon; pari-mutuel betting.

Skiing and climbing: Club Andino de Chile, Enrique Foster 29, ski club (open 1900-2100 on Mon and Fri). **Federación de Andinismo de Chile**, Almte Simpson 77A (T 222-0888, F 222-6285), open daily; see **Climbing** in **Adventure tourism**, page 18. It has the addresses of all the mountaineering clubs in the country. It has a mountaineering school. **Club Alemán Andino**, El Arrayán 2735, T 242-5453, open Tues and Fri, 1800-2000, May-June. Also try **Skitotal**, Apoquindo 4900, Oficina 32,33,43, T 246-0156, for 1-day excursions, and **Anke Kessler**, Arzobispo Casanova 25, T 737-1958, F 274-5146, for individually-tailored packages inc hotels and transport for budget skiers. Equipment hire is much cheaper in Santiago than in ski resorts. Sunglasses are essential. For ski resorts in the Santiago area see below page 106.

Skiing and climbing equipment: *Mountain Service*, Ebro 2805, Las Condes (Metro

Tobalaba) T 242-9723, English spoken, tents, stoves, clothing, equipment rental, rec; *Panda Deportes*, Paseo Las Palmas 2217 (Metro Los Leones), T 232-1840.

Swimming Pools: Tupahue (large pool with cafés, entry US$9 but worth it) and Antilen, both on Cerro San Cristóbal, open daily in summer except Mon 1000-1500 (check if they are open in winter, one usually is). In Parque O'Higgins, 1330-1830 summer only, US$3. Olympic pool in Parque Araucano (nr Parque Arauco Shopping Centre, closest Metro Escuela Militar), open Tues-Sat 0900-1900 Nov-March.

● **Tour companies & travel agents**
Wagons-Lits Cook, Carmencita, Providencia, T 233-0820, rec; *Turismo Cocha* (American Express representatives with mail service), Av El Bosque Norte 0430, PO Box 191035, Providencia, Metro Tobalaba, T 230-1000. *Pas-stours*, Huérfanos 886, Oficina 1110, T 639-3232, F 633-1498, many languages spoken, helpful, rec; *VMP Ltda*, Huérfanos 1160, Local 19, T/F 696-7829, for all services, German, English, French, Italian and Portuguese spoken, helpful, repeatedly rec; *Selec-*

tours, Agencia de Viajes, Las Urbinas 95, Providencia, T 252-0201/334-2637, F 234-2838; *All Travels*, Huérfanos 1160, local 10, T 696-4348, good for flight tickets; *Asatej Student Flight Centre*, Av Providencia 2594, Oficina 426, T 232-5388, 334-5166/7, F 233-3220, for cheap flights and youth travel; *Patagonia Connection SA*, Fidel Oteíza 1921, Oficina 1006, Providencia (Metro Pedro de Valdivia), T 225-6489, F 274-8111, for cruises to Patagonia; *Eurotur*, Huérfanos 1160, local 13, for cheap air tickets to Europe; *Blanco*, Pedro de Valdivia near Av Providencia, good for flight information and exchange; *Rapa-Nui*, Huérfanos 1160, specializes in trips to Easter Island; *Turismo Grace*, Victoria Subercaseaux 381, T 693-3740, good service. For local tours: *Ace Turismo*, O'Higgins 949, T 696-0391, city tour, US$12 for ½ day. *Maysa*, Paseo Ahumada 6, Of 43, T/F 696-4468, good tours of bodegas and Valparaíso, US$35.

For adventure tours and trekking: *Sport-stours*, Teatinos 330, p 10, T 696-8832/698-3058, German-run, helpful, 5 day trips to Antarctica (offices also at Hotels *Carrera*, and *San Cristóbal*); *Altue Expediciones*, En-

comenderos 83 P 2, Las Condes, T 232-1103/233-2964, F 233 6799, for wilderness trips inc tour of Patagonia, rec (above *Geo Pub*). Climbing and adventure tours in the Lake District and elsewhere, *Antu Aventuras*, Casilla 24, Santiago, T 271-2767, Tx 440019, RECAL CZ. *Andescape*, Santa Beatriz 84A, Providencia, T/F 235-5225, useful for information on Torres del Paine. *Azimut 360*, Monte Carmelo 360, Dept 36, T 777-2375, highly rec, low prices; *Mountain Service*, Ebro 2805, Las Condes, T 242-9723, F 234-3438, rec for climbing trips; *Racies*, Plaza Corregidor Zañartu 761, cultural tours, inc Robinson Crusoe Island and Antarctica, T/F 638-2904. *Turismo Grant*, Huérfanos 863, Oficina 516, T 639-5524, helpful, English spoken; *Patagonia Chile*, Constitución 172, Bellavista, T 351871, offer mountain trips, river rafting, trekking. *Turismo Cabo de Hornos*, Agustinas 814, Of 706, T 6338481, F 6338486, for DAP flights and Tierra del Fuego/Antártica tours. *Andina del Sud*, Bombero Ossa 1010, p 3, Of 301, T 697-1010, F 696-5121, for tours in the Lake District. Ask at *Hotel Maury*, address above, for tours with Fernández (Tony), who speaks English, inc riding, rafting and barbecue, US$50 pp, rec. For skiing in the Santiago area see below page 106.

Turismo Joven, Av Suecia Norte 0125, T 232-9946, F 334-3008, E-mail turjoven@mailent.rdc.cl, youth travel services for young people and students for travel, studies, leisure with links in Latin America and worldwide.

● **Tourist offices**
Servicio Nacional de Turismo (Sernatur – the national tourist board), Av Providencia 1550 (Casilla 14082), T 236-1416, Tx SERNA CL 240137, between metros Manuel Montt and Pedro de Valdivia, next to Providencia Municipal Library, open Mon-Fri 0900-1900, Sat 0900-1300. English and German spoken and maps (road map US$1.50), brochures and posters are available. Good notice board. Ask for the free booklet, *Paseos en Santiago* (City Walks in Santiago), which is very useful for those with time to explore on foot. Kiosk on Ahumada nr Agustinas (erratic opening times). Information office also at the airport, open 0900-2100 daily. Municipal Tourist Board, Casa Colorada, Merced 860, T 336700/330723, offers walking tours of the city, Wed 1500, or from kiosk on Paseo Ahumada. **NB** Many tourist offices outside Santiago are closed in winter,

so stock up on information here.

Excellent road maps (US$1.75) and information may be obtained from the **Automóvil Club de Chile**, Vitacura 8620, T 212-5702/3/4, F 229-5295 (Metro P de Valdivia then bus to Vitacura, or a US$6 taxi ride from the centre), which also gives discounts to members of affiliated motoring organizations; open Mon-Fri 0845-1815, Sat 0900-1300, very helpful. **Further reading** in the **Rounding up** chapter contains more information on maps and guide books.

Conaf (Corporación Nacional Forestal), Presidente Bulnes 259, oficina 206 (main office at No 285), T 696-0783/699-2833, publishes a number of booklets and has documents and maps about the national park system that can be consulted or photocopied (not very useful for walking). **CODEFF** (Comité Nacional Pro-Defensa de la Fauna y Flora), Sazie 1885, T 696-1268, can also provide information on environmental questions.

● **Useful addresses**
Immigration: Ministerio del Interior, *Extranjería* section, Moneda 1342, Mon-Fri 0830-1530, extension of tourist card US$8.

Policía Internacional: for lost tourist cards, etc, Santo Domingo y MacIver.

● **Transport**
Local Buses and taxis: destinations and fares of all buses are marked clearly on the front. There are three kinds of buses: the small fast kind called *liebres* (hares) which cost US$0.50 a ride; the regular buses at US$0.30, and the large buses marked Expreso, US$0.40. Taxis (black with yellow roofs) are abundant, and not expensive, with a minimum charge of US$0.40, plus US$0.12/200m. Taxi drivers are permitted to charge more at night, but in the day time check that the meter is set to day rates. At bus terminals, drivers will charge more – best to walk a block and flag down a cruising taxi. Large blue taxis do not have meters. Avoid taxis with more than one person in them especially at night. There are also colective taxis (*colectivos*) on fixed routes to the suburbs, US$0.70. For journeys outside the city arrange the charge beforehand. The private taxi service which operates from the bottom level of *Hotel Carrera* has been rec (same rates as city taxis), as has Radio Taxis Andes Pacífico, T 225-3064/2888; similarly Rigoberto Contreras, T 638-1042, ext 4215, available at *Holiday Inn Crowne Plaza*, but rates above those of city taxis.

Car hire: prices vary a lot so shop around

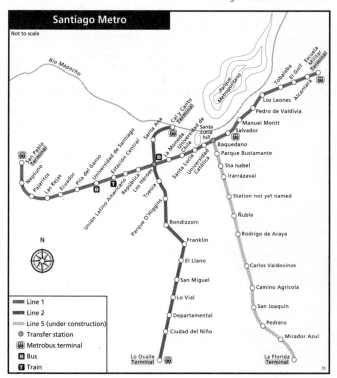

Santiago Metro

Not to scale

Río Mapocho

Parque Metropolitano

San Pablo Terminal
Neptuno
Pajaritos
Las Rejas
Ecuador
Pila del Ganso
Universidad de Santiago
Estación Central
Unión Latino Americano
República
Los Héroes
Toesca
Parque O'Higgins

Cal y Canto Terminal
La Moneda
Universidad de Chile
Santa Lucía hill
Santa Ana
Santa Lucía
Universidad Católica
Baquedano
Parque Bustamante
Sta Isabel
Irarrázaval
Station not yet named
Ñuble
Rodrigo de Araya
Carlos Valdovinos
Camino Agrícola
San Joaquín
Pedrero
Mirador Azul
La Florida Terminal

Manuel Montt
Salvador
Pedro de Valdivia
Los Leones
Tobalaba
El Golf
Alcántara
Escuela Militar Terminal

Rondizzoni
Franklin
El Llano
San Miguel
Lo Vial
Departamental
Ciudad del Niño
Lo Ovalle Terminal

N

Line 1
Line 2
Line 5 (under construction)
Transfer station
Metrobus terminal
Bus
Train

35

first. Hertz, Avis and Budget available from airport. **Hertz**, Av Andrés Bello 1469, T 225-9328, and airport, T 601-9262, has a good network in Chile and cars are in good condition. **Avis** at La Concepción 334, T 495-757, poor service reported. **Seelmann**, Antonio Varas 1472, of 156, T 225-2138, F 285-3222. **Automóvil Club de Chile** car rental, Marchant Pereira 122, Providencia, T 274-4167/6261, discount for members and members of associated motoring organizations. A credit card is usually asked for when renting a vehicle. Tax of 18% is charged but usually not included in price quoted. If possible book a car in advance. Remember that in the capital driving is restricted according to licence plate numbers; look for notices in the street and newspapers.

Metro: the first line of the underground railway system runs W-E between San Pablo and Escuela Militar, under the Alameda, and the second line runs N-S from Cal y Canto to Callejón Ovalle. The connecting station is Los Héroes. Line 5, from Baquedano S to La Florida is under construction. The trains are fast, quiet, and very full. The first train is at 0630 (Mon-Sat), 0800 (Sun and holidays), the last about 2245. Fares vary according to time of journey; there are 3 charging periods: high 0715-0900, 1800-1900, US$0.45; medium 0900-1800, 1930-2100 and weekends, US$0.40; low 0630-0715, 2100-2230, US$0.25. The simplest solution is to buy a *boleto valor*, US$3.50; a charge card from which the appropriate fare is deducted. Metrobus services connect with the metro at Lo Ovalle for southern Santiago and at Escuela Militar for Vitacura, Las Condes and Apoquindo.

Motorcycles: small BMW workshop, Av San Camilo 185, Sr Marco Canales. BMW car dealer *Frederic*, Av Portugal, has some spares. Also tyre shops in this area. BMW riders can also seek help from the *carabineros* who ride BMW machines and have a workshop with good mechanics at Av Rivera 2003.

Air International and domestic flights leave from Arturo Merino Benítez Airport at Pudahuel, 26 km NW of Santiago. There are two terminals: domestic and international. Airport information T 601-9709. On arrival get entry card from desk at entrance to arrivals hall before proceeding to immigration, otherwise you will be sent back. The international terminal is more modern and has most facilities, inc bank and Afex *cambio* (better rates, but not as good as in town), Sernatur office which will book accommodation and a fast-food plaza. The domestic terminal has a few shops, but they are very expensive, as are the bar and restaurant. Buy your wine etc in town. Left luggage US$2.50/bag/day.

Airport taxi, about US$15 but bargain hard and agree fare beforehand: more expensive with meter. Taxi to airport is much cheaper if flagged down in the street rather than booked by phone. Frequent bus services to/from city centre by 2 companies: *Tour Express* (Moneda 1529, T 671-7380) US$2.50, first bus from centre 0530, last from airport 0030; and *Centropuerto* (T 601-9883/695-8058), US$1.50, first from centre 0600, last from airport 2330. Buses leave from outside airport terminal and, in Santiago, from Moneda y San Martín calling at Plazoleta Los Héroes (near the yellow 'Línea 2' sign), Estación Central and the Terminal Santiago. (Beware the bus marked *Aeropuerto* which stops 2 km south of the Airport). *Empresa Turismo Bar-C* from your house or hotel to airport (or vice-versa), any time day or night, T 246-3600/1 for reservation (cheaper than taxi). *Empresa Navett*, Av Ejército Libertador 21 (nearest metro Los Héroes), T 695-6868 has a round-the-clock service, US$7. For schedules of domestic flights from Santiago, see under destinations.

Accommodation nearby at **B** pp *Hacienda del Sol y La Luna*, 4 Hijuela 9978, Pudahuel, T/F 601-9254, clean, English, German, French spoken, rec.

Trains No passenger trains to northern Chile. All trains leave from Estación Central at Alameda O'Higgins 3322. The line runs S to Rancagua, San Fernando, Curicó, Talca, Linares, Parral and Chillán, thereafter services go to 1) **Concepción**, 2) **Puerto Varas** (for Puerto Montt) via **Temuco**, with a bus connection to **Valdivia**. Schedules change with the seasons,

so you must check timetables before planning a journey. See under destinations for fares and notes on schedules. *Expreso* services do not have sleepers; some *rápidos* do (in summer *rápidos* are booked up a week in advance). *Dormitorio* carriages were built in Germany in 1930's, bunks (comfortable) lie parallel to rails, US-Pullman-style (washrooms at each end, one with shower-bath – often cold water only); an attendant for each car; bar car shows 3 films – no cost but you must purchase a drink ticket in advance. There is also a newer, *Gran Dormitorio* sleeping car (1984), with private toilet and shower, US$10 extra for 2, rec. For the *expresos* there are no reservations (get your ticket the morning of the day the train leaves and sit on the train as soon as you can get on; otherwise you'll stand for the whole journey). Free hot water supplied, so take own mug and coffee. Also a car-transporter service to Chillán, Temuco and Puerto Montt. Trains are still fairly cheap and generally very punctual, although 1st class is generally more expensive than bus; meals are good though expensive. Check for family, senior citizen and student discounts. Trains can be cold and draughty in winter and spring. There are also frequent local *Metrotren* services to Rancagua. Booking offices: for State Railways, Alameda O'Higgins 853 in Galería Hotel Libertador, Local 21, T 632-2801, Mon-Fri 0830-1900, Sat 0900-1300; or Metro Escuela Militar, Galería Sur, Local 25, T 228-2983, Mon-Fri 0830-1900, Sat 0900-1300; central station, open till 2230, T 689-5718/689-1682. For Calama-Oruro, contact Tramaca, Ahumada 11, Of 602, T 698-5536. Left luggage office at Estación Central.

A steam train runs tourist services between Santiago and Los Andes, 5-hrs' journey, T 698-5536 for details.

Buses There are frequent, and good, interurban buses to all parts of Chile. (**NB** Many leave early because of tight competition: arrive at bus station early.) Check if student rates are available (even for non-students), or reductions for travelling same day as purchase of ticket; it is worth bargaining over prices, especially shortly before departure and out of the summer season. Also take a look at the buses before buying the tickets (there are big differences in quality among bus companies); ask about the on-board services, many companies offer drinks for sale, or free, and luxury buses have meals and wine, colour videos, headphones. Reclining seats are common and there are also *salón cama* sleeper buses. Fares from/to the capital are given in the text. On Fri evening, when night departures are getting ready to go, the terminals are murder.

There are four bus terminals: 1) Terminal de Buses Alameda, which has a modern extension called Mall Parque Estación, O'Higgins 3712, metro Universidad de Santiago; all Pullman-Bus and Tur-Bus services go from here. 2). Terminal de Buses Santiago, O'Higgins 3878, one block W of Terminal Alameda, T 791-385, metro Universidad de Santiago; services to southern destinations; poorly organized. 3) Terminal San Borja, O'Higgins y San Borja, 1 block W of Estación Central, 3 blocks E of Terminal Alameda, metro Estación Central (entrance is, inconveniently, via a busy shopping centre); separate sections for buses to Region 5, inc Valparaíso and Viña del Mar and services to northern destinations; booking offices and departures organized according to destination. Left luggage US$1.50 per piece/day. 4) Terminal Los Héroes on Jiménez, just N of the Alameda, metro Los Héroes, has booking offices of about 10 companies for N and S routes as well as some international services. Varmontt buses, who run an expensive service to Puerto Montt, have their own terminal at Av 21 de Septiembre 2212 (office on 2nd floor), metro Los Leones.

See the note under **Taxis** about not taking expensive taxis parked outside bus terminals. Also, do not change money at the bus terminals; if coming from Argentina, try to get some Chilean pesos before you arrive.

International buses Most servies leave from Terminal Santiago, though there are also departures from Terminal Los Héroes.

Short distance: there are frequent services through the Cristo Redentor tunnel to **Mendoza** in Argentina, 6-7 hrs, US$15, many companies, departures around 0800, 1200 and 1600, touts approach you in Terminal Santiago. There are also collective taxis from the same terminal and from the 800/900 blocks of Morandé (Chi-Ar taxi company, Morandé 890, rec; Chile-Bus, Morandé 838; Cordillera Nevada, Morandé 870, T 698-4716), US$25, 5 hrs, shorter waiting time at customs.

Long distance: to Buenos Aires, US$65, 22 hrs (TAC and Ahumada rec); to **Montevideo**, most involving a change in Mendoza, eg Tas Choapa, 27 hrs, inc meals; to **Córdoba** direct, US$32, 18 hrs, several companies inc Turbus, Tas Choapa and TAC (El Rapido not rec); to **San Juan**, TAC, Tas Choapa, US$20; to **Bogotá** US$200, 7 days; to **Caracas** (Tues and

Fri 0900) US$230; to Lima, Ormeño, 51 hrs, US$70, it is cheaper to take a bus to Arica, a colectivo to Tacna (US$4), thence bus to Lima. Services also to **São Paulo** and **Rio de Janeiro** (eg Chilebus, Tues, Thur, Sat, US$100, 52 hrs); **Asunción** (4 a week, 28 hrs, US$75); **Guayaquil** and **Quito**. Tramaca, runs a *combinación* service which links with the train from Calama to **Uyuni** and **Oruro** in Bolivia. Géminis goes on Tues to **Salta**, Argentina, changing in Calama, US$60.

Hitchhiking To Valparaíso, take Metro to Pajaritos and walk 5 mins to W – no difficulty. Or, take bus 'Renca Panamericana' from MacIver y Monjitas. To hitch S, take Metro to Estación Central, then Buses del Paine at C Borja as far as possible on the highway to the toll area, about US$1, 75 mins. To hitch N take blue Metrobus marked 'Til-Til', frequent departures from near the Mercado Central as far as the toll bridge (*peaje*), 40 mins, US$60, then hitch from just beyond the toll-bridge. To Buenos Aires (and Brazil) take a bus to Los Andes, then go to Copec station on the outskirts (lots of trucks early morning).

Shipping Navimag, Av El Bosque Norte 0440, T 203-5030, F 203-5025, for services from Puerto Montt to Puerto Natales and viceversa. **Transmarchilay**, Agustinas 715, Oficina 403, T/F 633-5959, for services between Chiloé and the mainland, ferry routes on the Carretera Austral and on Lago General Carrera. M/n *Skorpios*: Augusto Leguía Norte 118, Las Condes, T 231-1030, F 232-2269 for luxury cruise out of Puerto Montt to Laguna San Rafael. Transmarchilay also sail to the Laguna San Rafael in summer. Check shipping schedules with shipping lines rather than Sernatur. **Patagonia Connection SA**, Fidel Oteíza 1921, Oficina 1006, Providencia (Metro Pedro de Valdivia), T 225-6489, F 274-8111, for services Puerto Montt-Coyhaique/Puerto Chacabuco-Laguna San Rafael.

Only posing Officer!

On 4 March 1997, London's *Financial Times* reported "Chilean Police stopped 49 motorists in Santiago for using cellular phones while driving, only to find that a third were pretending to talk on fake phones."

**DAY-TRIPS AND ACTIVITIES
OUTSIDE SANTIAGO**

SANTUARIO DE LA NATURALEZA YERBA LOCA

Situated 45 km NE of Santiago and reached by Route G21 (paved) towards Farellones, the park was founded in 1973. It covers 39,000 ha of the valley of the Río Yerba Loca ranging in altitude between 900 and 5,500m. Park administration is at Villa Paulina, 4 km N of Route G21, reached by a dirt road. From here a 4 hour walk leads N to Casa de Piedra Carvajal, which offers fine views. Further N are two hanging glaciers, La Paloma and El Altar.

Wildlife Native tree species include the mountain olive. Birdlife includes eagles and condors.

● **Park information** Open Sept to April (small entrance fee). No accommodation or transport. Maps and information available from Conaf in Santiago.

TERMAS DE COLINA

Situated 43 km N of Santiago, an attractive, popular spa in the mountains (915m). Take a bus from Cal y Canto metro station to the town of Colina (hourly in summer only, 40 mins), then another to the military base 1½ km from town. From here a rough road leads through beautiful countryside 6 km to **L3** *Hotel Termas de Colina*, T 844-1408, modern, thermal baths, beautiful swimming pool (closed Fri), formal restaurant; facilities open to public: swimming pool US$6 (crowded at weekends), thermal baths US$10; last return bus at 1900. On the walk to the hotel do not take photos or even show your camera when passing the military base. Taxi from Colina to the hotel, US$6.

The small towns in the Aconcagua Valley to the N – San Felipe, Jahuel and Los Andes – are described in the section 'To Argentina', page 108.

RESERVA NACIONAL RIO CLARILLO

45 km S of Santiago, reached by paved road via San Bernardo and Pirque, the park covers 10,185 ha and is situated in the precordillera at between 850 and 3,000m. Administration at entrance, 2 km SE of El Principal. Open all year.

● **Transport** Bus from Puente Alto to El Principal, US$2.50, 1 hr.

CAJON DEL MAIPO

Southeast of Santiago, in the Upper Maipo valley (Cajón del Maipo) are a number of resorts including: **San José de Maipo**, some 50 km from the capital, particularly beautiful in spring. The mountain town of **Melocotón** is 6 km further S, and **San Alfonso**, 4 km on. The walk from San Alfonso to the *Cascada de las Animas* is pleasant; ask permission to cross the bridge at the campsite (see below) as private land is crossed.

● **Accommodation** San José: **E** *Alojamento Inesita*, Comercio 301, good. **Melocotón**: **D** pp *Millahue*. **San Alfonso**: **B** *Posada Los Ciervos*, with breakfast and bath, **A** full board, good; **C** *Res España*, clean, comfortable, restaurant, also others; campsite at the *Comunidad Cascada de las Animas*, T 251-7506, also rents cabins (**C** for 4, hot water, cooking equipment etc) sauna, horseriding.

● **Places to eat** *Restaurant El Campito*, Camino al Volcán 1841, very good.

● **Transport** Buses leave Santiago from Metro Parque O'Higgins, Av Norte-Sur, or W side of Plaza Ercilla, every 30 mins to San José, US$2, 2 hrs.

31 km further SE is **El Volcán** (1,400m); there are astounding views, but little else (the village was wiped away in a landslide). **NB** If visiting this area or continuing further up the mountain, be prepared for military checks: passport and car registration numbers may be taken. From El Volcán the road (very poor condition) runs 14 km E to the **B** pp *Refugio Alemán Lo Valdés*, stone-built chalet accommodation, full board, own

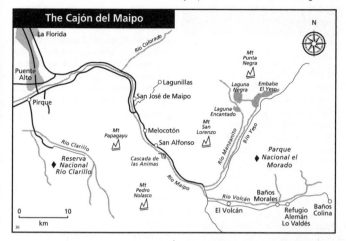

The Cajón del Maipo

generator, good food, rec, a good place to stay for mountain excursions, open all year. A splendid region which deserves the journey required to get there. Nearby are warm natural baths at **Baños Morales**, open from Oct, entry to baths, US$1. 12 km further E up the mountain is **Baños Colina**, not to be confused with Termas de Colina, see above; hot thermal springs, entry free, horses for hire. This area is popular at weekends and holiday times, but is otherwise deserted.

● **Accommodation & places to eat** At **Baños Morales**: D *Pensión Díaz*, friendly, good food, excellent café in the village, serving homemade jam, it closes at Easter for the winter; C pp *Refugio Baños Morales*, full board, hot water; D pp *Res Los Chicos Malos*, comfortable, fresh bread, good meals; free campsite. At **Baños Colina D** pp *Res El Tambo*, full board; restaurant, also camping. No shops so take food (try local goats cheese).

● **Transport** Buses from Metro Parque O'Higgins, to El Volcán 3 daily (US$2) and to Baños Morales daily in Jan/Feb, weekends only in March and Oct-Dec, at 0700, US$3, 3 hrs, returns at 1800; buy return on arrival to ensure seat back; alternatively, hitch back to Santiago on quarry lorries.

Parque Nacional El Morado
Situated N of Baños Morales, the park is reached by a turning off the main road from Puente Alto. It covers an area of 3,000 ha of the valley of the Río Morales, including the peaks of El Morado (5,060m) and El Mirador del Morado (4,320m), and El Morado glacier.

● **Park information** Administration is in Baños Morales. Park open Oct-April.

POMAIRE
A little town 65 km W of Santiago, where pottery can be brought and the artists can be observed at work. The area is rich in clay and the town is famous for its cider in the apple season (*chicha de uva*, 3 strengths: *dulce*, *medio* and *fuerte*) and Chilean dishes; highly rec: *Restaurant San Antonio*, welcoming, semi-outdoor, good food and service.

● **Transport** From Santiago take the Melipilla bus from C San Borja behind Estación Central metro station, every few minutes, US$1 each way, Rutabus 78 goes on the motorway, 1 hr, other buses via Talagante take 1 hr 25 mins (alight at side road to Pomaire, 2-3 km from town, colectivos every 10-15 mins – these buses are easier to take than the infrequent, direct buses); en route, delicious *pastel de choclo* can be obtained at *Restaurant Mi Ranchito*.

Climbing opportunities near Santiago (1)

🦶 The two main climbing areas are the *Grupo Loma Larga* and the *Grupo Plomo* (see Box **2**, below) each of which includes about a dozen peaks.

Grupo Loma Larga This massif, located around 100 km SE of Santiago, lies just N of the Parque Nacional el Morado and is reached via Baños Morales. The main peaks are El Morado (5,060m), Mesón Alto (5,297m), San Francisco (4,940m), Arenas (4,400m), the Mirador del Diablo and Cerro Unión. Cerro Morado, on the northern edge of the national park, is one of the most difficult climbs in Chile: the south face climb to the southern summit (5,000m) is particularly arduous involving 1,000m of vertical climbing, grade 9, on rock and ice.

VISITS TO VINEYARDS

The Maipo Valley is considered by many experts to be the best-wine producing area of Chile. Several vineyards in the Santiago area can be visited. *Cousiño-Macul*, Av Quilin on E outskirts of the city, offers tours Mon-Fri, phone first T 238-2855. *Concha y Toro* at Pirque, near Puente Alto, 40 km S of Santiago, T 850-3168, short tour (Spanish, English, French, German, Portuguese), Mon-Sat and Sun pm, free entry. Take 'La Puntilla' bus from Metro O'Higgins, 1 hr, US$1, asking to be dropped at Concha, or colectivo from Plaza Italia, US$2.50. The *Undurraga* vineyard at Santa Ana, SW of Santiago, T 817-2346, also permits visits with prior reservation only, 0930-1200, 1400-1600 on weekdays (tours given by the owner-manager, Pedro Undurraga). Take a Melipilla bus (but not Rutabus 78) to the entrance. *Viña Santa Carolina*, Rodrigo de Araya 1341, in Nuñoa, offers tours at weekends.

VISITS TO HACIENDAS

See under **Excursions**, San Fernando, for **Los Lingues**, page 209.

SKIING

There are six main ski resorts near Santiago, four of them around the mountain village of Farellones, 51 km E of the capital. All have modern lift systems, international ski schools, rental shops, lodges, mountain restaurants and first aid facilities. The season runs from June to

Sept/Oct, weather permitting, although some resorts have equipment for making artificial snow. Altitude sickness can be a problem, especially at Valle Nevado and Portillo: avoid overexertion on the first day or two.

Farellones, situated on the slopes of Cerro Colorado at 2,470m and reached by road in under 90 mins, was the first ski resort built in Chile. Now it is more of a service centre for the three other resorts, but it provides affordable accommodation, has a good beginners area and is connected by lift to El Colorado. Popular at weekends, it has several large restaurants. It offers beautiful views for 30 km across 10 Andean peaks and incredible sunsets. Daily ski-lift ticket, US$30; a combined ticket for all four resorts is also available, US$40-50 depending on season. 1-day excursions are available from Santiago, US$5; enquire Ski Club Chile, Goyenechea Candelaria 4750, Vitacura (N of Los Leones Golf Club), T 211-7341.

● **Accommodation** *Motel Tupungato* (Candelaria Goyenechea 4750, Santiago, T 218-2216), **A3** pp *Refugio Club Alemán Andino* (address under **Skiing and Climbing**, above), hospitable, good food; *Colorado Apart Hotel* (Av Apoquindo 4900, Oficina 43, Santiago, T 246-0660, F 246-1447); *Posada Farellones*, highly rec.

● **Transport** Buses from Santiago leave from from front of Omnium building, Av Apoquindo, 4 blocks from Escuela Militar Metro, daily at 0830, essential to book in advance, US$7. It is easy to hitch from the junction of

Av Las Condes/El Camino Farellones (petrol station in the middle): take a Las Condes bus from C Merced almost to the end of the line.

El Colorado

8 km further up Cerro Colorado has a large but expensive ski lodge at the base, offering all facilities, and a mountain restaurant higher up. There are 9 lifts giving access to a large intermediate ski area with some steeper slopes. *La Cornisa* and *Cono Este* are two of the few bump runs in Chile. A good centre for learning to ski. Lift ticket US$37.

● **Accommodation** *Edificio Los Ciervos* and *Edificio Monteblanco*, in Santiago, San Antonio 486, Oficina 151.

LA PARVA

6 km further E at 2,816m, is the upper class Santiago weekend resort with 12 lifts, 0900-1730. Accommodation is in a chalet village and there are some good bars in high season. Although the runs vary, providing good intermediate to advanced skiing, skiers face a double fall-line. Not suitable for beginners. Connections with Valle Nevado are good. Lift ticket, US$40; equipment rental, US$10-15 depending on quality.

In summer, this is a good walking area: a good trail leads to the base of Cerro El Plomo. Allow 3-4 days for the climb; ice axe and crampons necessary.

● **Accommodation** *Condominio Nueva Parva*, good hotel and restaurant, reservations in Santiago: Roger de Flor 2911, T 220-8510/206-5068. Three other restaurants.

VALLE NEVADO

16 km from Farellones, is owned by Spie Batignolles of France and was the site of the 1993 Pan American winter games. It offers the most modern ski facilities in Chile. "One has to imagine a deluxe hotel complex high up in the mountains with nothing else around" (Josselyn van der Pol and Leandro Yáñez). Although not to everyone's taste, it is highly regarded and and efficient. There are 25 runs accessed by 8 lifts. The runs are well prepared and are suitable for intermediate level skiers and beginners. There is a good ski school and excellent hell skiing is offered. Lift ticket US$30 weekdays, US$42 weekends.

● **Accommodation** *L1 Hotel Valle Nevado*, and more; *Hotel Puerta del Sol*; *Condominium Mirador del Inca*; 6 restaurants. *Casa Valle Nevado*, Gertrudis Echeñique 441, T 206-0027, F 228-8888.

PORTILLO

Situated at 2,855m, is 145 km N of Santiago and 62 E of Los Andes near the customs post on the route the Argentina. One of Chile's best-known resorts, Portillo lies near the Laguna del Inca, $5\frac{1}{2}$ km long and $1\frac{1}{2}$ km wide; this lake, at an altitude of 2,835m, has no outlet, is frozen over in winter, and its depth is not known. It is surrounded on three sides by accessible mountain slopes. From *Tío Bob's* there are magnificent views of the lake and surrounding area and condors may be spotted from the terrace. The runs are varied and well prepared, connected by 12 lifts, two of which open up the off-piste areas. This is an excellent family resort,

Climbing opportunities near Santiago (2)

Grupo Plomo Situated NE of Santiago, this group lies near the ski resort of La Parva. The main peaks are La Parva itself, El Plomo (5,430m), Paloma (4,930m) and El Altar (5,222m). El Plomo is not particularly difficult and is often used as an acclimatization climb before tackling Aconcagua or Ojos del Salado. It was the southernmost Inca sacrificial peak and the ruins near the summit are in good condition. Allow 3-4 days, ice axe and crampons essential. El Altar is one of the hardest climbs in Chile; particularly difficult is the very rarely scaled S face, grade 5.9 on loose rock.

with highly regarded ski school, and there are some gentle slopes for beginners near the hotel. The major skiing events are in Aug and September. Cheap packages can be arranged at the beginning and out of season. Lift ticket US$35, equipment hire US$22.

There are boats for fishing in the lake; but beware the afternoon winds, which often make the homeward pull 3 or 4 times as long as the outward pull. Out of season this is another good area for walking, but get detailed maps before setting out. Mules can be hired for stupendous expeditions to the glacier at the head of the valley or to the Cerro Juncal, to the pass in the W side of the valley.

● **Accommodation** **L2** *Hotel Portillo*, cinema, night club, swimming pool, sauna and medical service, on the shore of Laguna del Inca; accommodation ranges from lakefront suites, full board, fabulous views, to family apartments, to bunk rooms without or with bath (much cheaper, from C up), parking charges even if you go for a meal, jacket and tie obligatory in the dining room, self-service lunch, open all year. Reservations, Roger de Flor 2911, T 231-3411, F 699-2575, Tx 440372 PORTICZ, Santiago; **L3** *Hostería Alborada*, inc all meals, tax and service. During Ski Week (last in Sept), about double normal rate, all inclusive. Reservations, Agencia Tour Avión, Agustinas 1062, Santiago, T 72-6184, or C Navarro 264, San Felipe, T 101-R. Cheaper accommodation can be found in Los Andes but the road is liable to closure due to snow.

● **Places to eat** Cheaper than the hotels are *Restaurant La Posada* opp *Hotel Portillo*, open evenings and weekends only; and *Restaurant Los Libertadores* at the customs station 1 km away.

● **Transport** Except in bad weather, Portillo is easily reached by taking any bus from Santiago or Los Andes to Mendoza; you may have to hitch back.

Lagunillas

Lagunillas lies 67 km SE of Santiago in the Cajón del Maipo, 17 km E of San José de Maipo (see above for details of transport to San José de Maipo). Accommodation in the lodges of the Club Andino de

Chile (bookings may be made at Ahumada 47, Santiago). Tow fee US$20; lift ticket US$25; long T-bar and poma lifts; easy field. Being lower than the other resorts, its season is shorter, but it is also cheaper.

FROM SANTIAGO TO ARGENTINA

The route across the Andes via Los Andes and the Redentor tunnel is one of the major crossings to Argentina. Before travelling check on weather and road conditions beyond Los Andes. For buses on this route see under Santiago, **International Buses**.

Route 57 runs N from Santiago through the rich Aconcagua Valley, known as the Vale of Chile. North of Llaillay, at Km 69, the road forks – the W branch going to San Felipe, the E branch going to Los Andes.

SAN FELIPE

(*Pop* 42,000; *Alt* 635m; *Phone code* 034), the capital of Aconcagua Province, is 96 km N of Santiago and 128 km NE of Valparaíso. It is an agricultural and mining centre with an agreeable climate. Part of the Inca highway has recently been discovered in the city; previously, no traces had been found further S than La Serena. **Curimón**, 3 km SE of San Felipe, is the site of the Convento de Santa Rosa de Viterbo (1727) which has a small museum attached. A paved highway (13 km) runs N from San Felipe to the old town of **Putaendo**; in its church there is an 18th century baroque statue of Christ.

● **Accommodation** **C** *Hostería San Felipe*, Merced 204, T 510508.

TERMAS DE JAHUEL

Termas de Jahuel, high in the Cordillera (1,190m), is 18 km by road from San Felipe. The mountain scenery includes a distant view of Aconcagua.

● **Accommodation** **L2** *Termas de Jahuel*, T 511-240 or Santiago 393-810, thermal pool, tennis courts.

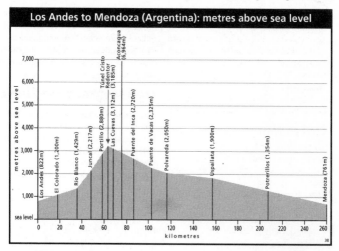

Los Andes to Mendoza (Argentina): metres above sea level

LOS ANDES

(*Pop* 30,500; *Alt* 730m; *Phone code* 034), 16 km SE of San Felipe and 77 km N of Santiago, is situated in a wealthy agricultural, fruit-farming and wine-producing area, but is also the site of a large car assembly plant. It is a good place for escaping from Santiago and a convenient base for skiing at nearby Portillo. There are monuments to José de San Martín and Bernardo O'Higgins in the Plaza de Armas, and a monument to the Clark brothers, who built the Transandine Railway to Mendoza (now disused). Good views from El Cerro de la Virgen, reached by a trail from the municipal picnic ground on Independencia (1 hr).

Museums Museo Arqueológico de los Andes, O'Higgins y Santa Teresa, 1030-1300, 1500-1830, entry US$0.60.

● **Accommodation A1** *Baños El Corazón*, at San Esteban, T 421371, with full board, use of swimming pool but thermal baths extra, take bus San Esteban/El Cariño (US$0.50); **B** *Plaza*, Esmeralda 367, T 421929, good but restaurant expensive; **D** *Central*, Esmeralda 278, T 421275, reasonable and very friendly (excellent bakery opp, try the *empanadas*); **E** *Alameda*, Argentina 576, T 422403, with-

out bath, clean; **F** pp *Res Maruja*, Rancagua 182, cheap, clean; **F** pp *Estación*, Rodríguez 389, T 421026, cheap restaurant; **F** *Valparaíso*, Sarmiento 160, clean.

● **Banks & money changers** Cambio Inter at *Plaza Hotel*, good rates, changes TCs.

● **Post & telecommunications Telephones**: CTC, O'Higgins 405.

● **Useful addresses Automovil Club de Chile** Chacabuco 33, T 422790.

● **Transport Trains** Rail service to Viña del Mar and Valparaíso (see under **Valparaíso**). **Buses** To Mendoza (Argentina) Tas Choapa, Fenix Pullman Norte, Cata and Ahumada. (Any of these will drop passengers off for Portillo, US$6). **Hitchhiking** Over the Andes possible on trucks from Aduana building in Los Andes.

EAST OF LOS ANDES

The road to Argentina follows the Aconcagua valley for 34 km until it reaches the village of **Río Blanco** (1,370m), where the Ríos Blanco and Juncal meet to form the Río Aconcagua. There is a fish hatchery with small botanical garden at the entrance to the Andina copper mine. East of Río Blanco the road climbs until Juncal where it zig-zags steeply through a series of 29 hairpin bends at the top of which is the ski resort of Portillo.

● **Accommodation** *Hostería Luna*, 4 km W of Río Blanco, good value, clean, helpful, good food; *Hostería Guardia Vieja*, 8 km E of Río Blanco, expensive but untidy, campsite. See above under skiing for services in Portillo.

● **Transport To Río Blanco**: buses run daily from Los Andes; from Santiago, Ahumada, at 1930 daily, direct, 2 hrs, US$2.

FRONTIER WITH ARGENTINA: LOS LIBERTADORES

The Redentor tunnel is open from 0800-1800 Chilean time, toll US$3. The old pass, with the statue of Christ the Redeemer (**Cristo Redentor**), is 8 km beyond the tunnel on the Argentine side. On the far side of the Andes the road descends 203 km to Mendoza.

● **Immigration & customs**
The Chilean border post is at Portillo. Bus and car passengers are dealt with separately. There may be long delays during searches for fruit, meat and vegetables, which may not be imported into Chile. All luggage entering Chile is X-rayed; remove all camera film before boarding bus as hand-luggage is not X-rayed.

● **Exchange**
Casa de Cambio in customs building in Portillo.

INTO ARGENTINA

The statue of El Cristo Redentor is at 3,854m. It was erected jointly by Chile and Argentina in 1904 to commemorate King Edward VII's decision in the boundary dispute of 1902. It is completely dwarfed by the landscape. As all transport across the frontier goes through 4-km tunnel, the statue can only be seen by taking a 12-hr excursion from Mendoza, or by walking from Las Cuevas (4½ hrs up, 2 down), a modern settlement being developed as a ski resort. The road from the tunnel to the statue is closed for the winter after the first snows of April.

Argentine customs are at Ingeniero Roque Carranza, 13 km from the tunnel. Just beyond is **Puente del Inca**, a sports resort named after the natural bridge which crosses the Río Mendoza. The bridge, apparently formed by sulphur-bearing hot springs, is 19m high, has a span of 21m and is 27m wide. At the resort is *Hostería Puente del Inca*, camping, transport to Mendoza and information and access for climbing **Aconcagua** (6,959m), the highest peak in the Americas. 17 km further E is **Punta de Vacas**, the Argentine immigration post, from where there is a good view of Tupungato (6,550m). The only town of any size between the frontier and Mendoza is **Uspallata** (accommodation, transport), from where two roads lead to Mendoza: the paved, southern branch of Route 7, via Potrerillos and Cacheuta, and the unpaved, northern branch via Villavicencio.

Valparaíso and Viña del Mar

PACIFIC BEACHES close to the capital include the international resort of Viña del Mar and a variety of others. On the same stretch of coast are the ports of Valparaíso and San Antonio.

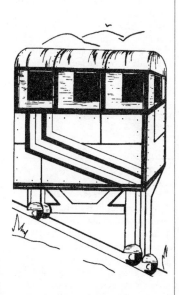

Ascensor

THE LAND

GEOGRAPHY

The coastal strip west of Santiago, stretching 130 km from the Río Petorca in the north to the Río Maipo in the south, includes two major cities, Valparaíso and Viña del Mar and a string of 24 other resorts, easily visited from Santiago. This proximity to the capital and a favourable climate make this the country's most popular coastal resort area attracting large numbers of Chileans and visiting Argentines.

This area is also one of the major economic centres of the country and its third most important industrial area. Valparaíso and San Antonio are major ports, between them handling much of the country's trade. Other facilities include an oil terminal and copper refinery at Quintero, an oil refinery at Concón and important chemical industries in Viña del Mar. It is also an impor-

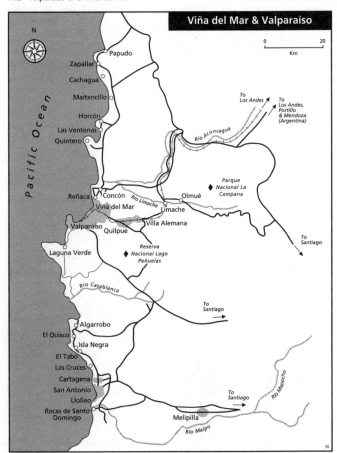

tant producer of agricultural products, particularly soft fruit such as grapes and peaches. Its population is over 90% urban.

CLIMATE

This coastline enjoys a Mediterranean-style climate; the cold sea currents and coastal winds produce much more moderate temperatures than in Santiago and the central valley. Rainfall is moderate in winter and the summers are dry.

HISTORY

This was one of the earliest areas settled by the Spanish, the lands being assigned to prominent conquistadores during the 16th century. For most of the colonial period this region was an important exporter of wheat and other foodstuffs to Peru. During the 19th century Valparaíso rose to become one of the most important ports on the Pacific coast of South America, but there were few other important centres along this coastline until the 1880s when the fashion for holidaying near the sea spread from southern Europe. Viña del Mar was established in 1880 and several other resorts followed between 1880 and 1900: Algarrobo, Cartagena, Las Cruces, Zapallar and Papudo, all owing part of their popularity to the building of railway lines linking them to the capital. Although the influence of European resorts can still be seen in some of the buildings, especially in Viña del Mar and Zapallar, most older buildings have not withstood earthquakes and bulldozers.

VALPARAISO

Valparaíso (*Pop* 277,000; *Phone code* 032) capital of V Región (Valparaíso), 90 km W of Santiago, is the principal port of Chile, and an important naval base. With the building of the new Congress building, it is also the seat of the Chilean parliament. The city is situated on the shores of a sweeping bay and on a crescent of hills behind. Seen from the ocean, it presents a majestic panorama: a great circle of hills is backed by the snowcapped peaks of the distant Cordillera.

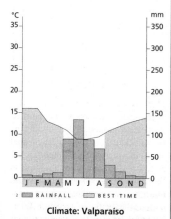

Climate: Valparaíso

History

Founded in 1542, Valparaíso became, in the colonial period, a small port used for trade with Peru. It was raided by pirates at least seven times in the colonial period. The city prospered from independence more than any other Chilean town. It was used in the 19th century by commercial agents from Europe and the United States as their trading base in the southern Pacific and became a major international banking centre as well as the key port for shipping between the northern Pacific and Cape Horn. Its decline was the result of the development of steam ships which stopped instead at the coal mines around Concepción and then to the opening of the Panama Canal in 1914. Since then it has declined further owing to the development of a container port in San Antonio, the shift of banks to Santiago and the move of the middle-classes to nearby Viña del Mar.

Little of the city's colonial past survived the pirates, tempests, fires and earthquakes of the period, but a remnant of the old colonial city can be found in the hollow known as El Puerto, grouped round the low-built stucco church of La Matriz. Most of the principal buildings date from after the devastating earthquake of 1906 (further serious earthquakes occurred in July 1971 and in March 1985) though some impression of its 19th century glory can be gained from the banking area of the lower town and from the mansions of wealthy merchants.

Places of interest

There are two completely different cities. The lower part, known as **El Plan**, is the business centre, with fine office buildings on narrow streets strung along the edge of the bay. Above, covering the hills ('cerros'), is a fantastic agglomeration of fine mansions, tattered houses and shacks, scrambled in oriental confusion along the narrow back streets. Superb views over the bay are offered from most

A walking tour of Cerros Alegre and Concepción

🏃 This is one of the best ways to view Valparaíso. From the Plaza de la Justicia a narrow passage (marked Museo de Bellas Artes) leads S to Ascensor El Peral. At the top end of the Ascensor turn left along Paseo Yugoslavo which offers superb views over the bay. On your right on the corner of Monte Alegre is the Palacio Baburrizza, formerly the residence of the nitrate barons, Ottorino Zanelli and Pascual Baburrizza, now housing the Museo de Bellas Artes.

The red and white mansion further along Monte Alegre on your left is now the Art Faculty of the University of Playa Ancha. At the end of the block turn left into C Leighton to reach a fork in the road over which towers an unusual building, 4-storeys high and 3m wide. Opposite is a passage, the Pasaje Bavestrello; at the other end of this turn left, cross C Urriola and climb the steps into Pasaje Galves. Take the first passage on your right (Pasaje Templeman) and you will emerge into C Templeman. About 50m along this is the Anglican church of **San Pablo**, built in 1858. From here follow Templeman 1 block NE, turn onto Abtao and you will reach the **Iglesia Luterano** (1897) from the base of which there are fine views over the Cerros. From the E end of the church follow Paseo Atkinson round (more fine views) and then turn right into C Papudo and right again into C Templeman. At the NE end of Templeman is the Paseo Gervasoni, from where you can return to the lower city via the Ascensor Concepción.

of the 'cerros'. The lower and upper cities are connected by steep winding roads, flights of steps and 16 *ascensores* or funicular railways dating from the period 1880-1914. The most unusual of these is **Ascensor Polanco** (entrance from C Simpson, off Av Argentina a few blocks SE of the bus station), which is in two parts, the first of which is a 160m horizontal tunnel through the rock, the second a vertical lift to the summit on which there is a *mirador*. Note that the lower entrance is in a slum area which is unsafe: do not go alone and do not take valuables.

The old heart of the city is the **Plaza Sotomayor**, dominated by the former **Intendencia** (Government House), now used as the Regional Naval Headquarters. Opposite is a fine statue to the 'Heroes of Iquique' (see page 225). The passenger quay is 1 block away (handicraft shops on quay) and nearby is the railway station, from which passenger services run on the metropolitan line to Los Andes. The streets of El Puerto run on either side from Plaza Sotomayor. C Serrano runs NW for 2 blocks to the

Plaza Echaurren, near which stands the church of **La Matriz**, built in 1842 on the site of the first church in the city. Further NW, along Bustamante lies the Plaza Aduana from where there is an *ascensor* to the bold hill of **Cerro Artillería**, crowned by the huge Naval Academy and a park.

Southeast of Plaza Sotomayor Calles Prat, Cochrane and Esmeralda run through the old banking and commercial centre to Plaza Aníbal Pinto, the most attractive square in Valparaíso around which are several of the cities oldest bars. Further E is the Plaza de la Victoria with the Cathedral; S of the Plaza on Cerro Bellavista and reached by C Molina is the Museo al Cielo Abierto, a collection of 20 murals on the exteriors of buildings. E of Plaza de la Victoria, reached by following C Pedro Montt is Plaza O'Higgins (flea market on Sat mornings), which is dominated by the imposing new **Congreso Nacional**.

To the W of **Cerro Artillería** the Av **Playa Ancha** runs to a stadium, seating

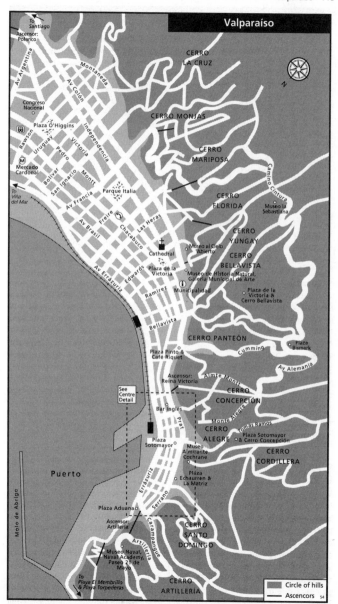

Valparaíso

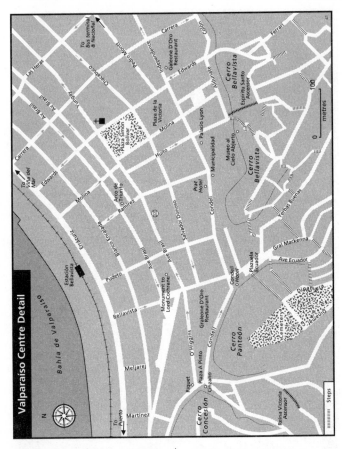

Valparaiso Centre Detail

20,000 people, on Cerro Playa Ancha. Avenida Altamirano runs along the coast at the foot of Cerro Playa Ancha to **Las Torpederas**, a picturesque bathing beach. The **Faro de Punta Angeles**, on a promontory just beyond Las Torpederas, was the first lighthouse on the W Coast; you can get a permit to go up. On another high point on the other side of the city is the **Mirador de O'Higgins**, the spot where the Supreme Dictator exclaimed, on seeing Cochrane's liberating squadron: 'On those four craft depends the destiny of America'.

The New Year is celebrated by a firework display on the bay, which is best seen from the Cerros.

Museums

Museo Municipal de Bellas Artes, with Chilean landscapes and seascapes and some modern paintings, housed in Palacio Baburizza, Paseo Yugoeslavo (free), open Tues-Sun 1000-1800; take Ascensor El Peral from Plaza Justicia, off Plaza Sotomayor.

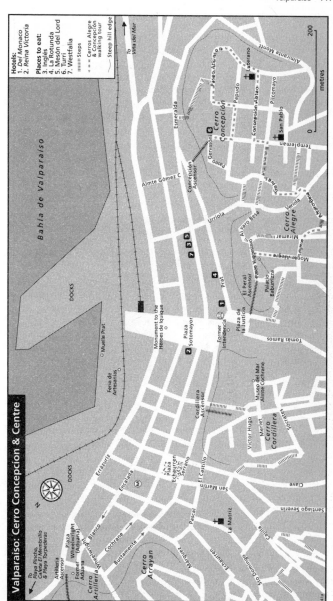

Valparaíso: Cerro Concepción & Centre

Hotels:
1. Del Monaco
2. Reina Victoria

Places to eat:
3. Inglés
4. La Rotunda
5. Mesón del Lord
6. Turri
7. Westfalia

▪▪▪ Steps
▪▪▪ Cerros Alegre & Concepción walking tour
—— Steep hill edge

Museo del Mar Almirante Cochrane, housing collection of naval models built by local Naval Modelling Club, good views over port, Tues-Sun 1000-1800, free, take Ascensor Cordillera from C Serrano, off Plaza Sotomayor, to Cerro Cordillera; at the top, Plazuela Eleuterio Ramírez, take C Merlet to the left.

Museo Naval, in the old Naval Academy on Cerro Artillería, Paseo 21 de Mayo, naval history 1810-1880, includes exhibitions on Chile's two naval heroes, Lord Cochrane and Arturo Prat, Tues-Sun 1000-1800, US$0.35 (take Ascensor Artillería from Plaza Aduana).

Museo de Historia Natural and **Galeria Municipal de Arte**, both in 19th-century Palacio Lyon, Condell 1546, Tues-Fri 1000-1300, 1400-1800, Sat/Sun 1000-1400.

Museo La Sebastiana, Pasaje Collado 1, Av Alemania, Altura 6900 on Cerro Florida, T 256606, former house of Pablo Neruda (see also his house at Isla Negra below), Tues-Sun 1030-1430, 1530-1800 (closes 1700 June-Aug), US$2 (take Verde Mar Bus O or D along Av Alemania).

Casa Mistral, Higueras 118, exhibition dedicated to life and work of Gabriela Mistral, Tues-Sun 1000-1330, 1530-1930.

Lord Cochrane

Lord Thomas Alexander Cochrane (1775-1860), born into a Scottish aristocratic family, began his career in the British navy during the Napoleonic Wars, rising rapidly as an officer, fighting a duel with a French officer in Malta and later being captured by the French and ransomed. He was elected to Parliament in 1806 as MP for Honiton and in 1807 as MP for Westminster. Although he had never been on good terms with his naval superiors, his use of the House of Commons to accuse the naval commander, Lord Gambier, of incompetence, led to his downfall. Gambier was court-martialled and acquitted; Cochrane was retired on half-pay and spent the next 3 years exposing corruption and abuses in the navy. His links with a financial scandal in 1814 provided his enemies with an opportunity for revenge: he was dismissed from the navy, expelled from Parliament and sentenced to 12 months imprisonment (he escaped and was recaptured).

Recruited for the armed forces by the Chilean agent in London, he quickly became friendly with O'Higgins and was put in command of the new republic's navy, a few ill-equipped vessels which relied on foreign adventurers for experienced sailors. With this fleet Cochrane harassed the Spanish-held ports along the Chilean coast; his audacious storming of the fortresses of Corral, San Carlos and Amargos led to the capture of the key Spanish base of Valdivia. Later that year Cochrane transported San Martín's troops along the Pacific coast to invade Peru, but his relations with San Martín were poor and he became very critical of the latter's cautious strategy. Afterwards he continued to attack Spanish shipping in the Pacific, in 1822 sailing as far N as Mexico.

In 1823 the new government of Brazil appointed him to head its navy in the struggle for independence from Portugal. Once again leading a motley collection of boats manned largely by foreigners, Cochrane drove a Portuguese fleet from Bahía and pursued it back to Portugal. In 1825 he fell out with the Brazilian government and returned to Britain. Two years later he volunteered to help the Greeks in their struggle for independence from Turkey. He was reinstated in the British navy in 1832, was promoted to Rear-Admiral and spent much of the rest of his life promoting developments in the use of steam power in shipping.

Sightseeing

Launches run trips in summer around the harbour from Muelle Prat, 30 mins, US$1.20, to Playa Las Torpederas and to Viña del Mar; other boats for hire for fishing. **NB** Don't photograph naval ships or installations. The **Camino Cintura**/Av Alemania is the only road which connects all the hills above Valparaíso; it affords constantly changing views, perhaps the best being from Plaza Bismark. No 9 'Central Placeres' bus gives a fine scenic drive over the hills to the port; also bus 'Mar Verde' (O) from Av Argentina near the bus terminal to Plaza Aduana.

Excursions

The **Reserva Nacional Peñuelas**, covering 9,260 ha surrounding the artificial Lago Peñuelas, is situated SE of Valparaíso near the main road to Santiago (Route 68). Much of the park is covered by mixed forest and shrubs. Access is permitted for walking and fishing; administration at park entrance, about 30 km from Valparaíso

● **Transport** Buses between Valparaíso and Santiago pass the entrance.

Laguna Verde, 18 km S of Valparaíso, is a picturesque bay for picnics, reached by a 2-hr dusty walk over the hills.

● **Accommodation** E pp *Posada Cruz del Sur*, also camping; *Camping Los Olivos*, good facilities, well run and friendly.

● **Transport** Bus No 3, marked 'Laguna Verde' from Victoria y Rancagua, hourly.

Quintay further S is a fishing village reached by turning left at Peñuelas on the main Santiago-Valparaíso road.

Local information
● **Accommodation**

B *Prat*, Condell 1443, T 253081, scruffy entrance but comfortable rooms, central, restaurant; under same management is **B** *Condell*, Pirámide 557, T 212788, similar.

C *Lancaster*, Chacabuco 2362, with bath and breakfast, clean; **C** *Reina Victoria*, Plaza Sotomayor 190, T 212203, D on top floors, without bath, with breakfast, poor beds, run down, clean.

D *Res Dinamarca*, Dinamarca 539 (from Plazuela Ecuador – just S of Condell y Bellavista – take any micro marked 'Cárcel'; or climb 10 mins up Av Ecuador), hot water, clean, good value, also short stay, parking, not nr restaurants but serves full breakfast and snacks; **D** *Garden*, Serrano 501, T 252776, friendly, hot water, use of kitchen; **D** *Res Lily*, Blanco Encalada 866, T 255995, 2 blocks from Plaza Sotomayor, clean, safe (despite no locks on doors); **D** *Enzo and Martina Tesser*, Av Quebrada Verde, T 288873, with breakfast, German spoken, friendly (reached by bus 1); **D** pp *María Pizarro*, Chacabuco 2340, Casa No 2, T 230791, clean, lovely rooms, central, quiet, kitchen, highly rec; her neighbours, Francisca Escobar and Guillermo Jones, Chacabuco 2326, T 214193, also rent rooms, same price, equally rec, English spoken.

E pp *Res Mi Casa*, Rawson 310, nr bus terminal, friendly, basic, fleas, also has rooms at Yungay 2842, quiet; **E** pp *Sra Mónica*, Av Argentina 322, Casa B, T 215673, 2 blocks from bus terminus, friendly; **E** pp *Sra Silvia*, Pje La Quinta 70, Av Argentina, 3 blocks from Congress, T 216592, clean, quiet, kitchen facilities, rec; **E** pp *Sra Anita*, Higuera 107, Cerro Alegre, with good breakfast, clean, hot water, wonderful views. Many of the 'cheap' hotels in the Chacabuco area are for short-term occupation only. Youth hostel office at Edwards 695, p 3, will extend membership; nearest hostel in Viña del Mar.

● **Places to eat**

Al Galeone D'Oro, Independencia 1766, Italian, not cheap but good; *Tentazione*, Pedro Montt 2484, good, cheap; *La Parrilla de Pepe*, Pedro Montt 1872, good food and service; *Hamburg*, O'Higgins 1274, German management, German beer, beware of overcharging; *Del Mónico*, Prat 669, good, cheap lunches, popular; *La Rotunda*, Prat 701, good food; *Nantón*, Brasil 1368, Chinese, good. Around the market there are lots of cheap lunch restaurants, specialising in seafood inc *Los Porteños*, Valdivia 169, very good. At Caleta Membrillo, 1 km NW of Plaza Sotomayor there are several good fish restaurants inc *Club Social de Pescadores*, Altamirano 1480, good; opp are *San Pedro*, shabby but friendly, and *El Membrillo*, more expensive. Other good places for lunch: *Nahuel*, Donoso 1498, popular, cheap; *Mesón del Lord*, Cochrane 859; *Bambú*, Pudeto 450, vegetarian.

Cafés and bars: two traditional bar/restaurants on Plaza Aníbal Pinto are: *Riquet*, traditional, comfortable, expensive, good coffee and breakfast, rec; *Cinzano*, popular. *Bar Inglés*, Cochrane 851 (entrance also on Blanco Encalada), good food and drink, traditional, rec, not cheap; *Westfalia*, Cochrane 847, coffee, breakfasts, vegetarian lunches; *Café do Brasil*, Condell 1342, excellent coffee, juices, sandwiches; *Turri*, Templemann 147, on Cerro Concepción, T 259196, overlooking port, good food and service.

● **Airline offices**
LanChile, Esmeralda 1048, T 251441; Ladeco, Blanco Encalada 951, T 216355.

● **Banks & money changers**
Banks open 0900 to 1400, but closed on Sat. Good rates at **Banco de Santiago**, Prat 816, and **Banco de Crédito e Inversiones**, Cochrane 820; **Fincard** (Mastercard), Esmeralda 1087; **Exprinter**, Prat 887 (the building with the clocktower at junction with Cochrane), good rates, no commission on TCs, open 0930-1400, 1600-1900; **Inter Cambios**, Errázuriz esq Plaza Sotomayor, good rates; **Gema Tour**, Esmeralda 940; **New York**, Prat 659, good rates for cash; **Afex**, Cochrane 828. When *cambios* are closed, street changers operate outside *Inter Cambios*.

● **Cultural centres**
Instituto Chileno-Norteamericano, Esmeralda 1069, shows foreign films.

● **Embassies & consulates**
British Consul, Blanco Encalada 725, oficina 26, T 256117, Casilla 82-V; Argentine Consul, Cochrane 867.

● **Entertainment**
Proa Al Canaveral, Errázuriz 304, good seafood restaurant downstairs, pleasant bar upstairs with dancing from 0100, poetry reading on Thur; several popular bars on Ecuador, some with live music and small entry charge.

● **Hospitals & medical services**
Dentist: *Dr Walther Meeden Bella*, Condell 1530, Depto 44, T 212233.

● **Laundry**
Las Heras 554, good and cheap

● **Post & telecommunications**
Telecommunications: VTR Telecommunications, Cochrane 825; CTC, Esmeralda 1054 or Pedro Montt 2023; Entel, Condell 1491.

● **Security**
Robbery is increasingly common in El Puerto and around the *ascensores*, especially on Cerro Santo Domingo.

● **Shopping**
Bookshop: *Librería Universitaria*, Esmeralda 1132, good selection of regional history; many others.

● **Tourist offices**
In the Municipalidad building, Condell 1490, Oficina 102, open Mon-Fri 0830-1400, 1530-1730. Kiosks at bus terminal (good map available), helpful, open 0900-1300, 1530-1930 (closed Thur, Mar-Nov), Muelle Prat, open Nov-March 1030-1430, 1600-2000, and in Plaza Victoria, open 1030-1300, 1430-2000 Nov-March.

● **Useful addresses**
YMCA: (Asociación Cristiana de Jóvenes), Blanco Encalada 1117. **YWCA**: (Asociación

Neruda on Valparaíso

"The hills of Valparaíso decided to dislodge their inhabitants, to let go of the houses on top, to let them dangle from cliffs that are red with clay, yellow with gold thimble flowers, and a fleeting green with wild vegetation. But houses and people clung to the heights, writhing, digging in, worrying, their hearts set on staying up there, hanging on, tooth and nail, to each cliff. The port is a tug-of-war between the sea and nature, untamed on the cordilleras. But it was man who won the battle little by little. The hills and the sea's abundance gave the city a pattern, making it uniform, not like a barracks, but with the variety of spring, its clashing colours, its resonant bustle. The houses became colours: a blend of amaranth and yellow, crimson and cobalt, green and purple."

Pablo Neruda, *Memoirs*, Penguin, 1978.

Cristiana Feminina), Blanco 967. **Valparaíso Seamen's Institute**: Blanco Encalada 394.

● **Transport**

Local Taxis: are more expensive than Santiago: a short run under 1 km costs US$1. **Buses** Buses and modern electric buses, US$0.20 within city limits. **Funiculares** US$0.30.

Trains Regular service on Merval, the Valparaíso metropolitan line between Valparaíso, Viña del Mar, Quilpué, Limache, Quillota, La Calera, Llaillay, San Felipe and Los Andes (and intermediate stations); to Viña del Mar every 15-30 mins, trains that run the entire route are 1800 daily, 1430 Mon-Fri (not holidays), 0805, Sat, Sun and holidays, fare to Los Andes US$1.50, 3 hrs. *El Porteño* tourist train runs on Sun, 1 Jan-28 Feb and on most public holidays.

Shipping For shipping services from Valparaíso to the Juan Fernández Islands and Easter Island see below under **The Chilean Pacific Islands**.

Buses Terminal is on Pedro Montt 2800 block, corner of Rawson, 1 block from Av Argentina; plenty of buses between terminal and Plaza Sotomayor. Excellent and frequent service to **Viña del Mar**, 25 min, US$0.25 from Plaza Aduana, passing along Av Errázuriz; colectivos to Viña US$0.40. To **Santiago**, 2 hrs, US$3-4, shop around, frequent (book on Sat to return to the capital on Sun); to **Concepción**, 11 hrs, US$12; to **Puerto Montt**, 17 hrs, US$18; to **La Serena**, 8 hrs, US$10; to **Calama**, US$35; to **Arica**, US$40, Fénix *salón cama* service, US$50. To Argentina: to **Mendoza**, 4 companies, 6-7 hrs, US$25; to **Córdoba**, US$40.

If driving to Santiago the main road passes through two tunnels, toll of US$3.25 paid at the first, but this can be avoided by turning off onto the old road over the mountains about 1 km before the tunnel; there is another toll just before the start of the motorway, 56 km from Santiago.

Hitchhiking To Santiago is easy from the service station on Av Argentina.

FROM VALPARAISO TO ARGENTINA

If driving from Valparaiso to the Argentine border, Route 62 runs through Viña del Mar, climbs out of the bay and goes through (16 km) **Quilpué**, 1½ km E of El Retiro, a popular inland resort with medicinal springs and a municipal zoo. It crosses a range of hills and reaches the Aconcagua Valley at **Limache**, a sleepy market town, 40 km from Valparaíso (*Pop* 22,511). Route 62 joins Route 60 just before **Quillota**, an orchard centre (**B** *Balneario El Edén*, 5 km out of town, cabins for rent, up to 6 people, very good restaurant in an old estate building, T 311963, F 312342, good swimming), continuing to La Calera (88 km from Valparaíso), where it joins the Pan-American Highway; turn SE and E for Llaillay, San Felipe, Los Andes and the Redentor tunnel to Mendoza.

PARQUE NACIONAL LA CAMPANA

Situated N of Olmué (8 km E of Limache), the park covers 8,000 ha and includes Cerro La Campana (1,828m) which Darwin climbed in 1836 and Cerro El Roble (2,200m). There are extensive views from the top of these Cerros, but a guide may be necessary because there are a number of ascents, some of which are very difficult.

Wildlife Much of the park is covered by native woodland. Near Ocoa there are areas of Chilean palms (*kankán*), now found in only two locations in Chile.

● **Access** There are three entrances: at Granizo, reached by paved road from Olmué, 5 km E; at Cajón Grande, reached by unpaved road which turns off the Olmué-Granizo road; at Palmar de Ocoa to the N reached by unpaved road (10 km) leading off the Pan-American Highway between Hijuelas and Llaillay. There is no public transport to the park.

VIÑA DEL MAR

(*Phone code* 032), 9 km NE of Valparaíso via Route 68 which runs along a narrow belt between the shore and precipitous cliffs. This is one of South America's leading seaside resorts. 6 km further N along the coast is the more exclusive resort of **Reñaca**.

Places of interest

The older part is situated on the banks of

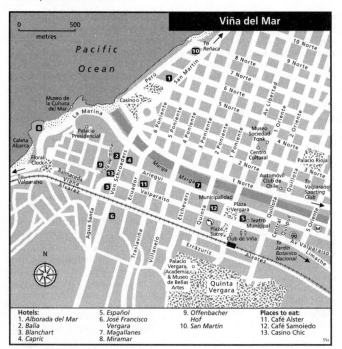

Viña del Mar

0   500
metres

Pacific
Ocean

Hotels:
1. Alborada del Mar
2. Balia
3. Blanchart
4. Capric
5. Español
6. José Francisco
   Vergara
7. Magallanes
8. Miramar
9. Offenbacher
   Hof
10. San Martín
Places to eat:
11. Café Alster
12. Café Samoiedo
13. Casino Chic

a lagoon, the Marga Marga, which is crossed by bridges. Around Plaza Vergara and the smaller Plaza Sucre to its S are the **Teatro Municipal** (1930) and the exclusive **Club de Viña**, built in 1910. The municipally owned **Quinta Vergara**, formerly the residence of the shipping entrepreneur Francisco Alvarez, lies two blocks S. The grounds are superb and include a double avenue of palm trees. The **Palacio Vergara**, in the gardens, houses the Museo de Bellas Artes and the Academia de Bellas Artes. Part of the grounds is a children's playground, and there is an outdoor auditorium where concerts and ballet are performed in the summer months, and in Feb an international song festival is held. (Tickets from the Municipalidad).

Further W on a headland overlooking the sea is **Cerro Castillo**, the summer palace of the Presidents of the Republic: its gardens can be visited. Just N, on the other side of the lagoon is the **Casino**, built in the 1930s and set in beautiful gardens, US$6 to enter, jacket and tie for men required (open all year).

The main beaches, Acapulco and Mirasol are located to the N but S of Cerro Castillo is Caleta Abarca, also popular. Beaches may be closed because of pollution. The coastal route N to Reñaca provides lovely views over the sea. East of the centre are the **Valparaíso Sporting Club** with a racecourse and playing fields. North of here in the hills are the Granadilla Golf Club and a large artificial lake, the **Laguna Sausalito**, adjacent to which is the Estadio Sausalito (home to Everton soccer team, among many other sporting facilities). It possesses an excellent tourist complex with swimming pools, boating, tennis courts, sandy beaches, water skiing, restaurants, etc. Entry US$2.50, children under 11, US$1.75; take colectivo No 19 from C Viana.

Museums

Museo de la Cultura del Mar, in the Castillo Wulff, on the coast near Cerro Castillo, contains a collection on the life and work of the novelist and maritime historian, Salvador Reyes, Tues-Sat 1000-1300, 1430-1800, Sun 1000-1400.

Museo de Bellas Artes, Quinta Vergara, Tues-Sun 100-1400, 1500-1800, US$0.25.

Palacio Rioja, Quillota 214, built in 1906 by a prominent local family and now used for official municipal receptions, ground floor preserved in its original state, open to visitors 1000-1400, 1500-1800, Tues-Sun, rec.

Museo Sociedad Fonk, C 4 Norte 784, archaeological museum, with objects from Easter Island and the Chilean mainland, including Mapuche silver, open Tues-Fri 1000-1800, Sat-Sun 1000-1400, entry US$0.20. An Easter Island statue stands on the lawn between the railway and the beach just beyond Caleta Portales, between Viña del Mar and Valparaíso.

Centro Cultural, Libertad 250, holds regular exhibitions.

Excursions

The **Jardín Botánico Nacional**, formerly the estate of the nitrate entrepreneur Pascual Baburizza, now administered by Conaf, lies 8 km SE of the city. Covering 405 ha, it contains over 3,000 species from all over the world and a collection of Chilean cacti but the species are not labelled. Take bus 20 from Plaza Vergara, entry US$1.

Local festivals

El Roto, 20 Jan, in homage to the workers and peasants of Chile.

Local information

● **Accommodation**

Many in **L3-A3** range, some with beach.

L3 *San Martín*, San Martín 667, T 689191, with breakfast.

A2 *Alborada del Mar*, San Martín 419, T 975274, tastefully decorated; **A2** *Español*, Plaza Vergara 191, T/F 685145, with bath, TV, phone and *Restaurante Colonial*; **A2** *José Francisco Vergara*, Dr von Schroeders 392, T 626022, has garden houses for up to 5; **A3** *Res Offenbacher Hof*, Balmaceda 102, T 621483, clean, friendly, rec; **A3** *Monte Carlo*, V MacKenna 136, 6 km N in Reñaca, T 830397, very modern, comfortable.

B *Alejandra*, 2 Poniente 440, T 974404, with shower and breakfast (C in low season); **B** *Balia*, von Schroeders 36, T 978310, F 680724, bath, TV, phone, parking; **B** *Petit Palace*, Paseo Valle 387, T 663134, small rooms, good, central, quiet; **B** *Quinta Vergara*, Errázuriz 690, T 685073, clean, friendly, large rooms, beautiful gardens, rec.

C *Capric*, von Schroeder 39, T 978295, with bath, TV, good value, **E** pp IYHA card holders; **C** *El Escorial*, two places: one at 5 Poniente 114, the other at 5 Poniente 441 (T 975266), with breakfast, shared bath, clean, central; **C** *Res Magallanes*, Arlegui 555, T 685101, with breakfast, clean, mixed reports; *Res Victoria*, Valparaíso 40, T 977370, without bath, with breakfast, clean, central; **C** *Res Villarica*, Arlegui 172, good, friendly.

D *Res Agua Santa*, Agua Santa 34, basic, hot shower; **D** *Res Blanchart*, Valparaíso 82, T 974949, clean, with breakfast, hot water, good service; **D** *Res Familiar*, Batuco 147, clean, friendly; **D** *Res France*, Montaña 743, clean, safe, helpful; **D** *Sra Nalda*, 2 Norte 849 (Pasaje Klamer), T 970488, good garden, cooking facilities, rec; **D** *Res Tajamar*, Alvarez 884, opp railway station, old-fashioned, central, huge rooms, atmospheric; **E** pp von Schroeder 151, T 971861, clean, safe, helpful. There are a great many more places to stay inc private accommodation (E pp). Out of season furnished apartments can be rented through agencies (with commission). In season it is cheaper to stay in Valparaíso and commute to the Viña beaches.

Camping: *Camping Reñaca*, Santa Luisa 401, expensive, dirty, also cabins.

Motels: several at Reñaca (6 km N of Viña del Mar).

Youth hostels: E pp *Res La Montaña*, Agua Santa 153, T 622230, for YHA card holders, with breakfast, other meals available, dingy, dirty bathroom, no cooking facilities, also family rooms; **E** pp *Lady Kinnaird Hostal*, 1 Oriente 1096, T 975413, YWCA, central, friendly, English spoken, women only, highly rec. See also *Hotel Capric* above.

● **Places to eat**
At hotels. *Cap Ducal*, Marina 51, expensive; *Raul*, Valparaíso 533, live music; *Casino Chico*, Valparaíso y von Schroeders, Chilean and international dishes; *Panzoni*, Pasaje Cousiño 12-B, good lunches, Italian; *Machitún Ruca*, San Martín 529, excellent. *Pizzería Mama Mía*, San Martín 435, good, reasonably priced; *Armandita*, San Martín 501, *parrilla*, large portions, good service; *El Encuentro*, San Martín 477, fish, very good; *Las Gaviotas*, 14 Norte 1248, Chilean meat dishes, not expensive, live music. Many restaurants on Av Valparaíso, try in the Galerías (arcades), eg *Café Big Ben*, No 469, good coffee, good food; *Alster*, No 225, expensive; *Samoiedo*, No 637, *confitería*, grill and restaurant. Several pleasant restaurants and cafés along the renovated Muelle Vergara inc *La Mía Pappa*, Italian, good lunches and evening buffets. *Centro Vital*, Av Valparaíso 376, vegetarian, excellent lunches.

In Reñaca: *El Pancho*, Av Borgoño 16180, excellent seafood and service; *Anastassia*, Av Borgoño 15000, excellent international menu, expensive; *Rincón Marino*, Av Borgoño 17120, good seafood, pricey; *Hotel Oceanic*, Av Borgoño, T 830006, very good, expensive.

● **Banks & money changers**
Many *casas de cambio* on Arlegui inc **Afex**, No 641 (open 0900-1400 Sat); **Cambio Norte**, No 610; **Cambio Andino**, No 644; also in the tourist office; **Fincard** (Mastercard), Ecuador 259.

● **Cultural centres**
Instituto Chileno-Británico, 3 Norte 824, T 971061; **Instituto Chileno – Norteamericano de Cultura**, 3 Norte 532, T 662145; **Casa Italia** (cultural centre, consulate, restaurant), Alvarez 398; **Goethe Institut**, El Salto, 20 mins from town; **Instituto Chileno-Francés**, Alvarez 314, T 685908.

● **Entertainment**
Discotheques: *Topsy Topsy*, Santa Luisa 501 and *La Cantina del Cocodrilo*, Av San Martín, both in Reñaca, expensive, rec; *El Gato de la Luna*, Arlegui 396, good bar, live music and dancing.

● **Post & telecommunications**
Telephone: CTC, Valparaíso 628; Global Telecommunications/Entel, 15 Norte 961.

● **Shopping**
Market: at intersection of Av Sporting and river, Wed and Sat.

● **Tourist offices**
Valparaíso 507, Of 303, T 882285. Arrangements may be made at the Tourist Office for renting private homes in the summer season. **Automóvil Club de Chile**: 1 Norte 901, T 689509.

● **Transport**
Local Car hire: Euro Rent-A-Car, in *Hotel O'Higgins*, clean cars, efficient.

Air Ladeco Santiago-Viña del Mar (to naval airfield nr Concón), several daily, 10 mins, US$15, T 978210; National T 883505; Alta, Av Libertad 22, local 1, T 692920, F 692917.

Trains Services on the Valparaíso Metropolitan line (Merval) stop at Viña (details under Valparaíso).

Buses Terminal at Av Valparaíso y Quilpué. To **Santiago**, US$3-4, 2 hrs, frequent, many companies, heavily booked in advance for travel on Sun afternoons, at other times some buses pick up passengers opposite the train station; to **La Serena**, 6 daily, 8 hrs, US$10, to **Antofagasta**, 20 hrs, US$35.

RESORTS NORTH OF VIÑA DEL MAR

North of Viña del Mar the coast road runs through Las Salinas, a popular beach between two towering crags, Reñaca and Cochoa, where there is a large sealion colony 100m offshore, to Concón. There is also a much faster inland road, between Viña del Mar and Concón.

CONCON

On the southern shore of a bay at the mouth of the Río Aconcagua, Concón is 18 km N of Viña del Mar. Main attractions: tennis, bathing, fishing, and riding. Main eyesore: an oil refinery (not visible from beach; some pollution). Near the Concón beach there is a pelican colony.

● **Accommodation L2** *Hostería Edelweis*, Av Borgoño 19200, T 903600, modern cabins, clean, comfortable, sea views, inc breakfast, excellent food in attached restaurant, German spoken, highly rec; several motels; **D** *Cabañas Koala Place*, Los Pescadores 41, T 813026, one-night stays unwelcome.

● **Places to eat** Good seafood *empanadas* at bars; *Vista al Mar*, Av Borgoño 21270, T 812-221, good fish restaurant, good value; *Don Chico*, Av Borgoño 21410, good seafood; *Mirador Cochoa*, Av Borgoño 17205, good, pricey.

QUINTERO

(*Pop* 16,000) another 16 km N of Concón, is a fishing town situated on a rocky peninsula with lots of small beaches. On the N shore of the bay at Las Ventanas are a power station and copper processing plant.

● **Accommodation A2** *Yachting Club*, Luis Acevedo 1736, T 930061; **D** *Isla de Capri*, 21 de Mayo 1299, T 930117, pleasant, sea views; **D** *Monaco*, 21 de Mayo 1530, T 930939, run down but interesting, good views. A number of *residenciales*.

HORCON

(Also known locally as Horcones) Horcón, set back in a cove surrounded by cliffs, is a pleasant small village, mainly of wooden houses. On the beach hippies sell cheap and unusual jewellery and trinkets. Vegetation is tropical with many cacti on the cliff tops. Seafood lunches with the catch of the day, sold at any number of stalls on the seafront, are recommended. It is best avoided in Jan-Feb when it is packed out. Drinking alcohol on the beach is forbidden – and enforced by the *carabineros*.

● **Accommodation B** *El Ancla*, cabañas, pleasant; **C** *Cabañas* on Playa Cau Cau, good; **C-B** *Aranciba*, with bath, **D** without, pleasant gardens, good food, friendly, rec; also rooms in private houses; no campsite but camping possible at private houses.

● **Places to eat** *El Ancla* rec; *Reina Victoria*, cheap, good.

Maitencillo (*Pop* 1,200), 19 km N of Las

Ventanas, consisting mainly of chalets, has a wonderful long beach. Just to the S is the tourist complex of Marbella, which has a hotel, conference centre, restaurants, golf course, tennis courts, pools.

● **Accommodation A3** *Cabañas Hermansen*; several hotels.

ZAPALLAR

(*Pop* 2,200) a fashionable resort 33 km N of Las Ventanas. A hint of its former glory is given by a number of fine mansions along Av Zapallar. At Cachagua, 3 km S a colony of penguins may be viewed from the northern end of the beach.

● **Accommodation A1** *César*, T 711313, very nice but expensive; **A3** *Isla Seca*, T 711508, small, pool, good restaurant; good, reasonably-priced food in *Restaurant César* (different management from hotel), on seafront; no *residenciales*, no campsite.

PAPUDO

(*Pop* 2,500), 10 km further N. This was the site of a naval battle in Nov 1865 in which the Chilean vessel *Esmeralda* captured the Spanish ship *Covadonga*. Following the arrival of the railway Papudo rivalled Viña del Mar as a fashionable resort in the 1920s but it has long since declined. Among the buildings surviving from that period is the Casa Rawlings, now the *Casa de la Cultura*.

● **Accommodation D** *Moderno*, F Concha 150, T 711496; **D'** *Peppino*, No 609, T 711482; many more.

● **Transport** Buses from Valparaíso and Viña del Mar: To **Concón** bus 9 or 10 (from Av Libertad between 2 and 3 Norte in Viña), US$0.50; to **Quintero** and **Horcón**, Sol del Pacífico, every 30 mins, US$1, 2 hrs; to **Zapallar** and **Papudo**, Sol del Pacífico, 4 a day (2 before 0800, 2 after 1600), US$3.

RESORTS NEAR THE MOUTH OF THE RIO MAIPO

This cluster of resorts stretches along the coast from the mouth of the Río Maipo

N towards Valparaíso. Although road links with the latter are poor, there are two good routes from Santiago, one leading from the main Santiago-Valparaíso highway to Algarrobo and the other, Route 78, direct to San Antonio.

SAN ANTONIO

(Pop 74,742; Phone code 035), 112 km S of Valparaíso and 113 km from Santiago near the mouth of the Río Maipo, is a container port and commercial centre for this part of the coast. It has a fishing port and fishmeal plants and is the terminal for the export of copper brought by rail from the large mine at El Teniente, near Rancagua. The town was badly damaged by the 1985 earthquake. Nearby to the S are two resorts: **Llolleo** (4 km), famous for the treatment of heart diseases, and 7 km further **Rocas de Santo Domingo**, the most attractive and exclusive resort in this area with 20 km of beaches and a golf course; even in high season it is not very crowded.

Museums Museo Municipal de Ciencias Naturales y Arqueología, Av Barros Luco, Mon-Fri 0900-1300, 1500-1900.

● **Accommodation At San Antonio:** C *Jockey Club*, 21 de Mayo 202, T 31302, best, good views, restaurant; **D** *Colonial*, Pedro Montt 196. **At Llolleo: D** pp *Oriente*, Inmaculada Concepción 50, T 32188; *Res El Castillo*, Providencia 253, T 373821. **At Santo Domingo: B** *Rocas de Santo Domingo*, La Ronda 130, T 231348; no cheap accommodation – try Llolleo.

● **Transport** Buses to Valparaíso, Pullman Bus, every 45 mins until 2000, US$2; to **Santiago**, Pullman Bus, every 20 mins, US$2.

CARTAGENA

(Pop 10,318), 8 km N of San Antonio, is the biggest resort on this part of the coast. In the early years of this century it was a fashionable summer retreat for the wealthy of Santiago: a number of mansions, notably the *Castillo Foster* overlooking the bay, survive. The centre lies

around the Plaza de Armas, situated on top of the hill. To the S is the picturesque Playa Chica, overlooked by many of the older hotels and restaurants; to the N is the Playa Larga. Between the two a promenade runs below the cliffs; high above hang old houses, some in disrepair but offering spectacular views. Cartagena is a very popular resort in summer, but out of season especially it is a good centre for visiting nearby resorts; there are many hotels and bus connections are good.

● **Accommodation D** *Biarritz*, Playa Chica, T 32246; **D** *La Bahía*, Playa Chica, T 31246; **D** *Violeta*, Condell 140, T 234093, swimming pool, good views; **E** pp *El Estribo*, just off Plaza de Armas, with breakfast, E pp full board, basic, cheap *comedor*; **E** pp *Res Carmona*, Playa Chica, T 212199, small rooms, basic, clean, good value.

NORTH OF CARTAGENA

There are several small resorts including **Las Cruces, El Tabo** and **El Quisco**, a small fishing port with 2 beautiful white beaches (crowded during Chilean holidays).

● **Accommodation At Las Cruces: C** *La Posada*, T 233520, with bath and breakfast, good birdwatching. **At El Tabo: C** *Hotel El Tabo*, T 33719, quite nice, and *Motel El Tabo*, T 212719, next door (overfull in Jan-Feb); 2 cheap and basic campsites. **At El Quisco** (accommodation generally expensive): **C** *Motel Barlovento*, T 481030; *Residenciales* 100-200m from beach in C range, eg *Res Oriental*, T 481662, with breakfast, good, clean, hot water; **D** pp *Cabañas del Irlandés Volador*, Aguirre 277, T 473464; **D** *Res Julia*, Aguirre 0210, T 481546, very clean, quiet, good value, rec; **D** *Cabañas Pozo Azul*, Capricornio 234, SE of town, quiet. Several on Dubournais (main street) inc **D** *El Quisco*, No 166, with breakfast, clean, open weekends only, with excellent seafood restaurant.

ISLA NEGRA

4 km S of El Quisco in the village of Isla Negra is the beautifully-restored **Museo-Casa Pablo Neruda**. Bought by Neruda in 1939 this house, overlooking

The Poet and the Sea 1

"The Sea"

The Pacific Ocean was overflowing the borders of the map. There was no place to put it. It was so large, wild and blue that it didn't fit anywhere. That's why it was left in front of my window.
The humanists worried about the little men it devoured over the years.
They did not count.
Not even that galleon, laden with cinnamon and pepper that perfumed it as it went down.
No.
Not even the explorers' ship – fragile as a cradle dashed to pieces in the abyss – which keeled over with its starving men.
No.
In the ocean, a man dissolves like a bar of salt. And the water doesn't know it.

Pablo Neruda (*The House in the Sand*, Prose Poems by Pablo Neruda, translated by Dennis Maloney and Clark M Zlotchew; Minneapolis: Milkweed, 1990, page 19).

the sea, was his writing retreat in his later years. It contains artefacts gathered by Neruda from all over the world. It is open for guided tours in Spanish, English or French (last two only after 1500), Tues-Sun 1015-1230, 1500-1800, in summer 1000-1745, US$2, T 035-212284 for opening hours or to book English guide (see also his house, La Chascona, under Santiago **Museums**, and La Sebastiaña, under Valparaíso **Museums**). Tours from Santiago, departing at 0900 from Plaza de Armas (Compañía y Ahumada), cost US$23.75 and include seaside resorts, T 232-2574.

The celebrated 1994 film **Il Postino** was based on Antonio Skármela's novel *Ardiente paciencia*, which is set in Isla Negra during the last years of Neruda's life. Skármeta himself adapted the book for the cinema in 1983, but after the 1994 success the novel was retitled *El cartero de Neruda* (*Neruda's postman*).

● **Accommodation**   **B** *Hostería Santa Elena*, beautiful building and location, restaurant, some rooms damp and gloomy.

ALGARROBO

29 km N of Cartagena, is the largest resort N of Cartagena and the most chic, with its large houses, yacht club and marina. Conveniently located for Santiago, it was, in the 1960s the retreat of politicians – both Salvador Allende and Eduardo Frei had summer residences here. From Playa Canelo there are good views of pelicans and boobies in a seabird colony on an offshore island (no entry). In summer there are boat tours round the island from the jetty.

● **Accommodation C** *Costa Sur*, Alessandri 2156, T481151; **D** *Uribe*, behind *Costa Sur*, T 481035, pleasant, quiet; **D** *Vera*, Alessandri 1521, with breakfast, good; **E** pp *Res San José*, Av Principal 1598, basic, no hot water.

● **Transport** Buses to Santiago, Pullman Bus, every 20 mins, 2 hrs, US$3, stopping in Cartagena and the resorts along the coast (but not San Antonio). Services to San Antonio by Empresa de Buses San Antonio (frequent, last bus around 2000) and Empresa Robles.

From Santiago to La Serena

THE CHIEF INTEREST lies along the coast; the land becomes less fertile as you go further North. The largest resort is La Serena, from where access can be made to the pisco-producing Elqui Valley and to one of the world's major astronomical centres.

THE LAND

GEOGRAPHY

This area, stretching from the Río Aconcagua to the Río Elqui is a transitional zone between the fertile heartland and the northern deserts. North of the Aconcagua the Andes and the coastal *cordillera* merge and are crossed by river valleys separated by mountain ridges. North of La Ligua, the Pan-American Highway mainly follows the coastline, which is relatively flat, passing many beautiful coves, alternatively rocky and sandy, with good surf, though the water is very cold. The valleys of the main rivers, the Choapa, Limarí and Elqui, are green oases; the land is intensively farmed using irrigation to produce fruit and vegetables. Elsewhere the vegetation is characteristic of semidesert (dry scrub and cactus), except in those areas where condensation off the sea provides sufficient moisture for woods to grow.

ECONOMY

Despite the dry climate agriculture is important, employing over a third of the labour force. Much of the region's industry is linked to its agricultural produce, notably the distilling of *pisco* from grapes. There are large fish-meal and processing plants in Coquimbo. Mining is also important: among the major mines are El Indio, inland from La Serena, the biggest gold producer in Chile as well as a source of copper and El Romeral, N of La Serena, the most important iron ore deposit in the country. Quartz and the precious stone lapis lazuli are also mined.

CLIMATE

Rainfall is rare and occurs only in winter. Temperatures are relatively stable, with little seasonal variation, especially on the coast where the average temperature is 14°C, morning mists are common and humidity is high; the interior is dry, with temperatures averaging 16-17°. The clear

From Santiago to La Serena

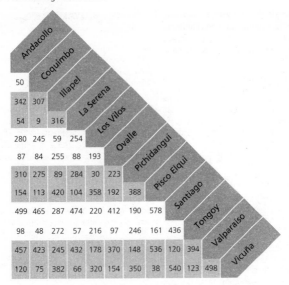

**From Santiago to La Serena:
distance chart (km)**

skies of the Elqui Valley have led to it becoming a major astronomical centre.

HISTORY

Archaeological finds indicate that the river valleys were inhabited at an early stage in pre-history; among the later peoples were the Diaguitas who crossed the Andes around 900AD and settled throughout the area.

Soon after the arrival of the Spanish and the foundation of Santiago, Pedro de Valdivia attempted to secure control over northern Chile by founding La Serena in 1544. Throughout the colonial period La Serena dominated the rest of the region; although small, it was the only city in the north and its leading families had close ties to the main Spanish landowners in the other valleys. After independence the area became an important mining zone producing large amounts of silver, copper and gold.

NORTH TO THE ELQUI VALLEY

The first stretch of the Pan-American Highway from Santiago is inland through green valleys with rich blue clover and wild artichokes. North of La Ligua it follows the coast. **Driving** See page 196 for list of service stations between Santiago and the Peruvian border.

LOS VILOS

Los Vilos (*Pop* 9,422; *Phone code* 051), 216 km N of Santiago, is a former mineral port, now a small seaside resort. Offshore are two islands reached by frequent launches: Isla de Los Huevos, situated in the bay, and, 5 km S, Isla de Los Lobos where there is a colony of seals. 26 km S is **Pichidangui** (*phone code* 053), a popular resort with a beautiful beach. **Los Molles**, 10 km S of Pichidangui is a small town where many wealthy residents of Santiago have their summer homes. There are two small hotels, one down at the beach and the other on the cliff overlooking the beach.

● **Accommodation** Los Vilos: **C** *Hostería Arrayán*, Caupolicán 1, T 541005, clean; **C** *Lord Willow*, Hostería 1444, T 541037, overlooking beach and harbour, with breakfast and bath, pleasant, parking, weekend disco next door; **D** *Bellavista*, Rengo 20, T 541073, with breakfast, without bath, hot water, clean; **F** pp *Res Angelica*, Caupolicán 627, central, warm water, restaurant attached, expensive camping (US$13/site). The *American Motel* is right on the highway, Km 224, T 541020, and is a convenient stopping place between Viña del Mar or Santiago and La Serena, quite good. **In Pichidangui**: *Motel El Bosque*, El Bosque s/n, T 541182, rec; **B** *Motel Pichidangui*, Francis Drake s/n, T 594010, swimming pool; **C** *Puquen*, 2 Poniente s/n, attractive, good value; various other hotels and *pensiones* in every price range. **Camping**: no campsite in Los Vilos; two good sites in Pichidangui, US$10 in season, bargain for lower price off season.

● **Places to eat** In Los Vilos *Restaurant Costanera*, good views over ocean, good meals, expensive. Restaurants in Pichindangui tend to be pricey although there is a food shop.

● **Transport** Only 1 bus daily Pichidangui-Santiago, but N-S buses (eg Inca Bus) on the Highway pass 3 km from the towns.

ILLAPEL

(*Pop* 18,900; *Alt* 350m; *Phone code* 053) 59 km NE of Los Vilos, 287 km N of Santiago, lies in the basin of the Río Choapa. Founded on its present site in 1788, it is a commercial centre for the valley.

Museums Museo Casa de la Cultura, on O'Higgins.

● **Accommodation** Several on Ignacio Silva inc *Domingo Ortíz de Rozas*, No 241, T 522127, 3 star; *Alemán*, No 45, T 522511; *Alameda*, No 20, T 522355; *Diaguitas*, Constitución 260, F 522587; *Londres*, Mackenna 21, T 211906.

(*Pop* 53,000; *Alt* 200; *Phone code* 053) 412 km N of Santiago, lies inland in the valley of the Río Limarí, a fruit, sheep-rearing, and mining district. Market days are Mon, Wed, Fri and Sat, till 1600; the market (*feria modelo*) is on Benavente. The town is famous for its *talabarterías* (leather workshops) and for its products made of locally-mined lapis lazuli. SE of the city, at the confluence of the Ríos Grande and Huatulame, is the Paloma reservoir, the largest in Chile.

Museums

Museo del Limarí, Independencia 329, open Tues-Sun 1000-1600, displays on petroglyphs and a good collection of Diaguita ceramics and other artefacts.

Excursions

The **Monumento Nacional Valle del Encanto**, located about 22 km SW of Ovalle, is one of the most important archaeological sites in northern Chile. Artefacts from hunting peoples from over 2,000 years ago have been found but the most visible remains date from the Molle culture (700 AD). There are over 30 petroglyphs as well as great boulders, distributed in 6 sites. Camping facilities.

● **Access** Mon-Fri 0900-1300, 1500-1900, Sat 0900-1300, 1500-1800, Sun 1000-1300, US$1). No local bus service; you must take a long distance bus and ask to be dropped off –

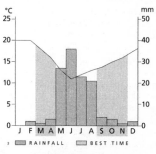

Climate: Ovalle

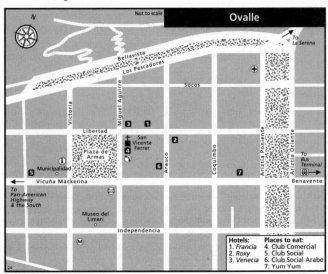

Not to scale

Ovalle

N

To La Serena

Bellavista
Los Pescadores

Socos

Victoria

Miguel Aguirre

Libertad

3 **1**

San Vicente Ferrer

2

Plaza de Armas

4

Arauco

Coquimbo

Ariztía Poniente

Ariztía Oriente

To Bus Terminal

5

Municipalidad

6

7

Vicuña Mackenna

Benavente

To Pan-American Highway & the South

Museo del Limarí

Independencia

M

Hotels:	Places to eat:
1. Francia	4. Club Comercial
2. Roxy	5. Club Social
3. Venecia	6. Club Social Arabe
	7. Yum Yum

5 km walk to the valley; flag down a bus to return.

Termas de Socos, situated 35 km SW of Ovalle on the Pan-American Highway, has fine thermal springs (entrance US$5), a good hotel (**A2**, T Ovalle 621373, Casilla 323) and a campsite (US$10 per tent, but bargain) nearby. Bus US$2.

Local information
● Accommodation
D *Res Bristol*, Araucano 224, pleasant spacious building, restaurant. On Libertad: **D** *Francia*, No 231, T 620828, pleasant, friendly, restaurant; **D** *Roxy*, No 155, T 620080, constant hot water, clean, friendly, patio, *comedor*, highly rec; **E** *Venecia*, No 261, T 620968, clean, safe, friendly, rec; **E** *Res Socos*, Socos 22, T 624157, clean, quiet, family run, rec. For cheaper accommodation try **G** *Res Lolita*, Independencia 274, without bath, **F** with, clean, basic, rec. Several other cheap *residenciales* in C Socos (short stay).

● Places to eat
Club Social, V MacKenna 400 block, excellent fish dishes though pricey; *Club Social Arabe*, Arauco 255, spacious glass-domed premises, limited selection of Arab dishes, good but not

cheap; *El Quijote*, Arauco 294, intimate atmosphere, good seafood, inexpensive; *Alamar*, Santiago 259, excellent seafood, good value. Good value *almuerzos* at *Casino La Bomba*, Aguirre 364, run by fire brigade. For drinks and snacks try *Café Caribe Express*, V MacKenna 241; *Yum Yum*, V MacKenna 21, good, cheap, lively; *D'Oscar Bar*, Plaza de Armas; *Pastelería Josti*, Libertad 427. *Club Comercial*, Aguirre 244 (on plaza), open Sun.

● Shopping
For articles made of Lapis Lazuli try Sr Wellington Vega Alfaro at kiosk on N outskirts (difficult to reach without transport), T 620797.

● Tourist offices
Two kiosks on the Plaza de Armas. **Automóvil Club de Chile**, Libertad 144, T 620011, very helpful, overnight parking.

● Transport
Buses to **Santiago**, several, 6½ hrs, US$7; to **La Serena**, 12 a day, 1¼ hrs, US$2; to **Antofagasta**, US$20.

LONGER EXCURSIONS FROM OVALLE

Parque Nacional Fray Jorge
Situated 90 km W of Ovalle and 110 km

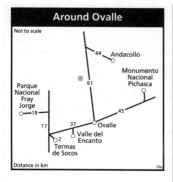

Around Ovalle

Not to scale

44 Andacollo

Monumento Nacional Pichasca

Parque Nacional Fray Jorge

61

45

18

17 37 Ovalle
   Valle del Encanto
2
Termas de Socos

Distance in km

S of La Serena at the mouth of the Río Limarí, the Park is reached by a dirt road leading off the Pan-American Highway. The entrance and administration are at Km 18, from which it is 10 km further to the summit of coastal hills known as the Altos de Talinay which rise to 667m.

The park covers 9,959 ha and contains original forests which contrast with the otherwise barren surroundings. Receiving no more than 113 mm of rain a year, the forests survive because of the almost constant fog and mist covering the hills.

● **Park information** Open Sat, Sun and public holidays only, entry 0830-1600, last departure 1800, US$4; visits closely controlled owing to risk of fire. Waterproof clothing essential. (Scientific groups may obtain permission to visit from The Director, Conaf, Córdovez 281, La Serena, T 211124.)

● **Transport** Round trip in taxi from Ovalle, US$30, Abel Olivares Rivera, T Ovalle 620352, rec.

Monumento Nacional Pichasca

Some 47 km NE of Ovalle at an altitude of 1,350, this is reached by an unpaved and largely winding road. It contains petrified tree trunks, archaeological remains, including a vast cave (comparable to the Cueva Milodón outside Puerto Natales) with remains of ancient roof paintings, and views of gigantic rock for-

mations on the surrounding mountains. Open 0830-1700, US$3.

● **Transport** Daily bus from Ovalle to Río Hurtado passes the turn off (to San Pedro) about 42 km from the city. From here it is 3 km to the park and about 2 km more to sites of interest.

ANDACOLLO

The good inland road between Ovalle and La Serena makes an interesting contrast to Ruta 5 (Panamericana), with a fine pass and occasional views of snow-capped Andes across cacti-covered plains and semi-desert mountain ranges. 61 km N of Ovalle a side road runs 44 km SE (last 20 km very bad) to **Andacollo** (*Pop* 10,216; *Alt* 1,050m). This old town situated in a gorge, in an area of alluvial gold washing and manganese and copper mining, is one of the great pilgrimage sites in Chile. In the enormous **Basilica** (1893), 45m high and with a capacity of 10,000, is the miraculous Virgen del Rosario de Andacollo. Nearby is the **Templo Antiguo**, smaller and dating from 1789.

Museums Museo de Andacollo, daily 0900-1300, 1500-1830.

Local holidays The Fiesta Grande from Dec 23 to 27 (most important day Dec 26) attracts 150,000 pilgrims from northern Chile. The ritual dances date from a pre-Spanish past. Colectivos run to the festival from C Benavente, near Colocolo, in La Serena, but 'purists' walk (torch and good walking shoes essential). 2 villages are passed on the route, which starts on the paved highway, then goes along a railway track and lastly up a steep, dusty hill. There is also a smaller festival, the Fiesta Chica on the first Sun of October.

● **Accommodation** No hotel, but some *pensiones*; during the festival private houses rent beds and some let you pay for a shower

● **Transport** To **Ovalle** colectivo, US$2.40; bus, US$1.70.

The legend of Fray Jorge

In 1627 an English sailor named Jorge (George) arrived in La Serena on a Spanish ship after his own vessel had been shipwrecked. He was a Catholic and during the storm which had sunk his ship he had promised that if he survived he would join the first religious order he set eyes on after reaching dry land. On landing in La Serena he saw a Franciscan monk and asked to join his order.

Thus Jorge reached the Monastery of San Franscisco and joined the community of monks. For six years he lived there, such a model of humility that he was considered a saint.

For many years the order had been building their church, but they had been unable to find wood long enough for the roof timbers. The community was desperate. One morning Jorge went to the Prior to tell him that he had been asking God for help to solve the problem of the church roof when he had experienced a kind of dream in which a voice had said "Tomorrow take a cart and follow the oxen wherever they lead". He asked the Prior for permission to leave with a cart and oxen.

The Prior agreed and he left next morning, following the oxen, who led him straight to a forest. Jorge loaded the cart with large pieces of timber and returned to the monastery. The monks were astonished and had no doubt that he was a saint. Since then the forest has had the name "Fray Jorge".

From Oreste Plath, *Geografía del Mito y la Leyenda Chilenos*,
quoted in *La Tierra En Que Vivimos*, Editorial Antártica, 1983.

THE ELQUI VALLEY

COQUIMBO

(*Pop* 106,000; *Phone code* 051) 84 km N of Ovalle and on the same bay as La Serena, this is a port of considerable importance. It has one of the best harbours on the coast and major fish-processing plants. The city is strung along the N shore of a peninsula. Most of the commercial life is centred on 3 streets which run between the port and the steep hillside on which are perched many of the poorer houses. On the S shore of the peninsula lies the suburb of Guayacán, with an iron-ore loading port, a steel church designed by Eiffel and an English cemetery. Nearby is **La Herradura**, 2½ km from Coquimbo which has the best beaches. Also nearby is a resort complex called *Las Tacas*, with beach, swimming pool, tennis, flats, *apart-hotel*, etc. At **Totoralillo**, 12 km S there are good beaches, ideal for swimming.

History
Coquimbo was used during the colonial period as a port for La Serena, attracting a lot of attention from English pirates including Drake, who visited in 1578. Legends of buried treasure at Bahía la Herradura de Guayacán persist. From these small beginnings Coquimbo grew into a city in the 19th century, when it and the separate centre of Guayacán became important in the processing of copper. By 1854 there were two large copper foundries in Coquimbo and in 1858 the largest foundry in the world was built in Guayacán.

Museums
In 1981 heavy rain uncovered 39 ancient burials of humans and llamas which had been sacrificed. A small museum has been built in the Plaza Gabriela Mistral to exhibit these.

Local information
● Accommodation
Generally much cheaper than in La Serena.

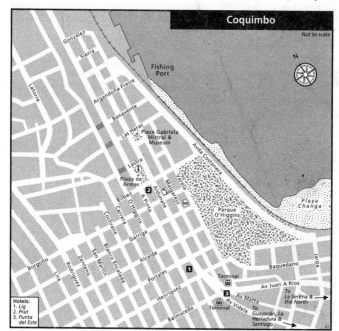

Coquimbo

Not to scale

Hotels:
1. Lig
2. Prat
3. Punta del Este

B *Lig*, Aldunate 1577, T 311171, comfortable, friendly, good value, nr bus terminus.

C *Prat*, Bilbao y Aldunate, T 311845, comfortable, pleasant; **C** *Iberia*, Bandera 206, p 8, T 671-4510, friendly, rec.

D *Punta del Este*, Videla 170, T 312768, nice rooms.

E *Claris*, Aldunate 669, run-down, old-fashioned, rambling hotel with bar and *comedor*, live music on Fri and Sat, popular with sailors; **E** *Mi Casa*, Varela 1653, clean, friendly, good value. Several hotels in La Herradura, inc **C** *Hotel La Herradura*, Costanera 200, T 321320.

Camping: *Camping La Herradura*, T 312084.

● **Places to eat**

Lots of good fish restaurants inc *Sal y Pimiento del Capitán Denny*, Aldunate 769, one of the best, pleasant, old-fashioned, mainly fish, US$12-20 pp; *La Picada*, Costanera nr statue of O'Higgins, excellent, pricey; *Crucero*, Aldunate 1326, excellent; *La Barca*, Ríos y Varela, modest but good; and *La*

Bahía, Pinto 1465, excellent, good value. Several good seafood restaurants (known as *pensiones*) at the municipal market, Melgarejo entre Bilbao y Borgoño (*El Callejón* rec); *Mai Lai Fan*, Av Ossandón 1, excellent Chinese, rec; *Tavola Calda*, Bilbao 451, good Italian, good value.

● **Post & telecommunications**
Telephones: CTC, Aldunate 1633.

● **Tour companies & travel agents**
Ingservitur, Los Lirios 300, Coquimbo, T 313821, F 312943, varied programme of tours, inc Parque Nacional Fray Jorge (see page 132), depending on demand.

● **Tourist offices**
Kiosk in Plaza de Armas (open summer only).

● **Transport**
Buses leave from the new bus terminal at Varela y Garriga. To **La Serena**, every few mins, US$0.30. To **Guanaqueros**, US$0.80, 45 mins, and to **Tongoy**, US$1, 1 hr, with Ruta Costera, frequency varies according to day (more on Sun) and season. Colectivos US$1.40 and US$1.70 respectively.

RESORTS SOUTH OF COQUIMBO

Guanaqueros, 37 km S, is a fishing village with beaches.

● **Accommodation** **D** *La Bahía*, clean, simple.

TONGOY

(*Pop* 3,350) 50 km S, is an old fishing port occupying the whole of a small peninsula. It is now a rapidly growing resort

and well worth a visit: to the S the Playa Grande is 14 km long; to the N the Playa Socos is 4 km in length.

● **Accommodation** **A1-B** *Hotel Yachting Club*, Costanera 20, T 391154, good; **A2** *Panorámico*, Mirador 455, T 391944, inc breakfast, all rooms with view of bay and fishing boats, excellent, clean, friendly; *Samay*, overlooking fishing port, T 391355; **E** *Plaza*, on main square, T 391184; several basic *residenciales*.

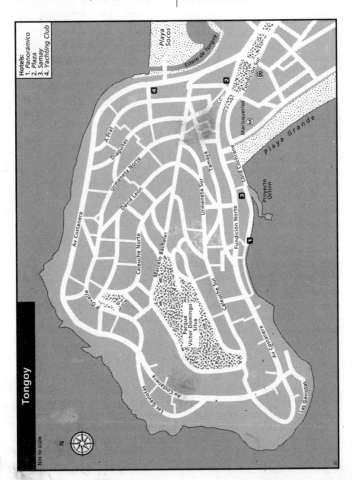

Hotels:
1. Panorámico
2. Plaza
3. Samay
4. Yachting Club

Tongoy

Not to scale

• **Places to eat** Try the *marisquerías* nr the fishing port, excellent value. *Restaurant El Buque*, Puesto 17 on seafront, nr fishing harbour, fish and meat with superb sauces, good service, highly rec.

LA SERENA

La Serena (*Pop* 120,000; *Phone code* 051), 12 km N of Coquimbo, 473 km N of Santiago, is the capital of IV Región (Coquimbo). Built on a hillside 2 km inland from Bahía de Coquimbo, it is an attractive city which has rapidly become a major tourist centre.

History

La Serena was founded by Juan de Bohón, aide to Pedro de Valdivia, in 1544, destroyed by Diaguita Indians in 1546 and rebuilt by Francisco de Aguirre in 1549. The city was sacked by the English pirate Sharpe in 1680. In the colonial period the city was the main staging-post on the route N to Peru. Many of the religious orders built churches and convents here providing accommodation for their members. In the 19th century the city grew prosperous from copper-mining; the neoclassical mansions of successful entrepreurs from this period can still be seen.

Places of interest

Around the attractive Plaza de Armas are most of the official buildings, including the Post Office, the **Cathedral** (built in 1844 and featuring a carillon which plays every hour) and the **Casa González Videla**, the great man's residence from 1927 to 1977, which now houses the Museo Histórico Regional (see below). There are 29 other churches, several of which have unusual towers. **San Francisco**, Balmaceda y de La Barra, built 1586-1627, has a baroque façade and faces a small plaza with arcades. **Santo Domingo**, half a block from the Plaza de Armas, built 1755 (the clock tower is from 1912) is fronted by a small garden with statues of sealions. **San Augustín**, Cantournet y Rengifo, originally a Jesuit church, dates from 1755 but has been heavily modified.

La Recova, the new market, at Cienfuegos y Cantournet, includes a large display of handicrafts and, upstairs, several good restaurants. On the W edge of the old city is the **Parque Pedro de Valdivia**, which includes a children's zoo and the Parque Japonés, open daily 1000-2000, US$1.25. A *moai* from Easter Island can be seen on Av Colo Colo, direction Vicuña, about 15 mins' walk from the centre; there is a view of the

González Videla and the Plan Serena

The present-day layout and architectural style have their origins in the 'Plan Serena' drawn up in 1948 on the orders of Gabriel González Videla, a native of the city. Born in 1898 González Videla was a lawyer, diplomat and Radical party politician who was elected President of Chile in 1946 as a result of deal with the Communist and Liberal parties. Once elected, he claimed to have discovered a left-wing plot, outlawed the Communist party and had many of its members imprisoned. Neruda, a member of the Communist party, was understandably scathing, describing him as "an irresponible and frivolous clown" and a "contemptible creature" with "an insignificant but twisted mind". It should be added that it was González Videla's government which gave the vote to women.

Eager to leave his mark on his native city, González Videla ordered the drafting of an urban plan. Under this Av Fransisco de Aguirre was modernised and the Pedro de Valdivia gardens, W of the city, were built. All new buildings in the centre were to be in Californian colonial style, though this regulation has since been modified permitting the construction of some modern buildings.

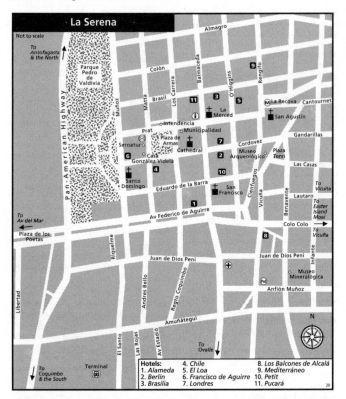

La Serena

Hotels:
1. Alameda
2. Berlín
3. Brasilia
4. Chile
5. El Loa
6. Francisco de Aguirre
7. Londres
8. Los Balcones de Alcalá
9. Mediterráneo
10. Petit
11. Pucará

city from here.

Av Francisco de Aguirre, a pleasant boulevard lined with statues and known as the **Alameda**, runs from the centre to the coast, terminating at the **Faro Monumental**, a neo-colonial mock-castle (US$0.45 entry). A series of beaches stretch from here to Peñuelas, 6 km S, linked by the Av del Mar. Many apartment blocks, hotels, *cabañas* and restaurants have been built along this part of the bay.

Museums

Museo Histórico Regional in the Casa González Videla on the Plaza de Armas, including several rooms on the man's life.

Open Tues-Sat 0900-1300, 1600-1900, Sun 1000-1300, entry US$0.60, ticket also valid for Museo Arqueológico.

Museo Arqueológico, Cordóvez y Cienfuegos, outstanding collection of Diaguita and Molle Indian exhibits, especially of attractively decorated pottery; open Tues-Sat 0900-1300, 1600-1900, Sun 1000-1300, entrance, US$0.30.

Museo De Arte Religiosa, in the San Francisco church, which includes the funeral mask of Gabriela Mistral.

Museo Mineralógico in the University of La Serena, A Muñoz between Benavente and Infante (for geologists, open Mon-Fri 0930-1200, free).

Local information

Note that O in front of an address indicates West of the centre and E indicates East.

● Accommodation

Accommodation in the centre of town is expensive. Route 5 from La Serena to Coquimbo is lined with cheaper accommodation, from hotels to *cabañas*, and restaurants. There are no buses along Av del Mar, but it is only ½ km off Route 5. The tourist office in the bus terminal has accommodation information, helpful.

L3 *El Escorial I*, Colón 617, T 224793, F 221433, good; **L3** *Los Balcones de Alcalá*, Av de Aguirre 452, T 225999, F 211800, comfortable, clean, TV; **L3** *Mediterráneo*, Cienfuegos 509, Casilla 212, T 225837, inc good breakfast, rec.

A2 *Francisco de Aguirre*, Córdovez 210, T 222991, with breakfast, shower, good rooms, reasonable restaurant; **A2** *Pucará*, Balmaceda 319, T 211966, F 211933, with bath and breakfast, modern, clean, quiet; **A3** *Berlín*, Córdovez 535, T 222927, F 223575, clean, safe, efficient, rec.

C *Londres*, Córdovez 550, T 214673, with bath, **D** without, restaurant, old fashioned; **C** *Brasilia*, Brasil 555, T 225248, friendly, small rooms, overpriced; **C** *Hostal Croata*, Cienfuegos 248, T/F 224997, with bath, **D** without, with breakfast, laundry facilities, cable TV, patio, hospitable, rec; **C** *Hostal Del Mar*, Cuatro Esquinas 0680 (nr beach), T 225816, also *cabañas*, clean, friendly.

D *Alameda*, Av de Aguirre 450, T 213052, run down, clean and comfortable; **D** *Hostal Santo Domingo*, Bello 1067, 10 mins' walk from bus station, with breakfast, highly rec; **D** *Lido*, Matta 547, T 213073, hot water, clean, friendly; **D** *Res Chile*, Matta 561, T 211694, basic, small rooms, clean, hot water am only; **D** *Casona de Cantournet*, Cantournet 815, T 226669, with bath, central; **D** *El Cobre*, Colón y Matta, large rooms, spotless, friendly owners, highly rec; **D** Edith González, Los Carrera 885, T 221941, cooking and laudry facilities, central, rec, also owns **D** Pení 321; **D** *Res El Loa*, O'Higgins 362, with shower, good inexpensive home cooking, friendly; **D** *Res Petit*, de la Barra 586, T 212536, hot water; **D** *Turismo 2000*, Lautaro 960, T 215793, hot water, bargain; **D** Lautaro 880, hot water, clean, rec; **D** *Gabriela Matos*, Cienfuegos 230 p 2, T 214588, in beautiful old building, use of kitchen, helpful, rec; **D** *Casa del Turista*, Colón 318, clean, back rooms better, laundry facilities, helpful; **D** *San Juan*, Balmaceda 827, clean, central.

E pp *Gregoria Fernández*, Andrés Bello 979A, T 224400, highly rec, clean, friendly, good beds, 3 blocks from terminal, excellent breakfast; **E** *Rosa Canto*, Cantournet 976, T 213954, hot water, kitchen, comfortable, family run, rec; **E pp** Las Rojas 21, T 215838, nr terminal, use of kitchen, clean, friendly; **E pp** *Alejandro Muñoz*, Brasil 720, T 211619, with breakfast, good showers, nice garden, English and French spoken, helpful, rec; **E** Adolfo Ballas 1418, T 223735; **E pp** *Ana Jofre*, Rgto Coquimbo 964 (entre Pení y Amunátegui), T 222335, kitchen facilities, nr bus terminal; **E/F** *Res Americana*, Bello 859 nr terminal, basic, cold water.

F pp unnamed *Residencial* at Av de Aguirre 411, in dormitories, clean.

Youth Hostel: **E** pp *Res Limmat*, Lautaro 914, T/F 211373, with breakfast, central, patio, tours offered, English and German spoken, IYHA reduction, rec.

Motels: **A1** *Canto del Agua*, Av del Mar 5700, T 242203, F 241767, very good, pleasant cabins; **A3** *Les Mouettes*, Av del Mar 2500, T 225665, F 226278, good restaurant, inc breakfast, rec; **B** *Cabañas Los Papayos*, Huerto 66, 2 km S of city (Vista Hermosa bus), much cheaper out of season, 2 bedroom cabins, rec, pool, gardens; **B** *La Fuente*, Av del Mar 5665, T 245755, F 541259, appartments, cable TV, parking, very good; several more motels along the beach.

Camping: *Camping Peñuelas*, Los Pescadores 795, T 313818. *Maki Payi*, 153 Vegas Norte, T 213628, about 5 km N of La Serena, nr sea, friendly, rec, self-contained cabins available. *Hipocampo*, 4 km S on Av del Mar (take bus for Coquimbo and get off at Colegio Adventista, US$2.50 pp by Playa El Pescador), T 214276.

● Places to eat

El Granero, Colón 360, excellent steaks, reasonably priced; *Club Social*, Córdovez 516, p 1, unpretentious but excellent value; *El Rincón Colonial*, Córdovez 578, good fish; *Hotel La Serena*, Córdovez 610, good meat. *Ciro's*, Aguirre 431, T 213482, old-fashioned, good lunch, rec; *El Cedro*, Prat 572, Arab cuisine, expensive; *Mesón Matias*, Balmaceda 1940, excellent Spanish, elegant, expensive but highly rec; *La Mía Pizza*, O'Higgins 460, Italian, good value, inexpensive (branch on Av del Mar in summer); *Pastissima Limitado*, O'Higgins 633, Italian, very good; *Mai Lai Fan*, Cordóvez 740, good Chinese, reasonably priced; *Salón Las Tejas*, Francisco de Aguirre 395, cheap, local dishes; *Chopería Don Antonio*, Vicente Zorrilla 837-9, 20m from *La Recova* market, friendly, good value. For good, fish lunches try the restaurants on the upper floor of the Recova market. Note that the quality of restaurants, especially on Av del Mar, varies considerably; often most dishes on the menu are not available.

Several good cafés: *Tito's*, O'Higgins y Cordóvez, popular meeting place; *Café do Brasil*, Balmaceda 461, good coffee; *Casa Miró*, Balmaceda 265, good for coffee and late evening drinks; *Café La Crêperie*, O'Higgins y de la Barra, crêpes, light meals, occasional live music; *Bocaccio*, Prat y Balmaceda, good cakes, modern, smart, popular; *Café del Patio*, Prat 470, sandwiches, cakes and coffee, English spoken, rec.

● **Airline offices**

LanChile, T 225981; **Ladeco**, Cordóvez 484, T 225753; **National**, Eduardo de la Barra 435, T 214460, F 232808; **Alta**, Los Carrera 515, T 212832, F 215671.

● **Banks & money changers**

Fincard (Mastercard), Balmaceda 383, Local 217, Mon-Fri 0900-1400, 1600-2030. **Banco Concepción**, O'Higgins 529, Visa. *Casas de Cambio*: **La Reconquista**, in a *galería* on Cordóvez between Balmaceda and O'Higgins, excellent rates; **US$100 Money Exchange**, Prat 645, Mon-Fri 0900-1400, 1600-2100, Sat 0900-1400; **Viajes Val**, Prat 540 (open Sat 1100-1400); **La Portada**, Balmaceda 515; **Serena Cambios** at bus terminal and airport, open 1100-2300 daily; **Cambio Fides**, Caracol Colonial, Balmaceda 460, good rates, changes TCs (another *cambio* in the basement, building closed 1400-1600). If heading N note that La Serena is the last place to change TCs before Antofagasta.

● **Laundry**

Ro-Ma, Los Carrera 654, open 0900-1300, 1600-2000; another at Balmaceda y Brasil.

● **Post & telecommunications**

Telecommunications: long distance calls from Cordóvez 446 and La Recova market. Entel, Prat 571. CTC administration on Plaza de Armas sells *Turistel*.

● **Shopping**

La Recova handicraft market, though many items imported from Peru and Bolivia; *Cema-Chile*, Los Carrera 562; *Las Brisas* supermarket, Cienfuegos y Cordóvez, food not as cheap as in *La Recova*. 24-hr supermarket on corner of Cienfuegos, 30m from *alojamiento* at No 324.

● **Sports**

Gimnasio GFU, Amunátegui 426, T 222420, and *Vitalia*, Cordóvez 756, T 221939.

● **Tour companies & travel agents**

San Bartolmé, Brasil 415, T/F 221992; *Gira Tour*, Prat 689, T 223535; *Turismo Elquitur*, Los Carrera 594, T 227875. See also *Ingservitur* under Coquimbo, above.

● **Tourist offices**

Main **Sernatur** office in Edificio de Servicios Públicos (next to the Post Office on the Plaza de Armas), T 225138, open Mon-Fri 0900-1300, 1500-1730 (0830-1800 in summer). Kiosks at bus terminal (summer only) and at Balmaceda y Prat (open in theory Mon-Sat 1100-1400, 1600-1900), helpful. **Automóvil Club de Chile**: Eduardo de la Barra 435, T 225279.

● **Transport**

Local Buses City buses US$0.25; taxis US$0.75 + US$0.10/every 200m. **Car hire**: Hertz, Av de Aguirre 0225, T 225471/226171, prices range from US$65 to US$110 per day; **Budget**, Av de Aguirre 0240; **Daire**, Prat 645, T 226149, rec, good service; **Oceanic**, Av de Aguirre 062, T 214007, cheapest; **Dollar**, O'Higgins 672, T 225714, cheapest; **Oceanic**, Av de Aguirre O240, good service. **Bicycle repairs**: **Green Go Club**, Panamericana Norte y Av de Aguirre, T 224454, North American run, good parts, information on local cycle routes.

Air Aeropuerto Gabriela Mistral, 5 km E of the city. Ladeco flies to **San Juan**, Argentina, in summer only. To **Santiago** and **Copiapó**, Lan Chile, Ladeco, National and Alta.

Buses Bus terminal, El Santo y Amunátegui (about 8 blocks S of the centre). Buses daily to **Santiago**, several companies, 7-8 hrs, US$14; to **Arica**, US$30; to **Calama**, US$23, 16 hrs. To **Valparaíso**, 7 hrs, US$10; to **Caldera**, 7 hrs, US$10; to **Antofagasta**, 11 hrs, several companies, US$20 (Flota Barrios cama US$38), and to **Iquique**, 17 hrs, US$25; to **Vicuña**, Frontera Elqui, Av Perú y Esmeralda, frequent service, 1 hr, US$2; *colectivo* to Vicuña, Empresa Nevada del Sol de Elqui, Domeyko 550, T 21450, others from Av Aguirre y Balmaceda, US$2.50; to **Pisco Elqui**, Vía Elqui, 4 a day from terminal, US$3, but other services run along Av Amunátegui outside terminal; to **Coquimbo**, bus No 8 from Av Aguirre y Cienfuegos, US$0.30, every few minutes.

OBSERVATORIES

The clear skies and dry atmosphere of the valleys around La Serena have led to the area becoming one of the astronomical centres of the world, with three observatories which may be visited:

El Tololo

Situated at 2,200m, 89 km SE of La Serena in the Elqui Valley, 51 km S of Vicuña, this belongs to Aura, an association of US and Chilean universities. It possesses the largest telescope in the southern hemisphere, seven others and a radio telescope. It is open to visitors by permit only every Sat 0900-1200, 1300-1600; for permits (free) write to Casilla 603, La Serena, T 051-225-415, then pick your permit up before 1200 on the day before (the office is at Colina Los Pinos, on a hill behind the new University – personal applications can be made here for all three observatories). During holiday periods apply well in advance; at other times it is worth trying for a cancellation the day before. They will insist that you have private transport; you can hire a taxi, US$33, but you will require the registration number when you book.

La Silla

Located at 2,240m, 150 km NE of La Serena, this belongs to ESO (European Southern Observatory), financed by 8 EU countries, and comprises 14 telescopes. Open first Sat of the month, 1430-1730; registration in advance in Santiago essential (Alonso de Córdoba 3107, Santiago, T 228-5006/698-8757) or write to Casilla 567, La Serena, T 224-527. From La Serena it is 114 km N along Route 5 to the turn-off (**D** *Posada La Frontera*, cabañas), then another 36 km.

Las Campanas

2,510m, 156 km NE of La Serena, 30 km N of La Silla, this belongs to the Carnegie Institute, has 4 telescopes and is altogether a smaller facility than the other two. It is open without permission every Sat 1430-1730, T 224680/211254, or write to Casilla 601, La Serena. Follow Route 5 to the same junction as for La Silla, take the turning for La Silla and then turn N after 14 km. La Silla and Las Campanas can be reached without private transport by taking any bus towards Vallenar (2 hrs, US$3.25) getting out at the junction (*desvío*) and hitch from there.

The Elqui Valley in the words of its poet

"It is a heroic slash in the mass of mountains, but so short as to be little more than a green-banked torrent, yet small as it is one comes to love it as perfect.

It contains in perfection all that man could ask of a land in which to live: light, water, wine and fruit. And what fruit! The tongue which has tasted the juice of its peaches and the mouth which has eaten of its purple figs will never seek sweetness elsewhere.

The people of the Elqui take remarkable pride in their green soil. Whenever there is a hump, a ridge or bare patch without greenery, it is because it is naked rock. Wherever the *Elquino* has a little water and three inches of soil, however poor, he will cultivate something: peaches, vines or figs. That the leafy, polished vines climb only a little way up the mountainsides is because, if they were planted higher, they would wither in the pitiless February sun."

Gabriela Mistral, quoted in Jan Read, *The Wines of Chile*, Mitchell Beazley, 1994.

Tours Travel agents in La Serena and Coquimbo inc Ingservitur, Gira Tour and Turismo Cristóbal, receive tickets from the observatories and arrange tours (to Tololo US$22 pp), though you may need to reserve several days in advance in holiday periods. Taxi-drivers will also do these trips: one rec as cheap and good is Cecilia Cruz, T 222529 (mobile 09-551-0579), US$63 to La Silla.

VICUÑA AND THE UPPER ELQUI VALLEY

The valley of the Río Elqui is one of the most attractive oases in this part of northern Chile. There are mines, orchards, orange groves and vineyards. The road up the valley is paved as far as Varillar, 24 km beyond Vicuña, the capital of the valley. Except for Vicuña, most of the tiny towns have but a single street. The Elqui Valley is the centre of *pisco* production : of the nine distilleries in the valley, the largest is Capel in Vicuña. Huancara, a delicious liqueur introduced by the Jesuits, is also produced in the valley.

VICUÑA

(*Pop* 7,716; *Alt* 610m; *Phone code* 051) 66 km E of La Serena, this small, clean, friendly, picturesque town was founded in 1821. On the W side of the plaza are the municipal chambers, built in 1826 and topped in 1905 by a medieval-German-style tower – the Torre Bauer – prefabricated in Germany and imported by the German-born mayor of the time. Inside the chambers is a gallery of past local dignitaries. Also on the plaza is the Iglesia Parroquial, dating from 1860. Tourist office on Plaza de Armas. There are good views from Cerro La Virgen, N of town. The Capel Pisco distillery is 1½ km E of Vicuña, to the right of the main road; guided tours (in Spanish) are offered Dec-Feb, Mon-Sat 0930-1200, 1430-1800, Sun 1000-1230; Mar-Nov, Mon-Fri 0930-1200, 1430-1800, Sat 1000-1230, free; no booking required.

Museums Museo Gabriela Mistral, C Gabriela Mistral y Riquelme (open Tues-Sat 0900-1300, 1500-1900, Sun 1000-1300, entry US$0.40); next door is the house where the poet was born.

Solar de los Madariaga, C Gabriela Mistral, former residence containing artefacts belonging to a prominent local family.

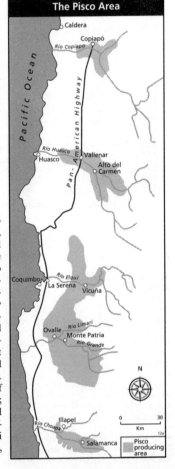

The Pisco Area

Pisco producing area

Pisco

The national strong spirit of Chile is *pisco*, a liquor made from grapes and known until the late nineteenth century as *aguardiente de vino*. Under a law of 1985 defining its demarcation, the term *pisco* is reserved for a spirit produced and bottled in Regions III and IV and made entirely by the distillation of wine grown in these regions. Although the Elqui Valley is the heartland of the *pisco* industry, the climate and soil being ideally suited to the cultivation of grapes with a high sugar-content, vines for *pisco* are grown in the valleys of rivers throughout these Regions, from the Copiapó in the north to the Choapa in the south.

After crushing and pressing the juice is fermented and then distilled, before being aged for 4-12 months in large oak barrels, stronger spirits spending more time in the wood: it is then diluted with water to the appropriate strength. There are four grades of strength: *Selección* (30%); *Especial* (35%); *Reservado* (40%) and *Gran Pisco* (43%).

The grapes for *pisco* are grown by smallholders, who, until the 1930s, sold their grapes to a number of private distilleries: dissatisfaction among the small-holders led to the establishment in 1931 of a cooperative, *Control* (full name *Cooperativa Agrícola Control de Elqui Limitada*) with modern equipment. Other groups of smallholders followed suit, setting up their own cooperatives. Today two cooperatives are responsible for the distillation of 95% of all *pisco*: *Control* based in La Serena, has 700 members; *Capel* (*Cooperativa Agrícola Pisquera de Elqui Limitada*) which has its headquarters in Vicuña, was established in 1942, and has 1,300 members.

Cooperativa Agrícola Pisquera Elqui Ltda. - CAPEL
Camino a Peralillo — Fono 411251 — Vicuña

• **Accommodation** **L3** *Hostería Vicuña*, Sgto Aldea 101, T 411301, F 411144, swimming pool, tennis court, excellent restaurant; **A2** *Yunkai*, O'Higgins 72, T 411195, F 411593, cabañas for 4/6 persons, pool, restaurant. On Gabriela Mistral: **C** *Valle Hermoso*, No 706, T 411206, clean, comfortable, parking, rec; **D** *Sol del Valle*, at No 743, hot water, TV, vineyard, restaurant; **E** *Hostal Michel*, No 573, large gardens; **E** *Res Moderna*, at No 718, full board available, no hot water, nothing modern about it, but quiet, clean, very nice; **E** pp *Res Mistral*, at No 180, restaurant, basic, hot water, clean. **Camping**: *Camping y Piscina Las Tinajas*, E end of Chacabuco, swimming pool, restaurant.

• **Places to eat** Mainly on G Mistral: *Club Social de Elqui*, at No 435, very good, attractive patio, good value *almuerzo*; *Mistral*, at No 180, very good, popular with locals, good value *almuerzo*; *Halley*, at No 404, good meat dishes, also *chopería*, swimming pool (US$5 pp); *Yo Y Soledad*, No 364, inexpensive, good value; *Pizzeria Virgos*, on plaza.

• **Transport** Buses to **La Serena**, about 10 a day, most by Frontera Elqui, first 0800, last 1930, 1 hr, US$2, *colectivo* from Plaza de Armas US$2.50; to **Santiago** via La Serena, Expreso Norte at 1145 and 2200; to **Pisco Elqui**, 4 a day, Vía Elqui and Frontera Elqui, 1 hr, US$2.

From Vicuña the road continues up the valley another 18 km to Rivadavia where it divides: the main route (Route 41) winding through the mountains to the Argentine frontier at Agua Negra (see below). At Juntas there is a turning to

Baños del Toro and the Mina el Indio, which can be visited only with a permit (obtainable from Compañía Minería del Indio, Baño Industrial Piñuelas, La Serena). The other branch of the road runs through Paihuano (camping) to Monte Grande, where the schoolhouse where Gabriela Mistral lived and was educated by her sister is now a museum. The poet's tomb is situated 1 km out of town. (Buses from the plaza in Vicuña). Here the road forks, one branch leading to El Colorado. Along this road are several Ashram places, some of which welcome visitors; camping allowed. The other branch leads to **Pisco Elqui**, an attractive town situated around a shady plaza. Here there are 2 *pisco* plants with another outside town.

● **Accommodation** C *Carillón*, A Prat s/n, pool, also cabanas (B); **E** pp *Hosteria de Don Juan*, with breakfast, fine views, noisy; **E** *El Elqui*, hot shower, good restaurant, rec, not always open; *Las Vegas* campsite, **F** pp *Sol de Barbosa*, also camping; **G** pp *Camping El Olivo*, small restaurant, pool, excellent facili-ties. Well-stocked supermarket one block from the plaza.

● **Useful information** CODEFF, the environmental organization, has an office on the outskirts of town.

● **Transport** Buses to La Serena, US$3, via Vicuña.

FRONTIER WITH ARGENTINA: PASO AGUA NEGRA

Paso Agua Negra (4,775m) is reached by unpaved road from Rivadavia, 18 km E of Vicuña.

● **Immigration**
Chilean immigration and customs at Juntas, 84 km W of the frontier, 88 km E of Vicuña. Open 0800-1700; US$2/vehicle, 1700-2200, Jan-April only.

● **Accommodation**
Basic accommodation at Huanta (Guanta on many maps) Km 46 from Vicuña,G, clean,ask for Guillermo Aliaga. Huanta is the last chance to buy food.

● **Transport**
No public transport. El Indio mine transport may give lifts to Juntas.

North of La Serena

S EMIDESERT continues as far North as the mining and agroindustrial centre of Copiapó, North of which the Atacama Desert begins, which is of little interest except after rain.

THE LAND

GEOGRAPHY

This part of the country can be divided into two: between the Río Elqui and the Río Copiapó the transitional zone continues; N of the Copiapó the Atacama desert begins. East of Copiapó the Andes divide: between the eastern range (Cordillera de Claudio Gay) and the western range (Cordillera de Domeyko) is a basin which collects the waters from the Andes but allows no escape. Here there are salt flats, the most extensive being the Salar de Pedernales. The eastern range rises to some of the highest peaks in Chile: Ojos del Salado (6,879m/6,864m – see below), Incahuasi (6,610m), Tres Cruces (6,330m) and San Francisco (6,020m). The valleys of the three main rivers, the Ríos Huasco, Copiapó and Salado, form oases in this barren landscape.

ECONOMY

Mining is a major economic activity: one

North of La Serena

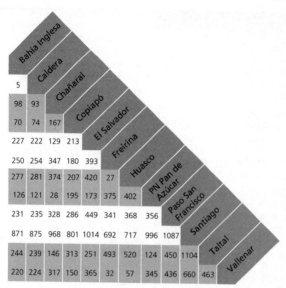

	Bahía Inglesa	Caldera	Chañaral	Copiapó	El Salvador	Freirina	Huasco	PN Pan de Azúcar	Paso San Francisco	Santiago	Taltal
Caldera	5										
Chañaral	98	93									
Copiapó	70	74	167								
El Salvador	227	222	129	213							
Freirina	250	254	347	180	393						
Huasco	277	281	374	207	420	27					
PN Pan de Azúcar	126	121	28	195	173	375	402				
Paso San Francisco	231	235	328	286	449	341	368	356			
Santiago	871	875	968	801	1014	692	717	996	1087		
Taltal	244	239	146	313	251	493	520	124	450	1104	
Vallenar	220	224	317	150	365	32	57	345	436	660	463

North of La Serena: distance chart (km)

of the largest state-owned copper-mines is at El Salvador and over 50% of all Chilean iron ore is mined around Vallenar. Other minerals include include gold and silver. Agriculture is mainly limited to the river valleys, but the Copiapó valley is an important producer of grapes, while the lower Huasco valley is Chile's biggest olive-growing area. Fishing, centred on Caldera, and on a smaller scale, Chañaral and Huasco, is also important.

CLIMATE

On the coast temperatures are moderated by the sea and mist is common in the mornings. Inland temperatures are higher by day and cooler by night. Rainfall is sparse and occurs in winter only. Amounts decrease as you go N: average annual rainfall in Vallenar is 64 mm, while in Copiapó it is 28 mm. Drivers should beware of high winds and blowing sand N of Copiapó.

HISTORY

Although small groups of Spanish settlers took over the fertile lands in the Huasco and Copiapó valleys in the sixteenth centuries, no towns were founded in this area until late in the colonial period. Even the valleys were sparsely populated until the 19th century when the development of mining led to the creation of the ports of Caldera, Chañaral and Huasco and encouraged the building of railways between the mines and the ports.

THE HUASCO VALLEY

The valley is an oasis of olive groves and vineyards. It is rugged and spectacular, dividing at Alto del Carmen, 30 km E of Vallenar, into the Carmen and Tránsito valleys. There are *pisco* distilleries at Alto del Carmen and San Félix (**F** *Res San Félix*, basic). A sweet wine known as Pajarete is also produced.

VALLENAR

(*Pop* 42,725; *Alt* 380; *Phone code* 051; airport) the chief town of the Huasco valley, is 194 km N of La Serena. Founded in 1789, its original name was San Ambrosio de Ballenary to mark the brithplace of Ambrosio O'Higgins.

Museums

Museo del Huasco, Sgto Aldea y Alonso de Ercilla, containing historic photos and artefacts from the valley (Tues-Fri 1030-1230, 1530-1900; Sat-Sun 1000-1230). Opposite is the northernmost Chilean palm in the country.

Excursions

To **Freirina**, 36 km W of Vallenar, easily reached by colectivo. Founded 1752, Freirina was the most important town in the valley, its prosperity based upon the nearby Capote goldmine and on later discoveries of copper. On the main plaza are the Municipalidad (1870) and the Santa Rosa church. No accommodation. To the **Humbolt Penguin Natural Reserve** on Isla Chañaral, where, besides penguins, there are seals, sea lions, a great variety of seabirds and, offshore, a colony of grey dolphin. Reached by following the Pan-American Highway to Domeyko, 51 km S where an unpaved road turns W for Caleta Chañaral. Permission to visit must be sought from Conaf in Caleta Choros.

Local information

● **Accommodation**

L3 *Hostería Vallenar*, Ercilla 848, T 614538, excellent, pool, Hertz car hire office, restaurant reputed to be among the best in Chile.

B *Cecil*, Prat 1059, T 614071, with bath and hot water, clean, rec; **B** *Real*, Prat 881, T 613963, parking.

C *Vall*, Aconcagua 455, T 611226, parking, rec.

D *Res La Oriental*, Serrano 720, T 613889, parking, rec; **D** *Viña del Mar*, Serrano 611, T 611478, clean, *comedor*, smoking disapproved of. Several *residenciales*.

● **Places to eat**

Bavaria, Santiago 678, good, not cheap; *El Fogón*, Ramírez 944, for meat dishes, *almuerzo* good value; *Shanghai*, Ramírez 1267, Chinese; cheap places along S end of Av Brasil.

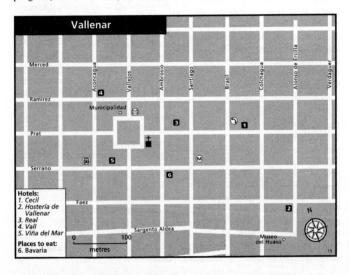

Vallenar

Hotels:
1. Cecil
2. Hostería de Vallenar
3. Real
4. Vall
5. Viña del Mar

Places to eat:
6. Bavaria

0   100
metres

HUASCO

(*Pop* 7,000) A pleasant town and port 56 km W at the mouth of the river. 1½ km S of Huasco is a terminal for loading iron ore from the deposits at Algarrobal, 52 km N of Vallenar.

● **Accommodation & places to eat** B *Hostería Huasco*, Craig y Carrera Pinto, T 531026; *Restaurant Escorial*, best; cheap seafood restaurants near port.

THE COPIAPO VALLEY

The valley of the Río Copiapó, generally regarded as the southern limit of the Atacama desert, is an oasis of farms, vineyards and orchards about 150 km long.

COPIAPO

Copiapó (*Pop* 100,000; *Alt* 400m; *Phone code* 052), capital of III Región (Atacama), lies 144 km N of Vallenar, 60 km inland. It is an important mining centre with a big mining school.

History

Founded in 1744, Copiapó became a prosperous town after the discovery in 1832 of the third largest silver deposits in South America at Chañarcillo. The wealth from Chañarcillo formed the basis of the fortunes of several famous Chilean families and helped finance the first railway line in South America, linking Copiapó to Caldera (1851). The journey from Copiapó to Chañarcillo was done by mule.

Places of interest

Several of Copiapó's churches will appeal to lovers of religious architecture. The **Cathedral**, on Plaza Prat, dating from 1851, was designed by the William Rogers. **San Francisco**, 5 blocks W of the Plaza, built in 1872 (the nearby convent is from 1662) is a good example of a 19th century construction using Oregon Pine and Guayaquil cane. **Belén**, Infante nr Yerbas Buenas, a colonial Jesuit church, was remodelled in 1856. The **Santuario**

The flowering of the desert

Although the semidesert between La Ligua and Chañaral appears to support only cacti and bushes, it occasionally breaks out into one of the world's most spectacular wildlife events. Rainfall is rare but if the winter rains are heavier than usual, spring brings the flowering of dormant seeds and bulbs while insects which normally hide underground emerge to enjoy the foliage. Between early Sept and mid Oct in a relatively wet year, look out for expanses of colour in unexpected places. As the brief spring unfolds the colours change as new plants push through to replace others. Although this flowering of the desert (*desierto florido*) can be found in many places N of La Ligua, it is particularly worth seeing around Vallenar, both along the Pan-American Highway N of the city and along the coastal road N of Huasco.

de la Candelaria, 3 km SE of the centre, is the site of two churches, the older built in 1800, the other in 1922; inside the latter is the Virgen de la Candelaria, discovered in the Salar de Maricunga in 1788. The wealth of the 19th century mining families is reflected in the **Villa Viña de Cristo**, built in Italian renaissance style, 1½ km N of the centre on Freire. The monument to Juan Godoy, the mule-driver, who, in 1832, discovered silver at Chañarcillo, formerly in the Plaza Prat, now stands at Matta y O'Higgins.

Museums

Museo Mineralógico, Colipí y Rodríguez, 1 block E from Plaza de Armas; Mon-Fri 1000-1300, 1500-1900, Sat 1000-1300, US$0.50, the best in Chile. Many ores shown are found only in the Atacama desert.

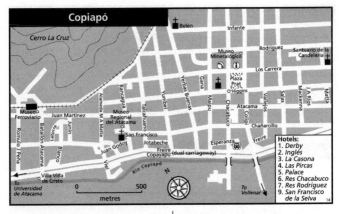

Copiapó

Hotels:
1. Derby
2. Inglés
3. La Casona
4. Las Pircas
5. Palace
6. Res Chacabuco
7. Res Rodríguez
8. San Francisco
   de la Selva

Museo Regional del Atacama, Atacama y Rancagua, entrance US$0.75 (free on Sun), interesting. Open Mon-Sat 0900-1245, 1500-1830, Sun 1000-1245.

The museum at the **railway station** is dull, but the Norris Brothers steam locomotive and carriages used in the inaugural journey between Copiapó and Caldera in 1851 can be seen at the Universidad de Atacama about 2 km N of the centre on C Freire.

Excursions

To the **Centro Metalúrgico Incaico**, a largely reconstructed Inca bronze foundry, 90 km SE up the Copiapó valley by paved road. By public transport: take Casther bus, 0845, to Valle del Cerro, US$1.50, 2 hrs and get off at Valle Hermoso (foundry is 1 km walk from main road). Return buses pass about 1400 and 1600. There is no accommodation in the nearby villages of Los Loros (site of a clinic for pulmonary diseases run by a Dr Wolman at the beginning of the 20th century, attended by the rich from Santiago), Villa Hermoso, Las Juntas.

59 km S of Copiapó on the Pan-American Highway is a signposted turning to the silver mine of **Chañarcillo**. Although the mine was closed in 1875, the tips are being reworked and this has destroyed much of the ruins.

Local festivals

Fiesta de la Candelaria, first Sun in Feb.

Local information
● **Accommodation**
A2 *Hostería Las Pircas*, Av Kennedy s/n, T 213220, bungalows, pool, dining room, out of town; **A2** *San Francisco de la Selva* Los Carrera 525, T 217013, modern.

C *Derby*, Yerbas Buenas, 396, T 212447, clean; **C** *Inglés*, Atacama 337, T 212797, old-fashioned, spacious; **C** *Palace*, Atacama 741, T 212852, patio, pleasant, parking; **C** *La Casona*, O'Higgins 150, T 217277/8, clean, friendly, tours organized; **C** *Marcoan*, Yumbel 351, T 211397, modern.

E pp *Res Chacabuco*, C Chacabuco 271, T 213428, nr bus terminal, quiet, clean; **E** *Res Nuevo Chañarcillo*, Rodríguez 540, T 212368, without bath, comfortable, rec; **E** *Res Rodríguez*, Rodríguez 528, T 212861, basic, friendly, good *comedor*, rec; **E** *Res Rocío*, Yerbas Buenas 581, T 215360, good value, clean, attractive patio, rec.

● **Places to eat**
La Carreta, on Carretera de Copayapu, 5 km S, ranch-style, very good meat and fish; *Bavaria*, on main plaza, good but not cheap. *Chifa Hao Hua*, Colipi 340, good Chinese; *Pampas*, Maipú y Atacama, smart, pleasant.

● **Banks & money changers**
Fincard (Mastercard), Chacabuco 389, open Mon-Fri 0900-1400, 1630-1930, Sat 1030-1300. Banco Concepción, cash advance on Visa.

The churches of Copiapó

👣 The "Age of Silver" which followed the discovery of Chañarcillo has left an unmistakable if subtle mark on the architecture of Copiapó's churches. New building materials, brought in to build railway stations and bridges, were used on houses and churches. Chief among these materials was *Pino Oregano*: neither a pine nor from Oregon (it is native to northern California), it offered the size and strength of timber required for the new buildings. Guayaquil cane, a type of large diameter bamboo from the Ecuadorean coast, was also introduced: sliced lengthways and flattened, it made strips of light fibre which could be used to make thin walls. At the same time, builders and carpenters from Britain and the United States, attracted by opportunities in railway and mine development, employed their skills on the new buildings of the city.

Church building in Copiapó was influenced by all these factors: architects such as the Englishman William Rogers designed churches which some have seen as reflecting English neoclassicism. Particularly noticeable is the design of the tower, positioned in the centre of the church and decorated with columns and wooden cornices. Built of wood or using strips of Guayaquil cane covered with clay, in an almost rainless climate they have withstood earthquakes to become the oldest buildings in Copiapó.

● **Post & telecommunications**
Telephones: CTC, Atacama 566.

● **Tour companies & travel agents**
Exploration and Adventure Tour, Rodríguez 771, T 212459, organizes a wide range of excursions.

● **Tourist offices**
Los Carrera 691, N side of Plaza de Armas, T 212838, helpful.

● **Transport**
Local Car hire: expensive: Av Kennedy 310, T 2964; **Hertz** at Copayapu 173, T 211333. **Cycle repairs**: *Biman*, Atacama 360B, T/F 217391, excellent.

Air LanChile, O'Higgins 640, T 213512, daily to/from Santiago, also to El Salvador; National (Colipi 350, T 218951) direct to La Serena and on to Santiago.

Buses Terminal 3 blocks SW of centre on Freire y Chacabuco. To **Santiago** US$15, 12 hrs; to **La Serena** US$7, 5 hrs; to **Caldera**, US$2, 1 hr.

FRONTIER WITH ARGENTINA: PASO SAN FRANCISCO

Paso San Francisco is reached either by unpaved road NE from Copiapó, via the Salar de Maricunga and Laguna Verde or by an unpaved road SE from El Salvador:

the two roads join near the Salar de Maricunga, 96 km W of Paso San Francisco. Officially open all year, this crossing is liable to closure in winter. On the Argentine side a poor road continues to Tinogasta (suitable only for 4WD vehicles).

● **Chilean immigration and customs**
Near the Salar de Maricunga, 100 km W of the frontier, open 0830-1830; US$2/vehicle charge for crossing Sat, Sun and holidays.

Ojos del Salado

Ojos del Salado, believed to be the third highest peak in the Americas, is situated S of the pass; its height is now thought to be 6,864m (although the latest Chilean IGM map says 6,879m – 1994; it seems to depend which side of the border you are on).

NORTH FROM COPIAPO

There are two alternative routes N: W to Caldera and then N along the coast to Chañaral, 167 km; the inland route via Diego de Almagro and then W to meet the Pan-American Highway near Chañaral, 212 km.

Climbing Ojos del Salado

Ojos del Salado is best climbed between Jan and Mar, though ascent is possible between Nov and April. In Nov, Dec and April it can be hit by the *Invierno Boliviano*, a particularly nasty weather pattern coming from the NE. Temperatures have been known to drop to -40°C with high winds up to 150 km/hr.

Access is by a road turning off the main Chile-Argentina road at *Hostería Murray* (burned down). Base camp for the climb is at the Argentine frontier post (4,500m). There are 2 refugios: *Refugio Atacama* (4-6 beds) at 5,200m and *Refugio Tejos* (better, 12 beds) at 5,700m. From the latter it is 10-12 hrs, climb to the summit, approx grade 3. The climb is not very difficult, except the last 50m, which is moderate climbing on rock to the crater rim and summit. There is little or no snow: water is available at *Hostería Murray* but it may be advisable to carry it from Copiapó. Large quantities must be taken on the ascent. Guides and equipment can be hired in Copiapó: try Rubén E Rubilan Cortes, O'Higgins 330, T 216535 and others (US$450-600).

Permits are required: obtainable free from the Dirección de Fronteras y Límites in Santiago (address under **Climbing** in **Adventure tourism**, or from the Municipalidad in Copiapó, which will fax Santiago).

CALDERA

(*Pop* 12,000; *Phone code* 052), 73 km W of Copiapó, is a port and terminal for the loading of iron ore. In the late 19th century it was a major railway engineering centre, but there are few reminders of this era; the **Iglesia de San Vicente** (1862) on the Plaza de Armas was built by English carpenters working for the railway company.

Bahía Inglesa, 6 km S of Caldera, 6 km W of the Highway, is popular with Chileans for its beautiful white sandy beaches and unpolluted sea (very expen-

sive and can get crowded Jan-Feb and at weekends). The climate is warm and dry the year round. It was originally known as Puerto del Inglés after the visit in 1687 of the English 'corsario', Edward Davis.

● **Accommodation In Caldera**: B *Hostería Puerta del Sol*, Wheelwright 750, T 315205, inc tax, cabins with bath and kitchen, view over bay; C *Costanera*, Wheelwright 543, T 316007, takes credit cards, simple rooms, friendly; A3 *Portal del Inca*, Carvallo 945, T 315252, shower, cabins with kitchen, English spoken, restaurant not bad, order breakfast on previous night; C *Pucará*, Ossa Cerda 460, T 315258; D *Res Fenicia*, Gallo 370, T 315594, eccentric owner, rec; E *Res Millaray*, main plaza, clean, friendly. **In Bahía Inglesa**: Very expensive in summer: cheaper to stay in Caldera. B *Los Jardines de Bahía Inglesa*, Av Copiapó, *cabañas*, T 315359, open all year, good beds, comfortable; *Camping Bahía Inglesa*, Playa Las Machas, T 315424, B/tent site, fully equipped *cabañas* for up to 5 persons, A3. *El Coral* restaurant has some cabins C, T 315331, Av El Morro, overlooking sea, good seafood, groups welcome, open all year.

● **Places to eat In Caldera**: *Miramar*, Gana 090, at pier, good seafood. *El Pirón de Oro*, Cousiño 218, good but not cheap; *Charles*, Ossa Cerda, good seafood, clean.

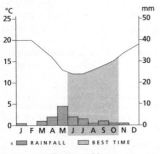

°C / mm graph with axes: °C (25, 20, 15, 10, 5, 0) and mm (50, 40, 30, 20, 10, 0), months J F M A M J J A S O N D

■ RAINFALL   □ BEST TIME

Climate: Caldera

● **Transport** Buses to **Copiapó** and **Santiago**, several daily; to **Antofagasta**, US$18, 7 hrs; to travel N, it may be better to take a bus to **Chañaral** (Inca-bus US$2), then change. Hourly buses between Bahía Inglesa and Caldera; taxis and colectivos US$1, all year; frequent micro service Jan-Feb US$0.25.

THE SALADO VALLEY

The valley of the Río Salado, 130 km in length, less fertile or prosperous than the Copiapó or Huasco valleys, is the last oasis S of Antofagasta.

CHAÑARAL

(*Pop* 12,000, *Phone Code* 052). A neglected looking town with wooden houses perched on the hillside is 93 km N of Caldera and 968 km N of Santiago. In its heyday it was the processing centre for ore from the nearby copper mines of El Salado and Las Animas, but it is now a base for visits to beaches and the Parque Nacional Pan de Azúcar.

● **Accommodation B** *Hostería Chañaral*, Miller 268, T 480055, excellent restaurant; **C** *Mini*, San Martín 528, T 480079, good value restaurant; **D** *Nuria*, Costanera 302, good; **D** *Jiménez*, Merino Jarpa 551, without bath, friendly, patio with lots of birds rec, restaurant good value; **E** *La Marina*, Merino Jarpa 562, basic.

● **Places to eat** In hotels; *Rincón Porteño*, Merino Jarpa 567, good and inexpensive. *San Remo*, Torreblanca, good seafood; *Restaurante de los Pescadores*, in La Caleta, good fish, clean, cheap, rec.

● **Banks & money changers** Poor rates for cash; nowhere to change TCs.

● **Tourist offices** Kiosk on the Pan-American Highway at S end of town (closed winter).

● **Transport** Bus terminal Merino Jarpa 854. Frequent services to **Antofagasta** US$11, 5 hrs, and **Santiago**.

PARQUE NACIONAL PAN DE AZUCAR

The park, N of Chañaral, consists of the Isla Pan de Azúcar on which Humboldt penguins and other sea-birds live, and some 43,700 ha of coastal hills rising to 900m. There are fine beaches (popular at weekends in summer). Fishermen near the Conaf office offer boat trips round Isla Pan de Azúcar to see the penguins, US$25, though these are sometimes visible from the mainland. **NB** There are heavy fines for driving in 'restricted areas' of the park.

Wildlife Vegetation is mainly cacti, of which there are 26 species, nourished by frequent sea mists (*camanchaca*). After rain in some of the gullies there are tall purple lilies. The park is home to 103 species of birds as well as guanaco and foxes.

● **Park information** Two entrances: N by good secondary road from Chañaral, 28 km to Caleta Pan de Azúcar; from the Pan-American Highway 45 km N of Cañaral, along a side road 20 km (road in parts deep sand and very rough, 4WD essential). Taxi from Chañaral US$20, or hitch a lift from fishermen at sunrise.

● **Conaf** office in Caleta Pan de Azúcar, maps available; park entry US$6, camping, US$10, no showers, take all food.

EL SALVADOR

(*Pop* 10,437; *Alt* 2,300) is a modern town, built near one of the biggest copper mines in Chile, 129 km E of Chañaral in the valley of the Río Salado, reached by a road which branches off the Pan-American Highway 12 km E of Chañaral. All along the valley there are people extracting metal ore from the water by building primitive settling tanks. Further E by unpaved road is the **Salar de Pedernales**, 30,000 ha of saltflats at an altitude of 3,350m.

● **Accommodation** *Hostería El Salvador*, Potrerillos 003, T 472492; *Camino del Inca*, El Tofo 333, T 472311; *Res Linari*, Potrerillos 705.

● **Transport Air** Lan Chile from Santiago and Copiapó (T 052-121-2590). **Buses** Pullman Bus daily to Santiago.

TALTAL

(*Pop* 9,000; *Phone code* 055) 146 km N of Chañaral, this is the only town between Chañaral and Antofagasta, a distance of 420 km. Along Av Prat are several wooden buildings dating from the late 19th century when Taltal prospered as a mineral port of 20,000 people, exporting nitrates from 21 mines in the area. It is now a fishing port with a mineral processing plant. There is an airport, but few flights. 72 km N is the Quebrada El Médano, a gorge with ancient rock-paintings along the upper valley walls.

Museums   Museo Arqueológico, on Av Prat.

● **Accommodation C** *Hostería Taltal*, Esmeralda 671, T 101, excellent restaurant, good value *almuerzo*; **C** *Verdy*, Ramírez 345,

T 105, with bath, **E** without, clean, spacious, restaurant, rec; opp is **E** *Taltal City*, clean, no hot water; **E** *San Martín*, Martínez 279, T 88, without bath, good *almuerzo*; **E** *Viña del Mar*, Serrano 762.

● **Places to eat** *Caverna*, Martínez 247, good seafood; *Club Social Taltal*, Torreblanca 162, excellent, good value.

● **Transport** Buses to **Santiago** 2 a day; to **Antofagasta** Tramaca, TurBus and Ramos, US$5.

77 km E of Taltal, and some 175 km S of Antofagasta, is Agua Verde, a fuel station and fruit inspection post. North of here, mining tracks lead off to the E, but there are no real signs. A good one leads E from Oficina Chile to Plato de Sopa, a camp built into caves above a salt flat.

Antofagasta, Calama and San Pedro

ANTOFAGASTA and Calama are export and service centres respectively for the copper industry in the area. Calama is also the starting point for one of the rail journeys to Bolivia. Around San Pedro de Atacama (which has remains of Atacameño culture) are superb Andean landscapes; San Pedro itself is growing increasingly as a tourist centre.

THE LAND

GEOGRAPHY

The Atacama Desert stretches 1,255 km N from the Río Copiapó to the Chilean frontier with Peru. The Cordillera de la Costa, at its highest in this region (the highest peak is Cerro Vicuña, 3,114m), runs close to the coast, an inhospitable pink cliff face rising to a height from 600m to 900m. Below this cliff, on the edge of the Pacific is a ledge on which are situated the city of Antofagasta, several smaller towns and a road connecting them. In the eastern branch of the Andes several peaks rise to around 6,000m: Llullaillaco (6,739m), Socompa (6,050m), Licancábur (5,916m), Ollagüe (5,863m). The western branch of the Andes ends near Calama. In between these two ranges the Andean Depression includes several

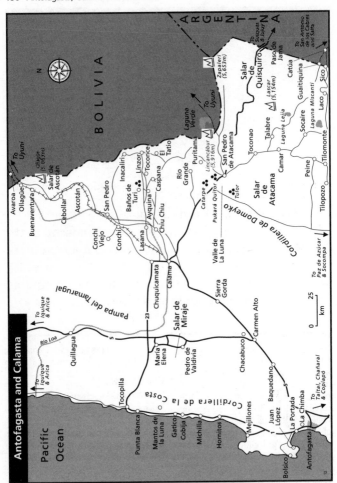

Antofagasta and Calama

BOLIVIA

A R G E N T I N A

Pacific Ocean

saltflats including the Salar de Atacama and the smaller Salar de Ascotán.

Although there are a number of small streams around San Pedro de Atacama, the only river in this part of Chile is the Río Loa, 440 km, the longest in the country. It has been dammed at Conchi to provide irrigation for several oases around Calama.

ECONOMY

Mining is the most important economic activity. The region includes large copper mines at Chuquicamata, Mantas Blancas, Escondida and La Exótica as well as new reserves at Zaldívar and El Abra and smaller-scale operations along the road between Antofagasta and Tocopilla. Two mines, María Elena and Pedro de Valdi-

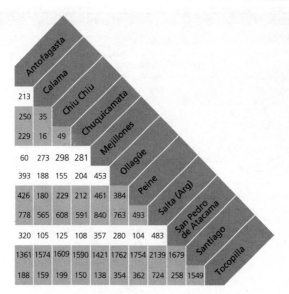

	Antofagasta	Calama	Chiu Chiu	Chuquicamata	Mejillones	Ollagüe	Peine	Salta (Arg)	San Pedro de Atacama	Santiago
Calama	213									
Chiu Chiu	250	35								
Chuquicamata	229	16	49							
Mejillones	60	273	298	281						
Ollagüe	393	188	155	204	453					
Peine	426	180	229	212	461	384				
Salta (Arg)	778	565	608	591	840	763	493			
San Pedro de Atacama	320	105	125	108	357	280	104	483		
Santiago	1361	1574	1609	1590	1421	1762	1754	2139	1679	
Tocopilla	188	159	199	150	138	354	362	724	258	1549

**Antofagasta, Calama and San Pedro:
distance chart (km)**

via produce nitrates and iodine, while the Salar de Atacama and the Salar de Ascotán contain respectively the world's largest known deposits of lithium and borax. Fishing is a major industry: the three main ports are Antofagasta, Mejillones and Tocopilla; there are 24 fish processing plants. Other industries include the manufacture of explosives at Calama and cement at Antofagasta. Agricultural activity is limited by the lack of water and poor soils. Apart from tropical fruit production on the coast S of Antofagasta, agriculture is limited to inland areas around the Río Loa and its tributaries.

The main towns, Antofagasta and Calama, account for 87% of the population of the area, 98.8% of which is urban. Other urban centres are mining towns with few economic activities not associated with the mining companies. Life in the area is artificial. Water has to be piped for hundreds of kilometres to the cities and the mining towns from the Cordillera; all food and even all building materials have to be brought in from elsewhere.

CLIMATE

There is some difference of climate between the coast and the interior. The coast is humid and cloudy; *camanchaca*, a heavy sea mist caused by the cold water of the Humbolt current, is common in the morning. In the interior the skies are clear day and night. The temperatures on the coast are fairly uniform; in the interior there is often a great difference in the temperature between day and night; the winter nights are often as cold as -10°C, with a cruel wind. Between Dec and March there are often violent storms of rain, snow and hail in the highlands, a phenomenon known as *invierno altiplánico* (highland winter) or *invierno boliviano* (Bolivian winter).

Nitrates

The rise and fall of the nitrate industry played an important part in opening up the northern desert areas between Iquique and Antofagasta to human settlement. In the second half of the 19th century nitrates became important in Europe and USA as an artificial fertilizer and for making explosives. The world's only known deposits of nitrates were in the Atacama desert provinces of Antofagasta in Bolivia and Tarapacá in Peru. After the War of the Pacific Chile gained control of all the nitrate fields, giving her a monopoly over world supply. Ownership was dominated by the British who controlled 60% of the industry by 1900. Taxes on the export of nitrates provided Chilean governments with around half their income for the next 40 years.

The processing of nitrates was labour-intensive: at its height over 60,000 workers were employed. Using a combination of dynamite and manual labour, the workers dug the nitrate ore from the desert floor. It was then transported to nitrate plants known as *oficinas,* crushed and mixed with water, allowing pure nitrates to be extracted. The mining and refining processes were dangerous and cost many lives, but wages were relatively high. Everything had to be brought in from outside the region, including food which was sold at the company stores using special tokens with which the workers were paid.

The development of the Haber-Bosch process, a method of producing artificial nitrates, in Germany during the First World War, dealt a severe blow to the nitrate companies and many mines closed in the 1920s. New techniques were introduced by the Guggenheim company, but the world depression after 1929 led to the collapse of demand for nitrates and with it the Chilean nitrate industry. Only two mines survive today, at María Elena and Pedro de Valdivia. Traces of the nitrate era can, however, still be seen: the mining ghost towns of Humberstone, near Iquique, and Chacabuco, N of Antofagasta, can be visited as can Baquedano, the most important junction of the nitrate railways; most of the other *oficinas* are marked only by piles of rubble at the roadsides north of Antofagasta.

HISTORY

The area around San Pedro de Atacama was one of centres of the Atacameño culture, until the arrival of the Incas around 1450. After the expeditions of Diego de Almagro in 1536 and Pedro de Valdivia in 1540, the early Spanish presence in this region was limited to the sharing out of productive lands among a few Spanish settlers and the foundation of a mission in San Pedro. By the end of the colonial period the Spanish had established urban settlements only in San Pedro and Chiu Chiu. At the time of independence most of the region became part of Bolivia though the frontier with Chile was ill-defined. Before the War of the Pacific deprived her of this coastal territory, Bolivia formally established several towns along the coast, notably Cobija (1825), Mejillones (1841), Tocopilla (1843) and Antofagasta (1872). Nevertheless by 1875 the total population of the region was under 10,000. After the War of the Pacific the exploitation of nitrates led to an increase in population, the building of railways and ports and the growth of Antofagasta into one of the most important cities in Chile.

ANTOFAGASTA

Antofagasta (*Pop* 185,000; *Phone code* 055), 1,367 km N of Santiago and 699 km S of Arica, is the largest city in Northern Chile and the fourth largest in the capital. It is the capital of the Second Region and is a major port for the export of copper from Chuquicamata. It is also a major commercial centre and home of two universities. The climate is delightful (apart from the lack of rain); the temperature varies from 16°C in June/July to 24°C Jan/Feb, never falling below 10°C at night.

History

Although used as a port throughout the 1860s, Antofagasta's existence was not officially recognised by the Bolivian government until 1869 (at first with the name Peñablanca). From a population at that time of about 300 it grew quickly as the terminal of the Antofagasta Nitrate and Railway Company, forerunner of the FCAB (see below).

Places of interest

In the main square, **Plaza Colón**, is a clock tower donated by the British community. **Paseo Prat**, which runs SE from Plaza Colón, is the main shopping street. Two blocks N of Plaza Colón, near the old port, is the **Ex-Aduana**, built as the Bolivian customs house in Mejillones and moved to its current site after the War of the Pacific. Opposite are two other buildings, the former **Capitanía del Puerto** (now occupied by the Fundación Andrés Sabella, which offers occasional workshops on weaving, painting, etc) and

the **ex-Resguardo Marítimo** (now housing Digader, the regional coordinating centre for sport and recreation). East of the port are the buildings of the **Antofagasta and Bolivia Railway Company** (FCAB) dating from the 1890s and beautifully restored, but still in use and difficult to visit. These include the former railway station, company offices and workers' housing. The former main square of the **Oficina Vergara**, a nitrate town built in 1919 and dismantled in 1978, can be seen in the campus of the University of Antofagasta, 4 km S of the centre (bus 3 or 4). Also to the S on a hill (and reached by Bus B) are the ruins of **Huanchaca**, a Bolivian silver refinery built after 1868 and closed in 1903. From below, the ruins resemble a fortress rather than a factory.

Museums

Museo Histórico Regional, in the former Aduana, Balmaceda y Bolívar, Tues-Sat 1000-1300, 1530-1830, Sun 1100-1400, US$0.80, children half-price, fascinating new displays (many in Spanish only) on life on land and in the oceans, development of civilization in South America, minerals, human artefacts, rec.

Museo Geológico of the Universidad Católica del Norte, Av Angamos 0610, inside the university campus, open Mon-Fri, 0830-1230, 1500-1800, free (colectivo 3 or 33 from town centre).

Excursions

The fantastic cliff formations and symbol of the Second Region at **La Portada** are 16 km N, reached by minibuses from Latorre y Sucre (US$2 return) or any bus for Mejillones from the Terminal Centro. Taxis charge US$11. Hitching is easy. From the main road it is 2 km to the beach which, though beautiful, is too dangerous for swimming; there is an excellent seafood restaurant (*La Portada*) and café (open lunch-time only). A number of bathing beaches are also within easy reach.

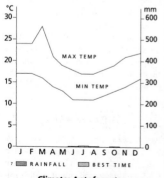

°C / mm

MAX TEMP

MIN TEMP

J F M A M J J A S O N D

RAINFALL   BEST TIME

Climate: Antofagasta

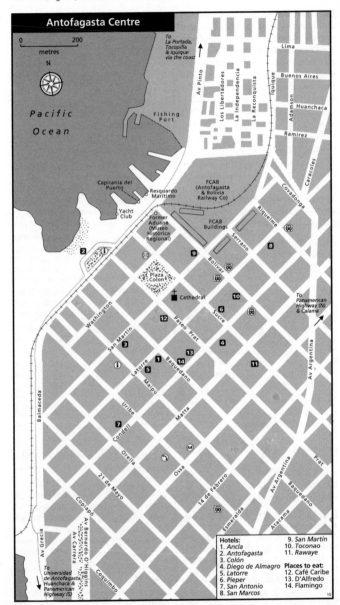

Antofagasta Centre

0 — 200 metres

N

Pacific Ocean

To La Portada, Tocopilla & Iquique via the coast

Av Pinto

Los Libertadores
La Independencia
La Reconquista

Lima
Buenos Aires
Adamson
Huanchaca
Ramirez
Caracoles
Iquique

Fishing Port

Covadonga

Capitanía del Puerto

Resguardo Marítimo

FCAB (Antofagasta & Bolivia Railway Co)

Yacht Club

Former Aduana (Museo Histórica Regional)

FCAB Buildings

Riquelme
Serrano

Bolívar

8

9

To Panamerican Highway (N) & Calama

Plaza Colón

Cathedral

Sucre

10

6

Washington

San Martín

12

3

Paseo Prat

Latorre

1

5

Baquedano

13

14

4

11

Av Argentina

Balmaceda

Maipú

Uribe

7

Condell

Matta

M

Orella

Ossa

21 de Mayo

14 de Febrero

Esmeralda

Av Argentina

Atacama

Baquedano

Prat

Coplapó

Av Bernardo O'Higgins

Av Carrera

Coquimbo

Av Grecia

To Universidad de Antofagasta, Huanchaca & Panamerican Highway (S)

Hotels:
1. Ancla
2. Antofagasta
3. Colón
4. Diego de Almagro
5. Latorre
6. Pieper
7. San Antonio
8. San Marcos
9. San Martín
10. Toconao
11. Rawaye

Places to eat:
12. Café Caribe
13. D'Alfredo
14. Flamingo

10

Juan López, 38 km N of Antofagasta, is a windsurfers' paradise (Hotel *La Rinconada*, T 268502; *Hostería Sandokan*, T 692031). Buses at weekends in summer only, also minibuses daily in summer from Latorre y Sucre. For those with their own transport, follow the road out of Juan López to the beautiful cove at Conchilla. Keep on the track to the end at Bolsico. The sea is alive with birds, including Humboldt penguins, especially opposite Isla Santa María.

72 km NE of Antofagasta (on the Pan-American Highway) is **Baquedano**, formerly an important railway junction. The old railway station (still used by goods trains) and a large and neglected collection of old (and rusting) locomotives with the grand title of Parque Histórico Ferrocarril, can be seen.

30 km further N and just off the Pan-American Highway is **Chacabuco**, a large abandoned nitrate town, opened in 1924, closed in 1938 and used as a concentration camp by the Pinochet government between 1973 and 1975. Workers' housing, the church, theatre, stores and the mineral plants can be visited. Free guided tour (in Spanish). Take any bus from Antofagasta towards Calama, get off at the Carmen Alto junction and walk the last 4 km.

Local festivals
29 June, **San Pedro**, patron saint of the fishermen: the saint's image is taken out by launch to the breakwater to bless the first catch of the day. On the last weekend of Oct, the foreign communities put on a joint festival on the seafront, with national foods, dancing and music.

Local information
● **Accommodation**
A1 *Nadine*, Baquedano 519, T 227008, F 265222, bath, TV, bar, café, parking, etc; opp is **A2** *Ancla*, Baquedano 508, T 224814, F 261551, bath, TV, bar, restaurant, exchange (see below); **A2** *Antofagasta*, Balmaceda 2575, T/F 268259, garage, swimming pool, lovely view of port and city, run down, with

breakfast (discount for Automóvil Club members), beach; **A2** *Diego de Almagro*, Condell 2624, T 268331, good for the money but a bit tatty; **A3** *Colón*, San Martín 2434, T 261851, F 260872,with breakfast, quiet, clean.

B *Pieper*, Sucre 509, T 263603, clean, modern, warmly rec; **B** *San Marcos*, Latorre 2946, T 251763, modern, comfortable, parking, avoid rooms at the back (loud music), overpriced; **B** *San Martín*, San Martín y Bolívar, T 263503, with bath, TV, parking, clean, safe and friendly; **B** *Tatio*, Av Grecia 1000, T 247561, modern building, out of old town on the beach, has buses converted into caravans, D, friendly, beautiful views, acts as youth hostel, no cooking facilities.

C *Latorre*, Latorre 2450, T 221886, pleasant; **C** *San Antonio*, Condell 2235, T 268857, clean, helpful, modern but noisy from bus station.

D *Res La Riojanita*, Baquedano 464, T 268652, basic, old-fashioned, hot water on demand, noisy; **D** *Res El Cobre*, Prat 749, T 225162, central, noisy, basic; **D** *Res O'Higgins*, Sucre 665, T 267596, big, old, dirty, no hot water; **D** *Rawaye*, Sucre 762, T 225399, without breakfast, basic, hot water am only, no towels; **D** *Res Toconao*,Bolívar 580, clean.

E pp *Brasil*, Bolívar 568,clean; **E** *Res Paola*, Prat 766, T 222208, without bath, noisy, poor bathroom facilities.

Camping: to the S on the road to Coloso are: *Las Garumas*, Km 9, T 247758, US$10 for tent (bargain for lower price out of season), US$15 for cabins; cold showers and beach (reservations Av Angamos 601, casilla 606). *Rucamóvil*, Km 13, T 231913 and 7 *cabañas*, T 221988. Both open year-round, expensive. To the N are: *La Gruta*, Km 12 and *La Rinconada*, Km 30, off road to Mejillones, between La Portada and Juan López, T 261139.

● **Places to eat**
Marina Club, Av Ejército 0909, good fish and seafood dishes and a view, expensive but worth it; *Tío Jacinto*, Uribe 922, friendly, good seafood; *El Arriero*, Condell 2644, good service, good set lunch otherwise pricey, live music; *Bavaria*, J S Ossa 2428, excellent meat and German specialities, not cheap; *Flamingo*, Condell y Baquedano, rec; *D'Alfredo*, Condell 2539, pizzas, good; *Chicken's House Center*, Latorre 2660, chicken, beef and daily specials, open till 2400; *Casa Vecchia*, O'Higgins 1456,

good value. Difficult to find coffee or breakfast before 0900. *Café Bahía*, Prat 452, and *Café Caribe*, Prat 482, good coffee, open 0900; *Piccolo Mondo*, Condell 2685, expresso coffee, snacks, drinks, opens 0930, good; ice cream at *Fiori di Gelatto*, Baquedano 519, in new *Hotel Nadine*, highly rec. Many eating places in the market; *Chico Jaime* above the market, surrealistic decor, seafood, *almuerzo* US$3, mixed reports; good reports of *El Mariscal* in same area. Good cheap lunches at *El Rincón de Don Quijote*, Maipú 642. Good fish restaurants in *terminal de pescadores*; also at Coloso, 8 km S nr the Playa Amarilla (take your own wine). *Chez Niko's*, Ossa 1951, restaurant, bar, bakery, *pastelería*, good pizzas, *empanadas* and bread. *Chifa Pekín*, Ossa 2135, Chinese, smart, reasonable prices.

● **Airline offices**
LanChile, Washington 2552, T 265151; Ladeco, Washington 2589, T 269170, F 260440; National, Latorre 2572, T 224418, F 268996; Alta, Balmaceda 2584, T 226089, F 282202.

● **Banks & money changers**
Banco de Concepción, Plaza Colón for Visa. Banco Edwards, Prat 461, TCs changed at high commission. Fincard, Prat 431, for Mastercard. Foreign money exchange (all currencies and TCs) is best at *Hotel Ancla*, Latorre 2478 y Baquedano 508, T 224814, open all day every day. **NB** Impossible to change TCs S of Antofagasta until you reach La Serena.

● **Embassies & consulates**
Bolivia, Av Grecia 563, Oficina 23, T 221403; France and Belgium, Baquedano 299, T 268669.

● **Entertainment**
Discotheques: *Con Tutti*, Av Grecia 421; *Popo's*, Universidad de Chile (far end from town); *Parador 63*, Baquedano 619, disco, bar-restaurant, live shows, good value.

Theatre: *Teatro Municipal*, Sucre y San Martín, T 264919, modern, state-of-the art; *Teatro Pedro de la Barca*, Condell 2495, run by University of Antofagasta, occasional plays, reviews.

● **Laundry**
París, Condell 2455, laundry and dry cleaning, expensive, charges per item; *Laverap*, 14 Febrero 1802.

● **Post & telecommunications**
Post Office: on Plaza Colón, 0830-1900, Sat 0900-1300.

Telephones: Entel Chile, Baquedano, 753; CTC, Condell 2529.

● **Shopping**
Galería del Arte Imagen, Uribe 485, sells antiques inc artefacts from nitrate plants.

Bookshop: *Librería Universitaria*, Latorre 2515, owner Germana Fernández knowledgeable on local history; opp is *Multilibro*.

Market: Municipal market, corner of Matta and Uribe.

● **Sports**
Swimming: Olympic pool at Condell y 21 de Mayo, US$1.20, open till 1800, best in am. Sauna: Riquelme y Condell.

Tennis: Club de Tenis Antofagasta, Av Angamos 906.

● **Tour companies & travel agents**
Many inc *Tatio Travel*, Latorre 2579, T 263532, Tx 225242 TATIO CL, English spoken, tours arranged for groups or individuals, highly rec. *Turismo Cristóbal* in *Hotel Antofagasta*, helpful. *Turismo Corssa*, San Martín 2769, T/F 251190, rec. Alex Joseph Valenzuela Thompson, Edif Bulnes, Sucre 220, p 4, Oficina 403, T 243322/F 222718, Aptdo Postal 55, offers to guide German speakers around the area.

● **Tourist offices**
Maipú 240, T 264044, Mon-Fri 0830-1300, Mon-Thur 1500-1930, Fri 1500-1930; kiosk on Balmaceda nr *Hotel Antofagasta* Mon-Fri 0930-1300, 1530-1930, Sat/Sun 0930-1300 kiosk at airport (open summer only). Automóvil Club de Chile: Condell 2330, T 225332.

Customs agent: Luis Piquimil Bravo, Prat 272, oficina 202, excellent, fast service, efficient.

● **Transport**
Local Car rental: Rent-a-Car, Prat 810, T 225200; Avis, Prat 272, T 221668; Budget, Prat 206, T 251745; Hertz, Balmaceda 2566 (T 269043), offer city cars and jeeps (group D, Toyota Landcruiser) and do a special flat rate, with unlimited mileage; Felcar, 14 de Febrero 2324, T 224468, English spoken, reported to be the cheapest.

Air Cerro Moreno Airport, 22 km N. Taxi to airport US$7, but cheaper if ordered from hotel. LanChile, Ladeco and National fly daily

The Poet and the Sea 2

"Monumento al mar/Monument to the Sea"

Here is the sea
The sea where the smell of the cities comes to be shivered
With its lap full of boats and fish and other cheerful things
Those boats which fish at the edge of the sky
Those fish which listen to each ray of light
Those algae with ageless dreams
And that wave which sings better than all the rest

Here is the sea
The sea which expands and anchors on its shores
The sea which wraps the stars in its waves
The sea with its martyred skin
and the shocks in its veins
With its days of peace and its nights of hysteria

He aquí el mar
El mar donde viene a estrellarse el olor de las ciudades
Con su regazo lleno de barcas y peces y otras cosas alegres
Esas barcas que pescan a la orilla del cielo
Esos peces que escuchan cada rayo de luz
Esas algas con sueños seculares
Y esa ola que canta mejor que las otras

He aquí el mar
El que se estira y se afierra a sus orillas
El mar que envuelve las estrellas en sus olas
El mar con su piel martirizada
Y los sobresaltos de sus venas
Con sus días de paz y sus noches de histeria

The Selected Poetry of Vicente Huidobro, edited with an introduction by David M Guss (New York: New Directions, 1981). Spanish version from *Ultimos poemas*, 1948.

to Santiago, Iquique and Arica.

Trains There are no passenger services from Antofagasta. The journey to Bolivia starts from Calama (see below) – tickets from Tramaca, Uribe 936 or in Calama.

Buses No main terminal; each company has its own office in town (some quite a distance from the centre). Buses for **Mejillones** and **Tocopilla**, operated by Barrios, Tramaca, Camus and others, depart from the Terminal Centro at Riquelme 513. Minibuses to Mejillones leave from Latorre 2730. Bus company offices as follows: Tramaca, Uribe 936, T 223624; Flota Barrios, Condell 2764, T 268559; Géminis, Latorre 3099, T 251796; Fénix Pullman Norte, San Martín 2717; Incatur, Maipú 554; Turis Norte, Argentina 1155; Libac,

Argentina 1155; Pullman Bus, Latorre 2805, T 262591; Chile-Bus (to Argentina and Brazil) and Tur-Bus, Latorre 2751. To **Santiago**, 18 hrs (Flota Barrios, US$60, *cama* inc drinks and meals); 30% reduction on Inca, Tramaca, and Géminis buses for students, but ask after you have secured a seat; many companies: fares US$35-40, book 2 days in advance. If all seats to the capital are booked, catch a bus to **La Serena** (13 hrs, US$20, or US$38 *cama* service), or **Ovalle**, US$20, and re-book. To **Valparaíso**, US$35. To **Arica**, US$16 (Tur-Bus), 13½ hrs, Tramaca, US$18. To **Chuquicamata**, US$6, frequent, 3 hrs. To **Calama**, several companies, US$5, Tramaca, 3 hrs; to **San Pedro de Atacama**, Tramaca direct service 0800 or go via Calama. Direct to **Copiapó** on Thur and Sat at 2230, US$10.50. Frequent buses to **Iquique**; US$13, 8 hrs.

Buses to Salta, Argentina Géminis, Wed, US$50, 22 hrs; via Calama, San Pedro and Paso Sico, immigration check at San Pedro de Atacama, then on to high Cordillera and to San Antonio de los Cobres (Argentine customs) all year round, although April-Sept dependent on weather conditions. Also Atahualpa/Tramaca joint service in summer only, Tues, Fri 0700 via Calama, San Pedro, Paso Sico and Jujuy US$50, student discount if you are persistent. Book in advance for these services, take food and as much warm clothing as possible. There is nowhere to change Chilean pesos en route. These services can be picked up in San Pedro, but book first in Calama or Antofagasta and notify bus company.

Hitchhiking If hitching to Arica or Iquique try at the beer factory a few blocks N of the fish market on Av Pinto, or the lorry park a few blocks further N. If hitching S go to the police checkpoint/restaurant/gas station La Negra, about 15 km S of the city.

MEJILLONES

(*Pop* 5,500; *Phone code* 055), 60 km N of Antofagasta, this little port stands on a good natural harbour protected from westerly gales by high hills. Until 1948 it was a major terminal for the export of tin and other metals from Bolivia: remnants of that past include a number of fine wooden buildings: the Intendencia Municipal, the Casa Cultural (built in 1866) and the church (1906), as well as the Capitanía del Puerto. Today the town lives mainly by fishing, coming alive in the evening when the fishermen prepare to set sail. The sea is very cold because of the Humboldt current. A Mediterranean-style tourist complex is planned for Mejillones Bay.

● **Accommodation A2** *Costa Del Sol*, M Montt 086, T 621590, 4-star, new; **D** *Res Marcela*, Borgoño 150, with bath, pleasant; **F** *Res Elisabeth*, Alte Latorre 440, T 621568, friendly, basic, restaurant. No campsite but wild camping possible on the beach.

● **Places to eat** *Juanito*, Las Heras 241, excellent *almuerzo*; *Sion-Ji*, Alte Latorre 718, Chinese, good value.

ROUTES NORTH FROM ANTOFAGASTA

There are two routes from Antofagasta N to Iquique.

1) Along the Pan-American Highway

The Highway continues N via Baquedano and Carmen Alto (Km 98), the turning to Calama. **María Elena**(*Pop* 7,700; *Alt* 1,250m) and **Pedro de Valdivia** (*Pop* 8,600), the two nitrate mines in Chile still functioning, are situated off a turning at Km 167. Both are clean modern mining towns. The **Museo Arqueológico y Histórico**, on the main plaza in María Elena, has exhibits on prehispanic cultures.

● **Accommodation María Elena: D** *Chacance*, T 632749, run down, but nicer rooms around the corner, clean; cheap meals at the *Casino Social*.

● **Transport** Buses to Iquique 6 hrs, US$10.

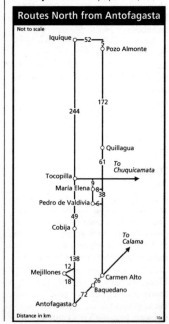

Routes North from Antofagasta

Not to scale

Distance in km

2) Along the coast road

From Antofagasta and Mejillones to Tocopilla, 187 km N, the road is paved all the way, but with no fuel N of Mejillones. The route runs at the foot of 500m cliffs, behind which are mountains which are extensively mined for copper, often by *piqueneros* (small groups of self-employed miners). There are larger mines, with the biggest concentration inland of Michilla (107 km N).

Reminders of the area's mining past can be seen at several points, principally the ruins of **Cobija** (127 km N), founded by order of Bolívar in 1825 as Bolivia'a main port. A prosperous little town handling silver exports from Potosí, it was destroyed by an earthquake in 1868 and again by a tidal wave in 1877 before losing out to the rising port of Antofagasta. Adobe walls, the rubbish tip (right above the sea) and the wreckage of the port are all that remains. The atmospheric ruins of the port of Gatico are at Km 144. About 5 km further N there is an amazing ransacked cemetery.

A zig-zag road (very steep) winds up the cliffs to the mine at Mantos de la Luna about 152 km N of Antofagasta. At the top there are rather dead-looking groves of giant cactus living off the sea mist which collects on the cliffs. Wildlife includes foxes (*zorros*).

There are good, weekend beach resorts at Hornitos (88 km N of Antofagasta) and Poza Verde (117 km N).

TOCOPILLA

(*Pop* 24,600; *Phone code* 055) is 187 km N of Antofagasta via the coastal road and 365 km via the Pan-American Highway. The town is dominated by a thermal power station, which supplies electricity to the whole of northern Chile, and by the port facilities used to unload coal and to export nitrates and iodine from María Elena and Pedro de Valdivia. There is a sports stadium and two good beaches: Punta Blanca (12 km S) and Caleta Covadonga. Tocopilla Yacht Club, 45 km S, has a good beach, restaurant and bar. There is also fine deep sea fishing if you can find a boat and a guide.

● **Accommodation** **C** *Chungará*, 21 de Mayo 1440, T 811036, comfortable, clean, rec; **C** *Vucina*, 21 de Mayo 2069, T 811571, modern, good restaurant; **C** *Casablanca*, 21 de Mayo 2054, T 813222, F 813104, friendly, helpful; **D** *Hostería Bolívar*, Bolívar 1332, T 812783, modern, helpful, meals, clean, friendly, highly rec; **E** *Hostal Central*, Aníbal Pinto 1241, friendly, clean; **F** *Res La Giralda*, 21 de Mayo 1134.

● **Places to eat** *Club de la Unión*, Prat 1354, good *almuerzo*, cheap; *Kong Jong*, 21 de Mayo 1833, reasonable value, Chinese; *El Pirata*, 21 de Mayo 1999, *parrilladas*. Good seafood at the Muelle Pesquero opp the old wooden clock tower.

● **Transport** Buses to **Antofagasta** 8 a day, several companies inc Barrrios, Tramaca and Camus, US$3, 2½ hrs; to **Iquique**, by bus and minibus along coastal road, Barrios, Tramaca and Turisnorte, 4 hrs, US$7, frequent. To **Chuquicamata** and **Calama**, Camus, 2 a day, 3 hrs, US$5. No direct services to **Santiago**, go via Antofagasta or take Tramaca or Flota Barrios to Vallenar or La Serena and change. Bus company offices are on 21 de Mayo.

Routes North and East of Tocopilla

East of Tocopilla a good paved road runs up the narrow valley 72 km to the Pan-American Highway. From here the road continues E in a very bad state (requires careful driving) to Chuquicamata.

81 km N of the crossroads is **Quillagua** (customs post, all vehicles and buses are searched) and 111 km further

Geoglyphs at Tillviche

is the first of three sections of the **Reserva Nacional del Tamarugal**. In this part are the **Geoglyphs of Pintados**, some 400 figures on the hillsides (3 km W of the highway). Beyond the Reserve are Pozo Almonte and the turn-off for Iquique. The second part of Tamarugal is near La Tirana (see page 188), the third 60 km N of Pozo Almonte.

The coastal road from Tocopilla N to Iquique, 244 km, offers fantastic views of the rugged coastline and tiny fishing communities. The customs post at Chipana-Río Loa (90 km N) searches all vehicles for duty-free goods; long delays. Basic accommodation is available at San Marcos, a fishing village, 131 km N. At Chanaballita, 184 km N there is a hotel, cabañas, camping, restaurant, shops. There are also campsites at the former

salt mining town of Guanillos, Km 126, Playa Peruana, Km 129 and Playa El Aguila, Km 160.

CALAMA

(*Pop* 106,970; *Alt* 2,265m; *Phone code* 055), lies 202 km NE of Antofagasta in the oasis of the Río Loa. Initially a staging post on the silver route between Potosí and Cobija, it has grown in this century as a commercial and residential centre for nearby Chuquicamata. It is an expensive modern town. Although there is little to do, it may be a useful point to stay for a day or 2 to get used to the altitude before going higher. It is the departure point for buses to San Pedro de Atacama and the weekly train to Bolivia.

Calama can be reached from the N by

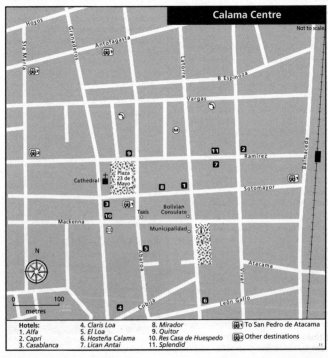

Calama Centre

Not to scale

Hotels:
1. Alfa
2. Capri
3. Casablanca
4. Claris Loa
5. El Loa
6. Hosteña Calama
7. Lican Antai
8. Mirador
9. Quitor
10. Res Casa de Huespedo
11. Splendid

To San Pedro de Atacama
Other destinations

a poor road via Chuquicamata, or, from the S, by a paved road leaving the Pan-American Highway 98 km N of Antofagasta at Carmen Alto (petrol and food). This road passes many abandoned nitrate mines (*oficinas*).

Places of interest

2 km from the centre on Av B O'Higgins is the **Parque El Loa** (open 1000-1800 daily), which contains a reconstruction of a typical colonial village built around a reduced-scale reproduction of Chiu Chiu church. Nearby in the park is the **Museo Arqueológico y Etnológico**, with an exhibition of pre-hispanic cultural history (open Tues-Fri 1000-1330, 1430-1800, Sat-Sun 1100-1830; colectivos 4, 5, 6 or 18 from the centre).

Local information
● Accommodation

L3 *Lican Antai*, Ramírez 1937, T 341621, with breakfast, good service and good restaurant, TV, phone, safe, rec.

A1 *Park*, Camino Aeropuerto 1392, T 319900, F 319901, 233-8509 in Santiago, first class, swimming pool, popular, bar and restaurant, rec; **A2** *Alfa*, Sotomayor 2016, T 342565, comfortable; **A2** *Hostería Calama*, Latorre 1521, T 341511, comfortable, good food and service; **A2** *Quitor*, Ramírez 2116, T 314159, good. **A3** *Mirador*, Sotomayor 2064, T/F 340329, with bath, **D** without, clean, helpful, rec.

B *Casablanca* on Plaza, Sotomayor 2160, T 312966, clean.

C *Res John Keny*, Ecuador 1991, T 211430, modern, clean, friendly, parking; **C** *Hostal Coco*, Sotomayor 2215, clean, hospitable.

D *El Loa*, Abaroa 1617, T 311963, English spoken; **D** *Res Splendid*, Ramírez 1960, T 211841, with bath, **E** without, clean, hot water, good; **D** *Res Internacional*, Velázquez 1976, T 211553, hot water, friendly but noisy; **D** *Genesis*, Granaderos 2148, T 212841, nr Tramaca and Geminis bus terminals, clean, kitchen, rec; **D** *Res Casa de Huéspedes*, Sotomayor 2079, poor beds, basic, clean, hot shower; **D** *Res Toño*, Vivar 1973, T 211185, next to Kenny bus, hot shower, basic, clean.

E *Universo*, Sotomayor 1822, T 313299, clean, friendly; **E** *Prat*, Vivar 1970, cheap, cold water; **E** *Res El Tatio*, P L Galo 1987, T 212284, basic, friendly, noisy, clean, reasonable; **E** pp *Capri 2*, Ramírez 1880, basic, safe; **E** *Los Andes*, Vivar 1920, T 341073, renovated, good beds, noisy; **E** *Luxor*, Vargas 1881, T 310292 basic, safe; **E** *Claris Loa*, Granaderos 1631, T 311939, clean, quiet, good beds.

● Places to eat

Bavaria, Sotomayor 2095, modern, clean, good coffee and delicatessen, open early morning; *Club Croata*, Abaroa 1869 (Plaza de Armas), serves good set lunches and evening meals. Good, cheap lunches at *Hotel Quitor*, *Comedor Camarino*, Latorre 2033, *Lascar*, Ramírez 1917, and in the market. *Mariscal JP*, Félix Hoyos 2127, good seafood. Good ice cream at *Fior di Gelato*, Plaza de Armas.

● Banks & money changers

Rates are generally poor especially for TCs. **Banco de Crédito e Inversiones**, Latorre, good rates, no commission (US$100 minimum); **Banco Osorno** (Visa), Sotomayor; **Fincard** (Mastercard), Latorre 1763, p 1, Mon-Fri 0900-1400, 1600-2000, Sat 1100-1300. *Casa de Cambio*, Sotomayor 1818, Mon-Fri, 0830-1400, 1500-1900 (closes 2300 for passengers on train to Bolivia). Try also shop at Ramírez 1434 and *La Media Luna* clothes store, Ramírez 1992 (poor rates). Money changers selling Bolivian money outside the railway station. At weekends try Tramaca or Morales Moralitos bus offices or *farmacias* (poor rates).

● Embassies & consulates

The Bolivian Consulate, Sr Reynaldo Urquizo Sosa, Bañados Espinoza 2232, Apdo Postal 85, T 341976, is open (in theory only) 0900-1230 and 1530-1830, Mon-Fri, friendly, helpful.

● Laundry

Laverap, Félix Hoyos y Abaroa; *París*, Vargas 2178 and Latorre 1955; *Universal*, Antofagasta 1313 (cheapest).

● Post & telecommunications

Post Office: Granaderos y V Mackenna, 0830-1300, 1530-1830, Sat 0900-1230, will not send parcels over 1 kg.

Telecommunications: CTC, Abaroa 1756; Entel, Sotomayor 2027.

● Shopping

Supermarkets, *El Cid*, Vargas 1942, *El Cobre*, Vargas 2148; market at Antofagasta between Latorre and Vivar.

The slow train to Oruro

The line between Calama and Oruro in Bolivia is the only section of the old Antofagasta and Bolivia Railway line still open to passenger trains. It is a long slow journey but well worthwhile for the scenery. The journey is very cold, both during the day and at night (-15°C). From Calama the line climbs to reach its highest point at Ascotán (3,960m); it then descends to 3,735m at Cebollar, skirting the Salar de Ascotán. Chilean customs are at Ollagüe, where there is a delay of 5-6 hrs while an engine is sent from Uyuni. The train is searched at Bolivian customs at Avaroa and passengers are required to disembark at both border posts for passport-control. There are money changers at Ollagüe and Avaroa. From the border the line runs NE to Uyuni, 174 km, crossing the Salar de Chiguana and running at an almost uniform height of 3,660m. Uyuni is the junction with the line S to the Argentine frontier at Villazón. Río Mulato is the junction for Potosí, but it is much quicker to travel by bus from Uyuni.

● **Tour companies & travel agents**

Several agencies run 1-day and longer tours to the Atacama region, inc San Pedro; these are usually more expensive than tours from San Pedro and require a minimum number for the tour to go ahead. Reports of tour quality are increasingly mixed – poorly maintained vehicles and poor guides. Those with positive recommendations inc: *Talikuna*, Gral Velázquez 1948, T 212595; *Turismo El Sol*, Abaroa 1796, T 210152; *Desierto Diferente*, Sotomayor 2261, T 315111; *Nativa*, Avaroa 1780, T 319834, F 340107; *Livia Tours*, Vivar 1960, T 211664, rec for their 3-day desert tour; *Moon Valley*, Sotomayor 1814, T/F 317456, very helpful, excursions, cycle rental.

● **Tourist offices**

Latorre 1689, T 211314. Map of town, helpful. Open Mon-Fri 0900-1300, 1430-1900 Sat-Sun (summer only) 0900-1300. **Automóvil Club de Chile**, Av Ecuador 1901, T 342770.

● **Transport**

Local Car hire: Comercial Maipo SA, Balmaceda 3950, T 212204; **Hertz**, Latorre 1510, T 211380; **Avis**, Granaderos 2895; **Avis**, Latorre 1512, T 319797; **Maxso**, Abaroa 1930, T 212194; **Budget**, Granaderos 2925, T 341076. A 4WD jeep (necessary for the desert) costs US$87-118 a day. Rates are sometimes much lower at weekends. A hired car or taxi, shared between several people, is an economic alternative for visiting the Atacama region. **NB** Car hire is not available in San Pedro de Atacama.

Air LanChile (Latorre 1499, T 341477/

341494), daily, and Ladeco (Ramírez 1858, T 312626/ 315183), to Santiago, via Antofagasta. Taxi to town US$6 (courtesy vans from Hotels *Calama*, *Alfa* and *Lican Antai*).

Trains To Uyuni and Oruro (Bolivia), weekly service, Wed 2300, US$12 to Uyuni, US$18 to Oruro, journey time to Oruro up to 48 hrs. Book seats in advance (passport essential) from Tramaca in Calama (Sotomayor 1961) or in Antofagasta. (The 2 offices sell tickets for different carriages and do not know of reservations made at the other office). Catch the train as early as possible: although seats are assigned, the designated carriages may not arrive; passengers try to occupy several seats (to sleep on) but will move if you show your ticket. Sleeping bag and/or blanket essential. Restaurant car; food is also available at Ollagüe and Río Mulato (only for the conditioned).

A freight train with one or two passenger cars attached leaves Calama for Ollagüe Sat 2300, return departure unknown, check details beforehand, buy ticket a few hours before departure, US$5 one way, not crowded. Note that there is no connecting passenger train and riding on goods trains from Ollagüe into Bolivia is not allowed. No accommodation in Ollagüe.

Buses No main terminal, buses leave from company offices: Tramaca, terminal at Granaderos 3048 (colectivo 1A from centre), office at Sotomayor 1961; Morales Moralitos, Sotomayor 1802; Yusmar, Antofagasta 2041, T 318543; Géminis, O'Higgins 078; Kenny Bus, Vivar 1954; Flota Barrios, Ramírez 2298. To **Santiago** 23 hrs, US$35-40; to **Arica**, Tramaca overnight, maybe more in summer, US$16, 8 hrs, or change in Antofagasta; to

Valparaíso/Viña del Mar, US$35; to Iquique, 8 hrs, US$13, overnight only (Geminis rec, Kenny Bus not rec). To La Serena, usually with delay in Antofagasta, 15 hrs, US$24. To Chuquicamata (see below). For services to San Pedro de Atacama and Toconao, see below; to Antofagasta, 3 hrs, several companies, eg Tramaca, hourly on the half-hour till 2130, US$5.

To Argentina Géminis services from Iquique and Antofagasta to Salta call at Calama, details above, book well in advance, US$39, 22 hrs. (Géminis service can also be picked up in San Pedro but book in Calama and tell the booking office). Also Tramaca, service from Antofagasta, dep Mon and Fri 1000, US$45, via Jujuy.

NB Remember that between Oct and March, Chilean time is 1 hr later than Bolivian.

CHUQUICAMATA

(*Pop* 13,000; *Alt* 2,800m; *Phone code* 055), 16 km N of Calama, is a clean modern town serving the world's largest opencast copper mine, employing 9,000 workers and operated by Codelco (the state copper corporation). Although copper has been mined here since pre-Inca times, it was the Guggenheim brothers who introduced modern mining and processing techniques after 1911 and made Chuquicamata into the most important single mine in Chile. Everything about Chuquicamata is huge: the pit from which the ore is extracted is 4 km long, 2 km wide and 630m deep; the giant trucks, with wheels over 3.5m high, carry 225 ton loads and work 24 hrs a day; in other parts of the plant 60,000 tons of ore are processed a day. Although the ore extracted is low grade, refined copper of 99.98% purity is produced. Since 1986 output has been over 500,000 tonnes a year.

Guided tours in Spanish (by bus, also in English if enough people) leave from the office of Chuqui Ayuda (a local children's charity) near the entrance at the top end of the plaza, Mon-Fri 1000 (though less frequently in low season – tourist office in Calama has details), 1 hr, US$2.50 donation, be there by 0915.

Register in the café near the entrance at least 30 mins in advance. Be in good time because space is sometimes limited; passport essential. No filming permitted, but photographs may be taken at specified points in the tour.

- **Places to eat** Cheap lunches available at the *Club de Empleados* and at *Arco Iris* both facing the bus terminal.

- **Transport** From Calama: yellow colectivo taxis (marked 'Chuqui') from the corner of the main plaza, US$0.75. Buses to Arica at 2200 (weekends at 2300), US$16, 9 hrs; to Antofagasta, 10 a day, US$6; to Iquique, US$14; to Santiago, US$28, 24 hrs.

NORTH ALONG THE RIO LOA

Near Calama there are several small towns and villages in the valley of the Río Loa.

Chiu Chiu, (*Pop* 300, *Alt* 2,500m) 33 km E of Calama, was one of the earliest centres of Spanish settlement in the area. The church of San Francisco, dating from 1611, has roof beams of cactus and walls over 1m thick. Nearby is a unique, perfectly circular, very deep lake, called Chiu Chiu or Icacoia. Ancient rock carvings are to be found a few kilometres N in the Río Loa valley.

At Lasana (*Pop* 800) 8 km N of Chiu Chiu, there are the ruins of a pre-Incaic *pukará*, a national monument, with explanatory tablets (soft drinks and beer on sale). At Conchi, 25 km N of Lasana, there is a spectacular view from the bridge over the Río Loa, but it is a military zone, so no photographs allowed. Access to the river is by side tracks, best at Santa Bárbara; interesting wildlife and flower meadows, trout fishing in season (permit from Gobernación in Calama).

From Chiu Chiu a road runs to Ollagüe, 240 km N on the Bolivian frontier. There is a *carabinero* checkpoint at Ascotán, the highest point of the road at 3,900m. North of Ascotán the road becomes worse, especially where it crosses the Salares de Ascotán and Ollagüe (ask

Copper: Chilean red gold

👞 Although copper was mined in Chile in pre-Inca times, it only became important after independence. For much of the 19th century Chile was the world's leading copper producer, until new technology helped the USA overtake her in 1882. After 1900 US investment and technology led to increased Chilean copper production, exploiting low-grade deposits through the use of large-scale open cast mining (as at Chuquicamata) and using new methods for separating the ore.

Copper was soon at the heart of a close relationship between Chile and the United States. During the First World War US demand for copper for arms manufacturing led to a 400% growth in Chilean copper production; by 1918 US investors controlled 87% of Chilean copper. Among the American corporations were the Chile Exploration Company, American Smelting, Kennecott and Braden, but by the 1960s two companies, Kennecott and Anaconda, dominated.

During the 1950s the role of the United States in the Chilean economy became a controversial issue in Chilean politics; US ownership of copper, which in 1970 accounted for 78.5% of Chilean commodity exports, was seen as a symbol of Washington's domination. The Christian Democrat government of Eduardo Frei (1964-1970) met the calls for nationalization with what it called Chileanization: under this the state took a controlling 51% share of the large companies. Complete nationalization was promised by Popular Unity in its 1970 election manifesto but nationalization was popular not only on the left; many conservatives supported it as a way of reducing US influence. The nationalization bill of 1971 passed through the Chilean Congress with the support of all parties. The large mines were taken over completely and placed under the control of CODELCO-Chile (Corporación Nacional del Cobre de Chile) which became the largest copper mining and refining company in the world.

Although the Pinochet government of 1973-1990 sold off most state-run industries to the private sector, CODELCO was not touched. However, since the 1980s new mining laws have encouraged private investment in new mines. This has led to the opening of large new private mines and an increase in Chilean copper output from 1.6 million to 2.2 million tonnes between 1990 and 1995. The biggest new mine is La Escondida, where production began in 1990 and an output of 800,000 tonnes is planned for 1996, making it the world's leading mine. At Collahuasi, projected to start production in 1998, output of 330,000 tonnes a year is expected. Although some of CODELCO's older mines are in decline, it too is opening new mines.

Since 1982 Chile has once again been the world's leading producer of copper. Despite the growth of new exports such as fruit and wine, copper is likely to remain of central importance to the Chilean economy, as it has been since the collapse of nitrates in the 1920s.

---

at Ascotán or Ollagüe before setting out about the conditions, especially in Dec/Jan or Aug). There are many llama flocks along this road and flamingoes on the salares. **NB** The desert to the eastern side of the road is extensively covered by minefields.

5 km S of Ollagüe is the sulphur

mining camp of Buenaventura. It is possible to camp here. The mine at 5,800m (only 150m short of the summit of Ollagüe Volcano) can be reached by hiring a 4WD vehicle or by walking. Amazing views of volcanoes and salt flats.

NB There is no petrol between Calama and Uyuni in Bolivia. If really short try buying from the *carabineros* at Ollagüe or Ascotán, the military at Conchi or the mining camp at Buenaventura. The only real answer is to take enough.

OLLAGÜE

(*Pop* 200; *Alt* 3,690m) 198 km N of Calama on the dry floor of the Salar de Ollagüe, surrounded by a dozen volcanic peaks of over 5,000m. The village has one basic *alojamiento*, one bus a week to Calama. Ollagüe can be reached by taking the Calama-Oruro train (see above) but, if you stop off, you will have to hitch back as the daily freight trains are not allowed to carry passengers. (Hitching is difficult but the police may help you to find a truck.)

A 77-km spur railroad of metre gauge runs to the copper mines of Collahuasi, and from there one can reach the highest mine in the world: the Aucanquilcha, at 5,580m. Its sulphur is taken to Aminchá, a town at the foot of the volcano, to be refined. The mine closes for Bolivian winter; it is served by road, which is sometimes impassable. On site are the ruins of an aerial tram system. From the mine you can scramble to the summit of Aucanquilcha at 6,176m, superb views. High clearance vehicle needed to drive to the mine. The highest passenger station on this spur is Yuma, at 4,400m.

At this altitude nights are cold, the days warm and sunny. Minimum temperature at Ollagüe is -20°C, and at the mine, -37°C. There are only 50 mm of rain a year, and water is very scarce.

An interesting excursion can be made N from Ollagüe to the village of **Coska** with its traditional agriculture and herds of llamas and alpacas.

FRONTIER WITH BOLIVIA: OLLAGÜE

Open 0800-2100; US$2 per vehicle charge for crossings 1300-1500, 1850-2100. A bad unmade road from Ollagüe runs into Bolivia. From the frontier it is 170 km to Uyuni, 591 km to Oruro. There is nowhere to stay in Ollagüe, but police and border officials will help find lodging. Hitchhikers will also be found transport on trucks, which take a more northerly route than the direct Ollagüe-Uyuni road. The scenery in this area is amazing, but it is remote and bitterly cold at night.

Motorists must be warned against the direct route from Chile to Uyuni by way of Ollagüe. There is the danger of getting lost on the many tracks leading over the deserted salt lakes, no gasoline between Calama (Chile) and Uyuni, and little hope of help with a breakdown on the Bolivian side unless you don't mind waiting for perhaps a week. After rain the route is impassable and even experienced guides get lost. Maps give widely differing versions of the route. Where the road has been built up, *never* forsake it for the appealing soft salt beside it. The salt takes a man's weight but a vehicle breaks through the crust into unfathomable depths of plasticine mud below.

SAN PEDRO DE ATACAMA

is 103 km SE of Calama by a paved road. There is no fuel, food or water along this road. At Paso Barros Arana (Km 58) there is an unpaved turning to the left which leads through interesting desert scenery to the small, mud-brick village of Río Grande. Look out for vicuñas and guanacos on the pass. The main road skirts the Cordillera de la Sal about 15 km from San Pedro. Spectacular views of sunset over to the Western Cordilleras. The old unmade road to San Pedro turns off the new road at Km 72 and crosses this range through the Valle de La Luna (see **Excur-**

sions below), but should only be attempted by 4WD vehicles. This road is partly paved with salt blocks.

San Pedro de Atacama is a small town (*Pop* 1,600; *Alt* 2,436m; *Phone code* 055) more Spanish-Indian looking than is usual in Chile, now attracting large numbers of visitors. Both Diego de Almagro and Pedro de Valdivia stopped in this oasis.

Places of interest

The **Iglesia de San Pedro**, dating from the 17th century, has been heavily restored (the tower was added in 1964). The roof is made of cactus; inside, the statues of Mary and Joseph have fluorescent light halos. Nearby, on the Plaza, is the **Casa Incaica**, the oldest building in San Pedro.

Museums

Museo Arqueológico, the collection of Padre Gustave Paige, a Belgian missionary who lived in San Pedro between 1955 and 1980, is now under the care of the Universidad Católica del Norte (Mon-Fri, 0800-1200, 1500-1900; Sat, and Sun, 1000-1200, 1500-1800; summer, Mon-Fri 0900-1200, 1400-1800, Sat-Sun 1000-1200, 1400-1800, entry US$4). It is a fascinating repository of artefacts, well organized to trace the development of

prehispanic Atacameño society. Labels on displays are good and there is a comprehensive booklet in Spanish and English. Graham Greene observed "the striking feature of the museum is ... the mummies of Indian women with their hair and dresses intact dating from before the Conquest, and a collection of paleolithic tools which puts the British Museum in the shade". There is no heating nor electricity: wear warm clothing even in warm weather and visit when sunlight is strongest.

Excursions

The **Valle de la Luna**, 12 km W of San Pedro, with fantastic landscapes caused by the erosion of salt mountains, is crossed by the old San Pedro-Calama road. Although buses on the new Calama-San Pedro road will stop to let you off where the old road branches off 13 km NW of San Pedro (signposted to Peine), it is far better to travel from San Pedro on the old road, either on foot (allow 3 hrs there, 3 hrs back; no lifts), by bicycle or by car. The Valle is best seen at sunset (provided the sky is clear). Take water, hat, camera and torch. Also consider spending the night to see the sunset (take warm clothes and plenty of water).

3 km N of San Pedro along the river is the **Pukará de Quitor**, a pre-Inca fortress restored in 1981. The fortress, which stands on the W bank of the river, was stormed by the Spanish under Pedro de Valdivia, 1,000 defenders being overcome by 30 horsemen who vaulted the walls (the path involves fording the river several times). A further 4 km up the river there are Inca ruins at Catarpe. At **Tulor**, 12 km SW of San Pedro, there is an archaeological site where parts of a stone-age village (dated 500-800 BC) have been excavated; worth a visit on foot (you can sleep in two reconstructed huts), or take a tour, US$5 pp. Nearby are the ruins of a 17th century Spanish-style village, abandoned in the 18th century because of lack of water. For

San Pedro de Atacama **173**

Toconao, 37 km S of San Pedro, see below.

Local information

San Pedro has electricity in the evening (until 2300/2400), but take a torch (flashlight) for walking at night. *Residenciales* supply candles, but better to buy them in Calama beforehand. Accommodation is scarce in Jan/Feb and expensive. Drink bottled water as the local supply is not drinkable.

● **Accommodation**

L3 *Hostería San Pedro*, on Solcor, T 11, reserve in advance, swimming pool (residents only), petrol station (leaded fuel only), tents for hire, cabins, hot water, electricity am-1200 and 1800-2300, restaurant (good lunch) and bar, rec, no credit cards or TCs; **C** *Kimal*, Atienza y Caracoles, T 30, F 52, good.

D *La Quinta Adela*, Toconao, friendly; **D** *Res Corvatch*, Antofagasta s/n, T 87, good rooms, good beds clean, friendly, German spoken highly rec; **D** *Res Juanita*, on the plaza, T 39, hot water on request, friendly, restaurant, rec; **D** *Hostal Takha-Takha*, on Caracoles, T 38 (F camping), hot water, very small rooms, some tents for rent, friendly and clean; **D** *Res Andacollo*, Tocopilla 11, T6, clean, basic, laundry facilities, cheap restaurant; **D** *Res Licancábur*, Toconao, T 7, clean, cooking facilities,safe, good.

E pp *Pensión Florida*, Tocopilla, temperamental hot water, basic, clean, laundry facilities, poor beds; **E** pp *Pukará*, Tocopilla 28, cold water, basic; **E** pp *Res Chiloé*, Atienza, T 17, hot water, good meals, laundry facilities, good beds, safe, popular; **F** pp *Res Solcor*, Atienza, dormitory accommodation, friendly; **E** pp *Camping Tulor*, off Atienza, T 27, good food, camping F pp, rents camping equipment, laundry facilities, rec; **E** pp

Archaeology of the Atacama

From very early times, people settled along the northern coast of Chile, sustained by the food supply from the Pacific Ocean. Since about 7,600 BC fisherfolk and foragers lived in relatively large groups in permanent settlements, such as the Quebrada de Conchas, just to the north of Antofagasta. They fished with fibre nets, sometimes venturing inland to hunt for mammals.

About 2,000 years later the successors of these people, the "Chinchorros", developed one of the deepest characteristics of Andean cultures, veneration for their ancestors. The role of the dead in the world of the living was vital to the earliest Andean people. As a link between the spiritual and the material world, the ancestor of each local kin group would protect his clan. The expression of these beliefs came in the form of veneration of the ancestors' bodies; sacrifices were made to them, funeral rites were repeated, and precious grave offerings were renewed. In the arid climate of the Atacama, the people observed how bodies were naturally preserved. The skilled practice of mummification was thus developed, over a period of 3,000 years, dedicated to preserving the dead as sacred objects and spiritual protectors.

Another major cultural practice of northern Chile was the use of hallucinogens. Grave remains found in the region, dating from about AD 1,000, include leather bags containing organic powder, wooden tablets and snuffer tubes. The tablets and snuffers were often decorated with supernatural figures, such as bird-headed angels, winged humans, star animals and other characters familiar in altiplano cultures. Although the origins and function of taking hallucinogens is not known for certain (see Chile prehistory above), it is thought that the practice may have been brought down to the coast by traders from the highlands. There were also "medicine men" who travelled throughout the central and south central Andes dispensing the drugs and healing the sick. As with cures still practised in the Andes and Amazonia, it is possible that the drugs were taken as part of religious rituals, and often for a combination of spiritual and physical healing.

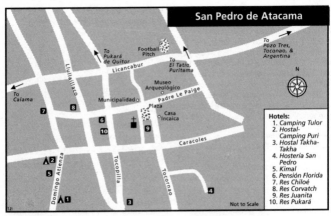

San Pedro de Atacama

Hotels:
1. Camping Tulor
2. Hostal-Camping Puri
3. Hostal Takha-Takha
4. Hostería San Pedro
5. Kimal
6. Pensión Florida
7. Res Chiloé
8. Res Corvatch
9. Res Juanita
10. Res Pukará

Not to Scale

Hostal-Camping Puri, Caracoles s/n, T 49, restaurant, clean, quiet, friendly, camping F, rental of camping and climbing gear.

● **Places to eat**
Best food in town at *Hostería San Pedro*. On Caracoles are *Estaka*, good set lunches and evening meals, popular; *Tambo Cañaveral*, live music at weekends, own generator, open late. Apart from these try *Residenciales*: *Juanita*, good set lunch and evening meal; *Andacollo*; *Chiloé* for cheap lunches. *Chañar Luminoso*, Caracoles, good coffee and juice. *Sonchek*, coffee, fruit juice, vegetarian dishes, also motorbikes for hire US$5/hr; *Chapaka*, opp Morales Moralitos bus stop sells health foods, bread, muesli.

● **Banks & money changers**
Cambio Atacama, Caracoles, open daily, poor rates, changes TCs, but often closed, best to change elsewhere. If stuck try *Hostería San Pedro* (worse rates still), or *Hostal Takha-Takha*.

● **Post & telecommunications**
Post Office: Granaderos y MacKenna sells excellent postcards.

Telephone: CTC, Caracoles y Gabriela Mistral; Entel on the plaza.

● **Sports**
Climbing: San Pedro is a good centre for climbing Mt Lincancábur (5,916m) and other peaks on the Chile/Bolivia border. Allow at least 8 hrs to climb Lincancábur and 4 hrs to descend. Take plenty of water and your passport and hire a 4WD vehicle in Calama.

Horse riding: *Galopea*, run by Eleanor Merrill and Roberto Plaza Castillo ('Guatita') run guided horseback tours, US$5/hr, speak 6 languages, ask in post office.

Swimming Pool: *Piscina Oasis*, at Pozo Tres, 3 km SE, was drilled in the late 1950s as part of a mineral exploration project, open all year 0500-1730 daily (except Mon). US$1.50 to swim, sometimes empty. Worth asking around before walking there. Camping US$3 and picnic facilities, very popular at weekends.

● **Tour companies & travel agents**
About 10 agencies, most charging the same rates and organizing joint tour groups. Agencies inc: *Nativa*, Toconao, T 44, rec; *Cosmo Andino Expediciones*, Caracoles s/n, T/F 340107, English, German, French and Dutch spoken, book exchange in the above languages, wide selection, owner Martin Beeris (Martín El Holandés), rec; *Atacama Inca Tour*, Toconao s/n, T 34, F 52, rec; *Desert Adventure*, Caracoles s/n; opp is *Merakopp*, rec; *Pachamama*, Toconao, rec; *Ochoa*, Toconao, Spanish only, rec; *Turismo Colque*, Caracoles s/n, T 851109; *Antai*, Caracoles s/n, English and French spoken, also sells handicrafts, rec; *Cactus* offers horseriding with good guides to Valle de la Luna and other sites. Tours are also run by several *Residenciales*. Usual tour rates: to Valle de la Luna (best at sunset) US$6; to Toconao and the Salar de Atacama (best at sunset) US$12; to el Tatio (begin at 0400) US$18 (take swimming costume and warm clothing), but shop around as different rates may be available. These run most days in

season, subject to demand at other times.

Turismo Colque run tours to Laguna Verde, Laguna Colorado, Uyuni and other sites in Bolivia, 3 days, changing vehicles at the border as the Bolivian authorities refuse permits for Chilean tour vehicles, US$65 pp, take own food and water and obtain passport stamps before departure.

There has been a boom in travel agencies since 1993, but many lack experience, dependable vehicles, suitable equipment (eg oxygen for El Tatio) or professionalism. Check that a guide speaks English if so advertised; ask to see the vehicle to be used (4WD land-cruisers are best); check if the company is recognized by the municipality. At the time of writing the first in the above list had formed the Asociación de Operadores Turísticos de San Pedro de Atacama; others are expected to join. Report any complaints to the municipality.

● **Transport**

Local Bicycle hire: from several places inc *Takha-Takha*; *Dada Atacama*, US$2.50/hr, US$10-12 a day; *Pangea*, Caracoles, English spoken, also cycle repairs. **Car hire**: is impossible. Try Calama. Pick up truck with 4WD best. Agency authorization essential to take a hired car into Bolivia.

Buses From Calama: two companies, both from Balmaceda y Sotomayor, opp railway station. Yusmar services leave **Calama** daily, 1100, 1600 and 1800, returning from San Pedro 0800, 1400 and 1800. Morales Moralitos buses 1000, 1530 and 1800, returning 0800, 1400 and 1800, 1½ hrs. Fare US$3 one way. Frequencies vary with more departures in Jan/Feb and some weekends, fewer out of season. Book in advance to return from San Pedro Sun pm. Both Morales Moralitos and Yusmar also run to Toconao. Géminis buses from Iquique and Antofagasta to Salta (Argentina) stop in San Pedro on Wed and Sat – book in Calama, Iquique or Antofagasta.

FRONTIER WITH BOLIVIA: HITO CAJONES

Hito Cajones is reached by a poor road E from San Pedro, 45 km. From the frontier it is 7 km N to Laguna Verde.

● **Immigration**

Chilean immigration and customs in San Pedro, open 0900-1200, 1400-1600. Incoming vehicles and passengers are searched for fruit and vegetables.

● **Bolivian consulate**

See under Calama.

● **Transport**

There are reports of a daily bus service from San Pedro to Hito Cajones to meet tour vehicles from Uyuni, US$10 pp. At Hito Cajones you may be able to find space in a tour vehicle (about US$20 to Uyuni). *Nativa* will take people to the frontier, US$120/vehicle.

INTO BOLIVIA

The wind-lashed, frothy jade waters of Laguna Verde (4,600m) are at the foot of Volcán Licancábur. There is a *refugio* at the lake (US$2, small, mattresses, running water). It is usually included on tours to the equally spectacular Laguna Colorada and the Salar de Uyuni, a vast salt lake. As well as Turismo Colque in San Pedro (see above), many Bolivian agencies run this tour, most out of the town of **Uyuni** (*pop* 10,000; *alt* 3,665m; accommodation, money exchange, transport to La Paz, Oruro and Potosí). If you intend to travel independently in this area, do not underestimate the dangers of getting stuck without transport or lodging at this altitude. Do not travel alone and seek full advice in advance.

FRONTIER WITH ARGENTINA: PASO DE JAMA AND PASO SICO

The Paso de Jama (4,200m) is reached by an improved road, suitable for all vehicles, which continues on the Argentine side to Susques and Jujuy. This is more popular than the Laguna Sico route but note but there is no accommodation in Susques.

Laguna Sico (4,079m) is reached by poor road which runs S and E of San Pedro, 207 km via Toconao. On the Argentine side this road continues to San Antonio de los Cobres and Salta.

● **Immigration**

Chilean immigration and customs in San Pedro. Incoming vehicles are searched for fruit.

● **Crossing by private vehicle**

Check road conditions before setting out as Paso de Jama can be closed by heavy rain in summer and blocked by snow in winter.

● **Transport**
For bus services from Antofagasta, Calama and San Pedro to Jujuy and Salta see above.

NORTH OF SAN PEDRO

El Tatio

(*Alt* 4,500m), the site of geysers, is a popular attraction. From San Pedro it is reached by a maintained road which runs NE, past the Baños de Puritama (28 km), then on a further 94 km. The geysers are at their best 0630-0830, though the spectacle varies: locals say the performance is best when weather conditions are stable. A swimming pool has been built nearby. There is a workers' camp which is empty apart from one guard, who will let you sleep in a bed in one of the huts, G pp, take food and sleeping bag. From here you can hike to surrounding volcanoes if adapted to altitude. There is no public transport and hitching is impossible. If going in a hired car, make sure the engine is suitable for very high altitudes and is

protected with antifreeze; 4WD is advisable. If driving in the dark it is almost impossible to find your way: the sign for El Tatio is N of the turn off. Tours arranged by agencies in San Pedro and Calama. **NB** People have been killed or seriously injured by falling into the geysers, or through the thin crust of the mud.

Routes From El Tatio To Calama

There are 3 alternatives:

1)   Direct, on an atrocious track, to **Caspana**, beautifully set among hills with a tiny church dating from 1641 and a museum with interesting displays on Atacameño culture, and then W along the valley of the Río Salado.

● **Accommodation G** pp At village stores, basic.

2)   N via Linzor to Inacaliri and the Ojo de San Pedro saltflat. Follow the road along the Río San Pedro Valley and cross the Río Loa at Conchi. The Río San Pedro has been a route for herders and silver caravans for centuries and there are many sites of interest, although access is on foot.

3)   North from El Tatio to Linzor and then W to **Toconce**, which has extensive prehispanic terraces set among interesting rock formations. Between Toconce and Caspana to the S are valleys of pampas grass with llama herds. If visiting Toconce, check in with the *carabineros* in the square. From Toconce follow the road W to Calama via Lasana and Chiu Chiu. For details on Conchi, Lasana and Chiu Chiu, see page 169 above.

20 km W of Toconce is **Ayquina**, in whose ancient church is enshrined the statue of the Virgin of Guadalupe. Her feast-day is 8 Sept, when pilgrims come from far and wide. There is day-long group dancing to Indian rhythms on flute and drum. Towards sunset the Virgin is carried up a steep trail to a small thatched shrine, where the image and the people are blessed before the dancing is renewed at the shrine and all the

North of Calama & San Pedro de Atacama

way back to the village. The poor people of the hills gather stones and make toy houses all along the route: miniatures of the homes they hope to have some day.

6 km N of Ayquina are the luke-warm thermal waters of the **Baños de Turi** and the ruins of a 12th-century *pukará* which was the largest fortified town in the Atacama mountains. Southwest of Ayquina is **Cupo**, which has a *fiesta* on 19 Mar (San José). Between this village and Turi is a large, ruined prehispanic settlement at **Paniri** with extensive field systems, irrigation canals (including aqueducts) and a necropolis. Some of the fields are still in use. The area around Cupo is one of the best for seeing the Atacama giant cactus (*Notocereus atacamensis*). Flamingos can be seen on the mudflats. The Vega de Turi is an important site for the llama and sheep herders, who believe it has curative properties. At several times in the year, especially Sept, herders from a wide area congregate with their flocks.

SOUTH OF SAN PEDRO

From San Pedro to Toconao, 37 km S, the road (well-surfaced) runs through groves of acacia and pepper trees. There are many tracks leading to the wells (*pozos*) which supply the intricate irrigation system. Most have thermal water but bathing is not appreciated by the local farmers. The groves of trees are havens for wildlife especially rheas (ñandu) and Atacama owls.

About 4 km before you reach Toconao, there are some vehicle tracks heading E across the sand. They lead to a hidden valley 2 km from the road where there is a small settlement called **Zapar**. Here are some well-preserved pre-hispanic ruins on the rocky cliffs above the cultivated valley. The sand is very soft and 4WD is essential.

Toconao, with some 500 inhabitants is on the eastern shore of the Salar de Atacama. All houses are built of bricks of white volcanic stone, which gives the

village a very characteristic appearance totally different from San Pedro. The 18th century church and bell tower are also built of volcanic stone. East of the village is an attractive oasis called the Quebrada de Jérez. The quarry where the stone (*sillar*) is worked can be visited, about 1½ km E (the stones sound like bells when struck). Worth visiting also are the vineyards which produce a unique sweet wine, and the tree-filled gorges with their hidden fields and orchards.

● **Accommodation** Three basic *residenciales* – ask around in the village. **Camping**: possible along the Quebrada de Jérez.

● **Transport** Yusmar buses daily from San Pedro, 1300, return 1645, US$1.30.

SALAR DE ATACAMA

South of Toconao is one of the main entrances to the Salar de Atacama, 300,000 ha, the third largest expanse of salt flats in the world. Rich in minerals including borax, potassium and an estimated 40% of world lithium reserves, the Salar is home to the pink flamingo and other birds (though these are usually only visible at a distance). The air is so dry that you can often see right across the Salar. Entry is controlled by Conaf in Toconao, US$1.50.

Three areas of the Salar form part of the **Reserva Nacional de los Flamencos**, which is in 7 sectors totalling 73,986 ha and administered by Conaf in San Pedro.

Routes South of Toconao

From Toconao the road heads S through the scenic villages of **Camar** (where handicrafts from cactus may be bought) and **Socaire** (which has domesticated llamas, knitwear for sale). 20 km S of Socaire is the beautiful **Laguna Miscanti** (*Alt* 4,350m) where wildlife abounds; 3 types of flamingo may be seen: Andean, Chilean (white and pink, no black) and James (small, with yellow legs). After Socaire the road goes on to

South of San Pedro de Atacama

the mine at Laco (one poor stretch below the mine), before proceeding to Sico, which has replaced the higher, more northerly Guaytiquina pass (4,295m, also spelt Huaytiquina) to Argentina.

10 km S of Toconao the old road branches E towards Guaytiquina. In a deep *quebrada* below Volcán Láscar is the small agricultural settlement of **Talabre**, with terracing and an ancient threshing floor. Above the *quebrada* is an isolated, stone-built cemetery. Large flocks of llamas graze where the stream crosses the road below the Láscar volcano (5,154m). After a steep climb, you reach the **Laguna Lejía** (4,190m), where flamingos abound. You then pass

through the high plains of **Guaytiquina** (4,275m), where only a few herdsmen are found. This crossing is not open for road traffic to Argentina.

67 km S from Toconao, on a road that runs along the eastern edge of the Salar de Atacama is the attractive village of **Peine**, which is the site of the offices of the lithium extraction company. There is also a pool filled by thermal springs where you can swim. Woollen goods and knitwear are made here. To the E of the village lies a group of beautifully coloured hills (colours best at sunset) with good views over the Salar de Atacama. A path leads across these hills to Socaire (allow 2 days). It is worth asking if the

company's access road can be used to visit the Salar de Atacama's spectacular salt formations. Other villages worth visiting include Tilomonte and Tilopozo, S and W of Peine.

From Peine a road (64 km) crosses the Salar de Atacama; it joins a road which runs from San Pedro down the W side of the Salar and continues S to Pan de Azúcar, an abandoned railway station. Here it meets the road which leads from the Pan-American Highway, 50 km S of Antofagasta via the modern copper mine of La Escondida to Socompa on the Argentine border. Between Pan de Azúcar and Socompa (poor road) is Monturaqui, the source of the green onyx which is much used for carving in northern Chile.

FRONTIER WITH ARGENTINA: SOCOMPA

● **Immigration**

Chilean immigration is at Socompa. The Chilean side is open 0800-2200. On the Argentine side the road carries on to San Antonio de los Cobres and Salta. Argentine immigration is at San Antonio de los Cobres.

● **Crossing with a private vehicle**

US$2 is charged for crossing between 1300-1500 and 1860-2100.

180

Iquique, Arica and the Far North

THE CONTINUATION of the desert zone to the Peruvian border. The main cities are Iquique and Arica; between them are old mineral workings and even older geoglyphs. Large areas of the Andean highland have been set aside as national parks.

THE LAND

GEOGRAPHY

The Atacama Desert extends over most of the Far North. The Cordillera de la Costa slowly loses height N of Iquique, terminating at the Morro at Arica: from Iquique North it drops directly to the sea and as a result there are few beaches along this coast. Inland the central depression (*pampa*) 1,000-1,200m is arid and punctuated by salt-flats S of Iquique. Between Iquique and Arica it is crossed from E to W by four gorges. East of this depression lies the *sierra*, the western branch of the Andes, beyond which is a high plateau, the *altiplano* (3,500m-4,500m) from which rise volcanic peaks, the highest of which include Parinacota (6,350m), Pomerape (6,250m), Guayatiri (6,064m), Acotango (6,050m), Capurata (5,990m), Tacora (5,988m) and Tarapacá (5,825m).

Northwards from Pisagua several rivers flow W from the *sierra*; the more

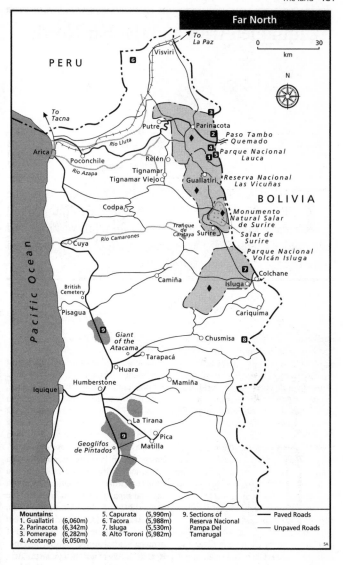

Far North

0   30
km

PERU

To La Paz

Visviri

6

N

To Tacna

Putre

Parinacota

2   Paso Tambo
     Quemado

4   *Parque Nacional*
5   *Lauca*

1

Arica

Poconchile

Río Lluta

Relén

Tignamar

Tignamar Viejo

Guallatiri

Reserva Nacional
Las Vicuñas

BOLIVIA

Río Azapa

Codpa

Tranque de
Caritaya

Río Camarones

Monumento
Natural Salar
de Surire

Cuya

Surire

Salar de
Surire

Parque Nacional
Volcán Isluga

Camiña

7   Colchane

British
Cemetery

Isluga

Pisagua

Cariquima

9   *Giant*
     of the
     Atacama

Chusmisa

8

Tarapacá

Pacific Ocean

Huara

Mamiña

Iquique

Humberstone

La Tirana

Geoglifos
de Pintados

9   Pica

Matilla

Mountains:
1. Guallatiri   (6,060m)
2. Parinacota   (6,342m)
3. Pomerape   (6,282m)
4. Acotango   (6,050m)

5. Capurata   (5,990m)
6. Tacora   (5,988m)
7. Isluga   (5,530m)
8. Alto Toroni   (5,982m)

9. Sections of
   Reserva Nacional
   Pampa Del
   Tamarugal

——— Paved Roads
——— Unpaved Roads

5A

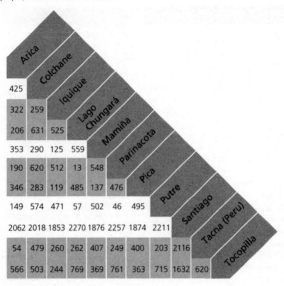

**Iquique, Arica & The Far North:
distance chart (km)**

northerly of these, the Ríos Lluta and San José, provide water for Arica. In the *altiplano* there are a number of lakes, the largest of which, Lago Chungará, is one of the highest lakes in the world. The main river draining the *altiplano*, the Río Lauca, flows eastwards into Bolivia.

ECONOMY

Over 90% of the population of this area lives in the two coastal cities, Arica and Iquique. The sea provides the main source of wealth. Iquique is the pricipal fishing port in Chile, unloading 35% of the total national catch. The city has important fish processing industries. Mining is much less important than in other parts of northern Chile, but silver and gold are mined at Challacollo and copper at Sagasca, near Tarapacá. Fruit is grown in the Valle de Azapa, the oasis formed by the Río San José, and in the *sierra* around Pica. The Azapa also produces olives.

Vegetables and alfalfa are grown in the oases of the *sierra*. Commerce is an important source of local employment: Arica benefits from its position as a port for Bolivian goods and its proximity to Peru, while Iquique is the site of a Free Zone.

CLIMATE

The coastal strip and the *pampa* are rainless; on the coast temperatures are moderated by the Pacific Ocean, but in the *pampa* variations of temperature between day and night are extreme, varying between 30°C and 0°C. In the *sierra* temperatures are lower, averaging 20°C in summer and 9°C in winter. The *altiplano* is much colder, temperatures averaging 10°C in summer and -5°C in winter. Both the *sierra* and the *altiplano* receive rain in summer. The Far North is also affected by *camanchaca* and *invierno boliviano* (see above).

John North, King of Nitrates

In the history of northern Chile few people have played a more controversial role than John North, the self-styled 'King of Nitrates'. Born in Liverpool in 1842, North arrived in Chile at the age of 24 and worked as a railway engineer in Iquique. In 1875 he founded the *Compañia de Agua de Iquique*, which brought water to the city by boat from Arica. After the defeat of Peru and Bolivia in the War of the Pacific, North bought large numbers of shares in Peruvian nitrate companies at low prices. North and his partner, John Harvey, a mining engineer, had inside knowledge that the Chilean government planned to recognize ownership of these shares; by the time this occurred North had acquired six nitrate mines and had made a fortune.

He returned to London and built a large financial empire in Chilean companies: by 1889 he controlled 15 nitrate mines, four railway companies including the Nitrate Railways Company which monopolized rail transport around Iquique, the Bank of Tarapacá and London and the Nitrates Provisions Company, which supplied food to the nitrate *oficinas*. North's efforts to establish a monopoly over nitrate transport were opposed by President Balmaceda; when Balmaceda came into conflict with the Chilean Congress in 1891, North provided £100,000 towards the Congressional war effort which overthrew the President. North had, however, also earned the opposition of the owners of other *oficinas* and this proved his undoing: by the time of his death in 1896 his business empire had collapsed.

HISTORY

As elsewhere in northern Chile, the early Spanish settler population was small in numbers. Settlement was concentrated largely in the oases of the *sierra*, where the climate was easier and malaria, the scourge of the coast, was not found. From an early date Arica became one of the principle ports for the silver trade from Potosí, but the coast remained sparsely inhabited until the 19th century. At the time of independence the whole of this area became part of Peru as the provinces of Tarapacá and Arica, coming under Chilean control as a result of the War of the Pacific. After the war Iquique and Tarapacá province shared in the nitrate boom of the late 19th century (see above).

IQUIQUE

Iquique (*Pop* 145,139; *Phone code* 057), the capital of I Región (Tarapacá) and one of the main northern ports, is 492 km N of Antofagasta. The name of the town is derived from the Aymara word *ique-ique*, meaning place of 'rest and tranquillity'. The city is situated on a rocky peninsula at the foot of the high Atacama pampa, sheltered by the headlands of Punta Gruesa and Cavancha.

A short distance N of town along Amunátegui is the Free Zone (Zofri), a giant shopping centre selling mainly imported electronic goods: it is worth a visit (much better value than Punta Arenas), good for cheap camera film (Fuji slide film available)(open Mon-Sat 0900-1330, 1630-2000). Colectivo taxi from the centre US$0.35. Limit on tax free purchases US$650 for foreigners, US$500 for Chileans. All vehicles travelling S from Iquique are searched for duty-free goods at Quillagua on the Pan-American Highway and at Chipana on Route 1, the coastal road.

History
Although the site was used as a port in

pre-hispanic times, it remained sparsely populated throughout the colonial period. Even in 1855, when the port had begun to export nitrates, the population was about 2,500. The nitrate trade transformed the town, bringing large numbers of foreign traders and creating a wealthy elite. The city, which was partly destroyed by earthquake in 1877, became the centre of this trade after its transfer from Peru to Chile at the end of the War of the Pacific.

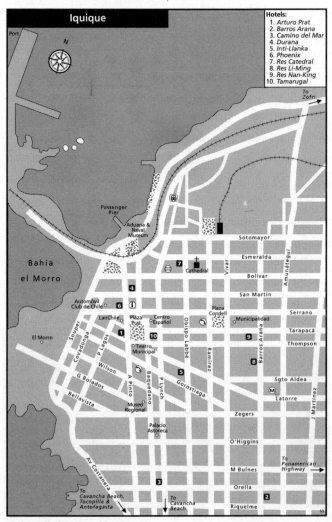

Iquique

Port

N

Bahia el Morro

Passenger Pier

Aduana & Naval Museum

To Zofri

Sotomayor

Esmeralda

Bolivar

San Martin

Cathedral

Vivar

Amunátegui

Plaza Condell

Serrano

Tarapacá

Thompson

Municipalidad

Automóvil Club de Chile

LanChile

Plaza Prat

Centro Español

Obispo Labbé

Ramirez

Barros Arana

El Morro

Teatro Municipal

Wilson

G Bolados

Bellavista

Souper

Covadonga

P. Lagos

A. Pinto

Baquedano

P. Lynch

Gorostiaga

Museo Regional

Palacio Astoreca

Sgto Aldea

Latorre

Zegers

O'Higgins

J. Martinez

To Panamerican Highway

Av Costanera

To Cavancha Beach, Tocopilla & Antofagasta

To Cavancha Beach

M Bulnes

Orella

Riquelme

Hotels:
1. Arturo Prat
2. Barros Arana
3. Camino del Mar
4. Durana
5. Inti-Llanka
6. Phoenix
7. Res Catedral
8. Res Li-Ming
9. Res Nan-King
10. Tamarugal

Places of interest

In the centre of the old town is **Plaza Prat** with a clock tower and bell dating from 1877. On the NE corner of the Plaza is the **Centro Español**, built in Moorish style by the local Spanish community in 1904; the ground floor is a restaurant, on the upper floors are paintings of scenes from Don Quijote and from Spanish history by the Spanish artist, Vicente Tordecillas. On the S side of the Plaza is the **Teatro Municipal**, built as an opera house in 1890; the façade features 4 women representing the seasons. Three blocks N of the Plaza is the old **Aduana** (customs house) built in 1871; in 1891 it was the scene of an important battle in the Civil War between supporters of President Balmaceda and congressional forces. Part of it is now the **Naval Museum**. Five blocks E along Sotomayor is the Railway Station, now disused, built in 1883 and displaying several old locomotives. Along C Baquedano, which runs S from Plaza Prat, are the attractive former mansions of the 'nitrate barons'. Adorned with columns and balconies, these date from between 1880 and 1903 and were constructed from imported Oregon Pine. The finest of these is the **Palacio Astoreca**, Baquedano y O'Higgins, built in 1903, subsequently the Intendencia and now a museum.

Sealions and pelicans can be seen from the harbour. There are cruises around the harbour from the passenger pier, US$2.65, 45 mins, minimum 10-15 people.

Museums

Museo Naval, Sotomayor y Baquedano, focussing on the Battle of Iquique, 1879 (see page 225), open Tues-Sat 0930-1230, 1430-1800, Sun and holidays 1000-1300, entry US$0.50.

Museo Regional, Baquedano 951, containing an archaeological section tracing the development of prehispanic civilizations in the region and a section devoted to the Nitrate Era which includes a model of a nitrate *oficina* and the collection of the nitrate entrepreneur, Santiago Humberstone, open Mon-Fri 0830-1300, 1500-1900, Sat 1030-1300, Sun (in summer) 1030-1300, US$0.50.

Palacio Astoreca, Baquedano y O'Higgins, fine late 19th century furniture and exhibitions of shells, open Tues-Sun 1000-1300, 1600-2000, entry free.

Excursions

To **Humberstone**, a large nitrate town, now abandoned, at the junction of the Pan-American Highway and the road to Iquique. At its height in 1940 the town had a population of 3,700. Though closed

Token paid to nitrate workers for use in company stores

since 1961, you can see the church, theatre, *pulpería* (company stores) and the swimming pool (built of metal plating from ships' hulls). Entry US$2.50, guided tours Sat-Sun, leaflets available. Nearby are the ruins of three other mining towns: Santa Laura, Peña Chica and Keryma, all of which can be visited. All four form the **Museo Arqueológico Industrial**; details from Salitreras Nebraska, T 751213, or Las Encinas 6141, Vitacura, Santiago, T 218-4161. Transport to/from Iquique: take any bus to/from Arica or Antofagasta, or a colective taxi for Pozo Almonte from Sgto Aldea y Barros Arana, US$2.

To Pintados (see page 189) take any bus S, US$2.50, and walk from the Pan-American Highway then hitch back or flag down a bus. Many other sites around Iquique, including the Giant of the Atacama (see page 189), are difficult to visit without a vehicle. Hire a car and drive S along the Pacific coast to see sealions, fishing villages and old salt mines, including the ghost town of Guanillos.

Local festivals
See below for the festival of the Virgen del Carmen in La Tirana, 70 km E of Iquique, 10-16 July.

Local information
● Accommodation
Accommodation is scarce in the weeks before Christmas as many Chileans visit Iquique to shop in the Zofri.

L3 *Hostería Cavancha*, Los Rieles 250, T 431007, 4-star, S of city, on water's edge.

A2 *Atenas*, Los Rieles 738, T 431100, F 424349, good service and food, rec; **A2** *Playa Brava*, Los Rieles 2503, T 431167, with breakfast, good; **A2** *Primeras Piedras*, street of same name, T 421358, 3 km from city, good food, friendly; **A3** *Tamarugal*, Tarapacá 369, T 424365, central, clean and modern, good restaurant.

B *Durana*, San Martín 294, T 412511, helpful; **B-C** *Inti-Llanka*, Obispo Labbé 825, T 412511, helpful.

C *Barros Arana*, Barros Arana 1330, T 412840, clean, modern, good value; **C** *Camino del Mar*, Orella 340, T 420465,

restored building, clean, simple; **C** *Hostal Cuneo*, Baquedano 1175, T 428654, modern, clean, pleasant; **C** *Phoenix*, Aníbal Pinto 451, T 421315, with bath and breakfast, old but pleasant, noisy juke box.

D *Res Condell*, Thompson 684, T 423079, with bath, clean, friendly; **D** *Plaza*, Plaza Prat, T 414268, clean, friendly; **D** *Res Nan-King*, Thompson 752, T 423311, clean, good value; **D** *España*, Tarapacá 465, nr Plaza Condell, without bath, friendly, warm water, dirty; **D** *Hostal América*, Rodríguez 550, T/F 427524, nr beach, clean, good value; **D** *Hostal San Francisco*, Latorre 990, clean, hot water, noisy; **D** *Res José Luis*, San Martín 601, spacious, clean; **D** *Res Marclaud*, Juan Martínez 753, rec, clean, motor-cycle parking.

E *Playa*, Gral Hernán Fuenzalida 938, T 22911, small, friendly; **E** *Res Araucano*, San Martín 777, T 420211, friendly, cooking facilities, grubby, noisy; **D** *Res Li Ming*, Barros Arana 705, T 421912, clean, good value; **E** *Res Centro*, Lynch 621, cheap, run down, basic; **E** *Res Sol del Norte*, Juan Martínez 852, T 421546, cold water, basic, small rooms.

F pp *Hosp Tarapacá*, Tarapacá 1348, T 426040, clean, friendly, no hot water; **F** pp *Centenario*, Amunátegui 845, clean.

Camping: no site but wild camping possible on La Brava beach. Equipment: *Tunset*, in Zofri; *Lombardi*, Serrano 447.

● Places to eat
Club de la Unión, Plaza Prat, roof terrace, good views, good, not cheap; *Sociedad Protectora de los Empleados de Tarapacá*, Plaza Prat, reasonable prices; *Centro Español*, Plaza Prat, good meals well served in beautiful building, attractive, expensive; *José Luis*, Serrano 476, good, pleasant atmosphere, good value *almuerzo*; *Bavaria*, Wilson y Pinto, good but not cheap; *Rapa Nui*, Amunátegui 715, for good, cheap, local food; *Grecia*, Thompson 865, cheap but good; *Balcón*, Lynch 656, snacks, live music; *Pizzería D'Alfredo*, Vivar 631, expensive, good coffee; *Italianissimo*, Edificio España, Vivar y Latorre, very good coffee. Several good, inexpensive seafood restaurants (eg *Bucanero*) can be found on the second floor of the central market, Barros Arana y Latorre; also cafés opp the bus station, on the wharf, sell good, cheap fish lunches. *Club de Yates* at the harbour serves very expensive meals. *El Rey del Pescado*, Bulnes y Juan Martínez, very nice local place with good

and cheap seafood dishes, *menú de la casa* a bargain; also *El Pescado Frito*, Bulnes y Juan Martínez, large portions. *Chifa Fu-Wa*, Barros Arana 740, Chinese.

Cafés: *Salón de Té Chantilly*, Tarapacá 520; *Café Diana*, Vivar 836; *Pinina*, Ramírez y Tarapacá, juices, ice-cream; *Samoa Grill*, Bolívar 396, good coffee and snacks.

● **Airline offices**
LanChile, Aníbal Pinto 641, T 414378; **Ladeco**, San Martín 428, T 413038; **National**, Galería Lynch, Local 1-2, T 427816, F 425158.

● **Banks & money changers**
National banks. **Fincard** (Mastercard), Serrano 372, open Mon-Fri 0900-1400, 1600-1800. Difficult to change TCs in town. Best rates for TCs and cash at *casas de cambio* in the Zofri.

● **Embassies & consulates**
Bolivia, Serrano Pasaje Alessandri 429, p 2, Of 300, Mon-Fri 0930-1400; **Peru**, Los Rieles 131, T 431116.

● **Entertainment**
Cinema: *Cine Tarapacá*, Serrano 202, shows foreign films.

● **Language schools**
Academia de Idiomas del Norte, Ramírez 1345, T 411827, F 429343, Swiss run, Spanish classes and accommodation for students.

● **Laundry**
Bulnes 170, expensive; Obispo Labbé 1446.

● **Post & telecommunications**
Post Office: Correo Central, Bolívar 458.

Telecommunications: CTC, Serrano 620, Ramírez 587; Entel, Gorostiaga 287; Diego Portales 840; Telegrams at TelexChile, Lynch y San Martín. **NB** Correos, Telex/Telefax and Entel all have offices in the Plaza de Servicios in the Zofri.

● **Sports**
Bathing: beaches at Cavancha just S of town centre, good, and Huaiquique, reasonable, Nov-March. Restaurants at Cavancha. Piscina Godoy, fresh water swimming pool on Av Costanera at Aníbal Pinto and Riquelme, open pm, US$1.

Fishing: equipment: *Ferretería Lonza*, Vivar 738; *Ferretería La Ocasión*, Sgto Aldea 890; fishing for broadbill swordfish, striped marlin, yellowfin tuna, oceanic bonito, Mar till end of August.

● **Tour companies & travel agents**
Iquitour, Lynch 563, Casilla 669, T 422009, no English spoken, tour to Pintados, La Tirana, Humberstone, Pica, etc, 0900-1900, lunch inc, a lot of time spent eating and bathing; *Lirima*, Baquedano 1035, rec; *Taxitur*, Sgto Aldea 791, 5-6 hr tour to local sites, maximum 5 passengers.

● **Tourist offices**
Aníbal Pinto 436, T 411523; open Mon-Fri, 0830-1300, 1500-1800, little information, poor maps. **Automóvil Club de Chile:** Serrano 154, T 426772.

● **Transport**
Local Car hire: expensive: **Hertz**, Souper 650, T 426316. **Continental**, Thompson 159, T/F 411426; **J Reategui**, Serrano 1058-A, T 429490/446079; **GP Car Rental**, O'Higgins 179. **Mechanic:** Sergio Cortez, *Givet*, Bolívar 684, highly rec for motorcycles. In the Zofri there is a wide range of motorcycle tyres.

Air Diego Aracena international airport, 35 km S at Chucumata, T 424577. Taxi from outside *Hotel Prat*, Plaza Prat, US$6, T 426184. Airport bus to city centre, US$2. LanChile, Ladeco and National all fly daily to Arica, Antofagasta and Santiago.

Buses Terminal at N end of Patricio Lynch (not all buses leave from here); bus company offices are nr the market on Sgto Aldea and B Arana. All luggage is searched for duty-free goods before being loaded onto buses; all southbound buses are then searched again, at Quillagua on the Pan American Highway and at Chipana on the coastal Route 1. To **Arica**, buses and colectivos, frequent, US$8, 4½ hrs; to **Antofagasta**, US$13, 8 hrs. To **Calama**, 8 hrs, US$13, Kennybus not rec. To **Tocopilla**

Routes around Iquique

Not to scale

Distance in km

along the coastal road, buses and minibuses, several companies, 4 hrs, US$7; to **La Serena**, 17 hrs, US$25; to **Santiago**, 28 hrs, several companies, US$30 (US$50 for Barrios *salón cama*).

International buses: Géminis (Obispo Labbé y Sotomayor) to **La Paz** (Bolivia) via Oruro, Thur and Sat 2300, 22 hrs, US$32; also Litoral, Esmeralda 974, T 423670, Tues, Sat, Sun 2300, US$32. To **Salta** (Argentina) via Calama and San Pedro, Géminis, once a week, US$50; Tramaca twice a week to Jujuy via Paso de Jama, US$50.

ROUTES AROUND IQUIQUE

Iquique lies 47 km W of the Pan-American Highway; 5 km S of the junction is Pozo Almonte (*Pop* 4,000).

INLAND TO PICA AND MAMIÑA

Inland from Iquique there are several small towns which were the early centres of Spanish colonial settlement. Note that the rainy season in this area is mainly in Jan.

MAMIÑA

(*Pop* 430; *Alt* 2,750m) is reached by a road which runs 74 km (first 54 km paved) from Pozo Almonte. Situated on a ridge and the site of thermal springs, the village has pre-colonial origins: there are ruins of a pre-hispanic *pukurá* (fortress). Legend has it that one of its thermal pools cured an Inca princess. The church, built in 1632, is the only colonial Andean church in Chile with two towers, each topped by a bell-tower. In the nitrate period its agreeable climate made it a resort for the wealthy: the Hotel Termas dates from this period. There is also a mud spring (Baño El Chino; open 0930-1300) and good accommodation. Electricity till 2230.

● **Accommodation** C pp *Termas de Salitre*, full board, thermal pool in each room, electricity till midnight, swimming pool open 0930-1300; **B** *Termal La Coruña*, T 796298, good, nice views; **C** *Tamarugal*, T 424365, thermal pool in each room; **D** *Res Sol de Ipla*, cheapest, 2 others; *cabañas* to let and camp-

site; basic accommodation may also be available at the military refuge.

● **Transport** Minibuses from Iquique leave B Arana y Latorre, Mon-Sat 1600; from Mamiña, 0800; Sun from Iquique 0930, from Mamiña 1600, US$4.50.

La Tirana

(*Pop* 550; *Alt* 995m) is famous for a religious festival to the Virgen del Carmen, held from 10 to 16 July, which attracts some 80,000 pilgrims. Over 100 groups dance night and day, starting on 12 July. All the dances take place in the main plaza in front of the church; no alcohol is served. Accommodation is impossible to find, other than in organized camp sites (take tent) which have basic toilets and showers. It is situated 10 km E of the Pan-American Highway, by a turning 9 km S of Pozo Almonte.

Matilla

(*Alt* 1,160m) 38 km E of La Tirana, is an oasis settlement founded in 1760. Its church (1887) is built of blocks of borax. Nearby is a **Museum** in the Lagar de Matilla, used since around 1700 for fermenting wine (open daily 0900-1700, key from the kiosk in the plaza).

PICA

(*Pop* 1,767; *Alt* 1,325m) 4 km NE of Matilla, was the most important centre of early Spanish settlement. In colonial times it produced a famous wine sold as far away as Potosí. Most older buildings including the church date from the nitrate period when it became a popular resort. The town is famous for its pleasant climate, its citrus groves and its two natural springs, the best of which is Cocha Resbaladero (open 0700-2000 all year, changing rooms, snack bar, beautiful pool, entry US$0.70).

● **Accommodation & places to eat** D *Resbaladero*, Ibáñez 57, T 741316, full pension, good pool; **D** *San Andrés*, Balmaceda 197, T 741319, with large breakfast, parking; **E** *O'Higgins*, Balmaceda 6, T 741322; **E** *El Tambo*, Ibáñez 60, T 741320, old fashioned, good restaurant; also *cabañas* for rent. Campsite at *Camping Miraflores*, T 741333. *Restaurant Palomar*, Balmaceda 74, excellent *almuerzo*.

● **Transport** Buses from Iquique operated by Santa Rosa, Latorre 973, daily 0930, 2 hrs; from Pica 1800, US$3. Several companies (Flonatur, Sgto Aldea 790; Julia, B Arana 965) operate minibuses from Iquique but services vary. There are two roads to Pica: note that only La Tirana-Pica is paved; the other route, Salar de Pintados-Pica, is unpaved and quite rough.

FROM IQUIQUE TO THE BOLIVIAN FRONTIER

At Huara, 33 km N of Pozo Almonte, a road turns off the Pan-American Highway to **Colchane**, 173 km NE on the Bolivian frontier. At Km 13 the road passes, on the right, the **Giant of the Atacama**, 86m high, reported to be the largest geoglyph in the world (best viewed from a distance).

At Km 23 a road branches off S to **Tarapacá** (*Alt* 1,350m), settled by the Spanish around 1560 and capital of the Peruvian province of Tarapacá until 1855, now largely abandoned. The major historic buildings, the Iglesia de San Lorenzo and the Palacio de Gobierno, are in ruins. From Km 25 the road is unpaved. At **Chusmisa** (*Alt* 3,650m), 3 km off this road at Km 77 there are thermal springs: the water is bottled and sold throughout northern Chile. Basic accommodation is available.

● **Transport** Colchane can be reached by Kennybus from Iquique, one a week, returns after 2 hrs. Géminis bus from Iquique to La Paz also passes through Colchane.

PARQUE NACIONAL VOLCAN ISLUGA

Situated NW of Colchane, the park covers 174,744 ha at altitudes above 2,100m of some of the best volcanic scenery in northern Chile. Apart from the still-smoking Isluga volcano (5,218m) the park includes three other peaks over 5,000m: Quimsachata (5,400m), Tatajachura (5,252m) and Latarama

(5,207m). The village of **Isluga**, near the park entrance, 6 km NW of Colchane, has an 18th century Andean walled church and bell tower.

Wildlife Varies according to altitude but includes guanacos, vicuñas, llamas, alpacas, vizcachas, condors and flamingoes.

● **Park information** Park Administration at Enquelga, 10 km N of the entrance, but *guardaparques* are seldom there. There is a campsite at Aguas Calientes, 2 km S of Enquelga.

Mountain roads in poor condition lead NW from Isluga across the Park to Camiña (see below), 171 km from Colchane. It is, in a 4WD vehicle, possible to drive N from Isluga through the Salar de Surire via Guallatiri to the Parque Nacional del Lauca, and from there to Bolivia, or via Putre and Poconchile to Arica or Peru.(Get good directions before setting out)

FRONTIER WITH BOLIVIA: COLCHANE

Open 0800-1300, 1500-1800 daily. On the Bolivian side an unpaved road leads to Oruro, 233 km NE.

SOUTH TOWARDS ANTOFAGASTA

South of Pozo Almonte, the Pan-American Highway runs to Quillagua, 172 km (customs post, all vehicles inc buses are searched) and on towards Antofagasta. At Km 24 the road runs through the largest section of the **Reserva Nacional Pampa del Tamarugal** (the other two sections are around La Tirana and N of Huara) which is administered by Conaf. Covering a total of 100,650 ha, the reserve includes plantations of tamaruga, a tree species adapted to saline soils. The **Geoglyphs of Pintados**, some 400 figures on the hillsides, representing humans, animals and birds as well as abstract designs, are situated some 3 km W of the Pan-American Highway (turn off at Km 43).

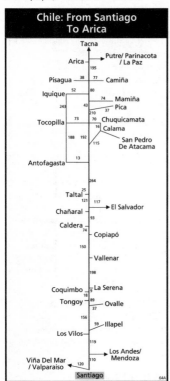

Chile: From Santiago
To Arica

important nitrate port, now a small fishing port. Several old wooden buildings here are National Monuments including the Municipal Theatre (1892) and the Clock Tower (1887), but it is now largely abandoned. There are fish restaurants and it makes a pleasant stop for a meal. Mass graves dating from just after the 1973 military coup were discovered near here in 1990.

Camiña (*Pop* 500; *Alt* 2,400m), a picturesque village in an oasis, lies 67 km E of Zapiga along a poor road (deep sand and dust). There is a basic hostal. 45 km further NE is the Tranque de Caritaya, a dam which supplies water for the coastal towns set in splendid scenery with lots of wildlife and interesting botany (especially *llareta*). From here mountain roads lead across the Parque Nacional Volcán Isluga to Colchane.

At Km 57 N of Huara there is an interesting British cemetery dating from 1876. The **Geoglifos de Chiza** (sign-posted, to left, and easily accessible), Km 121, can be seen from the highway. At Km 172 a road runs E to **Codpa**, an agricultural community in a deep gorge with interesting scenery. From Codpa poor roads lead N and E through **Tignamar** and Belén to Putre. **Belén** (*Alt* 3,240), a tiny village founded by the Spanish in 1625, was on the silver route between Potosí and the coast. It has two colonial churches: the older one, the Iglesia de Belén is one of the oldest (and smallest) churches in Chile; the other, the Iglesia de Carmen, dates from the 18th century. At Tignamar Viejo, an abandoned village 14 km S, there is another colonial church.

ARICA

(*Pop* 174,064; *Phone code* 058), Chile's most northerly city, 19 km S of the Peruvian border, built at the foot of the Morro headland, fringed by sand dunes. The Andes can be clearly seen from the anchorage.

NORTH TOWARDS ARICA

The Pan-American Highway runs across the Atacama desert at an altitude of around 1,000m, with several steep hills which are best tackled in daylight (at night, sea mist, *camanchaca*, can reduce visibility).

Huara (*Pop* 400), 33 km N of Pozo Almonte, once a town of 7,000 people, was the entertainment centre for the nearby nitrate towns but little remains from that period. (Last fuel before Arica).

● **Accommodation** *Restaurant Frontera*, basic.

At Zapiga, 47 km N of Huara there is a cross roads: one branch leads W for 41 km to **Pisagua** (*Pop* 200), formerly an

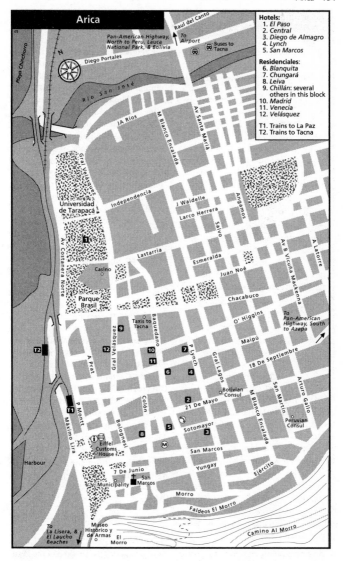

Arica

Pan-American Highway,
North to Peru, Lauca
National Park, & Bolivia

To Airport

Buses to Tacna

Diego Portales

Río San José

Gral Velásquez

JA Ríos

M Blanco Encalada

Av Santa María

Independencia

J Waidelle

Angamos

Universidad
de Tarapacá

Larco Herrera

Salvo

Av B Vicuña Mackenna

A Latorre

Lastarria

Esmeralda

Casino

Juan Noé

Parque
Brasil

Chacabuco

O' Higgins

To
Pan-American
Highway, South
to Azapa

Taxis to
Tacna

Maipú

P Lynch

Gral Lagos

18 De Septiembre

A Prat

Baquedano

Gral Velásquez

Bolivian
Consul

M Blanco Encalada

San Martín

Arturo Gallo

Colón

21 De Mayo

Peruvian
Consul

Bolognesi

P Montt

Máximo Lira

Sotomayor

Eiffel
Customs
House

San Marcos

Harbour

7 De Junio

San
Marcos

Yungay

Ejército

Municipality

Morro

To
La Lisera, &
El Laucho
Beaches

Museo
Histórico y
de Armas

El
Morro

Faldeos El Morro

Camino Al Morro

Hotels:
1. *El Paso*
2. *Central*
3. *Diego de Almagro*
4. *Lynch*
5. *San Marcos*

Residenciales:
6. *Blanquita*
7. *Chungará*
8. *Leiva*
9. *Chillán*: several others in this block
10. *Madrid*
11. *Venecia*
12. *Velásquez*

T1. Trains to La Paz
T2. Trains to Tacna

It is an important port and route-centre. A 448 km railway runs E to the Bolivian capital La Paz: about half the legal trade of Bolivia passes along this line. An oil pipeline also runs to La Paz. The completion of the international highway to the Bolivian frontier at Tambo Quemado has added to the city's importance. It is frequented for seabathing by Bolivians as well as the locals. A 63 km railway runs N to Tacna in Peru. Regrettably there are indications that Arica is also becoming a key link in the international drugs trade. There are large fishmeal plants and a car assembly factory.

History

During the colonial period Arica was important as the Pacific end of the silver route from Potosí. Independence as part of Peru and the re-routing of Bolivian trade through Cobija led to a decline from which the city recovered with the building of rail links with Tacna (1855) and La Paz (1913).

Places of interest

The **Morro**, with a good view from the park on top (10 mins' walk by footpath from the southern end of Colón), was the scene of a great victory by Chile over Peru in the War of the Pacific on 7 June 1880.

At the foot of the Morro is the Plaza Colón with the cathedral of **San Marcos**, built in iron by Eiffel. Though small it is beautifully proportioned and attractively painted. It was brought to Arica from Ilo (Peru) in the 19th century, before Peru lost Arica to Chile, as an emergency measure after a tidal wave swept over Arica and destroyed all its churches. Eiffel also designed the nearby **Aduana** (customs house) which is now the Casa de la Cultura (open Mon-Sat 1000-1300, 1700-2000.) Just N of the Aduana is the La Paz railway station; outside is an old steam locomotive (made in Germany in 1924) once used on this line. In the station is a memorial to John Roberts Jones, builder of the Arica portion of the railway, and a small museum (key at booking office).

Museums

Museo Arqueológico of the University of Tarapacá, see under **Excursions** below. **Museo Histórico y de Armas**, on the summit of the Morro, containing weapons and uniforms from the War of the Pacific.

Excursions

To the Azapa valley, E of Arica, by yellow colectivo from P Lynch y Chacabuco, US$1. At Km 13 is the **Museo Arqueológico de San Miguel**, part of the University of Tarapacá, containing an important collection of mummies from the Chinchorro culture, reputed to be the oldest collection in the world, as well as sections on Andean weaving, basketwork and ceramics (open Mon-Fri 0830-1300, 1500-1800, Sat, Sun, and holidays 1200-1800, Latin Americans US$1, others US$4, worth a visit). In the forecourt of the museum are several boulders with precolumbian petroglyphs. On the road between Arica and San Miguel images of humans and llamas ('stone mosaics') can be seen to the S of the road. On the opposite side of the valley at San Lorenzo are the ruins of a *pukará* (pre-Inca fortress) dating from the 12th century.

To the **Lluta valley**, N of Arica along Route 11, bus from MacKenna y Chacabuco, 4 a day: At Km 14 and Km 16

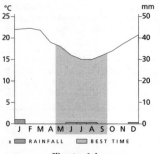

Climate: Arica

there are ancient images of llamas and humans on the hillside. The road continues through the Lauca National Park and on to Bolivia.

Local festivals

Fiestas for the **Virgen de las Peñas** at the Santuario de Livircar in the Azapa Valley are held on the first Sun in Oct and a lesser festival on 7-9 Dec (on 8 Dec the festival moves to Arica). Take a bus from Av Chacabuco y Vicuña Mackenna, then walk 12 km from where it stops to the sanctuary. The Dec festival is not particularly outstanding but it takes place in a part of the valley not normally accessible.

Local information

● **Accommodation**

NB In this area, *pensión* means restaurant, not hostel.

L3 *Arica*, San Martín 599, T 254540, F 231133, best, price depends on season, good value, good and reasonable restaurant, other services expensive, about 2 km along shore (buses No 7, 8, frequent), tennis court, pool, lava beach (not safe for swimming), good breakfast, poor water supply; **L3** *El Paso*, bungalow style, pleasant gardens, swimming pool, Gen Velásquez 1109, T 231965, with breakfast, good food; **L3** *San Marcos*, Sotomayor 382, T 232970, F 254815, clean, helpful, restaurant, parking.

A1 *Saint Georgette*, Camino a Azapa 3221, T 221914, F 223830, 5-star, pool, tennis court, restaurant, bar; **A2** *Azapa*, Sánchez 660, Azapa, T 222612, attractive grounds but several kilometres from beaches and centre, also cheaper cabins, restaurant; **A2** *Central*, 21 de Mayo 425, T 252575, central, nicely decorated; **A3** *Amadís de Gaula*, Prat 588, T/F 232994, central, modern; **A3** *Savona*, Yungay 380, T 232319, comfortable, friendly, quiet, highly rec.

B *Diego de Almagro*, Sotomayor 490, T 224444, F 221248, helpful, clean, comfortable, parking, rec, stores luggage; **C** *Lynch*, Lynch 589, T 231581, D without bath, pleasant but poor beds, clean, rec, parking; **C** *Res América*, Sotomayor 430, T 254148, clean, friendly, central.

D *Hostal 18 de Septiembre*, 18 de Septiembre 524, T 251727, clean, hot water, breakfast; **D** *Res Blanquita*, Maipú 472, T 232064,

clean, hot water; **D** *Res Caracas*, Sotomayor 867, T 253688, cheap, clean, hot water, TV, breakfast; **D** *Res Chungará*, Lynch 675, T 231677, without bath, clean, also meals; **D** *Res Ecuador*, Juan Noé 989, T 251573, clean, noisy, helpful, meals available; **D** *Res Las Condes*, Vicuña Mackenna 628, T 251583, helpful, hot water, rec; **D** *Res Real*, Sotomayor 578, T/F 253359, clean, very friendly and helpful, rec; **D** *Pensión Donoso*, Baquedano y Maipú, downstairs with bath, gloomy, E upstairs without bath, bright.

E *Casa Blanca*, Gen Lagos 557, modern, clean, rec; **E** *Hostal Raissa*, San Martín 281, T 251070, without bath, with breakfast; **E** *La Posada*, 21 de Mayo 186, small rooms, good beds, central, without bath; **E** *Res Española*, Bolognesi 340, T 231703, central, clean, basic, quiet; **E** *Res Las Vegas 120*, Baquedano 120, T 231355, basic, friendly, dark rooms, hot water, safe, central; **E** *Res Leiva*, Colón 347, T 232008, without bath, French spoken, cooking facilities, motorcycle parking with difficulty; **E** *Res Madrid*, Baquedano 685, T 231479, without bath, clean, good value but poor beds, reductions for IYHA cards; **E** *Res Maipú*, Maipú 479, T 252157, basic, clean, hot water, safe.

On Velásquez are: E *Res Chillán*, No 749, T 251677, noisy, poor beds; **E** *Res El Sur*, Maipú 516, very clean, small rooms, hot water, basic; **E** Gloria Martínez, pasaje 7, Población Juan Noé, T 241971, friendly, helpful; **E** *Res Ine'sa*, No 725, T 231609, comfortable, breakfast available, kitchen, laundry, good; **E** pp Raul del Canto 947, nice, friendly, clean, nr bus terminal; **E** pp Sra Leony Vidiella, Gonzalo Cerda 1030, close to bus station, with breakfast, cooking facilities, clean, safe, tepid water, English spoken; **E** *Res Tropical*, Gen Lagos 649, friendly, basic; **E** *Res Valencia*, No 719, T 253479, friendly, cooking and laundry facilties, motorcycle parking, rec; **E** *Res Velásquez*, No 685, T 231989, central, basic, friendly; **E** *Res Venecia*, Baquedano 739, T 252877, spotless, hot water, small rooms, rec; **F** pp Sra Eliana, Arteaga 50, T 232304, with breakfast, luggage stored, laundry facilities, rec. In Jan-Feb the municipality supplies cheap basic accommodation, ask at the tourist office.

Camping: *Gallinazos*, at Villa Frontera, 15 km N, T 232373, full facilities, pool; *El Refugio de Azapa*, 3.5 km from Arica, T 227545; at Playa Las Machas, 5 km N, no water or facilities and at Playa Corazones, 8 km S, no water.

● **Places to eat**

Acuario, Máximo Lira, Terminal Pesquero, for food and atmosphere, expensive; *El Rey del Marisco*, Maipú y Colón, seafood, pricey, rec; *Maracuyá*, San Martín 0321, seafood, splendid location on the coast, pricey; plenty of seafood lunch places in the market; *Los Aleros del 21*, 21 de Mayo 736, rec for seafood and service; *Don Floro*, V MacKenna y Chacabuco, steaks; *Snack Suceso Inn*, 18 de Septiembre 250, good set meal and coffee; *La Jaula*, 18 de Septiembre 293, cheap lunches; *Casanova*, Baquedano 397, excellent but not cheap; *Yuri*, Maipú 500, good service, cheap, rec; *Bavaria*, Colón 613, expensive, with delicatessen and expresso coffee, repeatedly rec; *Govinda*, Bolognesi 430, vegetarian, good value lunches, repeatedly rec; *Scala*, 21 de Mayo 201, excellent fruit juices; *Carpaccio*, Velásquez 510, restaurant and bar, live music from 2330 Wed-Sat; *El Tambo*, in Poblado Artesanal, Hualles 2025, for lunches, folk music and dancing on Sun; *La Picá del Muertito*, San Miguel de Azapa at entrance to cemetery, not far from the Museo Arqueológico, typical *norteño* food. Several good Chinese restaurants inc *Si Lom*, Sotomayor 593; *Chin Huang Tao*, Lynch 317. Several places for cheap breakfasts and set meals on Baquedano 700 block. *Casino de Bomberos*, Colón 357, at fire station, good value *almuerzo*; *Schop*, 18 de Septiembre 240, cheap sandwiches.

● **Airline offices**

LanChile, 7 de Junio 148, T 224738; **Ladeco**, 21 de Mayo 443, T 252021; **Lloyd Aéreo Boliviano**, P Lynch 298, T 251472; **AeroPerú**, 7 de Junio 148, T 232852; **National**, 21 de Mayo 627, T 253447, F 251283.

● **Banks & money changers**

Many money changers on 21 de Mayo and its junction with Colón, some accept TCs but with high commision. Banco Osorno, 21 de Mayo, cash on Visa, no commission; **Fincard** (Mastercard), 21 de Mayo 252, Mon-Fri 0900-1400, 1600-1730, only pesos given, at varying rates. *Casas de Cambio*: Inter-Santiago and Cambio Fides, Shopping Centre del Pacífico, Diego Portales 840; **Daniel Concha**, Chacabuco 300; **Sol y Mar**, Colón 610; **Tacora**, 21 de Mayo 171, good rates for cash; **Yanulaque**, 21 de Mayo 175, which stays open until 2000 but closes all day Sun. Most large hotels also change cash. Rates for TCs are generally poor, you may even get better rates in the street.

● **Embassies & consulates**

Brazil, Las Margaritas 717, Pob Prat, T 231142; **Bolivia**, 21 de Mayo 575, T 231030; **Peru**, San Martín 220, T 231020.

Denmark, 21 de Mayo 399, T 231399; Germany, 21 de Mayo 639, T 231551, open 0900-1300; **Italy**, San Martín y Chacabuco, T 229195; **Norway**, 21 de Mayo 399, T 231298; **Spain**, Santa María 2660, T 224655; **United Kingdom**, the only one in Chile N of Valparaíso, and Instituto Chileno – Británico de Cultura (library open Mon-Fri 0900-1200, 1600-2100), Baquedano 351, T 231960, Casilla 653.

Instituto Chileno-Alemán de Cultura, 21 de Mayo 816; **Instituto Cultural Chileno Norteamericano**, San Marcos 581.

● **Entertainment**

Cinemas: *Colón*, 7 de Junio 190, T 231165; *Cine Arte Universidad*, University Campus, T 251813.

Discotheques: 3 S of town along front, also *Sunset* and *Swing*, both 3½ km out of town in the Valle de Azapa, 2300-0430 weekends (taxi US$3).

Theatre: *Teatro Municipal de Arica*, Baquedano 234, new, wide variety of theatrical and musical events, exhibitions, rec.

● **Hospitals & medical services**

Dentist: *Juan Horta Becerra*, 18 de Septiembre 1154, T 252497, speaks English; *Rodrigo Belmar Castillo*, 18 de Septiembre 1051, T 252047.

Health: *Dr Juan Noé*, 18 de Septiembre 1000, T 231331 (T 232242 for urgent cases).

● **Laundry**

Lavandería La Moderna, 18 de Septiembre 457, per item, expensive; *Niko's*, 18 de Septiembre 188A, US$3/kilo, fast; *Americana*, Lynch 260, T 231808.

● **Post & telecommunications**

Post Office: Prat 375. To send parcels abroad, contents must be shown to Aduana (under main post office) on weekdays, except Tues, between 1500 and 1700. Your parcel will be wrapped, cheaply, but take your own carton.

Telephones: Entel-Chile, 21 de May 345, open 0900-2200; CTC, Colón 430 and at 21 de Mayo 211; VTR Telecommunications, 21 de Mayo 477, telex, fax, telegrams.

● **Shopping**

Poblado Artesanal, Plaza Las Gredas, Hualles

2025 (take bus 2, 3 or 7): local 2, expensive but especially good for musical instruments; *Mercado Central*, Sotomayor, between Colón and Baquedano, mornings only. *Feria Turística Dominical*, Sun market, W end of Chacabuco extending N on Av Costanera Norte, good prices for llama sweaters. Fruit, vegetable and old clothes market at Terminal Agropecuario at edge of town; take bus marked 'Terminal Agro'. Arica, as a duty free zone, is an important centre for cheapish electronic goods for Bolivian and Peruvian shoppers. Supermarket at San Martín y 18 de Septiembre.

● **Sports**

Bathing: Olympic pool in Parque Centenario, Tues-Sun, US$0.50; take No 5A bus from 18 de Septiembre. The best beach for swimming is Playa Chinchorro, N of town. Buses 7 and 8 run to beaches S of town – the first two beaches, La Lisera and El Laucho, are both small and mainly for sunbathing. Playa Brava is popular for sunbathing but not swimming (dangerous currents). Strong currents also at Playa Las Machas which is popular with surfers. Good surfing also beyond seawall at Club de Yates. Playa Corazones, 15 km to S (no buses, take taxi or hitch), rec, not for swimming but picnics and fishing.

Golf: 18-hole course in Valle de Azapa, open daily except Mon.

Tennis: *Club de Tenis Centenario*, Av España 2640, open daily.

● **Tour companies & travel agents**

Jurasi, Bolognesi 360 A, T 251696, will hold mail, helpful, good city tour; *Huasquitur*, Sotomayor 470, T 223875, helpful, English spoken, will cater for individual itineraries, rec for flights; *Vicuña Tour*, 18 de Septiembre 399, oficina 215, T 253773, F 252404, rec; *Globo Tour*, 21 de Mayo 260, T 232807, F 231085, very helpful; *Aricamundi*, Prat 358, T 252263, F 251797, for airline tickets; *Latinorizons*, O'Higgins 440, T/F 250007, specializes in tours to Lauca National Park, small groups in 4WD Landcruiser; *Parinacota Expeditions*, Lynch 731, T 251309, excellent day tour to Lauca, Arica city tour, archaeological tours of Azapa Valley. Agencies charge similar prices for tours: Lauca National Park US$20, Valle de Azapa US$12; city tour US$10. Alex Figares, Casilla 2007, T/F 213643, rec as guide, speaks English. One day tours to Lauca National Park are not really worthwhile: they involve a lot of travel at

high altitude and tour quality is often poor: shop around carefully.

● **Tourist offices**

Sernatur, Prat 375, p 2; open Mon-Fri 0830-1300, 1500-1830, T 232101. Very helpful, English spoken, good map; Kiosk on 21 de Mayo between Colón and Baquedano, open Mon-Fri, 0830-1300, 1500-1900; **Automobile Club** Chacabuco 460, T 252678; **Conaf**, Valle de Azapa 3444 (Km 1.5), T 231559, closed weekends (bus 8 to Azapa intersection).

● **Transport**

Local Bus: buses run from C Maipú, US$0.25. Collective taxis on fixed routes within city limit, US$0.30 pp (US$0.50 pp after 2000). **Car hire**: Hertz, *Hotel El Paso*, Gen Velázquez 1109, T 231487; **Budget**, 21 de Mayo 650, T 252978; **Klasse**, Velásquez 762, Loc 25, T 254498; **American**, Gen Lagos 559, T 252234; *GP*, Copacabana 628, T 252594; *Viva*, 21 de Mayo 821, T 251121; 4WD and antifreeze are essential for Lauca National Park.

Motoring Automóvil Club de Chile: Chacabuco 469, T 237780. **Car insurance**: at Dirección de Tránsito; may insist on car inspection. **Car service**: Shell, Panamericana Norte 3456; Esso, Portales 2462; Autocentro, Azola 2999, T 241241. **Bicycle parts**: *Bicicletas Wilson*, 18 de Sept 583, also Portales 1479.

Air Airport 18 km N of city at Chacalluta, T 222831. Taxi to town US$9, collective taxi US$4-5 pp from Lynch y 21 de Mayo. Flights: to **La Paz**, LanChile and LAB; to **Santiago**, Ladeco (via Iquique and Antofagasta), LanChile (via Iquique or Antofagasta), and National (via Iquique or Antofagasta). Book well in advance. To **Lima**, AeroPerú and others from Tacna (Peru), enquire at travel agencies in Arica.

Trains To **La Paz** (Bolivia): direct ferrobus services operated by Enfe (Bolivian Railways) leave Arica Tues and Sat at 0830, 12 hrs, US$52 (in clean US$ bills only) inc breakfast, lunch and drinks up to lunchtime (extra food and drinks sold). Book well in advance in Jan-Mar, tickets from the station at 21 de Mayo 51, T 232844. Baggage allowance, 25 kg plus hand luggage (luggage is weighed and searched at the station). Additional trains may run in Jan-Mar, reduced service off season. Local trains run to the frontier towns of Visviri (Chile) and Charaña (Bolivia) every other Tues (every Tues in Jan-Mar) at 2300, 9 hrs, US$12 1st class, US$7 2nd class; from Charaña a service runs at 1600 to Viacha, 32 km from La Paz, US$3.05 pullman. Check details in advance. On all journeys, take plenty of warm clothing; long delays, particularly at the frontier are common. Search for fruit, vegetables and dairy products at Arica station for passengers arriving from Bolivia.

The line from Arica skirts the coast for 10 km and passes into the Lluta Valley, whose vegetation is in striking contrast with the barrenness of the surrounding hills. From Km 70 there is a sharp rise of 2,241m in 42 km through a series of tunnels, Km 112, the plateau is reached at 4,168m. The line continues through Col Alcérreca (Km 140) and Villa Industrial (Km 165), before reaching its highest point at General Lagos (4,247m). In the distance can be seen the snowcapped heights of Tacora, Putre, Sajama, and their fellows. The frontier station of Visviri is at Km 205, with a customs house. Beyond, the train enters Bolivia and the station of Charaña. In summer a tourist train runs from Arica to Col Alcérreca and back on Sun, 0800, returning to Arica 2100.

See below for trains to Tacna, Peru.

Buses Bus terminal at Av Portales y Santa María, T 241390, bus or colectivo No 8 or 18 (US$0.15, or US$0.30), taxi to centre US$2 (terminal tax US$0.25). All luggage is carefully searched for fruit prior to boarding and is then searched again at Cuya on the Pan American Highway. All long-distance buses are modern, clean and air-conditioned, but ask carefully what meals are included. Bus company offices at bus terminal. Local services: Flota Paco (La Paloma), Germán Riesco 2071 (bus U from centre); Humire, P Montt 662, T 231891; Martínez, 21 de Mayo 575, T 232265; Bus Lluta, Chacabuco y V Mackenna.

To **Antofagasta**, US$18, 10 hrs. To **Calama** and **Chuquicamata**, 12 hrs, US$16, several companies, all between 2000 and 2200; to **Iquique**, frequent, US$8, 4½ hrs, also collective taxis, several companies, all with offices in the terminal; to **Santiago**, 28 hrs, a number of companies, eg Carmelita, Ramos Cholele, Fénix and Flota Barrios US$40-45, also *salón cama* services, run by Fichtur, Flota Barrios, Fénix and others, US$75, Tramaca rec (most serve meals and the more expensive, the more luxurious; student discounts available); to **La Serena**, 18 hrs, US$30; to **Viña del Mar** and **Valparaíso**, US$40, also *salón cama* service, US$50.

International buses: to **La Paz**, Bolivia, Internacional Litoral, Chacabuco 454, T 254702, Mon and Thur, 2400, US$22, no food; service via border towns of Chungará

(Chile) and Tambo Quemado (Bolivia, very cold at border – take blanket/sleeping bag, food, water and sense of humour). Also Géminis, Wed 2400, US$32, some food, via Huara and Challapata (Bolivia). To **Salta** (Argentina), Géminis, Tues 2130, US$50, connects at Calama next day with Antofagasta-Salta service. Computerized booking ensures seat reservation; passport details required, book in advance.

Motorists It is illegal to take fruit and dairy products S of Arica: all vehicles are searched at Cuya, 105 km S, and at Huara, 234 km S. **Service stations** between the Peruvian border and Santiago can be found at: Arica, Huara, Iquique, Pozo Almonte, Oficina Vitoria, Tocopilla, Oficina María Elena, Chuquicamata, Calama, Carmen Alto, Antofagasta, La Negra, Agua Verde (also fruit inspection post), Taltal, Chañaral, Caldera, Copiapó, Vallenar, La Serena, Termas de Soco, Los Vilos, and then every 30 km to capital.

Hitchhiking Not easy to hitch S: try the Terminal Agropecuario (trucks leave Mon, Thur and Sat before 0700) and the Copec station opp (bus from Arica marked 'Agro').

By road to Bolivia There are 2 routes:
1) Via Chungará (Chile) and Tambo Quemado (Bolivia). This, the most widely used route, begins by heading N from Arica on the Pan-American Highway (Route 5) for 12 km before turning right (E towards the cordillera) on Route 11 towards Chungará via Putre and Lauca National Park (see below). This road is now paved to La Paz (completed July 1996 on the Bolivian side), estimated driving time 6 hrs.
2) Via Visviri (Chile) and (Charaña) Bolivia, following the La Paz-Arica railway line. This route should not be attempted in wet weather.

FRONTIER WITH PERU: CHACALLUTA

● **Immigration**
Open 0800-2400; a fairly uncomplicated crossing.

NB Between Oct and Mar Chilean time is 1 hr later than Peruvian, 2 hrs later Oct to Feb or Mar, varies annually.

● **Crossing by private vehicle**
US$2/vehicle is charged for crossing 1300-1500, 1850-2400 and on Sat, Sun, holidays. Drivers entering Chile are required to file a form, *Relaciones de Pasajeros*, giving details of passengers, obtained from a stationery store

in Tacna, or at the border in a booth near Customs. You must also present the original registration document for your car from its country of registration. The first checkpoints outside Arica on the road to Santiago also require the *Relaciones de Pasajeros* form. If you can't buy the form, details on a piece of paper will suffice or you can get them at service stations. The form is *not* required when travelling S of Antofagasta.

● **Exchange**
Facilities at the frontier but reported better rates in Tacna.

● **Transport**
Local Collective taxis: run from the bus terminal and bus company offices in Arica to **Tacna**, US$4 pp, 1½ hrs, drivers take care of all the paperwork. Four companies: Chile Lintur, Baquedano 796, T 232048; Chasquitur, Chacabuco 320, T 231376; San Marcos, Noé 321, T 252528; Colectivo San Remo, Chacabuco 350, T 251925. Bus from the terminal, US$2, also Taxibus, 2 hourly, US$4. For Arequipa it is best to go to Tacna and catch an onward bus there.

Trains Services for passengers to Tacna leave Arica 3 times a week, US$1.60, 2½ hrs, from the station at Máximo Lira 889, T 231115. In Tacna there is a customs check at the station but no immigration facilities.

INTO PERU

Tacna is 36 km N of the frontier. The city was in Chilean hands from 1880 to 1929, when its citizens voted by plebiscite to return to Peru. There is a wide variety of hotels, restaurants, bus and air services to the rest of Peru, and a tourist office at Av Bolognesi 2088, T 3778. The Peruvian side of the border is open 0900-2200.

FRONTIER WITH BOLIVIA: VISVIRI

● **Immigration**
Open 0800-2400. Chilean formalities at Visviri, Bolivian formalities at Charaña, 10 km E.

● **Crossing with a private vehicle**
US$2/vehicle charge for crossing 1300-1500, 1850-2100 and Sat, Sun and holidays.

● **Transport**
Martínez buses from Arica to Visviri, Tues and Fri. Collective taxi from Arica US$10. In Visviri take a jeep across the border to Charaña. Bus from Charaña to La Paz, US$9.75, 7 hrs.

INTO BOLIVIA

In **Charaña** is **G** *Alojamiento Aranda*. Immigration is behind the railway station. Two routes go from Charaña to La Paz, both of which meet at Viacha.

Once in **La Paz**, at either the train or bus station, take a taxi to the hotel of your choice; among the micro bus services, nos 130 and M connect both stations with downtown. If arriving in La Paz direct from Arica, ie without stopping in the Parque Nacional Lauca, respect the altitude.

PARQUE NACIONAL LAUCA

The Parque Nacional Lauca, 176 km E of Arica stretching to the frontier with Bolivia, is one of the most spectacular National Parks in Chile. Acess is easy as the main Arica-La Paz road runs through the park and is paved. On the way, at Km 90 there is a pre-Inca *pukará* (fortress) and a few kilometres further there is an Inca *tambo* (inn). During the rainy season (Jan and Feb) roads in the park may be impassable, although the main road to La Paz is paved; check in advance with Conaf in Arica.

Situated at over 3,200m (beware of soroche unless you are coming from Bolivia), the park covers 137,883 ha and includes numerous snowy volcanoes including 10 peaks of over 6,000m, two large lakes (Cotacotani and Chungará) and lava fields at Cotacotani. A good base for exploring the park and for acclimatization is **Putre** (3,500m), a scenic village, 15 km before the entrance with a church dating from 1670 and surrounded by terracing dating from pre-Inca times, now used for cultivating alfalfa and oreg-

ano. From here paths provide easy walking and great views. Nearby there are 4,00 year old cave paintings and thermal baths.

At **Parinacota** (4,392m), at the foot of the Payachatas volcano, there is an interesting 17th century church – rebuilt 1789 – with frescoes and the skulls of past priests (Sr Sipriano keeps the key). Local residents knit alpaca sweaters, US$26 approx; weavings of wildlife scenes also available. Weavings are sold from a tin shed with an orange roof opposite the church. From here an unpaved road runs N to the Bolivian frontier at Visviri (see above). From the Conaf hut you can climb Guane Guane, 5,300m, in 2-3 hrs, ask the wardens. 20

The wildlife of Parque Nacional Lauca

Although the park lies very close to the lifeless Atacama desert, it receives more rain because of its altitude and the reward is a fairyland of volcanoes and highland lakes surrounded by brilliant green wetlands and vast expanses of *puna* grassland. The Río Lauca rises near Lago Chungará, then laces slowly through the park leaving marshy cushion bogs and occasional raceways, providing an array of habitats for the fauna of the altiplano.

The camelids are the stars of the park; thousands of domesticated llamas and alpacas, as well as the dainty, graceful, wild vicuña which now numbers over 18,000. The charming viscacha, seemingly a long-tailed rabbit, but in fact belonging to the chinchilla family, can be seen perched sleepily on the rocks, backside toward the morning sun. Pumas, huemules (deer), foxes, skunks and armadillos are the more elusive mammals, some nocturnal, occupying the more remote reaches.

Lauca birdlife is spectacular, with more than 120 species either resident or migrant. Lago Chungará is home to more than 8,000 giant coots, their bright orange legs, never-ending nest building, and primordial cackling entertains all. In addition to coots, ducks and grebes, the wetlands provide a fine habitat for the *puna* plover, the rare diademed sandpiper plover, the *puna* ibis, Andean species of avocet, goose and gull, and an assortment of migratory shorebirds. Occasionally one can see three species of flamingos at once, the Andean and the James (locally called *parinas*) and the more common Chilean Flamingo. Trips through the drier grasslands can produce glimpses of the *puna* tinamou (always in groups of three) and the *puna* rhea, seen in Oct and Nov with 20 or 30 miniatures scooting along behind. Passerines occupy all the habitats in the park, some to 5,000m and more, nearly to the snowline. Sierra finches, black siskins, tit-spinetails, earthcreepers, miners, canasteros, cinclodes, new names for most birders. After all this, don't forget to look up! Andean condors, mountain caracaras, aplomado falcons, black chested buzzard eagles and buteo hawks have all been seen in the skies above.

Barbara Knapton, *Birding Alto Andino*, Putre.

Parque Nacional Lauca

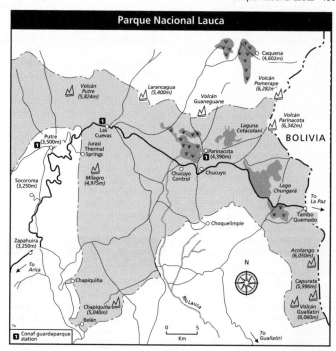

km SE of Parinacota is **Lago Chungará**, one of the highest lakes in the world at 4,600m, a must for its views of the Parinacota, Sajama and Guallatire volcanoes and for its varied wildlife. From here it is about 10 km to the Bolivian frontier at Tambo Quemado. About 30 km S of Parinacota by road is Choquelimpie, the highest gold mine in the world, with an attractive colonial church in the precinct.

Park information
● Accommodation

At Putre: **A2** *Hostería Las Vicuñas*, T 228564, bungalow-style, heating, good restaurant, does not accept TCs, US$ cash or credit cards; *Res La Paloma*, hot showers, no heating, good food; **E** pp *Res Rosamel*, clean, pleasant, hot water, restaurant; **F** pp *Res Oasis*, basic, no showers, cheap, good restaurant; Conaf also rent out 2 rooms, **E** pp basic, no

heating, clean. **Camping**: Sra Clementina Caceres, blue door on C Lynch, allows camping in her garden.

At **Chucuyo**: a village 30 km E of Putre, there are two shops/restaurants, one of which has 2 rooms to let, a good place to stock up on food.

In **Parinacota**: cheap accommodation at the local school, **G** pp, rec.

There are three Conaf refuges in the park, but check in advance with Conaf in Arica that they are open: at **Parincota** (there is supposed to be oxygen for those suffering from soroche, but it is often not available), at **Lago Chungará**, and at **Chucuyo**; all have cooking facilities, but no heating, US$12 pp, sleeping bag essential, take your own food, candles and matches. Camping US$6 tent. Advance booking rec. On arrival in Putre you are supposed to register with Conaf. Maps of the park (unreliable) are sometimes available from Conaf in Arica and from the tourist office.

● **Banks & money changers**
No facilities; buy pesos in Arica.

● **Shopping**
Food is available in Putre, which has several stores, 2 bakeries and where several private houses sell fresh produce. Fuel is much more expensive than in Arica but available in Putre from the Cali and Paloma supermarkets and from **ECA**, a government subsidized market on the plaza (cheapest). No food is available outside Putre.

● **Tours companies & travel agents**
Tours: *Birding Altoandino*, Baquedano 299 (Correo Putre) T 56-58-300013, F 56-58-222735, run general tours and specialist birdwatching tours to remote areas of the park and to the Salar de Surire and Parque Nacional Isluga; English spoken, owner is an Alaskan biologist, 1 day tour of Lauca US$100 for 4 people. *Turismo Taki*, is located in Copaquila, about 45 km W of Putre, 100 km E of Arica: restaurant, camping site and excursions to nearby *pucarás*, Inca *tambo* and cemetery, good local food, English and Italian spoken.

One-day tours are offered by most travel agencies in Arica (addresses above), daily in season, according to demand at other times, US$23 pp with breakfast and light lunch; but some find the minibuses cramped and dusty. You spend all day in the bus and, if not acclimatized, you will suffer from soroche. You can leave the tour and continue on another day as long as you ensure that the company will collect you when you want (tour companies try to charge double for this). For 5 or more, the most economical proposition is to hire a vehicle; fuel is available in Putre, ask at the shop, take at least one spare fuel can.

● **Transport**
Flota Paco buses (known as La Paloma) leave Arica for Putre daily at 0645, 4 hrs, US$4, returning Sun/Wed 1200, otherwise 1300; Jurasi collective taxi leaves Arica daily at 0700, picks up at hotels, T 222813, US$6.50. Bolivia Litoral bus from Arica to La Paz also runs along this route (charges full Arica-La Paz fare).Martínez buses run to Parinacota Tues and Fri.

Hitching back to Arica is not difficult; you may be able to bargain on one of the tour buses. Trucks from Arica to La Paz rarely give lifts, but a good place to try is at the Poconchile control point, 37 km from Arica. Most trucks for Bolivia pass Parinacota between 0700-1100.

FRONTIER WITH BOLIVIA: CHUNGARA

● **Immigration**
Open 0800-2100; US$2/vehicle crossing 1300-1500, 1850-2100 and Sat, Sun and holidays. Long delays are reported at this crossing.

● **Transport**
For details of through buses between Arica and La Paz see above under Arica.

INTO BOLIVIA

This road passes **Sajama**, Bolivia's highest mountain (6,530m), set in the Parque Nacional Sajama. At Sajama village (*pop* 500; *alt* 4,200m) there is basic accommodation and Peter Brunnhart (Señor Pedro) and Telmo Nina have information on routes to the summit. Beyond Sajama is Curahuara de Carangas, then Pata-

---

Travelling in the Northern Altiplano

🐾 "In all of the mountain areas of the N of Chile, it is important to note that weather and road conditions are very variable. The *carabineros* and military are very active trying to control the borders with Bolivia and Argentina, so they know about the conditions and are quite willing to tell, but only if asked. Some frontier areas are closed to visitors.

If you plan to stay in the mountains for any length of time, take small gifts for the locals, such as tea, sugar, coffee, salad oil, flour, or a few litres of fuel. Drivers should carry a tow-rope to assist other drivers. It is often possible to get people to bake bread etc for you, but you need to supply flour, yeast and salt. If you are planning to do much cooking, then a good pressure cooker is indispensible (remember water boils at only 90°C at these altitudes). You may also have problems with kerosene stoves; petrol ones, though rather dangerous, are much more reliable."

Dr Lyndsey O'Callaghan.

camaya, on the main La Paz-Oruro highway (104 km and 130 km respectively). At Patacamaya there is basic accommodation, also restaurants and Sun market.

RESERVA NACIONAL LAS VICUÑAS

South of Lauca is the beautiful **Reserva Nacional Las Vicuñas** at 4,300 to 5,600m, which is suitable for 'adventure tourism', to use Conaf's phrase. Be prepared for cold, skin burns from sun and wind, etc; there is no public transport. A high clearance vehicle is essential and, in the summer wet season, 4WD: take extra fuel. Administration is at **Guallatiri**, reached by turning off the Arica-La Paz road onto the A147 2 km after Las Cuevas, where there is also a Conaf office. Open Mar-November.

MONUMENTO NATURAL SALAR DE SURIRE

The same road leads into the **Monumento Natural Salar de Surire** (4,200m), which is open for the same months and for which the same conditions apply. Administration is in **Surire**, 45 km S of Guallatiri and 129 km S of Putre. This can be reached by getting a ride in a borax truck; these run every day between July and Nov from Zapahuira (a road junction between Bolivia and Arica).

● **Accommodation** At Surire there is a Conaf *refugio*, 4 beds, very clean, prior application to Conaf in Arica essential; Campsite at Polloquere, 16 km S of Surire, no facilities.

South through the
Central Valley

ONE of the world's most fruitful and beautiful countrysides, with the snowclad peaks of the Andes delimiting it to the east, the Central Valley contains most of Chile's population. It is a region of small towns, farms and vineyards, with several protected areas of natural beauty. To the south are the major city of Concepción, the port of Talcahuano and the main coal-mining area.

THE LAND

GEOGRAPHY

This section covers three of the administrative regions of Chile, Regions VI (O'Higgins), VII (Maule) and VIII (Biobío). The Central Valley is a wide depression located between the Andes to the E and the Cordillera de la Costa to the West. The Andes gradually lose height as they continue southwards, although there are a number of high peaks E of Rancagua: Alto de los Arrieros (5,000m), El Palomo (4,986m), Tinguiririca (4,280m). The Coastal Range is low (under 500m) but S of the Río Biobío

it forms a range of high peaks known as the Cordillera de Nahuelbuta. Five major rivers cross the Central Valley, cutting through the Coastal Range to reach the Pacific: from N to S these are the Ríos Rapel, Mataquito, Maule, Itata and Biobío. Of these the Biobío, one of the three largest rivers in Chile, is the most important.

ECONOMY

The Central Valley is the agricultural heartland of Chile, transformed in the past 20 years by the growth of commercial export agriculture: wheat, maize, rice, sugar, beans, vegetables and fruit are grown throughout this area, which also produces most of Chile's wine. Much of

South through the Central Valley

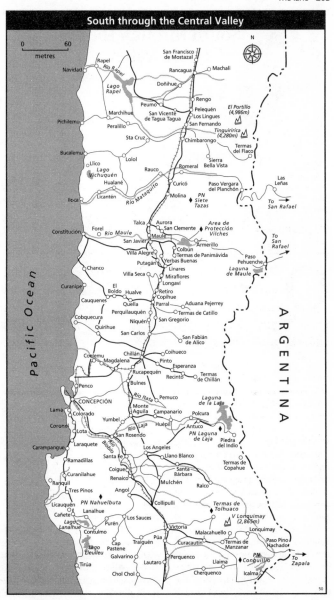

0 — 60
metres

N

Pacific Ocean

A R G E N T I N A

Navidad
San Francisco de Mostazal
Rancagua
Machalí
Rapel
Río Rapel
Lago Rapel
Doñihue
Peumo
Rengo
Peralillo
Marchihue
San Vicente de Tagua Tagua
Pelequén
Los Lingues
San Fernando
El Portillo (4,986m)
Pichilemu
Sta Cruz
Chimbarongo
Tinguiririca (4,280m)
Termas del Flaco
Bucalemu
Lolol
Rauco
Romeral
Sierra Bella Vista
Llico
Lago Vichuquén
Hualañé
Curicó
Paso Vergara del Planchón
Las Leñas
Iloca
Licantén
Río Mataquito
Molina
PN Siete Tazas
To San Rafael
Talca
Aurora
San Clemente
Area de Protección Vilches
Constitución
Forel
Río Maule
Maule
To San Rafael
San Javier
Armerillo
Villa Alegre
Colbún
Termas de Panimávida
Paso Pehuenche
Chanco
Putagán
Yerbas Buenas
Laguna de Maule
Villa Seca
Linares
El Boldo
Hualve
Miraflores
Curanipe
Cauquenes
Quella
Longaví
Retiro
Copihue
Cobquecura
Perquilauquén
Parral
Aduana Pejerrey
Quirihue
Niquén
Termas de Catillo
San Carlos
San Gregorio
San Fabián de Alico
Coelemu
Chillán
Coihueco
Magdalena
Pinto
Penco
Rucapequén
Esperanza
CONCEPCIÓN
Bulnes
Recinto
Termas de Chillán
Pemuco
Río Itata
Laguna de la Laja
Lama
Colorado
Monte Aguila
Campanario
Coronel
Yumbel
Polcura
Lota
Huépil
Antuco
Carampangue
San Rosendo
Río Laja
PN Laguna de Laja
Laraquete
Los Angeles
Piedra del Indio
Ramadillas
Santa Fe
Llano Blanco
Curanilahue
Coigue
Santa Bárbara
Termas de Copahue
Ranquil
Renaico
Mulchén
Tres Pinos
Angol
Ralco
Licauquén
Cañete
PN Nahuelbuta
Collipulli
Lago Lanalhue
Lanalhue
Los Sauces
Termas de Tolhuaco
Contulmo
Purén
Victoria
V Lonquimay (2,865m)
Cap Pastene
Púa
Malacahuello
Lonquimay
Lago Lleulleu
Traiguén
Curacautín
Termas de Manzanar
Paso Pino Hachado
Tirúa
Galvarino
Perquenco
Llaima
PN Conguillío
Lautaro
Chol Chol
Cherquenco
Icalma
To Zapala
Río Biobío

50

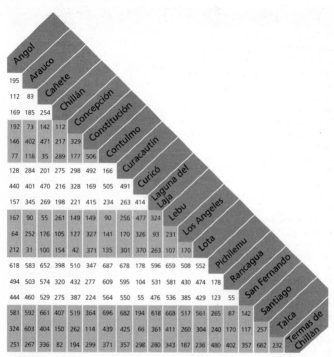

	Angol	Arauco	Cañete	Chillán	Concepción	Constitución	Contulmo	Curacautín	Curicó	Laguna del Laja	Lebu	Los Angeles	Lota	Pichilemu	Rancagua	San Fernando	Santiago	Talca
Arauco	195																	
Cañete	112	83																
Chillán	169	185	254															
Concepción	192	73	142	112														
Constitución	146	402	471	217	329													
Contulmo	77	118	35	289	177	506												
Curacautín	128	284	201	275	298	492	166											
Curicó	440	401	470	216	328	169	505	491										
Laguna del Laja	157	345	269	198	221	415	234	263	414									
Lebu	167	90	55	261	149	149	90	256	477	324								
Los Angeles	64	252	176	105	127	327	141	170	326	93	231							
Lota	212	31	100	154	42	371	135	301	370	263	107	170						
Pichilemu	618	583	652	398	510	347	687	678	178	596	659	508	552					
Rancagua	494	503	574	320	432	277	609	595	104	531	581	430	474	178				
San Fernando	444	460	529	275	387	224	564	550	55	476	536	385	429	123	55			
Santiago	581	592	661	407	519	364	696	682	194	618	668	517	561	265	87	142		
Talca	324	603	404	150	262	114	439	425	66	361	411	260	304	240	170	117	257	
Termas de Chillán	251	267	336	82	194	299	371	357	298	280	343	187	236	480	402	357	682	232

South of Santiago (the Central Valley): distance chart (km)

local industry is based on these products: rice mills, sugar mills, vegetable oil refineries and wineries are important sources of employment. While commercial forestry is based around the Biobío, it is important throughout the central valley. Fishing is of less importance, except around the Biobío: the coastline between Dichato and Arauco saw an important growth in large scale fishing and fish-processing in the 1980s.

The Biobío region is also a major industrial area. Concepcíon and the area around it have become the second most important industrial area in Chile, helped by the construction of the country's only steelworks at Huachipato in the 1950s and the development of major

hydroelectric power plants along the Río Laja. The coastal strip S of Concepción is still the most important coal producing area in Chile, while Talcahuano is the major port serving the region.

CLIMATE

The northern parts of this area enjoy a type of Mediterranean climate with a prolonged dry season, but with more rain than Santiago. In general rainfall increases gradually from N to S in amount and in duration, until around Concepcíon some rain falls in most months. The Central Valley itself receives less rain than the coastal range, but temperatures vary much more inland than in coastal areas.

HISTORY

At the time of the first Spanish incursions, the Río Biobío and the lands S were inhabited by the Mapuches. Further N, in the Central Valley, the indigenous inhabitants, linguistically and culturally related to the Mapuche, had been conquered by the Incas in about 1470. On his second visit to Chile Pedro de Valdivia led an expedition southwards, founding Concepción in 1550 and seven cities S of the Biobío. The Mapuche insurrection of 1598 and the Spanish defeat at Curalabo (1599) led to a Spanish withdrawal north of the Biobío.

The Mapuche uprising also led to the resettlement of many of the early Spanish settlers further N in the Central Valley where the land and inhabitants were divided up between the colonists. This was the origin of the hacienda which was to dominate social and economic life in the Central Valley for at least 200 years. The hacienda was a self-contained unit, producing almost everything needed and consuming its own produce. Until the 18th century there were no towns in the Central Valley, but from the 1740s the Spanish crown founded settlements in an attempt to increase its control. Towns were established at regular intervals along the main route S through the Central Valley: these included San Fernando (1742), Curicó (1743), Talca (1742), Cauquenes (1742) and Linares (1755).

After independence the Río Biobío continued to be the southern frontier of white settlement until in 1862 Col Cornelio Saavedra led an army S to build a line of 10 forts, each 4 km apart, between Angol and Collipulli. Following the occupation of the coast around Arauco in 1867 another line of forts was built across the Cordillera de Nahuelbuta. By 1881 the railway from Santiago had reached Angol, from where Chilean troops set out on the final campaign against the Mapuche.

ROUTES Road and railway run S through the Central Valley; the railway has been electrified from Santiago to just S of Temuco. Along the road from Santiago to Temuco there are several modern motels. From Santiago to San Javier (S of Talca), the highway is dual carriageway, with two tolls of US$3 to pay. The highway between Santiago and Rancagua is dangerous for cyclists (inattentive truck drivers).

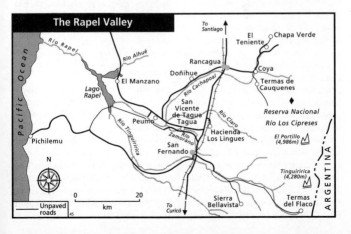

The Rapel Valley

THE RAPEL VALLEY

The Río Rapel is formed by the confluence of two much longer rivers, the Tinguiririca and the Cachapoal. The damming of the Rapel has produced Lago Rapel, the largest artifical lake in Chile. In the valleys of the rivers Cachapoal, Claro and Zamorano, the land is given over to fruit growing (including the estates of Viña Concha y Toro). Towns such as Doñihue, San Vicente de Tagua Tagua and Peumo have their roots in an Indian past which has been replaced by the *huaso* (cowboy) and, more recently, by agroindustry. The main towns in the valley are Rancagua and San Fernando.

RANCAGUA

(*Pop* 167,000; *Phone code* 072), the capital of VI Región (Libertador Gen Bernardo O'Higgins), lies 82 km S of Santiago, on the Río Cachapoal. Founded in 1743, it is a service and market centre for a rich agricultural area, easily visited from Santiago.

Places of interest

At the heart of the city is an attractive tree-lined plaza, the **Plaza de los Héroes**, and several streets of single-storey colonial-style houses. In the centre of the plaza is an equestrian statue of O'Higgins. The **Merced** church, 1 block N, several times restored, dates from 1758. The main commercial area lies along Av Independencia which runs W from the plaza towards the bus and rail terminals.

Museums

The **Museo Histórico**, Estado y Ibieta, housed in a colonial mansion, contains collections of religious art and late 19th century furniture.

Excursions

To the thermal springs of **Cauquenes**, 28 km E, reached by colectivo from Rancagua market (**A3** *Hotel Termas de Cauquenes*, T 297226, excellent, clean, excellent food, chapel, gardens, rec). 5 km N of Cauquenes is the village of **Coya**, where the Chilean President has a summer residence.

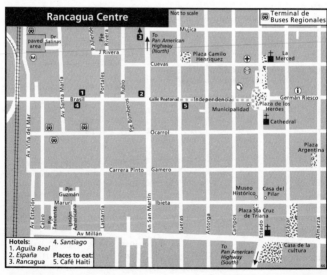

Rancagua Centre

Hotels:
1. Aguila Real
2. España
3. Rancagua
4. Santiago

Places to eat:
5. Café Haiti

The battle of Rancagua

Rancagua was the scene of an important battle during the Wars of Independence. On 1-2 Oct Bernardo O'Higgins and his 1,700 Chilean patriots were surrounded in the centre of the town by 4,500 Royalist (pro-Spanish) troops. O'Higgins, who commanded his forces from the tower of the Merced church, managed to break out and escape. Following this defeat he was forced into exile in Argentina, while the Royalists reestablished control over Chile. While in Argentina O'Higgins met up with San Martín who led the invasion force across the Andes which resulted in the final defeat of Spanish forces in Chile. Plaques in the centre of Rancagua mark the sites of the battle and a diagram in the Plaza de los Héroes shows the disposition of the troops. The battle resulted in the destruction of most of the buildings around the Plaza.

Local festivals

National Rodeo Championships, at the end of March (plenty of opportunities for purchasing cowboy items). **Festival del Poroto** (Bean Festival), 1-5 February.

Local information

● **Accommodation**

B *Aguila Real*, Brasil 1055, T 222047, inc breakfast; **B** *Santiago*, Brasil 1036, T 230855, poorly maintained, friendly; **B** *Rancagua*, San Martín 85, T 232663, F 241155, with bath, quiet, clean, secure parking, rec.

C *España*, San Martín 367, T 230141, with bath, less without, central, hot water, pleasant, clean. Many hotels do not accept guests before 2000, or may charge you double if you arrive in the afternoon. Some 50 km S (22 km N of San Fernando) is *Hacienda Los Lingues*, see page 209.

● **Places to eat**

Café Haiti, Paseo Independencia 690, p 2, lively at night; *Bravissimo*, Astorga 307, for ice cream; *Lasagna*, W end of Plaza, for bread and *empanadas*.

● **Banks & money changers**

Afex, Av Campos 363, for US$ cash; *Fincard*, Av Campos 376, Mon-Fri 0900-1400, 1530-1930, Sat 1000-1300, for Mastercard.

● **Tourist offices**

Germán Riesco 277, T 230413, helpful, English spoken. **Automóvil Club de Chile**: Ibieta 09, T 239930.

● **Transport**

Motorists For car parts try *Aucamar*, Brasil 1177, T 223594, and several others around Brasil 1100-1200, better selection and prices in Santiago.

Trains Main line services between Santiago and Concepción and Chillán stop here. Also regular services to/from Santiago on Metrotren, 1¼ hrs, 10-13 a day, US$2.

Buses Main terminal at Ocarrol y Calvo; local buses leave from the Terminal de Buses Regionales, just N of the market. Frequent services to Santiago, US$3, 1 hr 10 mins.

Lago Rapel, SW of Rancagua, is 40 km in length and feeds the Rapel hydroelectric plant. Although much of the N and S shores of the lake are inaccessible by road, it is rapidly becoming a popular Chilean holiday destination. Most facilities are on the E shore around El Manzano, the main town. There are watersports at Bahía Skorpios.

● **Accommodation A1** *Punta Verde*, Bahía Skorpios, T 591248; **C** *Hostería Playa Llallauquén*, T 751-5281 and many more. The E shore of the lake around El Manzano is lined with campsites (*Camping Punta Arenas*, 3 km N of El Manzano, basic, cheap).

East of Rancagua

The **El Teniente** copper mine, one of the biggest in the country, lies 67 km East. Owned by Codelco, it can only be visited by prior arrangement with the company. Nearby, on a private road above El Teniente, is the small **Chapa Verde** ski resort, owned by Codelco, but open to the public in season. It can only be reached by mine-transport bus (from Del Sol shopping centre, daily 0900,

Rodeo – coming of age as a cow

🐾 During the summer months rodeo is one of the most popular sports in central and southern Chile. Teams (or *colleras*) of two riders on horseback compete throughout the season which culminates in the national championships held in Rancagua at the end of March. Eliminatory rounds are held in Osorno, Temuco, San Carlos, San Fernando, Vallenar and Los Andes, but most small towns in central southern Chile have their own *media lunas* (stadia) which may be used once a year only.

Rodeo owes its origins to the colonial period, when cattle roamed the open spaces and were rounded up to be identified and marked by their owners once a year in a *rodeo*. Based on the traditional view that heifers need to be broken in, the modern sport of rodeo is a test of the ability of two horses and their riders to work together.

The event takes place inside a stockade of thick upright timbers; although now circular, this is known as a *media luna* (crescent) after the design of the early rings: at two points the walls of the ring are covered by padded sections with a flag at either end of the section. Each *collera* competes by manoeuvring a heifer around the edge of the ring between the padded sections, stopping it at each padded section by pinning its hindquarters against the fence, before turning it in the opposite direction. This is done three times before the animal is released from the ring. Three judges give points (on a scale of 1 to 7) for skills of horsemanship and elegance.

It is one of the principles of rodeo that no heifer should be put through this performance more than once; for the heifer the event should come as a complete surprise. Since there are far more heifers than rodeos to break them in, many farms have their own rings, where heifers are broken in without an audience.

Rodeo is a good opportunity to see traditional Chilean rural customs: the *huasos* (cowboys) in wide-brimmed hats, brightly coloured ponchos and the carved wooden stirrups which were common in the nineteenth century, the fine horses and the *cuecas* (traditional dances) which sometimes follow the event.

weekends in season every 15 mins between 0800 and 0930). Equipment can be hired, no accommodation, lift tickets US$18 weekdays, US$25 weekends, obtainable only from resort office in Del Sol shopping centre.

Reserva Nacional Río de los Cipreses

Situated 50 km SE of Rancagua and 22 km from the Termas de Cauquenes, the park covers 36,882 ha of the valley of the Río de los Cipreses at altitudes ranging from 900m to 4,900m. Park administration is at the entrance at the N end of the park, T 297505. There is a campsite at Los Maitenes, 12 km S of the entrance.

SAN FERNANDO

(*Pop* 44,500; *Alt* 460m; *Phone code* 072), lies on the Río Tinguiririca 51 km S of Rancagua. Founded in 1742, it is capital of Colchagua Province and a service town for this fertile valley. From San Fernando a road runs E towards the Cordillera and divides: the northern branch (75 km) runs to the **Termas del Flaco**, (*Alt* 1,720m) near the Argentine frontier (poor campsite, *cabañas* and hotels, but open only in summer when it attracts large numbers of visitors); the southern branch goes to the resort of **Sierra Bellavista**, a private *fundo* where many Santiago businessmen have holiday houses.

Rodeos in Oct and November.

Excursions Los Lingues is a private *hacienda* 20 km NE of San Fernando, 126 km S of Santiago, where, it is said, the best horses in Chile are bred. Rosie Swale was lent two of them for her epic ride from Antofagasta to Cape Horn, described in *Back to Cape Horn* (Collins, London, 1986). Visits can be arranged to the 17th century house, a gift of the King of Spain. One-day tours including transport, rodeo and lunch are available, also accommodation with extra charge for breakfast or full board, very expensive (the Hacienda is a member of the French Hotels et Relais et Chateaux). Contact: Hacienda Los Lingues, Torre C de Tajamar, Of 205, Santiago, T 235-2458/5446/7604, F 235-7604, Tx 346060 LINGUES CK. To 6060 LINGUE.

● **Accommodation** On Av Rodríguez: **C** *Español*, No 959, T 711098; **D** *Marcano*, No 968, T 714759; **E** *Imperio*, No 770, T 714595, with bath, clean; **D** *Pérez*, No 1028, T 713328, without bath.

Pichilemu

(*Pop* 6,827) 120 km W of San Fernando (road 86 km paved) is a coastal resort with a great many hotels and *residenciales* and several beaches, including the Punta Los Lobos beach, where international surfing competitions are held.

● **Accommodation** **B** *Chile-España*, Ortúzar 255, T 841270, friendly, helpful, excellent restaurant, good value; **C** *Rex*, Ortúzar 34, T 681003, good breakfast, good value; **E** *Bahía*, Ortúzar 262, with breakfast, clean. **Camping**: Campsites, US$15/site, more expensive than *residenciales*.

● **Transport** Andimar bus to **Santiago**, 4 hrs, US$5.50.

THE MATAQUITO VALLEY

The Río Mataquito, formed by the confluence of the rivers Lontué and Teno, flows through the heart of the Chilean wine country reaching the Pacific near Iloca.

CURICO

(*Pop* 103,919; *Alt* 200m; *Phone code* 075) 54 km S of San Fernando and 192 km from Santiago, Curicó lies between the Ríos Lontué and Teno. Founded in 1744, it is the only town of any size in the valley.

Places of interest

In the **Plaza de Armas** there are lovely fountains with sculptures of nymphs, black-necked swans and a monument to the Mapuche warrior, Lautaro, carved from the trunk of an ancient beech tree. There is a steel kiosk, built in New Orleans in 1904, which is a national monument. The church of **San Francisco** (1732), also a national monument, partly ruined, contains the 17th century Virgen de Velilla, brought from Spain. At the junction of Carmen and Av San Martín is the imposing **Iglesia del Carmen**. The fine, broad and tree-lined Av Manso de Velasco leads to **Parque Balmaceda**, in which is a bust of the poet, Gabriela Mistral. Overlooking the city, the surrounding countryside and with views to the distant Andean peaks is **Cerro Condell** (100m); it is an easy climb to the summit from where there are a number of walks.

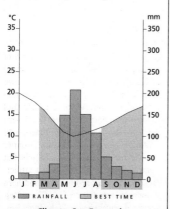

Climate: San Fernando

Excursions

To the **Torres wine bodega**, 5 km S of the city: take a bus for Molina from Henríquez y O'Higgins and get off at Km 195 on the Pan-American Highway, open 0900-1300, 1500-1800, no organized tour, Spanish only, worthwhile.

Local information

● Accommodation

B *Luis Cruz Martines*, Prat 301 y Carmen, T 310552, breakfast extra, overpriced.

C *Comercio*, Yungay 730, T 312442, rec.

D *Res Rahue*, Peña 410, T 312194, basic, meals, hot water, annex rooms have no ventilation.

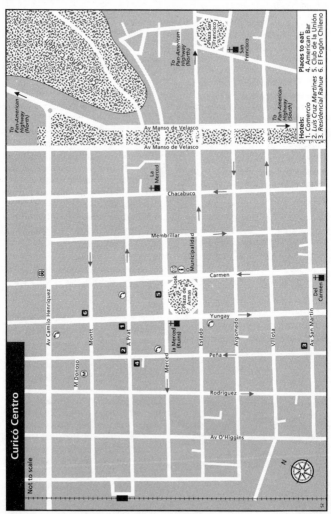

Curicó Centro

Not to scale

Hotels:
1. Comercio
2. Luis Cruz Martines
3. Residencial Rahue

Places to eat:
4. American Bar
5. Club de la Unión
6. El Fogón Chileno

D *Res Central*, Av Prat, 2 blocks from station, good value.

E *Prat*, Peña 427, T 311069, pleasant patio, friendly, clean, hot water, laundry facilities; **E** *Res Colonial*, Rodríguez 461, clean, patio, friendly.

● **Places to eat**
El Fogón Chileno, Yungay 802, good for meat and wines; *American Bar*, Yungay 647, coffee, small pizzas, good sandwiches, pleasant atmosphere, open early am to late pm inc weekends, rec; *Café-Bar Maxim*, Prat 617, light meals, beer and wine. *Club de la Unión*, Plaza de Armas, good; *Centro Italiano Club Social*, Estado 531, good, cheap meals.

● **Banks & money changers**
Fincard, Carmen 498, for Mastercard. **Casa de Cambio**, Merced 255, Local 106, no TCs.

● **Laundry & dry cleaners**
Limpiabien, Prat 454 (and other branches), quick, efficient.

● **Post & telecommunications**
Telephones: CTC, Peña 650-A.

● **Tourist offices**
Tourist information supplied by the Mayor's secretary, Gobernación building, p 2, Plaza de Armas, helpful, has street map. **Automóvil Club de Chile**: Chacabuco 759, T 311156. **Conaf**: Gobernación, p 1, Plaza de Armas.

● **Transport**
Trains Station is at the end of Prat, 4 blocks W of Plaza de Armas, T 310028. To/from Santiago, 5 a day, US$4 *económico*, US$5 *superior*. To/from Concepción 1 a day.

Buses Companies have their own terminals for interprovincial destinations. Local buses, inc to coastal towns, from Terminal Rural, O'Higgins y Prat, 1 block E of railway station. Many southbound buses by-pass Curicó, but can be caught by waiting outside town. To **Santiago** US$3, 3 hrs; to **Temuco**, LIT and Tur Bus, US$7.

ROUTES There is a toll (US$3) on the Longitudinal Highway S of Curicó. The city has a good road connection with Argentina, via Paso Vergara (Paso del Planchón, 92 km from Curicó) to San Rafael (transport schedules from Turismo Bucalemu, Yungay 621).

Area de Proteccíon Radal Siete Tazas

The park is in 2 sectors, one at Radal, 65 km E of Curicó, the other at Parque Inglés, 9 km further east. The most interesting sector is at Radal, where the Río Claro flows through a series of seven rock bowls (the *siete tazas*) each with a pool emptying into the next by means of a waterfall. The river then passes through a canyon, 15m deep but only 1½m wide, which ends abruptly in a cliff and a beautiful waterfall. The park is open Oct to March. Administration is in Parque Inglés.

● **Accommodation D** *Hostería La Flor de la Canela*, at Parque Inglés, inc breakfast, T 491613, good food, highly rec, camping, open summer only. **Camping**: campsites near entrance, dirty.

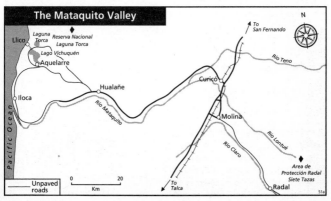

The Mataquito Valley
51a

● **Transport** Buses from Molina, 26 km S of Curicó to the Park, on Tues and Thur 1700, returning Wed and Fri 0800. Daily bus from Curicó in summer, 1545, 4½ hrs, returns 0745 (Sun 0700, returns 1900).

WEST OF CURICO

From Curicó a road runs W to the mouth of the Río Mataquito and the popular resort of **Iloca**.

● **Accommodation** C *Iloca*, T 887998; C *Hostería de Iloca*, T 671692. **Camping**: *La Puntilla*, 2 km N, good facilities; *El Peñon*, 6 km S, Reservations: Santiago, T 633-6099.

Llico, another resort, is N of Iloca, reached either by a coastal route or by an unpaved inland road which branches off at Hualañe (Km 74).

● **Accommodation** D *Res Atlántida 2000*, nr beach, good restaurant, bar, friendly, discount for *South American Handbook* readers; D *Hostería Llico*; *Res Miramar*, good seafood restaurant; D *Pensión Chile*, clean, friendly, rooms with bath have hot water, cheap meals.

● **Transport** Buses, from Terminal Rural in Curicó, by Bravo and Llomar companies, both daily 1230 and 1540, also Díaz, Mon-Sat 1530, 3 hrs.

Lago Vichuquén

A large lake surrounded by pine forest, 114 km W of Curicó, lies just E of Llico. It is very popular with the wealthy and with water-sports enthusiasts. Parts of the eastern shore of the lake are inaccessible by road, but there are full facilities on the western shore, particularly at Aquelarre.

● **Accommodation** A1-A2 *Hostería El Club de Yates*, well-equipped, restful, good food; other hotels. **Camping**: *Vichuquén*, on E shore, T 400062, full facilities; *El Sauce*, at N end of lake, F 75-400203, good facilities.

RESERVA NACIONAL LAGUNA TORCA

Situated just N of Lago Vichuquén, 120 km W of Curicó, this park, covering 604 ha, is a natural sanctuary for over 80 species of birds, especially black-necked

swans and other water fowl. Administration is 4 km E of Llico; campsite nearby. Open Sept-April.

● **Transport** Take any bus from Curicó to Llico and get out near Administration.

THE MAULE VALLEY

The Río Maule, 240 km long flows from Laguna Maule in the Andes to the sea at Constitución. Its waters have been dammed E of Talca, providing power and creating Lago Colbún.

TALCA

(*Pop* 160,000; *Phone code* 071) situated on the S bank of the Río Claro, a tributary of the Maule, lies 56 km S of Curicó (258 km from Santiago, all dual carriageway). The most important city between Santiago and Concepción it is a major manufacturing centre and the capital of VII Región (Maule). Founded in 1692, it was destroyed by earthquakes in 1742 and 1928.

Places of interest

In the **Plaza de Armas** are statues looted by the Talca Regiment from Peru during the War of the Pacific. Just off the Plaza at 1 Norte y 2 Oriente is the **Museo**

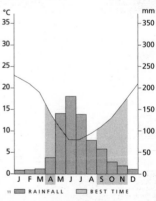

Climate: Talca

O'Higginiano (open Tues-Sat, 0915-1245, 1500-1845, US$1) located in a colonial mansion which belonged to Juan Albano Pereira, tutor to the young Bernardo O'Higgins who lived here between the ages of 4 and 10. The house was later the headquarters of O'Higgins' Patriot Government in 1813-14 (before his defeat at Rancagua). In 1818 O'Higgins signed the declaration of Chilean independence here: the room (Sala Independencia) is decorated and furnished in period style. 8 km SE is **Villa Huilquilemu**, a 19th century hacienda, now part of the Universidad Católica del Maule, housing four museums, of religious art, handicrafts, agricultural machinery and wine.

Local information
● **Accommodation**

On the Panamericana Sur, Km 250, are **A3** *Cabañas Entre Ríos*, T 223336, F 220477 (Santiago: San Antonio 486, of 132, T 633-3750, F 632-4791), very good value, excellent breakfast, pool, very helpful owner, highly rec. **A3** *Plaza*, 1 Poniente 1141, T 226150, good commercial standard; **C** *Amalfi*, 2 Sur 1265, T 225703, old-fashioned, central, very clean; **D** *Alcázar*, 2 Sur 1359, breakfast and meals available, rec as reasonable and clean; **D** pp

Cordillera, 2 Sur 1360, T 221812, F 233028, nr bus terminal.

● **Banks & money changers**
Edificio Caracol, Oficina 15, 1 Sur 898, for US$ cash; Fincard (Mastercard), 1 Sur 826.

● **Post & telecommunications**
Post Office: 1 Oriente s/n.
Telephones: CTC, 1 Sur 1156 and 1 Sur 835.

● **Tourist offices**
1 Poniente 1234, T 233669. **Automóvil Club de Chile**: 1 Poniente 1267, T 223-2774.

● **Transport**
Trains Station at 2 Sur y 11 Oriente, T 226254. To **Santiago**, 5 a day, US$5; to **Concepción**, 1 a day, to **Temuco** 1 a day.

Buses Terminal at 12 Oriente y 2 Sur. To **Chillán**, frequent service, US$2; also frequent to **Constitución**, 2 hrs, US$1.20.

EAST OF TALCA

A road from Talca runs 175 km SE along **Lago Colbún** and up the valley of the Río Maule, passing through some of the finest mountain scenery in Chile to reach the Argentine frontier at Paso Pehuenche.

● **Accommodation** *El Colorado*, on N shore of Lago Colbún, T/F 221750; **C** pp *Centro Portezuelo*, at Quinamávida, S of Lago Colbún on the road to Linares, T 09-7520510,

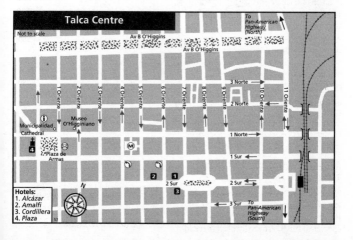

Talca Centre
Not to scale

Hotels:
1. Alcázar
2. Amalfi
3. Cordillera
4. Plaza

full board, large *estancia* offering forest trails, beaches, English spoken, highly rec.

VILCHES

63 km E of Talca, is the starting point for the climb to the volcanoes Quizapu and Descabezado (3,850m). For walks on Descabezado Grande and Cerro Azul (ice axe and crampons needed) contact recommended guide Carlos Verdugo Bravo, Probación Brilla El Sol, Pasaje El Nickel 257, Talca (Spanish only).

● **Accommodation C** pp *Hostería Rancho Los Canales*, with breakfast, use of kitchen, good food, log cabins C for 4 people, hospitable, pool, knowledgeable family (postal address: Casilla 876, Talca).

● **Transport** Two buses a day, US$1.50, 2-2½ hrs, leave Talca 1300 and 1650, leave Vilches 0700 and 1730.

The Area de Protección Vilches

2 km from Vilches, covers 16,684 ha and includes the peaks, El Peine (2,448m), El Picazo (2,322m) and El Afligido (2,290m), several small lakes, the Piedras Tacitas, a stone construction supposedly made by the aboriginal inhabitants of the region, and a visitors' centre. The administration is 1 km from the *Hotel Altos de Vilches* (closed).

FRONTIER WITH ARGENTINA: PASO PEHUENCHE

Paso Pehuenche (2,553m) is reached by unpaved road SE from Lago Colbún (see above). On the Argentine side the road continues to Malargüe and San Rafael. The border is open Dec-Mar 0800-2100, April-Nov 0800-1900.

CONSTITUCION

(*Pop* 28,748) lies W of Talca at the mouth of the Río Maule and is reached by road (89 km) from San Javier. Founded in 1794, it is an industrial town with naval shipyards and a cellulose factory; fishing is also important. Its main attraction is as a seaside resort, popular with Chileans in season. The beach, an easy walk from the town, is surrounded by very picturesque rocks. There are good views from Cerro Mutrún, at the mouth of the river (access from C O'Higgins).

● **Accommodation A2** *Hostería Constitución*, Echeverría 460, T 671450, best; **C** *Avendaño*, O'Higgins 681, pleasant patio, restaurant, friendly, safe; **D** *Res Urrutia*, Freire 238, inc breakfast, some rooms gloomy, laun-

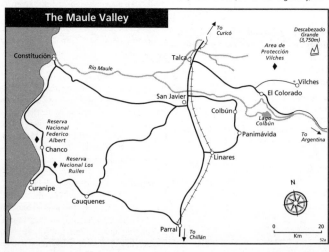

The Maule Valley

dry facilities; **D** *Res Fadiz*, Bulnes nr bus terminal, clean, laundry facilities; other *residenciales* in Freire 100-300 blocks, Portales 300 block and Rengifo 300 block. Many more hotels and *residenciales*, but book in advance from Jan to March.

SOUTH OF CONSTITUCION

A paved road runs along the coast to **Curanipe**, 83 km S, which has a beautiful beach. This area can also be rached by paved road from Parral via Cauquenes.

● **Accommodation** **C** *Pacífico*, Comercio 509, T 495903, pleasant, clean; **C** *La Bahía*, Comercio 438; several others; municipal campsite.

Nearby there are two **Reservas Nacionales: Los Ruiles**, off the road E to Cauquenes, covers 45 ha of native forest and flowers. Open Oct-March; daily buses from Constitución or Cauquenes. **Federico Albert**, on the coast ½ km N of Chanco, covers 145 ha of dunes and forest planted in experiments to control the shifting sand. It has a visitors' centre and campsite; open Oct-March.

PARRAL

(*Pop* 1,000; *Alt* 171m) 88 km S of Talca on the Pan-American Highway (342 km S of Santiago), is celebrated as the birthplace of the Nobel Prize-winning poet Pablo Neruda (see also under Santiago **Museums**, La Chascona, page 88, and Isla Negra, page 126. **NB** In late 1996 the Highway around Parral was being made into a dual carriageway.

● **Accommodation** **D** *Brescia*, Igualdad 195, T 422675, without bath, clean, good restaurant; **D** *Santiago*, opp station, large old-fashioned rooms, clean; **E** *Res do Brasil*, C 18, clean, quiet; campsite.

The Río Itata and its longer tributary, the Río Ñuble, flow W reaching the Pacific some 60 km N of Concepción.

CHILLAN

(*Pop* 146,000; *Alt* 118m; *Phone code* 042), 150 S of Talca, is capital of Ñuble province and a service centre for this agricultural area. Founded in 1580 and destroyed by the Mapuche, the city has been moved several times. Following an earthquake in 1833, the site was moved slightly to the NW, though the older site, now known as Chillán Viejo, is still occupied. Further earthquakes in 1939 and 1960 have ensured that few old buildings have survived. Chillán was the birthplace of Bernardo O'Higgins (Arturo Prat, Chile's naval hero, was born 50 km away at Ninhue).

Places of interest

Northwest of the Plaza O'Higgins, in the **Escuela México**, at Av O'Higgins between Vega de Saldías and Gamero, donated to the city after the 1939 earthquake, are murals by the great Mexican artists David Alvaro Siqueiros and Xavier Guerrero which present allegories of Chilean and Mexican history. The **San Francisco** church, 3 blocks NE of the Plaza, contains a **museum** of religious and historical artefacts; the adjoining **convent** (1835) was a big centre for missionary work among the Mapuche. The modern **Cathedral** on the Plaza O'Higgins is designed to resist earthquakes five streets W of the Plaza is the Iglesia Padres Carmelita. The **Mercado y Feria Municipal** (covered and open markets) sells regional arts and crafts and has many cheap, good restaurants, serving regional dishes; open daily, Sun until 1300. In **Chillán Viejo** (SW of the centre) there is a monument and park in honour of O'Higgins; it has a 60m long mural depicting his life (an impressive, but sadly faded, mosaic of various native stones), and a **Centro Histórico y Cultural**, with a gallery of contemporary paintings by regional artists (park is open 0900-1300, 1500-1900.

Museums

Museo Naval Arturo Prat, Collín y I Riquelme, contains naval artefacts and models Chilean vessels, Tues-Fri 0930-1200, 1500-1730.

Excursions

27 km SW of Chillán is **Quinchamalí**, a little village famous for the originality of its craftsmen in textiles, basketwork, black ceramics, guitars and primitive paintings (all on sale in Chillán market).

Local information
● **Accommodation**
A2 *Isabel Riquelme*, Arauco 600, T 213663.

B *Cordillera*, Arauco 619, on Plaza de Armas, T 215221, 3-star, small, all rooms with heating and bath, good; **B** *Rucamanqui*, Herminda Martín 590 (off Plaza de Armas), T 222927, clean, spartan; **B** *Floresta*, 18 de Septiembre, 268, quiet, old fashioned, friendly.

C *Quinchamalí*, El Roble 634, T 223381, central, quiet, clean, hot water, heated lounge; **C** *Nevado de Chillán*, O'Higgins 497, T 221013, with bath, D without, good value.

D *Libertador*, Libertad 85, T 223155, large rooms, clean, hot water; **D** *Real*, Libertad 219, T 221827, good; these two are a few minutes' walk from the railway station and are much better than the closer hotels such as *Chillán*, Libertad 85 (short-stay), and **E** *Bahía*, opp

station, no hot water, clean but basic, good restaurant below; **D** *Res Su Casa*, Cocharcas 555, T 223931, inc breakfast, clean, parking; **D** *Claris*, 18 de Septiembre 357, T 221983, 2 blocks from plaza, clean, friendly, good value, hot water, rec; **D** *Barcelona*, opp bus terminal, without bath, clean, friendly, above noisy restaurant; **E** *Hosp Sonia Segui*, Itata 288, T214879, good breakfast, small rooms, run down, but friendly.

● **Places to eat**
Centro Español, Plaza de Armas, separate bar with snacks, excellent; *Fuente Alemana*, Arauco 661, for *churrasco*, reasonable; *Café París*, Arauco 686, expresso coffee, fine restaurant upstairs, rec; *Club Comercial*, Arauco 745, popular at lunchtime, good value *almuerzo*, popular bar at night; *Quick Lunch*, El Roble 610, open 0800-2400 for good value meals with good service; *Arco Iris*, Plaza de Armas, vegetarian, lunches only, excellent; *O'Higgins*, O'Higgins y Libertad, good value; *Jai Yang*, Libertad 250, good Chinese; *La Copucha*, 18 de Septiembre y Constitución, inexpensive meals and sandwiches; *Café Madrid*, 5 de Abril 608, good for coffee; *La Masc'a*, 5 de Abril 544, excellent cheap meals, *empanadas de queso*, drinks, rec. In Chillán Viejo, *Los Adobes*, on Parque O'Higgins, good food and service, reasonable prices. The Chillán area is well-known for its *pipeño* wine (very young) and its *longanizas* (sausages).

● **Banks & money changers**
Both **Banco de Concepción** and **Banco Sudamericano** give poor rates. Better rates at

Chillán Cathedral 1870,
Iconografía de Chillán 1835-1939,
Marco Aurelio Reyes 1989

Modern Cathedral

Casa de Cambio, Constitución 550, or *Café París* on Arauco (ask for Enrique Schuler). **Fincard** (Mastercard), El Roble 553.

● Language schools

Interswop JB Turismo, Constitución 633, Of 03, T 223526, F 210744, offers exchange programmes with opportunities for work and language courses, US$180 for 25 hrs study. (Address in Germany: Bornstrasse 16, 20146 Hamburg, T/F 40-410-8029.)

● Tour companies & travel agents

JB Turismo, address above, has information and offers tours.

● Tourist offices

In Gobernación building on main plaza, central courtyard, left-hand gallery; street map of city, leaflets on skiing, Termas de Chillán, etc. **Automóvil Club de Chile**: O'Higgins 677, T 212550.

Two interesting publications on Chillán are: *Iconografía de Chillán, 1835-1939*, by Marco Aurelio Reyes (Universidad del Bío-Bío, 1989) which describes the history of Chillán up to the devastating 1939 earthquake with text, photographs and documents; and *Chillán me persigue*, by Luis Guzmán Molina, Sergio Hernández, Marco Aurelio Reyes and Norman

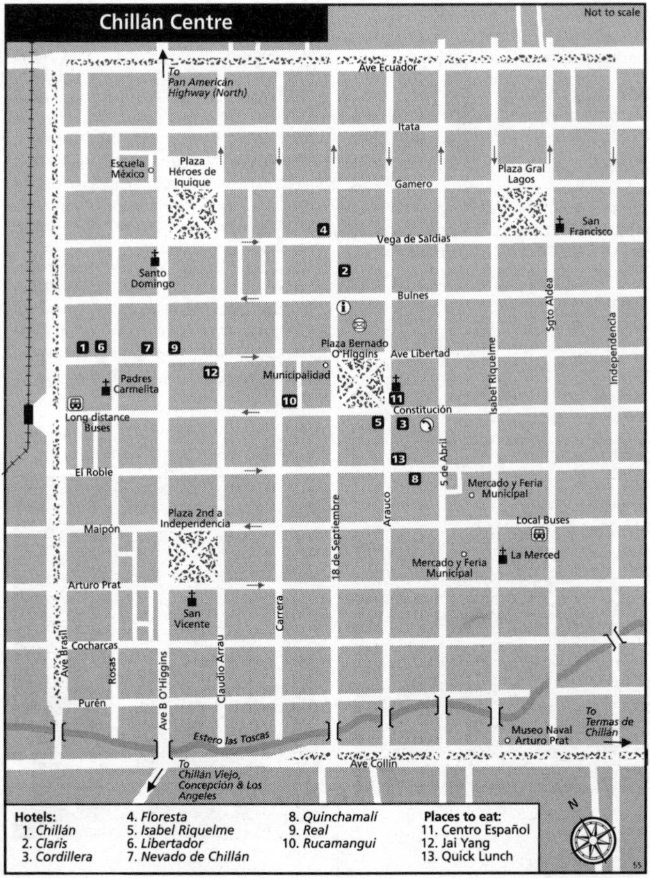
Chillán Centre
Not to scale
To Pan American Highway (North)
Ave Ecuador
Itata
Gamero
Vega de Saldias
Bulnes
Ave Libertad
Constitución
El Roble
Maipón
Arturo Prat
Cocharcas
Purén
Ave Collín
Escuela México
Plaza Héroes de Iquique
Plaza Gral Lagos
San Francisco
Santo Domingo
Plaza Bernado O'Higgins
Municipalidad
Padres Carmelita
Long distance Buses
Mercado y Feria Municipal
Local Buses
La Merced
Plaza 2nd a Independencia
San Vicente
Museo Naval Arturo Prat
To Termas de Chillán
Estero las Toscas
To Chillán Viejo, Concepción & Los Angeles
Ave Brasil
Rosas
Ave B O'Higgins
Claudio Arrau
Carrera
18 de Septiembre
Arauco
5 de Abril
Isabel Riquelme
Sgto Aldea
Independencia
Hotels:
1. Chillán
2. Claris
3. Cordillera
4. Floresta
5. Isabel Riquelme
6. Libertador
7. Nevado de Chillán
8. Quinchamalí
9. Real
10. Rucamangui
Places to eat:
11. Centro Español
12. Jai Yang
13. Quick Lunch

Violeta and the Parra family of Chillán

Violeta and Nicanor Parra were two of the 11 children of Nicanor and Clarisa Parra. The family was brought up in Chillán. Nicanor (father) was a music teacher, Clarisa, a seamstress who played the guitar and sang. Most of the children were artistic in some way. Violeta sang with her sister Hilda in Santiago bars for several years. She also worked in the circus. Nicanor (son) became a professor of maths and physics. His poetry is discussed elsewhere, as is that of Pablo de Rokha, who was a great friend of Violeta. Together Violeta and de Rokha travelled the length of Chile and abroad collecting material for and promoting their idea of Chilean-ness. While de Rokha expressed himself in the lyrical epic, Violeta sang, wrote songs, made tapestries, ceramics, paintings and sculpture. All her work was based on a philosophy of helping those in need. In France she was recognized as a great artist and her works were exhibited in the Louvre in 1964, but at home recognition was only grudgingly given. Neruda called her "Santa Violeta"; the Peruvian novelist José María Arguedas described her as "the most Chilean of all Chileans I could possibly know, but at the same time the most universal of all Chile". In the 1960s she set up her *La Carpa de la Reina* as a centre for popular art in the capital. It was here, in Feb 1967, that she committed suicide, her head resting on her guitar. The national grief at her funeral far outweighed the acclaim given her during her life. Her daughter Isabel was also a singer, as was her son, Angel, whose radical views prompted the military government to arrest him after the 1973 coup and imprison him in the Pisagua concentration camp.

For Violeta, folklore was a form of class struggle. Her influence on a whole generation of Latin American folk singers was enormous and, without her, Salvador Allende would not have had the folkloric backing of Victor Jara, Inti-Illimani, Los Quilapayún and Angel and Isabel Parra themselves. After her death, her brother, Nicanor, had published *Décimas*, a sort of autobiography in verse, full of simple humanity.

"Gracias a la vida"

Gracias a la vida que me ha dado tanto
Me dio dos luceros, que cuando los abro
perfecto distingo lo negro del blanco,
y en el cielo su fondo estrellado
y en las multitudes al hombre que yo amo.

Gracias a la vida que me ha dado tanto.
Me ha dado el oído, que en todo su ancho
graba noche y día grillos y canarios;
martillos, turbinas, ladridos, chubascos,
y la voz tan tierna de mi bienamado ...

Gracias a la vida que me ha dado tanto.
Me ha dado la risa y me ha dado el llanto,
así yo distingo dicha de quebranto,
los dos materiales que forman mi canto,
y el canto de ustedes que es el mismo canto
y el canto de todos que es mi propio canto.

"Thanks to Life"

I give thanks to life which has given me so much.
It gave me two eyes, and when I open them
I distinguish perfectly black from white,
and in the sky its starry depths
and in the crowds the man that I love.

I give thanks to life which has given me so much.
It has given me hearing, which in all its breadth
records night and day the crickets and canaries;
hammers, turbines, barks and squalls,
and the tender voice of my beloved ...

I give thanks to life which has given me so much.
It has given me laughter and it has given me tears,
so that I can tell good fortune from despair,
the two materials which make up my song,
and your song which is the same song
and everyone's song which is my own song.

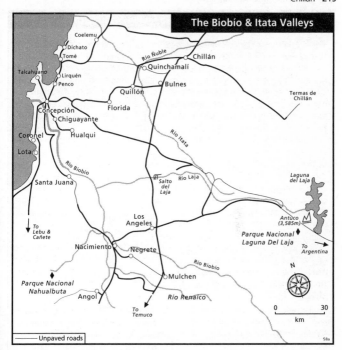

The Biobío & Itata Valleys

Unpaved roads

Ahumada, which contains images of Chillán in drawings, poetry and prose (1995).

● **Transport**

Trains Station, Brasil opp Libertad, 5 blocks from plaza, T 222424. To **Santiago**, 2 daily, 5½ hrs, *salón* US$7-7.35 depending on the service, *económico* US$5-5.35.

Buses Long distance buses leave from Constitución y Brasil (opp railway station). Local buses leave from Maipon y Sgto Aldea. To **Santiago**, 7 hrs, US$7.50; to **Concepción**, every 30 mins.

TERMAS DE CHILLAN

Situated 82 km E of Chillán by good road (paved for the first 50 km) 1,850m up in the Cordillera at the foot of the double-cratered Chillán volcano are thermal baths and, above, the largest ski resort in southern Chile. There are two open air thermal pools (officially for hotel guests only) and a health spa with jacuzzis, sauna, mud baths etc. The ski resort includes rental shops, restaurants, bars, ski-school, heli-skiing, first aid and nursery. Suitable for families and beginners and cheaper than centres nearer Santiago, Chillán is to be expanded in 1997 with a new luxury hotel and more lifts. Season: middle Dec to the end of March. Weekly packages are available (not cheap). Lift pass US$30/day, US$20/half-day. Information from Chillán Ski Centre, Barros Arana 261, or from Libertador 1042. Equipment hire also from Chillán Ski Centre (about US$25 pp).

● **Accommodation** Ski Club de Chile has a tourist centre with hotel (full board, T 223887 Chillán, Casilla 247, office at Arauco 600, or Santiago T 251-5776, Av Providencia 2237, locales 42-4). At Las Trancas on the road to the

The longest double chair in South America

🦶 "There are eight lifts, including what the proud locals announce as the 'longest double chair in South America', but is better known as the oldest and slowest ride in the continent. Chillán is a snowboarders and off-piste skiers paradise as the extensive slopes include natural half-pipes, shutes and cornices. The skiing can be superb but be prepared for the slow lifts. Piste preparation is haphazard. Despite this Chillán has a lot of potential, and soaking in the pools surrounded by trees after a hard day's skiing definitely makes up for all its shortcomings", Josselyn van der Pol and Leandro Yáñez.

Termas, 70 km from Chillán are **A2** *Hotel Los Pirineos*, T 293839, and **A2** *Parador Jamón, Pan y Vino*, 18 de Septiembre 661, oficina 23, T 492241, Casilla 22, Chillán (Don Emilio Chamorro), arranges rec horse riding expeditions. *Cabañas* also available in the village. **Camping**: 2 km from the slopes.

● **Transport** Ski buses run from Libertador 1042 at 0800 and from Chillán Ski Centre, subject to demand, US$30 (inc lift pass). Taxi US$30 one way, 1½ hrs. At busy periods hitching may be possible from Chillán Ski Centre.

ROUTES From Chillán there are various road routes to Concepción: (1) W to Tomé then S along the coast through Penco; (2) along the Longitudinal Highway to Bulnes, where a branch road goes SW to Concepción; or to Cabrero from where there is a paved road W to Concepción.

THE BIOBIO VALLEY

The Río Biobío, which flows NW from the Andes to reach the sea near Concepción, is 407 km long, the second longest river in Chile. Its more important tributaries include the Ríos Laja, Duqueco and Renaico. Apart from Concepción and Talcahuano on the coast, the valley includes several other important cities, notably Los Angeles.

Climate
The climate is very agreeable in summer, but from April to Sept the rains are heavy; the annual average rainfall, nearly all of which falls in those 6 months, is from 1,250 to 1,500 mm.

CONCEPCION

(*Pop* 326,784; *Phone code* 041) the capital of VIII Región (Bío-Bío), 15 km up the Biobío river and 516 km from Santiago, is the third biggest city in Chile. The most important city in southern Chile, it is one of the country's major industrial centres; to the S are coalfields and an important forestry area. Talcahuano, Chile's most important naval base is 15 km N.

History
Founded in 1550, Concepción became a frontier stronghold in the war against the Mapuche after 1600. Destroyed by an earthquake in 1751, it was moved to its present site in 1764.

Places of interest
In the attractive Plaza de Armas at the centre are the **Intendencia** and the **Cathedral**. It was here that Bernardo O'Higgins proclaimed the independence of

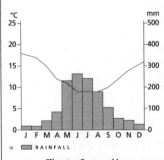

Climate: Concepción

Chile on 1 January 1818. Every Feb in the **Parque Ecuador** (on Victor Lamas, at the foot of Cerro Caracol), there is a craft fair. At the edge of the park is the Galería de la Historia (see below).

Cerro Caracol can easily be reached on foot starting from the statue of Don Juan Martínez de Rozas in the Parque Ecuador, arriving at the Mirador Chileno after 15 mins. From here it is another, 20 mins climb to **Cerro Alemán**. The Biobío and its valley running down to the sea lie below. On the far side of the river you see lagoons, the largest of which, **San Pedro**, is a watersport centre. On the city side, among cypress trees, is the modern **Barrio Universitario**. A stroll through the grounds, which are beautifully kept with geese, ducks, swans, hummingbirds and a small enclosure with *pudu-pudu* (miniature deer) is recommended. La Posada golf club, on the road to Coronel, is beside a picturesque lake.

Concepción is linked with Talcahuano, by two good roads, half-way along one of which is the Club Hípico's racetrack. Races are held on Sun and holidays. A branch road leads to good beaches, including Tomé (see below). Two other beaches are Las Escaleras (a private club) – a flight of natural stairs down a sheer 53m sea cliff leads to it – and Ramuntcho, named after a novel by a visitor in 1875: Pierre Loti (real name Julien Viaud, 1850-1923, French sailor and writer; *Ramuntcho* is about the French Basque country).

Museums

Museo de Concepción, near Barrio Universitario, Tues-Sat 1000-1300, 1400-1700, Sun 1430-1730; entrance US$0.50; interesting on history of the Mapuche nation.

The **Galería de la Historia**, Lincoyan y V Lamas, is an audiovisual depiction of the history of Concepción and the region; upstairs is a collection of Chilean painting, Mon 1500-1830, Tues-Fri

Extract from *Presencia de América Latina*

1000-1330, 1500-1830, Sat/Sun 1000-1400, 1500-1930, free.

The **Casa del Arte**, Roosevelt y Larena, contains the University art collection; the entrance hall is dominated by *La Presencia de América Latina*, by the Mexican Jorge González Camerena, (1965) an impressive allegorical mural depicting Latin American history. Note especially the pyramid representing the continent's wealth, the figures of an armoured warrior and an Indian woman and the wounded cactus with parts missing, representing Mexico's defeat by the USA in 1845-1848. Open Tues-Fri 1000-1800, Sat 1000-1600, Sun 1000-1300, entry free, explanations are given free by University Art students. There is another fine mural in the entrance hall of the railway station, *The History of Concepción* by Gregorio de la Fuente.

Excursions

To the **Museo y Parque Hualpén**, a house built around 1885 (now a national monument) and its gardens, donated to the city by Pedro del Río Zañartu; it contains beautiful pieces from all over the world, 2 hr visit, rec (open Tues-Sun 0900-1230, 1400-1800, free). The park also contains Playa Rocoto, which is at the mouth of the Río Biobío. Take a city bus to Hual-

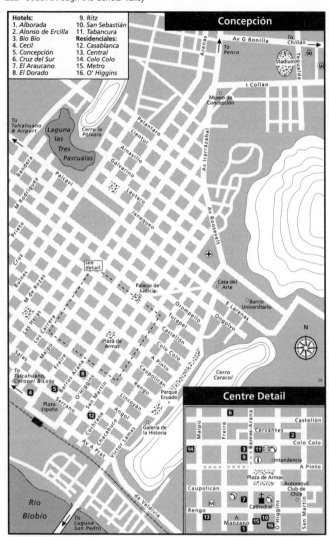

pencillo from Freire, ask the driver to let you out then walk 40 mins, or hitch. You have to go along Av Las Golondrinas to the Enap oil refinery, turn left, then right (it is signed).

To the **Museo Stom**, SE of Concepción, at Progreso 156, in Chiguayante, T 362014, Mapuche artefacts.

Local information
● Accommodation
A1 *Alborada*, Barros Arana 457, Casilla 176, T 242144, good; **A1** *Eldorado*, Barros Arana 348, T 229400, F 231018, comfortable, central, cafeteria, parking; **A2** *Concepción*, Serrano 512, T 228851, F 230948, central, comfortable, heating, English spoken, rec; **A3** *San Sebastián*, Rengo 463, T 244529, F 243412, with breakfast, parking.

B *Casablanca*, Cochrane 133, T 226576, with bath, **C** without, clean; **B** *Ritz*, Barros Arana 721, T 226696, reasonable; **B** *Tabancura*, Barros Arana 790, p 8, T 238348, clean, highly rec. *Cecil*, Barros Arana 9, T 226603, nr railway station, formerly great hotel, with breakfast, clean, quiet, highly rec.

C *Res Antuco*, Barros Arana 741, flats 31-33, T 235485, rec; **C** *Res San Sebastian*, Barros Arana 741, flat 35, T 242710, F 243412, rec, reductions for IYHA (both of these are entered via the Galería Martínez); **C** *Res Metro*, Barros Arana 464, T 225305, without bath, clean.

E pp *Pablo Araya*, Salas 643-C; **E** *Silvia Uslar*, Edmundo Larenas 202, T 227449, good breakfast, quiet, clean, comfortable. *El Naturista* restaurant lets out 2 rooms, **E** pp clean, central. Good budget accommodation is hard to find.

● Places to eat
El Rancho de Julia, Barros Arana 337, Argentine *parrillada*; *Piazza*, Barros Arana 323, good pizzas; *Rincón de Pancho*, Cervantes 469 (closed Sun), excellent meat, also pasta and congrio, good service and ambience; *Novillo Loco*, Portales 539, good, efficient service. *Le Château* Colo Colo 340, French, seafood and meat, expensive, closed Sun. Oriental: *Yiet-Xiu*, Angol 515, good, cheap; *Chungwa*, Barros Arana 270. *Big Joe Saloon*, O'Higgins 808, just off plaza, popular at lunchtime, closed Sun am but open in pm, good breakfasts, vegetarian meals, snacks and pizzas. *Saaya 1*, Barros Arana 899, excellent *panadería/pastelería/rotisería*, highly rec. Vegetarian:

El Naturista, Barros Arana 244, good fresh juices, soups and other dishes, closes 1800, highly rec. Several *fuentes de soda* and cafés on Caupolicán nr the Plaza de Armas inc: *Fuente Alemana*, No 654, rec; *Café El Dom*, No 415, and *Café Haiti*, No 515, both open Sun am, good coffee; *Royal Pub*, O'Higgins 790, a posh snack bar; *Nuria*, Barros Arana 736, very good breakfasts and lunches, good value; *QuickBiss*, O'Higgins between Tuscapel and Castellón, salads, real coffee, good service, good lunches; *Café Colombia*, Aguirre Cerda, good coffee, good atmosphere; *Treinta y Tantos*, Prat 356, nice bar, good music, wide selection of *empanadas*, rec; good breakfasts and lunches at the market.

● Airline offices
LanChile, Barros Arana 541, T 25014/240025; **Ladeco**, Barros Arana y Lincoyán, T 248824; **National**, Barros Arana 348, T 246710; **Alta**, Caupolicán 246, T 223371, F 223173; **Aerolíneas Argentinas**, O'Higgins 650, Of 602.

● Banks & money changers
Several *cambios* in Galería Internacional, entrances at Barros Arana 565 and Caupolicán 521: **Cambios Fides**, local 58, good rates for TCs; **Inter-Santiago**, local 31, T 228914; **Afex**, local 57, no commision on TCs. **Fincard** (Mastercard), O'Higgins 412, open 24 hrs. Banks such as **Banco Concepción** (which handles Visa) charge high commission on TCs.

● Cultural centres
Alliance Française, Colo Colo y Lamas, library, concerts, films, cultural events; **Chilean-British Cultural Institute**, San Martín 531 (British newspapers, library); **Chilean-North American Institute**, Caupolicán 301 y San Martín, has library; **Chileno-Italiano**, Barros Arana.

● Embassies & consulates
Argentine: San Martín 472; **British Consul**: Dr John F Pomeroy, Castellón 317, T 225655, Casilla 452.

● Laundry
Lincoyán 441; *Lavandería Radiante*, Salas 281, open 0900-2030, very good; *American Cleaning*, Freire 817.

● Post & telecommunications
Post Office: O'Higgins y Colo Colo.

Telephone CTC, Colo Colo 487, Angol 483. Entel, Barros Arana 541, Caupolicán 567, p 2; Colo Colo 487.

Forestry: from monkey-puzzles to woodchips

The Biobío is the heartland of Chilean commercial forestry. Although the Cousiño's Compañia Minera Lota experimented with new species and planted large areas for commercial foresty around Arauco in the 1880s, Chilean forestry owes its modern dynamism largely to a 1974 law which provided incentives for the development of the industry. Since 1974 over 1 million ha of trees have been planted in the VII, VIII and IX Regions, mostly of Monterrey Pine (*pinus radiata*), favoured for its fast growth and suitability for cellulose and construction timber. Normal growing periods are 10-15 years for trees destined for cellulose and 18-25 years for use as timber. Climatic conditions for forestry are particularly favourable in the area inland from Arauco, which has a high number of days of optimal temperatures and humidity for the growth of the Monterrey Pine, though this is now being replaced by faster growing species of eucalyptus.

Timber is a major industry in the Biobío region: there are four major cellulose plants in the Biobío valley, at La Laja, Concepción, Nacimiento and Mininco, as well as two more at Arauco on the coast. Timber trucks are a common feature on the roads of the region, and a common cause of traffic holdups.

Forestry development is not limited to the Biobío area: further S there are other signs of Chile's growing importance as a timber producer, for instance in the wood-chip mountains of Puerto Montt. While environmentalists voice concern at the disappearance of native species and particularly the threat to the ancient *araucaria araucana*, as well as the environmental damage produced by species such as the eucalyptus which extract most of the goodness from the soil, Chile is rapidly becoming one of the great powers of world timber production.

● **Shopping**
Main shopping area is N of Plaza de Armas. *Galería Internacional*, Caupolicán y Barros Arana is worth a visit (*El Naturista* vegetarian restaurant has a shop here at local 22). The market has excellent seafood, fruit and vegetables. *Las Brisas* supermarket, Freire y Lincoyán.

● **Sports**
Country Club: Pedro de Valdivia, outdoor swimming pool, tennis.

● **Tour companies & travel agents**
South Expeditions, O'Higgins 680, p 2, oficina 218D, T/F 232290, rafting and trekking expeditions, 1 and 2-day programmes.

● **Tourist offices**
Aníbal Pinto 460 on plaza, T 227976. Information on the more expensive hotels and *residenciales*. **Automóvil Club de Chile**: O'Higgins 630, Of 303, T 245884, for information and car hire (T 222070). **Codeff** (Comité Nacional pro Defensa de la Fauna y Flora) Caupolicán 346, Oficina E, p 4, T 226649.

● **Transport**
Local Bicycle repairs: *Martínez*, Maipú y Lincoyán, very helpful. **Car hire: Hertz**, Prat 248, T 230152; **Budget**, Arana 541, T 225377. **Automóvil Club de Chile**, Caupolicán 294, T 2250939.

Air Airport N of the city, off the main road to Talcahuano. In summer, flights daily to and from Santiago (fewer in winter) and connections to Temuco, Puerto Montt and Punta Arenas. Airlines run bus services to the airport from their offices, leaving 1 hr before flight, US$2.50, also meet flights. Taxi US$8.

Trains Station at Prat y Barros Arana, T 226925. Regular daily train to/from **Santiago**, plus Rápido del Bío Bío overnight service, 9 hrs; *salón* US$20, upper bunk US$30, lower bunk US$39; *departamento* US$80. Also local services to Laja and Yumbel. Booking offices at the station and at Galería Alessandri, Aníbal Pinto 478, local 3, T 225286.

Buses Main long distance terminal, known as Terminal Collao, is 2 km E, on Av Gen Bonilla, next to athletics stadium. (To the city centre take a Bus marked 'Hualpencillo' from outside the terminal and get off in Freire, US$0.40, taxi

A
journey of
1000 miles
begins with
your first
footprint...

With apologies to
Lao Tzu c.604 - 531 BC

Win two Iberia flights to Latin America

Welcome to Footprint Handbooks - the most exciting new development in travel guides since the original South American Handbook from Trade & Travel.

We want to hear your ideas for further improvements as well as a few details about yourself so that we can better serve your needs as a traveller.

We are offering you the chance to win two Iberia flights to Latin America. Iberia is the leading airline for Latin America, currently flying to 34 destinations. Every reader who sends in their completed questionnaire will be entered in the Footprint Prize Draw. 10 runners up will win an exclusive Footprint T-shirt!

Complete in a ball-point pen and return this tear-off questionnaire as soon as possible.

1 Title of this Handbook _____

2 **Age** Under 21 ☐   21 - 30 ☐ 31 - 40 ☐
          41 - 50 ☐   over 50 ☐

3 Occupation _____

4 Which region do you intend visiting next?
   North America ☐ India/S. Asia ☐ Africa ☐
   Latin America ☐ S.E. Asia   ☐ Europe ☐
   Australia   ☐

5 Which country(ies) do you intend visiting next?
   _____

6 There is a complete list of Footprint Handbooks at the back of this book. Which other countries would you like to see us cover?
   _____

Please enter your name and permanent address:

Name _____

Address _____
   _____
   _____

E-mail _____

Offer ends 30 November 1997. Prize Draw winners will be notified by 30 January 1998. Flights are subject to availability.

IBERIA Win two Iberia flights to Latin America

Footprint Handbooks
6 Riverside Court
Lower Bristol Road
Bath
BA2 3DZ
England

Affix
Stamp
Here

Footprint Handbooks

6 Riverside Court
Lower Bristol Road
Bath BA2 3DZ
T 01225 469141
F 01225 469461
handbooks@footprint.cix.co.uk

Andalucia Handbook
Zimbabwe & Malawi Handbook with Botswana, Mozambique, Zimbia
Caribbean Islands Handbook with the Bahamas
Morocco Handbook with Mauritania
Indonesia Handbook
Chile Handbook
Cambodia Handbook
India Handbook
Vietnam Handbook
Thailand Handbook
East Africa Handbook with Kenya, Tanzania, Uganda and Ethiopia
South Africa Handbook
Tibet Handbook with Bhutan
Peru Handbook
Malaysia & Singapore Handbook
Namibia Handbook
Myanmar (Burma) Handbook
Egypt Handbook
Ecuador & Galápagos Handbook
Mexico & Central America Handbook
Laos Handbook
South American Handbook
Tunisia Handbook with Libya

The Huáscar

At the outbreak of the War of the Pacific the Chilean navy blockaded Iquique, then an important Peruvian nitrate port. On 21 May 1879, the Peruvian Navy's huge ironclad, the *Huáscar*, and the smaller *Independencia* reached Iquique to lift the siege. Chile sent out two small wooden ships, the *Covadonga* and the *Esmeralda*, under Captain Arturo Prat to challenge them. Prat fought with ferocity. When his damaged vessel, the *Esmeralda*, was rammed by the *Huáscar*, Prat called upon his men to follow him, boarded the enemy and continued fighting until he was killed. Chile later captured the *Huáscar* at the battle of Angamos near Mejillones, on 8 October 1879.

US$4.) Tur Bus, Línea Azul and Buses Bío Bío services leave from Terminal Camilo Henríquez 2 km NE of main terminal on J M García, reached by buses from Av Maipú in centre. To **Santiago**, 8½ hrs, US$10; to **Valparaíso**, 9 hrs, US$12; to **Loncoche**, 7 hrs, US$6.50; to **Puerto Montt** several companies, US$15, about 12 hrs; to **Pucón**, 8 hrs, US$8; to **Valdivia**, US$10; to **Los Angeles**, US$2.50. Best direct bus to **Chillán** is Línea Azul, 2 hrs, US$2. For a longer and more scenic route, take the Costa Azul bus which follows the old railway line, through Tomé, Coelemu and Ñipas on to Chillán (part dirt-track, takes 5½ hrs). Services to **Coronel** (US$0.45), **Lota**, **Lebu**, **Cañete** and **Contulmo** are run by J Ewert (terminal next to railway station on Prat) and Los Alces (terminal at Prat y Maipú). To **Talcahuano** frequent service from Plaza de Armas (bus marked 'Base Naval'), US$0.20, 1 hr, express US$0.30, 30 mins.

NORTH OF CONCEPCION

A road runs N from Concepción along the coast through the suburbs of **Penco**, Km 12, and **Lirquén**, Km 15, a small, old, pretty town of wooden houses with a beach (walk along railway to reach it). Plentiful cheap seafood for sale.

Tomé, 13 km further N, is a small town set in a broad bay with long beaches. An interesting cemetery, Miguel Gulán Muñoz, is set on a cliff overlooking the ocean.

Dichato, 9 km further N along a hilly road offering fine views, is a beautiful fishing village and has the oceanographic centre of the University of Concepción. In summer it is a busy holiday resort. Private Museo del Mar, by Benjamín Ortega, interesting, free. Take a local bus to the tiny village of Cocholgüe.

● **Accommodation & places to eat** In **Penco**: **D** *Hotel La Terraza*, T 451422, **E** *Hosp Miramar*, good, and *Casinoriente*, good seafood restaurant. In **Tomé**: **D** *Hotel Roxy*, Sotomayor 1077, T 650729, and **E** *Linares*, Serrano 875, T 651284. 7 km before Tomé, on a hill, is *El Edén*, restaurant, bar and *cabañas*, **D**. In **Dichato**: **A3** *Chamaruk*, Daniel Vera 912, T 683022, with bath, **C** without, clean, pleasant; **A2** *Manantial*, on seafront, T 683003; **B** *Kalifa*, Casimiro Vera 766, T 681027, with bath, restaurant; **C** *Chicki*, Ugalde 410, T 683004, with bath, **D** without; **E** pp *Res Santa Inés*, República 540, without bath; *albergue* in the school in summer.

● **Transport** Línea Azul and Costa Azul buses from Concepción pass through all these villages, which can also be reached cheaply by collective taxi.

TALCAHUANO

(*Pop* 244,000), situated at the neck of a peninsula, has the best harbour in Chile. It is Chile's main naval station and an important commercial and fishing port.

Places of interest The **Huáscar**, a relic of the War of the Pacific, is in the naval base and can be visited, Tues-Sun 0900-1130, 1400-1700, US$1.25. Photography is permitted, but passports must be handed in at the main gate. On Península Tumbes is **Parque Tumbes**, owned by Codeff: paths lead along the coast, no services, no admission charge (details from Codeff office in Concepción).

● **Accommodation C** *De La Costa*, Colón 630; **D** *Res San Pedro*, Rodríguez 22, T 542145.

● **Places to eat** *Benotecas*, on seafront, a row of four restaurants sharing one window facing the harbour, superb fish and seafood in each one, rec, reasonable prices. *El Alero de los Salvo*, Colón 3396; *La Aguada*, Colón 912, shellfish dishes; *Domingo Lara*, Aníbal Pinto 450, seafood specialities, excellent.

THE COASTAL ROUTE SOUTH OF CONCEPCION

South of the Biobío is the **Costa del Carbón**, the main coal producing area of Chile, linked with Concepción by road and bridge. Between Concepción and Lota are the Lagunas San Pedro Chica (swimming) and Grande (watersports),

The Coastal Route south of Concepcion

just across the Río Biobío. Nearer Lota are Playa Negra (small, few people, black sand) and Playa Blanca (bigger, bars, cafés, crowded, white sand, free campsite), both on the Bahía de Coronel.

Coronel (*Pop* 80,000) in the heart of the coal area, 29 km from Concepción, was the scene of a British naval defeat in 1914 (the *Good Hope* and *Monmouth* were sunk by the *Scharnhorst* – a monument was dedicated in Nov 1989), which was later avenged at the Battle of the Falklands/Malvinas with the destruction of the German squadron.

LOTA

(*Pop* 52,000), 42 km S of Concepción, is the site of the most important coalmine in Chile, now state-owned, formerly the property of the Cousiño family. The town is in two parts: Lota Alto, on the hill, is the original mining town, while Lota Bajo, below, is more recent. In the church on the main plaza you can see a virgin made of coal.

The **Parque de Lota**, covering 14 ha on a promontory to the W of the town, was the life's work of Isadora Cousiño. Laid out by English landscape architects in the last century, it contains plants from all over the world, ornaments imported from Europe, romantic paths and shady nooks offering views over the sea, and peafowl and pheasants roaming freely. The mansion which was Isadora's home during her stays in Lota was destroyed in the 1960 earthquake. (Admission US$1.25, no picnicking; open 1000-1800 daily, till 2000 in summer.)

The Coalmine, the tunnels of which run almost entirely under the sea (the longest is of 11 km) can be visited. Guided tours (Spanish only) Tues-Sat 1000, 3 hrs (minimum party of 5) US$13 pp, meet at the Park entrance, tiring but highly rec. Advance booking advisable, T 876362 Anexo 204, or at Tourist Office in Concepción from whom further details can be obtained. Ask to see the miningmuseum before you leave.

● **Accommodation** *Res Rome*, Galvarino 233, clean, friendly.

● **Transport** Buses to **Concepción**, 1½ hrs, US$0.50. Many buses by-pass the centre: catch them from the main road.

South of Lota the road runs past the seaside resort of **Laraquete** where there are miles of golden sands. At Carampangue, Km 24, it forks, one branch running W to **Arauco** (*Pop* 12,000), the site of two cellulose factories. The other branch continues S, 52 km, to Tres Pinos, where there is a turning for Lebu.

● **Accommodation   In   Laraquete**: D *Laraquete*, on Gabriela Mistral, main street, friendly, small rooms, baths in poor repair; D *Hostería El Quinto*, helpful, basic, good breakfast. Several *residenciales* close to beach; campsite nr beach. **In Arauco**: B *Hostería Arauco*, P de Valdivia 80, T 551131. D *Plaza*, Chacabuco 347, T 551265.

LEBU

(*Pop* 20,000; *Phone code* 041) a fishing port and coal washing centre, lies at the mouth of the Río Lebu 149 km S of Concepción and is the capital of Arauco province. There are enormous beaches to both N and S, popular on summer weekends: 3 km N at Playa Millaneco are caves with steep hills offering good walks and majestic views.

● **Accommodation   A1** *Hostería Millaneco*, T 511540, T 511904 at Playa Millaneco, offers *cabañas*, sleep 7, good restaurant, rec; **C** *Central*, Pérez 183, T 511904, with bath, **E** pp without, clean, parking, rec; **D** pp *Gran* Pérez 309, T 511939, with bath, **E** pp without, old fashioned, clean, *comedor*; **E** *Res Alcázar*, Alcázar 144, with breakfast, cold water, friendly.

CAÑETE

(*Pop* 15,642; *Phone code* 041) 24 km S of Tres Pinos is **Cañete**, a small town on the site of Fort Tucapel where Pedro de Valdivia and 52 of his men were killed by Mapuche warriors in 1553.

Museums   Museo   Mapuche   de

Caupolicán

Caupolicán was a Mapuche chief who led the resistance to the Spanish after the death of Lautaro in Apr 1557, launching an unsuccessful attack on the recently built fort of Concepción. The following year he was captured in a surprise raid on his camp, his wife revealing his identity to the Spanish by reproaching him for allowing himself to be taken alive and dashing her infant son to the ground. He was executed by being impaled, supposedly on the site of the modern Plaza Caupolicán in Cañete.

Cañete, 3 km S on the road to Contulmo, in a modern building inspired by the traditional Mapuche *ruca*; includes Mapuche ceramics and textiles. Behind the museum is a reconstruction of a *ruca*. Open 0930-1230, 1400-1830, daily in summer, closed Mon in winter. Entry US$0.75.

● **Accommodation   C** *Alonso de Ercilla*, Villagrán 641, T 611974, with bath, clean; **D** *Derby*, Mariñán y Condell, T 611960, without bath, clean, basic, restaurant; **D** *Nahuelbuta*, Villagrán 644, T 611073, clean, pleasant, parking; **E** *Comercio*, 7° de la Línea, T 611218, very pleasant, rec; **E** *Gajardo*, 7° de la Línea 817 (1 block from plaza), without bath, old fashioned, friendly, pleasant.

● **Places to eat** *Don Juanito*, Riquelme 151, very good, friendly, rec by the locals; real coffee at *Café Nahuel*, off the plaza.

● **Transport** Buses leave from 2 diifferent terminals: J Ewert, Inter Sur and Thiele from Riquelme y 7° de la Línea, Jeldres, Erbuc and other companies from the Terminal Municipal, Serrano y Villagrán. To **Santiago**, Inter Sur, daily, 12 hrs; to **Purén**, US$1.50; sit on right for views of Lago Lanalhue; to **Concepción**, 3 hrs, US$2.50; to **Lebu** US$1.50; to **Angol** US$3.50; to **Tirúa**, Jeldres, frequent and J Ewert, 3 a day, 2 hrs, US$2.

LAGO LLEULLEU AND TIRUA

Lago Lleulleu, a peaceful lake covering

Fiesta de la Piedra Santa

The ancient festival of the Holy Stone is celebrated every year on 20 Jan though Mapuche families start to arrive on the previous day. The women dress in their traditional costumes, with colourful belts and silver jewelry. Each family carries a fowl which is sacrificed, covering the stone with blood, while they ask for favours or give thanks for favours received. A few drops of wine is also poured onto the stone before the rest is drunk. The stone is lit up by hundreds of candles and crosses made of straw or grass are placed over the blood, which sticks to them. Machis (priests), surrounded by people from their communities, go up to the stone and, accompanied on their sacred instrument, the kultrung, they sing, dance and recite, while passing their knives over the diseased parts of the bodies of the sick. The festival continues through the night with singing, dancing music and prayers.

Abridged and translated from *Lengua Y Costumbres Mapuches*
by Orietta Appelt Martín, Imprenta Austral, Temuco, 1995.

4,300 ha, lies 34 km S of Cañete (turn off at Peleco, Km 11). The lake offers sandy beaches, many opportunities for camping and fine views of the coastal mountain range, but there are few facilities.

Tirúa, at the mouth of the Río Tirúa, is 78 km S of Cañete. The island of **Mocha**, visited by Juan Bautista Pastenes in 1544 and later by Sir Francis Drake, lies 32 km offshore. Most of the island's 800 inhabitants live around the coast, the interior being forests. The main settlement is La Hacienda where accommodation is available with families. Transport from Tirúa: ferry daily 0600, US$14; plane US$56 (ask the police to radio the plane which is based on Mocha).

• **Accommodation in Tirúa** Three *hospedajes* all E.

• **Transport** Buses from Cañete.

LAGO LANALHUE

The lake, S of Cañete, is surrounded by forested hills from which there has been extensive logging. Much less popular than the Lake District this area offers good opportunities for walking. A road runs S from Cañete along the N side of the lake to Contulmo at its southern end. Playa Blanca, 10 km N of Contulmo, is a popular beach in summer (take any bus between Contulmo and Cañete). For further information on the area ask at the *Hostal Licahue*.

CONTULMO

(*Pop* 2,000; *Alt* 31m) is a sleepy village at the foot of the Cordillera which hosts a Semana Musical (music week) in January. The wooden Grollmus House and Mill, 3 km NW along the S side of the lake, are well worth a visit. The house, dating from 1918, has a fine collection of every colour of *copihue* (the national flower) in a splendid garden. The mill, built in 1928, contains the original wooden machinery. From here the track runs a further 9 km N to the *Posada Campesina Alemana*, an old German-style hotel in a fantastic spot at the water's edge. The **Monumento Natural Contulmo**, 8 km S and administered by Conaf, covers 82 ha of native forest.

• **Accommodation In Contulmo: C** *Contulmo*, Millaray 116, with bath, **E** pp without, an attractive retreat, friendly and hospitable, highly rec; **E** pp *Central*, Millaray 131, without bath, no sign, very hospitable. **On the lake**: **A3** *Posada Campesina Alemana*, open Dec-Mar, poor beds, own generator, fish come to hotel steps to be fed by guests, details from Millaray 135 in Contulmo; **B** *Hostal Licahue*, 4 km N towards Cañete (Casilla 644, Correo Contulmo) T Santiago 273-8417, with breakfast, also full board, attractively set overlooking lake, pool, highly rec, also *cabañas*, **A1**, sleep 8, on far side of lake (connected by boat); *Hostería Lanalhue*, reached from Tirúa road, on S lakeside. **Camping at Playa Blanca**: *Camping Elicura*, clean, rec, US$6; *Camping Playa Blanca*, clean; *Camping Huilquehue*, 15 km S of Cañete on lakeside.

● **Transport** Buses to **Concepción**, Thiele, US$4.50, 4 hrs; to **Temuco**, Thiele and Erbuc, US$4; to **Cañete**, frequent, US$1.

PUREN

(*Pop* 7,572) 20 km further S, is reached by crossing the Cordillera through dense forest (do this journey in daylight). Located in a major logging area, Purén was the site of a fortess built by Pedro de Valdivia in 1553 and destroyed soon after. It was key stronghold of the Chilean army in the last campaign against the Mapuche (1869-1881) and there is a full-scale reconstruction of the wooden fort on the original site. **Lumaco**, 21 km SE, is the site of a major Mapuche festival, the Piedra Santa (see box).

● **Accommodation** D *Hotel Tur*, Dr Garriga 912, T 22, clean, good; *Central Hotel*, on the plaza, meals excellent, rooms in tourist season only.

LOS ANGELES

(*Pop* 93,000; *Alt* 133m; *Phone code* 043) situated on the Pan-American Highway 110 km S of Chillán, is the capital of Bío-Bío province. Founded in 1739 as a fort, it was destroyed several times by the Mapuche. Located between the rivers Laja and Biobío at the heart of a wine, fruit and timber-producing district, it has become an important agroindustrial centre and is a pleasant, expanding city, with a large Plaza de Armas; Colón is the main shopping street. There is a good daily market. There is swimming in the Río Duqueco, 10 mins S by bus, US$0.80.

Local information
● **Accommodation**
A3 *Mariscal Alcázar*, Lautaro 385 (Plaza de Armas), T 311725.

B *Gran Hotel Müso*, Valdivia 230 (Plaza de Armas), T 313183, good restaurant open to non-residents.

C *Winser*, Rengo 138, overpriced but clean and friendly; **C** *Res Santa María*, Plaza de Armas, hot shower, TV, good beds.

Private house at Caupolicán 651, E, large breakfast, good value; opp is another, also No 651, basic, cheaper. **E** pp *Res Winser*, Colo Colo 335, T 323782, small rooms. 10 km N is **D** pp *Casa de familia/Cabañas El Rincón*, Panamericana Sur Km 494, Cruce La Mona 1 km E, T (09) 441-5019, F 043-317168, Elke and Winfried Lohmar, beautiful property beside a small river, restful, South American and European cuisine, inc vegetarian (**B** pp full board), tours arranged, English, French, German and Spanish spoken, highly rec ("one of the last corners in the garden of Eden"); *Antukelen*, Camino Los Angeles-Santa Bárbara-Ralco, 62.7 km SE on the Alto Bío-Bío, reservations Siegfried Haberl, Casilla 1278, Los Angeles, T 09-450-0210, camping, showers, German, English and French spoken, vegetarian food and other natural attractions; Spanish classes; *cabañas*, natural therapy centre and excursions to be developed in 1997.

● **Places to eat**
El Arriero, Colo Colo 235, T 322899, good *parrillas* and international dishes; *Di Leone*, Colón 265, good lasagna; *Julio's Pizzas*, Colón 542 and *Rancho de Julio*, Colón 720, excellent *parrilla*. *Bavaria*, Colón 357, good.

● **Banks & money changers**
Banco Santander, Colón 500, Mastercard; Banco Concepción, Colón 300; Banco Sudamérica, Valdivia 276.

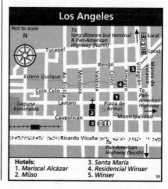

Los Angeles

Hotels:
1. Mariscal Alcázar
2. Müso
3. Santa María
4. Residencial Winser
5. Winser

Climate: Los Angeles

● **Cultural centres**
British Cultural Institute, Vicuña 648.

● **Post & telecommunications**
Post Office: on Plaza de Armas.

Telephone: CTC, Paseo Quilpué, or Valdivia 326; Entel, Colo Colo 393.

● **Tourist offices**
Proto-Turismo, Edif Cámara Comercio No 24, beside Lautaro 267. **Conaf**, Ercilla 936, 0900-1300. **Automóvil Club de Chile**: Villagrán y Caupolicán, T 322149.

● **Transport**
Long distance bus terminal on NE outskirts of town, local terminal at Villagrán y Rengo in centre. To **Santiago**, 9 hrs, US$12; to **Viña del Mar** and **Valparaíso**, 10 hrs, US$14; 4 daily to **Concepción**, US$2.50, 2¼ hrs; to **Temuco**, US$4, hourly; to **Curacautín**, daily at 0600, 3 hrs, US$4.

SALTO EL LAJA

25 km N of Los Angeles, is a spectacular waterfall in which the Río Laja plunges 47m over the rocks. It costs a few pesos to enter and walk up to the falls, or to walk on the hotel side.

● **Accommodation A3-B** *Motel Salto del Laja*, address: Casilla 562, Los Angeles, T 321706, F 313996 with fine restaurant, 2 swimming pools and chalet-type rooms on an island overlooking the falls; nearby are *Camping Los Manantiales*, T 323606, and Motels

El Pinar and *Los Coyuches*.

● **Transport** Buses (Bus Bío-Bío) from Los Angeles, US$1, 30 mins – frequent; to Chillán, frequent, US$2.

PARQUE NACIONAL LAGUNA DE LAJA

Covering 11,600 ha and situated 93 km E of Los Angeles by a road which runs past the impressive rapids of the Río Laja, the park is dominated by the Antuco volcano (2,985m), which is still active, and the glacier-covered Sierra Velluda. The Laguna is surrounded by stark scenery of scrub and lava. Trees include a few surviving araucarias. There are 46 species of birds including condors and the rare Andean gull. The Visitors' Centre is 1 km from park administration, which is 4 km from the entrance.

● **Access** Take a bus from Los Angeles (ERS Bus, Villagrán 507) to Abanico (**E** pp *Hostería del Bosque*, restaurant, also good campsite), 20 km past Antuco (US$1.35, 2 hrs, weekdays 5 daily, 2 on Sun and festivals, last return 1730), then 4 km to park entrance (details from Conaf in Los Angeles, Ercilla 936, 0800-1300, 1430-1800 Mon-Fri).

● **Accommodation** *Cabañas y Camping Lagunillas*, T 314275 (or Caupolicán 332, oficina 2, Los Angeles T 323-1066) 50m from the river, 2 km from park entrance, open all year, restaurant, poor campsite US$2.50 pp. Camping not permitted on lake shore. 21 km from the lake is the *Refugio Chacay* offering food, drink and bed (**B**, T Los Angeles 222651, closed in summer); two other *refugios*: *Digeder*, E, and Universidad de Concepción, both on slopes of Volcán Antuco, for both T Concepción 229054, office O'Higgins 740. Nearby is the Club de Esquí de los Angeles with two ski-lifts, giving a combined run of 4 km on the Antuco volcano (season, May-Aug).

SOUTH OF LOS ANGELES

The Pan-American (or Longitudinal) Highway (Ruta 5) bypasses **Mulchén**, a small, old-fashioned town (32 km; bus 45 mins). It continues via Collipulli (campsite), Victoria, Púa and Lautaro to Temuco.

ANGOL

(*Pop* 39,000; *Alt* 71m; *Phone code* 045), capital of the Province of Malleco, is reached by paved roads from Collipulli and Los Angeles. Founded by Valdivia in 1552, it was seven times destroyed by the Indians and rebuilt. The church and convent of **San Beneventura**, NW of the attractive Plaza de Armas, built in 1863, became the centre for missionary work among the Mapuche. Worth visiting is **El Vergel**, founded in 1880 as an experimental fruit-growing nursery; it now includes an attractive park with a wide range of trees and the **Museo Dillman Bullock** with precolumbian Indian artefacts (open daily 0830-1300, 1500-1800, US$1, a 5 km bus-ride from town, colectivo No 2).

• **Accommodation A1** *Millaray*, Prat 420, T 711570; **C** *Olimpia*, Lautaro 194, T 711517; **D** pp *La Posada*, at El Vergel, T 712103, full board, clean, friendly; **D** *Res Olimpia*, Caupolicán 625, T 711162, good; **D** pp *Casa Matriz*, Caupolicán 579, T 711771, with breakfast, clean, good food; **E** *El Parrón*, O'Higgins 345, T 711370; **E** Vergara 651, chaotic but cheap; **E** *Casa de Huespedes*, Dieciocho 465, with breakfast, friendly.

• **Places to Eat** *Carloncho*, Lautaro 447, popular with locals; *Flores*, Caupolicán 330.

• **Tourist offices** O'Higgins s/n, across bridge from bus terminal, T 711255, excellent.

• **Transport** Bus to **Santiago** US$6.50, **Los Angeles**, US$1.20, or **Collipulli**. To **Temuco**, Trans Bío-Bío, frequent, US$2.50.

PARQUE NACIONAL NAHUELBUTA

Situated in the coastal mountain range at an altitude of 800-1,550m, the park covers 6,832 ha of forest and offers views over both the sea and the Andes. Open all year (snow June-Sept).

Good walks include: to Piedra el Aguila, 1,400m, 4 km W of Visitors' Centre, where there is a *mirador* on top of a huge boulder; to Cormallín, 5 km N of Visitors' Centre, from where you may continue to Cerro Anay, 1,402m, another *mirador*.

Wildlife Although the forest includes many species of trees, the araucaria is most striking; some are over 2,000 years old, 50m high and 2m in diameter. There are also 16 species of orchids. Fauna include pudu deer, Chiloé foxes, pumas, black woodpeckers and parrots. There is a Visitors' Centre at Pehuenco, 5 km from the entrance, open summer only 0800-1300, 1400-2000, offering small displays on fauna and flora.

• **Access** Bus to Vegas Blancas (27 km from Angol) 0700 and 1600 daily, return 0900 and 1600, 1½ hrs, US$1.20, get off at *El Cruce*, from where it is a pleasant 7 km walk to park entrance (entry US$2.50). Access is also possible by dirt road from Cañete, 40 km W. Rough maps are available at the park entrance for US$0.25. **Conaf**, Prat 191, p 2, Angol, T 711870.

• **Accommodation Camping**: nr Visitors' Centre, US$9 – there are many free campsites along the road from *El Cruce* to the entrance. Also at Cormallín, no facilities.

The Lake District

YET MORE beautiful scenery: a variety of lakes, often with snow-capped volcanoes as a backdrop, stretch southwards to the salt water fjords which begin at Puerto Montt. There are a number of good bases for exploring (Valdivia has the added attraction of colonial forts a river trip away) and many national parks.

THE LAND

GEOGRAPHY

South from the Río Biobío to the Gulf of Reloncaví the same land formation holds as for the rest of Chile to the N: the Andes to the E, the coastal range to the W, and in between the central valley. The Andes and the passes over them are less high here, and the snowline lower. The coastal range also loses altitude: the Cordillera de Nahuelbuta stops N of the Río Imperial and the range then reappears intermittently, but at altitudes below 500m. Between Temuco and Puerto Montt is

The Lake District

65

National Parks:
1. Conguillío
2. Huerquehue
3. Villarrica
4. Puyehue
5. Vicente Pérez Rosales
6. Alerce Andino
7. Parque Nacional Tolhuaca
8. Reserva Nacional Malalcahuello Nalcas

To Concepción
Termas de Manzanar
Curacautín
Nehuentué
Carahue
Cherquenco
Pto Saavedro
Nueva Imperial
Vilcún
V Llaima
Lago Budi
Temuco
Lago Icalma
Melipeuco
Icalma
Barros Arana
Cunco
Teodoro Schmidt
Freire
Radal
Río Toltén
Lago Colico
Lago Caburga
Pacific Ocean
Toltén
Lago Villarrica
Pucón
Mehuin
Loncoche
Villarrica
Termas de Palguín
Lanco
Lican-Ray
V Villarrica (2,840m)
V Quetrupillán
Puesco
Paso Tromen
Lago Calafquén
Coñaripe
To Junín de Los Andes, San Martín de Los Andes and Bariloche
Río Cruces
Panguipulli
Liquiñe
Lago Neltume
Paso Carririñe
Valdivia
Antilhue
Lago Panguipulli
Niebla
Riñihue
Lago Riñihue
Choshuenco
Pto Fuy
To San Martín de los Andes
Corral
Los Lagos
Río Calle Calle
Lago Pirehueico
To San Martín de Los Andes
Paillaco
Futrono
Paso Huahum
Llifén
Río Bueno
Pto Nuevo
Lago Ranco
Lago Maihue
La Unión
CHILE
Trumao
Lago Ranco
Lago Huishué
Río Bueno
Lago Gris
Salto Pilmaiquén
Lago Puyehue
L Constancia
To Maicolpue & Pucatrihue
Osorno
Río Golgol
To Bariloche
Entre Lagos
Termas de Puyehue
Paso Puyehue
Río Negro
Rupanco
ARGENTINA
Lago Rupanco
Islote
Cerro Punteagudo
Pto Octay
V Osorno
Paso Pérez Rosales
N
Frutillar
La Picada
Lago Todos los Santos
To Bariloche
Lago Llanquihue
Petrohue
Peulla
Mt Tronador
Ensenada
Cayutué
Pto Varas
La Poza
V Calbuco
0   50
km
Río Petrohue
Pto Montt
Ralún
Lago Chapo
Cochamó
Río Maullín
I Tenglo
Maullín
I Huar
La Arena
Puelo
Calbuco
Puelche
Pargua
To Chaitén & Coyhaique

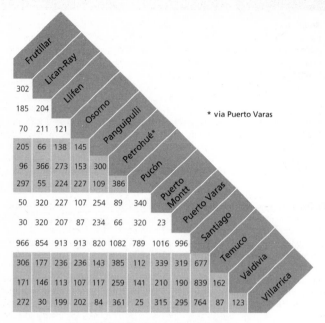

The Lake District: distance chart (km)

found one of the most picturesque lake regions in the world. There are some 12 great lakes of varying sizes, some set high on the Cordillera slopes, others in the central valley, as well as imposing waterfalls and snowcapped volcanoes.

This landscape has been created by two main geological processes: glaciation and volcanic activity. Several of the lakes are glacial in origin: Lago Villarrica, for example, is the result of a glacial morraine forming a barrier across the valley of the Río Maichín. Others are volcanic, such as Lago Pirehueico, formed by lava flows from the Choshuenco volcano having dammed the Río Fuy. The main mountain peaks are also volcanic: the highest are Lanín (3,747m) and Tronador (3,460m), both on the Argentine border, followed by Llaima (3,050m), Lonquimay (2,865m), Villarrica (2,840m) and Tolhuaca (2,806m). The most active volcanoes include Llaima and Villarrica, which have errupted 22 and 10 times respectively this century.

Seven main river systems drain the Lake District, from N to S the Ríos Imperial, Toltén, Valdivia, Bueno, Maullín, Petrohué and Puelo. Apart from the Imperial and the Puelo these gain much of their water from the lakes. The Río Bueno, 200 km long, drains Lago Ranco and is joined by the Ríos Pilmaiquén and Rahue, thus receiving also the waters of Lagos Puyehue and Rupanco: after the Ríos Simpson and Baker, it carries the third largest water volume of any Chilean river. In most of the rivers there is excellent fishing.

The 1960 earthquake

Southern Chile is highly susceptible to earthquakes: severe quakes struck the area in 1575, 1737, 1786 and 1837, but the tremor which struck around midday on 22 May caused extensive damage throughout Southern Chile and was accompanied by the erruption of four volcanoes. The resulting tidal wave was felt as far away as New Zealand and Japan.

Around Valdivia the land dropped 3m, creating new lagunas along the Río Cruces to the N of the city. The tidal wave destroyed all the fishing villages and ports between Puerto Saavedra in the N and Chiloé to the S. The earthquake also provoked several landslides. The greatest of these blocked the Río San Pedro near the point where it drains Lago Riñihue. The lake, which receives the waters of six other lakes, rose 35m in 24 hrs. Over the next 2 months all available labour and machinery was used to dig channels to divert the water from the other lakes and to drain off the waters of Lago Riñihue, thus averting the devastation of the San Pedro valley.

ECONOMY

Agriculture is the most important sector of the economy. Cereals, potatoes, beans and sugarbeet are grown throughout the region; cattle and sheep farming are more important further S than around Temuco. Despite the development of intensive fruit production since the early 1980s, much less fruit is grown than in the Central Valley. The farms are mostly medium sized, and no longer the huge haciendas found further N. The characteristic thatched or red tiled houses of the rural N disappear; they are replaced by the shingle-roofed frame houses typical of a frontier land rich in timber. Irrigation is unnecessary for agriculture. There is enough rainfall to maintain heavy forests, mostly of beech and native species, though increasingly of eucalyptus and other introduced varieties. Fishing is particularly important in the S of the region, where the growth of salmon farming is reflected in its presence on restaurant menus. Further N fishing is still largely small-scale, Puerto Saavedra and Quele being among the main fishing ports.

Industry has grown in importance in recent years, the main industries being connected to the region's produce, for example cereal mills, fish and meat processing plants, sugar beet plants, dairy processing and sawmills. Mining is of little significance, apart from small coal mines around Valdivia.

CLIMATE

The climate is cooler than further N; the summer is no longer dry, for rain falls all the year round, and more heavily further S. Rainfall decreases as you go inland: some 2,500 mm on the coast and 1,350 mm inland. Average daily temperatures in Valdivia are around 17°C in summer and 5°C in winter, with less variation between night and daytime than further inland.

Most parts of the Lake District attract fewer tourists than across the border in the Argentine lake district. Out of season many facilities are closed, in season (from mid-Dec to mid-Mar), prices are higher and it is best to book well in advance, particularly for transport. Between mid-Dec and mid-Jan enormous horse-flies (*tavanos*) are a problem – do not wear dark clothes.

HISTORY

After the Mapuche rebellion of 1598, Spanish settlement on the mainland S of the Río Biobío was limted to Valdivia. By the time of independence the only other Spanish settlement in this region was

Osorno, refounded in 1796. The Chilean government did not attempt to extend its control into the Lake District until the 1840s. In 1845 all land S of the Río Rahue was declared the property of the state and destined for settlement and three years later Bernardo E Philippi, a naturalist who had explored the lakes between Osorno and Lago Llanquihue between 1842 and 1845, was appointed coloniza- tion agent in Germany. In 1850 Vicente Pérez Rosales was sent to Valdivia to dis- tribute lands to arriving European colo- nists.

The southern Lake District including the lands around Lago Llanquihue were settled from the 1850s onwards. Further N Chilean troops began occupying lands S of the Biobío after 1862, but the de- struction of Mapuche independence did not occur until the 1880s when Chilean forces founded a series of forts in the area including Temuco (1881), Nueva Impe- rial (1882), Freire (1883) and Villarrica (1883). A treaty ending Mapuche inde- pendence was signed in Temuco in 1881.

White settlement in the area was fur- ther encouraged by the arrival of the railway, which reached Temuco in 1893, reducing the journey time from Santiago to 36 hrs; the line was later extended to Osorno (1902) and Puerto Montt (1912). Railways encouraged the production of new crops to feed the cities further N; some of the elegant wooden mansions built with the new wealth can still be seen.

CROSSING TO ARGENTINA

There are four main routes from the Chil- ean Lake District to Argentina:

1) The Tromen Pass, from Pucón and Curarrehue to Junín de los Andes (see page 255).

2) The Huahum Pass, from Pan- guipulli via Choshuenco and Lake Pire- hueico to San Martín de los Andes (see page 259).

3) The Puyehue Pass, from Osorno and Entrelagos via the Parque Nacional Puyehue to Bariloche (see page 272).

4) The Lakes Route, from Puerto Montt or Osorno via Ensenada, Petrohué and Lago Todos Los Santos to Bariloche (see page 292).

THE TEMUCO REGION

The northernmost city in the Lake Dis- trict is Temuco, situated on the Río Cautín, a tributary of the Río Imperial. North and E of Temuco are three national parks and several hot springs. Wheat, barley, oats, timber and apples are the principal products of the area.

TEMUCO

(*Pop* 225,000; *Alt* 107m; *Phone code* 045) founded in 1881 after the final treaty with the Mapuches, lies 679 km S of Santiago. The city is the capital of IX Región (Arau- canía) and one of the fastest growing commercial centres in the S.

Places of interest

The city is centred on the Plaza Aníbal Pinto, around which are the main public buildings including the cathedral and the municipalidad. On the plaza itself is a small Sala de Exposiciones, which stages exhibitions. The **cattle auctions** in the

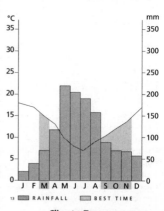

Climate: Temuco

stockyards behind the railway on A Malvoa, Thur mornings, are interesting; you can see the *huasos*, or Chilean cowboys, at work. There are also cattle sales at the Feria Agroaustral, just outside Temuco on the road to Nuevo Imperial, on Fri (take bus 4 from C Rodríguez), auction starts at 1400, and at Nuevo Imperial, 35 km away, on Mon and Tues. The **Municipal Cultural Centre** at the intersection of Balmaceda, Caupolicán and Prat houses the municipal library, a theatre, and art galleries. Temuco is the Mapuches' market town and you may see some, particularly women, in their typical costumes in the produce market next to the railway station (Lautaro y Pinto). Mapuche textiles, pottery, woodcarving,

The Mapuche

The largest indigenous group in southern South America, the Mapuche now live mainly in communities S of the Biobío especially around Temuco. There are also reserves in the Argentine cordillera around Lago Nahuel Huapi. The name *Mapuche* is derived from the Mapuche for 'land' (*mapu*) and 'people' (*che*). They were known as Araucanians by the Spanish.

Never subdued by the Incas, the Mapuche successfully resisted Spanish attempts at conquest. At the time of the great Mapuche uprising of 1598 they numbered some 500,000, concentrated in the area between the Río Biobío and the Reloncaví estuary and mainly settled in the lands around the present day cities of Temuco, La Unión and Osorno. After 1598 200 years of intermittent war were punctuated by 18 peace treaties. So great was the Mapuche threat considered to be that Concepción became the base of the only standing army in Spanish America.

Although tools and equipment were privately owned, the Mapuche held land in common, abandoning it when it was exhausted by repeated use. This relatively nomadic lifestyle helps explain their ability to resist the Spanish. Learning from their enemies how to handle horses in battle, they became formidable guerrilla fighters. They pioneered the use of horses by two men, one of whom handled the animal while the other was armed with bow and arrows. Horses also enabled them to extend their territory to the eastern side of the Andes. They also adopted aspects of Spanish life, adding wheat, oats and apples (used for brewing *chicha de manzana*) to their traditional crops.

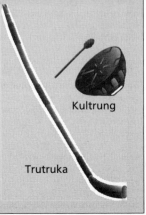

Kultrung

Trutruka

The conquest of the Mapuche after 1862 was made possible by several developments, including railways and new weapons such as the breach-loading rifle. The settlement of border disputes between Chile and Argentina enabled Argentine troops to occupy the border crossings while the Chilean army subjugated the Mapuche. After 1881 the Mapuche were confined to reservations, becoming, during the early twentieth century, steadily more impoverished and more dependent on the government.

For more information on musical instruments see page 48.

jewellery etc are also sold inside and around the **municipal market** in centre of town (corner of Aldunate and Diego Portales – it also sells fish, meat and dairy produce), but these are increasingly touristy and poor quality. The *Casa de la Mujer Mapuche*, Gen MacKenna 83, T 233886, F 236141, sells the textiles made by a co-operative of 135 Mapuche weavers; all items are 100% wool with traditional designs (spinning and weaving demonstrations are planned). Also highly recommended is the *Casa de Arte Mapuche*, Matta 25-A, T 213085, Casilla 1682, for information on Mapuche arts and crafts speak to the director Rayen Kvyeh. There is a good view of Temuco from **Cerro Ñielol**, a park (entry US$1),

where there is a fine collection of native plants in the natural state, including the national flower, the *copihue rojo*. There is also a bathing pool (US$0.40) and a restaurant (open 1200-2400). On Cerro Ñielol is also La Patagua, the tree under which the final peace was signed with the Mapuches in 1881.

Museums

Museo de la Araucanía, Alemania 84, a well-arranged collection devoted to the history and traditions of the Mapuche nation; also a section on German settlement. Open Tues-Sat 0800-1300, 1500-1800; Sun 1000-1400 (at some times of year Tues-Fri 0800-1300, 1500-1900), US$1.

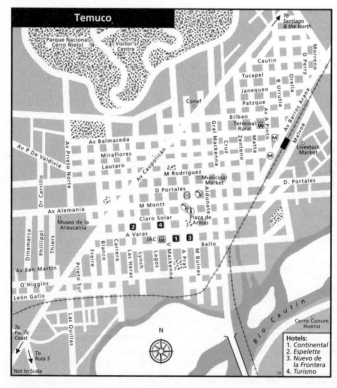

Temuco

Hotels:
1. Continental
2. Espelette
3. Nuevo de la Frontera
4. Turismo

Parque Museo Ferroviario, Av Barros Arana 3 km N of centre, contains 15 railway engines under restoration.

Excursions

To **Chol Chol**, a country town 30 km NW by unpaved road, providing a pleasant trip through Mapuche country. The trip traverses rolling countryside with panoramic views. On a clear day it is possible to see five volcanoes. Nearer Chol Chol, a few traditional round *rucas* can be seen. For an overnight stay and information, contact Sra Lauriza Norváez, C Luzcano (s/n), who prepares meals, and is very helpful. There are daily buses, laden with corn, vegetables, charcoal, animals as well as the locals, from Terminal Rural, Huincabus 1 hr, 4 times between 1100 and 1800, US$0.60, or García/Gangas 1000.

Local information

NB Do not confuse the streets Vicuña MacKenna and Gen MacKenna.

● **Accommodation**

A1 *Nuevo Hotel de la Frontera*, Bulnes 726, T 210718, inc breakfast, excellent; **A2** *Bayern*, Prat 146, small rooms, clean, helpful; **A2** *Apart Hotel Don Eduardo*, Bello 755, T 215554, parking, suites with kitchen, key; **A3** *C'Est Bayonne*, Vicuña MacKenna 361, T 235510, F 714915, with breakfast, modern, German and Italian spoken.

B *Continental*, Varas 708, T 238973, F 233830, popular with business travellers, clean, friendly, colonial-style wooden building, excellent restaurant, the bar is popular with locals in the evening, cheaper rooms without bath, rec; **B** *Turismo*, Claro Solar 636, T 210583, nr main square, slightly run-down, restaurant, good value, with bath, **C** without, good service, IYHA reductions.

C *Oriente*, M Rodríguez 1146, T 233232, clean, rec.

D *Hosp Adriane Becker*, Estébáñez 881, without bath, good breakfast, basic, friendly; **D** *Alba Jaramillo*, Calbuco 583, T 240042, by Av Alemania, with breakfast, clean; **D** *Hosp Aldunate*, Aldunate 187, T 213548, friendly, cooking facilities, also **E** dormitory accommodation; **D** *Casa Blanca*, Montt 1306 y Zenteno, T 212740, good breakfast, friendly, rec; **D** *Casa de huéspedes Centenario*, Aldunate 864, with breakfast, hot water, clean; **D** *Flor Acoca*, Lautaro 591, hot water, breakfast, clean; **D** *Hosp Millarey*, Claro Solar 471, simple, basic; **D** *Hostal Montt*, Manuel Montt 965, T 211856, parking, clean, friendly; **D** *Rupangue*, Barros Arana 182, hot shower, clean, good value. The following are in our **D** or **E** pp range: on Av Alemania, Sra Veronica Kiekebusch, No 0649, T 247287, with breakfast, clean, quiet, rec, buses No 1 or 9 from rural bus terminal; No 035, large rooms, hot water, use of kitchen, pleasant; Las Heras 810, without breakfast, basic, clean; Blanco Encalada 1078, T 234447, use of kitchen, friendly, rec; Bulnes 1006 y O'Higgins, good double rooms, hot water, above drugstore, ask for house key otherwise access limited to shop hours; on Claro Solar, No 151, with breakfast; No 483, clean, poor shower; Gen MacKenna 46, clean, Jan-Mar only; other private houses in same street; on Rodríguez, No 1311, friendly, clean, meals served; No 1341, *Res Temuco*, T 233721; Zenteno 486 (Sra Ruth Palominas), T 211269, friendly, clean, hot water, rec; **E** pp Zenteno 525, without breakfast, large rooms, clean, poor beds but good value; **E** *Res Ensueño*, Rodríguez 442, hot water, clean; **E** *Hosp González*, Lautaro 1160, p 2, friendly, safe, clean, rec; **E** San Martín 01760 (Sra Egla de González), T 246182, with breakfast, clean. Accommodation in private houses, category **D**, can be arranged by Tourist Office. Other *residenciales* and *pensiones* can be found in the market station area.

Camping: *Camping Metrenco*, 10 km S on Route 5.

● **Places to eat**

Café Marriet, Prat 451, Local 21, excellent coffee; on Bulnes: *Dino's*, No 360, good coffee; *Il Gelato*, No 420, delicious ice cream; *Julio's Pizza*, No 778, wide variety, not cheap; *Centro Español*, No 483; *Della Maggio*, No 536, good coffee and light meals. *D'Angelo*, San Martín 1199, good food, pleasant, pricey. For cheap lunches try eastern end of C Lautaro or inside the municipal market. *Pront Rapa*, Aldunate 421, for take-away lunches and snacks, rec; *Ñam-Ñam*, Portales 802, pizzas, sandwiches etc, good; *Café Artesanía Raíces Indoamericanas*, Manuel Montt 645, T 232434, specializes in Mapuche dishes, good coffee, adjoining shop sells handicrafts and textiles. *La Cumbre del Cerro Ñielol* (dancing), on top of Cerro Ñielol.

● **Airline offices**

LanChile, Bulnes 667, T 211339; Ladeco, Prat 565, Local 102, T 214325; **National**, Claro

Solar 780, Local 7, T 215764; **Varig**, MacKenna 763, T 213120; **TAN**, T 210500.

● **Banks & money changers**
Good rates for TCs at **Banco Osorno** and **Global** both on Plaza de Armas; also **Turcamb**, Claro Solar 733; **Christopher Money Exchange**, Prat 696, Oficina 419; also at Bulnes 667, Local 202; **Inter-Santiago**, Bulnes 443, local 2. All deal in dollars and Argentine pesos. **Fincard** (Mastercard), Claro Solar 922. **Banco Concepción** (for Visa), M Montt 901; **Banco de Chile**, Varas 818, rec for money transfers by Switch.

● **Embassies & consulates**
Netherlands, España 494, Honorary Consul, Germán Nicklas, is friendly and helpful.

● **Laundry**
Caupolicán 110, Nos 4 and 5, open 0900-2100 daily, good, cheap, quick; Portales 1185, expensive; automatic at M Montt between Las Heras and Lynch

● **Post & telecommunications**
Post Office: Portales 839.

Telephones: Centro de Llamadas CTC, A Prat just off Claro Solar and plaza, Mon-Sat 0800-2400, Sun and holidays 1030-2400. Entel, Bulnes 303, daily 0830-2200.

● **Shopping**
Cameras: *Ruka*, Bulnes 394, helpful, owner speaks German.

Crafts: best choice in the indoor municipal market at Aldunate y Portales.

Supermarket: *Las Brisas*, Carrera 899; *Frutería Las Vegas*, Matta 274, dried fruit (useful for climbing/trekking).

● **Tourist offices**
Bulnes 586, T 211969. Open 0830-2030, all week in summer, 0900-1200, 1500-1800 Mon-Fri in winter. Also at Balmaceda y Prat. **Automóvil Club de Chile**: Varas 687, T 213949. **Conaf**: Bilbao 931, T 234420.

● **Transport**
Local Car hire: Hertz, Las Heras 999, T 235385, US$45 a day. Budget, Lynch 471, T 214911; Automóvil Club de Chile, Varas 687, T 213949 and at airport; Puig, Portales, 779; Fatum, Varas 983, T 234199; Euro, MacKenna 426, T 210311, helpful, good value.

Air Manquehue Airport 6 km from the city. LanChile, Ladeco and National to Santiago. LanChile and Ladeco to Osorno and Valdivia; Na-

tional to Puerto Montt and once a week to Punta Arenas; TAN flies to Neuquén, Argentina.

Trains Station at Barros Arana y Lautaro Navarro, T 233416. To **Santiago**: 2 a day, 12 hrs: fares *económico* US$16, *superior/salón* US$22 (depending on service), sleeper US$24, double compartment, restaurant car expensive. To Osorno and **Puerto Montt** daily in summer 0850, 9 hrs. Ticket office at Bulnes 582, T 233522, open Mon-Fri 0900-1300, 1430-1800, Sun 0900-1300 as well as at station.

Buses No long-distance bus terminal – buses leave from company offices. Buses to neighbouring towns leave from Terminal Rural, Pinto y Balmaceda. Bus company offices: Igi Llaima and Narbus, Barros Arana y Miraflores; Erbuc, Miraflores y Bulnes; LIT, San Martín y Bulnes; Cruz del Sur, V MacKenna 671; JAC, MacKenna y Andres Bello; ETTA, Longitudinal Sur and Thiele, V MacKenna 600 block, nr Varas; Power, Bulnes 174; Pangui Sur, Miraflores 871.

Buses to **Santiago** US$16; to **Curacautín**, Erbuc, US$2, 7 daily, 2¾ hrs; to **Lonquimay**, Erbuc, 4 daily, 5¼ hrs, US$3; to **Laguna Captren**, Erbuc, Mon and Fri 1645, 4 hrs, US$3; to **Contulmo**, US$4, 2 hrs, **Cañete**, US$4 and **Lebu**, Erbuc and Thiele; Cruz del Sur, 3 a day to **Castro**, 10 a day to **Puerto Montt** (US$9, 5½ hrs), to **Valdivia** US$4; to **Osorno** US$6; to **Villarrica** and **Pucón** many between 0705 and 2045, 1½ hrs, US$3, and 2 hrs, US$3.50; to **Coñaripe**, 3 hrs, and **Lican Ray**, 2 hrs; to **Panguipulli**, Power and Pangui Sur at 0730, 3 hrs, US$2; Pangui Sur to **Loncoche**, **Los Lagos**, **Mehuin** in summer only; to **Concepción**, Bío Bío, US$5, 4½ hrs; to **Arica**, US$55 or US$70 *cama*; to **Antofagasta**, US$45.

Buses to Argentina: JAC from Terminal Rural to **Junín de los Andes** (US$25), San Martín de los Andes (US$25) and Neuquén (US$30), Wed and Fri 0400; also Igi Llaima and San Martín 3 a week each to **San Martín**, US$25. Nar Bus from Terminal Rural to San Martín and Neuquén, Mon-Fri (San Martín buses go via Villarrica and Pucón when the Tromen Pass is open); Ruta Sur, Miraflores 1151, to **Zapala** (US$22) and Neuquén (US$28),via Paso Pino Hachado, Wed and Sat 0400; La Unión del Sud, Miraflores 1285, same destinations Wed, Fri and Sat. Fénix (address above) to **Buenos Aires** and **Mendoza**.

ROUTES South of Temuco The Longitudinal Highway (Ruta 5) runs from Loncoche (81 km S of Temuco, good place for hitching) through Lanco to Paillaco and Osorno. At San José de la Mariquina, a road branches off Ruta 5 to Valdivia, 42 km from the Highway (bus Lanco-Valdivia, Chile Nuevo, US$0.85, 4 a day, fewer at weekends). The road from Valdivia to Ruta 5 going S is not in very good condition; the Highway is rejoined near Paillaco.

COASTAL RESORTS NEAR TEMUCO

Carahue (*Pop* 8,000), 55 km W by paved road is built on the site of the Spanish colonial city of Imperial which was destroyed by the Mapuche (accommodation available).

Puerto Saavedra, about 30 km further, S of the mouth of the Río Imperial, lies behind a black volcanic sandspit. In 1960 the town was destroyed by a tidal wave: few people were killed as they saw the water draining from the bay (the sign of a tidal wave) and fled to high ground. It comprises 3 distinct towns: the first administrative; the second, 2 km away, the fishing port with one poor *residencial*; the third, a further 2 km, the tourist area. From Puerto Saavedra a ferry crosses the river to Nehuentue, on the N bank of the river from where there are fine views of the bay, and to Trovolhue, reached by a specially chartered launch which takes 4 hrs to go up the Río Moncul.

● **Accommodation** E Sra Rita Sandoval Muñoz, Las Dunas 01511, lovely, knowledgeable; many *hosterías* in D-E category.

● **Transport** Buses to Temuco (Terminal Rural), Nar Bus, 3 a day, 3¼ hrs, US$2.50.

LAGO BUDI

Lago Budi, the only inland, salt-water lake in Chile, lies S of Puerto Saavedra. Over 130 species of water bird, including black-necked swans, visit it. On the E shore 40 km by road S of Carahue is **Puerto Domínguez**, a picturesque little town famous for its fishing. On the W shore is Isla Huapi (also spelt Guapi), a peninsula with a Mapuche settlement (also known as Isla Huapi) of traditional

thatched houses (*rucas*) and fine views of both the lake and the Pacific. Ideal for camping. Isla Huapi can be reached by ferry (*balsa*) either from about 10 km S of Puerto Saavedra or from Puerto Domínguez (see below).

● **Accommodation In Puerto Domínguez**: E pp *Hostería Rucaleufú*, Alessandri 22, with good meals, clean, lake views, highly rec.

● **Transport** Buses to Puerto Domínguez from Temuco, 3 hrs. **Ferries** The *Carlos Schalchli* ferry leaves Puerto Domínguez for Isla Huapi, Mon and Wed 0900 and 1700, returning 0930 and 1730, free, 30 mins.

Main routes from the Pan-American Highway to the Lakes

Not to scale

Distance in km

66a

EAST OF TEMUCO

CURACAUTIN

(*Pop* 12,737;*Alt* 400m) is small town situated 84 km NE of Temuco (road paved for the first 57 km) and 56 km SE of Victoria by paved road. Its main industry is forestry (there are several sawmills); it is a useful centre for visiting the nearby national parks and hot springs.

● **Accommodation** C *Hostería La Rotonda del Contiu*, restaurant; **D** pp *Plaza*, Yungay 157, T 56, main plaza, restaurant good but pricey; **E** pp *Hostería Abarzúa*, full board C pp, camping; **E** pp *Res Rojas*, Tarapacá 249, without bath, good meals, rec; **E** pp *Turismo*, Tarapacá 140, T 116, clean, good food, comfortable, best value; **E** pp Rodríguez 705 (corner of plaza) with breakfast, clean, kitchen facilities. *Camping Trahuilco*, 3 km S, expensive.

● **Places to eat** *El Refugio*, popular.

● **Transport** Bus terminal on the plaza. Buses to/from Temuco and Los Angeles.

HOT SPRINGS EAST OF CURACAUTIN

Termas de Manzanar, indoors, 18 km E of Curacautín (US$5, open all year) are reached by bus from Temuco and Victoria. The road passes the Salto del Indio (Km 14), before which is a turn-off to Laguna Blanca (25 km away, take fishing gear, ask Sernatur about trucks), and Salto de la Princesa, just beyond Manzanar.

● **Accommodation** B *Termas*, also simple rooms with bath; **E** *Hostería Abarzúa*, simple, friendly.

The **Termas de Río Blanco**, hotel, hot springs and mud baths, are 32 km SE at 1,046m on the slopes of the Sierra Nevada and near Lago Conguillio (bus to Conguillio National Park – see page 243 below – only at 1800).

The beautiful pine-surrounded **Termas de Tolhuaca** (open 1 Nov-30 April) are 35 km to the NE of Curacautín by unpaved road, or 57 km by unpaved road

from just N of Victoria (high clearance 4WD essential).

● **Accommodation** A2 *Termas de Tolhuaca*, with full board, inc use of baths and horse riding, very good, T 164, Casilla 48 Curacautín, or T Temuco 220975; **E** pp *Res Roja*, hot water, food, camping nr the river, good.

PARQUE NACIONAL TOLHUACA

The park, 2 km N of the Termas de Tolhuaca, covers 6,374 ha of the valley of the Río Malleco at altitudes of 850-1,830m, including the waterfalls of Malleco and Culiebra, and two lakes, Laguna Malleco and Laguna Verde. Superb scenery and good views of volcanoes from Cerro Amarillo. Park administration is near Laguna Malleco (open Dec-April), with a campsite nearby.

● **Access** The park is reached either from Curacautín via the Termas de Tolhuaca (route open all year) or by dirt road from the Pan-American Highway 5 km N of Victoria (4WD essential in winter and autumn). Bus from Victoria to San Gregorio (19 km from park entrance) Mon, Wed, Fri 1715, return same days 0645.

RESERVA NACIONAL MALALCAHUELLO-NALCAS

Situated NE of Curacautín, this 31,305 ha park on the slopes of the **Lonquimay volcano** which is a popular ski resort (season May-Nov) is much less crowded than nearby Parque Nacional Conguillio. The volcano begun erupting on Christmas Day 1988; the new crater is called Navidad. To see it, access is made from Malalcahuello, 15 km S and half-way between Curacautín and Lonquimay town. In Malalcahuello is a steam-powered carpenter's shop.

Climbing Lonquimay From the ski lodge it is a 1 hr walk to the base of the mountain. Walk towards the ski lift and from there head to the spur to the left. Allow 4 hrs for the ascent, 1 hr for the descent. Information from the Conaf lodge. Crampons and ice-axe are essential. The teacher at Malalcahuello school

Orllie Antoine de Tounens, King of Araucania

One of the more unusual European visitors to Southern Chile in the 19th century was Orllie Antoine de Tounens, a native of Périgueux in the Dordogne. His early reading of explorers' accounts of South America inspired Antoine to propose reuniting the 17 newly independent Spanish American states into a Monarchical Confederation with himself as king.

On arrival in South America in 1858 he decided instead to become King of the Mapuche. The widespread Mapuche belief that victory in their long struggle against the Chilean and Argentine governments would be brought about by the arrival of a new white chief, meant that Antoine, an imposing figure with long black hair who wore a French coat and poncho and carried a curved sabre, was received better than might be expected. Antoine's proposals for the new coat of arms, flag and constitution of Araucania or Nueva Francia appealed to Quilapan, one of the Mapuche chiefs, and Antoine was duly crowned. The Chilean government was less impressed: when Antoine led a band of armed Mapuche to the Río Biobío to negotiate a peace settlement, the Santiago authorities had him arrested. Antoine's claims that he merely intended to build schools and encourage education were rewarded with a 10 year prison sentence. French diplomats attempted to secure his release on the grounds of insanity. Eventually a compromise was arranged: the court ruled that although sane now, Antoine had been insane at the time of his offences so he was committed to an asylum in Santiago from which French diplomats were able to secure his release.

In France Antoine wrote his memoirs. His attempts to find benefactors to finance another visit to his kingdom were unsuccessful, but he returned secretly and penniless. With the Chilean government offering a reward for his head he was forced to flee. Back in France he sold bonds to finance another expedition, but the Chilean government objected to his activities and he was tried for selling fraudulent bonds. His final attempt to return was cut short when he was recognized disembarking at Bahía Blanca and deported by the Argentine government. Holding court in France, he sold specially minted coins, but was excommunicated by the Pope and the French government refused him the pension he claimed for services to his country of birth. Eventually his friends got him a job lighting street lamps. On his death in 1878 he left his crown to a cousin.

charges US$10 for transport to and from the volcano; Sra Naomi Saavedra at *Res Los Sauces* also arranges lifts

Fishing The Reserve is also a popular centre for fly-fishing: Sr Jorge Vio, at the ski lodge provides information and acts as guide, US$400 pp per day, inc transport but not equipment.

● **Accommodation** *Res Los Sauces*, **D** pp full board, or **E** pp with use of kitchen, hot water, good value; there is also a Conaf lodge. Accommodation is also available at the Centro de Ski Lonquimay, 10 km from the bus stop, **B** pp with breakfast, full board also available, free camping, open all year, ski pass US$17.

● **Transport** Bus Erbuc from Temuco, US$2 to Malalcahuello, 4 a day, 4 hrs, 5½ to Lonquimay town, US$3. There is accommodation in Lonquimay, but no public transport to the volcano.

PARQUE NACIONAL CONGUILLIO

Covering 60,833 ha, the park, situated 80 km E of Temuco, is one of the most popular in Chile, but is deserted outside Jan/Feb and weekends. In the centre is the 3,050m **Llaima volcano**, which is still active (the western side of the crater was completely blown out in 1994 and it began erupting again in Mar 1996). There

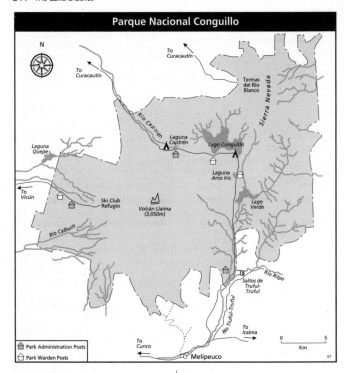

Parque Nacional Conguillo

N

To Curacautín

To Curacautín

Termas del Río Blanco

Río Captrén

Sierra Nevada

Laguna Quepe

Laguna Captrén

Lago Conguillo

Laguna Arco Iris

To Vicún

Ski Club Refugio

Volcán Llaima (3,050m)

Lago Verde

Río Calbuco

Río Rilpe

Saltos de Truful-Truful

Río Truful-Truful

To Icalma

🏠 Park Administration Posts
🏠 Park Warden Posts

To Cunco

Melipeuco

0   5
Km

67

are two large lakes, Laguna Verde and Laguna Conguillio, and two smaller ones, Laguna Arco Iris and Laguna Captrén. North of Laguna Conguillio rises the snow covered Sierra Nevada, the highest peak of which reaches 2,554m.

Wildlife This is the best place in Chile to see araucaria forest which used to cover an extensive area in this part of the country. Other trees include cypresses, lenga and cinammon. Birdlife includes the condor and the black woodpecker.

Climbing Llaima Crampons and ice-axe are essential. Climb NE from *Guardería Captrén*, avoiding the crevassed area to the left of the ridge and keeping to the right of the red scree just below the ridge. From the ridge it is a straight climb to the summit. Beware of sulphur fumes at the summit. Allow 5 hrs to ascend, 2 hrs to descend. Information on the climb is available from Sr Torres at *Guardería Captrén*.

Walking There is a range of trails, from 1 km to 22 km in length. Details are available from Park administration or Conaf in Temuco. The route through the park from the S end is as follows: from the entrance, 600m trail to Río Truful-Truful canyon and waterfall; 8 km to Laguna Verde; 3 km to Laguna Arco Iris; 3 km to Laguna Conguillio; 6 km from Centro de Información Ambiental on Conguillio to Laguna Captrén; 10 km to Park limits and *guardería*.

Skiing Llaima ski resort, one of the prettiest in Chile, reached by poor road from Cherquenco, 30 km W (high clearance vehicle essential).

Park Information Administration and information, open Nov-June, at Laguna Arco Iris, Laguna Captrén and at Truful-Truful. Out of season administration is at the western entrance. There is a Visitors' Centre at Laguna Captrén, open Dec-March. Conaf run a series of free lectures and short guided walks for adults and children during the summer, covering flora and fauna, Volcán Llaima and other subjects; details from the visitors centre. Entry US$4.

● **Access** There are three entrances:
1 From Curacautín, N of the park: take the Erbuc bus at 1830, Mon and Fri towards the park, 1 hr, US$1, or hitch (not difficult in summer). From the bus stop it is 10 km to Laguna Captrén.
2 From **Melipeuco**, 13 km S of the southern entrance at Truful-Truful.
3 From Cherquenco to the W entrance near the Llaima ski resort (see above). It is then a 2-3 day hike around Volcán Llaima to Laguna Conguillio, dusty, but beautiful views of Laguna Quepe, then on to the Laguna Captrén *guardería*.

● **Accommodation** In the park, **Laguna Captrén**: campsite US$20/site inc firewood but no other facilities. **Laguna Conguillio**: campsite (US$15/tent, hot water, showers, firewood), cheaper campsite (*camping de mochileros*, US$5 pp); *cabañas* (**A3** summer only, sleep 6, no sheets or blankets, gas stove, and café/shop). **In Melipeuco**: **E** *Germania*, Aguirre 399, basic, good food; **E** *Pensión Hospedaje*, Aguirre 729, more spacious, rec; **C** *Hostería Hue-Telén*, Aguirre 15, Casilla 40, T 693032 to leave message, good restaurant; free municipal campsite; also *Camping Los Pioneros*, 1 km out of town on road to the park, hot water. *Restaurant Los Troncos*, Aguirre 352, rec. Buy supplies in Temuco or Melipeuco: much cheaper than the shop in the park.

● **Transport** To the northern entrance: Bus from Temuco Terminal Rural, Nar Bus, 5 daily, 0900-1830, 4 hrs, US$1.30, ask driver to drop you at the road fork, 10 km from park entrance, last back to Temuco at 1630. Bus from Curacautín to Laguna Captrén, Erbuc,

Mon and Fri, 1730, summer only. To the western entrance: Daily buses from Temuco to Cherquenco, from where there is no public transport to the park. Transport can be arranged from Melipeuco into the park (ask in grocery stores and *hospedajes*, US$25 one way). For touring, hire a 4WD vehicle in Temuco.

FRONTIER WITH ARGENTINA: PASO PINO HACHADO

Paso Pino Hachado (1,884m) can be reached either by unpaved road, 77 km SE from Lonquimay or by unpaved road 103 E from Melipeuco. On the Argentine side this road continues to Zapala.

● **Chilean immigration & customs**
In Liucura, 22 km W of the frontier, open Dec-Mar 0800-2100, April-Nov 0800-1900. Very thorough searches and 2-3 hr delays reported.

● **Transport**
Buses from Temuco to Zapala and Neuquén use this crossing: see under Temuco.

FRONTIER WITH ARGENTINA: PASO DE ICALMA

Paso de Icalma (1,298m) is reached by unpaved road, 53 km from Melipeuco. On the Argentine side this road continues to Zapala.

● **Chilean immigration**
Open Dec-Mar 0800-2100, April-Nov 0800-1900.

LAGO VILLARRICA

Wooded Lago Villarrica, 21 km long and about 7 km wide, is one of the most beautiful in the region, with snow-capped Villarrica volcano (2,840m) to the SE.

VILLARRICA

(*Pop* 36,000; *Alt* 227m; *Phone code* 045), pleasantly set at the extreme SW corner of the lake, can be reached by a 63-km paved road SE from Freire (24 km S of Temuco on the Pan-American Highway), or from Loncoche, 54 km S of Freire, also paved. Less significant as a tourist resort than nearby Pucón, it is also cheaper. The *costanera* offers good views of the volcano. For good views over the lake go S along Aviador Acevedo and then Poniente Ríos towards the *Hostería La Colina*.

History

Founded in 1552, the town was besieged by the Mapuche in the uprising of 1599: after three years the surviving Spanish settlers, 11 men and 13 women, surrendered. The town was refounded in 1882.

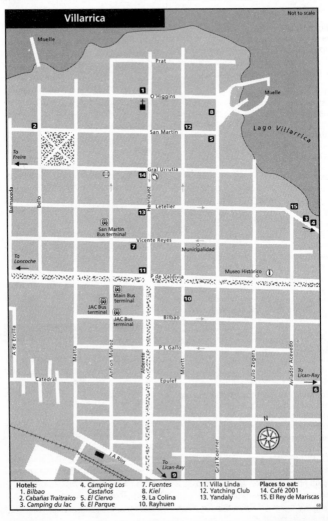

Villarrica

Not to scale

Hotels:	4. *Camping Los Castaños*	7. *Fuentes*	11. *Villa Linda*	Places to eat:
1. *Bilbao*	5. *El Ciervo*	8. *Kiel*	12. *Yatching Club*	14. *Café 2001*
2. *Cabañas Traitraico*	6. *El Parque*	9. *La Colina*	13. *Yandaly*	15. *El Rey de Mariscas*
3. *Camping du lac*		10. *Rayhuen*		

Museums

Museo Histórico, Pedro de Valdivia y Zegers.

Local festivals

Festival Cultural Mapuche, with market, usually in second week of Feb; enquire at the Santiago or Temuco tourist office.

Local information
● **Accommodation**

A3 *Hotel El Ciervo*, Gen Koerner 241, T 411215, German-run, beautiful location, pool, rec; **A3** *Yachting Club*, San Martín 802, T 411191, pleasant atmosphere, terraced gardens, swimming pool, restaurant, boating and fishing, cheaper rooms in motel annex; **A3** *Hostería la Colina*, Ríos 1177, overlooking town, T 411503, Casilla 382, run by North Americans, with breakfast, large gardens, good service, good restaurant, highly rec; **A3** *Hotel y Cabañas El Parque*, 3 km out of Villarrica on Pucón road, T 411120, Casilla 65, lakeside with beach, tennis courts, with breakfast, good restaurant set meals, highly rec.

B *Hostería Kiel*, Gen Koerner 153, T 411631, **D** off season, lakeside, clean, friendly, good; **B** *Cabañas Traitraico*, San Martín 380, T 411064, 100m from lake, cabins sleep 6, TV, heating, kitchenette, parking; **B** *Hostería Bilbao*, Henríquez 43, T 411452, clean, small rooms, pretty patio, good restaurant.

C *Rayhuen*, Pedro Montt 668, T 411571 (B in summer), clean, good restaurant, good breakfast, lovely garden, rec.

D *Yandaly*, Henríquez 401, T 411452, small rooms, good; **D** *Fuentes*, Vicente Reyes 665, T 411595, basic, clean, friendly, restaurant; **D** *Hosp Dalila Balboa*, San Martín 734, clean, cheap; **D** *Res Villa Linda*, Valdivia 678, T 411392, hot water, clean, basic, cheap, good restaurant.

E pp *Res Victoria*, Muñoz 530, friendly, cooking facilities; **E** pp Vicente Reyes 854, nr JAC terminal, good breakfast, poor bathroom facilities. Rooms in private homes, all **E** pp, incl several in Francisco Bilbao; Eliana Castillo, No 537, clean, friendly; Urrutia 407, large breakfast, kitchen, clean; Matta 469, cooking facilities, clean.

Youth hostel: **E** pp *Res San Francisco*, Julio Zegers 646, shared rooms.

Camping: 2 sites just outside town on Pucón road, *Los Castaños*, T 65-250183, and *du Lac*, quiet, but buy supplies at *Los Castaños* which is cheaper. Many more on S side of Lake Villarrica, see under Pucón (below). Summer houses available in Dec-February.

● **Places to eat**

Club Social, P de Valdivia 640, good; *El Rey de Mariscos*, Letelier 1030, good seafood; several good and cheap places for seafood in the market; *Rapa Nui*, V Reyes 678, good and cheap, closed Sun; *Hotel Yandaly*, Henríquez 401, good food, rec; *Café 2001*, Henríquez 379, coffee and ice-cream, good.

● **Banks & money changers**

Banco de Osorno changes TCs; *Casa de Cambio*, O'Higgins 210, poor rates for TCs; *Cristophe Exchange*, Valdivia 1061, good rates for TCs. Rates are generally poor.

● **Laundry**

Lavandería y Lavaseco Villarrica, Andrés Bello 348, T 411449.

● **Post & telecommunications**

Post Office: Muñoz y Urrutia, open 0830-1230, 1400-1800 (Mon-Fri), 0830-1230 (Sat).

Telephones: Entel, Reyes 721. CTC, C Henríquez 430.

● **Tourist offices**

Valdivia 1070; information and maps (open all day all week in summer).

● **Transport**

Buses to **Santiago**, 10 hrs, US$15-20. To **Pucón**, in summer every 30 mins, 40 mins' journey, US$1; to **Valdivia**, JAC, US$3.50, 3 a day, 2½ hrs; daily service to **Panguipulli** at 0700, US$2, scenic ride; to **Coñaripe** (US$1.50) and **Liquiñe** at 1600 Mon-Sat, 1000 Sun; to **Temuco**, JAC, US$3; to **Loncoche** (road and railway junction), US$1.50. **NB** JAC has 2 terminals: long distance at Bilbao y Muñoz, next to the main terminal, local is opp the main terminal.

To **Argentina** at 0615 on Tues, Thur and Sat with Empresa San Martín (Av A Muñoz 417) and at 0730 on Mon, Wed and Fri with Igi-Llaima, US$12, but if the Tromen pass is blocked by snow buses go via Panguipulli instead of Pucón.

PUCON

(*Pop* 8,000; *Alt* 280m; *Phone code* 045) is situated across the neck of a peninsula on the southeastern shore of Lago Villarrica,

26 km E of Villarrica. The major tourist centre on the lake, it is a pleasant town with a good climate and first-class accommodation. The black sand beach is very popular for swimming and watersports. Between 15 Dec to 15 Mar it is crowded and expensive; off season it is very pleasant but many places are closed. Apart from the lake, other attractions nearby include whitewater rafting. It is also a winter sports centre (see **Skiing** below).The town is scheduled for major development, with plans to build on La Península and around La Poza, the yacht harbour.

Places of interest

There is a pleasant walk to **La Península** for fine views of the lake and volcano, pony rides, golf, etc (private land owned by an Apart-Hotel, you must get permission first). There is another pleasant *paseo*, the **Otto Gudenschwager**, which starts at the lake end of Ansorena (beside *Gran Hotel Pucón*) and goes along the shore. Launch excursion from the landing stage at La Poza at the end of O'Higgins at 1500 and 1900, US$4 for 2 hrs. There is a large handicraft centre where you can see spinning and weaving in progress.

Excursions

Two excursions from Pucón close to Lago Villarrica: 2-km walk N along the beach to the mouth of the Río Pucón, with views of the volcanoes Villarrica, Quetrupillán and Lanín. To cross the Río Pucón: head E out of Pucón along the main road, then turn N on an unmade road leading to a new bridge, upstream from the old ferry crossing to La Reducción de Quelhue, near the N bank. This is supposed to be a Mapuche village, but no traditional dress, language or customs are used, and the children ask for money. From here there are pleasant walks along the N shore of the lake to Quelhue and Trarilelfú, or NE towards Caburga, or up into the hills through farms and agricultural land, with views of three volcanoes and, higher up, of the lake.

Local information
● Accommodation

In summer, Dec to Feb, add 20% to hotel prices; at this time rooms may be hard to find – plenty of alternatives (usually cheaper) in Villarrica. Off-season it is often possible to negotiate for accommodation.

L1 *Antumalal*, luxury class, 30m above the shore, 2 km from Pucón, T 441011, F 441013, very small, picturesque chalet-type, magnificent views of the lake (breakfast and lunch on terrace), lovely gardens, excellent, with meals, open year round, good beach, swimming pool and good fishing up the river; state owned **L3** *Gran Pucón*, Holzapfel 190, T 441001, half board, L2 full board, restaurant, shabby, disco, sports centre (swimming, gym, squash, etc) shared with **L3** *Condominio Gran Hotel* apartments; **L3** *Interlaken*, Caupolicán, on lakeside 10 mins from town, T 441276, F 441452, Swiss run, chalets, rec, water skiing, golf, pool, TCs changed, credit cards not accepted (open Nov-April), no restaurant.

A1 *Araucarias*, Caupolicán 243, T 441963, F 441286, clean, comfortable but not luxurious; **A2** *Gudenschwager*, Pedro de Valdivia 12, T 441904, classic Bavarian type, views over lake, volcano and mountains, attentive staff, comfortable, excellent restaurant (open in summer only); **A2** *Hostería El Principito*, Urrutia 291, T 441200, with bath, good breakfast, clean, very friendly, rec; **A3** *La Posada*, Valdivia 191, T 441088, with bath, cheaper without, full board available, also spacious cabins (C low season).

C *Hosp La Casita*, Palguín 555, T 441712, clean, laundry and kitchen facilities, English and German spoken, large breakfast, garden, motorcycle parking, ski trips, Spanish classes, **D** off season, rec; **C** *La Tetera*, Urrutia 580, T 441462, with bath and breakfast, German and English spoken, book swap, warmly rec; **C** *Salzburg*, O'Higgins 311, T 441907, with bath and breakfast, rec, German spoken, some rooms with view over volcano (possible to borrow crampons); **C** *Turista*, O'Higgins 136, T 441153 (D low season), with bath, friendly, clean.

D *Goldapfel*, O'Higgins 136A, clean, cooking facilities; **D** *Hosp De La Montaña*, O'Higgins 472, T 441267, good value, clean, TV, central, restaurant, next to JAC buses; **D** *Hostería Milla Rahue*, O'Higgins 460, T 441904, clean, good inexpensive restaurant, convenient for JAC; **D** *Res Lincoyán*, Av Lincoyán, T 441144, with bath, cheaper without, clean and comfortable; **D** pp *Saint John*, hostería and campsite, 2 km on Villarrica road, open Dec-Mar, full board available, Casilla 154, T 441165/92; **D** *Hosp Gerlach*, Palguín 460, clean, kitchen facilities, helpful.

D *Hostería ¡école!*, Urrutia 592, T 441675, F 441660, inc breakfast, run by Ancient Forest International, good vegetarian and fish restaurant, ecological shop, forest treks, information.

Accommodation in private houses, all **D** or **E**

pp unless stated: Familia Acuña, Palguín 233 (ask at *peluquería* next door), without breakfast, hot water, kitchen and laundry facilities, dirty, good meeting place. On Lincoyán: Juan Torres, No 445, T 441248, poor bathrooms, noisy, cooking facilities; *El Refugio*, No 348, with breakfast, good; *Hosp Sonia*, No 485, T 441269, hot showers, use of kitchen, very noisy and crowded, meals, friendly; No 630, friendly, clean; No 815, cooking facilities (information on climbing Villarrica); **F** pp Irma

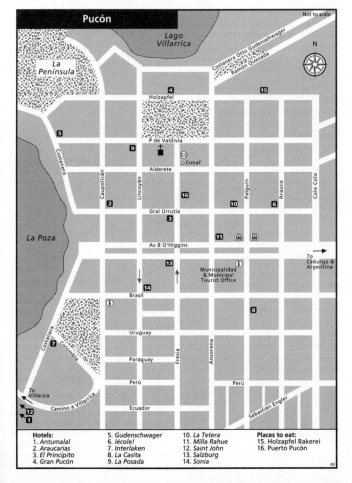

Hotels:
1. *Antumalal*
2. *Araucarias*
3. *El Principito*
4. *Gran Pucón*
5. *Gudenschwager*
6. *iécole!*
7. *Interlaken*
8. *La Casita*
9. *La Posada*
10. *La Tetera*
11. *Milla Rahue*
12. *Saint John*
13. *Salzburg*
14. *Sonia*

Places to eat:
15. *Holzapfel Bakerei*
16. *Puerto Pucón*

Torres, No 545, with breakfast, cooking facilities, clean; **F** pp No 565, friendly, clean, safe, quiet, rec, cooking facilities; next door is **Casa Eliana** (Pasaje Chile 225, T 441851), kitchen facilities, highly rec; **E** Adriana Molina, No 312, with breakfast, clean, helpful; **F** pp, on No 630, T 441043, kitchen facilities, good value; **Hosp Cherpas**, Fresia 161, T 441089, kitchen facilities, warm and friendly; **Hosp Graciela**, Pasaje Rolando Matus 521 (off Av Brasil), good food and atmosphere; Irma Villena, Arauco 460, clean, friendly, rec; Perú 720, use of kitchen, helps organize excursions to Volcán Villarrica and Huerquehue National Park; **F** pp Roberto y Alicia Abreque, Perú 170, basic, noisy, popular, kitchen and laundry facilities, information on excursions; **E** pp **Casa Richard**, Uruguay 539, behind service station on the edge of town, basic but friendly, cooking facilities, rec; **E** pp **Casa de Mayra**, Brasil 485, clean, helpful; many other families have rooms, especially on Calles Perú, Uruguay and Paraguay – look for the signs or ask in bars/restaurants.

Camping: buy supplies in Villarrica (cheaper). There are several campsites between Villarrica and Pucón: **Acapulco**, **Playa Linda** (Villarrica), **Suyay**, **Lorena**, 10 km from Villarrica (also rents *cabañas*); **Huimpalay**, 12 km from Villarrica; **Millaray**, 7 km S of Pucón; **Trancura** and **Saltos del Molco**; **La Poza**, 300m out of town on road to Villarrica, **E** pp, all facilities. In fact, there are so many establishments along the lake's southern shore that you cannot get to the water's edge unless staying in one. Camping is also possible in gardens, US$2.50 pp with use of bathroom. On the road to Tromen Pass, **Cabañas El Dorado**, US$18 for 2, good site, poorly maintained. Cheaper sites en route to Caburga. **Camping equipment**: *Eltit*, O'Higgins y Fresia; *Mawinda*, Ansorena 485.

● **Places to eat**
Pizzería Che Thomas, Palguín 465, good value, small place run by Jorge; *El Fogón*, O'Higgins 480, very good; *El Refugio*, Lincoyán 348, some vegetarian dishes, expensive wine; *Le Demago*, Lincoyán 361 (plus *Pub Naf-Naf*); *Carnes Orlando*, bar/restaurant/butcher's shop, Ansorena nr Urrutia; *Club 77*, O'Higgins, excellent trout; *Puerto Pucón*, on Fresia, Spanish, stylish; *Pastelería Suiza*, next to *Hostería Suiza*, O'Higgins 116, good; *Café de Brasil*, Fresia 477, for real coffee; *Holzapfel Backerei*, Clemente Holzapfel 524, German cafe; rec; *La Tetera*, Urrutia 580, wide

selection of teas, good coffee, snacks, German spoken, book exchange, rec; *Bar de Julio Parra*, Ansorena 370, English-style pub.

● **Banks & money changers**
Banco del Estado de Chile, O'Higgins casi Lincoyán, does not change cash or TCs. Many *casas de cambio* on O'Higgins, poor rates. Big supermarket on O'Higgins changes TCs.

● **Laundry**
Fresia 224; Colo-Colo 475 and 478.

● **Post & telecommunications**
Post Office: Fresia 813.

Telephone: CTC, Gen Urrutia 472; Entel, Ansorena 299.

● **Shopping**
Large supermarket on O'Higgins.

● **Sports**
Fishing: Pucón and Villarrica are celebrated fishing centres, for the lake and the very beautiful Lincura, Trancura and Toltén rivers. Local tourist office will supply details on licences and open seasons etc. Some tourist agencies also offer fishing trips, US$12-20.

Hiking: to the Cañi Forest Sanctuary, overnight hikes are rec; enquire at *Hostería ¡école!*

Horse riding: horse hire US$5/hr.

Skiing: on the slopes of the Villarrica volcano, see below.

Watersports: water-skiing, sailing, windsurfing at the beach by *Gran Hotel* and La Poza beach end of O'Higgins (more expensive than hotel, not rec); hotel rates: waterskiing US$10 for 15 mins, Laser sailing US$11/hr, sailboards US$6/hr, rowing boats US$3/hr.

Whitewater rafting: is very popular; many agencies offer trips (see below), basic course: US$9; advanced US$30.

● **Tour companies & travel agents**
Travel agents: on O'Higgins: *Sol y Nieve* (esq Lincoyán, also at *Grán Hotel Pucón*), excellent guides, frequently rec; *Altue*, No 371, *Nacional Travel Club*, No 323, *Trancura*, No 211, T 441959/441189 (good guides and equipment, some English spoken, rec); *Apumanque*, No 412, T 441085, poor equipment, good guides; *Turismo Florencia*, T/F 441267. All arrange trips to thermal baths, trekking to volcanoes, whitewater rafting, etc (prices: whitewater rafting and riding, see above; climbing Villarrica, US$40-45, 12 hrs, equipment provided; mountain bike hire from

US$5/hr to US$20/day; tours to Termas de Huife, US$20 inc entry). Shop around: prices vary at times, quality of guides and equipment variable. *Sergio Catalán*, T 441269 (office) or 441142, Gerónimo Alderete 192, tours, excursions and taxi service all year round. For falls, lakes and *termas* it is cheaper, if in a group, to flag down a taxi and bargain.

● **Tourist offices**
Sernatur, Caupolicán y Brasil, very helpful, ask here about all types of accommodation. Municipal Tourist Office at O'Higgins y Palguín provides information and sells fishing licences (US$1/month).

● **Transport**
Local Bicycle hire: *Taller el Pollo*, Palguín 500 block and *Trancura*, O'Higgins 261, US$20/day. Try also travel agencies, eg *Sol y Nieve* and *Andean Sports Tour* on O'Higgins. **Car hire:** Hertz, Fresia 220, US$65 for cheapest car (inc tax, insurance, and 200 km free); same prices/day at *Gran Hotel*. **Taxis**: Cooperative, T 441009; individual member Oscar Jara Carrasco, T 411992 (home in Villarrica).

Buses No main terminal: each company has its own terminal: JAC, O'Higgins 480, T 441923 (reputedly unreliable); LIT, O'Higgins y Palguín; Cordillera, Av Miguel Ansorena nr O'Higgins.

JAC to **Villarrica**, **Temuco** (frequent, US$3, 2 hrs, *rápido* US$3.50, 1 hr) and **Valdivia** (US$4.50); for **Puerto Montt** go to Valdivia and change; to **Santiago**, 10 hrs, US$18-25, many companies, Power cheapest (and least comfortable), overnight only; daytime go via Temuco; *cama* service by Tur-Bus; Cordillera, for **Paillaco** and **Lago Caburga** – see below. Colectivos to **Villarrica** from O'Higgins y Palguín. **Buses to Argentina**: Buses from Temuco to Junín pass through Pucón, fares are the same as from Temuco.

EAST OF LAGO VILLARRICA

Withing easy reach of Villarrica and Pucón are two more lakes, two National Parks and several hot springs.

PARQUE NACIONAL VILLARRICA

The park, which covers 61,000 ha, stretches from Pucón to the Argentine frontier near Puesco. There are three sectors: Villarrica Volcano, Quetrupillán Volcano and the Puesco sector which includes the slopes of the Lanín Volcano on the Argentine frontier. Each sector has its own entrance and ranger station.

The **Villarrica** volcano, 2,840m, 8 km S of Pucón (entry US$6) can be climbed up and down in 8-9 hrs (go in summer when days are longer), good boots, iceaxe and crampons, sunglasses, plenty of water and sun block essential. Beware of sulphur fumes at the top – take a cloth mask moistened with lemon juice.

● **Access** Following a number of deaths in recent years, restrictions on access to the park have been imposed: entry is permitted only to groups with a guide and to individuals who can show proof of membership of a mountaineering club in their own country. Several agencies offer excursions, US$40-50 (plus park entry) including guide, transport to park entrance and hire of equipment (no reduction for those with their own equipment); at the park entrance equipment is checked; entry is refused if the weather is poor. Note that travel agencies will not start out if the weather is bad and some travellers have experienced difficulties in obtaining a refund: establish in advance what terms apply in the event of cancellation and be prepared to wait a few days. Bargain for cheaper rate (US$30 pp for groups). Guides, see above under **Tour companies & travel agents**. Also Alvaro Martínez, Cristóbal Colón 430; Juan Carlos, at Oliva's *pensión*, or his pool room on main street, rec. Many others, all with equipment; beware charlatans, ask at the tourist office. Crampons, ice axe, sunglasses can be rented for US$4/day from the *Taller El Pollo* bicycle shop (address above).

● **Accommodation** There is a refuge without beds 4 km inside the Park, insecure and in desperate need of renovation. Campsite with drinking water, toilets, below refuge.

Skiing

The Pucón resort, owned by the *Gran Hotel Pucón*, is situated on the eastern slopes of the volcano and reached by a badly maintained track, 35 mins. A large modern base lodge offers equipment rental (US$15/day, US$82/week), ski instruction, first aid, restaurant and bar as well as wonderful views from the terrace. There are 8 lifts, though rarely do more than 2 or 3 work. Lift ticket US$12 full

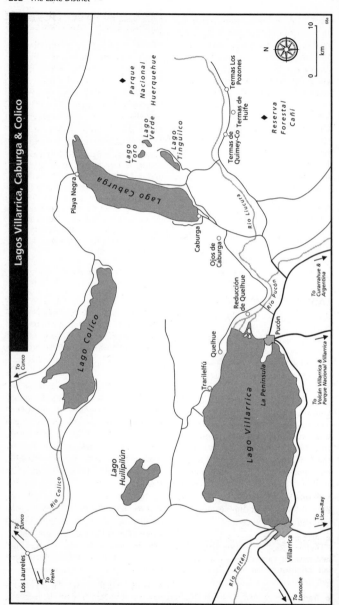

Lagos Villarrica, Caburga & Colico

day, US$18 weekends. Season is from July
to November. Piste preparation is at best
mediocre. Information on snow and ski-
lifts (and, perhaps, transport) from *Gran
Hotel Pucón*. The snow is generally soft.
Good for beginners, though more advanced skiers can try the steeper areas.

LAGO COLICO

One of the less accessible lakes, Lago
Colico lies N of Lago Villarrica in a wild,
remote setting. A road from Cunco runs
E along the lake's northern shore leading
to the northern tip of Lago Caburga (see
below).

● **Accommodation A2** *Trailanqui*, on
riverbank 20 km W of Lago Colico, luxury, also
suites and cabañas with kitchens. Booking:
Trailanqui, Portales 812A, Temuco, T/F 045-
214915. **Camping**: 2 sites about half way
along N shore: *Quichelmalleu*, Km 22 from
Cunco, T 573187; *Ensenada*, Km 26,
T 221441.

LAGO CABURGA

A very pretty lake in a wild setting 25 km
NE of Pucón at an altitude of 700m, Lago
Caburga (spelt locally Caburgua) is unusual for its beautiful white sand beach
(other beaches in the area are of black
volcanic sand). The E and W shores of
the lake are inaccessible to vehicles. The
N shore can be reached by a road from
Cunco via the N shore of Lago Colico.
The village of Caburga, at the southern
end is reached by a turning off the main
road 8 km E of Pucón. Around Caburga
the shore is lined with campsites. Rowing
boats may be hired US$2/hr. Just off the
road from Pucón, Km 15, are the **Ojos de
Caburga**, beautiful pools fed from underground, particularly attractive after rainfall (entry US$0.50).

● **Accommodation B** *Hostería Los Robles*,
3 km from village, lovely views, good restaurant; campsite, T 236989, expensive in season,
but cheap out of season. No shops, so take
own food.

● **Transport** Taxi day trips from Pucón,
US$25 return. Cordillera bus departs 1230 for

Pucón paradise

"There are not many days during the season when you can enjoy
skiing at Pucón in idyllic conditions,
but on a sunny, wind-free day with all
the lifts running, this is one of the most
mysterious and beautiful areas I have
skied in; smoke continuously bellow-
ing out of the crater, enormous lakes
and a national park down below."
Josselyn van den Pol and Leandro
Yáñez.

Caburga, returns 1400, 2nd bus (in summer
only) leaves 1700 and returns next morning
(US$1 single), but there are colectivos or you
can try hitching. If walking or cycling, turn left
3 km E of Pucón (sign to Puente Quelhue) and
follow the track for 18 km through beautiful
scenery, rec.

PARQUE NACIONAL HUERQUEHUE

Located a short distance E of Lago
Caburgo, the park, covering 12,500 ha at
altitudes of 700-2,000m, includes steep
hills, the highest of which is Cerro Araucano, and at least 20 lakes, some of them
very small (the shapes of many of these
are constantly changing). Tree species include araucaria and lenga. Entrance and
administration are near **Lago Tinguilco**,
the largest lake, on the western edge of
the park. From the entrance there is a
well-signed track N to three beautiful
lakes, Lagos Verde, Chico and Toro (for
those with cars there is a private car park,
US$0.50, 1½ km along the track). The
track zig-zags up (sign says 5 km, but
worth it) to Lago Chico, then splits left
to Toro, right to Verde. From Toro you can
continue to Lago Huerquehue and Lago
de los Palos (camping); there is no connecting path from Lago Toro to Lago
Verde, which is beautifully surrounded
by trees.

● **Access** Park entrance is 7 km (3 uphill, 3
down, 1 along Lago Tinquilco) from Paillaco,
which is reached by a dirt road (dusty in dry

weather, very slippery after rain) which turns off 3 km before Caburga. Entry US$2. The park is open officially only Jan-Mar, but you can get in at other times. Warden very helpful; people in the park rent horses and boats. Take your own food.

● **Accommodation** At the park entrance there are two campsites, US$8. 1½ km before the park entrance, two German speaking families, the Braatz and Soldans, offer accommodation, **E** pp, no electricity, food and camping (US$6); they also rent rowing boats on the lake; Nidia Carrasco Godoy runs a *hospedaje* in the park, T 09-443-2725, **E** pp, with breakfast, hot water, camping.

● **Transport** JAC bus from Pucón to Paillaco, 1½ hrs, US$1, Mon-Fri 1230, 1700, Sat/Sun 1600, returns immediately.

HOT SPRINGS SOUTH OF HUERQUEHUE

South of the Huerquehue Park on a turning from the Pucón – Caburga road there are three sets of thermal baths.

Termas de Quimey-Co, about 29 km from Pucón, are new, less ostentatious or expensive than Huife (see below), campsite, 2 cabins and *hostería* (*centro turístico* under construction). **Termas de Huife** (*Hostería Termas de Huife*, T 441222, PO Box 18, Pucón), Km 33, US$8, including use of one pool, modern, pleasant, picnicking not allowed (taxi from Pucón, US$23 return with taxi waiting, US$16 one way). **Termas los Pozones**, Km 35, are basic and lacking facilities.

RESERVA FORESTAL CAÑI

Situated S of Parque Nacional Huerquehue and covering 74,000 ha, this is a private park containing some of the oldest araucaria trees in Chile. From its highest peak, *El Mirador*, five volcanoes can be seen. For further information, including visiting arrangements, contact the *Hostería iécole!* in Pucón.

THE ROUTE TO ARGENTINA

From Pucón a road runs SE via Curarrehue to the Argentine frontier. At Km 18 there is a turning S to the **Termas de**

Palguín There are many hikeable waterfalls in the area; eg, 6-7 km from the turn-off for Termas de Palguín, Salto Palguín can be seen, but not reached, a further 2 km Salto China (spectacular, entry US$0.60, restaurant, camping); one more km to Salto del Puma (US$0.60) and Salto del León (US$1.25), both spectacular and 800m from the Termas.

● **Accommodation A1** *Termas*, address, Casilla 1D, Pucón, T 441968, full board, **B** in small huts with bath, run down, poor food, German-speaking owner, cool swimming pool, baths US$6. Nearby is the **D** *Rancho de Caballos*, offering accommodation, also *cabañas* and camping, good food, horse riding excursions (write to Cristina Bonninghoff, *Rancho de Caballos*, Casilla 142, Pucón).

● **Transport** From Pucón take Bus Regional Villarrica from Palguín y O'Higgins at 1100 to the junction (10 km from Termas); last bus from junction to the Termas at 1500, so you may have to hitch back. Taxi rates as for Termas de Huife.

Near Palguín is the entrance to the **Quetrupillán** section of the Parque Nacional Villarrica (high clearance vehicle necessary, horses best), free camping, wonderful views over Villarrica Volcano and six other peaks. Ask rangers for the route to the other entrance.

At Km 23 on the Curarrehue road a turning leads to **Termas de San Luis**, entry US$12.50, small hotel, 30 mins' walk to Lago del León (reached by Pucón-Curarrehue bus).

From Curarrehue the road turns S to Puesco and deteriorates (though work was in progress in Mar 1996 to improve parts of it). It climbs via **Lago Quellelhue**, a tiny gem set between mountains at 1,196m to reach the frontier at the Mamuil Malal or Tromen Pass.

The Lanín volcano

To the S of the pass rises the graceful cone of Lanín, 3,768m, one of the world's most beautiful mountains. Although extinct Lanín is geologically one of the youngest volcanoes in the Andes. It is climbed from the Argentine side. A 4-hr hike from the

Argentine customs leads to the *refugio* at 2,400m. The climb from here to the summit is not difficult but crampons and ice-axe are needed.

FRONTIER WITH ARGENTINA: PASO MAMUIL MALAL OR TROMEN

On the Argentine side the road runs S to Junín de los Andes, San Martín de los Andes and Bariloche.

● **Chilean immigration & customs**
At Puesco, open Dec-Mar 0800-2100, April-Nov 0800-1900, US$2/vehicle at other times.

● **Accommodation**
Conaf campsites at Puesco and 5 km from the frontier near Lago Tromen, free, no facilities.

● **Transport**
Daily bus from Pucón, 1800, 2 hrs, US$2.

THE SEVEN LAKES

This group of lakes, one of which – Lago Lacar – lies in Argentina, shares a common drainage system; five of the lakes empty their waters into Lago Panguipulli from where in turn they flow into Lago Riñihue. The three western lakes, Calafquén, Panguipulli and Riñihue, were created by glacial morraine forming a barrier across steep river valleys. After the final peace settlement of 1882 this became an area of Mapuche reservations.

LAGO CALAFQUEN

The most northerly of the lakes and dotted with small islands, Lago Calafquén is a popular tourist destination, readily accessible by paved road from Villarrica. The lake is reputedly one of the warmest and is good for swimming. Unpaved roads run round the lake.

LICAN-RAY

(*Pop* 1,700; *Alt* 207m) situated 30 km S of Villarrica on a peninsula on the N shore, Lican-Ray is the major resort on the lake. Boats can be hired from the beach (US$1.50 an hour). Although very crowded in season, most facilities close by the end of March. 6 km to the E is the river of lava formed when the Villarrica volcano erupted in 1971.

● **Accommodation A3** *Refugio*, Canadian-owned, on Playa Grande, open all year, has a Travellers' Exchange Library for English-language books, all donations of paperbacks (in reasonable condition) welcome; **E** pp *Res Temuco*, G Mistral 515, clean, hot water, good; **E** Hugo Linolilli 235; several motels (eg at **C** *Cabañas El Eden*, Huenuman 105, for a chalet for 6 with hot water; *El Conquistador*, Cacique Millaqueo s/n), *hosterías*, and camping sites (eg *Camping Las Gaviotas*, 3 km E).

● **Places to eat** *Café Ñaños*, Urrutia 105, very good, reasonable prices, helpful owner. Also on Urrutia, *Restaurant-Bar Guido's*, good value.

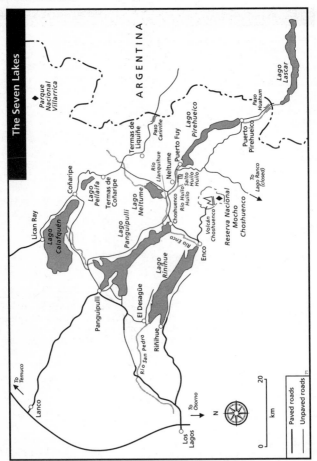

The Seven Lakes

ARGENTINA

Parque Nacional Villarrica

Lago Lascar

Paso Huahum

Termas de Liquiñe

Paso Carirriñe

Puerto Fuy

Lago Pirehueico

Puerto Pirehueico

Coñaripe

Lago Pellaifa

Termas de Coñaripe

Río Llanquihue

Neltume

Lago Neltume

Salto Huilo Huilo

Río Huilo Huilo

To Lago Ranco (closed)

Lican Ray

Lago Calafquén

Lago Panguipulli

Choshuenco

Volcán Choshuenco

Reserva Nacional Mocho Choshuenco

Río Enco

Enco

Lago Riñihue

Panguipulli

El Desagüe

Río San Pedro

Riñihue

To Temuco

Lanco

To Osorno

Los Lagos

N

20
km
0

Paved roads
Unpaved roads

● **Transport** Buses from Villarrica, 1 hr, US$1, several daily in summer from Villarrica (JAC – 7 a day, 3 on Sun – and García, Reyes y Henríquez, also frequent colectivos, US$0.60); in Jan-Feb, there are frequent direct buses from Santiago and Temuco; to Panguipulli, Mon-Sat 0730.

COÑARIPE

(*Pop* 1,253) 21 km SE of Lican-Ray at the eastern end of Lago Calafquén, is another popular Chilean tourist spot. At first sight the village is dusty and nondescript, but its setting, with a black sand beach surrounded by mountains, is very beautiful. There is a good walk from the left-hand side of the beach back through the fields to Coñaripe. From here a road around the lake's southern shore leads to Lago Panguipulli (see below) and offers superb views over Villarrica volcano.

● **Accommodation** **D** *Antulafquen*, homely; **E** pp *Hosp House*, with breakfast;

The legend of Lican-Ray

At the height of the wars between the Spanish and the Mapuche a young Spanish soldier lost the rest of his unit and strayed into the forests near Lago Calafquén. Suddenly he saw a beautiful young Mapuche woman drying her hair in the sun and singing. As he did not want to frighten her he made himself visible at a distance and began to sing along. Singing, smiling and exchanging glances, they fell in love. She called him *Allumanche* (white man in Mapuche) and, pointing to herself, indicated that her name was *Lican Rayan* (flower of magic stone). They began to live together near the lake.

Her father, Curtilef, a powerful and fearsome chief, feared she might be dead. One day a boy came to him and said: "Lican Rayan is alive. I have seen her near the lake with a white man but she is not a prisoner: it is clear they are in love".

Lican Rayan saw the warriors coming to look for her. Knowing her father, she feared what might happen, so she persuaded the soldier that they should flee. They escaped by riding on logs to one of the islands. There they felt safe, but they could not light a fire against the cold because the smoke would give them away. The weather grew colder, the North wind blew and it rained heavily. After several days, unable to put up with the cold and thinking that the warriors would have given up the search, they lit a fire. The smoke was spotted by Curtilef's men, so they fled to another island further away but again they were discovered and had to escape. This happened so many times that, although they were never caught, they were never seen again.

In the town of Lican-Ray, named after Curtilef's daughter, it is said that on spring afternoons it is sometimes possible to see a distant column of smoke from one of the islands, where Lican Rayan and the soldier are still enjoying their love of over 400 years.

Abridged and translated from *Lengua Y Costumbres Mapuches* by Orietta Appelt Martín, Imprenta Austral, Temuco, 1995.

E pp good *hospedaje* in bus terminal building, good meals; cheap campsites nr private houses (closed off season).

● **Transport** Buses to **Panguipulli**, 3 a day, US$1 and **Villarrica** US$1.50.

South East of Coñaripe

From Coñaripe a road runs SE over the steep Cuesta Los Añiques offering views of tiny **Lago Pellaifa**. The **Termas de Coñaripe**, with 4 pools, accommodation, restaurant, cycles and horses for hire, are at Km 16, 2 km from the lakeshore. Further S at Km 32 are the **Termas de Liquiñe** (hotel, B pp, cabins, restaurant, hot swimming pool, small native forest; accommodation in private houses, E pp; tours from Lican-Ray in summer, US$17, 0830-1830 with lunch). 8 km N of Liquiñe is a road going SW (20 km) along the SE shore of **Lago Neltume** to meet the Choshuenco-Puerto Fuy road (see below).

FRONTIER WITH ARGENTINA: PASO CARIRRIÑE

Paso Carirriñe is reached by unpaved road from Termas de Liquiñe. It is open 15 Oct-31 August. On the Argentine side the road continues to San Martín de los Andes.

LAGO PANGUIPULLI

The largest of the lakes, Lago Panguipulli is reached by paved road from Lanco on the Pan-American Highway or unpaved roads from Lago Calafquén. A road leads along the beautiful N shore, wooded with sandy beaches and cliffs. Most of the S shore is inaccessible by road.

PANGUIPULLI

(*Pop* 8,326; *Alt* 136m) Situated at the NW corner of the lake in a beautiful setting, is the largest town in the area. The site of a Mapuche settlement (the name is Mapuche for 'hill of lions'), the town grew as a railway terminal and port for vessels carrying timber from the lakesides. The streets are planted with roses: it is claimed that there are over 14,000. The **Iglesia Parroquial**, built by the Swiss Padre Bernabé, is in Swiss style; its belltower contains three bells from Germany. Fishing excursions on the lake are recommended. Excursions can also be made to Lagos Calafquén, Neltume, Pirehueico and to the northern tip of Lago Riñihue at **El Desagüe** (though this road was reported to be impassable owing to damaged bridges in Mar 1996). The road to Coñaripe, on Lago Calafquén, offers superb views of the lake and of Villarrica volcano.

Local festivals Last week of Jan, **Semana de Rosas**, with dancing and sports competitions.

● **Accommodation B** *Riñimapu*, in El Desagüe, T 388, comfortable, good value, excellent food; **C** *Hostería Quetropillán*, Etchegaray 381, T 348, comfortable, food; **D** *Central*, clean, hot water, friendly, good breakfast, rec; **E** pp *Res La Bomba*, quiet, friendly; **E** pp private house opp *Quetropillán*, clean, beautiful garden; **E** pp Etchegaray 464, for longer stays, clean, good breakfast; **E** pp Sra Pozas, Pedro de Valdivia 251, clean, clothes washing extra; **E** pp Olga Berrocal, JM Carrera 834, small rooms; **E** pp Eva Halabi, Los Ulmos 62, T 483, clean, good breakfast. **Camping**: *El Bosque*, P Sigifredo, US$7.50/site, clean, hot water; Municipal campsite 1½ km outside town, US$5 with all facilities, rec (closes at end-Feb); free camping on lakeside at Panguipulli possible.

● **Places to eat** *Didáctico El Gourmet*, restaurant of professional hotel school, excellent food and wine, pricey but high quality; *Café de la Plaza*, O'Higgins 816, good food and coffee; *Café Central*, M de Rosas 880, good cheap lunches, expensive evening meals; several cheap restaurants in O'Higgins 700 block.

● **Banks & money changers** In Pan-

guipulli: Banco de Crédito e Inversiones; Casa de Cambio, M de Rozas. Some shops accept US$ cash. Rates poor, TCs not accepted anywhere.

● **Tourist offices** In plaza next to police station.

● **Transport** Bus terminal at Gabriela Mistral y Portales. To **Santiago** daily at 1845, US$20; to **Valdivia**, frequent (Sun only 4), several lines, 2 hrs, US$3; to **Temuco** frequent, Power and Pangui Sur, US$2, 3 hrs; to **Puerto Montt**, US$5; to **Calafquén**, 3 daily at 1200, 1545 and 1600; to **Choshuenco** 1530, 1630 (reported as 0700 and 1100) US$2, 2½ hrs; to **Puerto Fuy**, 1800, 2½ hrs; to **Coñaripe** (with connections for Lican-Ray and Villarrica), 4 a day, 1½ hrs, US$2; to **Neltume**, **Choshuenco, Puerto Fuy** 1200, dep Puerto Fuy 1700 (means you can visit Huilo Huilo falls – see below – and return same day).

CHOSHUENCO

(*Pop* 622) lies 23 km E of Panguipulli at the eastern tip of the lake. To the S is the **Reserva Nacional Mocho Choshuenco** (7,536 ha) which includes two volcanoes: Choshuenco (2,415m) and Mocha (2,422). On the slopes of Choshuenco the Club Andino de Valdivia has ski-slopes and three *refugios*. This can be reached by a turning from the road which goes S from Choshuenco to Enco at the E end of Lago Riñihue (see page 259). Southeast of Choshuenco a road leads to Lago Pirehueico, via the impressive waterfalls of **Huilo Huilo**, where the river channels its way through volcanic rock before thundering down into a natural basin. The falls are 3 hrs' walk from Choshuenco, or take the Puerto Fuy bus and get off at *Alojamiento Huilo Huilo*, Km 9 (1 km before Neltume) from where it is a 1½-hr walk to the falls.

● **Accommodation** In Choshuenco **D** *Choshuenco*, run down, clean, good meal; various *hosterías*, inc **D** *Hostería Rayen Trai* (former yacht club), María Alvarado y O'Higgins, good food, open all year, rec; *Restaurant Rucapillán*, lets out rooms. **Camping**: on the beach. **In Neltume: E** *Pensión Neltume*, meals. **At Huilo Huilo: E** pp *Alojamiento Huilo Huilo*, basic but comfortable and well situated for walks, good food, highly rec.

● **Transport** Buses to Panguipulli 0645 and 0700.

LAGO PIREHUEICO

Situated 21 km SE of Choshuenco at 590m, Lago Pirehueico, is a long, narrow and deep lake, surrounded by virgin *lingue* forest, totally unspoilt except for some logging activity. (There are plans to build a huge tourist complex in Puerto Pirehueico). There are no roads along the shores of the lake.

There are two ports on the lake: **Puerto Fuy** (*Pop* 300) at the N end 21 km SE of Choshuenco, and **Puerto Pirehueico** at the S end. The two ports can be reached by a road from Neltume which links Puerto Pirehueico and the Argentine frontier crossing at Paso Huahum. The road S from Puerto Fuy around the Choshuenco volcano and through rainforest to the Río Pillanleufú, Puerto Llolles on Lago Maihue and Puerto Llifén on Lago Ranco (see below), one of the most beautiful in Chile, is privately owned and closed to all traffic.

● **Accommodation In Puerto Pirehueico and Puerto Fuy**: beds available in private houses inc the white house near bus terminal, very basic F pp. **Campsite**: Puerto Fuy on the beach (take your own food).

● **Transport Buses** Daily Puerto Fuy to Panguipulli, 3 daily, 3 hrs, US$3. **Ferries** From Puerto Fuy across the lake to Puerto Pirehueico US$3, 2-3 hrs. A beautiful crossing (to take vehicles reserve in advance at the *Hotel Quetropillán* in Panguipulli). Schedule varies according to season (Tues and Thur 0700 out of season).

FRONTIER WITH ARGENTINA: PASO HUAHUM

Paso Huahum (659m) is a 4-hr walk from Puerto Pirehueico. On the Argentine side the road leads to San Martín de los Andes and Junín de los Andes.

● **Chilean immigration**
Open summer 0800-2100, winter 0800-2000.

VALDIVIA

(*Pop* 110,000; *Phone code* 063), 839 km S of Santiago by road, lies at the confluence of two rivers, the Calle Calle and Cruces which form the Río Valdivia. Situated about 15 km inland and surrounded by hills, it is one of the most attractive cities in Chile. It is set in rich agricultural land receiving some 2,300 mm of rain a year and is the capital of Valdivia province. To the N of the city is a large island, Isla Teja, where the Universidad Austral de Chile is situated.

History

Valdivia was one of the most important centres of Spanish colonial control over Chile. Founded in 1552 by Pedro de Valdivia, it was abandoned as a result of the Mapuche insurrection of 1599 and the area was briefly occupied by Dutch pirates. In 1645 it was refounded as a walled city, the only Spanish mainland settlement S of the Río Biobío. The coastal fortifications at the mouth of the river also date from the 17th century. From independence until the 1880s Valdivia was an outpost of Chilean rule, reached only by sea or by a coastal route through Mapuche territory.

Places of interest

On the tree-lined, shady **Plaza de la**

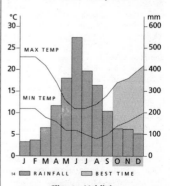

Climate: Valdivia

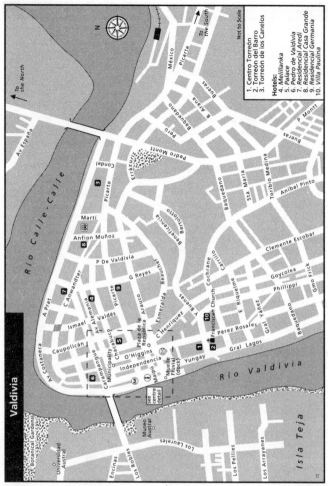

1. Centro Torreón
2. Torreón del Barro
3. Torreón de los Canelos

Hotels:
4. Melillanka
5. Palace
6. Pedro de Valdivia
7. Residencial Aredi
8. Residencial Casa Grande
9. Residencial Germania
10. Villa Paulina

República, a new cathedral is under construction. A pleasant walk is along **Avenida Prat** (or **Costanera**), which follows the bend in the river, from the bus station to the bridge to Isla Teja, the boat dock and the riverside market. On **Isla Teja**, near the library in the University, are a **botanic garden** and **arboretum** with trees from all over the world. **Lago de los Lotos** in Parque Saval on the island has beautiful blooms in Nov, entry US$0.30.

Museums

Museo Austral, on Isla Teja, run by the University, contains cartography, archaeology, history of German settlement (including cemetery), local Indian crafts, etc. Open Tues-Sun, 1000-1300, 1500-1800, US$1.

The German influence on Validiva

From 1849 to 1875 Valdivia was a centre for German colonization of the Lake District and a comparatively small number of German and Swiss colonists settled in the city, exerting a strong influence on architecture and on the agricultural methods, education, social life and customs of the area. They established most of the industries which made Valdivia an important manufacturing centre until the 1950s. According to an 1884 survey all the breweries, leatherworks, brickworks, bakeries, machine shops and mills in Valdivia belonged to families with German surnames.

"By the end of World War I, Valdivia was one of the most flourishing centres of German colonization in the South of Chile. O these earthy German gentleman farmers who dream and sing of their new world utopia before crackling fires of hawthorn and cinnamon wood, and toast it with fiery shots of homemade booze!

Cowboys, loggers, contractors, shipbuilders, industrialists, merchants; in half a century they turned the unruly, inhospitable country to the south into an exclusive society, firm and resilient. A rough-hewn frontier world, yet one of poetic beauty, where the winter rains blur the outlines of smoking pine cabins along the riverbanks, the lakeshores, and the tumbling sea." (Fernando Alegría, *Allende: A Novel*, Stanford Univ Press, 1993, page 9).

Little of the architectural heritage of this period survived the 1960 earthquake, but the city's German heritage can still be seen in some of its best cafés and restaurants and in the names of its streets.

Excursions

The district has lovely countryside of woods, beaches, lakes and rivers. The various rivers are navigable and there are pleasant journeys by rented motor boat on the Ríos Futa and Tornagaleanes around the Isla del Rey. Among the waterways are countless islands, cool and green.

The **Santuario de la Naturaleza Río Cruces**, flooded as result of the 1960 earthquake, where lots of bird species are visible, can also be visited; tours by boat. *Isla del Río*, daily 1415, 6 hrs, US$15 pp.

Local festivals

Semana Valdiviana, in mid Feb, culminates in Noche Valdiviana on the Sat with a procession of elaborately decorated boats which sail past the Muelle Fluvial. Accommodation is scarce at this time.

Local information

● **Accommodation**

L3 *Pedro de Valdivia*, Carampangue 190, T/F 212931, with bath, good; **A3** *Melillanca*,

Alemania 675, T 212509, F 222740, rec; **A2** *Naguilán*, Gen Lagos 1927, T 212851/52/53, F 219130, clean, quiet, swimming pool, good restaurant; **A2** *Villa del Río*, España 1025, T 216292, F 217851, with bath, restaurant expensive (try salmon in almond sauce), rents apartments with kitchen; **A3** *Palace*, Chacabuco y Henríquez, T 213319, F 219133, good, comfortable; **A3** *Villa Paulina*, Yerbas Buenas 389, T/F 216372, hot showers, clean, pool.

B *Raitúe*, Gen Lagos 1382, T 212503, with bath; **B** *Hostal Centro Torreón*, P Rosales 783, T 212622, with breakfast, shared bath, old German villa, nice atmosphere, car parking.

C *Hosp Turístico*, Henríquez 745, with bath, **E** pp without, lovely villa in large gardens, friendly, large rooms, kitchen and laundry facilities, English spoken, clean, highly rec.

Around the bus terminal: on Picarte, **C** *Hostal Montserrat*, No 849, T 215410, with breakfast, clean, comfortable, highly rec; **D** *Res Germania*, No 873, T 212405, with breakfast, poor beds, clean, German spoken, IYHA reductions, lovely garden; **E** pp *Hostal del 900*, No 953, with breakfast, good value, clean, heated lounge; **D** *Hosp Elsa Martínez*, No 737, T 212587, clean, friendly, highly rec;

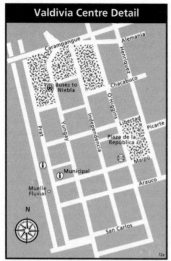

Valdivia Centre Detail

several others. On A Muñoz, outside terminal: **E** pp No 345, with breakfast, clean, friendly; **E** pp No 353, breakfast, hot water, rec. On C Anwandter: **E** pp *Hostal Casa Grande*, No 880, T 202035, attractive old house, laundry facilities, highly rec; **E** *Hosp Aredi*, No 624, Casa 2, T 214162, with breakfast, friendly, good value, *comedor*; **B** *Hostal La Terraza* No 624, Casa 4, T 212664, with breakfast, very comfortable, lovely views, parking; **E** pp *Hosp Andwandter*, No 482, clean, hot water; **F** pp No 490, without breakfast, use of kitchen.

Other, cheaper accommodation: **D** Arauco 935, clean, friendly; **D** *Prat*, Prat 595, T 222020, with good breakfast, clean; **D** *Unión*, Prat 514, T 213819, central, good value; **E** pp, Gen Lagos 874, T 215946, with breakfast, old German house, pleasant family atmosphere, rec; **E** *Hosp Universitaria*, Serrano 985, T 218775, breakfast, kitchen facilities, family atmosphere, clean, cheap meals, rec; **B** *Hosp Pérez Rosales*, Pérez Rosales 1037, T 215607, with bath, **E** pp without, modern, small rooms, good beds, overpriced; **E** pp *Hostal Cochrane*, Cochrane 595, with breakfast; **E** pp Baquedano 664, inc breakfast (but avoid laundry service); Aníbal Pinto 1335, friendly and cheap; **E** pp Riquelme 15, T 218909, with breakfast, friendly, clean, good value; **E** pp *Ana María Vera*, Beauchef 669, T 218542, clean, friendly, hot water, good

breakfast; **E** pp García Reyes 658, T 212015, Mario and Marcela, with breakfast, clean, helpful, English and German spoken, bikes to rent, use of kitchen, rec; Sra Paredes, García Reyes 244, **D** with breakfast, hot water, rec; **G** pp *Albergue Juvenil*, García Reyes s/n, off Picarte, Jan/Feb only.

Campsite: Camping Centenario, in Rowing Club on España, **E**/tent, overlooking river. Also in Parque Saval. White gas impossible to find, other than in pharmacies/chemists.

● **Places to eat**

Centro Español, Henríquez 436, good, lunch US$3.50; *Sociedad Protectora de EECC*, Independencia y Libertad, good seafood; *Dino*, Maipú y Rosales, good coffee; *Palace*, Arauco y P Rosales, popular, good atmosphere, expensive; *Pizzerón*, Henríquez 314, cheap, good, popular; *Delicias*, Henríquez 372, rec for meals and cakes, real coffee (open Sun am); *Selecta*, Picarte 1093, pleasant, excellent fish and meat, not cheap; *Shanghai*, Andwandter y Muñoz, pleasant Chinese, reasonably priced. *Fértil Provincia*, San Carlos 169, café, bookshop, cultural events, good meeting place, rec; *Café Haussmann*, O'Higgins 394, good tea and cakes; *Café Express*, Picarte 764, real coffee; *Phoenix Haus*, Av Viel s/n, on Isla Teja; restaurant in boat house, good seafood; several restaurants on the Costanera facing the boat dock, have good food and good atmosphere: *Bar Olimpia*, Libertad 28, always full, 24 hrs, cheap, good meeting point; *Entrelagos*, Pérez Rosales 622, ice cream and chocolates. Bakery: *La Baguette*, Libertad y Yungay, French-style cakes, brown bread, repeatedly rec.

● **Banks & money changers**

Banco del Estado at Arauca y Camilo Henríquez (huge commission on TCs). Good rates for cash at **Banco Osorno**, P Rosales 585, **Banco Concepción** (Visa), Picarte 370, will change cash and TCs. **Banco Santiago**, Arauco e Independencia, Mastercard. **Turismo Cochrane**, Arauco y Caupolicán. **Fincard** (Mastercard), Picarte 334, Mon-Fri 0900-1400, 1500-1930, Sat 0900-1330. *Casa de Cambio* at Carampangue 325, T 213305, open 0800-2100 Mon-Fri, 0930-1800 Sat, 0930-1400 Sun; *Turismo Austral*, Arauco y Henríquez, Galería Arauco, accepts TCs.

● **Entertainment**

Cinema in Chacabuco 300 block, also in University.

● **Laundry**
Au Chic, Arauco 436; *Lavazul*, Chacabuco 300, slow. Coin laundry *Lavamatic*, Schmidt y Picarte (Mon-Sat 0930-2030); *Manantial*, Henríquez 809, T 217609.

● **Shopping**
Supermarket: *Hiper-Unico*, Arauco 697.

Film: *Fotoquideon*, Picarte 417, for developing.

● **Sports**
Clubs: Santa Elvira Golf Club (9 holes); tennis, sailing, motor, and rowing clubs like Phoenix on Teja Island.

● **Tour companies & travel agencies**
Paraty Club, Independencia 640, T 215585; for excursions to Corral and Niebla, try the kiosks along the Muelle Fluvial.

● **Tourist offices**
Prat 555, by dock, T 213596. Good map of region and local rivers, list of hotel prices and examples of local crafts with artisans' addresses. Helpful kiosk in bus terminal, mainly bus information. **Conaf**: Ismael Váldez 431. **Automóvil Club de Chile**: Caupolicán 475, T 212378, also for car hire.

● **Transport**
Car hire: **Hertz**, Aguirre Cerda 1154, T 218316; **Turismo Méndez**, Gral Lagos 1249, T 233205.

Air LanChile (Arauco 159, of 201, T 213042) and Ladeco (Caupolicán 579, local 18, T 213392) to/from Santiago every day via Temuco.

Trains Station at Ecuador 2000, off Av Picarte,

T 214978. To **Santiago**, one a day, 14 hrs, bus Valdivia-Temuco 2¾ hrs, then change to train.

Buses Terminal at Muñoz y Prat, by the river. To **Santiago**: several companies, 13 hrs, most services overnight, US$12-17 (TurBus good) *salón cama* US$45; Pullman daily to and from central and southern towns. Half-hourly buses to **Osorno**, 2 hrs, several companies, US$5; to **Llifén**, 4 a day, US$2.50; to **Panguipulli**, US$3, Empresa Pirehueico, about every 30 mins, US$3; many daily to **Puerto Montt**, US$7, 3 hrs; to **Puerto Varas**, 2 hrs, US$6; to **Frutillar**, US$4, 3 hrs; to **Villarrica**, by JAC, 6 a day, 2½ hrs, US$3.50, continuing to Pucón, US$4.50, 3 hrs. Frequent daily service to Riñihue via Paillaco and Los Lagos.

To Argentina: to **Bariloche** via Osorno, 10 hrs, Bus Norte, US$20, and Tramaca; to **Zapala**, Igi-Llaima, Mon, Thur, Sat, 2300, change in Temuco at 0200, arrive Zapala 1200-1500, depending on border, US$34. To **Mendoza**, Fénix and Andesmar.

COASTAL RESORTS NEAR VALDIVIA

At the mouth of the Río Valdivia there are attractive villages which can be visited by land or by river boat. The two main centres are Niebla on the N bank and Corral opposite on the S bank.

NIEBLA

18 km from Valdivia is a resort with seafood restaurants and accommodation. To the W of the resort is the Fuerte de la Pura

Spanish forts in the Río Valdivia

The Spanish fortifications at the mouth of the Río Valdivia were among the strongest in the Empire. Although dating from just after the reoccupation of the city in 1645, they were greatly strengthened after 1760 owing to fears that Valdivia might be seized by the British. The main forts were rebuilt in brick and stone using the latest techniques of European military engineering. Large numbers of cannon were used to control access to the estuary. In all there were 17 forts: the main ones to see are at Niebla, Corral, Isla Mancera, Amargos and San Carlos. One other, San Luís de Alba de las Cruces, up the Río Cruces, can be visited by boat from Valdivia or by unpaved road from San José de la Mariquina.

These great fortifications were of little avail during the Wars of Independence: overnight on 2 February 1820 the Chilean naval squadron under Lord Cochrane seized San Carlos, Amargos and Corral and turned their guns on Niebla and Mancera which surrendered the following morning.

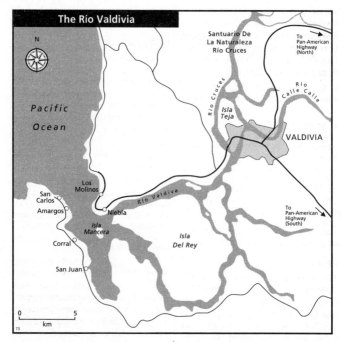

y Limpia Concepción de Monfort de Lemus, on a promontory. Partially restored in 1992, it has an interesting museum on Chilean naval history. Entry US$0.75, Sun free, open daily in summer 1000-1900, closed Mon in winter. Tourist information and telephone office nearby.

● **Accommodation D** *Hostería Riechers*; *Cabañas Fischers*, **C** per cabin; 2 campsites, worth bargaining out of season; **E** *Santa Clara*; *Las Delicias*, with restaurant with 'a view that would be worth the money even if the food weren't good', also *cabañas* and camping; *Hosp Plaza*.

Los Molinos, 6 km further round the coast is a seaside resort set among steep wooded hills (campsite, lots of seaside restaurants)

CORRAL

A fishing port with several good restaurants (eg *Español*, Av 6 de Mayo, good seafood), is 62 km by road from Valdivia. The Castillo de San Sebastián, with 3m wide walls was defended by a battery of 24 guns. It has a museum and offers a view upriver to Volcán Llaima in the distance, entry US$2.50. 3 km further N along the coast is the Castillo San Luis de Alba de Amargos in poor condition.

In midstream, between Niebla and Corral is **Isla Mancera** a small island, fortified by the Castillo de San Pedro de Alcántara, which has the most standing buildings. The island is a pleasant place to stopover on the boat trips, but it can get crowded when an excursion boat arrives. (**C** *Hosteria Mancera*, T/F 216296, open Dec-Mar, depending on weather; no singles, phone first: water not drinkable, electricity due to be connected in 1996/97).

● **Accommodation E** *Res Mariel*, Tarapacá

36, T 471290, modern, clean, friendly, good value; *Hostería La Nave*.

San Carlos, 4 km N along the coast from Corral is the site of the ruins of the Castillo de San Carlos. The coastal walks W and S of here are splendid.

● **Accommodation** E *Hostería Los Alamos*, a delightful hideout for those seeking a quiet life.

● **Transport** The tourist boats (*Neptuno* or *Calle-Calle*) to Isla Mancera and Corral, offer a guided half-day tour (US$20 with meals – cheaper without) from the Muelle Fluvial, Valdivia (behind the tourist office on Av Prat 555), 1330 daily. The river trip is beautiful, but you can also take a bus to Niebla from Chacabuco y Yungay, Valdivia, roughly every 20 mins between 0730 and 2100, 30 mins, US$0.75 (bus continues to Los Molinos), then cross to Corral by boat, frequent, US$1. There are occasional buses from Valdivia to Corral.

RESORTS FURTHER NORTH

The town of **San José de la Mariquina** (*Pop* 6,000) lies inland, 42 km N of Valdivia on the Río Cruces. From here an unpaved road leads S along the river to the Castillo de San Luis de Alba (22 km), a colonial fortification built in 1647 and largely rebuilt according to the original plans.

Mehuin

27 km NW of San José, is a popular resort and fishing port with a long beach. Bus from Valdivia 2 hrs, US$2.

● **Accommodation** C *Hostería Millalafquen*, T 279; D *Mehuin*, not very inviting; *Playa*; E *Hosp Marbella*, clean, cheapest.

Quele 6 km further N, has two simple *residenciales*. Good beach but bathing dangerous at high tide because of undercurrents; safer to bathe in the river near ferry.

INLAND FROM VALDIVIA

A beautiful, unpaved road runs 61 km E from Valdivia along the Río Calle Calle to **Los Lagos**, at the junction with the Pan-American Highway.

● **Accommodation** D *Roger*, Lynch 42, T 261, disco on Sat, rec; *Turismo Tell*, 10 km E, cabañas and campsite, T 09-653-2440, Eng-

lish, French and German spoken; 2 buses a day in summer.

LAGO RIÑIHUE

39 km further E, is the southernmost of the Seven Lakes. There is no road around the northern edge of the lake and the road around the southern edge of the lake from Riñihue to Enco is closed (except in jeeps in summer only), so Choshuenco at the SE end of Lago Panguipulli can only be reached by road from Panguipulli or Puerto Fuy. **Riñihue**, a beautiful but very small and isolated village at the western end of the lake, is worth a visit.

● **Accommodation** B *Hostería Huinca Quinay*, 3 km E of Riñihue, T 461347, F 461406, cabañas, restaurant; E *Restaurant del Lago* (no meals). Campsite by the lake.

LAGO RANCO

One of the largest lakes and starred with islands, this is also one of the most accessible as there is road round its edge. This road is terrible (lots of mud and animals, including oxcarts), but is worth taking to see an older lifestyle, the beautiful lake, waterfalls and sunsets on the distant volcanoes (if walking, beware the numerous guard dogs in the area). There is excellent fishing on the S shore and several hotels organize fishing expeditions.

From the N the lake can be reached from the Longditudinal Highway from Los Lagos or from a point 18 km S of Los Lagos, 11 km N of Paillaco. These two roads join and meet the road around the lake some 5 km W of Futrono. From the S access is from La Unión (*Hotel Club Alemán*, Letelier 497, T 322695), which is bypassed by the Longitudal Highway.

The main town on the northern shore is **Futrono** from where the road curves round the N of Lago Ranco to **Llifén**, 22 km, a picturesque place on the eastern shore. From Llifén, a visit can be paid to **Lago Maihue**, 33 km further E, the S shore of which is covered by native forests.

● **Accommodation In Futrono**: B *Hostería*

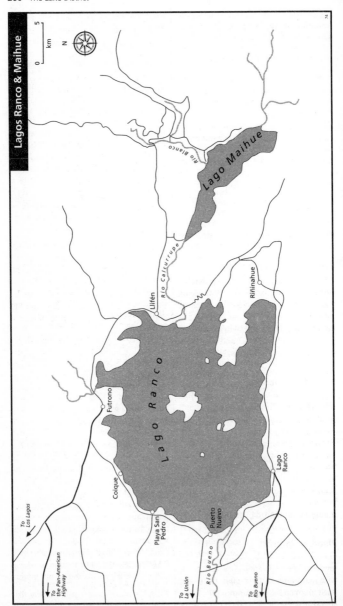

Rincón Arabe, T 481262, F 481330; *Puerto Futrono*, T 481281; **F** pp in the Casa Parroquial. **In Llifén A1** *Huequecura*, Casilla 4, T 09-653-5450, inc meals and fishing services, good restaurant; **B** *Hostería Chollinco*, 3 km out of town on the road towards Lago Maihue, T 0638-202, limited electricity, swimming pool; **C** *Hostería Lican*, T 09-653-5315, F Valdivia 218921. 4 campsites in the vicinity, eg at Chollinco.

From Llifén the road continues via the Salto de Nilahue (Km 14) to **Riñinahue**, Km 23, at the SE corner of the lake and **Lago Ranco**, Km 47, an ugly little town on the S shore, which has a museum with exhibits on Mapuche culture.

● **Accommodation In Riñinahue: A3** *Hostería Riñinahue*,Casilla 126, T 491379, organizes fishing expeditions; *Hosterá El Arenal del Nilahue*. **In Lago Ranco: B** *Hostería Parque Thule*, T 491293; **B** *Hostería Casona Italia*, T 491225; **B** *Hostería Phoenix*, T 491226; *Residenciales*, houses to let in summer.

On the western shore is **Puerto Nuevo** (hotel of same name, **A1**), very good, watersports, fishing on the Río Bueno. Further N, 10 km W of Futrono is **Coique** with the best beach on the lake.

● **Transport** Cordillera Sur bus from Valdivia to Llifén, twice daily, once Sun; from Osorno to Lago Ranco, Empresa Ruta 5, 6 daily.

OSORNO

(*Pop* 114,000; *Phone code* 064), 921 km from Santiago and 105 km N of Puerto Montt, is situated at the confluence of the Ríos Rahue and Damas and is a centre for visiting the lakes. Founded in 1553, it was abandoned in 1604 and was refounded by Ambrosio O'Higgins and Juan MacKenna O'Reilly in 1796. It later became one of the centres of German immigration; their descendants are still of great importance in the area.

Places of interest

On the large **Plaza de Armas** stands the modern, concrete and glass cathedral, with many arches, repeated in the tower, itself an open, latticed arch with a cross superimposed. West of the centre on a bend overlooking the river is the **Fuerte María Luisa**, named after the Spanish queen much painted by Goya, built in 1793, restored 1977, with only the river front walls and end turrets standing. East of the main plaza along MacKenna are a number of late 19th century mansions built by German immigrants, now preserved as National Monuments.

Museums

Museo Histórico Municipal, Matta 809. Entrance in Casa de Cultura, US$1; Mon-Fri 1000-1230, 1430-1800, also Sat 1000-1300, 1500-1800 and Sun 1500-1800 in summer. Includes displays on natural history, Mapuche culture, refounding of the city and German colonization.

Excursions

Drive or take bus (US$0.60, frequent) N of Osorno to Río Bueno, celebrated for its scenery and for fishing, to La Unión, and to **Trumao**, a river port on the Río Bueno, whence a launch may be taken to La Barra on the coast; leaves Wed and Sat only at 0900, 5 hrs, US$6; returns Sun at 0900, no service in winter.

The sea beaches at **Maicolpue** (60 km from Osorno – **D** *Hostería Müller*, on the beach, clean, good service, rec, campsite) and **Pucatrihue** (*Hostería Incalcar*, summer only) are worth a visit in the summer (daily bus service).

Local information

● **Accommodation**

L3 *Del Prado*, Cochrane 1162, T 235020, swimming pool, garden, good meals, well-located, charming.

A1 *Waeger*, Cochrane 816, T 233721, PO Box 802, F 237080, 4-star, restaurant, comfortable, rec; **A2** *Gran*, O'Higgins 615, T 233990, F 239311, cable TV, comfortable; **A3** *Inter-Lagos*, Cochrane 515, T 234695, F 232581, with breakfast, garage, restaurant; **A3** *Pumalal*, Bulnes 630, T 243520, F 242477, with breakfast, modern, airy, clean; **A3** *Res Riga*, Amthauer 1058, T 232945, clean, pleasant, highly rec but heavily booked in season; **A3** *Eduviges*, Eduviges 856, T/F 235023, spacious, clean, quiet, attractive, gardens, also *cabañas*, rec; **A3** *Res Rucaitué*,

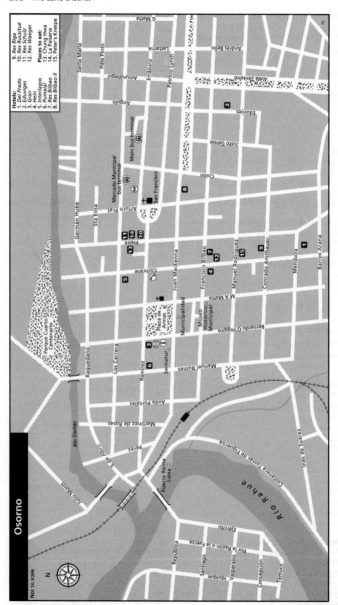

Osorno

Not to scale

N

Hotels:
1. Del Prado
2. Eduviges
3. Gran
4. Hein
5. Interlagos
6. Pumalal
7. Res Bilbao
8. Res Bilbao II
9. Res Riga
10. Res Rucatrué
11. Res Schulz
12. Res Waeger

Places to eat:
13. Chung Hwa
14. La Paisana
15. Peter's Kneipe

Freire 546, T 239922, with breakfast, cable TV, overpriced; **A3 Res Schulz**, Freire 530, T 237211, with bath, **B** without, cable TV.

B Millantúe, Errázuriz 1339, T 242072, opp bus terminal, with breakfast, parking; **B Res Hein**, Cochrane 843, T 234116, with bath, **C** without, old-fashioned, spacious, family atmosphere; **B Res Bilbao**, Bilbao 1019, T 236755, F 321111 and **Res Bilbao II**, MacKenna 1205, T 242244, with breakfast, parking, restaurant.

D Amunátegui 520, nr bus terminal, good; **D Germania**, Rodríguez 741, no hot water, cooking facilities; **D Res Ortega**, Colón y Errázuriz, 1 block from bus terminal, parking, basic, clean, toilet facilities limited; others nr bus terminal: at A Pinto 1758, E inc breakfast and hot water, T 238024.

E pp **Res Sánchez**, Los Carrera 1595, use of kitchen, hot showers, clean, noisy on ground floor, with breakfast; **E** pp **Hosp de la Fuente**, Los Carrera 1587, basic, friendly; **E** pp Colón 844, with breakfast.

F pp **Res Carillo**, Angulo 454, basic, clean; **La Paloma**, Errázuriz 1599, basic; **Richmond**, Lastarria 530, basic; **Silvane**, Errázuriz y Lastarria, T 234429, fairly basic. Private houses at Germán Hube, pasaje 1, casa 22, población Villa Dama, E pp, hot water, clean, use of kitchen, rec.

Camping: Municipal site at S entrance to city, open from Jan only, free.

● **Places to eat**
Peter's Kneipe, M Rodríguez 1039, excellent German restaurant, not cheap; **Dino**, Ramírez 898, on the plaza, restaurant upstairs, bar/cafeteria downstairs, good. **Los Troncos**, Cochrane 527, good pizzas, French spoken; **Chung Hwa**, Freire 543, Chinese, good value set menus; **Casa del Atillo**, MacKenna 1011, good food and service, pleasant atmosphere, rec; **La Paisana**, Freire 530, Arab specialities, not cheap; **Waldis**, O'Higgins next to **Gran Hotel**, good coffee; **Travels** in bus terminal for cheap snacks. Bakery at Ramírez 977 has good wholemeal bread.

● **Banks & money changers**
Fincard for Mastercard, MacKenna 877, Mon-Fri 0900-1400, 1530-1900, Sat 0930-1330. For good rates try **Cambio Tur**, MacKenna 1010, T 4846; **La Frontera**, Ramírez 949, local 5 (Galería Catedral); if stuck try **Travels** bar in bus terminal.

● **Laundry**
Prat 678 (allow at least a day).

● **Post & telecommunications**
Post Office: O'Higgins 645, also Telex.

Telephone: Ramírez at central plaza and Juan MacKenna y Cochrane.

● **Shopping**
Reinares and Thone, Ramírez 1100, for good fishing gear.

● **Sports**
Skiing: **Club Andino** O'Higgins 1073, for advice on possibilities.

● **Tourist offices**
Provincial government office, on Plaza de Armas, O'Higgins s/n, p 1, left, T 234104. **Automóvil Club de Chile**: Bulnes 463, T 232269, information and car hire.

● **Transport**
Local Garage: **Automotriz Salfa Sur SA**, Fco Bilbao 857; **Automotriz Amthauer**, Amthauer 1250.

Air LanChile, Matta 862, T 236688, Ladeco, MacKenna 975, T 234355; both operate daily flights Osorno-Santiago, via Temuco.

Trains Station at MacKenna 600, T 232992. Daily train to/from Santiago (18 hrs).

Buses Main terminal 4 blocks from Plaza de Armas at Errázuriz 1400. Left luggage open 0730-2030. Bus from centre, US$0.30. To **Santiago**, frequent, US$16, salón cama US$25, 16 hrs; to **Valparaíso** and **Viña del Mar**, Tas Choapa, US$25; to **Arica**, Tas Choapa, US$55; to **Concepción**, US$12; to **Temuco**, US$6; to **Pucón** and **Villarrica**, Tur Bus, frequent, US$6; to **Valdivia**, frequent, 2 hrs, several companies, US$5; to **Frutillar**, US$2.50, **Llanquihue, Puerto Varas** and **Puerto Montt** (US$5) services by Varmontt every 30 mins; to **Puerto Octay**, US$1.50, Vía Octay company 6 daily between 0815-1930 (return 0800-1930) Mon-Sat, 5 on Sun between 0800 and 2000 (4 return buses); to **Punta Arenas**, US$60-75, Cruz del Sur, Turisbus, Eurobus and Bus Norte, all twice a week.

Local buses to **Lago Ranco, Entre Lagos, Puyehue** and **Aguas Calientes** leave from the Mercado Municipal terminal, 1 block W of the main terminal. To Lago Ranco, 6 a day from 0810, Empresa Ruta 5, 2 hrs, US$1.50; to Entre Lagos frequent services in summer, Expreso Lago Puyehue and Buses Puyehue, 45 mins, US$1, reduced service off-season; some buses by both companies also continue to Aguas Calientes (off-season according to demand) 2 hrs, US$2; in summer there are also services Maicolpué on the coast if demand is sufficient.

EAST OF OSORNO

From Osorno Route 215 runs E to the Argentine frontier at the Puyehue Pass via the S shore of Lago Puyehue, Anticura and the Parque Nacional Puyehue.

LAGO PUYEHUE

(*Alt* 207m) is situated about 47 km E of Osorno, surrounded by relatively flat countryside. The S shore is much more developed than the N shore which is accessible only by unpaved road from the western end. At the western end is **Entre Lagos** (*Pop* 3,358) and the **Termas de Puyehue** are at the eastern end (entry US$15 pp, 0900-2000).

Local information
● **Accommodation & places to eat**

In Entre Lagos: C *Hosp Vista Hermosa*, with breakfast; D *Hostería Entre Lagos*, Ramírez 65, lake view, T 647225; D *Villa Veneto*, Gral Lagos 602, T 647203; D pp *Hosp Millarey*, with breakfast, excellent, clean, friendly; *Restaurant Jardín del Turista*, very good; *Pub del Campo*, highly rec restaurant, reasonable prices, owner is of Swiss descent.

On the S lakeshore: *Chalet Suisse*, Ruta 215, Km 55 (Casilla 910, Osorno, T Puyehue 647208, Osorno 064-234073), *hostería*, restaurant with excellent food; a few kilometres beyond, *Hosp y cabañas* at Almacén Valenciana; B *Posada Puntillo*, at Shell station, Km 62, before **A1** *Motel Ñilque*, T Santiago 231-3417, or (0647) 218, cabins, half-price May-Oct, fishing trips, watersports, car hire. B *Hostería Isla Fresia*, located on own island, T 236951, Casilla 49, Entre Lagos, transport provided.

At the Termas: L2-A1 pp *Gran Hotel Termas de Puyehue*, T 232157, F 371272 (cheaper May to mid-Dec) 2 thermal swimming pools (one indoors, very clean), theatre, conference centre, well maintained, meals expensive, in beautiful scenery, heavily booked Jan-Feb (postal address Casilla 27-0, Puyehue, or T Santiago 231-3417); accommodation also in private house nearby, **E** pp full board.

Camping: *Camping No Me Olvides*, Km 56, US$10; *Playa Los Copihues*, Km 56.5 (hot showers, good), all on S shore of Lake Puyehue; *Camping Playa Puyehue*, Km 75.

● **Transport**

Bus 2½ hrs, schedule under Osorno **Buses**; buses do not stop at the lake (unless you want to get off at *Gran Hotel Termas de Puyehue* and clamber down), but continues to Aguas Calientes.

PARQUE NACIONAL PUYEHUE

The Park, located E of Lago Puyehue and stretching to the Argentine frontier, covers 107,000 ha, much of it in the valley of the Río Golgol. On the E side are several lakes, including Lago Constancia and Lago Gris. There are two volcanic peaks: **Volcán Puyehue** (2,240m) in the N (access via a private road US$2.50) and **Volcán Casablanca** (also called Antillanca, 1,900m).

At **Aguas Calientes**, 4 km S of the Termas de Puyehue, there is an open air pool with very hot thermal water beside the Río Chanleufú, open 0830-1900, US$1.50, children US$1, and a very hot indoor pool, open Mon-Fri (in season only) 0830-1230, 1400-1800, Sat, Sun and holidays (all year) 0830-2030, US$5, children US$3.

From Aguas Calientes the road continues 18 km SE to **Antillanca** on the slopes of Volcán Casablanca, past three small lakes and through forests. (In winter a one way traffic system operates on the last 8 km: up 0800-1200 and 1400-1730, down 1200-1400 and after 1730). This is a particularly beautiful section, especially at sunrise, with the snow-clad cones of Osorno, Puntiagudo and Puyehue forming a semicircle. The tree-line on Casablanca is one of the few in the world made up of deciduous trees (southern beech). From Antillanca it is possible to climb Casablanca for even better views of the surrounding volcanoes and lakes, no path, 7 hrs return journey, information from Club Andino in Osorno. On the S side of the volcano there are caves (accessible by road, allow 5 hrs from *Hotel Antillanca*).

Skiing Attached to the *Hotel Antillanca* is one of the smallest ski resorts in Chile; there are 3 lifts, ski instruction and first aid available. Piste preparation is unre-liable. Skiing is not difficult but quality depends on the weather: though rain is common it often does not turn to snow.

In the Anticura section of the park, NE of Aguas Calientes, are three water-falls, including spectacular 40m wide

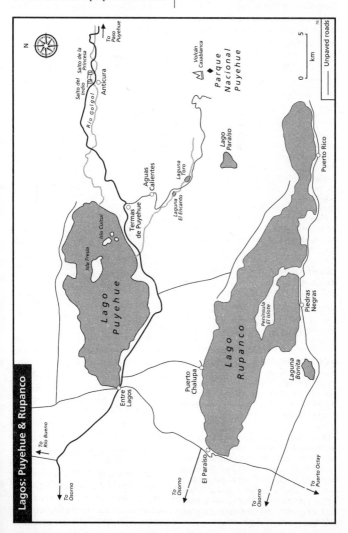

Lagos: Puyehue & Rupanco

Salto del Indio. Legend has it that an Indian, enslaved by the Spanish, was able to escape by hiding behind the falls. Situated just off the road, the falls are on a marked path through dense forest which includes a 800 year old Coihue tree known as 'El Abuelo'.

Park administration is at Aguas Calientes; there is also a ranger station at Anticura. Leaflets on walks and attractions are available.

● **Accommodation** A *Hotel Antillanca*, T 235114, inc free mountainbiking and parapenting, at foot of Volcán Casablanca, excellent restaurant/café, with pool, sauna, friendly club-like atmosphere. **Camping**: *Chanleufu*, in Aguas Calientes, with hot water, US$25/site, cabañas (**A3** in season, **C** off season) T 236988, a small shop – better to take your own food, and an expensive café; *Los Derrumbes*, 1 km from Aguas Calientes, no electricity, US$20/site. Conaf *refugio* on Volcán Puyehue, but check with Conaf in Anticura whether it is open.

● **Transport** See under Osorno for buses. No public transport from Aguas Calientes to Antillanca; try hitching – always difficult, but it is not a hard walk.

FRONTIER WITH ARGENTINA: PASO PUYEHUE

Paso Puyehue is reached by Route 215, paved most of the way, from Osorno via Entre Lagos and Lago Puyehue. On the Argentine side the road continues to Bariloche.

● **Chilean immigration**
Open second Sat in Oct-second Sat in Mar 0800-2100, otherwise 0800-1900. The Chilean frontier post is at **Anticura**, 22 km W of the border (*Hostería y Cabañas Anticura*; *Camping Catrue*).

NB This route is liable to closure after snow.

● **Crossing by private vehicle**
For vehicles entering Chile, formalities are quick (about 15 mins), but includes the spraying of tyres, and shoes have to be wiped on a mat; pay US$2 to 'Sanidad' and US$1.25 at the documents counter. Passage will be much quicker if you already have Chilean pesos and don't wait to change at the border.

● **Transport**
To Anticura, bus at 1620 from Osorno, 3 hrs. Several bus companies run daily services from Puerto Montt via Osorno to Bariloche along this route (see under Puerto Montt for details). Although less scenic than the ferry journey across Lake Todos Los Santos and Laguna Verde (see page 279) this crossing is cheaper, more reliable and still a beautiful trip.

LAGO RUPANCO

South of Lago Puyehue and considerably larger, this lake is very beautiful and much less developed than most of its neighbours. A 40 km dirt road runs along the S shore, passing through the village of **Piedras Negras**. South of the lake is Laguna Bonita, surrounded by forest. The N shore is accessible by a poor road S from Route 215. **El Paraíso** at the western end, can be reached by a 13 km road from Entre Lagos. Access from the S is best from the Osorno-Puerto Octay road, turning E after 33 km.

● **Accommodation El Paraíso** *Hostería y Cabañas El Paraíso*, T 236239. **In Piedras Negras**: *Hostería El Islote* 7 km E. **Camping**: several sites inc at Piedras Negras.

● **Transport** Buses from Osorno to Piedras Negras from either *Minimarket El Capricho*, MacKenna y Colón, or Estación Viejo (old railway station), leaves 1645, 1545 on Sat, returns from Piedras Negras 0700.

Hacienda Rupanco

Situated SE of Lago Rupanco and covering 47,000 ha, this hacienda, the largest milk-producing farm in Chile, invites visitors. Activities include horseriding, fishing, rafting, canoeing and sailing on Lago Rupanco. The main entrance is off the Osorno-Puerto Octay road. Accommodation **A3** in comfortable houses, full board, also camping, open all year.

LAGO LLANQUIHUE

The lake, covering 56,000 ha, is the second largest in Chile. Across the great blue sheet of water can be seen two snow-capped volcanoes: the perfect cone of Osorno (2,680m) and the shattered cone of Calbuco (2,015m), and, when the air is clear, the distant Tronador (3,460m).

The largest towns, Puerto Varas, Llanquihue and Frutillar are all on the western shore, linked by the Pan-American Highway. There are roads around the rest of the lake: from Puerto Octay the road along the eastern lakeside, with the Osorno volcano on your left, to Ensenada is very beautiful, but this road is narrow with lots of blind corners, necessitating speeds of 20-30 kph at best in places (see below). There is almost no public transport on this section and hitching is very difficult.

PUERTO OCTAY

(*Pop* 2,000; *Phone code* 064), 56 km SE of Osorno, is a small town at the N tip of the lake in a beautiful setting of rolling hills with German-style farmhouses. Founded by German settlers in 1851, the town enjoyed a boom period in the late 19th century when it was the northern port for steamships on the lake: a few buildings survive from that period, notably the church and the enormous German-style former convent. Since the arrival of railways and the building of roads it has declined. 3 km S along an unpaved road is the Peninsula of **Centinela** with lodging, camping, a launch dock, bathing beaches, watersports. From the headland are fine views of the volcanoes Osorno, Calbuco, Puntiagudo and the Cordillera of the Andes; a very popular spot in good weather (taxi US$2.50 one way). The **Hotel Centinela**, idyllically situated, was built in 1913 as a summer mansion. Much less frequented by visitors than Frutillar or Puerto Varas, Puerto Octay offers an escape for those seeking peace and quiet.

Museums Museo el Colono, Independencia 591, with displays on Ger-

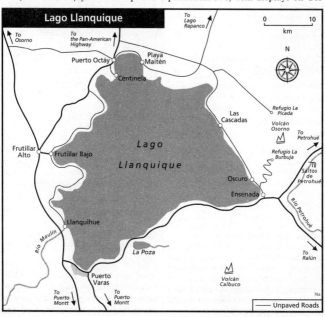

Lago Llanquique

To Lago Rapanco

To Osorno

To the Pan-American Highway

Playa Maitén

Puerto Octay

Centinela

Las Cascadas

Refugio La Picada

Volcán Osorno

To Petrohué

Refugio La Burbuja

Lago Llanquique

Frutillar Alto

Frutillar Bajo

Oscuro

Saltos de Petrohué

Ensenada

Río Petrohué

Río Maulín

Llanquihue

La Poza

To Ralún

Puerto Varas

Volcán Calbuco

To Puerto Montt

To Puerto Montt

Unpaved Roads

man colonization, open Tues-Sun 0900-1300, 1500-1900, Dec-Feb only; another part of the museum, housing agricultural implements and machinery for making chicha, is just outside town on the road to Centinela.

● **Accommodation & places to eat** **B** *Haase*, Pedro Montt 344, T 193, with breakfast, attractive old building; **C** *Posada Gubernatis*, Santiago s/n, lakeside, clean, comfortable; **E** pp *Hosp La Naranja*, Independencia 361, without bath, with breakfast, restaurant; **E** pp *Hosp Fogón de Anita*, 1 km out of town, T 34523, good breakfast; **F** pp *Hosp Raquel Mardorf*, Germán Wulf 712, with enormous breakfast, clean, comfortable, owners have *Restaurante La Cabaña* at No 713, good; *Restaurante Baviera*, Germán Wulf 582, cheap and good. **Camping**: *El Molino*, beside lake, US$5 pp, clean, friendly, rec. **Centinela**: *Hotel Centinela*, T Santiago 234-4010, sadly neglected, meals available, friendly staff, also has *cabañas*; **E** pp *Hostería La Baja*, Casilla 116, T 391269, beautifully situated at the neck of the peninsula, with breakfast and bath. **Camping**: Municipal site on lakeside, US$15/site.

● **Tourist offices** Pedro Montt s/n, T 276, open Dec-Feb daily 0900-2100.

● **Transport** Buses to Osorno 7 a day; to Frutillar (1 hr), Puerto Varas (2 hrs) and Puerto Montt (3 hrs) Thaebus, 8 a day; to **Las Cascadas** (see below) Mon-Fri 1700, return next day 0600. Bus to Ensenada 0600, daily in season, less frequent out of season.

East of Puerto Octay 10 km E of Puerto Octay is Playa Maitén, 'highly recommended, nice beach, marvellous view to the Volcán Osorno, no tourists'. 24 km further on is **Las Cascadas**, surrounded by picturesque agricultural land, old houses and German cemeteries.

● **Accommodation** *Centro de Recreación Las Cascadas*, T 235377; **E** *Hostería Irma*, on lake, 2 km past Las Cascadas, run by Tres Marías, attractive former residence, good food, very pleasant. Several farms on the road around N and E side of the lake offer accommodation, look for signs. **Camping**: *Centro de Recreación Las Cascadas* and Villa Las Cascadas picnic area (free); at Playa Maitén, rec.

FRUTILLAR

(*Pop* 5,000; Phone code 065) Lying about half-way along the W side of the lake, Frutillar is in fact two towns: Alto Frutillar, with a railway station, just off the main highway, and Bajo Frutillar beautifully situated on the lakeside, 4 km away. (Colectivos run between the two towns, 5 mins, US$0.50.)

Places of interest

Bajo Frutillar is possibly the most attractive – and expensive – town on the lake: from its **costanera** there are superb views over the water with the forms of Calbuco and Osorno in the background. There is a large open-air chess board in the square outside the Club Alemán. At the N end of the town is the **Reserva Forestal Edmundo Winckler**, run by the Universidad de Chile, 33 ha, with a guided trail through native woods.

Museums

Museo Colonial Alemán, including watermill (which does not turn), replicas of two German colonial houses with furnishings and utensils of the period, a blacksmith's shop (personal engravings for US$5), and a *campanario* (circular barn with agricultural machinery and carriages inside), gardens and handicraft shop. Well worth a visit. Open daily 0930-1900 summer, Tues-Sun 0930-1400, 1530-1800 winter, US$2.

Local festivals

In late Jan to early Feb there is a highly-regarded classical music festival (accommodation must be booked well in advance).

Local information
● **Accommodation**
North of Frutillar Bajo: **L3** *Salzburg*, T 421589 or Santiago 2061419, new, excellent, country style, restaurant, sauna, mountain bikes, arranges tours and fishing; *Hostal Cinco Robles*, Casilla 100, T 421351, with bath, breakfast, other meals on request, parking. In Frutillar Bajo: **B** *Casona del 32*, Caupolicán 28, T 421369, Casilla 101, with bath

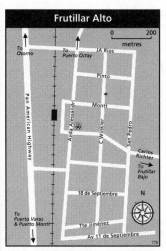

Frutillar Bajo

To Reserva Forestal Edmundo Winkler

To Puerto Octay

Caupolicán

S Junginger

18 de Septiembre

C Richter

Museo Colonial Alemán

Prat

Balmacada

San Martín

Municipalidad Public Toilets

O'Higgins

M Montt

Las Piedras

Pérez Rosales

M Rodríguez

P Aguirre

21 de Mayo

To Llanquihue

Av Alemana

Av Philippi

Lago Llanquihue

N

0   200
metres

Hotels:
1. *Am See*
2. *Casona del 32*
3. *El Arroyo*
4. *Kaisersseehaus*
5. *Salzburg*
6. *Trayén*
7. *Vivaldi*
8. *Winkler*

Places to eat:
9. *Bierstube*
10. *Casino de Bomberos*
11. *Club Alemán*

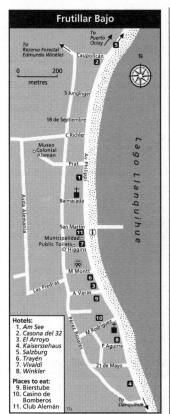

Frutillar Alto

To Osorno

To Puerto Octay

JA Ríos

Pinto

Montt

Pan American Highway

Avda Alessandri

C Winkler

San Pedro

Carlos Richter

To Frutillar Bajo

18 de Septiembre

Tte Jiménez

Av 11 de Septiembre

To Puerto Varas & Puerto Montt

N

0   200
metres

bach), No 1333 (Casilla 13, T 421387), hot water, good, cheap food, welcoming, English, German, Spanish spoken, poor beds; **D** Pérez Rosales 590, excellent breakfast. In Frutillar Alto: **D** *Faralito*, Winkler 245, hot water, cooking facilities (owner can be contacted at shop at Winkler 167, T 421440).Several along Carlos Richter (main street). Cheap accommodation in the school in Frutillar Alto, sleeping bag required.

Camping: *Playa Maqui*, 7 km N of Frutillar, T 421139, fancy, expensive; *Los Ciruelillos*, 2 km S, T 9123, most services. Try also Sr Guido González, Casa 3, Población Vermont, T 421385, G pp, rec.

● **Places to eat**

Club Alemán, Av Philippi 747, good but not cheap, hostile to backpackers; Bar Restaurant upstairs at the Fire Station, *Bomberos*, opp *Hotel Frutillar* (which burnt down in 1993), best value, open all year, memorable painting caricaturing the firemen in action. *Bierstube*, Varas, open 1600-2400. Many German-style cafés and tea-rooms on C Philippi (the lakefront) eg *Salón de Te Frutillar*, No 775. *Der Volkladen*, O'Higgins y Philippi, natural products, chocolates and cakes, natural cosmetics. *Café Hermosa*, good breakfast. Budget travellers should eat at *Kaisersseehaus* (see **Accommodation**) 'and explode'.

and breakfast, comfortable old house, central heating, English and German spoken; **C** *Hosp El Arroyo*, Philippi 989, T 421560, with breakfast, highly rec; **C-D** *Hosp Costa Azul*, Philippi 1175, T 421388, mainly for families, good breakfasts; also on Philippi: **C** *Winkler*, No 1155, T 421388, discount to YHA members, cabins, friendly, rec; **D** pp *Hosp Vivaldi*, No 851, T 421382, Sra Edith Klesse, quiet, comfortable, excellent breakfast and lodging, also family accommodation, rec; **D** *Las Rocas*, No 1235, T 421397, with breakfast; **D** *Residenz/Café am See*, No 539, good breakfast; **C** No 451, T 421204, clean, good breakfast; **D** *Hotel Philippi*, on lake shore, good rooms, rec; **D** *Hosp Trayén*, No 963, T 421346, basic, clean; **E** pp *Hosp Kaisersseehaus* (Viola Her-

● **Useful services**
Toilet, showers and changing cabins for beach on O'Higgins. *Cema-Chile* shop, Philippi y O'Higgins.

● **Tourist offices**
On lakeside opp *Club Alemán*, helpful; *Viajes Frutillar*, Richter y Alissandre in Alto Frutillar, run tours.

● **Transport**
Buses to **Puerto Varas** (US$0.75) and **Puerto Montt** (US$1.25), frequent, Varmontt and Full Express; to **Osorno**, Varmontt 1¼ hrs, US$3; to **Puerto Octay**, Thaebus, 6 a day. Most buses leave from opp the Copec station in Alto Frutillar.

LLANQUIHUE

(*Pop* 9,422; *Phone code* 065) 20 km S of Frutillar at the source of the Río Maullín. Perhaps the least interesting town on the lake, it offers a cheaper alternative to Puerto Varas and Frutillar. There is a German style beer festival at the end of Jan with German music.

● **Accommodation A3** *Siete Lagos*, Errázurriz 132, T 242020; **B** *El Cisne*, M Montt s/n, T 242726, cabañas; *Posada Alemana*, Bulnes 517, T 242629; several hospedajes.

PUERTO VARAS

(*Pop* 16,000; *Phone code* 065) This beauty spot is the commercial and tourist centre of the lake and a residencial centre for Puerto Montt 20 km to the S. In the 19th century, it was the southern port for shipping on the lake. The Catholic church, in monumental Baroque style, built by German Jesuits in 1918, is a copy of the church in Marieenkirche in the Black Forest; worth a visit. North and E of the **Gran Hotel Puerto Varas** (1934) are a number of German style mansions dating from the early 20th century: there are plans to turn one of these, the **Casa Kuschel**, into a museum. **Parque Philippi**, on top of hill, is a pleasant place to visit; walk up to *Hotel Cabañas del Lago* on Klenner, cross the railway and the gate is on the right. The views are a bit restricted by trees and the metal cross at the top is unattractive (so is the electric clock which chimes the quarter-hours in town).

Excursions

Puerto Varas is a good base for trips around the lake. On the S shore two of the best beaches are Playa Hermosa (Km

---

German colonization in Llanquihue

The most important area of German agricultural colonizaton in Chile was around Lago Llanquihue. In 1845, when the Chilean government declared the area to be destined for colonization, it knew little about the area which was covered by dense virgin forest. Vicente Pérez Rosales, appointed to encourage settlement travelled to Lago Llanquihue in 1851 and tried to sail around the lake in a dugout; it sank and, though Rosales swam to safety, his companion drowned.

To encourage settlement and help the new arrivals get started the government gave each adult male 75 *cuadras* of land plus an extra 12 *cuadras* for each son, a milking cow, 500 planks of timber, nails, a yoke of oxen, a year's free medical assistance and medicines and Chilean citizenship on request.

The first groups of German colonists arrived in the area in 1852: one group settled around Maitén and Puerto Octay, another helped found Puerto Montt. The lives of these early settlers were hard and the risks great: in cutting a path between Puerto Montt and Lago Llanquihue, two young settlers strayed from the others and were never seen again. Yet within 10 years they had cleared much of the forest round the lake and soon they were setting up small industries. In 1880, when the offer to colonists ended, unsettled land was auctioned in lots of 400-800 ha. By then the lake was ringed by a belt of smallholdings.

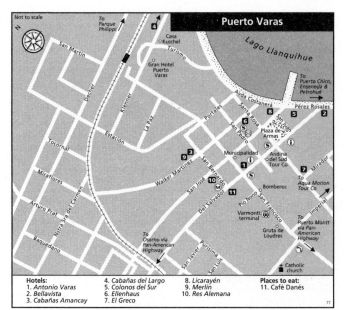

Puerto Varas

Not to scale

Lago Llanquihue

Hotels:
1. Antonio Varas
2. Bellavista
3. Cabañas Amancay
4. Cabañas del Largo
5. Colonos del Sur
6. Ellenhaus
7. El Greco
8. Licarayén
9. Merlín
10. Res Alemana

Places to eat:
11. Café Danés

7) and Playa Niklitschek (entry fee charged). **La Poza**, at Km 16, is a little lake to the S of Lago Llanquihue reached through narrow channels overhung with vegetation; **Isla Loreley**, an island on La Poza is very beautiful (frequent boat trips); a concealed channel leads to yet another lake, the Laguna Encantada. At Km 21 there is a watermill being converted into a museum.

Buses from Puerto Montt run every day on the southern side of the lake between Puerto Varas and Ensenada, in the S-eastern corner of the lake, continuing to Ralún, Cochamó and Río Puelo (see below). In summer, buses go daily from Puerto Montt and Puerto Varas in the morning to Ensenada, Laguna Verde, Petrohué Falls and Lago Todos Los Santos, US$7, good value.

Local information
● **Accommodation**

Accommodation is expensive, it is cheaper to stay in Puerto Montt.

L3 *Los Alerces*, Pérez Rosales 1281, T 233039, 4-star hotel, with breakfast, new cabin complex, attractive.

A1 *Colonos del Sur*, Del Salvador 24, T 233369, F 233394, with bath, good views, good restaurant, tea room; **A1** *Cabañas del Lago*, Klenner 195, T 232291, F 232707, on Phiippi hill overlooking lake, spacious rooms with good breakfast, restaurant with superb views; also self-catering cabins sleeping 5 (good value for groups), cheaper rates in low season, heating, sauna, superb location; **A1** *Antonio Varas*, Del Salvador 322, T 232375, F 232352, very comfortable; **A2** *Bellavista*, Pérez Rosales 60, T 232011, F 232013, cheerful, rec, restaurant, overlooking lake; **A3** *Cabañas Ayentemo*, Pérez Rosales 1297, clean, comfortable cabins, friendly, T/F 232270; **A3** *Licarayén*, San José 114, T 232305, F 232955, with bath, overlooking lake, comfortable, 'enthusiastically rec', book in season, C out of season, clean, friendly, 'the perfect place for bad weather or being ill'.

B *Merlín*, Walker Martínez 584, T/F 233105, quiet, excellent restaurant, highly rec; **B** *Motel Altué*, Pérez Rosales 1679, T 232294, inc breakfast. **C** *El Greco*, Mirador 134, T 233388, modern, good; **B** *Hosp Loreley*, Maipo 911, T 232226, rec, homely, quiet.

D María Schilling Rosas, La Quebrada 752, rec; **D** pp *Hosp Las Carmelas*, Imperial y Rosario, new, excellent, helpful, good meals, lends books inc some in English, highly rec; **D** pp *Cabañas Amancay*, Martínez 564, with breakfast, German spoken, rec; **D** pp Andrés Bello 321, nice atmosphere, good breakfast; **D** *Res Alemana*, San Bernardo 416, T 232419, with breakfast, without bath, clean; **D** *Hosp Don Raúl*, Salvador 928, laundry and cooking facilities, very friendly, clean, rec, camping F pp; **C** Imperial 8 (opp *Motel Trauco*), good breakfast, good views, highly rec; other family *hospedajes* on same street inc **D** *Hosp Imperial*, No 653, T 232451, clean, inc breakfast, central, rec; **F** pp Pío Nono 489, T 233172, with breakfast; **E** pp Elsa Pinto, Verbo Divino 427, clean; **E** *Hosp Ellenhaus*, Martínez 239, T 233577, use of kitchen, lounge, hospitable, highly rec.

Camping: on S shore of Lago Llanquihue starting at Puerto Varas: Km 10, Playa Hermosa, T Puerto Varas 8283, Puerto Montt 252223, fancy, rec, take own supplies. Km 11, Playa Niklitschek, full facilities; Km 20, Playa Venado; Km 49, Conaf site at Puerto Oscuro, beneath road to volcano, very good.

● **Places to eat**
Donde El Gordito, downstairs in market, immense portions, very popular, good value; *Domino*, Del Salvador 450, good, cheap; *Café Danés*, Del Salvador 441, good coffee and cakes; *El Amigo*, San Bernardo 240, large portions, good value. At the Puerto Chilo end of Pérez Rosales are *Costa Azul*, No 01071, rec and *Ibis*, No 1117, warmly rec, expensive motel restaurants just beyond it aren't worth visiting, although service is friendly. *Café del Turismo*, next to Cruz del Sur office, cheap, good; *El Molino*, café next to an old water mill, on road to Ensenada 22 km from Pto Varas.

● **Banks & money changers**
Turismo Los Lagos, Del Salvador 257 (Galería Real, local 11), open daily 0830-1330, 1500-2100, Sun 0930-1330, accepts TCs, good rates. Banco Osorno, Del Salvador 399, good rates.

● **Laundry**
Del Salvador 553.

● **Post & telecommunications**
Post Office: San José y San Pedro.

Phone Office: Del Salvador y Santa Rosa.

● **Shopping**
VYH Meistur Supermarket, Walker Martínez, good selection, reasonably priced.

● **Sports**
Fishing: the area around Puerto Varas is popular for fishing. A licence costs US$2.50 a year, obtainable from the Municipal offices.

Cycle hire: *Travel Art*, Imperial 0661, T 232198, but check equipment carefully.

● **Tour companies & travel agents**
Andina del Sud, Del Salvador 243, T 232511, operate 'lakes' trip to Bariloche, Argentina via Lago Todos los Santos, Peulla, Cerro Tronador (see under Puerto Montt, **To Argentina**), plus other excursions, good. Also *Eco Travel*, Av Costanera s/n, T 233222, *Turismo Nieve* (on San Bernardo, rec), *Aqua Motion*, Imperial 0699, T/F 232747, for trekking, rafting and climbing, German and English spoken, good equipment; several others. Most tours operate in season only (1 Sept-15 April).

● **Tourist offices**
Del Salvador 328, T 232402, F 233315, 0900-2100 in summer, helpful, find cheap accommodation; also art gallery.

● **Transport**
Trains To Santiago daily, 1600, details under Puerto Montt.

Buses Varmontt terminal, San Francisco 500 block. To **Santiago**, Varmontt, Igi Llaima and others, US$20; to **Puerto Montt**, 30 mins, Varmontt and Full Express every 15 mins, US$0.50; same companies, same frequency to Frutillar (US$0.75, 30 mins) and **Osorno** (US$3.50, 1¼ hrs); to **Valdivia** US$6. To **Bariloche**, Andina del Sud, see above. Minibuses to Ensenada and Petrohué leave from San Bernardo y Martínez, Buses JM and Varastur.

ENSENADA

47 km E of Puerto Varas, is beautifully situated at the SE corner of Lago Llanquihue and a good centre for excursions. A half-day trip is to Laguna Verde, about 30 mins from *Hotel Ensenada*, along a beautiful circular trail behind the lake (take first fork to the right behind the information board), and then down the

road to a campsite at Puerto Oscuro on Lago Llanquihue. The site is quiet and secluded, a good spot for a picnic

● **Accommodation A2** *Hotel Ensenada*, Casilla 659, Puerto Montt, T 232888, with bath, olde-worlde, good food (closed in winter), good view of lake and Osorno Volcano, runs tours, hires mountain bikes (guests only); also *hostal* in the grounds, cooking facilities, much cheaper but not that cheap. **B** *Hosp Ensenada*, T 8278, very clean, excellent breakfast, **D** off-season, rec; **C** *Cabañas Villa Ensenada*, sleep 4, bargain off season; **C** *Hostería Los Pumas*, 3 hrs up the hill, also highly rec, in season only; about 2 km from town is **C** *Pucará*, also with good restaurant (the steaks are rec); **C** *Ruedas Viejas*, T 312, for room, or **D** in cabin, about 1 km W from Ensenada, IYHA reductions, basic, damp, hot water, restaurant; **C** *Hosp Arena*, on same road, with breakfast, rec; **D** *Cabañas Brisas del Lago*, T 252363, chalets for 6 on beach, good restaurant nearby, highly rec for self-catering, supermarket next door; **D** *Moteles Hostería*, with breakfast, clean, poor service, comfortable; **D** *Hosp Opazo*, with breakfast, friendly; **E** pp *Hosp* above Toqui grocery, cheapest in town, basic, quiet, hot water, use of kitchen, beach in the back yard, rec. **Camping**: *Camping Montaña*, opp *Hotel Ensenada*, US$10, fully equipped, highly rec; also at Playa Larga, 1 km beyond *Hotel Ensenada*, US$10 and at Puerto Oscuro, 2 km N, US$8.

● **Places to eat** *Canta Rana* rec for bread and *kuchen*; *Ruedas Viejas*, the cheapest; most places closed off season, a few pricey shops; take your own provisions.

● **Tour companies & travel agents Guide**: Ludwig Godsambassis, owner of *Ruedas Viejas*, who works for *Aqua Motion* in season, works independently as a trekking guide out of season and is very knowledgeable about flora and fauna.

● **Transport** Minibuses run from Puerto Varas, frequent in summer (see above). Hitching from Puerto Varas is difficult.

VOLCAN OSORNO

Volcán Osorno, situated N of Ensenada, can be reached either from Ensenada, or from a road branching off the Puerto Octay-Ensenada road at Puerto Klocker, 20 km SE of Puerto Octay.

Climbing Weather permitting, *Aqua Motion* (address under Puerto Varas), organize climbing expeditions with local guide, transport from Puerto Montt or Puerto Varas, food and equipment, US$150 pp payment in advance (minimum group of 2, maximum of 6 with 3 guides) all year, setting out from the *refugio* at La Burbuja. *Aqua Motion* check weather conditions the day before and offer 50% refund if climb is abandoned due to weather. From La Burbuja it is 6 hrs to the summit. Conaf do not allow climbing without a guide and insist on 1 guide to every two climbers. Only experienced climbers should attempt to climb right to the top, ice climbing equipment essential.

"Unlike many other volcanoes Osorno has some interesting ice-climbing on crevasse walls and between high seracs (although you avoid the technical stuff if you go on a tour). Best for this are the southern and southeastern slopes. *Aqua Motion* guide Marcelo Soto will take more experienced climbers on 2/3 day climbs on these slopes. There is a large ice-cave on the N slope." Simon Harvey.

● **Accommodation** The Club Andino Osorno (address under Osorno) has three shelters (US$3 pp): to the N at La Picada (20 km SE of Puerto Klocker) at 950m; to the S at *Las Pumas*, 12 km from Ensenada at 900m, with plenty of beds and cooking facilities, very friendly guards (apply at the Oficina de Turismo de Osorno); also to the S, 1.5 km from Ensenada at 1,200m. **Refugio Teski Club**, E, bunk accommodation, restaurant and bar, sleeping bag useful, bleak site above the tree line; a good base for walking.

PARQUE NACIONAL VICENTE PEREZ ROSALES

This park, covering 251,000 ha and stretching E from Lago Llanquihue to the Argentine frontier, contains Lago Todos Los Santos and three major volcanic peaks, Osorno, Puntiagudo and Tronador.

Lago Todos los Santos is a long

irregularly shaped sheet of water, the most beautiful of all the lakes in southern Chile. There are no roads round it and only people with houses on the lake are allowed boats on it. The waters are emerald green; the shores are deeply wooded and several small islands rise from its surface. In the waters are reflected the slopes of Volcán Osorno. Beyond the hilly shores to the E are several graceful snow-capped mountains, with the mighty Tronador in the distance. To the N is the sharp point of Cerro Puntiagudo, and at the northeastern end Cerro Techado rises cliff-like out of the

water. The ports of **Petrohué** at its western and **Peulla** at its eastern ends are connected by boat. Trout and salmon fishing are excellent in several parts including Petrohué

The only scheduled vessel on the lake is the Andino del Sud service with connections to Bariloche (Argentina), but private launches can be hired for trips. Isla Margarita, the largest island on the lake, with a lagoon in the middle, can be visited (in summer only) from Petrohué, boats by Andino del Sud leave 1500, US$30.

Petrohué, 16 km NW of Ensenada, is

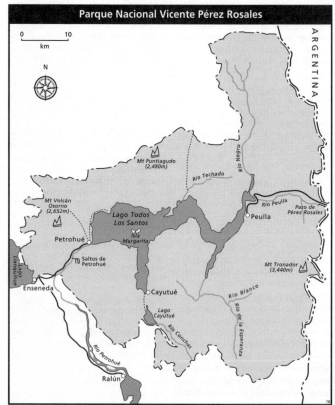

Parque Nacional Vicente Pérez Rosales

Climbing Puntiagudo and Tronador

Tronador, 3,460m, offers many technical possibilities, with both easy and difficult stretches on the upper slopes. It is usually climbed from the Argentine side. There is no road on the Chilean side so a 4-5 day hike is required. Moreover glaciers on the western (Chilean) slopes make climbing difficult and pose safety problems. There is a basic hut on the Chilean side.

Puntiagudo, 2,490m, is the most distinctive peak in the Lake District as a result of its sharp volcanic plug summit which is much steeper than the lower slopes. Only ever climbed a few times, it poses considerable climbing problems because of the 75-90° upper slopes and the very poor loose rock, though it may be easier in winter when there is more snow and ice. The southern side is the most difficult. Access is from the northern side of Lago Todos Los Santos or from the southern side of Lago Rupanco.

a good base for walking tours around the foot of Osorno Volcano, or for lookouts over it, eg Cerro Picada. The **Salto de Petrohué** (entrance, US$1.50) is 6 km (unpaved) from Petrohué, 10 km (paved) from Ensenada (a much nicer walk from Petrohué). Near the falls is a snackbar; there are also two short trails, the Senderos de los Enamorados and Carileufú.

Peulla, is a good starting point for hikes in the mountains. The Cascadas Los Novios, signposted above the *Hotel Peulla*, are a steep walk, but are stunning once you reach them. Good walk also to Laguna Margarita, 4 hrs, take water.

On the S shore of Lago Todos Los Santos is the little village of **Cayutué**, reached by hiring a boat from Petrohué, US$30. From Cayutué it is a 3-hr walk to Laguna Cayutué, a jewel set between mountains and surrounded by forest. Good camping and swimming. From here it is a 5 hr hike S to Ralún on the Reloncaví Estuary (see below). This is part of the old route used by missionaries in the colonial period to travel between Nahuel Huapi in Argentina and the island of Chiloé. It is now part of a logging road and is good for mountain bikes.

North of the lake are the **Termas de Callao**, reached by hiring a boat to El Rincón (uninhabited) from Petrohué (arrange for the boat to wait or collect you later). "It is 3½-4 hrs walk through

virgin forest beside the Río Sin Nombre. The path twice crosses the river by rickety hanging bridges. The slopes immediately beside the river and path are steep, giving the impression that the forest is even more gigantic than it actually is. Just before the baths is a house: collect the keys and pay. The Termas are two large Alerce tubs in a cabin." (Simon Harvey). Nearby is a modern comfortable *refugio*.

The park is infested by *tavanos* in Dec and Jan: cover up as much as possible with light-coloured clothes which may help a bit.

Park Administration Conaf office in Petrohué with a visitors centre, small museum and 3D model of the park. There is a *guardaparque* office in Puella.

● **Accommodation   At   Petrohué**: **A2** *Hostería Petrohué*, T/F 258042, with bath, excellent views, log fires, cosy; owner, Franz Schirmer, a former climbing guide, can advise on activities around the lake; **A3** *Fundo El Salto*, near Salto de Petrohué, very friendly, run by New Zealanders, mainly a fishing lodge, good home cooking, fishing trips arranged, Casilla 471, Puerto Varas; **E** pp *Familia Küschel* on other side of river (boat across), with breakfast, meals available, electricity only 3 hrs in pm, dirty, noisy, poor value, camping possible. Albergue in the school in summer. Conaf office can help find cheaper family accommodation. There is a shop with basic supplies in the village.

At Peulla: **A1** *Hotel Peulla*, PO Box 487, Puerto Montt, T 253253 (inc dinner and breakfast, direct personal reservations A3, PO Box 487, Puerto Montt, cheaper out of season), beautiful setting by the lake and mountains, restaurant and bar, good but expensive meals, cold in winter, often full of tour groups (tiny shop at back of hotel); **D** pp *Res Palomita*, 50m W of Hotel, half board, family-run, simple, comfortable but not spacious, separate shower, book ahead in season, lunches; accommodation is also available with local residents: Elmo and Ana Hernández Maldonado (only house with a balcony), **D** with breakfast, use of kitchen, helpful, clean. Small shop in Andino del Sud building but best to take your own food. **Camping**: at Petrohué on far side beside the lake, US$4/site, no services (local fishermen will ferry you across, US$0.50). At Peulla, opp Conaf office, US$1.50. Ask the commander of the military garrison at the beach nearest the hotel if you can camp on the beach; no facilities. Good campsite 1¾ hrs' walk E of Peulla, take food.

● **Transport Minibuses** from Puerto Varas to Ensenada continue to Petrohué, frequent in summer.

The **boat** between Petrohué and Peulla costs US$25 day return or one way (book in advance); it leaves Petrohué at 1030, Peulla at 1500 (not Sun, 2½ hrs – most seating indoors, no cars carried, cycles free), commentaries in Spanish, English and German plus loud music. This is the only public service across the lake and it connects with the Andina del Sud tour bus between Puerto Montt and Bariloche (see under Puerto Montt). Local fishermen make the trip across the lake, but charge much more than the public service. If planning to go to Bariloche in stages, book through to Bariloche in Petrohué, not Peulla because onward connections from Peulla may be full and the accommodation is not so good there.

FRONTIER WITH ARGENTINA: PASO PEREZ ROSALES

● **Chilean immigration**

In Peulla, 30 km W of the frontier, open summer

Parque Nacional Pérez Rosales & The Lakes route to Argentina

To Osorno

Parque Nacional Puyehue

Volcán Puntiagudo

Volcán Osorno

Río Negro

Puerto Blest

Lago Nahuel Huapi

Llao Llao

Peulla

Lago Frías

Paso Pérez Rosales

Petrohué

Lago Todos Los Santos

Puerto Frías

Lago Llanquihue

Saltos de Petrohué

Ensenada

Parque Nacional Pérez Rosales

Volcán Tronador

Bariloche

Cayutué

To Puerto Varas

Río Petrohué

Laguna Cayutué

ARGENTINA

Ralún

Río Cochamó

N

Lago Chapo

Cochamó

Reloncaví Estuary

Río Puelo

Lago Tagua Tagua

0   15

km

Puelo

0800-2100, winter 0800-2000.

NB It is impossible to do this journey independently out of season as then there are buses only as far as Ensenada, there is little traffic for hitching and none of the ferries takes vehicles.

The Reloncaví estuary, the northernmost of Chile's glacial inlets, is recommended for its local colour, its sealions, dolphins and its peace.

RALUN

A small village situated at the northern end of the estuary, is 31 km SE from Ensenada by a paved road along the wooded lower Petrohué valley. The road continues, unpaved, along the E side of the estuary to Cochamó and Puelo. In Ralún there is a village shop and post office, with telex. The road which goes to the *Hotel Ralún* continues round the base of the mountains to Lago Chapo, giving access at the eastern end to Parque Nacional Alerce Andino (see page 315). There is, as yet, no connection between the eastern and western shores of Lago Chapo.

● **Accommodation E** pp *Restaurant El Refugio* rents rooms; **E** pp *Navarrito*, restaurant and lodging; **F** pp *Posada Campesino*, simple, clean, without breakfast, very friendly; **E** pp *El Encuentro*; the *Hotel Ralún*, at S end of the village, which burnt down in 1992, has cabins.

● **Transport** Bus from Puerto Montt, 5 a day, Bohle, between 1000 and 1930, 4 on Sat, return 0700-1830, US$2. Also bus from Ensenada daily, US$1.

COCHAMO

17 km S of Ralún on the E shore of the estuary is a pretty village, with a fine wooden church similar to those on Chiloé, built in 1900 and situated in a striking setting, with the estuary and volcano behind.

● **Accommodation D** *Cochamó*, T 212, basic but clean, friendly, often full with salmon

The legend of Cochamó

🪂 It is said that when the Jesuits were expelled from Chile, many hid in Ancud, later to make their way across the Gulf of Ancud and up the Reloncaví Estuary and then overland via Cochamó to Bariloche. Along the way they buried the valuables they were carrying, including hoards of gold, silver and coin.

farm workers, good meals, rec, and a large number of *pensiones* (just ask), eg **E** pp *Mercado Particular Sabin*, Catedral 20, next to *Hotel*; **E** pp Sra Flora Barrientos offers floorspace in her bar/restaurant/drugstore, same street No 16; **E** pp *Restaurant Copihue*; **E** pp *Res Gato Blanco*; cheapest accommodation at Catedral 2, by the pier (floor space only). *Camping Los Castaños*, T 214 (Reservations Casilla 576, Puerto Montt).

● **Places to eat** *Reloncaví*, next to *Hotel*; *Donde Payi* opp church.

● **Horseriding (trekking with packhorses)**: *Campo Aventura* (Casilla 5, Correo Cochamó) T/F 232747, offer accommodation at their base camp 2 km S of Cochamó (**E** pp, kitchen, sauna, camping) and at their other base, a renovated mountain house in the valley of La Junta. Specialize in horseback and trekking expeditions between the Reloncaví Estuary and the Argentine frontier, 2-10 days.

● **Transport** Bus Fierro to Ralún, Ensenada, Puerto Varas and Puerto Montt, 3 daily; to Puelo 2 daily

The **Gaucho Trail** E to Paso León on the Argentine frontier was used in the colonial period by indians and Jesuit priests and later by gauchos. The route runs along Río Cochamó to La Junta, then along the N side of Lago Vidal, passing waterfalls and the oldest surviving Alerce trees in Chile at El Arco, 3-4 days by horse, 5-6 days on foot, depending on conditions (best done Dec-Mar). From the border crossing at Paso León it is a 3-hr walk to the main road to San Carlos de Bariloche.

PUELO

Further S, on the S bank of the Río Puelo, is a most peaceful place (ferry crossing); lodging is available at the restaurant (**F** pp) or with families – try Roberto and Olivia Telles, simple, clean, no bath/shower, meals on request, or Ema Hernández Maldona; two restaurants.

● **Transport** Buses Fierro services from Puerto Montt, Mon-Sat 1230 and 1600, Sun 0900 1500 (from Puerto Varas 30 mins later). Daily buses from Cochamó Mon-Sat 0800 and 1730, Sun 1130 and 1700. From here the road continues to Llaguepe. In summer boats sail up the Estuary from Angelmó. Tours from Puerto Montt US$30. Off season the *Carmencita* sails once a week, leaving Puelo Sun 1000 and Angelmó Wed 0900 (advisable to take warm clothes, food and seasickness pills if windy).

PUERTO MONTT

(*Pop* 110,139; *Phone code* 065) The capital of X Región (Los Lagos), 1,016 km S of Santiago, lies at the N end of the Seno de Reloncaví. It was founded in 1853 on the site of a Mapuche community known as Melipulli (meaning four hills) as part of the German colonization of the area. Good views over the city and bay are offered from outside the Intendencia Regional on Av X Region. The port is used by fishing boats and coastal vessels, and is the departure point for vessels to Puerto Chacabuco, Laguna San Rafael and for the long haul S to Punta Arenas. A paved road runs 55 km SW to Pargua, where there is a ferry service to Chiloé.

Places of interest

The **Iglesia de los Jesuitas** on Gallardo, dating from 1872, has a fine blue-domed ceiling; behind it on a hill is the **campanario** (clock tower). The little fishing port of **Angelmó**, 2 km W, has become a tourist centre with many seafood restaurants and handicraft shops (reached by Costanera bus along Portales and by collective taxi Nos 2, 3, 20 from the centre, US$0.30pp).

Puerto Montt at the time of the arrival of the first German immigrants
Transitarios y Turismo, March 1990

Museums

Museo Regional Juan Pablo II, Portales 997 near bus terminal, local history and a fine collection of historic photos of the city; also memorabilia of the Pope's visit. Open daily 1030-1800, US$0.50.

Excursions

Puerto Montt is a popular centre for excursions to the Lake District. The wooded **Isla Tenglo**, close to Puerto Montt and reached by launch from Angelmó (US$0.30), is a favourite place for picnics. Magnificent view from the summit. The island is famous for its *curantos*, a local dish. **Chinquihue** (the name means "place of skunks") W of Angelmó, has many seafood restaurants, with oysters as a speciality. East of Puerto Montt, **Chamiza**, up the Río Coihuin, has fine fishing. There is a bathing beach with black sand (polluted) at **Pelluco**, 4 km E of Puerto Montt (accommodation including *cabañas*; several good seafood restaurants, including *Pazos*, best *curanto* in Puerto Montt, rec). **Isla Guar** may be visited by boat from Angelmó harbour (1600, 2 hrs); boat returns from the other end of the island at 0730. The N shore is rocky. Accommodation, if lucky, at the church; best to camp.

West of Puerto Montt the Río Maullín, which drains Lago Llanquihue, has some attractive waterfalls and good fishing (salmon). The little fishing village of **Maullín**, founded in 1602 (**B** *Motel El Pangal*, 5 km away, T 244), at the mouth of the Río Maullín, is worth a visit. Southeast of here, on the coast, is Carelmapu; 3 km away is an excellent beach, Playa Brava. **Calbuco**, centre of the fishing industry (*Restaurant San Rafael*, rec) with good scenery, is on an island linked to the mainland by a causeway. It can be visited direct by boat or by road (the old coast road from Puerto Montt is very beautiful).

Local information

● **Accommodation**

Accommodation is expensive in season, much cheaper off season. Check Tourist Office.

A1 *Vicente Pérez Rosales*, Varas 447, T 252571, with bath and breakfast, some rooms noisy, excellent restaurant, seafood, tourist and climbing information, rec; **A1** *O'Grimm*, Gallardo 211, T 252845,

F 258600, with breakfast, cosy restaurant with occasional live music, central; **A2** *Burg*, Pedro Montt y Portales, T 253813, modern, central heating, centrally located, good, interesting traditional food in restaurant; **A1** *Club Presidente*, Portales 664, T 251666, 4-star, with breakfast, very comfortable, also suites, rec; **A1** *Don Luis*, Urmeneta y Quillota, T 259001, F 259005, heating, very good, no restaurant; **A3** *Montt*, Varas y Quillota, T 253651, with bath, C without, clean, friendly, good value, good restaurant; **A3** *Raysan*, Benavente 480,

T 256151, helpful; **A2** *Viento Sur*, Ejército 200, T 258701, F 258700, excellent, good restaurant, sauna, gym, excellent views; **A3** *Millahue*, Copiapó 64, T 253829, F 253817, and apartments at Benavente 959, T/F 254592, with breakfast, modern, good restaurant.

B *Colina*, Talca 81, T 253813, with bath, clean, restaurant, bar, car hire, rec; **B** *Le Mirage*, Rancagua 350, T 255125, F 256302, with breakfast, small rooms, clean; **B** *El Candil*, Varas 177, T 253080, clean, attractive; also has **C** *Res Candil*, Illapel 87 nearby.

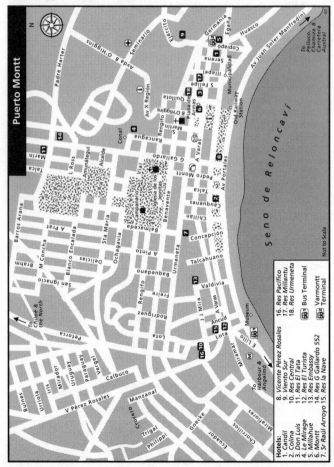

Puerto Montt

Hotels:
1. Candil
2. Colina
3. Colina
4. Don Luis
5. Le Mirage
6. Millahue
7. Sr Raúl Arroyo
8. Vicente Pérez Rosales
9. Viento Sur
10. Res Central
11. Res El Tata
12. Res El Turista
13. Res Embassy
14. Res G Gallardo 552
15. Res la Nave
16. Res Pacífico
17. Res Millantu
18. Res Urmeneta

🚌1 Bus Terminal
🚌2 Varmontt Terminal

C pp *Hostal Pacífico*, J J Mira 1088, T 256229, with bath, **D** pp without, with breakfast, cable TV, parking, comfortable, rec; **C** *Res Embassy*, Valdivia 130, T 253533, with bath, **E** pp without, clean, stores luggage, rec; **C** pp *Res Urmeneta*, Urmeneta 290, T 253262, with bath, **D** pp without, clean, comfortable, rec, IYHA reductions; **C** pp *Res La Nave*, Ancud y Varas, T 253740, with bath, **E** pp without, clean, pleasant, inexpensive restaurant.

Near the bus terminal: **C** *Hosp Polz*, J J Mira 1002, T 252851, with breakfast, clean, warm, good beds, rec; **D** *Res El Turista*, Ancud 91, T 254767, with and without bath, with breakfast, clean, comfortable, rec; **D** *Res El Talquino*, Pérez Rosales 114, T 253331, hot water, clean; **D** *Res Punta Arenas*, J J Mira 964, with breakfast, hot water, basic but clean; **E** pp *Casa Gladis*, Ancud y Mira, dormitory style, kitchen and laundry facilities, crowded; **E** pp *Walglad*, Ancud 112, with breakfast, clean, friendly; **E** pp *Hosp Leticia*, Lota 132, basic, safe, cooking facilities, rec; **E** pp *Res Central*, Lota 111, T 257516, clean, use of kitchen, rec; **E** pp Goecke 119, T 266339, with breakfast, clean, cooking facilities, poor bathroom.

Near the Plaza de Armas: **D** *Res Calipso*, Urmeneta 127, T 254554, without bath, clean IYHA accepted; **D** *Res La Alemana*, Egaña 82, T 255092, with breakfast, German spoken, run down; in C Huasco: **E** pp No 16, with breakfast, basic; **E** pp No 126, friendly, better, rec; **E** pp No 130, hot showers, cooking facilities, rec; **E** pp Sr Raúl Arroyo, Concepción 136, T 262188 (go to the 'inland' end of Concepción, turn right to end of alley), with breakfast, basic, crowded, run down, poor kitchen and bathroom facilities, English spoken, also has a cabaña 3 km away, sleeps 10; **D** Varas 840, basic, inc breakfast; cheaper.

Other cheaper accommodation: **D** *Casa Haraldo Steffen*, Serrano 286, T 253823, with breakfast, 15 mins' walk from centre, small clean rooms, run down, only 1 bathroom; **D** pp *Alda González*, Gallardo 552, T 253334, with bath, **E** pp without, with breakfast, cooking facilities, clean, popular; **F** pp *El Tata*, Gallardo 621, floor space, very basic, popular, packed in summer; **D** Aníbal Pinto 328, with breakfast, popular, laundry facilities, 10 mins' walk from centre, rec; **E** pp, Balmaceda 300, with breakfast, clean, friendly; **E** pp Balmaceda 283, clean, hospitable; **E** pp Balmaceda y Vial, reached by steep path behind Balmaceda 283, very friendly, good breakfast,

safe, clean, rec; **E** pp *Vista Hermosa*, Miramar 1486, with bath, quiet, helpful; **E** pp Trigal 309, T 259923, use of kitchen, clean, with breakfast; **E** pp *Casa Perla*, Trigal 312, T 262104, with breakfast, French, English spoken, helpful, friendly, meals, Spanish classes offered off season, rec; **E** pp *Hosp Reina*, Trigal 361, family run, clean, welcoming; **E** pp Bilbao 380, T 256514, hot water, very clean, comfortable; **E** pp Sra María Oyarzo, Subida Miramar 1184, T 259957, inc breakfast, friendly, basic (no heating, hot water next door), clean, good beds; **E** pp *Res Emita*, Miraflores 1281, inc breakfast with homemade bread, clean, friendly, safe; **E** pp Vivar 1141, T 255039, inc breakfast, hot water; **E** pp Baquedano 247, T 252862, friendly, clean; **D** pp *Suiza*, Independencia 237, with breakfast, clean, German spoken; on Petorca: **E** pp No 119, T 258638, clean, friendly, rec; **E** pp *Hosp Montesinos*, No 121, T 255353, with breakfast, clean, rec; **E** pp No 132, clean; **E** pp Colo Colo 1350, T 263342, with good breakfast, very clean; *Albergue* in disused school opp bus station, sleeping bag on floor, very cheap, but no security.

Camping: 'wild' camping possible along the sea front. Several sites W of Puerto Montt: *Camping Municipal* at Chinquihue, 10 km W (bus service), open Oct-April, fully equipped with tables, seats, barbecue, toilets and showers. Small shop, no kerosene. *Camping Anderson*, 11 km W, American run, hot showers, private beach, home-grown fruit, vegetables and milk products. *Camping Los Alamos*, T 256067, 13 km W, nice views, poor services, stray dogs, US$17/site; *Camping Metri*, 30 km SE on Carretera Austral, T 251235, Fierro bus, $2/tent.

● **Places to eat**

Embassy, Ancud 106, very good, pricey; *Club de Yates*, Juan Soler s/n, excellent, expensive seafood; *Centro Español*, O'Higgins 233, expensive but very good; *Super Yoco*, Quillota 259, good value; *Kiel*, Capilla 298, excellent food and atmosphere, not cheap; *Club Alemán*, Varas 264, old fashioned, good food and wine; *Café Real*, Rancagua 137, for *empanadas*, *pichangas*, *congrío frito*, and cheap lunches; *Costa de Reloncaví*, Portales 736, good, moderate prices; *Café Central*, Rancagua 117, good atmosphere, meals and pastries; *Suerte Rincón*, Talca, excellent lunches, large portions, popular with locals. *Dino*, Varas 550, restaurant upstairs, snacks downstairs (try

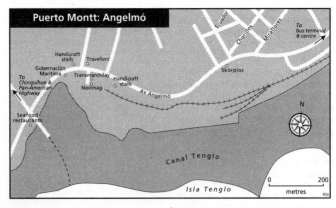

Puerto Montt: Angelmó

the lemon juice). *Don Pancho*, by the sea, in railway station, good. *Di Napoli Pizzas*, Gallardo 119, limited choice; *Café Amsel*, Pedro Montt y Portales, superb fish but not cheap; *Plato's*, Portales 1014, Galería Comercial España, cheap, good; also in the Galería is *El Rinconcito*, a good bar. *Super Dragon*, Benavente 839, Chinese, not cheap. Excellent and cheap food at bus terminal (all credit cards accepted). In **Angelmó**: many small seafood restaurants in the old fishing port, very popular, lunches only, ask for *té blanco* (white wine – they are not legally allowed to serve wine); *Asturias*, Angelmó 2448, limited menu, often rec.

Bakery: *La Estrella*, Varas 984, self-service, good. Local specialities inc *picoroco al vapor*, a giant barnacle whose flesh looks and tastes like crab, and *curanto*.

● **Airline offices**
LanChile, San Martín 200, T 253141/253315; **Ladeco**, Benevente 350, T 253002; **National**, Benevente 305, T 258277, F 250664; **Aerosur**, Urmeneta 149, 252523; **TAN**, T 250071; **Don Carlos**, Quillota 127, T 253219.

● **Banks & money changers**
Impossible on Sun (but try *Hotel Pérez Rosales*). Exorbitantly high commission and low rates at **Banco del Estado**. For Visa try **Banco Concepción**, Pedro Montt y Urmeneta, good rates. **Banco Osorno**, Varas y Garrardo, good for Visa cash, but does not change TCs. Commission charges vary widely. Good rates at **Galería Cristal**, Varas 595, **El Libertador**, Urmeneta 529-A, local 3, and **Turismo Latinoameri-** cano, Urmeneta 531; *Travellers* travel agent in Angelmó (address below) has exchange facilities. **Fincard** (Access), Varas 437. **La Moneda de Oro** at the bus terminal exchanges Latin American currencies (Mon-Sat 0930-1230, 1530-1800). Obtain Argentine pesos before leaving Chile.

● **Embassies & consulates**
Argentine, Cauquenes 94, p 2, T 253996, quick visa service; **German**, Varas y Gallardo, p 3, of 306, Tues/Wed 0930-1200; **Spanish**, Rancagua 113, T252557; **Dutch**, Seminario 350, T 253428.

● **Entertainment**
Casa del Arte Diego Rivera, off Plaza de Armas, temporary exhibitions, concerts, plays.

● **Laundry**
Center Varas 700; *Lavatodo*, O'Higgins 231; San Martín 232; *Unic*, Chillán 149; *Yessil't*, Edif Caracol, Urmeneta 300; *Nautilus*, Av Angelmó 1564, cheaper, good service; also in *Las Brisas* supermarket. Laundry prices generally high (US$7 for 3 kg).

● **Post & telecommunications**
Post Office: Rancagua 120, open 0830-1830 (Mon-Fri), 0830-1200 (Sat).

Telephone Office: Pedro Montt 114 and Chillán 98.

● **Shopping**
Woollen goods and Mapuche-designed rugs can be bought at roadside stalls in Angelmó and on Portales opp the bus terminal. Prices are much the same as on Chiloé, but quality is often lower. Supermarkets: *Las Brisas* opp bus

terminal, very good, open 0900-2200 daily; *Mondial*, 2 blocks W is cheaper with better selection. *Libros*, Portales 580, small selection of English novels, also maps.

● **Sports**

Aerial Sports: Felix Oyarzo Grimm, owner of the *Hotel O'Grimm* can advise on possibilities, esp parachuting.

Fishing: Luis Wellman, at the *Hotel Don Luis* is very knowledgeable about fishing in the area.

Football: stadium opp Marina del Sur yacht club.

Gymnasium: Urmeneta 537.

Sailing: two Yacht Clubs in Chinquihué: Marina del Sur (MDS), T/F 251958, modern, bar and restaurant, sailing courses, notice board for crew (*tripulante*) notices, MDS Charters office (also Santiago T/F 231-8238) specializes in cruising the Patagonian channels. Charters US$2,200-8,500/week depending on size of boat. Club de Desportes Náuticas, founded by British and Americans in 1940s, more oriented towards small boat sailing, windsurfing, water sports.

● **Tour companies & travel agents**

Andina del Sud, very close to central tourist kiosk, Varas 437, T 257797, sells a daily tour at 0830 (not Sun) to Puerto Varas, Parque Nacional V Pérez Rosales, Petrohué, Lago Todos los Santos, Peulla and back (without meals US$27, with meals US$37), and to other local sights, as well as skiing trips to the Osorno volcano (see below for trip to Bariloche); *Travellers*, Av Angelmó 2456, PO Box/Casilla 854, T 262099, F 258555, e-mail gochile@chilepac.net, close to 2nd port entrance and Navimag office, open Mon-Fri 0900-1330,1500-1830, Sat 0900-1400 for booking for Navimag ferry *Puerto Edén* to Puerto Natales, Osorno volcano trips and other excursions, money exchange, flights, also sells imported camping equipment and runs computerized tourist information service, book swap ('best book swap S of Santiago'), map display, TV, real coffee, English-run, rec; *Petrel Tours*, San Martín 167, of 403, T/F 255558, rec. Many other agencies. Most offer 1-day excursions to Chiloé and to Puerto Varas, Isla Loreley, Laguna Verde, and the Petrohué falls: both these tours are much cheaper from bus company kiosks inside the bus terminal, eg

Bohle, US$15 to Chiloé, US$11 to the lakes.

● **Tourist offices**

Sernatur is in the Intendencia Regional, Av Décima Región 480 (p 3), Casilla 297, T 254580/256999, F 254580, Tx 270008. Open 0830-1300, 1330-1730 Mon-Fri. Ask for information on Chiloé as this is often difficult to obtain on the island. Also kiosk on Plaza de Armas run by the municipality, open till 1800 on Sat. Town maps available, but little information on other places. Telefónica del Sur and Sernatur operate a phone information service (INTTUR), dial 142 (cost is the same as a local call). Dial 149 for chemist/pharmacy information, 148 for the weather, 143 for the news, etc. The service operates throughout the Tenth Region. Sernatur in Puerto Montt has a reciprocal arrangement on information with Bariloche, Argentina. **Conaf**: Ochogavia 458, but cannot supply details of conditions in National Parks. **Automóvil Club de Chile**: Esmeralda 70, T 252968.

● **Transport**

Local Car hire: Hertz, Varas 126, T 259585, helpful, English spoken; **Automóvil Club de Chile**, Ensenada 70, T 254776, and at airport. Others are **Avis**, Egaña 64, T 256575 and at airport; **Budget**, San Martín 200 and at airport; **Dollar** (Hotel Vicente Pérez Rosales), Varas 447; **First**, Varas 437; **Formula Uno**, Santa María 620, T 254125, highly rec; **Autovald**, Portales 1330, T 256355, cheap rates; **Travicargo**, Urmeneta 856, T 257137/256438; **Automotric Angelmó**, Talca 79, cheap and helpful. **Famas**, Portales y Gallardo, friendly, helpful, good value, has vehicles that can be taken to Argentina.

Air El Tepual Airport, 13 km NW of town. ETM bus from terminal 1½ hrs before departure, US$2. To Santiago at least 2 daily flights by LanChile, Ladeco and National (cheaper). To Punta Arenas, LanChile, Ladeco and National (both cheaper) daily; in Jan, Feb and Mar you may well be told that flights are booked up; however, cancellations may be available from the airport. National also flies to Concepción and Temuco. Flights to Bariloche and Neuquén (Argentina), TAN, twice a week, 40 mins. To Balmaceda, LanChile and Ladeco, daily. To Coyhaique, LanChile daily. Don Carlos flies to Chaitén, 1115 and 1515 Mon-Fri, Sat 1115 (fares under Chaitén), and runs regular charters for 5 passengers to Bariloche, Chaitén, and Coyhaique. Alta to Chaitén and to Balmaceda, Puerto Natales (3 hrs, US$70, highly rec for

views) and Punta Arenas. Aerosur, also flies to Chaitén, daily except Sun and to Futaleufú and Palena on Tues and Fri.

Trains New station under construction at Alerce, 10 km N of town. Old station at San Felipe 50, T 254908, functions only as ticket office (0830-1130, 1300-1700). Daily service in summer to **Santiago** departs from Puerto Varas, 1600, Rápido with 1930s German-built sleepers, 19 hrs. Seats: turista US$21, salón US$35; sleepers: US$44 lower bunk, US$59 upper bunk, US$130 double compartment, bicycles US$10, restaurant car, car transporter, book 3 days in advance, but 2 weeks in advance in high season

Buses Terminal on sea front at Portales y Lota, has telephones, restaurants, casa de cambio (left luggage, US$1/item for 24 hrs). Varmontt has its own terminal at Copiapó y Varas, but Varmontt buses also call at main terminal. To **Puerto Varas** (US$0.50), **Llanquihue**, **Frutillar** (US$1.25) and **Osorno** (US$5) every 30 mins, Varmontt and Full Express. To **Ensenada** and **Petrohué** Buses JM at least 3 a day. To Pucón, US$7. To **Santiago**, express 15 hrs, US$18-25, cama US$45, Tur-Bus, very good, 14 hrs, Tas Choapa Royal Class US$33; to **Punta Arenas**, Austral, Turbus and Ghisoni, between 1 and 3 times a week, US$60-75 depending on company, departing either 0800 or 1100 (bus goes through Argentina via Bariloche – take US$ cash to pay for meals etc in Argentina), 32-38 hrs; book well in advance in Jan-Feb and check if you need a multiple-entry Chilean visa; also book any return journey before setting out; to **Temuco** US$9, to **Valdivia**, US$7; **Concepción**, US$15. For services to **Chiloé**, see page 301.

Buses to Argentina via Osorno and the Puyehue pass Daily services to Bariloche on this route via Osorno, US$20-25, 6-10 hrs, are run by Cruz del Sur, Andesmar, Turismo Lanín (not rec), Tas Choapa and Bus Norte. Tas Choapa services also run to Mendoza, Buenos Aires, Montevideo and Rio de Janeiro. Out of season, services are reduced. Buy tickets for international buses from the bus terminal, not through an agency. If intending to return by this route, buy an open return ticket as higher fares are charged in Argentina. Book well in advance in Jan and February. Hitchhiking on this route is difficult and may take as long as 4 days. For the route to Argentina via Lago Todos Los Santos see below.

Motoring: when driving N out of Puerto

Chile: From Santiago To Puerto Montt

the Paso Pérez Rosales to Argentine customs in Puerto Frías, 20 min boat trip across Lago Frías to Puerto Alegre and bus from Puerto Alegre to Puerto Blest. From Puerto Blest it is a beautiful 1½ hr catamaran trip along Lago Nahuel Huapi to Puerto Panuelo, from where there is a 1 hr bus journey to Bariloche (bus drops passengers at hotels, camping sites or in town centre). Out of season this trip is done over 2 days with overnight stay in Peulla, add about US$89 to single fare for accommodation in *Hotel Peulla*. (Baggage is taken to *Hotel Peulla* automatically but for alternative accommodation see under Peulla above.)

● **Transport** The route is operated only by Andino del Sud (address above). Bus from company offices daily at 0800; the fare is US$104 one way. Note that the trip may be cancelled if the weather is poor; there are reports of difficulty in obtaining a refund. Try both Puerto Montt and Puerto Varas offices if you want to take the Andina del Sud trip in sections.

Montt (or out of Puerto Varas, Frutillar, etc), look for signs to 'Ruta 5'.

Boat hire: Lucinda Cárdenas, Manuel Montt Pasaje 7, Casa 134, Angelmó, for trips around the harbour or to Tenglo island.

Shipping offices in Puerto Montt: Navimag (Naviera Magallanes SA), Terminal Transbordadores, Angelmó 2187, T 253318, F 258540; **Skorpios 1** and **2** of **Constantino Kochifas C**, Angelmó 1660 y Miraflores (Castilla 588), T 252619, Tx 370161 NATUK CL; **Transmarchilay Ltda**, Angelmó 2187, T 254654, F 253683; **Patagonia Connection**, Portales 872, T 259790.

TO ARGENTINA VIA LAGO TODOS LOS SANTOS

This popular route to Bariloche, involving ferries across Lago Todos Los Santos, Lago Frías and Lago Nahuel Huapi is outstandingly beautiful whatever the season, though the mountains are often obscured by rain and heavy cloud. The route is via Puerto Varas, Ensenada and Petrohué falls (20 mins stop) to Petrohué, where it connects with catamaran service across Lago Todos Los Santos to Peulla. Lunch stop in Peulla 2 hrs (lunch not inc in fare: *Hotel Peulla* is expensive, see page 282 for alternatives). Chilean customs in Peulla, followed by a 2 hr bus ride through

SAN CARLOS DE BARILOCHE

San Carlos de Bariloche (*Pop* 77,750; *Phone code* 0944), on the S shore of Lago Nahuel Huapi, founded 1898, is the best centre for exploring the Parque Nacional Nahuel Huapi. Renowned for its chocolate industry, it is a beautifully-situated, Swiss-looking town of steep streets, its wooden chalets perched upon a glacial moraine at the foot of Cerro Otto. The place is full of hotels and *hosterías*. To the S lie the heights of the Ventana and the Cerro Colorado (2,135m). The forests are particularly beautiful around May. Major fires in Jan 1996 burned some 2,000 ha of forest S of the city.

The town has experienced phenomenal growth and can be very busy. The best time to visit it is out of season either in the spring or autumn, although the weather is unpredictable Mainly in July, Bariloche is a major destination for secondary school students, who come to complete courses, ski and enjoy themselves in the evening. The main road into Bariloche from the E is paved and in good condition.

Places of interest

The **cathedral**, built in 1946, dominates the town; interior unfinished. There is a **belvedere** at the top of Cerro Otto with wide views over the town and the lake and mountain. The **Lido swimming pool** on the lake shore is beautifully sited but somewhat run down. The clock in the **Centro Cívico** has four figures which rotate at noon; photos with St Bernard dogs (including brandy keg) may be taken in the Centro Cívico plaza and on 12 de Octubre above the Lido.

Museums

The **Museo de La Patagonia** in the Centro Cívico has nice collections of stuffed animals and Indian artefacts, open 1000-1200, 1400-1900 Tues-Fri, 1000-1300, Sat US$2.50; the attached **Biblioteca Sarmiento** is open Mon-Fri, 1100-2200.

Llao-Llao

The 24 km road to the resort of Llao-Llao (bus No 20, 45 mins) is largely ribbon-developed. Hotels on this road and in the resort are given below. At Km 17.7 on the road to Llao-Llao there is a chairlift to Cerro Campanario (0900-1200, 1400-1800 daily, US$5), from the top of which there are fine views of Isla Victoria and Puerto Pañuelo. At Km 18.3 begins the Circuito Chico, a 60 km circular route around Lago Moreno Oeste, past Punto Panorámico and through Puerto Pañuelo and Llao-Llao itself. Tour companies do the circuit and it can be driven in half a day. It can be extended to a full day: Bariloche-Llao Llao-Bahía-Colonia Suiza (on Lago Moreno Este)-Cerro Catedral-Bariloche; the reverse direction misses the sunsets and afternoon views from the higher roads, which are negotiable in winter (even snow-covered). The surrounding countryside offers beautiful walking, eg to Lago Escondido on a 3½ km trail off the Circuito Chico.

Boat excursions

A ½-day excursion (1300-1830) may be taken from Bariloche to Puerto Pañuelo, then by boat to Isla Victoria. The full-day excursion (0900-1830, or 1300 till 2000 in season) at US$28 includes the Arrayanes forest on the Quetrihue peninsula further N, and 3 hrs on Isla Victoria, picnic lunch advised. It is best to book this trip through an agency, as the boat fare alone is US$21. Some boats going to Arrayanes call first at Isla Victoria, early enough to avoid boat-loads of tourists. These boats carry the names of Paraná river provinces – *Corrientes*, *Misiones*, *Santa Fe* – and they have no open deck. (Turisur have four catamarans with a bar and cafeteria.) All boats are very crowded in season, but operators have to provide seating for all passengers.

Tours

There are numerous tours: most travel agencies charge the same price. It is best to buy tours on the spot rather than in advance, although they get very booked up in season. Whole-day trip to Lagos Gutiérrez, Mascardi, Hess, the Cascada Los Alerces and Cerro Tronador (950m) leaves at 0800, US$29, and involves 1 hr walk to the Black Glacier, interesting but too much time spent on the bus. Catedral and Turisur have a 9-hr excursion, leaving at 0900 (afternoon dep also Dec-Mar), to Puerto Pañuelo, sailing down to Puerto Blest and continuing by bus to Puerto Alegre and again by launch to Puerto Frías (US$19.50). A visit to the Cascada de los Cántaros is made (stay off the boat at the Cascada and walk around to Puerto Blest through beautiful forest, 1 hr, recommended). Several 12-hr excursions to San Martín de los Andes, US$34, recommended, through two national parks, passing seven lakes, returning via Paso de Córdoba and the Valle Encantado.

If one is staying only 1-2 days in the area the best excursions are to Cerro Tronador the 1st day, and on the 2nd to Cerro Catedral in the morning and Isla

Victoria in the afternoon (possible only Dec-Mar when there are afternoon departures for the island).

Local information

● Accommodation

The most complete listing with map is published by the Oficina Municipal de Turismo, which you are advised to consult if you arrive in the high season without a reservation. Out of season, prices are reasonable, in all ranges, but in season everything is very expensive. Most hotels outside the town inc half-board, and those in the town inc breakfast. Hotels with lake views normally charge US$3-4 extra/room/day, for the view in high season; the following selection gives lake-view high-season prices where applicable.

● Banks & money changers

There are several banks and exchange shops, which buy and sell virtually all European and South American currencies, besides US dollars; Sat is a bad day.

● Embassies & consulates

Consulates: **Chilean** JM de Rosas 180, friendly, helpful; **German**, Ruiz Moreno 45, T 25695; **Swiss**, Quaglia 342, T 26111.

● Post & telecommunications

Post Office: Centro Cívico (same building as tourist office). *Poste Restante* US$2.50/letter.

Telecommunications: San Martín e Independencia and Elflein y Frey (3 mins minimum charge); cheaper from *Hotel Bariloche*, San Martín 127. Outside the phone office is a telephone with links to several countries (eg UK, Chile, Japan).

● Sports

Apart from sailing and boating, there are golf, mountaineering, walking, birdwatching, skiing, and fishing (for which you need a permit). Excellent trout fishing Nov-Mar; boat hire arranged with tackle shops.

● Tourist offices

Oficina Municipal de Turismo in Centro Cívico, open in skiing season Mon-Fri 0800-2000, Sat 0900-1900. Daily at those times in summer but check times out of season (April, Oct-Nov) when closed at weekends. Has full list of city buses, and details of hikes and campsites in the area and is very helpful in finding accommodation. The book, *Guía Busch, Turismo y Comercio*, useful, is available free at the Río Negro or national tourist offices

in Buenos Aires, but is not free in Bariloche. National Park information (scanty) at San Martín 24, open 0800-2000. Information also from Sociedad Profesional de Guías de Turismo, Casilla de Correo 51, 8400 SC de Bariloche (President: Ama Petroff).

● Useful addresses

Immigration Office: next to *Hostería Tirol*, Libertad 175.

● Transport

Air Airport, 15 km from town. Taxi to or from airport, US$12; bus US$3 from Austral or Aerolíneas office. Many flights to **Buenos Aires**, with AR, Austral and Lapa. Austral also flies to **Viedma**. TAN and Kaiken fly to **Comodoro Rivadavia** and **Neuquén**; TAN also to **Puerto Deseado**, **San Martín de los Andes** and, in summer only, to **Puerto Montt** (Chile). Kaiken also serves **Esquel** and **Trelew**.

Trains The railway station is 5 km E of centre, reached by local buses 70 and 71, or taxi, US$5-6. The trains run to Buenos Aires via Bahía Blanca.

Buses The bus station is 3 km E of the centre (buses 20 and 21). There are services to all parts of the country.

SEA ROUTES SOUTH OF PUERTO MONTT

Taxi from centre to ferry terminal, US$2. All shipping services should be checked in advance; schedules change frequently.

To Puerto Natales

The dramatic 1,460 km journey first goes through Seno Reloncaví and Canal Moraleda. From Bahía Anna Pink along the coast and then across the Golfo de Peñas to Bahía Tarn it is a 12-17 hrs sea crossing, usually rough. The journey continues through Canal Messier, Angostura Inglesa, Paso del Indio and Canal Kirke (one of the narrowest routes for large shipping). The only regular stop is made off Puerto Edén (1 hr S of the Angostura Inglesa), where there are 3 shops, with scant provisions, one off-licence, one café, but no hotel or camping facility, nor running water. Population is 180, plus 5 *carabineros* and the few remaining Alacaluf Indians. It is, though, the drop-off point for exploring Isla Wellington,

The Poet and the Sea 3

"We sing to the Sea"

At that time I was unaware,
Frankly, even of my own name,
I hadn't written my first poem,
Nor shed my first tear;
My heart was nothing more, nothing less
Than a forgotten kiosk in a square.
It so happened that one day my father
Was exiled to the South, to far off
Chiloé Island where the winter
Is like an abandoned city.
I left with him and without thinking we arrived
In Puerto Montt one clear morning.
My family had always lived
In the Central Valley or in the mountains,
So that never, in our house, did we think about
Or talk about the sea.
On this point I only knew
what was taught in public school ...
We got down from the train among flags
And a solemn fiesta of bells
When my father took me by the arm
And turning his eyes to the white,

Free and eternal foam which navigates
In the distance towards some nameless country,
Said to me as if uttering a prayer
In a voice which still rings in my ear:
"That, my boy, is the sea." ...
I began to run, headlong,
As if desperate towards the beach
And for an unforgettable moment I stood
In front of that great lord of battles ...
How long our greeting lasted
I cannot put into words.
I can only add that on that day
The need and the anguish was born in my mind
To create in verse what in wave after wave
God created ceaselessly in my vision ...
It is, in truth, that since the world began,
The voice of the sea has been in my being.

Translated from "Se canta al mar", Nicanor Parra, *Obra gruesa* (Santiago: Editorial Andrés Bello, 1983), pages 18-20.

---

which is largely untouched, with stunning mountains. If stopping here, take all food; maps (not very accurate) are available in Santiago.

Navimag's *Puerto Edén* sails **to Puerto Natales** every 8 days, taking 4 days and 3 nights; the fare ranges from US$160 pp economy (inc meals) to US$660 pp in various classes of cabin (also inc meals); 10% discount on international student cards in cabin class only. Payment by credit card or foreign currency generally not accepted. Economy class accommodation is basic, in 24-berth dormitories and there is limited additional space for economy class passengers when weather is bad. Apart from videos, entertainment on board is limited. Economy class and cabin passengers eat in separate areas. Some report good food, others terrible. Standards of service and comfort vary, depending on the number of passengers and

weather conditions. Take seasickness tablets.

Another Navimag vessel, the *Amadeus*, carries cargo between Puerto Montt, Puerto Chacabuco and Puerto Natales, with a few passengers, same price as cheaper cabins on the *Puerto Edén*, no fixed timetable.

● **Booking** Economy class can only be booked, with payment, through Navimag offices in Puerto Montt and Puerto Natales. Economy tickets are frequently sold just before departure. Cabin class can be booked in advance through *Travellers* in Puerto Montt or Puerto Natales (see **Tour companies**, above), through Navimag offices in Puerto Montt, Puerto Natales and Punta Arenas, or through Cruceros Austalis (Navimag parent company) in Santiago. All of these have their own ticket allocation: once this is used up, they have to contact other offices to request spare tickets. Book well in advance for departures between mid-Dec and mid-Mar especially for the voyage S (Puerto Natales to Puerto Montt is less heavily booked). It is well worth going to the port on the day of departure if you have no ticket. Note that departures are frequently delayed – or even advanced.

To Puerto Chacabuco
● **Shipping services**
The roll on/roll off vehicle ferry m/n *Evangelistas* of Navimag, runs twice weekly to Puerto Chacabuco (80 km to the W of Coyhaique), usually Wed and Sat, returning from Puerto Chacabuco on the following day. From end-Dec to mid, or end-Mar the schedule changes to include a Sun-Tues trip from Puerto Chacabuco to Laguna San Rafael, so Pto Montt to Pto Chacabuco is Wed and Sat, but return to Pto Montt is Tues and Thur. The cruise to Puerto Chacabuco lasts about 24 hrs. First class accommodation includes 2 cabins with bath (US$125-250 depending on which cabin and number of occupants); tourist class, 14 bunks (about US$145 double); and third class, 400 reclining seats (US$68, type 'B', US$40, type 'A'). Fare to Laguna San Rafael US$155-220, reclining seat, or US$285-510 in cabin. First class reservations must be made in advance at the Santiago offices (see page 103). There is a small canteen; long queues if the boat is full. Food is expensive so take your own.

The *Colono* of Transmarchilay sails to Puerto Chacabuco on Tues and Fri between 1 Jan and early Mar, 26 hrs; passengers US$24-164 pp, vehicles US$165. Transmarchilay also runs a ferry service on the route Quellón (Chiloé)-Chaitén-Puerto Montt-Chaitén-Quellón (see under Quellón and Chaitén for details). Overbooking and long delays reported.

To Laguna San Rafael
● **Shipping services**
The m/n *Skorpios 1* and *2* of Constantino Kochifas C leave Pto Montt on Sat at 1100 for a luxury cruise with stops at Puerto Aguirre, Melinka, Laguna San Rafael, Quitralco, Castro (each ship has a slightly different itinerary) and returns to Puerto Montt on Fri at 0800. The fare varies according to season, type of cabin and number of occupants: a double ranges from US$465 (low) to US$660 (high) on *Skorpios 1* and from US$770 (low) to US$1,100 (high) on *Skorpios 2*, which is the more comfortable of the two. It has been reported that there is little room to sit indoors if it is raining on *Skorpios 1*, but generally service is excellent, the food superb and at the glacier, you chip your ice off the face for your whisky. (After the visit to San Rafael the ships visits Quitralco Fiord where there are thermal pools and boat trips on the fiord.)

Patagonia Connection SA, Fidel Oteíza 1921, Oficina 1006, Providencia, Santiago, T 225-6489, F 274-8111, operates *Patagonia Express*, a catamaran which runs from Puerto Chacabuco to Laguna San Rafael via Termas de Puyuhuapi, see page 321. Tours lasting 4 to 6 days start from Puerto Montt and include the catamaran service, the hotel at Termas de Puyuhuapi and the day excursion to Laguna San Rafael. High season 20 Dec-20 Mar, low season 11 Sept-19 Dec and 21 Mar-21 April. High season fares for a 4-day tour from US$940, all inclusive, highly rec.

Other Routes
The m/n *Bohemia* makes 6 day/5 night trips from Puerto Montt to Río Negro, Isla Llancahué, Baños Cahuelmó and Fiordo Leptepu/Coman, US$545-720 pp depending on season (Antonio Varas 947, T 254675, Puerto Montt).

See also under Chaitén for passenger services on Terminales Marítimos Chilenos.

Chiloé

THE CULTURE of Chiloé has been strongly influenced by isolation from Spanish colonial currents, the mixture of early Spanish settlers and Mapuche indians and a dependence on the sea. Religious and secular architecture, customs and crafts, combined with delightful landscapes, all contribute to Chiloé's uniqueness.

THE LAND

The island of **Chiloé**, officially known as Chiloé Grande, is 250 km long, 50 km wide and covers 9,613 sq km. The Cordillera de la Costa, the coastal mountain range, runs down the island from N to S, though at altitudes below 1,000m. South of Castro there is a gap in the range where two lakes, Lago Huillinco and Lago Cucao, are situated. Thick forests cover most of the western side. The hillsides in summer are a patchwork quilt of wheat fields and dark green plots of potatoes. Most of the population of 116,000 live on the sheltered eastern side of Chiloé Grande. There are two main towns, Ancud and Castro, and many fishing villages. East of the island are several groups of smaller islands; the largest of these, Quinchao, Lemuy and Mechuque are described below.

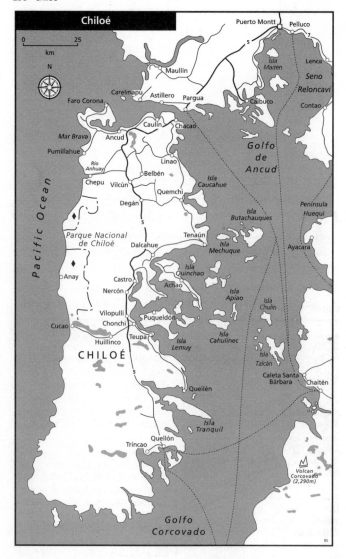

Chiloé

Puerto Montt
Pelluco
7
5
Isla
Maiten
Lenca
Seno
Reloncavi
Maullín
Calbuco
Contao
Carelmapu
Astillero
Pargua
Faro Corona
Caulín
Chacao
Mar Brava
Ancud
Golfo
de
Ancud
Pumillahue
Río
Anhuay
Linao
Chepu
Belbén
Vilcún
Isla
Caucahue
Quemchi
Peninsula
Huequi
Degán
5
Isla
Butachauques
Parque Nacional
de Chiloé
Tenaún
Dalcahue
Ayacara
Isla
Mechuque
Anay
Isla
Quinchao
Castro
Achao
Nercón
Isla
Apiao
Isla
Chulin
Vilopulli
Puqueldón
Cucao
Chonchi
Teupa
Isla
Cahulinec
Huillinco
Isla
Lemuy
Isla
Talcán
CHILOÉ
Caleta Santa
Bárbara
Chaitén
5
Queilén
Isla
Tranquil
Volcán
Corcovado
(2,290m)
Trincao
Quellón

Golfo
Corcovado

Pacific Ocean

0   25
km
N

85

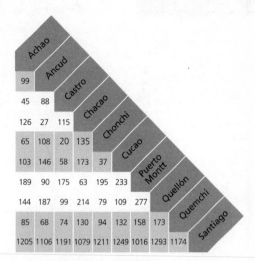

	Achao	Ancud	Castro	Chacao	Chonchi	Cucao	Puerto Montt	Quellón	Quemchi	Santiago
Ancud	99									
Castro	45	88								
Chacao	126	27	115							
Chonchi	65	108	20	135						
Cucao	103	146	58	173	37					
Puerto Montt	189	90	175	63	195	233				
Quellón	144	187	99	214	79	109	277			
Quemchi	85	68	74	130	94	132	158	173		
Santiago	1205	1106	1191	1079	1211	1249	1016	1293	1174	

Chiloé : distance chart (km)

CLIMATE

The West coast, exposed to strong Pacific winds, is wet for most of the year. The sheltered east coast and the offshore islands are drier, though frequently cloudy.

HISTORY

The original inhabitants of Chiloé were the Chonos, who were pushed S by the Mapuches invading from the N. The first Spanish sighting was by Francisco de Ulloa in 1553; a Spanish expedition was despatched from the mainland 5 years later and in 1567 Martín Ruiz de Gamboa took possession of the islands on behalf of Spain. The small Spanish settler population divided the indigenous population and their lands between them. The rising of the Mapuche after 1598 which drove the Spanish out of the mainland S of the Río Biobío left the Spanish community on Chiloé (some 200 settlers in 1600) isolated. Much of Chiloé's distinctive character derives from its 200 years of isolation from the mainstream of Spanish colonial development. During the 17th century Chiloé was served by a single annual ship from Lima, though on occasions even this failed to arrive. In 1600 and 1642 the island was attacked by Dutch pirates. Following a violent earthquake in 1646 the Spanish population asked the Viceroy in Lima for permission to leave, but this was refused.

The islanders were the last supporters of the Spanish Crown in South America. When Chile rebelled the last of the Spanish Governors fled to the island and, in despair, offered it to Britain. Canning, the British Foreign Secretary, turned the offer down. The island finally surrendered to the patriots in 1826.

ART AND ARCHITECTURE

The availability of wood and the lack of metals have left their mark on the architecture of Chiloé. Some of the earliest of the island's churches were built entirely of wood, using wooden pegs instead of nails. These early churches often dis-

The Jesuits in Chiloé

The Jesuits arrived in Chiloé in 1608 and the first Jesuit residence was established 4 years later. Although in Chiloé they established few of the missions for which they became famous in other parts of the continent, by the time they were expelled in 1767 there were 79 churches on the island. The key to their influence lay in their use of *fiscales*, indigenous people freed from the duty to work for the Spanish and trained to teach Christian doctrine and ensure that everyone observed prayers and other religious duties. One *fiscal* was appointed for every 50 inhabitants. On 17 Sept each year, two missionaries set sail from Castro in small boats, taking with them statues of saints and other essential supplies. They spent the next 8 months sailing round the islands, visiting all the parishes in a set order. In each parish they spent 3 days, carrying out weddings and baptisms, hearing confessions and reviewing the work of the *fiscales*.

Most of the old churches for which Chiloé is famous date from after the expulsion of the Jesuits, but some writers claim that their influence can still be seen, for example in the enthusiasm for education in the island which has long boasted one of the lowest illiteracy rates in the world. Meanwhile many villages still have *fiscales* who are, by tradition, responsible for keeping the church keys.

Stamps depicting Chiloé churches

played some German influence as a result of the missionary work of Bavarian Jesuits. Three notable features were the *explanada* or porch which ran the length of the front of the church, the not-quite semi-circular arches and the central position of the tower directly above the door. In the 19th century the original design was often modified. Few of the oldest churches have survived the ravages of fire, earthquakes and the weather, but there are still over 150 churches mostly built of wood.

The houses (*rucas*) of the indigenous population were thatched and throughout the 19th century thatch continued in widespread use. Two features of local architecture often thought to be traditional are in fact late 19th century in origin. The use of thin tiles (*tejuelas*) made from alerce wood was partly the result of the influence of the German settlers around Puerto Montt. These tiles, which are nailed to the frame and roof in several distinctive patterns, overlap to form an effective protection against the wet climate. *Palafitos* or wooden houses built on stilts over the water, were once popular in the main ports, but are now mainly found in Castro.

The island is also famous for its traditional handicrafts, notably woollens and basket ware, which can be bought in the main towns and on some of the off-shore islands, as well as in Puerto Montt.

MODERN CHILOE

Although the traditional mainstays of the economy, fishing and agriculture, are still important, salmon farming has become an important source of employment. Seaweed is harvested for export to Japan. Tourism provides a seasonal income for a growing number of people, especially in Castro. The relatively high birth rate and the shortage of employment in Chiloé have led to regular emigration. Chilotes have settled throughout Chile, were prominent as shepherds in late 19th century Patagonia and are an important source of labour for the Argentine oil industry.

Chiloé's distinctive history and its maritime traditions are reflected in the strength of its unique folklore, much of which is in the form of traditional tales.

TRANSPORT TO CHILOE

Regular ferries cross the straits of Pargua between **Pargua**, 55 km SW of Puerto Montt on the mainland, and **Chacao** on Chiloé.

● **Accommodation** At **Pargua**: *Hotel La Ruta*; *Res El Porvenir*. At **Chacao**: **E** pp *Pensión Chiloé*; **E** pp *Hosp Angelino*.

● **Buses** From Puerto Montt, frequent, US$2, 1 hr, though most buses go right through to Ancud (3½-4 hrs) and Castro. Transport to the island is dominated by Cruz del Sur, who also own Trans Chiloé and Regional Sur and have their own ferries. Cruz del Sur run frequent services from Puerto Montt to Ancud and Castro, 6 a day to Chonchi and Quellón; their fares are highest (Trans Chiloé lowest but sell out quickly) but in busy periods they are faster (their buses have priority over cars on Cruz del Sur ferries). Fares from Puerto Montt: to Ancud, Cruz del Sur US$$5.75,Trans Chiloé US$4.50; to Castro, Cruz del Sur US$7.50, Trans Chiloé US$6; to Chonchi, US$7, Quellón, US$9. Note that there are direct bus services from Santiago, Osorno, Valdivia, Temuco and Los Angeles to Chiloé. Buses drive on to the ferry (passengers can get out of the bus). **Ferries** About 24 crossings a day, 30 min crossing, operated by several companies inc Transmarchilay and Cruz del Sur; all ferries carry buses, private vehicles (cars US$10 one way) and foot passsengers (who travel free).

ANCUD

(*Pop* 23,148; *Phone code* 065), lies on the N coast of Chiloé 30 km W of the Straits of Chacao at the mouth of a great bay, the Golfo de Quetalmahue. Founded in 1767 to guard the shipping route around Cape Horn, it was defended by two fortresses, the Fuerte San Antonio and Fuerte Ahui on the opposite side of the bay. Less

The legend of the potato

🐾 A chief on Chiloé, a place populated by seagulls, wanted to make love like the gods.

When pairs of gods embraced, the earth shook and tidal waves were set moving. That much was known, but no one had seen them.

Anxious to surprise them, the chief swam out to the forbidden isle. All he got to see was a giant lizard, with its mouth wide open and full of foam and an outsized tongue that gave off fire at the tip.

The gods buried the indiscreet chief in the ground and condemned him to be eaten by the others. As punishment for his curiosity, they covered his body with blind eyes.

Oreste Plath, *Geografía Del Mito Y La Leyenda Chilena*, Santiago, 1973, quoted in Eduardo Galeano, *Genesis*, Methuen, 1986.

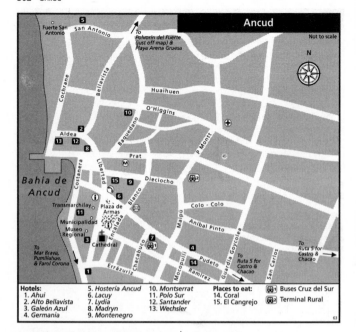

Hotels:
1. Ahui
2. Alto Bellavista
3. Galeón Azul
4. Germania
5. Hostería Ancud
6. Lacuy
7. Lydia
8. Madryn
9. Montenegro
10. Montserrat
11. Polo Sur
12. Santander
13. Wechsler

Places to eat:
14. Coral
15. El Cangrejo

🚌1 Buses Cruz del Sur
🚌2 Terminal Rural

important than Castro, it is a good centre for visiting the villages of northern Chiloé.

Places of interest

The port is dominated by the **Fuerte San Antonio**, built in 1770, the site of the Spanish surrender of Chiloé to Chilean troops in 1826. Close to it are the ruins of the **Polvorín del Fuerte** (a couple of cannon and a few walls). 1 km N of the fort is a secluded beach, **Arena Gruesa**. 2 km E is a **Mirador** offering good views of the island and across to the mainland.

Museums

Near the Plaza de Armas is the **Museo Regional** (open summer daily 1100-1900, winter Tues-Fri 0900-1300, 1430-1830, Sat 1000-1330, 1430-1800, US$1), with an interesting collection on the early history of Chiloé as well as replicas of a traditional Chilote thatched wooden house and of the small sailing ship *Ancud*.

Excursions

To **Faro Corona**, the lighthouse on Punta Corona, 34 km W, along the beach, which, though unsuitable for swimming, offers good views with interesting birdlife and dolphins. To **Pumillahue**, 27 km SW, and **Mar Bravo** on W coast, bus 1230 Mon-Fri. Near Pumillahue (bus daily 0700, details from tourist office) there is a penguin colony: hire a fishing boat to see it, US$2.50 pp.

Local information

● **Accommodation**

A1 *Hostería Ancud*, San Antonio 30, T/F 622340/622350, overlooking bay, attractive, very comfortable, friendly and helpful, restaurant; **A3** *Galeón Azul*, Libertad 751, T 622567, F 622543; **A3** *Lydia*, Pudeto y Chacabuco, T 622990, F 622879, with bath, **B** without bath, poor beds, small rooms, overpriced; **A3** *Lacuy*, Pudeto 219 near Plaza de Armas, T/F 623019, with breakfast, restaurant, rec; **A3** *Montserrat*, Baquedano 417, T/F 622957, with breakfast, clean, good views, attractive.

The voyage of the *Ancud*

The opening of regular steamship services through the Straits of Magellan in the early 1840s and the seizure of the Falkland Islands/Islas Malvinas by the British in 1833 revived European interest in the route to the Pacific. Alarmed at reports of a French expedition to claim the Straits, President Bulnes ordered the dispatch of the *Ancud*. The vessel, which sailed from Ancud on 23 May 1843, was captained by John Williams of Bristol, who was accompanied by the naturalist Bernardo Philippi, 11 sailors, 8 soldiers, 2 women, 3 dogs, 2 pigs and a pregnant goat. After a three month voyage the party landed at Puerto Hambre, one day before the arrival of a French warship. Williams's voyage was later commemorated by the naming of the Chilean naval base on Isla Navarino *Puerto Williams* in his honour.

B *Cabañas Las Golondrinas*, end of Baquedano at Arena Gruesa, T 622823, superb views, with bath, hot water and kitchenette; **B** *Hostería Ahui*, Costanera 906, T 622415, with bath and breakfast, modern, clean, good views; **B** *Polo Sur*, Costanera 630, T 622200, with bath, hot water, good seafood restaurant, not cheap, avoid rooms overlooking disco next door; **B** *Res Weschler*, Cochrane 480, T 622318, with bath, **D** without, clean, view of bay; **B** *Res Germania*, Pudeto 357, T/F 622214, with bath, **C** without, parking, comfortable, clean; **C** *Madryn*, Bellavista 491, T 622128, with bath, also meals, clean.

D *Caleta Ancud*, Bellavista 449, good breakfast, good restaurant; **D** *Hosp Alto Bellavista*, Bellavista 449, T 622384, with sleeping bag on floor much cheaper; **D** *Hosp Capri*, Ramírez 325, good breakfast; **D** *Hosp Alinar*, Ramírez 348, clean, hot water, hospitable; **D** *Hosp Santander*, Sgto Aldea 69, with bath, **E** without, clean, rec; **D** *Res MaCarolina*, Prat 28, with breakfast; **E** pp *Res Montenegro*, Blanco Encalada 531, T 622239, fair, no hot water; **E** pp Edmundo Haase Pérez, Ramírez 295, with breakfast, clean, basic, good value; **E** pp Errázuriz 442, with breakfast, cold water; **E** pp Elena Bergmann, Aníbal Pinto 382, clean, friendly, use of kitchen, parking; **E** pp Pudeto 331, T 622535, without bath, old fashioned; **E** pp Lautaro 947, T 2980, clean, friendly; **E** pp Sra Lucía, San Martín 705; **E** pp Familia Reuter-Miranda, Errázuriz 350, T 622261, good breakfast, clean, spacious, opp Cruz del Sur terminal, rec; Errázuriz 395, T 622657, without bath, clean; **F** pp Pudeto 619, with breakfast, clean, friendly. In summer the school on Calle Chacabuco is used as an *albergue*.

Camping: *Arena Gruesa* at N end of Baquedano; *Playa Gaviotas*, 5 km N; *Playa Larga Huicha*, 9 km N, E per site, bath, hot water, electricity.

● **Places to eat**

Seafood restaurants in market area. Good lunches at *Hotel Polo Sur*. On Pudeto: *Carmen*, No 159, Chilean cooking, *pasteles*; *Coral*, No 346, good, not cheap; *Jardín*, No 263, good local food, not cheap; *Lydia*, No 254, Chilean and international. *Macaval*, Chacabuco 691; *El Trauco*, Blanco y Prat, seafood excellent, highly rec; *La Pincoya*, next to harbour, friendly, good seafood; *El Cangrejo*, Dieciocho 155, seafood highly rec; *Hamburguería*, Av Prat, much better than name suggests, good seafood; *Mar y Velas*, Serrano 2, p 2, beautiful views, good food.

● **Post & telecommunications**

Post Office: On corner of Plaza de Armas at Pudeto y Blanco Encalada.

Telephone: Plaza de Armas, open Mon-Sat 0700-2200.

● **Tour companies & travel agents**

Turismo Ancud, Pudeto 219, Galería Yurie, T 2235, Tx 297700 ANCD CL; *Paralelo 42*, Prat 28, T 2458, F 2656, rec for tours to the Río Chepu area, inc 2-day kayak trips, guide Carlos Oyarzun (also at *Res MaCarolina*) rec.

● **Tourist offices**

Sernatur, Libertad 665, T 622665, open Mon-Fri 0900-1300, 1430-1800.

● **Transport**

Buses Cruz del Sur, Trans Chiloé and Regional Sur use the terminal at Errázuriz y Los Carrera; local buses leave from municipal terminal at Pedro Montt 538 though a new terminal is under construction on the E outskirts at Aníbal Pinto y Marcos Vera. To **Castro**, US$3, frequent (see below), 1½ hrs. To **Puerto Montt**, 2 hrs, Cruz del Sur 10 a day, Trans Chiloé 3 a day, Varmontt 3 a day from *Hotel Polo Sur*. To Quemchi via the coast 2 hrs, US$1.50.

Shipping Transmarchilay Libertad 669, T 622317/622279, Tx 375007 MARCHI CK.

Longer excursions

Chepu, on the coast SW of Ancud, famed for its river and sea fishing, is a base for exploring the drowned forest and river environment of the Río Chepu and its tributaries, inhabited by a wide range of birds. (It is also the entrance to the N part of the Parque Nacional Chiloé, see under Cucao.) At **Río Anhuay** (also known as **Puerto Anhuay**) there is a camping site and *refugio*. From here it is a 1½ hr walk to Playa Aulén which has superb forested dunes and an extinct volcano.

Activities Boat trips can be organized in Río Anhuay to Laguna Coluco, 1 hr up the Río Butalcura (a tributary of the Río Chepu). Longer trips, navigating the Ríos Grande, Carihueco and Bu-

Ancud to Castro

Ancud —11— —16— Chacao
26
41   ○ Linao
27
○ Quemchi
24
25   ○—7—○ Mechuque
         Tenaun
33
16   ○ Dalcahue
   15   ferry crossing —22—
6   ○ Achao
○ Castro

86a   Not to scale

talcura usually start further inland and finish at Río Anhuay, 2 days, arrange in Ancud (*Paralello 42* rec). This area offers great opportunities for horse-riding with long beaches for galloping. Try Sr Zuñipe or Sr Uroa (rec), US$5 per hr (ask at the *refugio* in Río Anhuay).

• **Access** From Route 5, 26 km S of Ancud by a 24 km dirt road. Alternatively there is a 2 day coastal walk from Ancud: you can take the daily bus to Pumillahue (0700, return 1330) or hitch. The route is difficult to follow so take food for 3 days and wear light-coloured clothes in summer to protect against *tavanos*. No public transport.

East of Ancud on the N coast is **Caulín**, with good beaches; fresh oysters in *Hotel Lyon*. The road goes along the beach, only passable at low tide.

ANCUD TO CASTRO

There are two alternative routes: direct along Route 5, the Pan-American Highway, crossing rolling hills, forest and agricultural land, or via the E coast along unpaved roads passing through small farming and fishing communities and offering good views of rural life in Chiloé. The two main towns along the coastal route, Quemchi and Dalcahue, can also be reached by roads branching off Route 5.

QUEMCHI

(*Pop* 2,000) 68 km S of Ancud via Route 5 is a quiet town with long beaches.

• **Accommodation** F pp *Hosp El Embrujo*, Pedro Montt 431, T 262; **F** pp *Hosp La Tranquera*, Yungay 40, T 250, without bath, basic.

DALCAHUE

(*Pop* 2,300) 74 km S of Ancud, is more easily reached from Castro, 30 km further S. It is one of the main ports for boats to the offshore islands, inc Quinchao and Mechuque (see below). The wooden church on the main square dates from the 19th century. The market is on Sun, from 0700 to 1300; good quality, but bargaining practically impossible. Tourist kiosk in season. Tenaún, 40 km E of Dalcahue, is an interesting fishing village with a good 18th-century church.

● **Accommodation D/E** *La Feria*, Rodríguez 17, T 641293, without bath, basic; **D/E** *Res Playa*, Rodríguez 9, basic; **E** *Hosp Puteman*, Freire 305, T 330, clean, basic; **E** *Res San Martín*, San Martín 1, T 641207, basic, clean, also meals.

● **Places to eat** *Restaurant La Dalca*, Freire 502, good food and service, rec.

● **Transport** Buses to Castro, hourly, 40 mins, US$1. Also collective taxis.

QUINCHAO

The island of Quinchao is a short ferry journey from Dalcahue. Its main settlement is **Achao**, 25 km SE of Dalcahue, a quiet, pretty fishing village and market town serving the smaller islands offshore. Its wooden church, built in 1730 and saved by a change of wind from a fire which destroyed much of the town in 1784, is a fine example of Chilote Jesuit architecture. The original construction was without use of nails. There is a small museum, entry US$1.

● **Accommodation D** *Plaza*, Plaza de Armas, T 661283, with bath and breakfast, clean, good; **D/E** *Hosp Chilhue*, Zañartu 021, without bath, with breakfast, clean; **D** pp *Hosp Achao*, Serrano 061, T 661373, with bath, good, clean; **E** pp *Hosp Sao Paulo*, Serrano 52, basic, poor beds, hot water; **D** pp *Hostería La Nave*, Prat y Aldea, T 661219, with bath, **E** pp without bath, with breakfast, restaurant with fine views over bay.

● **Places to eat** *Arrayan*, Zañartu 19; *Restaurant Central*, Delicias, simple, cheap, good; *Restaurant Mar y Velas*, on waterfront, good fish, cheap, rec.

● **Tourist offices** Serrano y Progreso (Dec-Mar only).

● **Transport Ferry**: from Dalcahue, frequent, free for pedestrians and cyclists.

MECHUQUE

The island of Mechuque, E of Dalcahue, has one village and offers splendid walking country.

● **Accommodation** with the schoolteacher's son or with Sra Dina del Carmen Paillacar, **E**, good meals, rec.

● **Transport Boat**: from Dalcahue, dep Tues and Thur 1330, return Mon and Wed 1000, 2½ hrs, US$2.50 one way.

CASTRO

(*Pop* 20,000; *Phone code* 065) the capital of Chiloé lies 88 km S of Ancud on a fjord on the E coast. Founded in 1567, the centre is situated on a promontory, from which there is a steep drop to the port. Castro is the major tourist centre of the island; its central location and good communications make it a good base for excursions to Dalcahue and the offshore islands and to Chonchi and the Parque Nacional Chiloé.

Places of interest

On the Plaza de Armas is the large **Cathedral**, strikingly decorated in lilac and

---

Curantos

Particularly associated with Puerto Montt and Chiloé, *curantos* is a very filling fish, meat and seafood stew, which is delicious despite the rather odd combination of ingredients. Though of prehispanic origins, it has developed over generations by adding new ingredients. In its original pre-conquest form a selection of fish was wrapped in leaves and baked over hot stones in a hole. Could this way of cooking have come from the Pacific islands where pit baking is still practised? With the arrival of the Spanish, the dish was modified to include pork, chicken and white wine. Nowadays it is usually cooked in a large pan and then it is often advertised as *pullmay* to distinguish it from the pit-baked form.

Jaime Baez

orange, with a splendid wood panelled interior, built by the Italian architect, Eduardo Provosoli and dating from 1906. S of the Plaza on the waterfront is the **Feria**, or Mercado Municipal de Artesanía, where local woollen articles (hats, sweaters, gloves) can be found. Nearby are several *palafito* restaurants, built on stilts above the water. More *palafitos* can be seen on the northern side of town and by the bridge over the Río Gamboa. There are good views of the city from **Mirador La Virgen** on Millantuy hill above the cemetery.

Museums

Museo Regional on Esmeralda, opp *Hotel La Bomba*, contains history, folklore, handicrafts and mythology of Chiloé and photos of the 1960 earthquake, open summer Mon-Sat 0930-2000, Sun 1030-1300; winter Mon-Sat 0930-1300, 1500-1830, Sun 1030-1300; **Museo de Arte Moderno**, near the Río Gamboa, in the Parque Municipal, about 3 km NW of the centre, reached by following C Galvarino Riveros up the hill W of town, T 632787, F 635454 (open 1000-2000).

Excursions

To **Puntilla Ten Ten** and the Peninsula opposite Castro, a pleasant walk through woods and fields, 2 hrs round trip, turn off Route 5, 2 km N of town.

Local information
● **Accommodation**

A1 *Unicornio Azul*, Pedro Montt 228, T 632359, F 632808, good views over bay, comfortable, restaurant; **A2** *Cabañas Centro Turístico Nercón*, 5 km S, T 632985, rooms with bath, hot water, heating, restaurant, tennis court; **A3** *Hostería Castro*, Chacabuco 202, T 632301, F 635668 with bath and breakfast, hot water, good restaurant, attractive building, wonderful views; **A3** *Cabañas Truyen*, 5 km S of Castro, B off season, lovely views; **A2** *Gran Alerce*, O'Higgins 808,

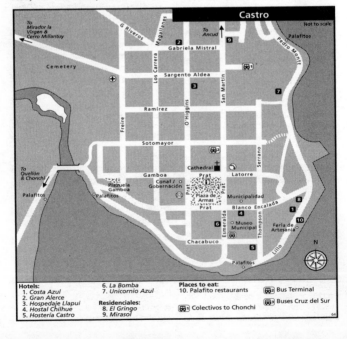

Hotels:
1. Costa Azul
2. Gran Alerce
3. Hospedaje Llapui
4. Hostal Chilhue
5. Hostería Castro

6. La Bomba
7. Unicornio Azul

Residenciales:
8. El Gringo
9. Mirasol

Places to eat:
10. Palafito restaurants

Colectivos to Chonchi

Bus Terminal

Buses Cruz del Sur

T 632267, with bath, heating, helpful, breakfast, also has *cabañas* and restaurant 4 km S of Castro.

B *Casita Española*, Los Carrera 359, T 635186, heating, TV, parking, rec; **B** *Chilhue*, Blanco Encalada 278, T 632956, with bath, good; **B** *Moteles Auquilda*, Km 2, Panamericana Norte, T 632458; **C** *Quinta Niklitschek*, Panamericana Norte 331 (3 km N), T 632137, better inside than out; **C** *Costa Azul*, Lillo 67, T 632440, with bath, **D** without, friendly.

Cheaper accommodation On San Martín (convenient for bus terminals): **D** *Res Mirasol*, No 815, basic, friendly, noisy; **E** pp *Hosp Chiloé*, No 739, breakfast, clean, rec; **E** pp *Hosp Angie*, San Martín 747, small rooms, clean, pretty; **E** pp *Hosp Guillermo*, No 700, clean, cheap; **E** pp *Res Capullito*, No 709, clean, friendly, quiet; **F** pp No 879, with big breakfast, central, clean, highly rec; **F** pp Lidia Low, No 890, with good breakfast, warm showers, use of kitchen; **E** pp No 638, clean; **E** pp No 581, helpful.

Other Budget accommodation: **D** *Hilton*, Ramírez 385, good value, friendly, restaurant; **E** pp *Hosp* of Jessie Toro, Las Delicias 287, with good breakfast, hot water, helpful, clean, spacious, good bathrooms, also cabins, warmly rec; **D** *La Bomba*, Esmeralda 270, T 632300, without bath, cheaper on 3rd floor, clean, good value, hot water, good 3 course *menú*; **E** pp *Casa Blanca*, Los Carrera 300, inc breakfast, clean, modern, warm; **D** Los Carrera 658, no sign, with breakfast, clean, friendly, rec; **E** pp *Res La Casona*, Serrano 488, above TV shop, with breakfast, rec; **E** Serrano 407, breakfast, clean, warm water; **D** *Res El Gringo*, Lillo 51, without bath, good views, overpriced; **E** *Hosp Llapui*, O'Higgins 657, run down, with breakfast; **E** pp Eyzaguirre 469, comfortable, rec; **E** pp María Zuñiga, Barros Arana 140, T 635026, inc breakfast, clean, comfortable, cooking facilities, friendly, secure, rec; **E** pp, Freire 758, breakfast, clean, good value; **E** pp O'Higgins 415, Dpto 41, quiet, very clean, hot water; **E** pp O'Higgins 865, clean, friendly, hot water; **E** pp Chacabuco 449, good beds, clean, quiet, friendly, water only warm; **E** pp Los Carrera 560, T 632472, clean, hot water; **D** *Hosp Sotomayor*, Sotomayor 452, T 632464, with breakfast, quiet, small beds; **E** pp *Hosp Tonque*, Pasaje Díaz 170, T 632773, without breakfast, clean, hot water; **E** pp *Hospedaje El Mirador*, Barros Arana

127, T 633795, friendly, good breakfast; **F** pp *Hosp Polo Sur*, Barros Arana 169, T 635212, clean, safe, cooking facilities, wonderful views. Basic accommodation Dec-Feb in the Gimnasio Fisical, Freire 610, T 632766, **F** with breakfast, clean.

Camping: *Camping Pudú*, Ruta 5, 10 km N of Castro, T 635109 cabins, showers with hot water, sites with light, water, children's games. Several sites on road to Chonchi.

● **Places to eat**
Palafito restaurants near the Feria Artesanía on the waterfront offer good food and good value, inc *Brisas del Mar, Mariela* and *La Amistad*; *Gipsy*, O'Higgins 548, Chinese; *Sacho*, Thompson 213, good sea views, clean; *Don Camilo*, Ramírez 566, good food, not expensive, rec; *Pizzería La Nona*, Serrano 380, good pizzas, welcoming staff; *Stop Inn Café*, Prat y Chacabuco, good coffee; *Chilo's*, San Martín 459, good lunches; *El Curanto*, Lillo 67, seafood inc *curanto*, rec. *Maucari*, Lillo 93, good seafood, not expensive. In the market, try *milcaos*, fried potato cakes with meat stuffing; also *licor de oro*, like Galliano; *La Brújula del Cuerpo*, Plaza de Armas, good coffee, snacks; breakfast before 0900 is difficult.

● **Banks & money changers**
Banco del Estado de Chile, Plaza de Armas, accepts TCs (at a poor rate). BCI, Plaza de Armas, Mastercard and Visa ATM. Better rates from Julio Barrientos, Chacabuco 286, cash and TCs.

● **Hospitals & medical services**
Doctor: *Muñoz de Las Carreras*, near police station, surgery 1700-2000 on weekdays, rec.

● **Laundry**
Lavandería Adolfo, Blanco Encalada, quick, reasonably priced.

● **Post & telecommunications**
Phone Office: Latorre 289.

Post Office: on W side of Plaza de Armas.

● **Shopping**
See above for market. Cema-Chile outlet on Esmeralda, opp *Hotel La Bomba*. *Libros Chiloé*, Blanco Encalada 204, books in Spanish on Chiloé. Cassettes of typical Chilote music are widely available.

● **Sports**
Bicycle hire: San Martín 581.

● **Tourist offices**
Kiosk on Plaza de Armas opposite Cathedral; **Conaf** in Gamboa behind the Gobernación building.

● **Tour Companies and travel agents**
Pehuén Expediciones, Thompson 229, T 635254; *Chiloé Tours*, Blanco Encalada 318, T 635952; *Turismo Queilén*, Gamboa 502, T 632776 good tours to Chonchi and Chiloé National Park, rec. **LanChile** agency, Thompson 245. **Ladeco** agency on Serrano, opp *Hostería Castro*. *Transmarchilay* agency at Suzuki Car Hire, San Martín y Blanco Encalada. Local guide Sergio Márquez, Felipe Moniel 565, T 632617, very knowldegeable, has transport. Tour prices: to Parque Nacional Chiloé US$25, to Mechuque US$37.

● **Transport**
Local Buses: frequent services to Chonchi, choose between buses (Cruz del Sur, Queilén Bus and others), minibuses and collective taxis (from Esmeralda y Chacabuco). Arroyo and Ocean Bus both run to Cucao, 1 a day off season, 0945 and 1600 in summer, US$2. To Dalcahue frequent services by Gallardo and Arriagada, also collective taxis from San Martín 815. To Achao via Dalcahue and Curaco de Vélez, Arriagada, 4 daily, 3 on Sun, last return from Achao 1730. To Puqueldón on the island of Lemuy, Gallardo, Mon-Fri 1315, US$2. To Quemchi, 2 a day, 1½ hrs, US$2.50; to Quellón, Regional Sur and Trans Chiloé, frequent; to Queilén, Queilén Bus; to Quemchi, 2 a day, Queilén Bus.

Buses leave from 2 terminals: Cruz del Sur, T632389, Trans Chiloé and Arriagada from Cruz del Sur terminal on San Martín behind the cathedral. Other services leave from the Municipal Terminal, San Martín, 600 block (2 blocks further N). Frequent services to Ancud and Puerto Montt by Cruz del Sur and Trans Chiloé. Cruz del Sur also run to Osorno, Valdivia, Temuco, Concepción and Santiago. Bus Norte to Ancud, Puerto Montt, Osorno and Santiago daily; to Punta Arenas, Tur Bus, Ghisoni and Austral.

CASTRO TO QUELLON

Route 5 continues S to Quellón, the southernmost port in Chiloé. There are side roads to Chonchi (paved) and to Cucao and Parque Nacional Chiloé (unpaved). From Chonchi an unpaved road runs S to Queilén. This road, winding across forested hills, is the probably the most attractive in Chiloé especially in autumn.

CHONCHI

(*Pop* 3,000; *Phone code* 065) is a picturesque fishing village 25 km S of Castro. From the plaza Calle Centenario, with several attractive but sadly neglected wooden mansions, drops steeply to the harbour. Fishing boats bring in the early morning catch which is carried straight into the nearby market. The wooden church, on the plaza, was built in 1754, remodelled in neo-classical style in 1859 (key from handicraft shop next door). There is another 18th century church at Vilopulli, 5 km N.

Museums Museo de las Tradiciones Chonchina, Centenario 116, artefacts donated by local families reflecting life in the early 20th century.

● **Accommodation A3** *Posada Antiguo Chalet*, Irarrazával, T 671221, **B** in winter, charming, beautiful location, very good; **B** *Cabañas Amankay*, Centenario 421, T 671367, homely, kitchen facilities, rec; **C** *Hostería Remis*, Irarrazával 27, T 671271, with bath, **E** without, lovely position on waterfront, good food, rec; **D** *Hosp Chonchi*, O'Higgins 379, T 671288, full board available, good value, rec; **D** *Esmeralda By The Sea*, on waterfront 100 m E of *Restaurant La Costanera* (Casilla 79), T 671328, with breakfast, attractive, welcoming, English spoken, boat trips offered, information, highly rec;

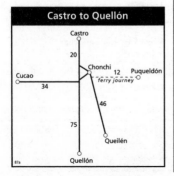
Castro to Quellón

D *Huildin*, Centenario 102, T 671388, without bath, old fashioned, good beds, also *cabañas* **A3**, garden with superb views, parking; *Res Los Tres Pisos*, Centenario 330, without bath, basic, overpriced; **D** *Hosp Mirador*, Alvarez 198, with breakfast, friendly, clean, rec; **E** pp Alvarez 891, clean, noisy, friendly, good breakfast; **E** *Res Turismo*, Andrade 299, T 257, without bath, with breakfast; **E** Baker at Andrade 184, clean, friendly; **E** Cerda 160.

● **Places to eat** *La Parada*, Centenario 133, very friendly, good selection of wines, often closes evenings, rec; *El Alerce*, Aguirre 106, excellent value; *El Trébol*, waterfront; *La Quila*, Andrade 183. Cheapest place for lunch is *La Costanera*, on waterfront.

● **Banks & money changers** Nicolás Alvarez, Centenario 429, cash only.

● **Shopping** Handicrafts from *Opdech* (Oficina Promotora del Desarrollo Chilote), on the waterfront, and from the *parroquia*, next to the church (open Oct-March only).

● **Tourist offices** Kiosk on the main plaza in summer.

● **Transport** Buses and taxis to Castro, frequent, US$0.75, from main plaza. Services to Quellón and Queilén from Castro and Puerto Montt also call here.

LEMUY

(*Pop* 4,200) an island, 97 sq km, with one main village, **Puqueldón**, lies offshore opposite Chonchi and offers many good walks along quiet unpaved roads through undulating pastures and woodland.

● **Accommodation** **E** pp *Restaurant Le-* *muy* and *Café Amancay*, both clean, without bath, good.

● **Transport Buses** Once a day from Castro. **Ferry** service from Puerto Huicha, 4 km S of Chonchi, approx every 30 mins, foot passengers free (from here it is 8 km to Puqueldón).

Queilén, 46 km by unpaved road SE of Chonchi, is a pretty fishing village with long beaches and wooden pier.

● **Accommodation & places to eat** **F** pp *Pensión Chiloé*, without bath, basic; *Restaurant Melinka*, friendly.

● **Transport** Buses to Castro, Queilén Bus, 6 a day, 4 on Sat, 3 on Sun, 2 hrs, US$2.50.

CUCAO

From Chonchi an unpaved road leads W to **Cucao**, 40 km, one of two settlements on the W coast of Chiloé. At Km 12 is Huillinco, a charming village on Lago Huillinco (**E** pp *Residencia*, good food, or stay at the Post Office). At Cucao there is an immense 15 km beach with thundering Pacific surf and dangerous undercurrents.

● **Accommodation & places to eat** **E** pp *Hosp Paraíso*, friendly; **E** pp *Posada Cucao*, with breakfast, hot water, meals, friendly; **E** pp with full board or *demi-pension* at *Provisiones Pacífico* (friendly, good, clean, candles provided, no hot water), Sra Boreuel or with Sra Luz Vera, next to school, meals and good homemade bread, rec; **E** pp *Casa Blanca*, with breakfast. **Camping**: several campsites inc *Parador Darwin*, check prices carefully first. *Las Luminarias* sells excellent *empanadas de machas* (*machas* are local shell fish).

When Cucao had everything

'Long ago', Don Antonio began, 'Cucao had everything – cows, horses, sheep, goats, everything – and the rest of Chiloé had nothing. One day a sheep was born with three horns, and its fame spread. A stranger came to see the sheep and stayed the night. In the morning the people woke to find all their animals gone. They followed the tracks and came to a river. There was an old man sitting on the bank.

'"Have you seen the thief who stole our animals?" they asked.

'"That was no thief", the man said. "That was the King of the Land."

'And ever since the people of Cucao have nothing and the rest of the island is rich.'

Bruce Chatwin, *What Am I Doing Here?* Picador, 1989.

● **Transport** For buses from Castro see above; in season as many as 4 buses a day, last departure 1600, reduced service off-season; hitching is very difficult.

PARQUE NACIONAL CHILOE

The Park, which is in 3 sections, covers 43,057 ha. The northern sector, covering 7,800 ha, is reached by a path which runs S from Chepu (see page 304). The third section is a small island, Metalqui, off the coast of the N sector. The southern sector, 35,207 ha, is entered 1 km N of Cucao, where there is an administration centre (limited information), small museum and guest bungalow for use by visiting scientists (applications to Conaf via your embassy). Park entry US$2.50. No access by car. Maps of the park are available. (**NB** *Refugios* are inaccurately located.)

A path runs 3 km N from the administration centre to Laguna Huelde (many camp sites) and then N a further 12 km to Cole Cole (*refugio*, key kept at Conaf office at entrance, free camping, dirty) offering great views, best done on horseback (return journey to/from Cucao 9 hrs by horse). The next *refugio* is at Anay, 9 km further N across the Río Anay (crossed by ferry, US$10). There are several other walks but signposting is limited. Many houses in Cucao rent horses at US$2.50/hour, US$22/day. If you hire a guide you pay for his horse too. Horseflies are bad in summer (wear light clothing).

Wildlife Much of the park is covered by evergreen forest. The Park marks the southern limit of the Chilean Alerce. Fauna include the Chiloé fox and pudú deer. There are over 110 species of birds inc cormorants, gulls, penguins and flightless ducks.

● **Accommodation** No accommodation in the Park, but several places in Cucao. There is a campsite near the administration centre and other sites nearby. *Refugios* at Cole Cole and Anay are desribed above.

● **Transport** For transport to N sector see above under Chepu; for S sector see under Cucao.

QUELLON

(*Pop* 7,500; *Phone code* 065) the southernmost port in Chiloé, 92 km S of Castro, is the departure point for ferries to Chaitén. There are pleasant beaches nearby at Quellón Viejo (old wooden church), Punta de Lapa and Yaldad. The launch *Puerto Bonito* sails 3 times daily in summer from the pier, US$12.50 to tour the bay passing Punta de Lapa, Isla Laitec and Quellón Viejo. A trip can also be made to Chaiguao,11 km E, where there is a small Sun morning market; horses can be hired US$2.50/hr. Also kayaks with a guide, US$2.50/hr; camping US$3.50.

Museums

Museo de Nuestros Pasados, Ladrilleros 215, includes reconstructions of traditional Chilote house and mill; **Municipal**, on Gómez García.

Local information
● **Accommodation**

A1 *Golfo Corcovado*, Vargas 680, T 681528, F 681527, overlooking town, fine views, very comfortable, English spoken; **B** *Melimoyu*, P Montt 369, T 681250, clean, good beds, parking; **D** *Playa*, P Montt 427, T 681278, with breakfast, without bath, clean; **E** pp *Leo Man*, P Montt 445, T 681298, without bath, pleasant, good value, friendly; **E** pp *Res Estrella del Mar*, Gómez García 18, without bath, basic, poor value; **E** pp *El Colono*, Freire y Ladrillero, without bath; **E** pp *El Chico Leo*, Aguirre Cerda 20, T 681567, without bath, basic; **E** pp *Res Esteban*, Cerda 155; **C/D** *Res El Tráfico*, P Montt 115, with bath, **E** pp without, with breakfast, parking; **E** pp *La Pincoya*, La Paz 422, T 681285; **E** pp *Hosp La Paz*, La Paz 370, with breakfast, hot water; **F** pp *Las Brisas*, P Montt 555, T 681413, without bath, basic; **F** pp *Turino Club Deportes*, La Paz 24, floor space and camping, cold water, kitchen facilities, basic, open Dec-Feb only. *Albergue*, Ladrilleros, nr Carrera Pinto, **G** pp locals, **F** pp foreigners; dormitory accommodation. At Punta de Lapa, 7 km W are: *Leo Man*, chalets and *cabañas*; *Cabañas y Camping Las Brisas*.

● **Places to eat**

Rucantú on waterfront, good food, good value; *El Coral*, 22 de Mayo, good, reasonably

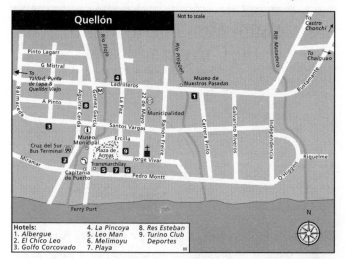

Hotels:
1. Albergue
2. El Chico Leo
3. Golfo Corcovado
4. La Pincoya
5. Leo Man
6. Melimoyu
7. Playa
8. Res Esteban
9. Turino Club
   Deportes

priced, superb views; *Fogón Las Quilas*, La Paz 053, T 206, famous for lobster, rec; *Hotel Leo Man* serves good coffee, pleasant *comedor*; *Nuevo Amanecer*, 22 de Mayo 201, cheap, clean.

● **Banks & money changers**
Banco del Estado, US$12 commission on TCs, credit cards not possible, no commision on US$ cash.

● **Tourist offices**
Kiosk on the park, open mid-Dec to mid-March. Ask about *hospedajes* not listed in their information leaflet.

● **Transport**
Buses To Castro, 2 hrs, frequent, Cruz del Sur, US$4, Trans Chiloé US$3; also services to Ancud and Puerto Montt.

Ferries: in summer only (2 Jan-8 Mar), the Transmarchilay ferry *Pincoya* sails to Chaitén on the mainland, Mon and Wed 1600, return departure Wed and Sat 0900, 5 hrs crossing, US$70-80 per car, US$11 pp. The ship continues from Chaitén to Puerto Montt. The *Pincoya* also sails from Quellón to Puerto Chacabuco Sat 1600, all year round, 18 hrs, cars US$110, passengers US$20-27. If you take this ferry when heading S you miss a large section of the Carretera Austral; if you wish to see the Carretera's scenery, take the ferry to Chaitén. From 15 Mar to 29 Dec ferries go only from Pargua to Chaitén and Puerto Chacabuco. **Transmarchilay** office, Pedro Montt 451, Quellón, T 681331. Enquire first, either in Santiago or Puerto Montt.

South from Puerto Montt: the Carretera Austral

THE CONSTRUCTION of the Carretera Austral has opened up the impressive landscapes of this wet and windy region of mountains, channels and islands. The main town is Coyhaique. A boat journey, either as a means of access, or for viewing the glacier at Laguna San Rafael gives an equally magnificent, but different perspective.

THE LAND

A third of Chile lies to the south of Puerto Montt, but its land and climate are such that, until recently, it has been put to little human use: less than 3% of the country's population lives here.

South of Puerto Montt the sea has broken through and drowned the central valley between the Andes and the coastal mountain range. The higher parts of the latter form a maze of islands, stretching for over 1,000 km and separated from the coast by tortous fjord-like channels. It is fortunate for shipping that this maze has a more or less connected route through it: down the channel between Chiloé and the mainland, across about 290 km of open sea beyond the southern tip of Chiloé and then down the Moraleda, Mesier, Inocentes and Smyth channels into the

Straits of Magellan. In some places along this route the tide levels change by 12m. In one particular place two sharp-cut walls, 900m high, enclose the constricted channel which leads to Puerto Natales; here the waters are deeper than the cliffs are high and slack water lasts for 30 mins only. The Smyth Channel enters the Straits of Magellan at Cape Thamar.

The Andes are much lower than further N and eroded by glacial action: towards the coast they rise in peaks such as San Valentín (4,058m), the highest mountain S of Talca; inland they form a high steppe around 1,000m. The other mountain peaks in this area include Fitzroy (3,340m), Lautaro (3,380m), Maca (2,960m), Hudson (2,600), Jeinimeni (2,600m) and Alesna (2,480m). To the S of Coyhaique are two areas of high land covered by ice and glaciers, known

The Carretera Austral: Puerto Montt to Puerto Cisnes

Not to scale

- Puerto Montt
- Parque Nacional Andino Alerce
- La Arena
- Puelche
- Río Negro/Hornopirén
- Parque Nacional Hornopirén
- Isla Llancahue
- Fiordo Leptepu
- Fiordo Reñihue
- Leptepu
- Golfo de Corcovado
- Fiordo Largo
- Caleta Gonzalo
- Santa Barbara
- Chaitén
- Amarillo
- Lago Espolón
- Futaleufú — To Esquel
- Río Yelcho
- Puerto Cárdenas
- Lago Yelcho
- Villa Santa Lucía
- Puerto Ramírez
- Palena — To Route 40
- Río Palena
- La Junta
- Reserva Nacional Rosselot
- Río Figueroa
- Lago Rosselot — To Route 40
- Termas de Puyuhuapi
- Lago Risopatrón
- Lago Verde
- Puyuhuapi
- Parque Nacional Quelat — To Route 40
- Parque Nacional Isla Magdalena
- Río Cisnes
- Puerto Cisnes
- Villa Amengual
- Lago Las Torres
- Reserva Nacional Lago Las Torres — To Coyhaique
- Canal Puyuguapi

ARGENTINA

N

90

The Carretera Austral: Mañihuales to Puerto Yungay

- Mañihuales
- Fiordo Aisén
- Puerto Aisén
- Río Simpson
- Coyhaique Alto — To Route 40
- Puerto Chacabuco
- Coyhaique
- Lago Atravesado
- Lago Frío
- Lago Castor
- Lago Pollux
- El Blanco
- Balmaceda — To Route 40
- Lago Elizalde
- Río Ibáñez
- Villa Cerro Castillo
- Puerto Ibáñez — To Perito Moreno
- Bahía Murta
- Lago General Carrera
- Lago Buenos Aires
- Río Tranquilo
- Chile Chico — To Perito Moreno
- Lago Bertrand
- Puerto Guadal
- El Maitén
- Cochrane
- Lago Cochrane
- Río Baker
- Lago Pueyrredón
- Tortel
- Puerto Yungay
- Villa O'Higgins

ARGENTINA

N

Not to scale

90b

as *campos de hielo* (ice fields). The Campo de Hielo Norte, over 100 km from N to S and some 50 km from E to W, includes the glaciers San Rafael, San Quintin and Steffen. The Campo de Hielo Sur covers a larger area, stretching S from the mouth of the Río Baker towards Puerto Natales.

Five main rivers flow westwards: from N to S these are the Futaleufú or Yelcho, the Palena, the Cisnes, the Simpson or Aisén and the Baker. The latter, 370 km long, is the third longest river in Chile. Only the Cisnes and the Simpson are entirely in Chile, the other three being largely fed from Argentina. The three largest lakes in this region, Lago

Gen Carrera (the largest in Chile), Lago Cochrane and Lago O'Higgins are also shared with Argentina.

ECONOMY

Agriculture is limited by the climate and poverty of the soil. Potatoes and cereals are among the major crops, while sheep farming is more important than cattle. Chile Chico and the shores of Lago Gen Carrera enjoy a warm microclimate which allows the production of fruit. Fishing remains important as a source of employment in the inland channels. Forestry plays a growing role in the economy: wood is used for construction and in towns such as Coyhaique is in such

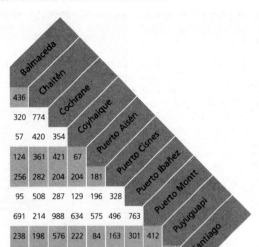

Carretera Austral: distance chart (km)

demand in winter for fuel that it costs as much as petrol. It is also increasingly exported, often as woodchips. Zinc, lead and copper are mined, but of these only zinc is produced in major quantities. Manufacturing is mainly restricted to processing local agricultural produce.

CLIMATE

There is no real dry season. On the offshore islands and the western side of the Andes annual rainfall is over 2,000 mm. Westerly winds are strong especially in summer. Temperatures vary little between day and night. Inland on the steppelands the climate is drier and colder. Jan and Feb are probably the best months for a trip to this region.

HISTORY

The original inhabitants were Tehuelches (Tzónecas, or Patagones), who lived on the pampa hunting guanacos, ñandúes (rheas) and huemules (a large indigenous deer, now almost extinct), and Alacalufes (Kaweshour, or Canoeros), who were coast dwellers living off the sea. See **Archaeology and Prehistory**, page 36 and **The original Patagonians** box, page 341. There is archaeological evidence, notably cave paintings, in the vicinity of Lago General Carrera, eg at Cueva de la Guanaca, near Lago Lapparent, and Cueva de las Manos, near Chile Chico. The arrival of the Spaniards, who called the region Trapananda, led to little more than exploration of the coast by navigators and missionaries.

This was the last territory to be occupied by the Chilean state after independence from Spain. In the late 19th century expeditions up the rivers led by George Charles Musters (1869) and Enrique Simpson Baeza (1870-72) were followed by a failed attempt to found a settlement at the mouth of the Río Palena in 1884. Fearing that Argentina might seize the territory, the Chilean government appointed Hans Steffen to explore the area. His seven expeditions

(1892-1902) were followed by an agreement with Argentina to submit the question of the frontier to arbitration by the British crown.

Chile's first attempt to occupy the area was by granting concessions to three large cattle companies. Although the companies undertook to export their produce through Chile and to encourage settlement, it was much easier to use routes through Argentina and they had little interest in colonization. Until the 1920s there were few settlers and few towns; early pioneers settled along the coast and supplied themselves from Chiloé. The first estimate, in 1907, gave the population of Aisén as 197. By 1920 this had risen to 1,660 and by 1930, 8,886

inhabitants in the region. Although the first town, Balmaceda was founded in 1917, followed by Puerto Aisén in 1924, the first road, between Puerto Aisén and Coyhaique, was not built until 1936. It was not until the 1960s when new roads were built and airstrips were opened in small towns that the integration of this region with the rest of the country began to take place.

PUERTO MONTT TO CHAITEN

This section of the Carretera Austral, 242 km, includes two ferry crossings. Before setting out, it is imperative to check when the ferries are running and, if driving, make a reservation: do this in Puerto Montt, rather than Santiago, at the Transmarchilay office, Angelmó 2187, T 254654. The alternative to this section is by ferry from Puerto Montt or Quellón to Chaitén.

The road (Ruta 7) heads E out of Puerto Montt, through Pelluco and after an initial rough stretch follows the shore of the beautiful Seno Reloncaví passing the southern entrance of the Parque Nacional Alerce Andino.

PARQUE NACIONAL ALERCE ANDINO

The park situated between the Seno Reloncaví to the S and W and Lago Chapo to the NE covers 39,255 ha of steep forested valleys rising to 1,500m, small lakes and waterfalls. It contains one of the best surviving areas of alerce trees, some over 1,000 years old (the oldest is estimated at 4,200 years old). Wildlife includes pudú, pumas, vizcachas, condors and black woodpeckers. There are four ranger posts: at Río Chaicas, Lago Chapo, Sargazo and at the N entrance. There are basic *refugios* at Río Pangal, Laguna Sargazo and Laguna Fría and camping sites at Río Chaicas and the N entrance. Very little information at ranger posts; map available from Conaf in Puerto Montt.

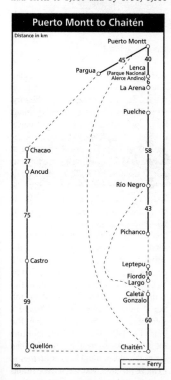

Puerto Montt to Chaitén

Distance in km

Puerto Montt
45 / 40
Pargua — Lenca (Parque Nacional Alerce Andino)
6
La Arena
Puelche
Chacao
27
Ancud
58
Río Negro
75
43
Pichanco
Castro
Leptepu
10
Fiordo Largo
Caleta Gonzalo
99
60
Quellón — Chaitén
90a

----- Ferry

● **Access** There are two entrances: 2.5 km

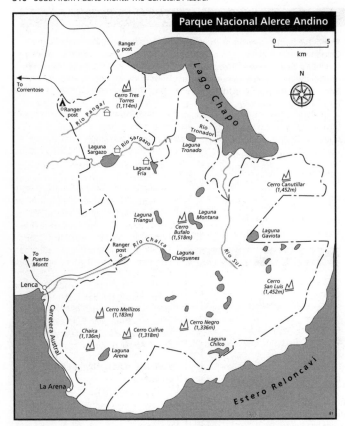

Parque Nacional Alerce Andino

from Correntoso (35 km E of Puerto Montt) at the northern end of the park and 7 km E of Lenca (40 km S of Puerto Montt) at the southern end.

● **Transport** To N entrance: take Fierro or Río Pato bus to Correntoso (or Lago Chapo bus which passes through Correntoso), several daily except Sun, then walk. To S entrance: take any Fierro bus to Chaicas, La Arena, Contau and Hornopirén, US$1.50, getting off at Lenca sawmill, then walk (signposted).

LA ARENA

46 km from Puerto Montt (allow 1 hr), this is the site of the first ferry, across the Reloncaví Estuary to Puelche.

● **Ferries** 30 mins, US$4.65 for a car, 7 crossings daily. Ferry leaves Puelche for La Arena 45 mins before it returns from La Arena. Arrive at least 30 mins early to guarantee a place; buses have priority. Roll-on roll-off type operating all year.

RIO NEGRO

(*Pop* 1,100) also called **Hornopirén** after the volcano above it, lies 58 km S of Puelche. From here you catch the second ferry, to Caleta Gonzalo. At the mouth of the fjord is **Isla Llancahué**, good for hiking in the forests amid beautiful scenery. *Hotel Termas de Llancahué* charges C pp

The Carretera Austral

Before the opening of the **Carretera Austral** (Southern Highway), the Chilean mainland between Puerto Montt and Punta Arenas had been poorly connected to the rest of the country, relying on overland transport through Argentina, limited airline services and irregular coastal shipping. Communications between communities in this area were also poor: roads ran E-W linking up with the Argentine road system.

Begun in 1976 the central section of the Carretera Austral, from Coyhaique to Chaitén, was opened in 1983. Five years later the northern section, linking Chaitén to Puerto Montt, and the southern section, between Coyhaique and Cochrane, were officially completed. Since then work has continued, taking the road further S towards its final destination, Villa O'Higgins, beyond which the icefields of the Campo de Hielo Sur prevent construction.

Although the new road has helped transform the lives of many of the inhabitants of the small towns and villages of the S, the motivation behind it was mainly geopolitical: since independence Chilean military and political leaders have stressed the importance of occupying the southern regions of the Pacific coast and preventing any incursion by Argentina. The Carretera Austral is a means of occupying and securing territory, just as colonization in the area was in the early part of this century.

The highway can be divided into three major sections: Puerto Montt-Chaitén (242 km) with 2-3 ferry crossings (see below); Chaitén-Coyhaique (435 km); and Coyhaique-Puerto Yungay (421 km). It is described on Chilean maps as a "camino ripio" (paved with stones). Most of the villages along the Carretera are of very recent origin and consist of a few houses which offer accommodation and other services to travellers. Although tourist infrastructure is growing rapidly, motorists should carry adequate fuel and spares, especially if intending to detour from the highway itself, and should protect their windscreens and headlamps. Unleaded fuel is available as far S as Cochrane. Cyclists should note the danger of stones thrown up by passing vehicles.

---

full board (excellent food), hot spring at the hotel. To get there, make arrangements by phoning 0965-38345. The hotel will send an open boat for you; the 1 hr crossing affords views of dolphins and fur seals. Efforts are under way to preserve areas of ancient emerald araucaria and alerce forest E of Volcán Hornopirén, co-ordinated by Ancient Forest International and Codeff, the Chilean environmental organization.

● **Accommodation** Electricity 1900-0100. *Cabañas* at Copec service station; **B** *Perlas del Reloncaví*, clean, pleasant, good restaurant, English and German spoken, highly rec; the cabins are usually taken before the rooms in the two other hotels, the **D** pp *Holiday Country*, on the road to Pichanco, hot shower,

restaurant, and the *Hornopirén*, at the water's edge, next to the sawmill, highly rec, T Puerto Montt 255243.

● **Transport Buses** Fierro run daily 0800 and 1500 from Puerto Montt. There are no buses S from Río Negro. **Ferries** Río Negro – Caleta Gonzalo, Transmarchilay, Wed 1600, Thur-Sun 1500, 5 hrs (may be much longer if the ferry cannot dock in rough weather). Going N the ferry leaves Caleta Gonzalo at 0900, Mon, Thur, Fri, Sat, Sun. Fare for vehicles over 4m US$88, under 4m US$75, passengers US$14, bicycles, US$9. Ferry operates Jan/Feb only and can be very busy; there can be a 2-day wait to get on the ferry.

The Río Negro-Caleta Gonzalo trip may also use two ferry stages, the first, from Pichanco up the Fiordo Leptepu, passing a narrow channel in which the

German light cruiser *Dresden* hid from the British fleet in 1915. The crew was protected by the local German community. The second stage, after a 10 km stretch of road from Leptepu to Fiordo Largo, crosses the Fiordo Reñihue to Caleta Gonzalo.

South of Caleta Gonzalo there is a steep climb on a coarse gravel surface to Laguna Blanca. Caleta Santa Bárbara, a black sand beach with nice camping and swimming, is at Km 48. (**NB** Do not camp close to the water.) It is a further 12 km to Chaitén.

CHAITEN

(Pop 3,258; Phone code 065), the capital of Palena province, is important as a port for ferries to Puerto Montt and Quellón. There are good views over the Corcovado Bay from the Costanera. Fuel is available.

Local information
● Accommodation
A2 *Mi Casa*, Av Norte, T 731285 – on a hill – rec, with bath, comfortable, or **E** in youth hostel, negotiable, the owners prefer you to eat in their restaurant.

B *Hostería Schilling*, Corcovado 230, T 731295, on waterfront, with bath and heating (hot water is turned on or off on the intuition of the landlady, check your shower before entering), no restaurant.

D *Continental*, Juan Todesco 18, T 731312, no heating nor private bath, but good meals, very helpful and friendly, rec; **D** *Hostería Los Alerces*, Av Norte s/n, F 731266, hot water, clean, restaurant; **D** *Res Astoria*, Corcovado 442, T 731263, with breakfast, shared bath, clean, bar downstairs.

E pp *Hosp Lo Watson*, Ercilla 580, use of kitchen, clean, friendly; **E** pp *Casa Rita*, Rivero y Prat (**F** pp for floor space, F pp for camping), use of kitchen, clean, open all year, heating, rec; **E** pp Corcovada 466, family atmosphere, hot shower extra; **E** pp Martín Ruiz, Carretera Austral 1 km N, inc breakfast, friendly, nice views; **E** pp *Hosp Recoba*, Libertad 432, T 731390, with breakfast, clean, friendly, good meals. *Los Arrayanes* campsite 4 km N, with hot showers and close to sea, good.

● Places to eat
Flamengo, Corcovado, T 314, excellent, popular with travellers; *Mahurori*, Independencia 141.

● Sports
Fishing: there is excellent fishing nearby, especially to the S in the Ríos Yelcho and Futaleufú and in Lagos Espolón and Yelcho. Fishing licences are sold at the Municipalidad.

● Tour companies & travel agents
Chaitur, in bus terminal, friendly and helpful.

● Transport
Air Flights Puerto Montt-Chaitén-Puerto Montt with Don Carlos, Juan Todesco 42, T 275, 1220 and 1600, Mon-Fri, 1220 on Sat, US$35. Also Aerosur daily except Sun, same fare.

Buses Artetur (Av Costanera) runs microbuses between Chaitén and Coyhaique, 3 a week in summer, Wed and Sat off-season (US$30, 12-14 hrs). The service depends very much on demand and in winter especially may not run all the way (ie only to La Junta). On the full service, the bus stops overnight in La Junta in winter but only briefly in summer. Other stops

Chaitén

Not to scale

Hotels:
1. Los Alerces
2. Mi Casa
3. Schilling

Places to eat:
4. Flamengo

The Carretera Austral by bike

🐾 "I would highly recommend cycling the Carretera Austral, but give yourself plenty of time to be able to enjoy it. Going by bus is way too fast and hitching can be frustrating: you can easily wait a day and a half for a ride and in the high season hitching can be competitive, with up to 20 people trying to get a ride out of the same place. In emergencies or if time gets away from you, it is fairly easy to catch a bus, although you may need to wait a day to make a connection. Buses charged up to US$12.50 extra for the bikes. Stock up on provisions in major towns. Bread is generally available in small towns or houses *en route*. 'Free' camping is fairly easy to find and water is easily available from small streams or by asking at nearby houses.

"If you have to stop riding for a section, Puerto Cisnes to Coyhaique is a long stretch of tree 'cemeteries' as a result of massive burning by the original colonists of the area. The road conditions of the Carretera vary, but the uphill stretches ('cuestas') are manageable. An especially rainy section is through the Parque Nacional Queulat. If it looks like rain, try to head for the camping areas which have covered spaces for fires and picnic tables. There may be a charge for camping. The circuit around Lago General Carrera [via Puerto Ibáñez and Chile Chico] can be done by bus or by bicycle; the scenery is spectacular but there are some very challenging passes on the southern shore of the lake. If possible travel from Cochrane towards Chile Chico to take advantage of the spectacular views of the Andes. Hitching this section is close to impossible; hitching S of Cochrane would be a lost cause." Carrie Wittner, San José, California.

on request, but it is easier to go right through than pick up a bus on route. Similar services by Transportes San Rafael, Mon and Thur 1200, and B and V Tours (Libertad 432) summer only. Hitching the whole route takes about a week, but you must be prepared for a day's wait if you find yourself out of luck.

Ferries Port about 1 km from town. The Transmarchilay ferries *Pincoya* and *Mailen* run between Chaitén, Puerto Montt and Quellón on Chiloé: sailings for Puerto Montt are on Mon 2200, Mon 2400, Thur 0900 and Fri 0900, 11 hrs; from Puerto Montt to Chaitén Tues 1200, Tues 1400, Thur 2200 and Fri 2000. Fares to Puerto Montt US$100/car over 4m, US$88 under 4m, US$16/deck passenger, seat US$20, bunk US$31, bicycle US$11. To Quellón Wed and Sat 0900 in Jan-early March, otherwise Sat 0900 only, fares under Quellón. The Navimag ferry *Alejandrina* sails between Chaitén and Puerto Montt, no bunks, no fixed schedule. Check in advance for exact times; office Av Corcovado 266, T 731272. There is also a ferry to Puerto Montt for trucks, Ro-Ro *Mercedes*, Terminales Marítimos Chilenos, which will also take passengers but with no shelter, standing only, unless someone lets you get in their vehicle, once a week (twice a week Jan-Feb), 12 hrs, US$8. Office is in a hardware store (*ferretería*) on Juan Todesco, T 731333; in Puerto Montt, Chorillos y Pudeto, T 257259.

CHAITEN TO COYHAIQUE

This section of the Carretera Austral, 422 km, runs through small villages and passes through the Parque Nacional Queulat; roads branch off E to the Argentine frontier and W to Puerto Cisnes.

AMARILLO

At Amarillo, 25 km S of Chaitén there is a turning to the **Termas de Amarillo**, 5 km E (2 wooden sheds with a very hot pool inside, US$3 pp, also outdoor swimming pool). From here it is possible to hike along **the old trail to Futaleufú**, 4-7 days, not for the inexperienced, be prepared for wet feet all the way. The trail follows the Río Michinmawida (passing the volcano of the same name) to Lago Espolón. A sporadic ferry crosses the lake taking cargo only to Futaleufú. Campsite

Climbing volcanoes along the Carretera Austral

The many volcanoes along the Carretera Austral offer climbing opportunities of varying degrees of difficulty, though in this part of the country most climbs usually take only 1 or 2 days and there are no problems with *soroche*. Corcovado (2,600m), a beautiful mountain with a sharp summit situated 40 km S of Chaitén and visible from parts of Chiloé, is particularly difficult. Most are much easier, eg Volcán Yates, further N near Puelche.

at this end of the lake also has bungalows (see below). There is superb salmon fishing in the rivers, and the local people are very friendly.

● **Accommodation** **B** *Termas de Amarillo*, at the Termas, T 731326, also camping and *cabañas*. In the village: **E** *Res Marcela*; **E** *Hosp Las Rosas*.

PUERTO CARDENAS

Situated 46 km S of Chaitén, Puerto Cárdenas lies on the northern tip of **Lago Yelcho**, a beautiful lake on Río Futaleufú surrounded by hills and frequented by anglers. The *Isla Monita Lodge* offers packages for anglers and non-anglers on a private island in the lake, as well as fishing in many nearby locations; contact *Turismo Grant*, PO Box 52311, Santiago, T 639-5524, F 633-7133. Further S at Km 60, a path leads to **Ventisquero Yelcho** (2 hrs' walk).

● **Accommodation** Two *residenciales* inc **C** *Res Yelcho*, clean, full board available; *Cabañas Cavi*, 7 km S on lakeshore, also camping, cafeteria.

THE ROUTE TO FUTALEUFU

The Argentine frontier is reached in two places, Futaleufú and Palena by a road which branches off at **Villa Santa Lucía** (Km 81), where there are 30 houses, a military camp, one small shop and bread is available from a private house. The road to the border is single track, gravel, passable in a regular car, but best with a good, strong vehicle; the scenery is beautiful. At **Puerto Ramírez** at the southern end of **Lago Yelcho** the road divides: the N branch runs along the valley of the Río

Futaleufú to **Futaleufú** and the southern one to Palena. **Lago Espolón**, W of Futaleufú, reached by a turning 41 km NE of Villa Santa Lucía, is a beautiful lake in an area enjoying a warm microclimate: 30°C in the day in summer, 5° at night. The lake is warm enough for a quick dip but beware of the currents. There are *cabañas* (**E** pp, US$3.75 for a motorhome) and a campsite; Aníbal, who owns the campsite, sells meat, bread, beer and soft drinks and will barbecue lamb. The Río Futaleufú and Lago Espolón provide excellent fishing (ask for the Valebote family's motorboat).

● **Accommodation** At Villa Santa Lucía: several places on main street: at No 7 (Sra Rosalía Cuevas de Ruiz, basic, meals available), No 13 (breakfast extra) and No 16 (not bad), all F pp, none has hot water. At Puerto Piedra: *Pensión Alexis*; campsite nearby; At Puerto Ramírez: *Hostería Río Malito*, rooms, camping, fishing. At Futaleufú: **D** *Res Carahue*, O'Higgins 322, T 221; **E** pp *Hotel Continental*, Balmaceda 597, T 222, basic, hot water, clean, rec, cheap restaurant. At Palena: *La Frontera*, T 741240; *Res La Chilenita*, T 258633.

● **Transport** **Air** Aerosur flights from Chaitén to Futaleufú, Tues and Fri, US$62. **Buses** A microbus runs from Chaitén to Futaleufú on Tues, at least.

FRONTIER WITH ARGENTINA: FUTALEUFU

● **Chilean immigration**
In Futaleufú, 9 km W of the frontier. Allow 1½ hrs for formalities. The border is at the bridge over the Río Grande.

NB Only transit visas for Argentina are issued, which can cause problems. You must either leave within 10 days or renew your entry stamp at an immigration office

● **Entering Chile**

Continue from Futaleufú towards Puerto Ramírez, but outside Ramírez, take the unsigned right turn to Chaitén (left goes to Palena)

● **Exchange**

Change money in Futaleufú (poor rates); nowhere to change at the border.

● **Transport**

From Futaleufú a bus runs to the border, Tues and Fri 1300, 1300 approx, US$3, 30 mins (ask at the small grey store, Kitty, at the school corner on Balmaceda).

FRONTIER WITH ARGENTINA: PALENA

● **Chilean immigration**

At Palena, 8 km W of frontier.

NB Only transit visas are issued (see above under Futaleufú crossing).

● **Accommodation**

Several *pensiones* in Palena.

● **Transport**

Expreso Yelcho bus from Chaitén twice a week, US$12, 5½ hrs.

INTO ARGENTINA

Both crossings lead to **Trevelin**, which is 45 km from Futaleufú, 95 km from Palena. Trevelin is an offshoot of the Welsh Chubut colony on the Atlantic side of Argentine Patagonia. It has accommodation, restaurants, tea rooms and a tourist office, but many more services will be found at **Esquel**, 23 km NE. This town (*pop* 18,800) is modern, with a reasonable supply of amenities.

LA JUNTA

From Villa Santa Lucía the Carretera Austral follows the Río Frío and then the Río Palena to La Junta (*Pop* 736), a drab, expensive village at the confluence of Río Rosselot and Río Palena, 151 km S of Chaitén. **Lago Rosselot**, surrounded by forest and situated in the **Reserva Nacional Lago Rosselot**, 9 km E of La Junta, can be reached by a road which heads E, 74 km, to Lago Verde and the Argentine frontier.

Chaitén to Coyhaique

Not to scale

Chaitén
25
Amarillo
21
Puerto Cárdenas
35
Villa Santa Lucía — 31 — 47 — Futaleufú
Puerto 51
Ramírez — Palena
70
La Junta
46
Puyuguapi
59
Puerto Cisnes — 35
33
Villa Amangual
3 — 104 → To Argentina
49
Villa Mañihuales
13
To Puerto Aisén — 49
30
Villa Ortega
34
Coyhaique

Distance in km   92a

● **Accommodation** C *Hostería Valdera*, Varas s/n, T 314105, inc breakfast, with bath, very good value; C *Cabañas Espacio Tiempo*, T 314141, restaurant, fishing expeditions; **E** pp *Copihue*, Varas 611, T 314140, few rooms but clean, without bath, hot water, good meals, changes money at very poor rates; **D** *Café Res Patagonia*, Lynch 331, T 314115, good meals, small rooms, limited bathrooms. At Lago Risopatrón is a Conaf campsite.

● **Banks & money changers** If desperate to change money try the hotels, but bargain hard.

● **Transport** Fuel is available. Buses to Coyhaique, Artetur (Diego Portales 183), US$14.30, twice a week, also Transaustral twice a week US$15.

PUYUGUAPI

From La Junta the Carretera Austral runs S along the W side of Lago Risopatrón, to Puyuguapi (also spelt Puyuhuapi; *Pop* 500; *phone code* 068), 45 km further S. Located at the end of the Puyuguapi

Channel, the village was founded by four Sudeten German families in 1935. The famous carpet factory can be visited. 18 km SW, accessible only by boat, are **Termas de Puyuhuapi**, several springs with 40°C water filling three pools near the beach (baths cost US$15 pp, children under 12 US$10, take food and drink). Sr Alonso runs day-trips from Puyuguapi, US$30. Daily visits from Carretera Austral, just to hot spring pools are possiblem boat transfer included in price. This resort can be visited with 4 and 6-day tours run by *Patagonia Connections SA* (see page 296, To Laguna San Rafael, shipping services).

● **Accommodation** L3-A1 *Hotel Termas de Puyuhuapi* (price depends on season and type of room), inc use of baths and boat transfer to hotel, full board US$40 extra, good restaurant, rec. For reservations: *Patagonia Connection SA*, Fidel Oteíza 1921, Oficina 1006, Providencia, Santiago (Metro Pedro de Valdivia), T 223-6489, F 274-8111 or directly at the *Hotel Termas de Puyuhuapi*, T 325 103. (See also under Puerto Montt **Shipping**.) Boat schedule from jetty, 2 hrs' walk from town, 0930, 1000, 1200, 1230, 1830, 1900, residents only, US$3 each way, 10 mins crossing. **A3** *El Pangue*, 17 km N on Lago Risopatrón, T/F 325128, cheaper off season, *cabañas*, camping, restaurant; **B** *Res Alemana*, Otto Uebel 450, T 325118, a large wooden house on the main road, owned by Sra Ursula Flack Kroschewski, comfortable, highly rec; **C** pp *Hostería Ludwig*, on the road S, T 325131, excellent, often full; **E** pp *Hosp El Pino*, Hamburgo s/n, T 325117, homemade bread, friendly; **E** pp *pensión* of Sra Leontina Fuentes, Llantureo y Circunvalación, clean, hot water, good breakfast for US$1; **E** pp *Res Elizabeth*, Llantureo y Henríquez, inc breakfast, clean; **E** pp *pensión* at Tureo 18. **A3** *Cabañas Fiordo Queulat* (T Coyhaique 233302), rec. There is a dirty campsite by the sea behind the general store. The store is behind the service station, which sells fuel until 1930.

● **Places to eat** *Café Rossbach* with limited menu, not cheap, excellent salmon. There are 2 bars.

● **Transport** Bus transport out of Puyuguapi is very scarce. Artetur (O'Higgins 039, T 325101) to Coyhaique and La Junta twice a week, to Chaitén once a week (Tues), Transaustral twice a week to Coyhaique.

PARQUE NACIONAL QUEULAT

The park, which covers 154,093 ha, lies N and E of Puyuguapi and is, according to legend, the place where the rich town of Césares once was. In the N of the park is **Lago Risopatrón**; 24 km S of Puyuguapi, is the beautiful Ventisquero Colgante (hanging glacier), with the Salto del Cóndor waterfall a further 29 km S. Boat trips can be made on Lago Risopatrón and Laguna Tempano. Administration is in the Conaf office in La Junta; entry US$1.

● **Access** The Carretera Austral runs through the W of the park.

● **Accommodation** **A3** *Cabañas El Pangue*, at N end of Lago Risopatrón, F 325128, also camping; *Cabañas Lago Queulat*, on Seno Queulat, campsite nearby, US$3.50.

PUERTO CISNES

At the southern end of Parque Nacional Queulat, 59 km S of Puyuguapi, a road branches W and follows the Río Cisnes 35 km to **Puerto Cisnes** (*Pop* 1,784) at the mouth of the river. Fuel is available.

The Río Cisnes, 160 km in lengrh, is rec for rafting or canoeing, with grand scenery and modest rapids except for the horrendous drop at Piedra del Gato; there is a 150m cliff at Torre Bright Bank. Good camping in the forest.

● **Accommodation** **B** *Manzur*, E Dunn 75, T 346453, *cabañas*; **D** pp *Hostal Michay*, Mistral 112, T 346462; **D** pp *Res El Gaucho*, Holmberg 140, T 346483, with breakfast, dinner available, welcoming, hot water; *pensión* at Carlos Condell y Dr Steffen, **D** pp, with breakfast, hot shower, friendly.

● **Transport** Buses Wed and Sun at 1100 to Coyhaique with Litoral, 5½ hrs, US$14, Trans Mañihuales daily US$14; Colectivos Basoli 2 a week, US$12.

RIO CISNES TO COYHAIQUE

89 km S of Puyuguapi is Villa Amengual (accommodation, food); at Km 92 a road branches E, 104 km to La Tapera and to the Argentine border. Chilean immigration is 12 km W of the frontier, open daylight hours only. On the Argentine side the road continues to meet up with Ruta 40, the N-S road at the foot of the Andes.

The **Reserva Nacional Lago Las Torres**, at Km 98, covering 16,516 ha, includes the wonderful Lago Las Torres, which offers good fishing and a small Conaf campsite. Further S at Km 125 a road branches E to El Toqui copper mine.

Villa Mañihuales(*Pop* 1,339) at Km 148 is near the **Reserva Forestal Mañihuales**; the forests are largely destroyed by forest fires in the 1940s, but the views are good. Entry US$1.

● **Accommodation** There are at least 3 *pensiones*, inc **E** pp *Pensión Bienvenido*, clean, friendly, and restaurant; **E** pp *Villa Mañihuales*, friendly, breakfast, *cabañas* **A** (both right-hand side of road going S at southern end).

● **Transport** Bus to Coyhaique, Trans Mañihuales, one a day except Sun.

13 km S of Villa Mañihuales the road forks W to Puerto Aisén, E to Coyhaique. At Villa Ortega on the Coyhaique branch, the *Restaurant Farolito* takes guests, **E** pp, rec.

COYHAIQUE

(*Pop* 36,367; *Phone code* 067), is located 420 km S of Chaitén in the broad green valley of the Río Simpson surrounded by mountains. Founded in 1929, it is the administrative and commercial centre of the XI Region. It provides a good base for hiking, skiing and fishing excursions in the area.

Places of interest

The town is centred around an unusual pentagonal plaza, on which stand the Cathedral, the Intendencia, the Liceo San Felipe Benicio and a handicraft market. Outside the city on the W bank of the Río Simpson is the **Piedra del Indio**, a rock outcrop which looks like a face in profile (if arriving from the airport, look left from the bridge over the Río Simpson).

Museums

Museo Regional de la Patagonia Central in the Casa de Cultura, Baquedano 310 (US$0.75, Tues-Sun 0900-1300, 1500-2000), containing photos of early settlers, history, paleontology, fauna and archaeology, good.

Excursions

To the **Reserva Nacional Coyhaique**, 5 km NW off the Carretera Austral, which covers 2,150 ha of mixed forest. Park administration is at the entrance. There are campsites at Laguna Verde (basic), 4 km from the entrance and at Casa Bruja, 2½ km from entrance, US$4, and a *refugio* 3½ km from entrance. Entry US$1.

Southwest to **Lagos Atrevesado** (20 km) and **Elizalde** which offers good fishing, yachting and camping. Southeast to **Lagos Frío**, **Castor** and **Pollux**, all of which offer good fishing. At El Fraile, 29 km SE near Lago Frío, there is skiing: there are 5 pistes and 2 lifts, cafeteria, equipment hire (season June to Sept). The **Monumento Natural Dos Lagunas**, 21 km E on the Coyhaique Alto road, is a small park which includes Lagos El Toro and Escondido, worth a visit. Entry US$1; camping US$12 per site.

Local information
● **Accommodation**
In summer rooms are in very short supply; the tourist office has a full list of all types of accommodation, but look out for notices in windows since any place with less than 6 beds does not have to register with the authorities (several on Baquedano and Almte Simpson).

A2 *Los Ñires*, Baquedano 315, T 232261, with breakfast, comfortable, parking; **A2** *Cabañas La Pasarela*, T 234520, Km 1.5

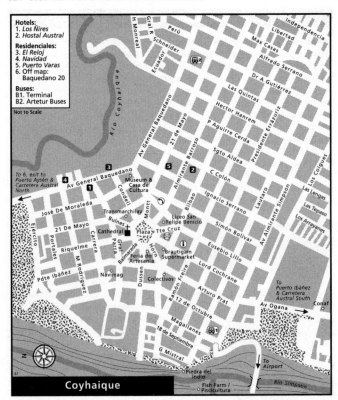

Hotels:
1. Los Ñires
2. Hostal Austral

Residenciales:
3. El Reloj
4. Navidad
5. Puerto Varas
6. Off map:
   Baquedano 20

Buses:
B1. Terminal
B2. Artetur Buses

Not to Scale

Coyhaique

Carretera a Aisén, good atmosphere, *comedor*;
A2 *Cabañas Río Simpson*, T 232183, Km 3
road to Pto Aysén, cabins for 5, or 2, fully-
equipped, horse hire, fishing; **A3** *Cabaña
Abedules*, 18 de Septiembre 463, F 232396,
at Plaza Angol, price/cabin for 5, hot water,
heating, kitchen, TV, suitable for families;
A3 *Austral*, Colón 203, T 232522, hot water,
clean, English spoken, tours arranged, friendly,
rec.

B *Cabaña San Sebastián*, Freire 554,
T 231762, with bath and breakfast; **B** *Res El
Reloj*, Baquedano 444, T 231108, with restau-
rant.

C *Licarayen*, Carrera 33A, T 233377 (Santiago T 743-1294) with bath and breakfast, rec;
C *Res Puerto Varas*, Serrano 168, T 233689,
without bath, check which of the bathrooms

has hot water, restaurant and bar, basic, tatty.
D pp *El Serrano*, Serrano 91, T 235522, with
breakfast, friendly, clean, rec.

E pp *Hosp* at Baquedano 20, T 232520, Patricio y Gedra Guzmán, room in family home
(also 3 flats), use of kitchen, breakfast with
homemade bread, tent sites with bathroom
and laundry facilities down by the river, English
spoken, most hospitable, rec; **D** *Hosp Her-
mina Mansilla*, 21 de Mayo 60, with breakfast, highly rec; **E** pp Manuel Torres, Barroso
957, hot water, use of kitchen, good; **F** pp *Res
Navidad*, Baquedano 198, T 235159, without
bath or breakfast, *comedor*, hot showers, use
of kitchen, clean; **E** pp *Hosp Pierrot*,
Baquedano 130, T 221315 with breakfast,
clean, quiet. Several cheap places on Av Simpson, eg **E** *Casa El Fondo*, No 417, clean,

Coyhaique: The Angler's Paradise

Coyhaique is the greatest centre for fishing in Chile; each summer the international fishing fraternity converge on the town for the season which runs from 15 Nov to 15 April. The weather is changeable, with hot sunshine (20-30°C) interspersed with showers; evenings are cool and the wind can lower temperatures particularly when fishing in river gorges. A warm jersey and lightweight waterproofs are advisable as well as total sun block protection.

Rivers range from the typically English slow chalk stream to the fast flowing Andean snowmelt torrents, requiring a variety of angling techniques. On the outskirts of Coyhaique, the spectacular Río Simpson teems with both Rainbow and Brown trout. The Simpson offers over 60 km of world class angling. It is renowned for its exciting evening hatches (sedge and mayfly) which take place throughout the season. Anglers will find that, pound for pound, these are some of the best fighting fish to be found anywhere. Catches in excess of 5 lbs are frequent and last season's record Rainbow tipped the scales at over 12 lbs.

Located near the Argentine border a scenic one hour drive from Coyhaique, the Río Nirehuao is a fly-fisher's dream. Throughout the season the Brown trout feed voraciously on grasshoppers and dragonfly. The easy wading and moderate casting distances make this river an all-time favourite.

South of Coyhaique the Río Baker, rising from South America's second biggest lake, Lago Gen Carrera, offers anglers a unique fishing experience in its turquoise blue water. The Baker is huge and intimidating, as are its fish: rainbows up to 12 lbs lurk in its deep blue depths and anglers regularly take fish in the 4-7 lb range. The Río Cochrane, a tributary of the Baker, also holds large Rainbows and if it were possible for a river to be clearer than 'gin-clear' this would be it. The Cochrane is mainly a 'sight-fishing' experience which requires skill, patience and an experienced guide.

Major JA Valdés-Scott.

friendly; **F** pp at No 649; **E** pp *Los Cuatro Hermanos* Colón 495, T 232647, without breakfast (more with), hot water, clean; **E** pp Baquedano 274, small rooms, very good; **E** pp *Hosp Lautaro*, Lautaro 532, T 231852, clean, comfortable, kitchen facilities, large rooms, rec. Youth hostel in summer at one of the schools (it changes each year), F pp with sleeping bag.

Camping: at Baquedano 20, see above. There are many camping sites in Coyhaique and on the road between Coyhaique and Puerto Aisén, eg at Km 1, 2 (*Camping Alborada*, US$8.50, T 231014, hot shower), 24, 25, 35, 37, 41, 42 (*Camping Río Correntoso*, T 232005, US$15/site, showers, fishing, Automobile Club discount) and 43. Sernatur in Coyhaique has a full list of all sites in XI Región.

● **Places to eat**
Loberías de Chacabuco, Barroso 553, good seafood, slow service; *La Olla*, C Parra be-

tween Riquelme and Moraleda, popular, good lunches; *Café Oriente*, 21 de Mayo y Condell 201, good bakery, tea; *Café Kalu*, Prat 402, serves set meals, hamburgers; *Café Ricer*, Horn 48, good food; *Cafetería Alemana*, Condell 119, nice, excellent cakes and coffee, vegetarian dishes; *Lito's*, Lautaro 147, next to Bus Terminal, good food and atmosphere; *Casino de Bomberos*, Gen Parra 365, wide range, cheap. A good bar is *Pub*, 12 de Octubre 361, nice atmosphere and music; around the corner is *Bar West*, Western style.

● **Airline offices**
LanChile, Gen Parra 215, T 231188; Ladeco, Dussen y Prat 188, T 231300; Don Carlos, Cruz 63, T 231981.

● **Banks & money changers**
Banco Osorno, Prat 340, T 232214, for cash advance on Visa, and Turismo Prado, 21 de Mayo 417, T/F 231271, both accept TCs. Banco Santander, Condell 100, Mastercard

ATM. For dollars TCs and Argentine pesos *Lavaseco* on Gen Parra. **Fincard** (Mastercard), Prat 340, local 1, T 233026, Mon-Fri 0900-1400, 1530-1900, Sat 0930-1330; at same address, oficina 208, *El Libertador*, T 233342.

● **Language schools**
Baquedano International Language School, Baquedano 20, at *Hosp* of Sr Guzmán (see **Accommodation** above), T 232520, F 231511: US$300/week course inc lodging and all meals, 4 hrs a day person-to-person tuition, other activities organized at discount rates.

● **Laundry**
Lavamatic, Bilbao 198; *QL*, Bilbao 160; *Universal*, Gen Parra 55; *Lottie*, Baquedano 1259.

● **Post & telecommunications**
Post Office: Cochrane 202, open Mon-Fri 0830-1230, 1430-1800, Sat 0830-1200.

Telephone Office: at Barroso 626, open till 2200, opens on Sun about 0900.

● **Shopping**
Feria de Artesanía on the plaza; *Cema-Chile* on plaza, between Montt and Barroso. Large well-stocked supermarkets: *Brautigam*, Horn, Prat y Bilbao; *Central*, Magallanes y Bilbao, open daily till 2230; 2 small ones on Prat, Nos 480 and 533, open Sun. Food, especially fruit and vegetables, is more expensive than in Santiago but cheaper than Argentina.

● **Sports**
Excellent opportunities for fishing in the Coyhaique area.

● **Tour companies & travel agents**
Turismo Prado, address in **Banks & money changers** above; *Expediciones Coyhaique*, Bolívar 94, T/F 232300. Both offer tours of local

lakes and other sights, arrange Laguna San Rafael trips, etc; *Prado* does historical tours, while *Expediciones* does fishing trips and excursions down the Río Baker. *Turismo Queulat*, 21 de Mayo 1231, T/F 231441, trips to Queulat glacier, adventure and nature tourism, fishing, etc. *Res Serrano*, C Serrano, organizes trips to Lago Elizalde and Lago Atrevesado, US$15 pp. *Aventura*, Bilbao 171, T 234748, offers rafting; *45 Sur*, 12 de Octubre 253, T 234599, horseriding, good value; *Alex Prior*, T 234732, for fly fishing. Tours only operate in season.

● **Tourist offices**
Cochrane 320, T 231752. **Conaf**: office, Ogana 1060. Maps (photocopies of 1:50,000 IGM maps) from Dirección de Vialidad on the square.

● **Transport**
Local Bicycle rental: *Figón*, Simpson y Colón, check condition first. Bicycle spares from several shops on Simpson. **Car hire**: **Automóvil Club de Chile**, Bolívar 254, T 231649, rents jeeps and other vehicles. **Budget**, Parra 215; **Traeger-Hertz**, Baquedano 457; **Economy**, Carrera 339, T 233363, cars may be taken across Argentine border and may be returned to a different office; **Automundo AVR**, Bilbao 509. 4WD rec for Carretera Austral. Buy fuel in Coyhaique, several stations. **Taxis**: US$5 to airport (US$1.65 if sharing); fares in town US$1.35. 50% extra after 2100. Colectivos congregate at Prat y Bilbao, average fare US$0.50.

Air Airport, Tte Vidal, about 5 km SW of town (inc a steep climb up and down to the Río Simpson bridge). Served by local airlines; larger planes use Balmaceda (see below). Air taxi to visit glaciers, US$350 (5 passengers), also to southern archipelagic region. Don Carlos to

The price of settlement

Two legacies of the Chilean government's attempts to encourage settlement in this area are the large expanses of burnt tree stumps to be seen especially around the Río Palena and Mañinhuales and the shifting of the port facilities from Puerto Aisén to Puerto Chacabuco. A law of 1937 offered settlers ownership of land provided it was cleared of forest: smoke from the forest fires which followed could be seen from the Atlantic coast. So much soil was washed into the rivers that the Río Aisén silted up preventing vessels reaching Puerto Aisén.

Chile Chico (Tues, Thur, Sat), and Cochrane (Wed, Fri, 45 mins, rec only for those who like flying, with strong stomachs, or in a hurry).

Buses Terminal at Lautaro y Magallanes; most buses leave from here, but not all. Bus company offices: Turibus, Baquedano 1171, T 231333; Transaustral, Baquedano 1171, T 231333; Don Carlos, Subteniente Cruz 63, T 232981; Litoral, Baquedano e Independencia, T 232903; Artetur, Baquedano 1347, T 233768, F 233367; Transportes San Rafael, 18 de Sept 469, T 233408; B and V Tours, Simpson 1037.

To/from **Puerto Montt**, via Bariloche, all year, Turibus, Tues and Fri 1600, US$28.50, with connections to Osorno, Valdivia, Temuco, Santiago and Castro, often heavily booked. To **Puerto Aisén**, Transaustral, 4 a day, 5 on Sun, La Cascada (T 231413), 4 daily, and Don Carlos taxi-bus, US$3, 8 a day, 3 on Sun; to **Puerto Chacabuco**, Transaustral Thur and Sun, La Cascada 3 times daily, US$3.25. **Puerto Cisnes** daily with Litoral, Tues and Sat at 1130, or Colectivos Basoli, T 232596, Thur and Sun 1200, US$13. There are daily buses to **Mañihuales**, Trans Mañihuales (daily 1700) and Litoral. To **Balmaceda** and **Puerto Ibáñez**, Buses Ruta Sur, T 232788.

To **Puerto Ibáñez** on Lago Gen Carrera, colectivos (connect with *El Pilchero* ferry to Chile Chico) from *El Gran Calaforte*, C Prat, 3 hrs, book the day before, US$7; to Bajada Ibáñez, Aerobus from bus terminal, Mon, Wed, Fri 1000, return next day, US$5.45, and Pudú, T 231000/6, Tues and Sat 0815.

Buses on the **Carretera Austral** vary according to demand: N to **Chaitén**, with Artetur, Wed 0700, US$30, overnight stop in La Junta, extra service on Sat in summer, in winter may go only as far as La Junta, US$14.30. Similar service by Transportes San Rafael, Mon and Thur 0900 in summer, 11 hrs, US$30, Transaustral, Tues and Sat 0900 and B and V Tours. Transaustral goes to La Junta via Puyuguapi, US$15, Tues and Sat. To **Puerto**

Montt, Tues and Fri US$35. South to **Cochrane** Pudú, at terminal, T 231008, Don Carlos and Río Baker Taxis (T 231052), all 3 times a week, charging US$23, 10-12 hrs.

To Argentina: options are given below and under Balmaceda, Chile Chico and Cochrane. Many border posts close at weekends. If looking for transport to Argentina it is worth going to the local Radio Santa María, Bilbao y Ignacio Serrano, and leaving a message to be broadcast.

Shipping: Transmarchilay, 21 de Mayo 147, T 231971, Tx 377003 MARCHI CK. **Navimag**, Ibáñez 347, T 233306, F 233386. **Patagonia Connection SA**, Fidel Oteíza 1921, Oficina 1006, Providencia, Santiago, T 225-6489, F 274-8111, operates *Patagonia Express*, a catamaran which runs from Puerto Chacabuco to Laguna San Rafael via Termas de Puyuhuapi, see page 296 for further details.

FRONTIER WITH ARGENTINA: COYHAIQUE ALTO

On the Argentine side the road leads through Río Mayo and Sarmiento to Comodoro Rivadavia on the Atlantic seaboard.

● **Chilean immigration**

At Coyhaique Alto, 43 km E of Coyhaique, 6 km W of the frontier, open May-Aug 0800-2100, Sept-April 0700-2300.

● **Transport**

To **Comodoro Rivadavia**, Empresa Giobbi, Coyhaique bus terminal, T 232067, Tues, Thur, Sat 0830, US$30, 12-13 hrs, also service by Turibus, 2 a week.

PARQUE NACIONAL RIO SIMPSON

Situated 37 km W of Coyhaique on the paved road to Puerto Aisén, the park covers 40,827 ha of valleys and hills rising to 1,878m. There are beautiful waterfalls and good views of the river and very good fly-fishing. Wildlife includes *pudú*, condors and *huemul*. Administration is at the entrance; campsite near the turning to Santuario San Sebastián US$5.

● **Transport** Take any bus between Coyhaique and Puerto Aisen.

PUERTO AISEN

(*Pop* 13,050; *Phone code* 067), is situated 57 km W of Coyhaique and 426 km S of Chaitén, quite an attractive town at the meeting of the rivers Aisén and Palos. They say it rains 370 days a year here. Formerly the region's major port, it has been replaced by Puerto Chacabuco, 15 km to the W. There are few vestiges of the port left, just some boats high and dry on the river bank when the tide is out and the foundations of buildings by the river, now overgrown with fuchsias and buttercups. To see any maritime activity you have to walk a little way out of town to Puerto Aguas Muertas where the fishing boats come in.

A new bridge over the Río Aisén and a paved road lead to **Puerto Chacabuco**; a regular bus service runs between the two. The harbour is a short way from the town.

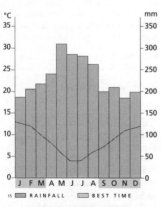

● RAINFALL   ● BEST TIME

Climate: Puerto Aisén

Excursions

There is a good walk N to Laguna Los Palos, 2 hrs from Puerto Aisén. In season the *Apulcheu* sails regularly to **Termas de Chiconal**, about 1 hr from Puerto Chacabuco, offering a good way to see the fjord, US$28, take own food.

Local festivals

Local festival of folklore, 2nd week in November.

Local information

Services given below are in Puerto Aisén unless stated otherwise.

● **Accommodation**
Hard to find, most is taken up by fishing companies in both ports.

In Puerto Aisén: D *Plaza*, O'Higgins 237, T 332784, without breakfast; **D** *Res Aisén*, Av Serrano Montaner 37, T 332725, good food, clean, full board available; **D** *Roxy*, Aldea 972, T 332704, friendly, clean, large rooms, highly rec, restaurant; **E** pp unnamed *hospedaje* at Serrano Montaner 471, T 332574, very pleasant and helpful, rec; **E** pp *Yaney Ruca*, Aldea 369, T 332583, clean, friendly. No campsite but free camping easy.

In Puerto Chacabuco: A2 *Parque Turístico Loberías de Aisén*, Carrera 50, T 351115, F 351188, accommodation overpriced, best food in the area, climb up steps direct from port for drink or meal overlooking boats and mountains before boarding ferry; **D** *Moraleda*, O'Higgins, T 331155. No other places to buy food or other services.

● **Places to eat**
Gastronomía Carrera, Cochrane 465, large, very good, popular.

● **Banks & money changers**
Banco de Crédito, Prat, for Visa; **Banco de Chile**, Plaza de Armas only changes cash, not TCs.

● **Post & telecommunications**
Post Office: on other side of bridge from Plaza de Armas.

Telephone Office: on S side of Plaza de Armas, next to *Café Rucuray*, which posts boat information.

● **Tourist offices**
In Municipalidad, Prat y Sgto Aldea, 1 Dec to end-Feb only, helpful.

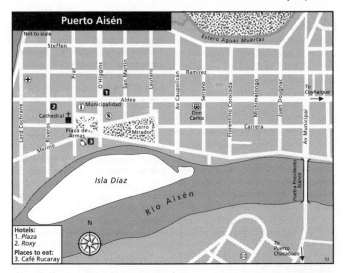

Puerto Aisén

Not to scale

Estero Aguas Muertas

Steffen

Prat · O'Higgins · San Martín · Lautaro · Aldea · Ramírez · Av Caupolicán · Serrano · Florentino Coroceda · Michimalongo · Juan Dougnac · Av Municipal

Municipalidad

Cathedral

Carrera

Plaza de Armas

Cerro Mirador

Lord Cochrane · Rivero · Merino

Don Carlos

To Coyhaique →

Puerta Presidenta Ibáñez

Isla Díaz

RÍO AISÉN

N

To Puerto Chacabuco

Hotels:
1. Plaza
2. Roxy

Places to eat:
3. Café Rucaray

● **Transport**

Buses to **Puerto Chacabuco**, La Cascada on Serrano Montaner, to left of Sgto Aldea (main street) walking away from Plaza de Armas, 6 a day between 0800-1730, 30 mins, US$1, return 0830-1800; colectivo US$1.50 pp. La Cascada to **Coyhaique**, 4 a day between 0830-1900 (Sun and holidays between 0845 and 1930), US$3, 1½ hrs; Transaustral, Sgto Aldea 348, 4 a day; Don Carlos taxi-bus, 8 a day, US$3. Transaustral and La Cascada have daily buses between Coyhaique and Puerto Chacabuco.

Ferries Transmarchilay's *Colono* runs from Puerto Chacabuco via the Canal Moraleda to Puerto Montt, Mon 1400 and Wed 2200, 26 hrs, all year service (fares under Puerto Montt); meals are available. From Jan to early March the ship also makes an excursion from Puerto Chacabuco to Laguna San Rafael each Sat at 2100, returning Mon 0800 (fares, inc food, US$105-225 pp, ranging from economy class to cabin). Transmarchilay's *Pincoya* sails to Quellón on Chiloé Sun 1600, all year round (fares under Quellón) stopping at Melinka and Puerto Aguirre. Navimag's *Evangelistas* sails each Thur and Sun from Puerto Chacabuco to Puerto Montt, taking about 24 hrs (fares under Puerto Montt, the *pionero* seats are quite spacious and comfortable and there is a cafeteria selling burgers, sandwiches, soft drinks,

beer, hot beverages, etc); it too diverts from its schedule in summer to run a 5-day trip to Laguna San Rafael, leaving Sat, from US$250. See under Puerto Montt **Shipping** for *Patagonia Express*. **Shipping Offices**: Agemar, Tte Merino 909, T 332716, Puerto Aisén; **Navimag**, Terminal de Transbordadores, Puerto Chacabuco, T 351111, F 351192; **Transmarchilay**, Av O'Higgins s/n, T 351144, Puerto Chacabuco. It is best to make reservations in these companies' offices in Puerto Montt, Coyhaique or Santiago (or, for Transmarchilay, in Chaitén or Ancud). For trips to Laguna San Rafael, see below; out of season, they are very difficult to arrange, but try Edda Espinosa, Sgto Aldea 943, or ask at *Restaurant Yaney Ruca* or *Restaurant Munich*.

SOUTH OF COYHAIQUE

The southernmost section of the Carretera Austral, 443 km, currently ends at Puerto Yungay. Branch roads run off to Balmaceda and Puerto Ibañez and Chile Chico on Lago General Carrera. The section around the W of Lago Gen Carrera is reckoned by some to be the most spectacular.

El Blanco (Km 35) is a hamlet with *pensión* at *Restaurant El Blanco* (or

South of Coyhaique

Distance in km

Coyhaique
35
El Blanco
6
15 — Balmaceda
56
Villa Cerro Castillo 8 — 31 — Puerto Ibáñez
93
5 — Bahía Murta
25
Río Tranquilo
50
El Maitén — 128 — Chile Chico
11
Puerto Bertrand
59
Cochrane
100
Puerto Yungay
To
Villa O'Higgins
94b

F pp *El Nuevo* – breakfast extra) and shop. At Km 41 a branch road runs E to **Balmaceda** on the Argentine frontier at Paso Huemules (no accommodation). Chilean immigration is open May-July 0800-2100, Sept-April 0700-2100.

● **Transport Air** Balmaceda airport is used by LanChile, Ladeco and National for flights from Santiago via Puerto Montt for Coyhaique. Taxi from airport to Coyhaique, 1 hr, US$6, minibus US$4.50. **Buses** Daily to Coyhaique, 0800, US$1.70.

LAGO GENERAL CARRERA

Straddling the frontier, Lago General Carrera (Lago Buenos Aires in Argentina), covers 2,240 sq km. The lake itself

is a beautiful azure blue; the Chilean end is predominantly Alpine and the Argentine end dry pampa. The major eruption of Volcán Hudson in 1991, polluted parts of the lake and many rivers, but the waters are now clear. The effects can still be seen in a metre-thick layer of ash on the ground. Sheltered from the prevailing W winds by the Campo de Hielo Norte, the region prides itself in having the best climate in Southern Chile with some 300 days of sunshine; much fruit is grown as a result especially around Chile Chico. Rainfall is very low for this area. The main towns, Puerto Ibáñez on the N shore and Chile Chico on the S, are connected by a ferry, the *Pilchero*. There are two alternative routes to Chile Chico: through Argentina or on the Carretera Austral which runs W around the lake.

Puerto Ibáñez

(*Pop* 800), the principal port on the Chilean section of the lake, is reached by taking a branch road, 31 km long, from the Carretera Austral 97 S of Coyhaique. There are some fine waterfalls, the Salto Río Ibañez, 6 km N.

● **Accommodation E** pp *Ibáñez*, Bertrán Dixon 31, T 423227 clean, warm, hot water; **D** *Hostería Doña Amalia*, Bajada Río Ibañez. Fuel (sold in 5 litre containers) available at Luis A Bolados 461 (house with 5 laburnum trees outside).

● **Transport Minibus**: to Coyhaique, 2½ hrs, US$7. There is a road to Perito Moreno, Argentina, but no public transport. **Ferries** The car ferry, *El Pilchero*, sails between Puerto Ibañez and Chile Chico, 4 times a week. Fares for cars US$33, for passengers US$3.50, 2¾ hr crossing, bicycles US$2.50. Number of passengers limited to 70; reservations possible. Buses and jeeps meet the ferry in Puerto Ibáñez for Coyhaique.

The Carretera Austral to Cochrane

From the turning to Puerto Ibáñez the Carretera Austral goes through Villa Cerro Castillo (Km 8) which has a small supermarket and three *residenciales* (inc one at Aguirre Cerda 35, **D** with good

Lago General Carrera

meals). The **Reserva Nacional Cerro Castillo** nearby, is named after the fabulous mountain (2,675m), which looks like a fairytale castle, with pinnacles jutting out of thick snow. The park, 179,550 ha, includes several other peaks in the northern wall of the Río Ibáñez valley. *Guardería* on the Senda Ibáñez, opp Laguna Chinguay, open Nov-Mar, camping US$4. The Carretera climbs out of the valley, passing the aptly-named Laguna Verde and the Portezuelo Cofré. It descends to the boggy Manso valley, with a good campsite at the bridge over the river, watch out for mosquitoes (this area was seriously affected by the ash from Volcán Hudson).

Bahía Murta, 5 km off the Carretera, lies at Km 198, on the northern tip of the central 'arm' of Lago General Carrera. From here the road follows the lake's western shore; the colour of the water is an unbelievable blue-green, reflecting the mountains that surround it and the clouds above

● **Accommodation E** pp *Res Patagonia*, Pasaje España; **E** pp *Hostería Lago Gen Carrera*, Av 5 de Abril, welcoming, excellent meals, also has cabin with own store; free camping by lake, good view of Cerro Castillo.

Río Tranquilo, Km 223, is where the buses stop for lunch: fuel is available at the ECA store from a large drum (no sign). Nearby is the Catedral de Mármol,

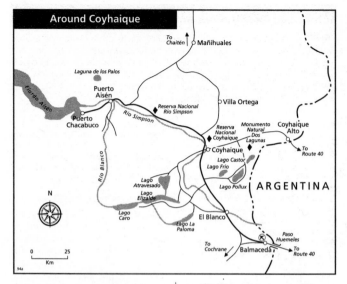

Around Coyhaique

a peninsula made of marble, with caves which can be visited by boat.

● **Accommodation D** pp *Res Los Pinos*, 2 Oriente 41, basic; **D/E** pp *Cabañas Jacricalor*, 1 Sur s/n; **E** pp *Res Carretera Austral*, 1 Sur 223.

El Maitén, Km 273, is at the SW tip of Lago Gen Carrera: here a road branches off E along the S shore of the lake towards Chile Chico (see below). South of El Maitén the Carretera Austral becomes steeper and more bendy (in winter this stretch, all the way to Cochrane, is icy and dangerous).

Puerto Bertrand, Km 284, is a good place for fishing. Nearby is a sign to the Nacimiento del Río Baker: the place where the Río Baker is reckoned to begin (it flows out of Lago Gen Carrera).

● **Accommodation A3** *Hostería Campo Baker; Casa de Huéspedes*, dormitory accommodation; one small shop.

Beyond the road climbs up to high moorland, passing the confluence of the Ríos Neff and Baker, before winding into Cochrane. The scenery is splendid all the way; in the main the road is rough but not treacherous. Watch out for cattle on the road and take blind corners slowly.

THE SOUTH COAST OF LAGO GEN CARRERA TO CHILE CHICO

At **Puerto Guadal**, 10 km E, there are shops, a post office and petrol.

● **Accommodation & places to eat E** pp *Hostería Huemules*, Magnolia 382, T 411212, with breakfast, good views; **E** pp *Res Maitén*, Las Magnolias. *Restaurant La Frontera*, Los Lirios y Los Pinos.

Further E along the shore are the villages of Mallín Grande and **Fachinal** (no accommodation though people will let you stay for free if you have a sleeping bag). Parts of this road were built into the rock face, giving superb views over the lake and the Andes, but also dangerous, unprotected precipices.

CHILE CHICO

(*Pop* 2,200) A quiet, friendly but dusty town on the lake shore which has an annual festival at end-January.

The War of Chile Chico (1917)

Chile Chico dates from 1909 when Chilean settlers crossed from Argentina and occupied the land. In the previous year the Chilean government had granted 80,000 ha of land between Lago Gen Carrera and Lago Cochrane to cattle ranchers from the Sociedad Explotadora Río Baker. In the showdown which followed the ranchers were driven out by the settlers, but it was not until 1931 that the Chilean government finally recognized the town's existence.

● **Accommodation** B *Hostería de la Patagonia*, Camino Internacional s/n, full board, clean, excellent food, English, French and Italian spoken, trekking, horse-riding and white-water rafting organized (Casilla 91, Chile Chico, XI Region, T 411337, F 411444), rec; **E** pp *Casa Quinta No me Olvides/Manor House Don't Forget Me*, *hospedaje* and camping, Camino Internacional s/n, clean, cooking facilities, warm, bathrooms, hot showers, honey, eggs, fruit and vegetables for sale, rec, tours arranged to Lago Jeinimeni and Cueva de las Manos; **E** pp *Plaza*, O'Higgins y Balmaceda, basic, clean, rec; **E** pp *Hosp Don Luis*, Balmaceda 175, clean, meals available. **Camping**: free campsite at Bahía Jarra, 15 km E.

● **Places to eat** Apart from *Residenciales*: *Cafetería Elizabeth y Loly* on Plaza serves coffee and delicious icecream and cakes, expensive. Supermarket on B O'Higgins.

● **Banks & money changers** It is very difficult to change dollars (*Café Elizabeth y Loly* changes dollars at bank rate in small amounts); change Argentine pesos in shops and cafés on main street (very poor rates).

● **Tourist offices** On O'Higgins; ask here or at the Municipalidad for help in arranging tours.

● **Transport Minibuses**: are run by 3 companies along the S side of the lake between Chile Chico and Puerto Guadal, up to 3 times a week each, US$9. These connect in Puerto Guadal with Pudú service for Cochrane. Minibus to Coyhaique, frequency varies, US$9, 2¾ hrs. Flights to/from Coyhaique (see above).

FRONTIER WITH ARGENTINA: CHILE CHICO

● **Chilean immigration**
open Sept-April 0700-2300, May-Aug 0800-2100.

● **Transport**
Minibuses run from Chile Chico to Los Antiguos on the Argentine side, US$3, ¾ hr inc formalities, ask around for times; from here connections can be made to Perito Moreno and to Caleta Olivia on the coast.

INTO ARGENTINA

Perito Moreno (*pop* 1,700; *alt* 400m) has a few hotels, a campsite, a restaurant and money exchange services. The bus service to Caleta Olivia on the Atlantic is only daily in Feb. There is one flight a week Perito Moreno-Río Gallegos. 118 km S of Perito Moreno is the famous **Cueva de las Manos** where the walls of a series of galleries are covered with painted human hands and animals, 10,000 years old.

Reserva Nacional Lago Jeinimeni

J M Bibby (The Wirral) writes: "60 km S of Chile Chico lies the **Reserva Nacional Lago Jeinimeni**, covering breathtaking snow-capped peaks, impressive cliffs, waterfalls, small glaciers and Lakes Jeinimeni and Verde. The reserve contains huemul deer, pumas and condors. Activities include fishing for salmon and rainbow trout, trekking and rowing. A good map is essential. Entrance fee US$1, camping US$2.75 (take all your requirements). Access only between Nov and Mar owing to high river levels. Lifts may be possible from Chile Chico: try Juan Núñez, Hernán Trizzando 110, for a lift on a timber truck, or ask in the Conaf office."

The country to the S and W of Chile Chico, with weird rock formations and dry brush-scrub, provides good walking for the mountaineer. The northern and higher peak of Cerro Pico del Sur (2,168m) can be climbed by the agile from Los Cipres (beware dogs in farmyard). You will need a long summer's day and the 1:50,000 map. Follow the horse trail until it peters out, then navigate by compass or sense of direction until the volcano-like summit appears. After breaching the cliff ramparts at an obvious point, there is some scrambling and a 10-ft pitch to the summit: indescribable views of the Lake and Andes. (Brian Spearing).

COCHRANE

Cochrane (*Pop* 2,000), 343 km S of Coyhaique, sits in a hollow on the Río Cochrane. It is a simple place, sunny in summer, good for walking and fishing. The **Reserva Nacional Lago Cochrane**, which surrounds Lago Cochrane, 12 km E, includes a few surviving huemules (deer). Campsite at Playa Vidal. Northeast of Cochrane is the **Reserva Nacional Tamango**, with lenga forest and guanaco, foxes and lots of birds including woodpeckers and hummingbirds. It is inaccessible in the four winter months. Ask in the Conaf office on the square (T 422164) about visiting because some access is through private land and tourist facilities are rudimentary, entry US$1. The views from the reserve are superb, over the town, the nearby lakes and to the Campo de Hielo Norte to the W.

● **Accommodation B** pp *Hostería Wellmann*, Las Golondrinas 36, T 522171, hot water, comfortable, warm, good meals, rec; **D** pp *Res Rubio*, Tte Merino 04, T 522173, Sra Elva Rubio, very nice, breakfast inc, lunch and dinner extra; **E** pp *Res Austral Sur*, Sra Sonia Salazar, Prat s/n, T 522150, breakfast inc, hot water, also very nice; **D** *Residencia Cero a Cero*, Lago Brown 464, T 522158, with breakfast, welcoming. In summer it is best to book rooms in advance. **Camping**: ask for Washington Baez, speaks English.

● **Places to eat** *Belén*, Esmeralda 301; *Café* at Tte Merino 502.

● **Transport** Bus company agencies: **Pudú** at *Botillería Quiaco* on Tte Merino; **Don Carlos**, *Res Austral Sur*; **Río Baker Taxis**, Río Colonia. All run 3 buses a week to Coyhaique, US$23. Petrol is available, if it hasn't run out, at the Empresa Comercial Agrícola (ECA) and at the Copec station. Horses can be hired for excursions in the surrounding countryside, ask around, eg at *Hostería Wellmann*.

To Argentina: 17 km N of Cochrane, a road through Villa Chacabuco and Paso Roballos (78 km), enters Argentina (and continues to Bajo Caracoles); no public transport, road passable in summer but often flooded in spring. If hitching, allow a week.

SOUTH OF COCHRANE

The Carretera Austral has been constructed a further 122 km S of Cochrane to Puerto Yungay, with 50 km of the final stretch to Villa O'Higgins completed. En route, it bypasses **Tortel**, a village built on a hill at the mouth of the Río Baker. It has no streets, no proper plan, only wooden walkways ('no hay ni una bicicleta'). It trades in wood with Punta Arenas and fishes for shellfish (such as *centolla* and *loco*).From here you can hire a boat to the **Glaciar Jorge Montt**; contact Don Juan Nahuel by leaving a phone message at the Municipality in Tortel or by Radio Santa María in Coyhaique or Cochrane. Three day trip, US$250, take sleeping bag, also one day trips.

● **Accommodation** Ask for Doña Berta Muñoz, **D** pp full board. "Expect fresh mutton meals and if you are squeamish about seeing animals killed don't look out of the window when they butcher the 2 lambs a day on the front porch." Carrie Wittner.

● **Transport Air** Don Carlos five-seater plane (every Wed from Cochrane, US$12, book well in advance.) **Land** By horse, mountain bike or on foot, several days journey from Cochrane on a good track by the Río Baker (several river crossings by boat). **Boat** From Vagabundo, 2 hrs, book in advance. Hire of private boat, US$85. Or by kayak down the Río Baker.

PARQUE NACIONAL LAGUNA SAN RAFAEL

Some 150 nautical miles S of Puerto Aisén is the **Laguna San Rafael**, into which flows a glacier, 30m above sea level, and 45 km in length. It calves small icebergs, carried out to sea by wind and tide. The thick vegetation on the shores, with snowy peaks above, is typical of Aisén. The glacier is one of a group of four that flow in all directions from Monte San Valentín. This icefield is part of the **Parque Nacional Laguna San Rafael** (1.74 million ha), regulated by Conaf.

Park entry fee is US$4.65. At the glacier there is a small ranger station which gives information; a pier and two paths have been built. One path leads to the glacier. The rangers are willing to row you out to the glacier in calm weather, a 3-hr trip.

Robert af Sandeberg (Lidingö, Sweden) describes this journey as follows: "The trip in the rowboat is an awesome venture. At first it is fairly warm and easy to row. Gradually it gets colder when the wind sweeps over the icy glacier (be sure to take warm clothes – a thick sweater, and waterproof jacket are rec – Ed). It gets harder to row as small icebergs hinder the boat. Frequently somebody has to jump onto an icefloe and push the boat through. The glacier itself has a deep blue colour, shimmering and reflecting the light; the same goes for the icebergs, which are an unreal, translucent blue. The glacier is very noisy; there are frequent cracking and banging sounds, resembling a mixture of gun shots and thunder. When a hunk of ice breaks loose, a huge swell is created and the icebergs start rocking in the water. Then great care and effort has to be taken to avoid the boat being crushed by the shifting icebergs; this is a very real danger."

In the national park are puma, pudú (miniature deer), foxes, dolphins, occasional sealions and sea otters, and many species of bird. Walking trails are limited (about 10 km in all) but a lookout platform has been constructed, with fine views of the glacier.

● **Transport** The only way there is by plane or by boat: Air Taxi from Coyhaique (Don Carlos), US$110 each if party of 5; some pilots in Puerto Aisén will fly to the glacier for about US$95, but many are unwilling to land on the rough airstrip. The glacier is best seen from the sea: the official cruises are: *Skorpios I* and *II* (see under Puerto Montt); Navimag's *Evangelistas* and Transmarchilay's *Colono* (see under Pto Chacabuco); *Patagonia Express* a catamaran which runs from Puerto Chacabuco to Laguna San Rafael via Termas de Puyuhuapi, in tours lasting 4-6 days, from Puerto Montt over Coyhaique including the catamaran service, the hotel stay at Termas de Puyuhuapi and the day excursion to Laguna San Rafael (see page 296); *Pamar*, Pacheco Altamirano 3100, T 256220, Puerto Montt, Sept-Mar only; Compañía Naviera Puerto Montt has 2 vessels: the *Quellón*, with 6-day, 6-night tours to the Laguna from Puerto Montt via various ports and channels (US$900 not inc flight from Santiago); Puerto Montt, Diego Portales 882, T/F 252547; Puerto Chacabuco T 351106. *Odisea* and *Visun*, motorized sailing boats, Dec to Mar, in Santiago, Alameda B O'Higgins 108, local 120, T 633-0883, in Puerto Aisén, Sgto Aldea 679, T 332908, 6-day trips from Puerto Chacabuco to Laguna San Rafael. Various private yachts can be chartered in Puerto Montt for 6-12 passengers to Laguna San Rafael. Local fishing boats from Chacabuco/Puerto Aisén take about 18-20 hrs each way, charging the same as the tourist boats. Ask for Jorge Prado at the port (he takes a minimum of 7, more expensive than others); Andino Royas, Cochrane 129; Justiniano Aravena, Dr Steffen 703; Rodrigo Azúcar, Agemar office, T 332716; or Sr Ocuña, ask at the port. These unauthorized boats may not have adequate facilities.

NB If you plan to go to Laguna San Rafael by boat, check first with the Gobernación Marítima in Puerto Aisén that the boat is licensed for the trip (very few are).

Chilean Patagonia

THE GLACIAL regions of southern Patagonia and Chilean Tierra del Fuego. Punta Arenas and Puerto Natales are the two main towns, the latter being the gateway to the Torres del Paine and Balmaceda national parks. In summer, a region for climbing, hiking, boats trips and the southernmost crossings to Argentina.

THE LAND

GEOGRAPHY

This section covers Region XII (Magallanes) which stretches S from the icefields of the Campo de Hielo Sur to the Chilean part of Tierra del Fuego and, still further S, Isla Navarino, on which is situated the naval base of Puerto Williams. The coastline is indented by fjords and offshore are numberous islands, few of which are inhabited. The large island of Tierra del Fuego, shared with Argentina, is separated from the mainland by the *Estrecho de Magallanes* (Straits of Magellan), which are reached by two ferry crossings: between Punta Arenas and Porvenir and, further W between Punta Delgada and Punta Espora. The remnants of the Andes stretch along the coast, seldom rising above 1,500m. Mountains above this altitude include

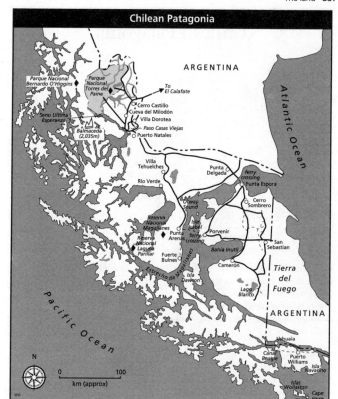

Chilean Patagonia

the Cordillera del Paine (several peaks over 2,600m) and Cerro Balmaceda (2,035). Vegetation varies from thick rainforest on the wet W coast to grassland further E.

This area is sparsely populated: although it covers 17.5% of Chilean territory, its population is around 171,000, under 1% of the Chilean total. This population is overwhelmingly urban: 160,000 live in towns, most of them in Punta Arenas, the main settlement.

LOCAL ECONOMY

Sheep farming is still important to the local economy; much of the meat is ex-ported to Islamic countries, whereas lo-cally produced beef is mainly sold do-mestically. Potatoes are an important crop, but owing to the climate most other vegetables are grown under cover. Fish-ing is a traditional activity, though chang-ing with the growth of salmon farming. Forestry has grown in importance and become controversial as a result of the use of native forests for woodchips for export to Japan, Taiwan and Brazil. Al-though oil production has declined as reserves have become depleted, large quantities of natural gas are now pro-duced. About 33% of Chilean coal comes from large open cast coal mines on the

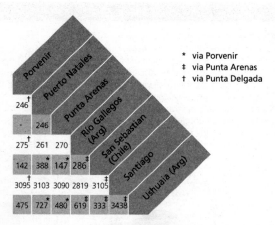

Porvenir					
246†	Puerto Natales				
-	246	Punta Arenas			
275†	261	270	Río Gallegos (Arg)		
142*	388*	147*	286‡	San Sebastián (Chile)	
3095	3103	3090	2819	3105‡	Santiago
475	727*	480‡	619‡	333‡	3438‡	Ushuaia (Arg)

* via Porvenir
‡ via Punta Arenas
† via Punta Delgada

Chilean Patagonia: distance chart (km)

Brunswick Peninsula, NW of Punta Arenas; most of it is shipped to the thermal power stations of northern Chile. Tourism is growing rapidly, making an increasingly important contribution to the local economy.

CLIMATE

Strong, cold, piercing winds blow, particularly during the spring, when they may exceed 100 km an hour. These bring heavy rain to coastal areas, over 4,000 mm a year on the offshore islands. Further E the winds are much drier; annual rainfall at Punta Dungeness at the E end of the Straits of Magellan is only 250 mm. Along the coast temperatures are moderated by the sea: summer temperatures are more variable, though seldom rising above 15°C. In winter snow covers the country, except those parts near the sea, making many roads more or less impassable, except on horseback. The winds parch the ground and prevent the growth of crops, except in sheltered spots and greenhouses. When travelling in this region, protection against the sun's ultraviolet rays is essential.

HISTORY

Although southern Patagonia was inhabited from the end of the ice ages, the first Europeans did not visit until the 16th century. In 1519 Hernando de Magallanes, a Portuguese sailor serving the Spanish crown, sailed through the Straits that bear his name. The strategic importance of the Straits, connecting Europe with the Pacific, was quickly recognized: soon Spanish naval and merchant ships were using the route, as were others such as Francis Drake on his world voyage (1578). However the route became less important after 1616 when the Dutch sailors Jacob le Marie and Cornelius van Schouten discovered a quicker route round Cape Horn.

Although at independence Chile claimed the far southern territories, little was done to carry out this claim until 1843 when, concerned at British activities in the area and at rumours of French plans to start a colony, President Bulnes ordered the preparation of a secret mission. The expedition established Fuerte Bulnes on a rocky point; the fort was abandoned in 1848 in favour of the new settlement of Punta Arenas.

Sheep

Although Bernardo Philippi, Governor of Punta Arenas, imported a few sheep from Chiloé in 1852, sheep-farming did not become big business until the 1880s. In 1877 Governor Diego Almeyda brought 300 sheep from the Falkland Islands/Islas Malvinas; they were sold to a British merchant who left them on Isabel Island in the Magellan Straits. Other merchants established sheep on other islands, where they could not stray and could be easily protected from Tehuelche hunters.

Sheep-farming was not without risks: up to 50% of the sheep died on the voyage from the Falklands/Malvinas, while fencing and other equipment were expensive. However the high price of wool made it worth while especially once the settlement of frontier disputes with Argentina in 1881 enabled the Chilean government to distribute land around Punta Arenas and on Tierra del Fuego. In 1884 alone 570,000 ha were handed out in 90 lots in the Punta Arenas area. The main beneficiaries were a few local families, whose names are recalled in the streets, names of Punta Arenas Their newly-acquired lands were converted into sheep *estancias*, the equipment and many of the shepherds and other workers being brought from the Falklands/Malvinas, New Zealand and Britain.

PUNTA ARENAS

(*Pop* 110,000; *Phone code* 061), the most southerly city in Chile, and capital of XII Región, 2,140 km S of Santiago, lies on the eastern shore of the Brunswick Peninsula facing the Straits of Magellan at almost equal distance from the Pacific and Atlantic oceans. It is a centre for the local sheep farming and fishing industries and exports wool, skins, and frozen meat. It is also the home of La Polar, the most southerly brewery in the world. Although it has expanded rapidly, particularly in recent years, it remains tranquil and pleasant. Several new hotels have been built in response to increased tourism. Good roads connect the city with Puerto Natales, 247 km N, and with Río Gallegos in Argentina. Punta Arenas has certain free-port facilities; the Zona Franca is 3½ km N of the centre, on the righthand side of the road to the airport. **NB** Calle Pedro Montt runs E-W, while Calle Jorge Montt runs N-S.

History

After its foundation in 1848, Punta Arenas became a penal colony modelled on Autralia. In 1867 it was opened to foreign settlers and given free port status. From the 1880s it prospered as a refuelling and provisioning centre for steam ships and whaling vessels. It also became a centre for the new sheep estancias since it afforded the best harbour facilities. The city's importance was reduced overnight by the opening of the Panama Canal in 1914.

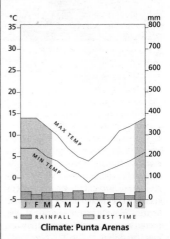

Climate: Punta Arenas

Punta Arenas

Hotels:
1. *Cabo de Hornos*
2. *Hostal de la Patagonia*
3. *Los Navegantes*
4. *Mercurio*
5. *Plaza and Residencial París*
6. *Residencial Sonia Kuscevic*
7. *Ritz*
8. *Savoy*

Buses:
1. Austral
2. Fernández & Pingüino
3. Sur

Places of interest

Around the **Plaza Muñoz Gamero** are a number of former mansions of the great sheep ranching families of the late 19th century. See the **Palacio Sara Braun**, which dates from 1895. In the centre of the plaza is a statue of Magellan with a mermaid and 2 Fuegian Indians at his feet. According to local wisdom those who rub the big toe of one of the Indians will return to Punta Arenas. Just N of the plaza on C Magallanes are the **Palacio Braun Menéndez** (see below) and the **Teatro Cervantes** (now a cinema): the interiors of both are worth a visit. Further N, at Av Bulnes 929, is the **Cemetery**,

even more fantastic than the one at Castro (Chiloé), with a **statue of Indiecito**, the little Indian (now also an object of reverence, bedecked with flowers, the left knee well-rubbed, NW side of the cemetery), cypress avenues, and many memorials to pioneer families and victims of shipping disasters (open 0800-1800 daily).

East of the Plaza Muñoz Gamero on C Fagnano is the **Mirador Cerro de La Cruz** offering a view over the city. Nearby on Waldo Seguel are two reminders of the British influence: the **British School** and **St James' Church** next door. The **Parque María Behety**, S

The original Patagonians

Southern Patagonia was originally inhabited by four indigenous groups, all of whom followed nomadic lifestyles. The *Tehuelches*, who lived along the E side of the Andes as far N as modern-day Bariloche, were hunters of *guanaco* and *rheas*. In the 18th century they began to domesticate the wild horses of the region and sailed down the Patagonian rivers to reach the Atlantic coast. They were very large: it is said that the name Patagonia originates from the Spanish *qué patagón* (what a large foot) on discovering Tehuelche footprints in the sand. The *Onas*, also hunter-gatherers, lived further S on Tierra del Fuego which they reached at the end of the final ice age when the island was still connected to the mainland. The *Yaganes* (or Yahgan), who lived largely by fishing further S around the Beagle Channel, traded with the *Onas* and sailed as far S as Cape Horn. The final group, the *Alacalufes* lived on the islands along the W coast between the Magellan Straits and the Golfo de Penas further north. They surivived in these inhospitable conditions by fishing and hunting seals. A small community survives at Puerto Edén.

The fate of all these groups was very similar. The granting by the Chilean government of large land concessions in the late 19th century ended the nomadic life-style of the Tehuelches and the Onas. The Yaganes and the Alacalufes were killed by diseases and alcohol introduced by whalers and sealers. The fate of the Onas was particularly tragic. Many were hunted down and slaughtered by gunmen employed by goldminers and ranchers: the gunmen were paid for each pair of ears they presented. José Fagnano, a Salesian missionary, attempted to save them by taking them to the missions which he founded on Dawson Island in 1888 and near Río Grande (Argentina) 5 years later. Few survived diseases and the change of lifestyle.

of town along 21 de Mayo, features a scale model of Fuerte Bulnes and a campsite, popular for Sun picnics.

Museums
Museo Regional Salesiano Mayorino Borgatello, in the Colegio Salesiano, Av Bulnes 374, entrance next to church, covering history of the indigenous peoples, sections on local animal and bird life, and other interesting aspects of life in Patagonia and Tierra del Fuego, excellent. Tues-Sat 1000-1200 and 1500-1800, Sun 1500-1800, hours change frequently (entry US$1.25).

Museo de Historia Regional Braun Menéndez, Magallanes 949, off Plaza de Armas, T 244216, located in the former mansion of Mauricio Braun, built in 1905, recommended. Part is set out as room-by-room regional history, the rest of the house is furnished (guided tours in Spanish only). Closed Mon, otherwise open 1100-1600 (summer) and 1100-1300 (winter, entry US$1), free booklet in English.

The **Instituto de la Patagonia**, Av Bulnes Km 4 N (opp the University), T 244216, houses the **Museo del Recuerdo**, an open air museum with artefacts used by the early settlers, pioneer homes, a naval museum and botanical gardens. Outdoor exhibits open Mon-Fri 0800-1800, indoor pavillions: 0830-1115, 1500-1800.

Naval and Maritime Museum, Pedro Montt 981, open Mon-Fri 0930-1230, 1500-1800, Sat 1000-1300, 1500-1800.

Excursions
The **Reserva Forestal Magallanes**, 7 km W of town and known locally as the Parque Japonés, extends over 13,500 ha and

rises to 600m. Follow Independencia right through town and up the hill, 3 km from the edge of town is the turnoff for Río de las Minas to the right. The entrance to the reserve is 2 km beyond, there you will find a self-guided nature trail, 1 km, free leaflet. The road continues through the woods for 14 km, passing by several small campgrounds. From the top end of the road a short path leads to a lookout over the Garganta del Diablo (Devil's Throat), a gorge formed by the Río de las Minas, with views over Punta Arenas and Tierra del Fuego. From here a slippery path leads down to the Río de las Minas valley and thence back to Punta Arenas. Administration at Conaf in Punta Arenas. *Turismo Pali Aike* offers tours to the park, US$ 3.75 pp.

Local information
● **Accommodation**
Most hotels include breakfast in the room price. Hotel prices are substantially lower during winter months (April-Sept).

L2 *Hotel José Nogueira*, Plaza de Armas, Bories 959 y P Montt, in former Palacio Sara Braun, T 248840, F 248832, beautiful loggia, good food, lovely atmosphere, rec; **L3** *Cabo de Hornos*, Plaza Muñoz Gamero 1025, T/F 242134, rec; **L3** *Finis Terrae*, Colón 766, T 228200, F 248124, modern, some rooms small but all very nice, safe in room, rooftop café/bar with lovely views, parking; **L3** *Isla Rey Jorge*, 21 de Mayo 1243, T 222681, F 248220, modern, pleasant, pub downstairs; **L3** *Los Navegantes*, José Menéndez 647, T 244677, F 247545; **L3** *Tierra del Fuego*,

Colón 716, T/F 226200, good breakfast, parking, rec, *Café 1900* downstairs.

A2 *Hostería Yaganes*, Camino Antiguo Norte Km 7.5, T 211600, F 211948, cabins on the shores of the Straits of Magellan, nice setting; **A1-A2** *Apart Hotel Colonizadores*, Colón 1106, T 243578, F 244499, clean, fully furnished apartments (2 bedrooms **A1**, 1 bedroom **A2**) discounts for long stay; **A3** *Hostal de la Patagonia*, O'Higgins 478, T 241079, with bath (**B** without), good breakfast, excellent; **A3** *Colonizadores*, 21 de Mayo 1690, T 244144, F 226587, with bath; **A3** *Hostal Carpa Manzano*, Lautaro Navarro 336, T/F 248864, rec; **A3** *Cóndor de Plata*, Colón 556, T 247987, F 241149, very good; **A3** *Mercurio*, Fagnano 595, T/F 242300, bath, TV and phone, good restaurant and service, rec; **A3** *Plaza*, Nogueira 1116, p 2, T 241300, F 248613 (B without bath), pleasant, good breakfast.

B *Savoy*, Menéndez 1073, T 241951, F 247979, pleasant rooms but some lack windows, good place to eat; **B** *Ritz*, Pedro Montt 1102, T 224422, old, clean and cosy, rec; **B** *Hotel El Pionero*, Chiloé 1210, T 248851, F 248263, with bath; **C** *Res Central*, No 1 España 247, T 222315, No 2 Sanhueza 185, T 222845, with bath (**D** without), comfortable; **B** *Chalet Chapital*, Sanhueza 974, T 242237, F 225698 (cheaper without bath), good, comfortable, doubles only, welcoming; **B** *Hostal de la Avenida*, Colón 534, T 247532, good breakfast, friendly, safe, rec; **B** *Hostal Del Estrecho*, Menéndez 1048, T/F 241011, with breakfast and bath.

C *Albatros*, Colón 1195, T 223131, without bath, good; **C** *Res Sonia Kuscevic*, Pasaje Darwin 175 (Angamos altura 550), T 248543,

The Braun-Menéndez Empire

🐾 Among the people who benefitted most from the Chilean government's distribution of lands in the Punta Arenas area after 1881 were José Menéndez, whose *estancia* at San Gregorio covered 90,000 ha, his neighbours Sara Braun and her brother Mauricio at the Pecket Harbour Estancia, and José Nogueira, who married Sara Braun. After Nogueira's death in 1893, the Brauns built his *Sociedad Explotadora Tierra del Fuego* into the largest commercial landowner in Chile: their factory at Puerto Bories, N of Puerto Natales, processed meat from all over southern Chile and Argentina.

After years of rivalry the Braun and Menéndez were linked in 1908 when Mauricio Braun married José Menéndez's daughter Josefina. The two families formed a joint company, the *Sociedad Anónima Importadora Y Exportadora de Patagonia*, with interests in shipping, banking, department stores and coalmining. Although José Menéndez died in 1918, leaving some of his money to King Alfonso XIII of Spain, the Braun and Menéndez families, now closely linked by marriage, continued to dominate the local economy of southern Chile and Argentina for several decades.

popular, IYHA accepted, with bath, breakfast, hot water, heating, parking.

D *Casa Dinka*, Caupolicán 169, T 226056, with breakfast, use of kitchen, noisy, very popular; **D** pp *Res Roca*, Roca 1038, T 243903, without bath, clean; **D** pp *Res Rubio*, España 640, T 226458, with bath, helpful. Accommodation available in many private houses, usually E pp, ask at tourist office; **D** *Hosp Lodging*, Sanhueza 933, T 221035, good value, clean, heating, modern; **D** Sra Carolina Ramírez, Paraguaya 150, T 247687, nice and friendly, hot water, safe motorcycle parking, meals, rec.

E pp Caupolicán 99, T 222436, with breakfast, clean; **E** pp *Casa Deportista*, O'Higgins 1205, T 225205, F 243438, cheap meals, cooking facilities, dormitory style, noisy; **E** pp *Casa Roxas*, Angamos 971, very good, clean, with bath; **E** pp *Hostal Paradiso*, Angamos 1073, T 224212, with bath, breakfast, parking, use of kitchen, rec; **E** pp *Backpackers' Paradise*, Carrera Pinto 839, T 222554, F 226863, hot water, popular, large dormitories, cooking facilities, limited bathroom facilities, good meeting place, luggage store, rec; **E** pp Sra Lenka, José Miguel Carrera 1270, heating, clean, use of kitchen, rec; **E** Nena's, Boliviana 366, T 242411, friendly, with breakfast, highly rec; **E** pp, España y Boliviana, T 247422, without bath, clean, friendly, use of kitchen; **E** Sanhueza 750, homely, rec.

F pp *Alojamiento Prat*, Sgto Aldea 0520,

clean, rec; **F** pp Sanhueza 712, T 225127, basic, use of kitchen; **F** pp Bellavista 577, dormitory accommodation, kitchen, hot showers, clean.

Camping: in Reserva Forestal Magallanes (no public transport, see **Excursions** above). *Camping Pudú*, 10.5 km N on Route 9, G pp, pleasant, good facilities.

● **Places to eat**
Main hotels: good value set lunches and dinners at *Cabo de Hornos*, excellent restaurants at *Los Navegantes* and *José Nogueira*.

Many places closed on Sun. *El Mercado*, Mejicana 617, open 24 hrs, reasonably-priced set lunch, expensive à la carte; *Centro Español*, Plaza Muñoz Gamero 771, above Teatro Cervantes, large helpings, reasonable selection, reasonably priced; *El Mesón del Calvo*, Jorge Montt 687, excellent, seafood, lamb, small portions, pricey, rec; seafood at *Sotitos*, O'Higgins 1138, good service and cuisine, excellent, rec; *La Mama*, Sanhueza 700 block, little Argentine-style pasta house, rec; *Lucerna*, Bories 624, excellent meat, reasonably priced, good; *Dino's Pizza*, Bories 557, cheap, good, big pizzas; *Café Garogha*, Bories 817, open Sun pm, busy at night, smoky; *Bianco's Pizza*, Bulnes 1306, excellent pizzas, rec; *El Quijote*, Lautaro Navarro 1087, good sandwiches, highly rec; *Asturias*, Lautaro Navarro 967, good food and atmosphere; *Venus*, Pedro Montt 1046, good food, service and atmosphere, reasonable prices; *La Casa de*

Juan, O'Higgins 1021, Spanish food; *El Estribo*, Carrera Pinto 762, good grill, also fish; *Yaganes*, Camino Antiguo Norte Km 7.5, beautiful setting, weekend buffet; *Golden Dragon*, Colón 529, Chinese, good, expensive; *La Terraza*, 21 de Mayo 1288, sandwiches, *empanadas* and beer, cheap and good; *La Taberna del Club de la Unión*, Plaza Muñoz Gamero y Seguel, for drinks. For economic set lunches several along Chiloé: *Restaurant de Turismo Punta Arenas*, No 1280, good, friendly, rec; *Los Años 60 The Mitchel*, No 1231, also serves beer and 26 varieties of sandwiches, open 24 hrs; *Parrilla Apocalipsis*, Chiloé esq Balmaceda; *Carioca*, Menéndez 600 esq Chiloé, *parrilla*, snacks and beer, very friendly; *Lomit's*, Menéndez 722, cheap snacks and drinks, open when the others are closed; *Kiosco Roca* (no sign), Roca 875, early morning coffee. Cheap fish meals available at stalls in the *Cocinerías*, Lautaro Navarro S of the port entrance. Excellent *empanadas*, bread and pastries at *Pancal*, 21 de Mayo 1280; also at *La Espiga*, Errázuriz 632; excellent pastries at *Casa del Pastel*, Carrera Pinto y O'Higgins. Lobster has become more expensive because of a law allowing only lobster pots. *Centolla* (king crab) is caught illegally by some fishermen using dolphin, porpoise and penguin as live bait. There are seasonal bans on *centolla* fishing to protect dwindling stocks, do not purchase *centolla* out of season. At times *centolla* fishing is banned because the crabs can be infected with a disease which is fatal to humans. If this ban refers to the *marea roja* (red tide), it does not affect crabs, only bivalve shellfish. Mussels should not be picked along the shore owing to pollution and the *marea roja*.

● **Airline offices**
LanChile, Lautaro Navarro 999, T 241232, F 222366; Ladeco, Lautaro Navarro 1155, T/F 241100/223340. National, Bories 701, T 221634. Aerovías DAP, O'Higgins 899, T 223340, F 221693, open 0900-1230, 1430-1930; Kaiken, Magallanes 974, T 242134 ext 106, F 241321.

● **Banks & money changers**
Banks open Mon-Fri 0830-1400. *Casas de cambio* open Mon-Fri 0900-1230, 1500-1900, Sat 0900-1230; outside business hours try Buses Sur, Colón y Magallanes, kiosk at *Garogha Café*, Bories 817 and the major hotels (lower rates). Fincard (Mastercard), Pedro Montt 837, T 247864, Mon-Fri 0900-1400,

1530-1730. Banco Concepción, Magallanes y Menéndez, for Visa. Banco O'Higgins, Plaza de Armas, changes TCs, no commission. Argentine pesos can be bought at *casas de cambio*. Good rates at *Cambio Gasic*, Roca 915, Oficina 8, T 242396, German spoken; *La Hermandad*, Lautaro Navarro 1099, T 243991, excellent rates, US$ cash for Amex TCs; *Sur Cambios*, Lautaro Navarro 1001, T 225656 accepts TCs. *Kiosco Redondito*, Mejicana 613 in the shopping centre, T 247369.

● **Embassies & consulates**
Argentine, 21 de Mayo 1878, T 261912, open 1000-1400, visas take 24 hrs, US$25; Brazilian, Arauco 769, T 241093; Belgian, Roca 817, Oficina 61, T 241472; British, Roca 924, T 247020; Danish, Colón 819, Depto 301, T 221488; Dutch, Sarmiento 780, T 248100; Finnish, Independencia 660, T 247385; German, Pasaje Korner 1046, T 241082, Casilla 229; Italian, 21 de Mayo 1569, T 242497; Norwegian, Independencia 830, T 242171; Spanish, J Menéndez 910, T 243566; Swedish, Errazúriz 891, T 224107.

● **Entertainment**
Discotheques: discos in the city centre often have a young crowd: *Gallery*, J Menéndez 750, T 247555; *Yordi*, Pedro Montt 937; *Borssalino*, Bories 587. On the outskirts of town, to the S: *Club Boulevard*, Km 5.5, T 265807; *Torreones*, Km 5.5, T 261985; *Salsoteca*, Km 5. To the N: *Drive-In Los Brujos*, Km 7.5, T 212600; *Salsoteca*, Km 6.

Nightlife: *The Queen's Club*, 21 de Mayo 1455. Lots of *Whiskerías*: *Sexywoman*, Av España, and *Tentación*, Av Colón, rec.

● **Hospitals & medical services**
Dentists: *Dr Hugo Vera Cárcamo*, España 1518, T 227510, rec; *Rosemary Robertson Stipicic*, 21 de Mayo 1380, T 22931, speaks English.

Hospitals: *Hospital Regional Lautaro Navarro*, Angamos 180, T 244040, public hospital, for emergency room ask for *La Posta*; *Clínica Magallanes*, Bulnes 01448, T 211527, private clinic, medical staff is the same as in the hospital but fancier surroundings and more expensive.

● **Laundry**
Lavasol, the only self-service, O'Higgins 969, T 243067, Mon-Sat 0900-2030, Sun (summer only) 1000-1800, US$6/machine, wash and

dry, good but busy; *Lavaseco Josseau*, Carrera Pinto 766, T 228413; *Lavanderia Limpec*, 21 de Mayo 1261, T 241669.

● **Post & telecommunications**

Post Office: Bories 911 y J Menéndez, Mon-Fri 0830-1930, Sat 0900-1400.

Telecommunications: for international and national calls and faxes (shop around as prices vary): *CTC*, Nogueira 1106, Plaza de Armas, daily 0800-2200, *CTC*, Roca 886, loc 23, daily 0900-2030; *Entel*, Lautaro Navarro 957, Mon-Fri 0830-2200, Sat-Sun 0900-2200; *Telex-Chile/Chile-Sat*, Bories 911 and Errázuriz 856, daily 0830-2200, also offers telex and telegram service. *VTR*, Bories 801, closed Sat afternoon and Sun. For international calls and faxes at any hour *Hotel Cabo de Hornos*, credit cards accepted, open to non-residents.

● **Shopping**

For leather goods and sheepskin try the Zona Franca; quality of other goods is low and prices little better than elsewhere; Mon-Sat 1030-1230, 1500-2000 (bus E or A from Plaza de Armas; many colectivo taxis; taxi US$3). Handicrafts at *Pingüi*, Bories 404, *Artesanía Ramas*, Independencia 799, *Chile Típico*, Carrera Pinto 1015, *Indoamérica*, Colón y Magallanes and outdoor stalls at the bottom of Independencia, by the port entrance. **Supermarkets**: *Listo*, 21 de Mayo 1133; *Cofrima*, Lautaro Navarro 1293 y Balmaceda, *Cofrima 2*, España 01375; *Marisol*, Zenteno 0164.

Cameras: wide range of cameras but limited range of film, from Zona Franca. *Foto Arno*, Bories 893, for Kodak products. *Foto Sánchez*, Bories 768, for Fuji film and *Fotocentro*, Bories 789, for Agfa: all have same day print-processing service.

Chocolate: hand made chocolate from *Chocolatería Tres Arroyos*, Bories 448, T 241522 and *Chocolatería Regional Norweisser*, José Miguel Carrera 663, both good.

● **Sports**

Golf: 9-hole golf course 5 km S town on road to Fuerte Bulnes.

Skiing: Cerro Mirador, only 9 km W from Punta Arenas in the Reserva Nacional Magallanes, the most southerly ski resort in the world and one of the few places where one can ski with a sea view. Transtur buses 0900 and 1400 from in front of *Hotel Cabo de Hornos*, US$3, return, taxi US$7. Daily lift-ticket, US$7; equip-

ment rental, US$6 per adult. Mid-way lodge with food, drink and equipment. Season June to Sept, weather permitting. Contact the Club Andino, T 241479, about crosscountry skiing facilities. Also skiing at Tres Morros.

● **Tour companies & travel agents**

Turismo Lazo, Angamos 1366, T/F 223771, wide range of tours, highly rec; *Turismo Aventour*, J Nogueira 1255, T 241197, F 243354, English spoken, helpful, good, specializes in fishing trips, organize tours to Tierra del Fuego. *Turismo Comapa*, Independencia 840, T 241437, F 247514, tours to Torres del Paine, Tierra del Fuego, also trips to the Falklands/Malvinas, charter boats to Cape Horn and Isla Magdalena, *Turismo Runner*, Lautaro Navarro 1065, T 247050, F 241042, adventure tours; *Arka Patagonia*, Ignacio Carrera Pinto 946, T 248167, F 241504, all types of tours, rafting, fishing, etc; *Turismo Pehoé*, Av Colón 782, T 244506, F 248052, organizes tours and hotels, enquire here about catamaran services; *Turismo Aonikenk*, Magallanes 619, T 228332, rec; *Turismo Pali Aike*, Lautaro Navarro 1129, T 223301; *El Conquistador*, Menéndez 556, T 222896, rec; *Turismo Viento Sur*, Fagnano 565, T/F 225167, for camping equipment; *Turismo Patagonia*, Bories 655 local 2, T 248474, F 247182, specializes in fishing trips. And others. Most organize tours to Torres del Paine, Fuerte Bulnes and *pingüineras* on Otway sound: shop around as prices vary; Sr Mateo Quesada, Chiloé 1375, T 222662, offers local tours in his car, up to 4 passengers.

In-Tur is an association of companies which aims to promote tourism in Chilean Patagonia. The members are *Arka Patagonia*, *Turismo Aventour*, *Turismo Pehoé*, *Turismo Runner*, *Aerovías DAP* and *Hostería Las Torres* (in the Parque Nacional Torres del Paine). The head office is at Errázuriz 840, p 2, Punta Arenas, T/F 229049, which contacted for information. See **Bus services**, below, for In-Tur's SIB bus to Torres del Paine.

● **Tourist offices**

Sernatur, Waldo Seguel 689, Casilla 106-D, T 241330, at the corner with Plaza Muñoz Gamero, 0830-1745, closed Sat and Sun. Helpful, English spoken. Kiosk on Colón between Bories and Magallanes Mon-Fri 0900-1300, 1500-1900, Sat 0900-1200, 1430-1730, Sun (in the summer only) 1000-1230. Turistel Guide available from kiosk belonging to *Café Garogha* at Bories 831. **Conaf**, Menéndez 1147, p 2, T 223841, open Mon-Fri.

● **Transport**

NB All transport is heavily booked from Christmas through to March: advance booking strongly advised.

Local Car hire: Hertz, Colón 798 and Carrera Pinto 770, T 248742, F 244729; **Australmag**, Colón 900, T 242174, F 226916; **Autómovil Club**, O'Higgins 931, T 243675, F 243097, and at airport; **Budget**, O'Higgins 964, T 241696; **Internacional**, Sarmiento 790-B, T 228323, F 226334, rec; **Willemsen**, Lautaro Navarro 1038, T 247787, F 241083, highly rec; **Lubac**, Magallanes 970, T/F 242023/247060; **Todoauto**, España 0480, T 212492, F 212627. **NB** You need a hire company's authorization to take a car into Argentina. **Car repair**: *Automotores del Sur*, O'Higgins 850, T 224153. **Taxis**: ordinary taxis have yellow roofs. Collective taxis (all black) run on fixed routes, US$0.25 for anywhere on route. Reliable service from *Radio Taxi Austral*, T 247710/244409.

Air Carlos Ibáñez de Campo Airport, 15 km N of town. Bus service by Austral Bus, J Menéndez 565, T 247139, F 241708, between the airport and Plaza Muñoz Gamero scheduled to meet flights, US$2.50. LanChile, DAP and Ladeco have their own bus services from town, US$2.50; taxi US$10. The airport restaurant is good. To **Santiago**, LanChile, Ladeco, DAP and National daily US$220, via Puerto Montt (sit on right for views), some National flights also stop in Concepción. When no tickets are available, go to the airport and get on the standby waiting list. To **Porvenir**, Aerovías DAP daily at 0815 and 1730, return 0830 and 1750 (US$20), plus other irregular flights, with Twin-Otter and Cessna aircraft. (Heavily booked with long waiting list so make sure you have your return reservation confirmed.) Military (FACh) flights approx twice a month to Puerto Montt US$30, information and tickets from airforce base at the airport, Spanish essential, T 213559; need to book well in advance. It is very difficult to get space during the summer as all armed forces personel and their families have priority over civilians.

Services to Argentina: To Ushuaia, Aerovías DAP twice a week, also Kaiken in summer (schedules change frequently). To Río Grande, Kaiken 5 a week. Reserve well in advance from mid-Dec to February.

Buses Company offices: Pingüino and Fernández, Sanhueza 745, T 242313, F 225984; **Ghisoni**, Lautaro Navarro 975, T 223205; **Pacheco**, Colón 900, T 242174; **Bus Sur**, Colón y Magallanes, T 244464; **Austral Bus**, Menéndez 565, T 247139, T/F 241708. **Los Carlos**, Plaza Muñoz Gamero 1039, T 241321. **Turbus**, Errázuriz 932, T/F 225315. **Gesell**, José Menéndez 556, T 222896. Bus timetables are printed daily in *La Prensa Austral*.

Bus services: buses leave from company offices. To **Puerto Natales**, 3½ hrs, Fernández, Austral Bus, and Buses Sur, several every day, last departure 1800, US$6. *In-Tur* (see **Tour companies**, above) runs a twice daily circuit Punta Arenas-Puerto Natales-Torres del Paine in minibuses with snack, English-speaking guide and inc National Park entry; service runs mid-Oct to mid-April. Turbus, Ghisoni and Austral have services through Argentina to **Osorno**, **Puerto Montt** and **Castro**. Fares: to Puerto Montt or Osorno US$60-75 (cheaper off season) 36 hrs; to Castro US$ 67-83; Turbus continues to **Santiago**, US$95 (cheaper in winter), 46 hrs.

To **Río Gallegos**, Argentina, Pingüino daily 1200, return 1300; Ghisoni, daily except Fri, 1000; Mansilla Fri 1000, US$22, Magallanes Tour, Tues 1000. Fares US$20-22, officially 5 hrs, but can take up to 8, depending on customs, 15 mins on Chilean side, up to 3 hrs on Argentine side, inc 30 mins lunch at Km 160. All customs formalities now undertaken at the border, but ask before departure if this has changed (taxi to Río Gallegos US$130). To **Río Grande**, Hector Pacheco, Mon, Wed, Fri 0730 via Punta Delgada, return Tues, Thur and Sat, 0730, 10 hrs, US$27, heavily booked. To **Ushuaia** via Punta Delgada, Los Carlos, Tues and Sat, 0700, return Mon and Fri, 0300, 14 hrs, US$48, book any return at same time. Alternatively, Tecni Austral runs daily from Río Grande to Ushuaia at 0730 and 1800, 4 hrs, US$20.

Ferries For services to Porvenir (Tierra del Fuego), see page 360.

Shipping Offices Navimag, Colón 521, T 244400, F 242003; **Comapa** (Compañía Marítima de Punta Arenas), Independencia 830, T 244400, F 247514.

Shipping Services For Navimag services Puerto Montt – Puerto Natales, see under Puerto Montt (confirmation of reservations is advised). Visits to the beautiful fjords and glaciers of Tierra del Fuego are highly rec. Comapa runs a once a fortnight 22-hr, 320-km round trip to the fjord d'Agostino, 30 km long, where many glaciers come down to the sea. The luxury cruiser, *Terra Australis*, sails from Punta Arenas on Sat via Ushuaia and Puerto Williams; details from Comapa. Advance booking (advisable) from Cruceros Australis SA, Miraflores 178, p 12, Santiago, T 696-3211, F 331871. Government supply ships are rec for the young and hardy, but take sleeping bag and extra food, and travel pills. For transport on navy supply ships to Puerto Williams, enquire at Tercera Zona Naval, Lautaro Navarro 1150, or ask the captain direct, but be prepared to be frustrated by irregular sailings and inaccurate information. All tickets on ships must be booked in advance Jan-February.

● **To the Falkland Islands/Islas Malvinas**
Punta Arenas is now the main South American link with the islands. Aerovías DAP (address above) fly the following schedule: depart Santiago Wed 1300, arrive Punta Arenas 1600, dep 1700, arrive Mt Pleasant, Falklands/Malvinas 1815; depart Mt Pleasant Thur 1530, arrive Punta Arenas 1700, depart 1800, arrive Santiago 2100, all year. Book well in advance.

● **To Puerto Williams**
For details of sea and air service, see page 368.

● **To Antarctica**
Other than asking in agencies for possible free berths on cruise ships, the only possibility is with the Chilean Navy. The Navy itself does not encourage passengers, so you must approach the captain of the vessel direct. Spanish is essential.

● **Overland to Argentina**
From Punta Arenas there are 3 routes to Calafate and Río Gallegos: 1) NE via Route 255 and Punta Delgada to the frontier at Kimiri Aike and then along Argentine Route 3 to Río Gallegos. 2) N along Route 9, turning 9 km before Puerto Natales for Dorotea (good road) and then NE via La Esperanza (fuel, basic accommodation). 3) Via Puerto Natales and Cerro Castillo on the road to Torres del Paine joining the road to La Esperanza at Paso Cancha.

LONGER EXCURSIONS

Fuerte Bulnes

56 km S, is a replica of the wooden fort erected in 1843 by the crew of the Chilean vessel *Ancud*. Nearby is Puerto Hambre. Tours by several agencies, US$12. At the intersection of the roads to Puerto del Hambre and Fuerte Bulnes, 51 km S of Punta Arenas, is a small marker with a plaque of the Centro Geográfico de Chile, ie the midway point between Arica and the South Pole.

Port Famine (Puerto Hambre)

In 1582 Felipe II of Spain, alarmed by Drake's passage through the Straits of Magellan, decided to establish a Spanish presence on the Straits. A fleet of 15 ships and 4,000 men, commanded by Pedro Sarmiento de Gamboa, was despatched in 1584. The ships were scattered by storms, only 3 arriving with 300 men on board. With his small force Sarmiento founded two cities: *Nombre de Jesús* on Punta Dungeness at the eastern entrance to the Straits and *Rey Felipe* near Puerto Hambre.

Disaster struck when their only remaining vessel broke its anchorage in a storm; the ship, with Sarmiento on board was blown into the Atlantic. After vain attempts to re-enter the Straits, Sarmiento set sail for Rio de Janeiro where he organized two rescue missions: the first ended in shipwreck, the second in mutiny. Captured by English corsairs, Sarmiento was taken to England where he was imprisoned. Released by Elizabeth I, he tried to return to Spain via France, where he was gaoled again. Until his death in 1608, Sarmiento besieged Felipe II with letters urging him to rescue the men stranded in the Straits.

When the English corsair Thomas Cavendish sailed through the Straits in 1587 he found only one survivor at *Rey Felipe*, the remainder having hanged themselves, or starved owing to the lack of supplies and the inhospitable climate. Cavendish named the place Port Famine.

Reserva Forestal Laguna Parrillar

53 km S, covering 18,814 ha, has older forest than the Magallanes Reserve and sphagnum bogs. There is a 3-hr walk to the tree-line along poorly-marked paths. (No public transport, radio taxi US$60.)

Otway Sound

60 km N of Punta Arenas, is the site of a small colony of Magellanic penguins which can be visited (Nov-Mar only); following the attentions of some tourists, chasing the birds or trampling over the hatcheries, visitors are only allowed to see the penguins at a distance (there are a fence and bird-hides). Patience is required to see the penguins since they nest in burrows underground (tread carefully on the soft ground so as not to damage the nests), in the late afternoon they can be seen by the beach where screens have been built to facilitate viewing. Rheas and skunks can also be seen. Tours by several agencies, US$12, entry US$4; taxi US$35 return.

Isla Magdalena

A small island 25 km NE, is the location of the **Monumento Natural Los Pingüinos**, a colony of 150,000 penguins. Deserted apart from the breeding season (Nov-Jan), the island is administered by Conaf. Magdalena is one of a group of three islands (the others are Marta and Isabel), visited by Drake, whose men killed 3,000 penguins for food. It can be visited by boat with Comapa (address above): Tues, Thur, Sat, 0800 (Dec-Feb), 2 hrs each way, with 2 hrs on the island, returns 1400, coffee and biscuits served, US$60, rec.

NORTH FROM PUNTA ARENAS

From Punta Arenas a gravel road runs N to Puerto Natales; beside it, the southbound lane is paved. Fuel is available in Villa Tehuelches, 100 km from Punta Arenas.

● **Accommodation** Along this road are several hotels, inc **B** *Hostal Río Penitente*, Km 138, T 331694, in an old *estancia*, rec; **C** *Hotel Rubens*, Km 183, T 226916, popular for fishing; *Hostería Llanuras de Diana*, Km 215, T 248742, F 244729 (Punta Arenas), T 411540 (Puerto Natales) hidden from road, highly rec; **C** *Hostería Río Verde*, Km 90, E off the highway on Seno Skyring, T 311122, F 241008, private bath, heating.

PUERTO NATALES

Puerto Natales (*Pop* 15,000; *Phone code* 061) is 247 km N of Punta Arenas and close to the Argentine border at Río Turbio. It stands on the Ultima Esperanza gulf amid spectacular scenery and is the jumping-off place for the magnificent Balmaceda and Torres del Paine national parks. Very quiet in the winter, packed with tourists in the summer. Puerto Bories, 6 km N, was the site of the biggest meatpacking factory in Patagonia; though much of the old plant was destroyed by fire, the administration buildings and housing can be visited.

Museums

Museo De Agostini, in the Colegio Salesiano at Padre Rossa 1456, 1 room, Tierra del Fuego fauna, free.

Museo Histórico Municipal, Bulnes 285, Tues-Sun 1500-1800.

Excursions

A recommended walk is up to **Cerro Dorotea** which dominates the town, with superb views of the whole Ultima Esperanza Sound. Take any bus going E and alight at the jeep track for summit (Km 9.5).

Local wildlife

'A good place to photograph rheas (ñandúes) is a few kilometres N of the checkpoint at Kon Aiken, near the turnoff for Otway. Antarctic cormorants can be seen sitting on offshore rocks from the road to Fuerte Bulnes. The local skunk (chingüe) is apparently very docile and rarely sprays. Also look out for foxes and the Great Horned Owl.' Arthur Shapiro (Dept of Zoology, Univ of California, Davis).

Puerto Natales

Hotels:
1. Austral
2. Blanquita
3. Bulnes
4. Costa Australis
5. Eberhard
6. Glaciares
7. Juan Ladrilleros
8. Lady Florence Dixie
9. Laury
10. Melissa
11. Natalino
12. Palace
13. Res Carahue
14. Res Grey
15. Sir Francis Drake
Places to eat:
16. El Marítimo
17. La Burbuja
18. La Costanera
19. La Tranquera
20. La Ultima Esperanza

The **Monumento Natural Cueva Milodón** (50m wide, 200m deep, 30m high), 25 km N, contains a plastic model of the prehistoric ground-sloth whose bones were found there in 1895. Evidence has also been found here of occupation by early Patagonian humans some 11,000 years ago. (Free camping once US$4 entrance fee has been paid.)

● **Transport** Buses J and B regular service US$7.50; taxi US$15 return or check if you can get a ride with a tour; both Adventur and Fernández tour buses to Torres del Paine stop at the cave.

Local information
● **Accommodation**

In season cheaper accommodation fills up quickly after the arrival of the *Puerto Edén* from Puerto Montt. Most prices include breakfast.

L3 *Eberhard*, Pedro Montt 58, T 411208, F 411209, excellent views, restaurant; **L3** *Costa Australis*, Pedro Montt 262, T 412000, F 411881, new in 1994, modern, good views, popular cafetería.

A1 *Palace*, Ladrilleros 209, T 411134, good food, overpriced; **A2** *Juan Ladrilleros*, Pedro Montt 161, modern, with bath, good restaurant, clean, T 411652, F 412109, rec; **A2** *Glaciares*, Eberhard 104, T 412189, F 411452, new, snack bar; **A2** *Hostal Sir Francis Drake*, Phillipi 383, T/F 411553, good views, snack bar, rec; **A3** *Hostal Lady Florence Dixie*, Bulnes 659, T 411158, F 411943, modern, friendly, rec; *Martín Guisinde*, Carlos Bories 278, T 412770, F 412820, phone, TV, tourist information, parking, pub, restaurant, new.

B *Blanquita*, Carrera Pinto 409, quiet, rec; **B** *Hostal Melissa*, Blanco Encalada 258, T 411944, private bath; **B** *Natalino*, Eberhard 371, T 411968, clean and very friendly (tours to Milodón Cave arranged), C without bath, parking.

C *Hostal Los Antiguos*, Ladrilleros 195 y Bulnes, T/F 411488, shared bath, pleasant; **C** *Res Carahue*, Bulnes 370, T 411339, with breakfast, laundry facilities, nice; **C** *Bulnes*, C Bulnes 407, T 411307, with breakfast, good, stores luggage; **C** *Hostal Puerto Natales*, Eberhard 250, T 411098, private bath.

D pp *Lago Sarmiento*, Bulnes 90, T 411542, hot water, some rooms with heating, very friendly, good dinners; **D** *Res Centro*, Magallanes 258A, T 411996, private bath; **D** *Res Sutherland*, Barros Arana 155, with and without bath, welcoming, clean, kitchen facilities.

E pp *Hosp La Chila*, Carrera Pinto 442, use of kitchen, welcoming, luggage store, bakes bread, rec; **E** pp *María José*, Magallanes 646, cooking facilities, helpful; **E** pp *Hostal Famatina*, Ladrilleros 370, T 412067, clean, friendly; **E** pp *Hosp Gamma/Milodón*, El Roble 650, T 411420, cooking and laundry facilities, evening meals, tours; **E** pp *Los Inmigrantes*, Carrera Pinto 480, good breakfast, clean, kitchen facilities, luggage store, rec; **E** pp *Res El Mundial*, Bories 315, T 412476, large breakfast, use of kitchen, good value meals, luggage stored, rec; **E** pp *Tierra del Fuego*, Bulnes 29, clean, family of Juan Osorno, will store luggage, good; **E** pp *Casa de familia Bustamente*, Bulnes 317, T 411061, clean, good breakfast, helpful, luggage store, rec; **E** pp *Casa de familia Elsa Millán*, O'Higgins 657, good breakfast, homemade bread, dormitory-style, popular, hot water, warm, friendly, cooking facilities, rec (latest reports say it has moved, new address not known Nov 96); **E** pp *Casa de familia Dickson*, Bulnes 307, T 411218, good breakfast, clean, helpful, cooking and laundry facilities, rec; **E** pp *Pensión Ritz*, Carrera Pinto 439, full pension available, friendly; **E** pp *Res Temuco*, Ramírez 310, T 411120, friendly, reasonable, good food, clean; **E** pp *Hosp Laury*, Bulnes 222, with breakfast, cooking and laundry facilities, clean, warm, friendly; **E** pp *Bories*, Bories 206, hostel type, use of kitchen, sleeping bag necessary, good meeting place, friendly; **E** pp *Casa Cecilia*, Tomás Rogers 60, T/F 411797, backpackers' annexe **F** pp, clean, cooking and laundry facilities, only one bathroom, English, French and German spoken, rents camping equipment, information on Torres del Paine, organizes tours; **E** pp *Patagonia Adventure*, Tomás Rogers 179, T 411028, dormitory style, and private rooms, friendly, clean, use of kitchen, breakfast, English spoken, camping equipment for hire, book exchange, rec; **E** pp Sra Bruna Mardones, Pasaje Don Bosco 41 (off Philippi), friendly, meals on request; **E** pp *Casa de familia Alicia*, M Rodríguez 283, with breakfast, clean, spacious, luggage stored, helpful, rec; **E** pp *Don Bosco*, Padre Rossa 1430, good meals, use of kitchen, helpful, rec, motorcycle parking, luggage store; **E-F** pp Sra Teresa Ruiz, Esmeralda 463, good value, warm, cheap meals, quiet, friendly, rec, tours to Torres

del Paine arranged; **F** pp *Res Lago Pingo*, Bulnes 808, T 411026, basic, breakfast extra, hot water, laundry, use of kitchen, will store luggage; similar at O'Higgins 70, 431 and Perito 443; **F** pp private house at Magallanes 1, friendly, cheap meals.

North of Puerto Natales are: **L3-A2** *Cisne de Cuello Negro*, a former guest house for meat buyers at the disused meat packing plant, T 411498 (Av Colón 782, Punta Arenas, T 244506, F 248052), friendly, clean, reasonable, excellent cooking, rec, 5 km from town at Km 275 nr Puerto Bories; **A2** *Patagonia Inn*, Km 26 N, reservations Hotel Cabo de Hornos, T/F 242134, Punta Arenas, private bath, restaurant; **C** Hotel 3 Pasos, 40 km N, T 228113, simple, beautiful. In Villa Cerro Castillo, 63 km N: **B** Hostería El Pionero, T/F 411646, with bath, country house ambience, good service. For accommodation in the Torres del Paine area, see below. **NB** Hotels in the countryside open only in summer months: dates vary.

● **Places to eat**

Don Alvarito, Blanco Encalada 915, hospitable; *El Marítimo*, Pedro Montt 214, seafood and salmon, good views, popular, slow service; *Mari Loli*, Baquedano 615, excellent food, good value; *La Ultima Esperanza*, Eberhard 354, rec for salmon, seafood, enormous portions, not cheap but worth the experience; *La Costanera*, Bories y Ladrilleros, good food, superb views; *Andrés*, Ladrilleros 381, excellent, good service; *La Burbuja*, Bulnes 371, huge portions, reasonably priced; *Tierra del Fuego*, Bulnes 29, cheap, good, slow service; *Café Josmar*, Yungay 743, only cafe open every day, packed lunches sold for boat trips; *Melissa*, Blanco Encalada, good coffee and cakes; *Centro Español*, Magallanes 247, reasonable; *La Frontera*, Bulnes 819, set meals and à la carte, good value; *La Tranquera*, Bulnes y Blanco Encalada, popular. Cheap meals at *Club Deportivo Natales*, Eberhard 332. *Cristal*, Bulnes 439, good sandwiches and salmon; *Tío Cacho*, Phillipi 553, pizzas and sandwiches; *Delicatessen Pollo Loco*, Baquedano 330, T 411393, good, does packed lunches, rec.

● **Banks & money changers**

Poor rates for TCs, which cannot be changed into US$ cash. **Banco O'Higgins**, Bulnes 655, Mastercard, ATM. *Casas de cambio* on Blanco Encalada 226 (Andes Patagónicos) and 266 (Enio América) where Argentine pesos can be changed. **Cambio Stop**, Baquedano 380, good for cash (also arranges tours). Another two at Bulnes 683 and 1087 (good rates; also Argentine pesos); others on Prat. Shop around as some offer very poor rates.

● **Language schools**
Natalis English Centre, Bulnes 1231, T 411193, F 411300, one to one tuition US$4/hr, good.

● **Entertainment**
Discos: *El Cielo*, Esmeralda y Ramírez; *Milodón*, Blanco Encalada.

● **Laundry**
Lavandería Papaguayo, Bulnes 518; *Tienda Milodón*, Bulnes, cheap; *Liberty*, Bulnes 513, or try Sra María Carcamo (at Teresa Ruiz's *Hospedaje* at 1000-1200, 1800-2200), good service, more expensive.

● **Post & telecommunications**
Post Office: Eberhard 417, open Mon-Fri 0830-1230, 1430-1745, Sat 0900-1230.

Telephones: CTC, Blanco Encalada 23 y Bulnes, phones and fax.

● **Shopping**
Shoe repairs: *París*, Miraflores between Blanco Encalada and Baquedano.

Supermarket: *El Favorito*, Bulnes 1008; 24 hr supermarket Bulnes 300 block; markets good; food prices variable so shop around; cheaper in Punta Arenas.

● **Sports**
Camping equipment: *Patagonia Adventures*, see **Hotels** above; *Casa Cecilia*, Tomás Rogers 54, German, French and English spoken, imported gear, also for sale, rec; *Patagonia Adventures*, Tomás Rogers 179. Check all equipment and prices carefully. Average charges, per day: tent US$6, sleeping bag US$3-5, mat US$1.50, raincoat US$0.60, also cooking gear, US$1-2. (**NB** Deposits required: tent US$200, sleeping bag US$100.) Camping gas is widely available in hardware stores, eg at Baquedano y O'Higgins and at Baquedano y Esmeralda.

Fishing: tackle for hire at *Andes Patagónicos*, Blanco Encalada 226, T 411594, US$3.50/day for rod, reel and spinners; if you prefer fishing with floats, hooks, split shot, etc, take your own. Other companies up to 5 times as expensive.

● **Tour companies & travel agents**
Turis Ann, Tomás Rogers 255, T/F 411141, very helpful, accommodation arranged, tours, equipment hire; *San Cayetano*, Eberhard 145, T 411112; *Michay*, Baquedano 388, T 411149/411957 (Pedro Fueyo rec); *Andescape*, Pedro Montt 308, next to harbour, T 412592; *Knudsen Tours*, Encalada 284, T 411531, rec; *Onas*, Bulnes 453, T 412707 (Casilla 78); *Servitur*, Pratt 353, T 411028; *Turismo Zalej*, Bulnes 459, rec, T 412260, F 411355. Patricio Canales, Eberhard 49, rec as a good guide; *Turismo Cabo de Hornos*, Pedro Montt 380; *Turismo Tzonka*, Carrera Pinto 626, T 411214. Reports of the reliability of agencies, especially for their trips to Torres del Paine National Park, are very mixed. It is better to book tours direct with agents in Puerto Natales than through agents in Punta Arenas.

Several agencies offer tours to the Perito Moreno glacier in Argentina, 1 day, US$70 without food or park entry fee. The agencies are reluctant to let tourists leave the tour in Calafate and continue into Argentina.

● **Tourist offices**
Offices in kiosk on waterfront, Av Pedro Montt y Phillipi; maps for US$1 from Eberhard 547. **Conaf**: Carrera Pinto 566.

● **Transport**
Local Bicycle hire: *Onas*, Bulnes 453, US$10 a day; also try *Hotel Eberhard*. **Bicycle repairs**: *El Rey de la Bicicleta*, Arauco 779, good, helpful. **Car hire**: Andes Patagónicos, Blanco Encalada 226, T 411594, helpful, US$85/day inc insurance and 350 km free; **Todoauto**, Bulnes 20, T 412837. US$110/day for high clearance vehicle, others US$80/day, or US$85 with driver. Hire agents can arrange permission to drive into Argentina, but this is expensive and takes 24 hrs to arrange. **Mechanic**: Carlos González, Ladrilleros entre Bories y Eberhard, rec.

Air Alta from Puerto Montt, fine views, 3 hrs, US$50, a rec alternative to the ferry. (In late 1996, Alta was planning a Puerto Natales-Calafate service.)

Buses To Punta Arenas, several daily, 3½ hrs, US$6. Bus Fernández, Eberhard 555, T 411111, Bus Sur, Baquedano 534, T 411325 and Austral Bus, Baquedano y Valdivia, T 411415. Book in advance. To Coyhaique via Calafate, Urbina Tours, 4 days, US$120 (Nov-March). Out of season the only service to rest of Chile: Austral Bus, Tues to Pto Montt, US$150, book days in advance.

  To Argentina: to **Río Gallegos** direct, Bus Sur, US$22, Tues and Thur 1830 and El Pingüino, Wed and Sun 1200, US20; hourly to **Río Turbio**, Lagoper, Baquedano y Valdivia, and other companies, US$3, 2 hrs (depending on Customs – change bus at border). To **Calafate**, Río Turbio bus from Onas, Bulnes 453, 0630, US$17.50, otherwise travel agencies run several times a week depending on demand, 7 hrs, US$50, shop around, reserve 1 day ahead.

Shipping See page 292 on services from Puerto Montt. Navimag office: Pedro Montt 262 Loc B, Terminal Marítimo, T/F 411421.

FRONTIER WITH ARGENTINA

There are three crossing points:

1) PASO CASAS VIEJAS

16 km E of Puerto Natales. On the Argentine side the road continues to a junction, with alternatives S to Río Turbio and N to La Esperanza and Río Gallegos.

● **Chilean immigration**
Open all year 0800-2000.

2) VILLA DOROTEA

16 km NE of Puerto Natales. On the Argentine side this joins the Río Turbio-La Esperanza road.

● **Chilean immigration**
Open all year daytime only.

3) CERRO CASTILLO

65 km N of Puerto Natales on the road to Torres del Paine. On the Argentine side, Paso Cancha Carrera (14 km), the road leads to La Esperanza and Río Gallegos.

● **Chilean immigration**
open 0830-1200, 1400-2000, Nov-March or April only.

● **Accommodation**
2 *hospedajes* in Cerro Castillo.

INTO ARGENTINA

The Río Turbio-La Esperanza road, Route 40, goes NE from Cancha Carrera to Fuentes del Coyle (Hotel, **D** pp, dirty, cold; small bar/confitería with 2-3 rooms) and then to the Río Coyle. Here Route 40 continues NE unpaved and difficult, especially after heavy rain (2 fjords may be impassible), to a point 90 km SE of El Calafate, while gravel Route 7 goes to La Esperanza (petrol pump; large *confitería*). At La Esperanza the paved road heads either NW to El Calafate and the famous Ventisquero Moreno (the glacier on Lago Argentino), or SE to Río Gallegos, capital of Santa Cruz Province.

PARQUE NACIONAL BERNARDO O'HIGGINS

Usually referred to as the **Parque Nacional Monte Balmaceda**, lies at the N end of Ultima Esperanza Sound and can be reached by sea only. Two boats *21 de Mayo* and *Alberto de Agostini* sail daily from Puerto Natales in summer and on Sun only in winter (minimum 10 passengers), when weather conditions may be better with less cloud and rain, US$38.

After a 3-hr journey up the Sound, the boat passes the Balmaceda Glacier which drops from the eastern slopes of Monte Balmaceda (2,035m). The glacier is retreating; in 1986 its foot was at sea level. The boat docks 1 hr further N at Puerto Toro, from where it is a 1-km walk to the base of Serrano Glacier on the N slope of Monte Balmaceda. On the trip dolphins, sea-lions (in season), black-necked swans, flightless steamer ducks and cormorants can be seen.

Bookings through *Andes Patagónicos* (address above) or other agencies, expensive lunch extra, take own food, drinks available on board. Take warm clothes, hat and gloves. This trip can also be combined with a visit to Torres del Paine. You have to pay full fare on the boat and you need a permit from Conaf. The 35 km walk from Puerto Toro along the Río Serrano to the Torres del Paine administration centre is hard going with no clear path; it is not an authorized route and the *guardaparques* in Torres del Paine discourage its use.

PARQUE NACIONAL TORRES DEL PAINE

Situated 145 km NW of Puerto Natales and covering 181,414 ha, this national park is a 'must' for its wildlife and spectacular scenery. In the centre of the park is a granite *massif* from which rise the *Torres* (Towers) and *Cuernos* (Horns) of Paine, oddly shaped peaks of over 2,600m. The valleys are filled by beautiful lakes at 50m to 200m above sea level. There are 15 peaks above 2,000m, of which the highest is Cerro Paine Grande (3,050m). On the W edge of the Park is the enormous *Campo de Hielo Sur* icecap; 4 main glaciers (*ventisqueros*), Grey, Dickson Zapata and Tyndall, branch off this and drop to the lakes formed by their meltwater. Two other glaciers, the *Francés* and *Los Perros* descend on the W side of the central *massif*.

The scenery in the Park is superb, with constantly changing views of fantastic peaks, ice-fields, vividly coloured lakes of turquoise, ultramarine and grey and quiet green valleys. The park enjoys a micro-climate especially favourable to wildlife and plants: there are 105 species of birds including 18 species of waterfowl and 11 birds of prey. Particularly noteworthy are condors, black-necked swans, rheas, kelp geese, ibis, flamingos and austral parrots. There are also 25 species of mammals including *guanaco*, hares, foxes, *huemules* (a species of deer), pumas and skunks. Over 200 species of plants have been identified. The Park is open all year round, although snow may prevent access in the winter: warmest time is Dec-Mar, although it can be wet and windy. It is also more crowded at this time. Oct-Nov can be very nice. In winter there can be good, stable conditions and well-equipped hikers can do some good walking.

Torres del Paine has become increasingly popular with foreigners and Chileans alike: in 1996 it received 51,000 visitors, most during the summer. Despite the best efforts to manage this large influx of visitors rationally, their impact is starting to show. Litter has become a problem especially around the *refugios* and camping areas. Please take all your rubbish out of the park and remember that toilet paper is also garbage.

The park is administered by Conaf: the Administration Centre is in the S of the park at the N end of Lago del Toro (open 0830-2000 in summer, 0830-1230, 1400-1830 off season). The Centre provides a good slide show at 2000 on Sat and Sun and there are also exhibitions, but no maps or written information to take away. For information (in Spanish) on weather conditions phone the Administration Centre (T 691931). There are six ranger stations (*guarderías*) staffed by rangers (*guardaparques*) who give help and advice and will also store luggage (except at Laguna Amarga where they have no room). Rangers keep

Torres del Paine

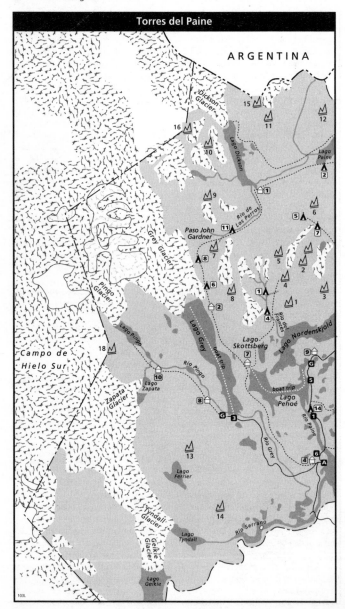

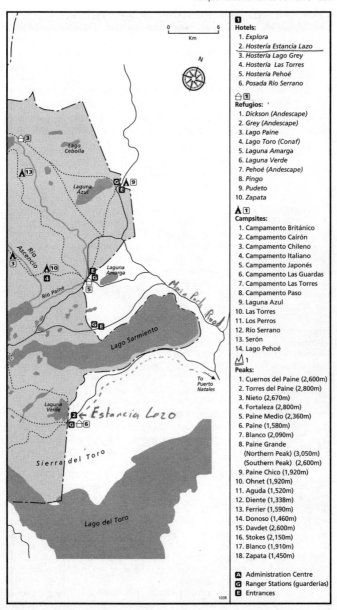

Hotels:
1. *Explora*
2. *Hostería Estancia Lazo*
3. *Hostería Lago Grey*
4. *Hostería Las Torres*
5. *Hostería Pehoé*
6. *Posada Río Serrano*

Refugios:
1. *Dickson (Andescape)*
2. *Grey (Andescape)*
3. *Lago Paine*
4. *Lago Toro (Conaf)*
5. *Laguna Amarga*
6. *Laguna Verde*
7. *Pehoé (Andescape)*
8. *Pingo*
9. *Pudeto*
10. *Zapata*

Campsites:
1. Campamento Británico
2. Campamento Caírón
3. Campamento Chileno
4. Campamento Italiano
5. Campamento Japonés
6. Campamento Las Guardas
7. Campamento Las Torres
8. Campamento Paso
9. Laguna Azul
10. Las Torres
11. Los Perros
12. Río Serrano
13. Serón
14. Lago Pehoé

Peaks:
1. Cuernos del Paine (2,600m)
2. Torres del Paine (2,800m)
3. Nieto (2,670m)
4. Fortaleza (2,800m)
5. Paine Medio (2,360m)
6. Paine (1,580m)
7. Blanco (2,090m)
8. Paine Grande
   (Northern Peak) (3,050m)
   (Southern Peak) (2,600m)
9. Paine Chico (1,920m)
10. Ohnet (1,920m)
11. Aguda (1,520m)
12. Diente (1,338m)
13. Ferrier (1,590m)
14. Donoso (1,460m)
15. Davdet (2,600m)
16. Stokes (2,150m)
17. Blanco (1,910m)
18. Zapata (1,450m)

A Administration Centre
G Ranger Stations (guarderías)
E Entrances

a check on the whereabouts of all visitors: you are required to register and show your passport when entering the park. You are also requested to register at a ranger station before setting off on any hike. There are entrances at Laguna Amarga, Lago Sarmiento and Laguna Azul. Entry for foreigners: US$12 (proceeds are shared between all 35 Chilean National Parks) climbing fees US$800. Allow a week to 10 days to see the park properly.

Warning It is vital not to underestimate the unpredictability of the weather (which can change in a few minutes), nor the arduousness of some of the stretches

An impression of Torres del Paine

Torres del Paine is one of the most impressive mountain areas on Earth. There are few comparable sites with almost 1,000m vertical shafts of basalt with concial caps atop steep forested talus slopes. These are the remains of frozen magma in ancient volcanic throats, everything else having been eroded; the highest is 3,248 and may be seen from near sea-level. As well as these spectacular mountains the surrounding forest, with lakes, glaciers and open country is truly magnificent. Although outposts of civilization exist near the edges of the park it is quite easy to escape its influences in a few hours trekking. One consideration is, however, the Patagonian winter; although the park may be visited throughout the year, those going in the cold months should be well prepared. Even in summer the weather may change at short notice. Spectacular displays of snow plumes blowing from the mountain tops are well known in summer, and occur at least a thousand metres above the observer. The weather is changeable: if unpleasant conditions occur they will not last long.

Wildlife abounds; guanacos and condors are common, and other mammals and birds quite abundant. I recall a very peculiar scratching sound on the corrugated iron roof of a hut one morning, and emerged to find a large condor was roosting on the ridge for the night but having difficulty securing a good grip with its claws. The region is sufficiently S for the worst of the biting invertebrates to be only a minor problem.

Vegetation is typical South Andean. Although few trees reach great size, several valleys are thickly forested and little light penetrates. The grassland is distinct from the monotony of the pampa and dispersed sclerophyl forest. A complex series of lakes and streams leads into fjords extending sinuous distances from the sea. These are another attraction; many are glacial fed (and thus very cold); fortunately some strategic footbridges exist. It is quite unnecessary to carry water when trekking.

Much of the park was once a cattle ranch. This explains some of the older *refugios* which were huts where gauchos lived during round-up. Most cattle have now gone leaving the few hotels as the only commerce.

Time to enjoy such a place is important. The writer (a trekker) suggests at least 10 days which will allow a comfortable circumnavigation with plenty of time to do side tracks (and some to spare in case of a windy and wet day). To some extent you can live off the land; there is a Chilean legend that one who eats the Calafate berry is sure to return. This fruit is delicious and I suggest that you eat a lot if you are fortunate to be there during the correct season (late summer); in my case the legend was certainly true.

RK Headland, Scott Polar Research Institute, Cambridge.

on the long hikes. Rain and snowfall are heavier the further W you go, and bad weather sweeps off the *Campo de Hielo Sur* without warning. It is essential to be properly equipped against cold, wind and rain. The only means of rescue are on horseback or by boat; the nearest helicopter is in Punta Arenas and high winds usually prevent its operation in the park.

Hikes

There are about 250 km of well-marked trails. Visitors must keep to the trails: cross-country trekking is not permitted. **NB** The times indicated should be treated with caution: allow for personal fitness and weather conditions.

El Circuito The most popular hike is a circuit round the Torres and Cuernos del Paine: usually it is done either anticlockwise starting from the Laguna Amarga *guardería* or clockwise from the administration centre. From Laguna Amarga the route is N along the W side of the Río Paine to Lago Paine, before turning W to follow the Río Paine to the S end of Lago Dickson. From here the path runs along the wooded valley of the Río de los Perros before climbing steeply to Paso John Gardner (1,241m, the highest point on the route), then dropping to follow the Grey Glacier SE to Lago Grey, continuing to Lago Pehoé and the Administration Centre. There are superb views, particularly from the top of Paso John Gardner.

Although some people complete the route in less, it normally takes 5-6 days. Lone walkers are not allowed on this route and camping gear must be carried. The circuit is often closed in winter because of snow. The longest lap is 30 km, between Refugio Laguna Amarga and Refugio Dickson (10 hrs in good weather), but the most difficult section is the very steep slippery slope between Paso John Gardner (1,241m) and *Campamento Paso*. Although most people go anti-clockwise round the circuit, some

advise doing it clockwise so that you climb to Paso John Gardner with the wind behind. The major rivers are crossed by footbridges, but these are occasionally washed away.

The Valley of the Río del Francés From *Refugio Pehoé* this route leads N across undulating country along the W edge of Lago Skottberg to *Campamento Italiano* and then follows the valley of the Río del Francés which climbs between (to the W) Cerro Paine Grande and the Ventisquero del Francés and (to the E) the Cuernos del Paine to *Campamento Británico*. Allow 2½ hrs from Refugio Pehoé to *Campamento Italiano*, 2½ hrs further to *Campamento Británico*. The views from the *mirador* above *Campamento Británico* are superb.

To Lago Pingo From *Guardería Grey* (18 km W by road from the Administration Centre) follow the Río Pingo, via *Refugio Pingo* and *Refugio Zapata* (4 hrs), with views S over Ventisquero Zapata (plenty of wildlife, icebergs in the lake) to reach the lake (5 hrs from *Guardería Grey*). Ventisquero Pingo can be seen 3 km away over the lake.

To the base of the Torres del Paine From *Refugio Laguna Amarga* the route follows the road W to *Hostería Las Torres* before climbing along the W side of the Río Ascensio via *Campamento Chileno* to *Campamento Las Torres*, close to the base of the Torres and near a small lake. Allow 1½ hrs to *Hostería Las Torres*, then 2 hrs to *Campamento Chileno*, 2 hrs further to *Campamento Torres* where there is a lake: the path is well-marked, but the last 30 mins is up the morraine; to see the towers lit by sunrise (spectacular but you must have good weather), it's well worth humping camping gear up to *Campamento Torres* and spending the night. 1 hr beyond *Campamento Torres* is the good site at *Campamento Japonés*.

To Laguna Verde From the administation centre follow the road N 2 km, before taking the path E over the Sierra del Toro and then along the S side of Laguna Verde to the *Guardería Laguna Verde*. Allow 4 hrs. This is one of the easiest walks in the park and may be a good first hike.

To Laguna Azul and Lago Paine This route runs N from Laguna Amarga to the W tip of Laguna Azul, from where it continues across the sheltered Río Paine valley past Laguna Cebolla to the *Refugio Lago Paine* at the W end of the lake. Allow 8½ hrs.

Equipment

A strong, streamlined, waterproof tent is preferable to the *refugios* and is essential if doing the complete circuit. Also essential are protective clothing against wind and rain, strong waterproof footwear, compass, good sleeping bag, sleeping mat, camping stove and cooking equipment. In summer take shorts and sunscreen also. Equipment is checked at the entrance. Take your own food: the small shops at the Andescape *refugios* (see below) and at the *Posada Río Serrano* are expensive and have a limited selection. Note that rats and mice have become a major problem around camping sites and the free *refugios*. Do not leave food in your pack (which will be chewed through): the safest solution is to hang food in a bag on wire. Maps (US$3), are obtainable at Conaf offices in Punta Arenas or Puerto Natales. Most maps are unreliable but the one produced by Sociedad Turística Kaonikén, US$5, has been recommended as more accurate than the Conaf map (available at *Nandú Artesanía* at port end of Bulnes).

Park information

● **Accommodation**

Hotels: **L1** *Hotel Explora*, new, luxurious and comfortable, at Salto Chico on edge of Lago Pehoé, T 411247, offering spectacular views, pool, gym, tours (reservations: Av Américo Vespucci 80, p 7, Santiago, T 228-8081, F 208-5479); **L3** *Hostería Pehoé*, T 411390, 60 rooms, private facilities, cheaper off season, 5 km S of Pehoé ranger station, 11 km N of park administration, on an island with spectacular

view across the Lake to Cerro Paine Grande and Cuernos del Paine, good meals (reservations: *Turismo Pehoé* in Punta Arenas or Antonio Bellet 77, office 605, T 235-0252, F 236-0917, Santiago); **L3** *Hostería Las Torres*, head office Lautaro Navarro 1125, Punta Arenas, T/F 222641, new, modern conveniences, separate restaurant, English spoken at reception, horse-riding, transport from Laguna Amarga ranger station, rec; **L3** *Hostería Lago Grey*, T/F 227528, or Punta Arenas T/F 241042/248167, good food, new, on edge of Lago Grey (reservations through *Arka Patagonia* or *Turismo Runner* in Punta Arenas); **A1** *Hostería Estancia Lazo*, on the E edge of the park, 8 cabins beautifully situated on Laguna Verde with spectacular views, very friendly, comfortable, excellent food, very highly rec (reservations: *Operatur Patagónia SA*, Av Colón 568, T/F 61-221130/240056, Punta Arenas); **A2** pp *Posada Río Serrano*, an old *estancia*, some rooms with bath, some with shared facilities, breakfast extra, nr park administration, with expensive but good restaurant and a shop (reservations advisable: run by *Turismo Río Serrano*, Prat 258, Puerto Natales, T 410684).

Refugios: **F** pp *Refugio Lago Toro*, nr administration centre, run by Conaf, hot showers, cooking facilities, good meeting place, sleeping bag and mattress essential, no camping, open summer only – in the winter months another more basic (free) *refugio* is open nr administration centre. The following are run by Andescape (addresses under Puerto Natales and Santiago): *Refugio Lago Pehoé*, on the NE arm of Lago Pehoé; *Refugio Grey*, on the eastern shore of Lago Grey; *Refugio Lago Dickson*; all **D** pp, modern, closed in winter until 10 Sept, clean, with dormitory accommodation (sheets not provided) hot showers (US$2 for non-residents) cooking and laundry facilities, meals served, kiosk with basic food and other supplies, rental of camping equipment, campsite (US$3 pp). **D** pp *Refugio Las Torres*, is owned by *Hostería Las Torres*, meals served.

In addition there are 6 free *refugios*: Zapata, Pingo, Laguna Verde, Laguna Amarga, Lago Paine and Pudeto. Most have cooking areas (wood stove or fireplace) but Laguna Verde and Pingo do not. These are now in very poor condition and are very crowded in summer (rangers know how many people are on each route and can give you an idea of how busy refugios will be).

Camping: in addition to sites at the Andescape *refugios* there are the following sites: *Camping Serón* and *Camping Las Torres* (at *Hostería Las Torres*) both run by Estancia Cerro Paine, US$4, hot showers; *Camping Los Perros*, run by Andescape, US$3 pp, shop and hot showers; *Camping Lago Pehoé* and *Camping Serrano*, both run by Turismo Río Serrano (address above), US$20/site at former (max 6 persons, hot showers) and US$15/site at latter (max 6 persons, cold showers, more basic); *Camping Laguna Azul*, hot showers, **D**/site. Free camping is permitted in seven other locations in the park: these sites are known as *campamentos*. Fires may only be lit at organized *camping* sites, not a *campamentos*. The *guardaparques* expect people to have a stove if camping. (**NB** These restrictions should be observed as forest fires are a serious hazard.) Beware mice, which eat through tents. Equipment hire in Puerto Natales (see above).

● **Boat trips**
From *Hostería Grey* at the S end of Lago Grey to the Grey Glacier, minimum 8 passengers, US$25 inc refreshments, 2-3 hrs, a stunning trip. From *Refugio Lago Pehoé* to *Refugio Pudeto*, US$12 one way daily, from Pudeto 1030, 1600, from Pehoé 1200, 1530, 1 hr, in high season reserve in advance at the *refugios* at either end or at *Turismo Tzonka* in Puerto Natales. Off-season, radio for the boat from *Refugio Pehoé*.

● **Transport**
Car hire: hiring a pick-up from Budget in Punta Arenas is an economical proposition for a group (up to 9 people): US$415 for 4 days. If driving there yourself, the road from Pto Natales is being improved and, in the Park, the roads are narrow, bendy with blind corners, use your horn a lot; it takes about 3½ hrs from Pto Natales to the administration, 3 to Laguna Amarga. Petrol available at Río Serrano, but fill up in case. **Horse hire**: Baquedano Zamora, Blanco Encalada 226, Puerto Natales, T 411592.

Buses San Cayetano, Servitur and JB Buses (addresses above) run daily bus services to the park from Puerto Natales leaving between 0630 and 0800, returning between 1300 and 1500, 3½ hrs' journey, US$8.75 one way, US$12.50 open return (return tickets are not interchangeable between different companies, buy single ticket), from early Nov to mid April. See also under Punta Arenas **Buses** for the daily In-Tur minibus service from Punta

Arenas. Buses pass *Guardería Laguna Amarga* at 1030, *Guardería Laguna Amarga* at 1130, arriving at Admin at 1230, leave Admin at 1400 (in high season the buses fill quickly so it is best to board at the Administration). All buses wait at *Refugio Pudeto* until the 1430 boat from *Refugio Lago Pehoé* arrives. Travel between two points within the park (eg Pudeto-Laguna Amarga) US$1.25. At other times services by travel agencies are dependent on demand: arrange return date with driver and try to arrange your return date to coincide with other groups to keep costs down. Luis Díaz has been rec, about $12 pp, min 3 persons. A new road to the Park from Puerto Natales has been built to the southern entrance, at Lago Toro, although in March 1996, a bridge over the Río Serrano was still missing.

To go from Torres del Paine to Calafate (Argentina) either return to Pto Natales and go to Río Turbio for bus to La Esperanza, or take a bus or hitch from the park to Villa Cerro Castillo border point (106 km S of the administration), cross to Paso Cancha de Carreras and try to link with the Río Turbio-La Esperanza-Río Gallegos bus schedule, or hitch. (See Accommodation **North of Puerto Natales**, above.)

Tours Several agencies in Puerto Natales including *Servitur, Scott Tours* and *Luis Díaz* offer 1-day tours by minibus, US$37.50 (some travellers report that these are a waste of time as you need to stay overnight to appreciate the park). José Torres of *Sastrería Arbiter* in C Bulnes 731 (T 411637) rec as guide. *Enap* weekend tours in summer cost US$45 including accommodation and meals. *Buses Fernández* offer 2-day tours, US$132 and 3-day tours (which includes trip to the Balmaceda Glacier) US$177. Before booking a tour check carefully on details and get them in writing: increasingly mixed reports of tours. Many companies who claim (you see the Grey Glacier only visit Lago Grey (you see the Grey Glacier in the distance). Taxi costs US$80 per day, run by *Zalej* (Arturo Prat 260), but may be cheaper if you catch him when he's going to the Park anyway. After mid-Mar there is little public transport (ask *San Cayetano*) and trucks are irregular.

Onas Turismo (address under Puerto Natales **Tour companies**) runs trips from the Park down the Río Serrano in dinghies to the Serrano glacier and from there, on the *21 de Mayo* or *Alberto de Agostini* tour boats to Puerto Natales, US$90 pp all inclusive. Book in advance.

TIERRA DEL FUEGO

The largest island off the extreme S of South America, Tierra del Fuego is surrounded by the Magellan Strait to the N, the Atlantic Ocean to the E, the Beagle Channel to the S – which separates it from the southern islands – and by the Whiteside, Gabriel, Magdalena and Cockburn channels etc, which divide it from the islands situated to the W. The western side belongs to Chile and the eastern to Argentina. It produces most of Chile's oil.

History

Until the 1880s the small Chilean colony at Punta Arenas made no effort to settle on Tierra del Fuego, which was inhabited by the Onas. In 1879 Ramón Serrano explored the interior of the island and reported that the land was ideal for cattle and sheep. The following year an expedition led by Jorge Porter discovered gold in the Sierra Boquerón, sparking off a gold rush from Europe and the United States.

The arrival of gold mining and ranching led to the rapid extermination of the Onas.

FERRIES TO TIERRA DEL FUEGO

There are two ferry crossings to Tierra del Fuego.

Punta Arenas to Porvenir The *Melinka*, sails from Tres Puentes (5 km N of Punta Arenas, bus A or E from Av Magallanes, US$1; taxi US$3) at 0930 daily except Mon in season, less frequently off season, 2½ hr crossing (can be rough and cold), US$6 pp, US$5 per bike, US$30 per vehicle. Return from Porvenir 1400 (1700 Sun). Timetable dependent on tides and subject to change: check in advance. Reservations essential especially in summer (at least 24 hrs in advance for cars), obtainable from *Agencia Broom*, Bulnes 05075, T 218100, F 212126. The ferry company accepts no responsibility for damage to vehicles on the crossing.

Punta Delgada to Punta Espora This crossing is via the *Primera Angostura* (First Narrows), 170 km NE of Punta Arenas. There are several crossings a day; schedules vary with the tides. Price US$1 pp (cycles free) and US$14 per car, one way. The ferry takes about 4 trucks and 20 cars; before 1000 most space is taken by trucks. There is no bus service to or from this crossing. If hitching, this route is preferable as there is more traffic.

- **Accommodation** In Punta Delgada: **E** pp *Hotel El Faro*; **C** *Hostería Tehuelche*, T 061-694433 at Kamiri Aike 17 km from port, with restaurant.

PORVENIR

(*Pop* 4,500, several hundred from former Yugoslavia; *Phone code* 061) is the only town in Chilean Tierra del Fuego. There is a small museum, the **Museo Fernando Cordero Rusque**, Samuel Valdivieso 402, with archaeological and photographic displays on the Onas.

- **Accommodation Porvenir: A2** *Los Flamencos*, Tte Merino, T 580049, best; **C** *Central*, Phillippi 298, T 580077, hot water; **C** *Rosas*, Phillippi, T 580088, with bath, hot water, heating, restaurant and bar, rec; **E** pp *Res Colón*, Damián Riobó 198, T 580108, also full board; **C** *España*, Santos Mardones y Croacia, good restaurant with fixed price lunch; *Res Los Cisnes*, Soto Salas 702, T 580227; **E** pp *Res* at Santos Mardones 366 (**D** with full board), clean, friendly, heaters in rooms, hot water, good; many good *pensiones*, D, with full board, but they are often fully occupied by construction workers. **Elsewhere in Chilean Tierra del Fuego**: at Cerro Sombrero, 46 km S of Primera Angostura: **E** pp *Hostería Tunkelen*, rec; **F** *Pensión del Señor Alarcón*, good, friendly; *Posada Las Flores*, Km 127 on the road to San Sebastián, reservations via *Hostal de la Patagonia* in Punta Arenas; *Refugio Lago Blanco*, on Lago Blanco, T Punta Arenas 241197. For accommodation at San Sebastián see below.

- **Places to eat** *Croacia Club* does wholesome and reasonable lunch (about US$5), also *Restaurante Puerto Montt*, Croacia 1169, for seafood, rec. Many lobster fishing camps where fishermen will prepare lobster on the spot.

● **Banks & money changers** At *Estrella del Sur* shop, Santos Mardones.

● **Transport Air** From Punta Arenas – weather and bookings permitting, Aerovías DAP, Oficina Foretic, T 80089, Porvenir, fly daily except Sun at 0815 and 1730 to Porvenir, return at 1000 and 1930, US$20. Heavily booked so make sure you have your return reservation confirmed. **Buses On Tierra del Fuego** 2 a week between Porvenir and Río Grande (Argentina), Tues and Sat 1400, 5 hrs, Transportes Gessell, Duble Almeyda 257, T 580488, US$20 heavily booked, buy ticket in advance, or phone; Río Grande-Porvenir, Wed and Sun 0800. **Ferries** Terminal at Bahía Chilota, 7 km W, see above for details. From bus terminal to ferry, taxi US$6, bus (if running) US$1.50. **Motorists** All roads are gravel. Fuel is available in Porvenir, Cerro Sombrero and Cullen. **Hitchhiking** Police may help with lifts on trucks from Porvenir to Río Grande; elsewhere is difficult as there is so little traffic.

Cameron, 149 km SE of Porvenir on the opposite shore of Bahía Inútil, can be reached by bus from C Manuel Señor, Porvenir, Mon and Fri, 1700, US$10; from here a road runs SE to Estancia Vicuña. East of Vicuña is Lago Blanco, surrounded by trees, good fishing; in the centre of the lake is Isla Victoria, with accommodation (see above). Beyond Vicuña a horse trail leads across the Darwin Range to Yendegaia. From there you will have to retrace your steps as it seems impossible to get permission to cross the unmanned border to Ushuaia or to get a Chilean exit stamp.

FRONTIER WITH ARGENTINA: SAN SEBASTIAN

The only legal frontier crossing between the Chilean and Argentine parts of Tierra del Fuego is 142 km E of Porvenir. On the Argentine side the road continues to Río Grande.

NB There are two settlements called San Sebastián, one on each side of the frontier but they are 14 km apart; taxis are not allowed to cross.

An early map of Tierra del Fuego with, underneath, a portrait of Magellan and the *Victoria*, one of the ships in Magellan's flotilla.

NB Argentine time is 1 hr ahead of Chilean time, March-October.

● **Entering Chile**
No fruit, vegetables, dairy produce or meat permitted.

● **Accommodation**
E pp *Hostería de la Frontera*, in the annex which is 1 km away from the more expensive main building.

● **Transport**
Minibus from Porvenir to San Sebastián, US$14. For transport between Porvenir and Río Grande, see above.

ARGENTINE TIERRA DEL FUEGO

Río Grande (*Pop* 35,000) is 97 km SE of San Sebastián. It has several hotels and places to eat, a tourist office at the Municipalidad (closed at weekends), banks, and air services to Buenos Aires, Río Gallegos and Ushuaia (also buses). This port is in windy, dust-laden sheep-grazing and oil-bearing plains.

USHUAIA

The most southerly town in Argentina, and among the most expensive, **Ushuaia** (*Pop* 50,000; *Phone code* 0901) is 236 km SW of Río Grande by a new road via Paso Garibaldi. Its steep streets overlook the green waters of the Beagle Channel, named after the ship in which Darwin sailed the Channel in 1832, on Captain Fitzroy's second expedition. The people are engaged in timber cutting, fishing and, nowadays, in the electronics industry. The tourist industry is also expanding rapidly.

Places of interest

The old prison, **Presidio**, at the back of the Naval Base can be visited, interesting: tours start from the Museum daily 1600-2300, US$3 (not including tip for guide). There are impressive views of the snow-clad peaks, rivers, waterfalls and dense woods. There is a naval station at **Isla Redonda**. Ushuaia and its environs are worth a 2-3 day visit.

Museums

Museo Territorial, Maipú y Rivadavia, T 21863, open Mon-Sat 1600-2000, US$2, small but interesting display of early photos and artefacts of the local Indian tribes; relics from the missionaries and first settlers, etc. Known as the 'museum at the end of the world' (you can get a stamp in your passport). Highly rec. The building also contains an excellent library with helpful staff, a good bookshop with books in English, and post office, open afternoons when the main one is closed.

Excursions

To the **Cerro Martial** and the glacier (itself unspectacular but fine views down the Beagle Channel and to the N) about 7 km behind the town; to reach the chairlift (US$5) follow Magallanes out of town, allow 1½ hrs, or take Turismo Pasarela minibus, several departures daily in summer, US$5 return. The glacier is a 3-hr walk from town. In winter the Cerro is inaccessible, even on foot.

Other excursions include: to the **Río Olivia** falls; to **Lagos Fagnano** and **Escondido** (tours depart 0930, 5-6 hrs, US$5; Los Carlos bus to Lago Fagnano, 2½ hrs, US$10, then from Lake to Río Grande 2 hrs, US$11). A bus runs to **Puerto Almanza** on the Beagle Channel, 75 km, 4-5 hrs, US$18.

The Estancia **Harberton**, the oldest on the island, now run by descendents of a British missionary, Mr Bridges, offers guided walks through protected forest (not Mon) and tea, in Manacatush *confitería* (T 22742). You can camp. It can be reached by rented car from Ushuaia and by boat. By car, leave Ushuaia on Route 3, after 40 km fork right on Route J, passing Lago Victoria, then 25 km through forest before the open country around Harberton (85 km in all). Some parts of the road are bad; tiring driving, 5 hrs there and back. Agency tours by land cost US$30 plus US$6 entrance; take your own food if not wishing to buy

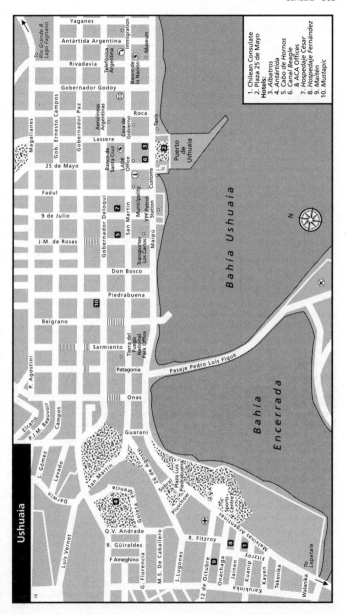

Ushuaia

1. Chilean Consulate
2. Plaza 25 de Mayo

Hotels:
3. Albatros
4. Antártida
5. Cabo de Hornos
6. Canal Beagle & ACA Offices
7. Hospedaje César
8. Hospedaje Fernández
9. Maitén
10. Mustapic

meals at the Estancia. Tours to the Estancia and to the penguin colony by boat and bus, Mon, Tues, Fri, Sun, US$72 plus US$6 entrance, 12 hrs, from all agents, take own food (the sea can be very rough). Some tour agencies in Ushuaia imply that their excursions go to the Estancia though in fact they only go to the bay; others go by inflatable launch from main boat to shore. Check thoroughly in advance.

Sea Trips

Rumbo Sur does a whole-day trip by catamaran down the Beagle Channel to see wildlife, with return by bus, highly rec (see below under **Travel Agents**). Similar tours operated by Aventura Travel, US$70. *Tres Marías* is a fishing boat, tours are 4 hrs, twice a day, maximum 8 passengers, snack included, through agencies Antartur, All Patagonia, Caminante. In summer, chartered trips may be taken to see the sealions on Isla de Los Lobos, 4-5 hrs, or by catamaran, dep 0930, 1430, 2½ hrs. Ask at Rumbo Sur; the *Ana B* leaves 0930 and 1430 daily, English and Spanish-speaking guide. Catamaran trips cost US$40-60 depending on duration. Take food and drinks on all these trips as those sold on board are expensive.

Local festivals

12 Oct: *Founding of Ushuaia*.

Local information

NB Prices double on Dec 12 and accommodation may occasionally be hard to find Dec-Mar – the tourist office will help with rooms in private homes and with campsites. Hotel prices are higher than on the mainland. It is best not to drink tap water in Ushuaia.

● Accommodation

L3 *Canal Beagle*, Maipú 590, T 21117, restaurant (catering usually for tour groups), overpriced; **L3** *Tolkeyen*, at Estancia Río Pipo 5 km from town, T 22637, with rec restaurant Tolkeyen, 100m (see below); **L3** *Albatros*, Maipú 505, T 33466, F 30636, clean, modern, inc breakfast, but rooms a bit cold; **L3** *Las Lengas*, Florencia 1722, T 23366, superb setting, heating, good dining room.

A2 *Malvinas*, Deloqui 615, T 22626, with bath, inc breakfast, pleasant, helpful, central heating, rec; **A2** *Antártida*, San Martín 1600, T 21896, friendly, restaurant with fine views, rec; **A2** *Cabo de Hornos*, San Martín y Rosas, T 22187, F 22313, comfortable, often full, TV, spotless, good value, restaurant not open to non-residents; **A2** *César*, San Martín 753, T 21460, F 32721, with bath, comfortable, often full (book in advance), friendly, clean, inc breakfast, rec; **A3** *Fernández*, Onachaga y Fitzroy, T 21192, very friendly, hot water, good but expensive meals, cheaper in bunk-bed accommodation (dank and dirty); **A3** *Maitén*, 12 de Octubre 140, T 22745, good value, clean, but 2 km from centre, 10% discount for ISIC and youth card holders; **A3** *Monte Cervantes*, San Martín y Sarmiento, T 30600, rec; **A3** *Mustapic*, Piedrabuena 230, T 21718, multi-lingual owner (Sr Miro, from Croatia, his daughter runs travel agency next door, T 23557, rec), 10% discount for ISIC card holders, no singles, highly rec, exceptionally clean, can leave luggage, rooftop restaurant for breakfast; **A3** *Posada Fin del Mundo*, Valdez 281, T 22530, family atmosphere, rec; **A3** *Hosp Turístico*, Deloqui 271, T 21316, with private bath, very clean, friendly, parking, TV, kitchen, English spoken, rec.

B *Garbin-Casalaga*, Gob Paz 1380, clean, comfortable, friendly, heating, good breakfast, no sign, rec; **B** *Hostal Julio Linares*, Deloqui 1522, nr airport, new, clean good value; **B** *Hosp María Cristina Navarrete*, 25 de Mayo 440, T 23068, clean, friendly, cooking facilities; **B** *Familia Cárdenas*, 25 de Mayo 345, T 21954, nr top of hill, rec; **B** *Sra Marta Loncharich*, Magallanes 229, T 24150, shared bathroom, good food and comfort, clean, but overpriced.

D pp *Alojamiento Internacional*, Deloqui 395, 1st floor, T 23483/23622, spartan, scruffy, friendly, dormitory, take sleeping bag, no security, good meeting place, changes money; **C** pp *María Guercio*, Kuanip 67, T 22234, also large chalet outside town to let; **D** pp *Hosp Torres al Sur*, Gob Paz 1437, T 30745, heating, clean, hot water, kitchen facilities; **C** rooms, at home of Ismael Vargas, Kayen 394 (T 21125) 15 mins from centre, clean, doubles only, Sra Vargas speaks English.

Accommodation in private homes (all **B-C**): *Familia Beltrame*, Gob Valdez 311, T 22819, rec; *Familia Galeazzi*, Gob Valdez 323, T 23213, speak English and French, rec; *Familia Velásquez*, Fadul 361, T 21719, dormitory accommodation, clean, warm, helpful, not enough showers, skimpy breakfast, can leave luggage when hiking. *Zulema R Saltzmann*, Roca 392 (esq Campos), **C** pp, clean and friendly; *Sr Ueno*, 12 de Octubre 432, T 24661, full board US$10 pp, rec. *La Fiaka*, Deloqui 641, T 22669, **C** pp, clean, warm, cooking facilities, rec.

There is no YHA in Ushuaia. Hostel for sporting groups only at Sports Complex. Many people go to the airport to offer rooms in private houses, in our **E** pp range (minimum).

At Lago Escondido: **B** *El Petrel Inn*, 54 km from Ushuaia after a spectacular climb through Garibaldi Pass, on the road to Río Grande (bus dep 0900, returns 1500, US$17 return, minimum 4 people), T 24390, trout fishing possible, boat rides, friendly staff.

At Lago Fagnano: **C** *Hostería El Kaiken*, T 0964-24427 (ACA) also bungalows, nice site, well-run facilities, cheap drinks, on a promontory 93 km from Ushuaia, has real bath.

Facilities at *Kaiken* and *Petrel* are open all year round. These inns are rec for peace and quiet.

Camping: none in town. East of Ushuaia are: *Ushuaia Rugby Club Camping* (Km 3) US$4-5/tent, restaurant and good facilities; *Ushuaia Camping Municipal* (Km 8) free; *Camping Río Tristen*, in the Haruwen Winter Sports complex (Km 19), T/F 24058, US$5/tent, electricity, bar, restaurant. Inside the Parque Nacional Tierra del Fuego (entry fee US$5) are 3 free sites: *Camping Río Pipo*, 10 km from Ushuaia, no facilities; *Ensenada Camping*, 15 km from Ushuaia, no facilities; *Camping Lago Roca*, 18 km from Ushuaia, at Lapataia, by forested shore of Lago Roca, with good facilities, dirty, showers (US$3), noisy, reached by bus Jan-Feb, small shop, cafeteria.

● **Places to eat**
Tía Elvira, Maipú 349, very popular, make advance booking, good seafood; *Asturias*, Rosas 45, pleasant, reasonable, open 1200-1500, 2030-2300; *Barcleit 1912*, Fadul 148, cordon bleu cooking at reasonable prices; *Kaupé*, Roca 470, English spoken, excellent food and wine, rec, expensive. Best place to eat lamb is at *Tolkeyen*, Estancia Río Pipo, 5 km from town, meal US$15, taxi US$7; *El Viejo Marino*, Maipú 229, nice ambience; *Mi Viejo*, Campos 758, good *parrillada* and buffet, highly rec; *Pizzería Ideal*, San Martín 393, good, cheap, *tenedor libre* US$13, very popular with travellers, 10% discount for ISIC card holders; *Los Amigos*, San Martín 130, quick service, some cheap dishes; *Volver*, Maipú 37, interesting decor, good food and service, not cheap; *El Aborigen*, Antártida Argentina 75, inexpensive; *Quick*, San Martín 130, clean, good service, rec, 10% discount for ISIC card holders; also *Split*, Piedrabuena 238, pizzería, offers same discount, cheap; *Turco*, San Martín between Onas y Patagonia, cheap, popular with locals. *Café de la Esquina*, San Martín y 25 de Mayo, rec; *Der Garten*, confitería, San Martín 638, in Galería shopping arcade. Excellent homemade chocolate sold at a shop at San Martín 785. *Helados Massera*, San Martín 270-72, good. The coffee bar at the airport is very expensive. Ask around for currently available *centolla* (king crab) and *cholga* (giant mussels). Food and drink (apart from the duty-free items) in Ushuaia are very expensive.

● **Airline offices**
LADE, Av San Martín 542, T 21123, airport T 21700; **Austral**, Barberis agency, Av San Martín 638, T 23235; **Aerolíneas Argentinas**, Roca 160, T 21218, airport 21265; **LAPA**, Av Malvinas Argentinas 120, T/F 22150/22637; **Kaiken**, San Martín 857, T 23663, or at airport, T 22620/23049; **DAP**, Agencia Akawala, 25 de Mayo 64.

● **Banks & money changers**
Banks open 1000-1500 (in summer). Useful to have credit cards here as difficult to change cheques and very high commission (up to 10% reported), but **Banco del Sud**, Maipú 600 block, only place for changing TCs (downstairs).Cash advance on Mastercard at **Banco de Tierra del Fuego**, San Martín 1044. Tourist agencies and the *Hotel Albatros* also give poor rates. *Listus* record shop, San Martín 973, sweet shop next door, or *Caminante* travel agency for better rates for cash.

● **Embassies & consulates**
Chile, Malvinas Argentinas y Jainen, Casilla 21, T 21279; **Finland**, Paz y Deloqui; **Germany**, Rosas 516; **Italy**, Yaganes 75.

● **Entertainment**
A popular spot at night is the disco *Extasis* at 9 de Julio y Maipú; another disco is *Barny's*, Antártida Argentina just off San Martín. *Café Latino*, Deloqui y Rivadavia, bar with live music (Argentine and contemporary), in summer gets going around 0200, great atmosphere, high standard.

● **Laundry**
Rosas 139, between San Martín and Deloqui, open weekdays 0900-2100, US$8.

● **Post & telecommunications**
Post Office: San Martín y Godoy, Mon-Fri 0900-1300 and 1700-2000, Sat 0830-1200.

Telephones: and fax on Roca next to Aerolíneas Argentinas.

● **Shopping**
Good boots at *Stella Maris*, San Martín 443. Bookshop at San Martín y 9 de Julio (Lapataia Arcade). Film is cheaper in Chile. Supermarkets: *Surty Sur* (with clean toilets, San Martín y Onas) and *Sucoop*, Paz 1600. Most things are more expensive than elsewhere but some cheap imported goods, eg electrical equipment and cigarettes.

● **Sports**
Sports Centre on Malvinas Argentinas on W side of town (close to seafront). Ice skating rink at Ushuaia gymnasium in winter (when lagoon is frozen). Beachcombing can produce whale bones.

Fishing: trout, contact Asociación de Caza y Pesca at Maipú y 9 de Julio, with small museum. Fishermen may be interested in visiting the fish hatchery 7 km E of Ushuaia, visiting hours daily 1400-1700. There are brook, rainbow and brown trout and land-locked salmon. Take No 1 bus east-bound on Maipú to the end of the line and continue 2 1/2 km on foot to the hatchery. Birdwatchers will also find this ride rewarding.

Skiing, hiking, climbing: contact Club Andino, Solís 50, or *Caminante*. **Skiing**: A downhill ski run (beginner standard) on Cerro Martial. There is another ski run, Wallner, 3 km from Ushuaia, open June-Aug, has lights for night-skiing and is run by Club Andino. The area is excellent for cross country skiing; *Caminante* organizes excursions 'off road'. 20 km E of Ushuaia is Valle Tierra Mayoria, a large flat valley with high standard facilities for cross country skiing, snow shoeing and snowmobiling; rentals and a cafeteria; bus am and 1400 from *Antartur*, San Martín 638. The Haruwen Winter Sports complex is 21 km E on Route 3.

● **Tour companies & travel agents**
All agencies charge the same fees for excursions; with 3 or 4 people it is often little more expensive to hire a *remise* taxi. *Rumbo Sur*, San Martín 342, T 21139, runs a range of tours on water and on land and offers a 2-day

package to Cafayate, US$150 inc transport and hotel, good value. Also organizes bus to ski slope, very helpful; *Antartur*, San Martín 638, T 23240; *All Patagonia*, 25 de Mayo 31, of A, T 24432, F 30707, Amex agent; *Onas Tours*, 25 de Mayo 50, T 23429, just off main street, very friendly; *Aventura Austral*, Maipú 237, catamaran trip to Estancia Harberton, highly rec. *Tolkeyen*, 12 de Octubre 150, T 22237, rec; *Caminante*, Don Bosco 319, T 32723, F 31040, organizes walking, climbing tours and horse riding to suit all levels of experience, provides food, tents, equipment, outdoor clothing, detailed map, very friendly and helpful, English and German spoken, highly rec; *Kilak*, Kuanip 67, T 22234, for horse-riding tours. Recommended guide: Domingo Galussio, Intervú 15, Casa 211, 9410 Ushuaia, bilingual, not cheap (US$120), rec.

● **Tourist offices**
San Martín 660, T/F (0901) 24550, 'best in Argentina', literature in English, German and Dutch, helpful, English spoken. Large chart of hotels and prices and information on travel and staying at Estancia Harberton. Has noticeboard for messages. Open Mon-Fri 0830-2030, Sat and Sun 0900-2000. **National Park Office**, on San Martín between Patagonia y Sarmiento, has small map but not much information. The **ACA** office on Maipú also has maps and information.

● **Transport**
Local Car hire: Tagle, San Martín y Belgrano, T 22744, good, also *Río Grande*, Elcano 799, T 22571, and *Localiza*, in *Hotel Albatros* and at airport, rec, T 30663.

Air The airport was upgraded in late 1995. Taxi to airport, US$3, or 30 mins' walk (no bus). Services are more frequent in high season; in winter weather often impedes flights. In the summer tourist season it is sometimes difficult to get a flight out. Aerolíneas Argentinas (AR) and LAPA to Buenos Aires via Río Gallegos and/or Trelew, all year round, over 4 1/2 hrs. To Río Grande, AR and Kaiken. To Río Gallegos, LADE once a week, Kaiken, LAPA and AR. Kaiken daily to Calafate. LADE to Comodoro Rivadavia via Río Grande, Río Gallegos, Calafate/Lago Argentino, Gob Gregores and Perito Moreno on Thur (to Calafate only in summer). To Punta Arenas, Aerovías DAP twice a week.
   At the airport ask around for a pilot willing to take you on a 30 mins flight around Ushuaia, US$38 pp (best to go in pm when wind has dropped). Alternatively ask about flights at the

tourist office in town. Aerial excursions over the Beagle Channel with local flying club, hangar at airport, 3-5 seater planes, 30 mins: Lago Fagnano, Lapataia and Ushuaia Bay.

Trains A Decauville gauge train for tourists runs along the shore of the Beagle Channel between the Fin del Mundo station in Ushuaia to the boundary of the Tierra del Fuego National Park, 4.5 km, 3 departures daily, US$15 (tourist), US$27 (first class), plus US$5 park entrance and US$3 for bus to the station; it is planned to continue to Lapataia. Run by Ferrocarril Austral Fueguino with new locomotives and carriages, it uses track first laid by prisoners to carry wood to Ushuaia; tickets from Tranex kiosk in the port, T 30709. Sit on left outbound.

Buses Run daily between Ushuaia and Río Grande 4 hrs, times vary, US$21, Transportes Los Carlos, Rosas 85, T 22337, and Tecni Austral (summer only), San Martín 657, T 21945. There is a twice-weekly service to Punta Arenas on Mon and Fri, dep 0300 with Transportes Los Carlos, 14 hrs, US$58, a comfortable and interesting ride via Punta Delgada. Trucks leave Ushuaia for the refinery at San Sebastián Mon-Fri, but hitching is very difficult (easier via Bahía Azul and Punta Delgada where there is more traffic). A good place to hitch is from police control on Route 3.

PARQUE NACIONAL TIERRA DEL FUEGO

12 km W is the entrance to the park, which stretches to the Chilean frontier. At Km 30 from Ushuaia is **Lapataia Bay**. US$5 National Park fee (free before 31 Oct).

In winter the temperature drops to as low as -12°C, in summer it goes up to 25°C. Even in the summer the climate can often be cold, damp and unpredictable.

Beaver inhabit the Parque Nacional near the Chilean border; one may see beaver dams and with much luck and patience the beavers themselves. Stand still and down-wind of them: their sense of smell and hearing are good, but not their eyesight. There are many beautiful walks. No maps of the Park are available and hiking can be interrupted by the

Chilean border. Good climbing on Cerro Cóndor, rec. It is reported that most of the park has been closed off to preserve nature.

● **Access** Minibus to National Park from Turismo Pasarela, Fadul 40, T 21735, US$5 one way, 4 times a day from YPF service station (Maipú y Fadul, first at 1000, last back 2000 from Lago Roca in the Park). In summer Caminante run minibuses to the National Park, departing from Don Bosco 319, 2 or 3 a day, US$15 return. A similar service is operated by two other agencies. Caminante also runs a 1 day excursion to the Parque Nacional, including trek, canoeing, *asado* lunch, US$70 inclusive (small groups, book early). Ask at the tourist office about cycling tours in the park, US$65 full day, also 'Eco Treks' available and cultural events. It is possible to hitchhike, as far as Lapataia. A ranger truck leaves Ushuaia every weekday at 1300 and picks up hitchhikers.

● **Accommodation** See above for **Camping** possibilities. Rangers in the park are friendly and will sometimes put people up for a couple of days (as will police) and help with places to visit.

Argentina apparently has plans for tourist developments in **Antarctica** (accommodation at Marambio and Esperanza stations). Flights can be arranged in Buenos Aires in Jan-Feb through Surexpress, Esmeralda 629, 4th floor, T 325-0252. The plane goes to Ushuaia and you take a boat from there. Also try Andy Macfarlane at Macren Travel, T 322-7988. Complete trips for US$6,000-8,000 for 11 days can be booked at Corrientes 536, 10th floor, T 394-5399. The National Institute of the Antarctic is at Cerrito 1248, T 816-6313/1689, 0900-1500.

PUERTO WILLIAMS

(*Pop* 1,500; *Phone code* 061) is a Chilean naval base on **Isla Navarino**, S of the Beagle Channel. Situated about 50 km E of Ushuaia (Argentina) at 54° 55' 41" S, 67° 37' 58" W, Puerto Williams is the most southerly place in the world with a permanent population. It is small, friendly and remote (it suffered a serious fire in 1994). The island is totally unspoilt and beautiful, with a chain of rugged snowy peaks, magnificent woods and many animals, including large numbers of beaver which were introduced to the island and have done a lot of damage.

Excursions

Sights include beaver dams, cascades, the Villa Ukika, 2 km E of town, the place where the last descendants of the Yaganes people live, and the local *media luna* where rodeos are held. For superb views, climb Cerro Bandera (3-4 hrs round trip, steep, take warm clothes). No equipment rental on island; buy food in Punta Arenas.

Museums

Museo Martín Gusinde, known as the *Museo del Fin del Mundo* ('End of the World Museum') is full of information about vanished Indian tribes, local wildlife, and voyages including Charles Darwin and Fitzroy of the *Beagle*, a 'must'. Open 1000-1300, 1500-1800 (Mon-Thur); 1500-1800 (Sat-Sun), Friday closed (subject to change). Admission US$1.

Local information
● Accommodation
A3 *Hostería Walla*, on the edge of Lauta bay, T 223571, 2 km out of town (splendid walks), very hospitable, good food; **E** pp *Res Onashaga* (run by Señor Ortiz – everyone knows him), cold, run down, good meals, helpful, full board available; **D** pp *Pensión Temuco*, Piloto Pardo 224, also half board, comfortable, hospitable, good food, hot showers, rec; you can also stay at private houses. You can camp nr the *Hostería*: collect drinking water from the kitchen. Aeropetrel will charter a plane, if a sufficiently numerous party is raised, to Cape Horn (US$2,600 for 8-10 people).

● Airline offices
Aerovías DAP, LanChile, Ladeco in the centre of town.

● Post & telecommunications
Post Office: closes 1900

Telephone: CTC, Mon-Sat 0930-2230, Sun 1000-1300, 1600-2200). **Telex**.

● Tourist offices
Near the museum (Closed in winter). Ask for details on hiking. Maps available.

● Transport
Air From Punta Arenas by air, Aerovías DAP (details under Punta Arenas) on Mon and Fri 1400, Wed 0830, return Mon and Fri 1800, Wed 1000, US$64 single. Book well in advance; 20 seater aircraft and long waiting lists (be persistent). The flight is beautiful, with superb views of Tierra del Fuego, the Cordillera Darwin, the Beagle Channel, and the islands stretching S to Cape Horn. Also army flights available (they are cheaper), but the ticket has to be bought through DAP.

Ferries From Ushuaia (Argentina), the *Tres Marías*, once a week in summer, 3-4 hrs crossing, US$65 pp, take own lunch; irregular service in winter, and frequent schedule changes.

Boats from Punta Arenas: *Ñandú* or *Ultragas* leaves on a fixed schedule every 10 days, about midnight, arrives 1700 each way, reclining chairs, no food, US$45 one way. Enquire at the office, Independencia 865, next to service station. The *Navarino* leaves Punta Arenas in 3rd week of every month, 12 passengers, US$150 pp one way; contact the owner, Carlos Aguilera, 21 de Mayo 1460, Punta Arenas, T 228066, F 248848 or via *Turismo Pehoé*. The *Beaulieu*, a cargo boat carrying a few passengers, sails from Punta Arenas once a month, US$300 return, 6 days. Juanita Cofre, Boliviana 533, Punta Arenas, frequently rec as knowledgeable and helpful in arranging transport to Puerto Williams. Navy and port authorities in Puerto Williams may deny any knowledge, but everyone else knows when a boat is due.

Boat trips: ask at the yacht club on the off chance of hitching a ride on a private yacht. Luxury cruises around Cape Horn are run by *Tierra Austral* for US$800, 6 days. Captain Ben Garrett offers recommended adventure sailing in his schooner *Victory*, from special trips to Ushuaia to cruises in the canals, Cape Horn, glaciers, Puerto Montt, Antarctica in Dec and January. Write to Victory Cruises, Puerto Williams (slow mail service); Fax No 1, Cable 3, Puerto Williams; phone (call collect) asking for Punta Arenas (Annex No 1 Puerto Williams) and leave message with the Puerto Williams operator.

Falkland Islands/ Islas Malvinas

T HE FALKLAND Islands/Islas Malvinas comprise about 420 islands in two groups: East Falkland (Isla Soledad) with its adjacent islands, about 2,600 km^2; and West Falkland (Gran Malvina), with its islands, about 2,100 square miles. Approximately 480 miles NE of Cape Horn, the Islands lie between latitudes 51° and 53° S and between longitudes 57° and 62° W. Nearly all land combat during the 1982 war was confined to the northern half of East Falkland; its southern peninsula of Lafonia, and West Falkland were little affected. According to the 1991 census, slightly less than two-thirds of the 2,050 residents are Falklands-born; another quarter were born in the United Kingdom. Slightly more than a quarter live and work on sheep farms. During the past decade, land reform through sale and subdivision of traditional large stations has resulted in more broadly based local ownership of pastoral land.

In accordance with the practice suggested by the UN, we are calling the Islands by both their English and Spanish names.

THE LAND

CLIMATE

Although the *Sunday Express* once referred to a mutton freezer in the Falklands as a 'Colonial Development project

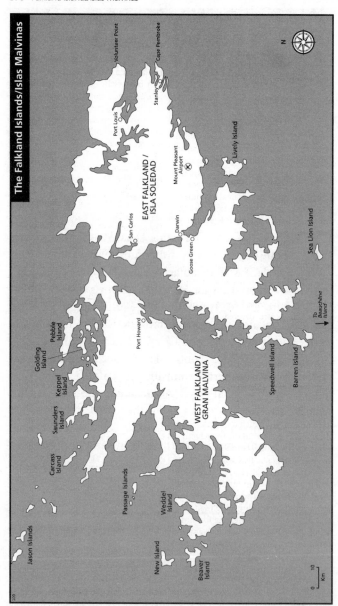

The Falkland Islands/Islas Malvinas

near the South Pole' (8 March 1953), the Islands are in the same latitude S as London is N. The climate is cool and oceanic, dominated by persistent westerly winds which average 16 knots. Long periods of calm are rare except in winter. Though not always inclement, weather is very changeable but temperatures vary relatively little. At Stanley the mean month temperature in summer (Jan/Feb) is 10°C and in winter (June/July) 7°C. Stanley's annual rainfall of about 630mm is slightly higher than London's. In the drier camp, outside Stanley, summer drought sometimes threatens local water supplies. Snowfall is rare although a dusting may occur at any time of the year. Spring, autumn and winter clothing, as used in the United Kingdom, is suitable.

FLORA AND FAUNA

The main islands are covered by acidic peaty soil of low fertility, though at higher elevations (over 500m) the peat gives way to stony and clay soils. Large areas of the major islands are covered by oceanic heathlands, consisting of White Grass, dwarf shrubs, Mountain Berry and Christmas Bush. These heathlands support little fauna, but where they are crossed by small streams the valleys are covered by rich grasslands which attract several species, among them Upland and Ruddy Headed Geese.

Tussock grass, which was common on the larger islands until the introduction of livestock farming, covers about 270 of the smaller islands. Tussock grass, which grows to 3m in height and has leaves up to 2m long, thrives in marine environments subject to sea spray and moisture laden atmospheres with a high salt content. It provides ideal nesting for birds: 46 of the 62 species which regularly breed on the islands use tussock grass as a nesting or feeding habitat.

There are few trees on the islands and only where these have been introduced and carefully cultivated at settlements such as Hill Cove.

EARLY HISTORY

Records of early voyages are ambiguous, but Dutchman Sebald de Weert made the first universally acknowledged sighting in 1598. The Englishman Strong landed in 1690 and named the Falkland Sound for a British peer; this name was later applied to the entire group. The Islands acquired their French appellation, Iles Malouines, from 17th century seafarers from the channel port of St Malo. This in turn became the Spanish Islas Malvinas.

In 1764 France established a small colony of Acadians at Port Louis under Bougainville. 2 years later France sold the settlement to Spain, under which it became a military garrison and penal colony. At about the same time as France, Britain had built an outpost at Saunders Island, West Falkland, whose occupants Spain discovered and expelled in 1770. Restored in the following year after threat of war, the post was abandoned in 1774.

Deserted by Spain in 1811, during the South American wars of independence, the Islands lacked formal authority until 1820, when the United Provinces of the River Plate (later part of Argentina) raised their flag at Port Louis (Soledad). In 1831, a United States warship destroyed a promising colonization project under the auspices of a German-born merchant from Buenos Aires, who had arrested and imprisoned United States sealers operating in the area. After British warships expelled a token Buenos Aires force in 1833, the Islands experienced nearly 150 years of stability until April 1982, when Argentina invaded and occupied. Britain's counter-invasion recaptured the Islands by June of that year.

Since the declaration of a 150 nautical mile fisheries protection zone in 1986, the economy has been transformed.

License fees from Asian, South American and European fleets exploiting the Islands' squid, hake, and whiting have quadrupled Government revenue, to about £25 million a year. Revenues began to fall in 1993 following Argentina issuing cut-price fishing licences in neighbouring waters and the Falkland Islands Government lowering the price of its own licences. Much of the revenue is being used to fund overdue improvement in education and infrastructure, as well as social expenditures for increased pensions. A new telephone system has been installed and a community school has been built. The housing stock has doubled since the 1982 war, roads have been improved and there are many more vehicles in use. A new swimming pool has been constructed in Stanley.

Most of the camp, as the countryside is known locally, is devoted to sheep grazing. There are some 600,000 sheep, all of whose wool is exported to the United Kingdom.

ADMINISTRATION

The Islands' Constitution provides for a Governor, appointed from London, an Executive Council composed of appointed and elected members, and an elected Legislative Council.

EDUCATION

A Junior and Senior Community School in Stanley cater to the needs of town children and rural children who board in the School Hostel. Instruction to GCSE Level is available locally (compulsory to the age of 16), but higher education requires overseas travel, usually to Britain. Rural children receive attention from settlement instructors or travelling teachers. Radio is used to keep in contact with the more isolated farms.

STANLEY

The capital, Stanley, on East Falkland, is the major population centre. Its 1,557 residents live mostly in brightly-painted houses, many of which have corrugated iron roofs. Port Stanley, surrounded by rolling moorland, resembles parts of the Hebrides. The outer harbour of Port William is larger but less protected. East Cove, 30 miles SE of the capital, is the principal port for the new military installations at Mount Pleasant.

Places of interest and events

The Museum at Britannia House, Ross Road West, merits a visit (Tues-Fri, 1030-1200, 1400-1600, also Wed, 1800-2000, Sun, 1000-1200). Mr John Smith, the curator, is knowledgeable on the Islands' maritime history. Government House, the Anglican Cathedral (most southerly in the world, built in 1890), and monuments commemorating the naval battle of 1914 and the 1982 liberation are also worth seeing. During the December holidays, the annual sports meeting at the race course attracts visitors from all over the Islands. The equally popular West and East Falkland sports, at the end of the shearing season in February or March, rotate among various settlements.

Local information

● Accommodation & places to eat

Upland Goose Hotel, Ross Road, T 21455, F 21520, from £49.50 bed and breakfast, to £72.50 d full board, evening meal £14.95; *Emma's Guest House*, Ross Road, T 21056, F 21573, from £30.50 bed and breakfast; *Malvina House Hotel*, 3 Ross Road, T 21355, F 21357, from £47.50 bed and breakfast. Prices subject to change. Full meals at all three, with reservations rec at *Upland Goose* and *Malvina* (restaurant is smart with good food, book 36 hrs in advance). *Warrah Guest House*, John Street, T 21252, from £25 bed and breakfast. Fish and chips and pizza at *Woodbine Cafe*, 29 Fitzroy Road, T 21102, closed Sun and Mon. *Monty's/Deano's* bistro, bar snacks on John Street, inc vegetarian menu; *Boathouse Café*, Ross Road, Mon-Fri 0930-1600; *Clayton's Bakery*, T 21273, Mon-Sat, 0730-1230; *Stanley Bakery*, T 22692, Mon-Fri, 0830-1530, Sat 0900-1230; *R'lett's Café*, Philomel Hill, open daily except Wed, 0900-2200.

On Sea Lion Island: *Sea Lion Lodge*,

T 32004, £50 full board. **At Port Howard:** *Port Howard Lodge*, T 42150, £49 full board. **On Pebble Island:** *Pebble Island Hotel*, T 41097, £47.50 full board. Each lodge has a long wheelbase Land Rover for transport to the airstrip and points of interest nearby. The comfortable tourist lodges at Sea Lion Island, the most southerly inhabited island of the group (35 mins flight fom Port Stanley), and Pebble Island (40 mins flight) are good bases to view wildlife. Also on Pebble Island *Marble Mountain Shanty*, at NW of the island, T 41098, Mr R Evans, self-catering, £15/night and room for up to 4. It is 12 miles from the rest of the population so is peaceful with plenty of wildlife (3 types of penguin within ½ hr walk). Bring food and bedding, all else provided. Scenic Port Howard's lodge on West Falkland, offers excellent trout fishing, a small but interesting war museum, and an opportunity to see the operations of a traditional large sheep station. *Blue Beach Lodge*, **San Carlos**, East Falkland, £49 full board. *Carcass Island Cottages*, Mr and Mrs McGill, Ross Road East, T 41106, £25/night/cottage, both on West Falkland. Further self-catering at Fox Bay Village and Fox Bay West, prices from £7.50 pp/night to £25/group/night. Also *Salvador* (Gibraltar Station, East Falkland, T 31199/31193, F 31194), £10/night (adult), £5/night (child).

Camping is not encouraged on the islands; there is a very real risk of fire and of disturbance to wildlife.

● **Services**

Stanley has an excellent new civilian-military hospital, replacing the one damaged by fire early in 1984. Dental services are also available. Post Office, Philatelic Bureau, library and some other Government services are in Town Hall, Ross Road. Other Government offices are in the nearby Secretariat. Cable and Wireless, Ross Road, operate overseas telephone, fax, telegraph and telex services. The islands' telephone system has been completely replaced, with direct dialling worldwide. There are some well-stocked stores, open Mon to Sat. The few pubs, the *Globe* near the public jetty, the *Rose*, on Dury St, the *Victory* on Philomel Hill, *Deano's* on Dean St, the *Stanley Arms* at W end of Stanley, John Biscoe Rd, and the *Ship* behind the *Upland Goose Hotel* are popular meeting places (open all day, except Sun only from 1200 to 1400, and 1900-2200).

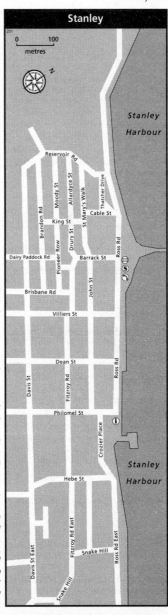

● **National Tourism Bureau**

Falkland Islands Tourist Board (FITB), representative, Cherilyn King, Ross Road, Stanley, T (010500) 22215/22281, F 22619, will provide all information on holidays on the islands. Bookings for lodgings and for fishing, riding, Range Rover hire, tours, inter-island travel are handled by Stanley Services Ltd, Airport Road, Stanley, T 22622, F 22623, Tx 2438. See below under communications for the Falklands Islands Tourist Board's London Office.

● **Transport**

Rentals: The Falkland Islands Company, Stanley, rents Fiat Strada 4 x 4 cars for about £125/week, for road use only. Dave Eynon, South Atlantic Marine Services, PO Box 140, Stanley, T 21145/22667, Tx 2413, hires a Land Rover and his dinghy *Zodiac* with diving equipment, also arranges diving and fishing trips. Ian Bury on Davis Street rents Land Rovers for £30-50 a day. Insurance is extra from the Falkland Islands Company. The *Malvina House Hotel*, T 21355, Mel Lloyd, Swan Inlet (rec as good value, experienced driver, 8-seater vehicle) and Tony Smith, T 21027 (or try at Ian Bury's House), offer overland Land Rover excursions from Stanley. Boats may be hired from Sullivan Shipping, T 22626, or the FIC, T 27630.

OUTSIDE STANLEY

For wildlife enthusiasts, especially birders, the Islands are an exceptional destination. The small islands to the W and SE have concentrations of the local wildlife (approximately 70 species of breeding birds and approximately 27 species of marine mammals). Several of these islands offer guest facilities; a wonderful opportunity to experience the wild and beautiful nature of the islands, while enjoying their renowned warm hospitality. Visiting each of these islands involves short flights on the local twin-engine Islander aircraft. For up-to-date information on how to make bookings and availability contact the Falkland Islands Tourism Board. On arrival, visitors are given a guide to respecting the Falklands wildlife and its habitat, with a checklist of breeding birds and mammals. Best months to visit are October to March. Make allowance for unpredictable

weather. Always wear or carry waterproof clothing; wear good boots and a peaked hat to protect the eyes from rain or hail. Outside Stanley, there is a major road to the airport at Mount Pleasant, but great care should nevertheless be taken on it. Roads connect Stanley with San Carlos (70 miles) and Goose Green (64 miles). On West Falkland a new road connects most of the settlements. Elsewhere, tracks require Land Rovers or motorbikes. Remember to phone farms in the camp for permission to drive across private land. Off-road driving in the boggy terrain is a skill not easily learned by short-term visitors. Near Stanley and a few farm settlements there are still unexploded mines, but hazardous areas are clearly marked and fenced. Visitors should *never* enter these areas, and should report suspicious objects to the police or military authorities in Stanley. Free minefield maps are available from the Bomb Disposal Office, Ross Road, Stanley. (In April 1994 the Falklands Island government accepted Argentine proposals for the clearance of about 30,000 mines but this has yet to begin.) Ordnance Survey maps of the Islands are available from the Secretariat, £2.50 each for the 1:50,000 sheets; there is also a two-sheet, 1:250,000 map suitable for most purposes.

Travel outside the vicinity of Stanley and the road to Goose Green is mainly by air. The Falkland Islands Government Air Service (FIGAS) operates three Islander aircraft to farm settlements and settled outer islands according to bookings, seat availability, and weather. To book a seat, visitors should telephone FIGAS no later than the morning of the day before travelling; flight schedules are announced that evening on local radio (airfares are about £1 per minute for non-islanders, luggage limit 14 kg/30 lbs, high excess charge). FIGAS tickets are also available from Stanley Services Ltd, Airport Road, Stanley, T 22622. Regular service operates 7 days a week. Flights leave from Stanley Airport, three miles E of town on the Cape Pembroke peninsula.

Places of interest

Sparrow Cove, Kidney Cove, and adjacent areas, only a short distance across Stanley Harbour by boat and out into Port William, are good areas to see penguins and other wildlife; dolphins often follow in the wake of your boat near The Narrows. Gypsy Cove, walking distance from Stanley, features a colony of burrowing Magellanic penguins and other shorebirds. Leopard seals, elephant seals and the occasional killer whale visit the area. Observe minefield fences which prevent close inspection of the penguins (they are not unduly inhibiting, though). At Cape Pembroke, around the town airport and the recently renovated lighthouse one can see Gentoo penguins and ground-nesting birds such as dotterels, snipe, and Upland geese.

Of particular interest are the hulks of old sailing ships at Stanley and Darwin.

Examples at Stanley are the *Jhelum* (built in 1839 for the East India Company) near Government House, the *Charles Cooper* (the last US sailing packet to sail out of New York Harbour; in the Islands since 1866), and the iron-built *Lady Elizabeth* at the far end of the harbour (228 ft long, with three masts still standing). *Snow Squall*, one of the last American clipper ships, was removed by a team of marine archaeologists from Harvard University in 1987. A Maritime History Trail has been set up around Port Stanley (self-guided with interpretive panels at key points, and guide book available at FITB; a book describing the Stanley wrecks is sold by the museum). At Darwin are the *Vicar of Bray* (last survivor of the California Gold Rush fleet), and another old iron ship, the *Garland*. Some of these hulks are still used for storage. There are interesting old French buildings and ruins at Port Louis (the road between Stanley and Port Louis is a boulder-strewn

Sea Lion Island

Sea Lion Island in the SE, is a delightful place to explore and relax. Throughout the austral summer accommodation is available at the lodge (7 rooms, maximum 15 visitors) run by David and Pat Gray. This island is aptly named as many Southern Sea Lions breed on the beaches. An adjacent cliff offers spectacular overviews of the great bull Sea Lions with their harems, and pups. As well as the Sea Lions, countless juvenile Southern Elephant Seals snooze on the white sandy beaches. Early in the season the pups are very appealing with their fawn coloured coats and large inquisitive eyes. These pups are weaned at 23 days, after which their parents are offshore feeding on the squid and fish resources so abundant in the Falklands. Later in the season the adults come ashore to moult contentedly in pungent wallows. A pod of Orca whales is seen almost daily cruising the kelpbeds in search of an unsuspecting meal. The island also has magnificent birdlife. Gentoo, Magellanic and Rockhopper Penguins all breed on the island, and one or two King Penguins can be seen cosily nesting in amongst the Gentoos. Giant Petrels (known locally as 'stinkers'), King Cormorants, the incredible flightless Steamer Duck, Black-crowned Night Herons, the friendly Tussock Bird, and Oystercatcher (Magellanic and Black) are all found breeding on the island. The rare Striated Caracara can be found sitting solemnly on fence posts overlooking meadows of small blossoming plants, including the characteristic Diddle-dee from which the Kelpers (a local name for Falklanders) make tea and jam.

Kim Crosbie, Scott Polar Research Institute, Cambridge.

clay track, very tricky when wet).

Neil Rogers of New Brighton, Merseyside, has suggested the following walk: From the 'Beaver' hanger opposite 'Strathcarron', Ross Road W, walk past the various ships and monuments, along the harbour, up to the Falkland Islands Company offices. Here it is possible to walk onto the jetty and visit the after section of a 19th century sailing vessel that is still being used as a warehouse. Also below the jetty you will see a couple of 19th century Welsh colliers. From here go E until you reach B slip, used by the British Forces during the 1982 conflict. Carry on E, past the floating harbour and around the head of the bay to the iron barque *Lady Elizabeth*. At low tide it is possible to walk out to her. Follow the bay round and eventually you will come to various penguin rookeries and Gypsy Cove.

Volunteer Point, N of Stanley, is a wildlife sanctuary. Permission to visit must be obtained from the manager, Mr George Smith, at Johnson's Harbour, T 31398; he charges £5 to visit – the fee goes towards looking after the penguins. By arrangement with Mr Smith it is possible to camp at the shepherd's house at Volunteer Point (you must take your own food and sleeping bag – don't drink the stream water, it is polluted by the penguins). Stanley Services occasionally arranges tours; overland guided tours are also conducted by the *Malvina House Hotel* and Tony Smith, T 21027. On other occasions, the farmer will drive you to the point if he is not busy; otherwise it is a 10 mile walk. Contact Mike Rendell for transport, T 21084. Volunteer contains the only substantial nesting colony of King penguins in the Falklands. Gentoo penguins, Magellanic penguins, geese, ducks, and elephant seals are very tame and easily

Carcass Island and New Island

On Carcass Island the farm at Settlement Harbour is home to the McGills. The farm is surrounded by an arbour, alive with Black-crowned Night Herons. A group of Dusky Dolphins often play in the harbour. Patagonian Crested Ducks, with their deep wine-red eyes, can be seen spinning in courtship displays in the shallows while brilliant white male Kelp Geese and their less conspicuous female partners pick their way along the shore. Like the other islands, Carcass is an idyllic place to explore on foot; the long white beaches and colonies of penguins and albatrosses, Upland Geese grazing in the fields and Military Starlings, with their crimson breasts, marching among the tussock. Anyone who pauses will soon be befriended by the small brown tussock bird, indigenous to the Falklands. There are lovely views to West Falkland.

The tussock grass in the southern sector of New Island is home to one of the largest colonies of Prions; it is magical at nightfall when the prions return in huge, cackling, flocks to feed their young. There is also a colony of Black-browed Albatrosses. These birds once seen are never forgotten, overwhelmingly graceful in flight, endearingly serene on the nest or in courtship, and amazingly comical when landing. Adjacent to the albatrosses there is a colony of Rockhopper Penguins. These aptly named birds are often considered the punks of the penguin world with erect yellow crests. Both of these species are at present declining: Rockhoppers are being considered for the globally threatened list; and Black-browed Albatross populations are being closely monitored. It is a privilege and incredibly rewarding to sit quietly near the edge of one of these colonies.

Kim Crosbie, Scott Polar Research Institute, Cambridge.

photographed. An exceptional wildlife hike is along the N coast of East Falkland, from Seal Bay to Volunteer Point. Ask permission of the manager of Port Louis as well, and allow three to 4 days. Battlefield visits, to some of the sites associated with the 1982 conflict, can be arranged.

The smaller islands off West Falkland, such as Carcass and New Island, are the most spectacular and attractive for wildlife and scenery. The southern half of New Island, on the extreme W of the archipelago, is run as a nature reserve by Ian and Maria Strange. The northern half, owned by Tony and Annie Chater, has a small sheep farm. The island has a grass airstrip and is served by FIGAS on flights limited to three passengers (owing to the length of the strip). There are basic self-catering facilities on the island and enquiries should be addressed to Ian and Maria Strange, Snake Hill, Stanley, T 21185, F 21186; on New Island 42017. Carcass can be visited more easily and has two self-catering cottages (see above). Saunders Island, besides a representative sample of wildlife, contains the ruins of the 18th century British outpost at Port Egmont and an accessible albatross colony.

Fishing Sea-trout fishing is excellent on the islands. The season runs from 1 September to 30 April. For information in the UK on fishing in the Falklands/Malvinas, contact Go Fishing Falklands (Maggi Smit), 6 Barons Gate, 33/35 Rothschilds Road, Chiswick, London W4 5HT, T 0181-742 3700, F 0181-994 7388; or Sport Elite Tours (J A Valdes Scott), Woodwalls House, Corscombe, Dorchester, DT2 0NT, England, T (0935) 891477, F (0935) 891797.

ANTARCTICA

Antarctica, the 5th largest continent, is 99.6% covered with perpetual ice. Although very inaccessible, approximately 8,000 tourists visit annually and it is well known for extraordinary scenery, wildlife, scientific stations, and historic sites. The weather may also be spectacularly severe, thus visits are confined to the brief summer. Presently 18 countries operate 42 scientific stations with wintering personnel there, and about a dozen summer stations also function. A wintering population of about 1,200 lives in a continent larger than Europe. These governmental stations are expensive to maintain thus, with only minor exceptions, they make no provision for visitors not connected with their work.

Governance of Antarctica is principally through the Antarctic Treaty (1959) signed by all countries operating there (43 countries were parties to the Treaty in 1997, these represent about 75% of the Earth's population). Most visitors will be affected by several provisions of the Treaty, in particular those of the Environmental Protocol made in Madrid in 1992. Seven countries have territorial claims over parts of Antarctica and three of these overlap (Antártida Argentina, British Antarctic Territory, and Territorio Chileno Antártico); the Treaty has neutralized these

with provision of free access to citizens of contracting states. Some display of sovereignty is legitimate; many stations operate a Post Office where philatelic items and various souvenirs are sold.

The region S of South America is the most accessible part of the Antarctic, therefore over half the scientific stations are there and on adjacent islands. Fortuitously it is one of the most spectacular areas with many mountains, glaciers and fjords closely approachable by sea. One ice-breaker, other large ships, several private yachts, and an air company carry passengers there every austral summer. Three ports are used: Stanley (Falkland Islands/Malvinas), Punta Arenas (Chile), and Ushuaia (Argentina). Vessels sailing from one may return to another or go farther to South Africa, New Zealand, or Australia. Most are fully booked well in advance by luxury class passengers but sometimes late opportunistic vacancies can be secured by local agencies (on the basis that any vacant cabin is a loss). During the 1996-97 austral summer 18 passenger vessels made several voyages each to Antarctica carrying an average of about 100 tourists.

Voyages from South America and the Falkland Islands involve at least 2 days each way, crossing the Drake Passage where sea conditions may be very uncomfortable. No guarantee of landings, views or wildlife is possible and delays due to storms are not exceptional. Conversely, on a brilliant day, some of the most spectacular sights and wildlife anywhere can be seen. All visitors should be well prepared for adverse conditions with warm clothing, windproofs and waterproofs, and good boots for wet landings. Weather and state of the sea can change quickly without warning.

In 1991 the International Association of Antarctica Tour Operators was formed (contact Mr Darrel Schoeling, International Association of Antarctica Tour Operators, 111 East 14th St, Suite 110, New York, United States, 10003; T +1 212 460-8715, F +1 212 529-8684) which represents the majority of companies and can provide details of most Antarctic voyages planned during an austral summer (annual variation of these is great). Many vessels have a principal contractor and a number of other companies bring smaller groups, thus it is advantageous to contact the principal. Adventure Network International (Canon House, 27 London End, Beaconsfield, Buckinghamshire, United Kingdom, HP9 2HN; T +44 1494 671808, F 671725), provides commercial flights landing in Antarctica which depart from Punta Arenas where there is a local office (935 Arauco, Punta Arenas, Chile; T +56 61 247735, F 226167). Wheeled aircraft fly as far as a camp at Patriot Hills (80° 19'S, 81° 20'W) whence ski-aircraft proceed to the South Pole, vicinity of Vinson Massif (4,897m, Antarctica's highest peak), and elsewhere. Tickets start at about US$8,000. 1 day overflights are operated only by *Qantas* from Australia. More such flights are expected to operate in the future.

More opportunistic travel is possible with certain private yachts which have carried passengers for several summers. These are not coordinated but inquiries on the waterside of the ports listed may secure transport. Similarly opportunities to travel with the Argentine or Chilean navy occur but are virtually impossible to arrange other than in Ushuaia or Punta Arenas. Neither navy encourages passengers so your only chance is by approaching the captain of the vessel. No advance booking, fares about US$100 pp per day. Levels of comfort and prices are usually much lower than for the cruise ships. Many tourist ships and some yachts also visit South Georgia; there are other possibilities for reaching this Antarctic island from the Falkland Islands/Islas Malvinas.

RK Headland, Scott Polar Research Institute, Cambridge.

INFORMATION FOR TRAVELLERS

BEFORE TRAVELLING

● Entry requirements

All travellers must have full passports to visit the Falkland Islands/Islas Malvinas. Generally, visa requirements are the same as for the UK, but at present Argentine citizens are not permitted to visit unless they have relatives on the islands. If going to the islands from Argentina via Chile, check entry procedures. All visitors require a 4-month visitor permit, normally provided on arrival upon presentation of a return ticket. Visitors are also asked to have pre-booked accommodation and sufficient funds to cover their stay. Work permits are not available. Do not stay beyond the valid period of your visa without applying to the Immigration Office for an extension.

● Currency

The local £ is on a par with sterling. Local notes and coins. UK notes and coins are (except the new small 10p and 5p, Falkland Island coins are the old larger ones) also legal tender. Currency from Ascension Island, where the RAF Tri-Star stops for refueling, or Santa Helena, is not accepted, nor are Falklands notes or coins legal in the United Kingdom. Foreign currency may be changed at Standard Chartered Bank, Ross Road, Stanley.

● Cost of living

About the same as in Britain. Freight adds to the price of imported groceries. Since the construction of a hydroponic market garden near Stanley, fresh produce such as lettuce, tomatoes and aubergines are available year-round. Potatoes and other vegetables are grown in gardens and conservatories for household use, but are not readily purchased.

There is no value-added tax; only tobacco, wine, spirits and beer pay import duty. Small luxury goods on which freight is correspondingly low are sometimes cheaper than in the UK. Colour slide film, which can be scarce, should be brought from outside the islands.

● Postal services

Since the opening of Mount Pleasant, there is direct and dependable air mail service from the United Kingdom. Heavy parcels come by sea from the UK 4 or 5 times a year. Inter-island mail service is carried out by FIGAS and by the vessels *Tamar* (see above) and *Forrest*.

GETTING THERE

The RAF usually operates two Tri-Star flights a week from Brize Norton, Oxfordshire, to Mount Pleasant airport (every Mon and most Thur, returning to UK every Wed and most Sat). The fare is £2,180 return, but there are also cheaper APEX (£1,340) and group rates. Falkland Islands residents receive a discount (£940). Confirm your seat 12 hrs before departure to avoid disappointment from overbooking or lost reservations. Flight time is 18 hrs, but diversions to Montevideo owing to bad weather are not uncommon. Enquiries about passages can be addressed to Miss Jenny Smith, Falkland Islands Government London Office, Falkland House, 14 Broadway, Westminster, London SW1H 0BH, T 0171-222 2542, F 222 2375. The Falkland Islands Tourist Board (same address and phone number) answers enquiries about the islands themselves and gives information on organized tours.

Aerovías DAP of Chile operate a weekly schedule Santiago-Punta Arenas-Stanley, departing Wed, arriving in Stanley at 1815, returning from Stanley about 1530 on Thur. These flights connect with British Airways' London-Santiago service (overnight stop on Stanley-Santiago-London route). The plane is a Boeing 707; fares are Santiago-Stanley US$528 business, US$396 economy, US$316 tourist; Punta Arenas-Stanley US$316, US$158, US$140 respectively, all one way. Booking offices: Aerovías DAP, O'Higgins 899, Punta Arenas, T (56-61) 243958/223340, F 221693; Falkland Islands Co, Crozier Place, Stanley, T (500) 27600, F 27603, or 94a Whitechapel High St, London E1 7RH, T (0171) 377 0566, F 377 6194 (all 3 offices accept credit cards: Visa, Mastercard, Eurocard). MV *Tamar FI*, of Byron Marine Ltd, Stanley, T 22245 makes unscheduled sailings to Punta Arenas, £125 single, 2 cabins, 2 passengers per cabin, cramped though the ship is, 'relatively modern and a good sea-goer'. *Tamar* will take passengers around the islands.

ON ARRIVAL

● Airport information

Mount Pleasant, 35 miles from Stanley, is built to international specifications. C and M Travel, James Street, Stanley, T 21468, transports passengers and luggage to and from the capital for £12 single. Departing passengers should make reservations. Also, Lowes Taxi, T 21381, for transport between Stanley and the airport, and within Stanley (Mon-Fri, 0800-2000), and Ben's Taxi, Ross Road East, T 21437.

The Chilean Pacific Islands

TWO NATIONAL park possessions in the Pacific: Juan Fernández Islands, a little easier to reach (and leave) now than in Robinson Crusoe's time, and the unique Easter Island.

JUAN FERNANDEZ ISLANDS

THE LAND

(*Pop* 500) Situated 667 km W of Valparaíso, this group of small volcanic islands is a national park administered by Conaf. There are three islands, Robinson Crusoe, the largest, which was the home (1704-09) of Alexander Selkirk (the original of Defoe's *Robinson Crusoe*), Alejandro Selkirk and Santa Clara, the smallest. Selkirk's cave on the beach of Robinson Crusoe is shown to visitors. The only settlement is San Juan Bautista, a fishing village of simple wooden frame houses, located on Bahía Cumberland on the N coast of Isla Robinson Crusoe: it has a church, schools, post office, and radio station. The islands are famous for *langosta de Juan Fernández* (a pincerless lobster) which is sent to the mainland. In summer, a boat goes once a month between Robinson Crusoe and Alejandro

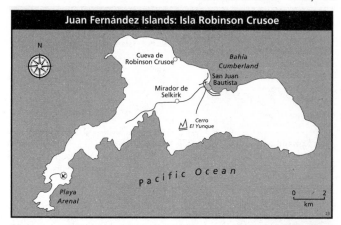

Juan Fernández Islands: Isla Robinson Crusoe

Cueva de
Robinson Crusoe

Bahía
Cumberland

San Juan
Bautista

Mirador de
Selkirk

Cerro
El Yunque

N

Pacific Ocean

Playa
Arenal

0   2
km

Selkirk if the *langosta* catch warrants it, so you can visit either for a few hours or a whole month.

CLIMATE

The islands enjoy a mild climate and the vegetation is rich and varied: the Juan Fernández, previously used widely for handicrafts, is now a protected species, but the *sandalo* (sandalwood tree), once the most common tree on the islands, is now extinct owing to its overuse for perfumes. Fauna includes wild goats, humming birds and seals. The islands were declared a UN World Biosphere Reserve in 1977. Best time for a visit: Oct-March. **Take insect repellent**.

HISTORY

The islands are named after Joao Fernández, a Portuguese in the service of Spain, who was the first European to visit in 1574. Although they were frequented by pirates and corsairs over the following 150 years, it was not until after 1750 that the Spanish took steps to defend them, founding San Juan Bautista and building seven fortresses. During the Wars of Independence the islands were used as a penal colony, the Spanish deporting here Chilean independence leaders captured after the Battle of Rancagua. In 1915 two British destroyers, HMS *Kent* and *Glasgow* cornered the German cruiser, *Dresden*, in Bahía Cumberland. The German vessel, which was scuttled, still lies on the bottom; a monument on shore commemorates the event and, nearby, unexploded shells are embedded in the cliffs. Some of the German crew are buried in the cemetery.

PLACES OF INTEREST

The remains of the **Fuerte Santa Bárbara**, the largest of the Spanish fortresses, overlook San Juan Bautista. Nearby are the **Cuevas de los Patriotas**, home to the deported Chilean independence leaders. South of the village is the **Mirador de Selkirk**, the hill where Selkirk lit his signal fires. A plaque was set in the rock at the look-out point by British naval officers from HMS *Topaze* in 1868; nearby is a more recent plaque placed by his descendents. Selkirk, a Scot, was put ashore from HMS *Cinque Ports* and was taken off 4 years and 4 months later by a privateer, the *Duke*. The Mirador is the only easy pass between the N and S sides of the island. Further S is the anvil-shaped **El Yunque**, 915m, the highest peak on the island, where Hugo Weber, a survivor from the *Dresden,* lived as a hermit for 12 years: some remains of his dwelling can be seen. The only sandy beach on Robinson Crusoe is **Playa Arenal**, in the extreme SW corner, 2 hrs by boat from San Juan Bautista.

LOCAL INFORMATION

● **Accommodation**
C pp *Hotel Selkirk*, clean, good food, full board A pp, rec (T Santiago 531-3772); **A3** *Hostería Robinson Crusoe*, full board, plus 20% tax, about 1 hr walk from the village; **A1** *Daniel Defoe Hotel*, at Aldea Daniel Defoe (T Santiago 531-3772); *Hostería Villa Green*, good. Lodging with villagers is difficult.

● **Banks & money changers**
There are no exchange facilities. Only pesos and US$ cash accepted. No credit cards, no TCs.

● **Transport**
Air Air taxi daily in summer (subject to demand) from Santiago (Los Cerrillos airport, US$395 round trip), by Transportes Aéreas Isla Robinson Crusoe, Monumento 2570, Maipú, Santiago, T 531-4343, F 531-3772, and by Lacsa, Av Larraín 7941, La Reina, Santiago, T 273-4354, F 273-4309; also from Valparaíso. The plane lands on an airstrip in the W of the island; passengers are taken by boat to San Juan Bautista (1½ hrs, US$2 one way).

Sea The boat service, about every 3 weeks from Valparaíso on the *Río Baker* and *Charles Darwin*, is for cargo and passengers, modest accommodation, 36-hr passage; *Agentur*, Huérfanos 757, oficina 601, T 337118, Santiago. *Pesquera Chris*, Cueto 622, Santiago, T 681-1543, or Cochrane 445 (near Plaza Sotomayor), Valparaíso, T 216800, 2 week trips to the island (5 days cruising, a week on the island), from US$200 return. No fishing or cargo boats will take passengers.

EASTER ISLAND

Easter Island (Isla de Pascua, Rapa Nui; *phone code* 108) is just S of the Tropic of Capricorn and 3,790 km W of Chile; its nearest neighbour is Pitcairn Island.

THE LAND

The island is triangular in shape, 24 km across, with an extinct volcano at each corner. The original inhabitants called the island Te Pito o te Henua, the navel of the world. The population was stable at 4,000 until the 1850s, when Peruvian slavers, smallpox and emigration to Tahiti (encouraged by plantation-owners) reduced the numbers. Now it is about 2,800, of whom about 500 are from the mainland, mostly living in the village of Hanga Roa. About half the island, of low round hills with groves of eucalyptus, is used for horses and cattle, and nearly one-half constitutes a National Park (entry US$10, payable at Orongo). The islanders have preserved their indigenous songs and dances, and are extremely hospitable. Tourism has grown rapidly since the air service began in 1967. Paid work is now more common, but much carving is still done. The islanders have profited greatly from the visits of North Americans: a Canadian medical expedition left a mobile hospital on the island in 1966, and when a US missile-tracking station was abandoned

Yachting

Each Feb, a yachting regatta visits the islands; setting out from Algarrobo, yachts sails to Isla Robinson Crusoe, thence to Talcahuano and Valparaíso. At this time Bahía Cumberland is full of colourful and impressive craft, and prices in restaurants and shops double for the duration.

Thomas G Lammers, Department of Botany, University of Miami.

in 1971, vehicles, mobile housing and an electricity generator were left behind.

CLIMATE

Average monthly temperatures vary between 15-17°C in Aug and 24°C in Feb, the hottest month. Average annual rainfall is 1,100 mm. There is some rain throughout the year, but the rainy season is Mar-Oct (wettest in May). The tourist season is from Sept to April.

HISTORY

It is now generally accepted that the islanders are of Polynesian origin. Thor Heyerdahl's theories, as expressed in *Aku-Aku, The Art of Easter Island* (New York: Doubleday, 1975), are less widely accepted than they used to be, and South American influence is now largely discounted (see below).

European contact with the island began with the visit of the Dutch admiral, Jacob Roggeven, on Easter Sunday 1722, who was followed by the British James Cook in 1774 and the French Le Perouse in 1786. Between 1859 and 1862 over 1,000 islanders were transported as slaves to work in the Peruvian guano trade. The island was annexed by Chile in 1888. Until 1952 most of Easter Island was leased to a private company which bred sheep on its grasslands: a wall was built around the Hanga Roa area and the islanders were forbidden to cross.

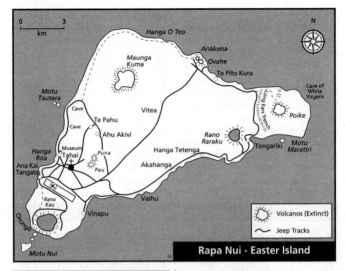

Rapa Nui - Easter Island

PLACES OF INTEREST

The unique features of the island are the 600 (or so) *moai*, huge stone figures up to 9m in height and broad in proportion. One of them, on Anakena beach, was restored to its (probably) original state with a plaque commemorating Thor Heyerdahl's visit in 1955. Other *moai* have since been re-erected.

A tour of the main part of the island can be done on foot, but this would need at least 2 days, either camping at Anakena or returning to Hanga Roa and setting out again the next day (but most correspondents agree that this is far too quick). To see more, hire a vehicle. From Hanga Roa, take the road going SE past the airport; at the oil tanks turn right to Vinapu, where there are two *ahu* and a wall whose stones are joined with Inca-like precision. Head back NE along the S coast, past Vaihu (an *ahu* with eight broken *moai*; small harbour); Akahanga (*ahu* with toppled *moai*); Hanga Tetenga (1 toppled *moai*, bones can be seen inside the *ahu*), Ahu Tongariki (once the largest platform, damaged by a tidal wave in 1960, being restored with

Japanese aid). Turn left to Rano Raraku (20 km), the volcano where the *moai* were carved. Many statues can be seen. In the crater is a small lake surrounded by reeds (swimming possible beyond the reeds). Good views.

The road heads N past 'the trench of the long-ears' and an excursion can be made to Poike to see the open-mouthed statue that is particularly popular with local carvers (ask farmer for permission to cross his land). On Poike the earth is red; at the NE end is the cave where the virgin was kept before marriage to the victor of ceremonies during the birdman cult (ask directions). The road along the N coast passes Ahu Te Pito Kura, a round stone called the navel of the world and one of largest *moai* ever brought to a platform. It continues to Ovahe. At Ovahe, there is a very attractive beach with pink sand and some rather recently carved faces and a cave.

From Ovahe, one can return direct to Hanga Roa or continue to Anakena, site of King Hotu Matua's village and Thor Heyerdahl's landing place. From Anakena a coastal path of variable quality passes interesting remains and beautiful cliff scenery. At Hanga o Teo, there appears to be a large village complex, with several round houses, and further on there is a burial place, built like a long ramp with several ditches containing bones. From Hanga o Teo the path goes W then S, inland from the coast, to meet the road N of Hanga Roa.

A 6-hr walk from Hanga Roa on the W coast passes Ahu Tahai (a *moai* with eyes and top knot in place, cave house, just outside town). Two caves are reached, one inland appears to be a ceremonial centre, the other (nearer the sea) has 2 'windows' (take a strong flashlight and be careful near the 'windows'). Further N is Ahu Tepeu (broken *moai*, ruined houses). Beyond here you can join the path mentioned above, or turn right to Te Pahu cave and the seven *moai* at Akivi. Either return to Hanga Roa, or go to Puna Pau crater (2 hrs), where the topknots were carved (good views from the three crosses at the top).

Rano Kau, S of Hanga Roa, is another important site to visit; one finds the curious Orongo ruins here. The route S out of Hanga Roa passes the two caves of Ana Kai Tangata, one of which has

The cultural development of Easter Island

"Far from being the passive recipient of external influences, Easter Island shows the extent of unique development possible for a people left wholly in isolation. It is believed to have been colonized from Polynesia about AD 800: its older altars (*ahu*) are similar to those of (French) Polynesia, and its older statues (*moai*) similar to those of the Marquesas Islands. The very precise stone fitting of some of the *ahu*, and the tall gaunt *moai* with elongated faces and ears for which Easter Island is best known were later developments whose local evolution can be traced through a comparison of the remains. Indigenous Polynesian society, for all its romantic idylls, was competitive, and it seems that the five clans which originally had their own lands demonstrated their strength by erecting these complex monuments. The *moai* were sculpted at the Rano Raraku quarry and transported on wooden rollers over more or less flat paths to their final locations; their red topknots were sculpted at and brought from the inland quarry of Puna Pau; and the rounded pebbles laid out checkerboard fashion at the *ahu* all came from the same beach at Vinapu. The sculptors and engineers were paid out of the surplus food produced by the sponsoring family: Rano Raraku's unfinished *moai* mark the end of the families' ability to pay. Over several centuries from about AD 1400 this stone work slowed down and stopped, owing to the deforestation of the island caused by roller production, and damage to the soils through deforestation and heavy cropping. The birdman cult represented at Orongo is a later development after the islanders had lost their clan territoriality and were concentrated at Hanga Roa, but still needed a non-territorial way to simulate inter-clan rivalry." David Bulbeck, Adelaide.

The central feature of the birdman cult was an annual ceremony in which the heads of the lineages, or their representatives, raced to the islets to obtain the first egg of the sooty tern (known as the Manutara), a migratory seabird which nests on Motu Nui, Motu Iti and Motu Kao. The winning chief was named Bird Man, Tangata Manu, for the following year. It appears that, in the cult, the egg of the tern represented fertility, although it is less clear what the status of the Tangata Manu actually was. The petroglyphs at Orongo depict the half-man, half-bird Tangata Manu, the creator god Make Make and the symbol of fertility, Komari.

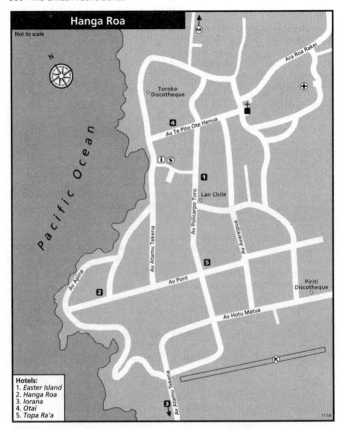

Hanga Roa

Not to scale

Pacific Ocean

Toroko Discotheque

Av Te Pito Ote Henua

Ara Roa Rakei

Lan Chile

Av Policarpo Toro

Av Atamu Tekena

Av Avareipua

Av Apina

Av Pont

Piriti Discotheque

Av Hotu Matua

Av Atamu Tekena

Hotels:
1. *Easter Island*
2. *Hanga Roa*
3. *Iorana*
4. *Otai*
5. *Topa Ra'a*

paintings. If on foot you can take a path from the Orongo road, just past the Conaf sign, which is a much shorter route to Rano Kau crater. 200m below is a lake with many reed islands. On the seaward side is Orongo (entrance US$11), where the bird-man cult flourished, with many ruined buildings and petroglyphs. Out to sea are the 'bird islets', Motu Nui, Motu Iti and Motu Kao. It is very windy at the summit; good views at sunset, or under a full moon (it is easy to follow the road back to Hanga Roa in the dark).

In Hanga Roa is Ahu Tautira, next to a swimming area marked out with concrete walls and a breakwater (cold water). Music at the 0900 Sun mass is 'enchanting'. Museum near Tahai, US$1, most objects are reproductions because the genuine articles were removed from the island, but it has good descriptions of island life. There is a cultural centre next to the football field, with an exhibition hall and souvenir stall.

LOCAL FESTIVALS

Tapati, or *Semana Rapa Nui*, end-Jan/beginning-Feb, lasts one week. Dancing competitions, singing, sports (horse racing, swimming, modified decathlon), body-painting, typical foods (lots of small booths by the football field), necklace-making, etc. Only essential activities continue outside the festival.

Recommended Reading There is a very thorough illustrated book by J Douglas Porteous, *The Modernization of Easter Island* (1981), available from Department of Geography, University of Victoria, BC, Canada, US$6. See also Thor Heyerdahl's work, details above; *Easter Island, Earth Island*, by Paul Bahn and John Flenley (Thames and Hudson, 1992) for a comprehensive appraisal of the island's archaeology. *Islas Oceánicas Chilenas*, edited by Juan Carlos Castillo (Ediciones Universidad Católica de Chile, 1987), contains much information on the natural history and geography of Juan Fernández and Easter Islands.

Anyone continuing into Polynesia or Melanesia from Easter Island will find David Stanley's *South Pacific Handbook* (Moon Publications Inc, PO Box 3040, Chico, CA 95927, USA, F 1-916-345-6751) a useful guidebook.

LOCAL INFORMATION

Time zone: Easter Island is always 2 hrs behind the Chilean mainland, summer and winter time.

● Accommodation

The accommodation list at the airport information desk only covers the more expensive places. Flights are met by large numbers of hotel and *residencial* representatives but it is cheaper to look for yourself. Accommodation ranges from US$10-200. Note that room rates, especially in *residenciales* can be much cheaper out of season and if you do not take full board. Unless it is a particularly busy season there is no need to book in advance; mainland agencies make exorbitant booking charges.

L3 *Hanga Roa*, Av Pont, inc all meals (120 beds), no credit cards, T 223299 (Santiago 633-9130, F 639-5334); **L3** *Iorana Hotel*,

Ana Magara promontory, 5 mins from airport, T 223312 (Santiago 633-2650), friendly, excellent food, convenient for visiting Ana Kai Tangata caves.

A1 *Easter Island*, Policarpo Toro, Hanga Roa, breakfast and dinner (excellent restaurant), good service, nice garden, T 223294, or Santiago 211-6747; **A1** *Otai*, Te Pilo Te Henua, T 223250, comfortable, friendly, family run, rec; **A1** *Victoria*, Av Pont, T 223272, friendly, helpful owner arranges tours; **A1** *Topo Ra'a*, Atamu Kekena, T 223223, 5 mins from Hanga Roa, very good, helpful, excellent restaurant; **A3** *Poike*, Petero Atamu, T 223283, homely, hot water.

Homes offering accommodation and tours (rates ranging from US$18 to US$35, inc meals): **A1** *Res Pedro Atán*, T 223329, full board, Policarpo Toro; **A1** *Res Apina Nui*, Hetereki, T 223292 (C low season, but bargain), good food, helpful, English spoken; Yolanda Ika's **A2** *Res Taire Ngo Oho*, T 223259, with breakfast, rec, modern; Krenia Tucki's **A2** *Res Kai Poo*, Av Pont, small, clean, friendly with hot water; **A2** *Res Hanga Roa Reka*, T 223276, full board, good, friendly, camping US$5; María Georgina Hucke, of Tiki Tours, **B** with half board, rec; *Res El Tauke*, Te Pito Te Henua s/n, T 223253, same rates as *Hanga Roa Reka*, excellent, airport transfers, tours arranged; *Res Taheta One One*, T 223257, same rates, motorbike rental; **B** *Res Tahai*, Simón Paoa s/n, T 223338, with breakfast, A2 full board, nice garden, rec; **B** pp *Res Holiday Inn*, T 223337, half board, excellent food, hot water, rec; **C** Anita and Martín Pate's guesthouse, opp hospital in Hanga Roa, half board in high season, less low season, clean, good food; **D** pp *Res Taniera*, T 223290, also camping, horses; **D** pp María Cecilia Cardinale, nr Tahai Moai, half board, speaks English and French, excellent food, camping US$5; **D** María Goretti, rooms with breakfast, camping US$6; **D** pp *Ana Rapu*, C Apina, T 223540, F 223318, inc breakfast, evening meal US$7, camping US$5, comfortable, family-run, hot water (except when demand is heavy), English spoken; **C** pp *Res Viaka Pua*, Simón Paoa, Hanga Roa, T 223377, full board, comfortable, friendly, rec. **A3** Emilio and Milagrosa Paoa, with full board, rec accommodation and tours.

Camping: free in eucalyptus groves near the Ranger's house at Rano Raraku (with water tank), and at Anakena, no water, make sure your tent is ant-proof. Officially, camping is not allowed anywhere else, but this is not apparently strictly enforced. Many people also offer campsites in their gardens, US$5-10 pp (Ana Rapu rec), check availability of water first; some families also provide food. Several habitable caves around the coast: eg between Anakena beach and Ovahe. If you must leave anything behind in a cave, leave only what may be of use to other campers, candles, oil, etc, certainly not rubbish. **NB** There is no camping equipment for hire on the island.

● **Places to eat**

Mama Sabina, Av Policarpo Toro, clean, welcoming; *Ave Rei Pua*, limited menu; good; *Tarake* near municipal market (which does not sell food); *Pizzería*, opp post office, moderately priced. Several others. *Le Pecheur*, French run, unfriendly, expensive; *Kona Koa*, not cheap but good. Most *residenciales* offer full board. Coffee is always instant. Beware of extras such as US$3 charge for hot water.

● **Banks & money changers**

Best done in Santiago. Bank next to Entel, open 0900-1200 daily, charges US$12 commission on changing TCs, but you can change as many TCs for this fee as you like (and they can be in different names). Cash can be exchanged in shops, hotels, etc, at about 3% less than Santiago. Good rates on Amex TCs at Sonoco service station. Amex TCs also changed by Kia-Koe Land Operator, *Hanga Roa Hotel*. Prices are often quoted in dollars, but bills can be paid in pesos. Amex credit cards are accepted on the island, but cannot be used to obtain cash (but enquire at Sonoco service station).

● **Entertainment**

Discotheques: there are three in Hanga Roa: *Maitiki* (open daily), E side of town, with pool table; *Toroko*, near harbour (open Thur-Sat), US$1.25, and *Piditi*, near airport (open Thur-Sat). Also *Maitaka* at Tararaina, only one open Wed. Action begins after 0100. Drinks are expensive: a bottle of pisco costs US$9, canned beer US$2.

● **Hospitals & medical services**

There is a 20-bed hospital as well as 2 resident doctors, a trained nurse and 2 dentists on the island.

● **Post & telecommunications**

Post Office: 0900-1700.

Telephones: phone calls from the Chilean mainland are subsidized, at US$0.35/minute.

Calls to Europe cost US$10 for 3 mins, cheap rate after 1400.

● **Shopping**

On Av Policarpo Toro, the main street, there are lots of small shops and market stalls (which may close during rain) and a couple of supermarkets, cheapest *Kai Nene* or *Tumukai*. Local produce which can be found free (but ask) inc wild guava fruit, fish, 'hierba luisa' tea, and wild chicken. Food, wine and beer are expensive because of freight charges, but local fish, vegetables, fruit and bread are cheap. Average prices: coffee/tea US$0.50, meals about US$7.50, snacks US$1, bread US$2/kg, beer/cola US$1.50 in most bars and restaurants. Bring all you can from the mainland, but not fruit. Vegetarians will have no problems on the island.

Handicrafts: wood carvings, stone moais, best bought from the craftsmen themselves, such as Antonio Tepano Tucki, Juan Acka, Hipolito Tucki and his son (who are knowledgeable about the old culture). The municipal market, left of church, will give you a good view of what is available – no compunction to buy. The airport shop is expensive. Good pieces cost between US$30 and 150. Souvenirs at *Hotu Matuu's Favorite Shoppe* have been described as 'top dollar and she will not bargain', but she does have the best T-shirts. There is a *mercado artesanal* next to the church and people sell handicrafts at Tahai, Vaihu, Rano Raraku and Anakena. Bargaining is only possible if you pay cash.

● **Sports**

Hiking: allow at least a day to walk the length of the island, one way, taking in all the sites. It is 5 easy hrs from Hanga Roa to Rano Raraku (camp at ranger station); 5 hrs to Anakena (camp at ranger station, but ask first). You can hitch back to Hanga Roa, especially at weekends though there are few cars at other times. Anyone wishing to spend time exploring the island would be well-advised to speak to Conaf first (T 223236); they also give good advice on special interests (biology, archaeology, handicrafts, etc). **Horseback**: the best way to see the island, provided you are fit, is on horseback: horses, US$20-25 a day. A guide is useful. Try Emilio Arakie Tepane, who also leads horseback tours of the island (Spanish only) T 504.

● **Tour companies & travel agents**

Mahinatur Ltda, vehicle reservations in advance. Their guide, Christian Walter, is rec;

Kia-Koe, at *Hanga Roa Hotel*, **Schmidt Oster-insel Reisen**, office in *Hanga Roa Hotel*, T 223600, F 223532, English, French and German spoken, offers tours around the island and to caves, both US$15. Maps are sold on Av Policarpo Toro for US$15-18, or at the ranger station at Orongo for US$10. LanChile office on Av Policarpo Toro provides tours of the island (inc during stop-overs). Many agencies, *residenciales* and locals arrange excursions around the island, eg: *Aku-Aku Tours*, Krenia Tucki of *Res Kai Poo*, Michel Fage, Fernando and Marcelo León (Pai Tepano Rano, rec), Hugo Teave (good English, well-informed, polite), Charles Wilkins, **Agencia de Viajes Mahinatur Ltda**, T 20, English-born guide, rec, as is Victoriano Giralde, *Kia-Koe Tours*. Some go in jeeps, others will accompany tourists in hired vehicles (eg US$130 for 8), prices up to US$30 pp/day. The English of other tour guides is often poor.

● **Transport**
Local There is one taxi and in summer a bus goes from Hanga Roa to Anakena on Sun at 1300, returning 1400 (unreliable). **Vehicle rental**: a high-clearance vehicle is better-suited to the roads than a normal vehicle. If you are hiring a car, do the sites from S to N since travel agencies tend to start their tours in the N. Jeep hire at **Sunoco service station**, Vaihu, T 223325 or 223239, on airport road, US$10/1 hr, US$20/4 hrs, US$50/day. **Hertz**, opp airport, US$50/day. Many other vehicle hire agencies on the main street. Chilean or international driving licence essential. There is no insurance available, drive at your own risk (be careful at night, many vehicles drive without lights). **Motorbike rental**: about US$35 a day inc gasoline (Suzuki or Honda 250 rec because of rough roads). Rentals from Av Policarpo Toro, T 223326. **Bicycles**: some in poor condition, are available for rent for US$15 on main street or from *residenciales*, or you can buy a robust

one in Santiago (LanChile transports bikes free up to a limit of 20 kg) and sell it on the island after 4 days.

Transport to Easter Island Air LanChile fly 4 days a week in high season (Sat, Sun, Tues, Thur), 2 days a week low season (Sun, Thur) 3 hrs 25 mins. Return to Santiago is Mon, Tues, Fri and Sat (Mon, Fri out of season). Most flights continue to Papeete, Tahiti. LanChile office on Av Policarpo Toro, T 223279, reconfirm flights here – imperative; do not fly to Easter Island unless you have a confirmed flight out (planes are more crowded to Tahiti than back to Santiago) and reconfirm your booking on arrival on the Island. For details of LanChile air passes which inc Easter Island and which must be purchased outside Chile, see **Information for travellers**. The fare in 1996 was US$812 return. Special deals may be available on flights originating outside Chile. Get to airport early and be prepared for a scramble for seats. Students studying in Chile eligible for 30% discount. If flying to, or from Tahiti, check if you can stay over till another flight or even if there is time for sightseeing before the flight continues – US$10 stop-over sightseeing tours can be arranged (in either case it won't be long enough to take it all in properly). Don't take pesos to Tahiti, they are worthless in French Polynesia. The airport runway has been improved to provide emergency landing for US space shuttles. **Airport tax**: flying from Santiago to Easter Island incurs the domestic tax of US$5; if flying to Tahiti without stopping on Easter Island you pay the international departure tax of US$12.50. The airport tax for international flights from Easter Island to Tahiti is US$5.

Sea There are no passenger services to Easter Island. Freight is brought by sea 3 times a year.

Information for travellers

BEFORE TRAVELLING

ENTRY REQUIREMENTS

● **Documents: tourist cards**

Passport (valid for at least 6 months) and tourist card only are required for entry by all foreigners except citizens of New Zealand, Guyana, Haiti, Kuwait, African countries, Cuba and some ex-Communist countries, who require visas. It is imperative to check visa requirements before travel. These details were correct in Jan 1997 according to the Chilean Consul in London, but regulations change. National identity cards are sufficient for entry by citizens of Argentina, Brazil, Colombia, Paraguay, and Uruguay. Tourist cards are valid for 90 days (except for nationals of Greece, Indonesia and Peru where their validity is 60 days); they can be obtained from immigration offices at major land frontiers and Chilean airports; you must surrender your tourist card on departure and it is essential that you keep it safe. If you wish to stay longer than 180 days (as a tourist), it is easier to make a day-trip to Argentina and return with a new tourist card, rather than to apply for a visa, which involves a great deal of paperwork. An onward ticket is officially required but is seldom asked for. 90-day extensions (US$8) are obtained from any local Gobernación office, which will require proof of funds, then you have to go to Investigaciones for an international record check. Tourist card holders are not allowed to change their status to enable them to stay on in employment or as students: to do this

you need a visa, obtained from a Chilean consulate. On arrival you will be asked where you are staying in Chile.

Visas For some nationalities a visa will be granted within 24 hrs upon production of an onward ticket, for others (eg Guyana), authorization must be obtained from Chile. For visitors from New Zealand, single or multiple entry visa costs US$45. For other nationalities who need a visa, a charge is made, but it varies from country to country. Note that to travel overland to or from Tierra del Fuego a multiple entry visa is essential since the Argentine-Chilean border is crossed more than once (it is advisable to get a multiple entry visa before arriving, rather than trying to change a single entry visa once in Chile). A student card is sometimes useful for obtaining discounts on buses, etc.

Chilean officials are very document-minded. You should always carry your passport in a safe place about your person, or if not going far, leave it in the hotel safe. If staying for several weeks, it is worthwhile registering at your Embassy or Consulate. Then, if your passport is stolen, the process of replacing it is simplified and speeded up. Keeping photocopies of essential documents, including your flight ticket, and some additional passport-sized photographs, is recommended.

Remember that it is your responsibility to ensure that your passport is stamped in and out when you cross frontiers. The absence of entry and exit stamps can cause serious difficulties: seek out the proper migration offices if the stamping process is not carried out as you cross. Also, do not lose your entry card; replacing one causes a lot of trouble, and possibly expense. Citizens of countries which oblige visitors to have a visa can expect more delays and problems at border crossings.

Students If planning to study in Chile for a long period, make every effort to get a student visa in advance. Student cards can be obtained from Providencia 2594, Local 421 and cost US$8, photo and proof of status required.

If you are in full-time education you will be entitled to an International Student Identity Card, which is distributed by student travel offices and travel agencies in 77 countries. The ISIC gives you special prices on all forms of transport (air, sea, rail etc), and access to a variety of other concessions and services. If you need to find the location of your nearest ISIC office contact: The ISIC Association, Box 9048, 1000 Copenhagen, Denmark T (+45) 33 93 93 03.

Identity and membership cards Membership cards of British, European and US motoring organizations have been found useful for discounts off hotel charges, car rentals, maps, towing charges, etc. Student cards must carry a photograph if they are to be of any use in Latin America for discounts. (If you describe yourself as a student on your tourist card you may be able to get discounts, even if you haven't a student card). Business people should carry a good supply of visiting cards, which are essential for good business relations in Latin America.

● **Tourist information**

The national secretariat of tourism, *Sernatur*, has offices throughout the country (addresses are given in the text). City offices provide town maps, leaflets and much useful information. See the **Further reading** section, below, and the **Adventure tourism** section at the beginning of the book for useful organizations and their publications. Ancient Forest International, Box 1850, Redway, CA 95560, T/F 707-323-3015, USA, can be contacted regarding Chilean forests.

MONEY

● **Currency**

The unit is the peso, its sign is $. Notes are for 500, 1,000, 5,000 and 10,000 pesos and coins for 1, 5, 10, 50 and 100 pesos. There is a shortage of change so keep a supply of small denomination coins.

● **Exchange**

Travellers' cheques are accepted at reasonable rates if exchanging them for pesos, though rates are better in Santiago than in most other places and this has become more difficult in most towns apart from Arica, Antofagasta and Puerto Montt. TCs can be changed into dollars in Santiago, but is much more difficult elsewhere: check if a commission is charged as this practice seems to vary. Even slightly damaged US dollar notes may be rejected for exchange. Exchange shops (*casas de cambio*) are open longer hours and often give slightly better rates than banks. It is always worth shopping around. Rates tend to get worse as you go N from Santiago. Official rates are quoted in *El Economista* and *El Mercurio*.

Prices may be quoted in US dollars; check if something seems ridiculously cheap. Remember that foreigners who pay with US dollars cash or TCs are not liable for VAT.

The easiest way to obtain cash is by using ATMs (in major cities) which operate under the sign Redbank; they take Cirrus, Visa and Mastercard and permit transactions up to US$250. Diners' Club, Visa and Mastercard are common in Chile (Bancard, the local card, is affiliated to the last two), offices can be found in most cities and will give cash against the cards: Fincard handles Mastercard and Banco Concepción takes Visa, but American Express is less useful (use in American Express banks does not incur commission). US dollars cash are very rarely given against cards or cheques. For Western Union, T (02) 696-8807.

● **Cost of living**

Shops throughout Chile are well stocked and there is a seasonal supply of all the usual fruits and vegetables. Milk in pasteurized, evaporated, or dried form is obtainable. Chilean tinned food is dear. Food is reasonable, but food prices vary tremendously. Santiago tends to be more expensive for food and accommodation than other parts of Chile. Slide film is very expensive, much cheaper in Bolivia.

In 1995-96 the average cost for a traveller on an economical budget was about US$250/week. Cheap accommodation in Santiago costs over US$10 pp while N and S of the capital rates are US$6-10 pp. Breakfast in hotels, if not inc in price, is about US$2 (instant coffee, roll with ham or cheese, and jam). *Alojamiento* in private houses (bed, breakfast and often use of kitchen) costs US$7-10 pp (bargaining may be possible). Southern Chile is more expensive between 15 Dec and 15 March.

Stop Press Since the calculations for prices in this *Handbook* were made, the peso has continued to appreciate against the dollar. Unless government policy alters the exchange rate, travellers will find that Chile will become more expensive for those carrying dollars.

● **General tips**
Low-value US dollar bills should be carried for changing into local currency if arriving in the country when banks or *casas de cambio* are closed. They are also useful for shopping. If you are travelling on the cheap it is essential to keep in funds; watch weekends and public holidays carefully and never run out of local currency. Take plenty of sucres, in small denominations, when making trips away from large cities.

It is a good idea to take 2 kinds of travellers' cheque: if large numbers of one kind have recently been forged or stolen, making people suspicious, it is unlikely to have happened simultaneously with the other kind.

There are two international **ATM** (automatic telling machine) acceptance systems, Plus and Cirrus. Many issuers of debit and credit cards are linked to one, or both (eg Visa is Plus, Mastercard is Cirrus). Look for the relevant symbol on an ATM and draw cash using your PIN. Frequently, the rates of exchange on ATM withdrawals are the best available. Find out before you leave what ATM coverage there is in Ecuador and what international 'functionality' your card has. Check if your bank or credit card company imposes handling charges. Obviously you must ensure that the account to which your debit card refers contains sufficient funds. With a credit card, obtain a credit limit sufficient for your needs, or pay money in to put the account in credit. If travelling for a long time, consider a direct debit to clear your account regularly. Do not rely on one card, in case of loss. If you do lose a card, immediately contact the 24-hr helpline of the issuer in your home country (keep this number in a safe place).

Money can be transferred between banks. A recommended method is, before leaving, to find out which local bank is correspondent to your bank at home, then when you need funds, telex your own bank and ask them to telex the money to the local bank (confirming by fax). Give exact information to your bank of the routing number of the receiving bank. Funds can be received within 48 banking hrs.

BY AIR

● **From Europe**
To Santiago: British Airways from London via Rio or São Paulo (3 times a week); Air France from Paris (3 per week); from Madrid LanChile and Iberia (4 a week each); KLM from Amsterdam (3), Lufthansa (3) and LanChile from Frankfurt (4 a week), Alitalia from Rome (2) and Aeroflot from Moscow (2). Connections from Europe can be in Buenos Aires.

● **From North America**
American Airlines fly daily from Miami direct. LanChile also has daily flights from Miami. Also from Miami, United flies daily, and AeroPerú via Lima. From New York, United and LanChile. From Los Angeles there are flights with LanChile via Mexico City and Lima, Lacsa via Mexico City, San José and Lima, and Mexicana via Mexico City and Bogotá. From Dallas with American. From other US cities, connect with LanChile flights in Miami, New York or Los Angeles. CP Air have 2 flights per week from Toronto (changing planes in São Paulo).

● **Transpacific routes**
LanChile flies once or twice a week, depending on season, between Tahiti (making connections from Japan, Australia and New Zealand) and Santiago; they stop over at Easter Island. Air New Zealand and LanChile have a cosharing agreement on weekly flights between Auckland, Sydney and Santiago. For excursion fares between Australia/New Zealand and Chile, the stopovers at Easter Island now carry a surcharge of about US$125.

● **Within Latin America**
To/from Buenos Aires (about 75/week) by LanChile, Aerolíneas Argentinas, Air France, Alitalia, KLM, Swissair, American, or Avianca (many depart at the same time, check carefully); from Mendoza by LanChile or National. From Montevideo (8 per week) by LanChile and Pluna; from Asunción 6 times a week by National, 4 days a week with Lapsa; from Rio de Janeiro with British Airways (once) and Iberia direct (4 a week), LanChile, or Varig via São Paulo; from São Paulo non-stop by LanChile, Varig, British Airways; from La Paz 5 per week by Lloyd Aéreo Boliviano (LAB) and daily with LanChile (LAB also from Cochabamba and Santa Cruz, LanChile 3 a week from Santa Cruz); from Caracas, LanChile and Viasa; from

Lima (23/week) by Aero-Perú, Lacsa, United and LanChile; from Bogotá (12) by Avianca, Mexicana and LanChile; from Ecuador, Lan-Chile, Tame and Saeta non-stop from Guayaquil (Saeta and Tame's flights start in Quito).

To Arica and Iquique, from La Paz and Santa Cruz by LAB and LanChile. National flies from Arequipa to Arica and Iquique, also to Iquique from Asunción.

● **General tips**

Airlines will only allow a certain weight of luggage without a surcharge; this is normally 30 kg for first class and 20 kg for business and economy classes, but these limits are often not strictly enforced when it is known that the plane is not going to be full. On some flights from the UK via Paris special outbound concessions are offered (by Iberia, Viasa, Air France, Avianca) of a 2-piece allowance up to 32 kg, but you may need to request this. Passengers seeking a larger baggage allowance can route via USA, but with certain exceptions, the fares are slightly higher using this route. On the other hand, weight limits for internal flights are often lower; best to enquire beforehand.

● **Prices and discounts**

1. It is generally cheaper to fly from London rather than a point in Europe to Latin American destinations; fares vary from airline to airline, destination to destination and according to time of year. Check with an agency for the best deal for when you wish to travel.

2. Most airlines offer discounted fares of one sort or another on scheduled flights. These are not offered by the airlines direct to the public, but through agencies who specialize in this type of fare. In UK, these include *Journey Latin America*, 14-16 Devonshire Road, Chiswick, London W4 2HD (T 0181-747 3108); *Trailfinders*, 48 Earl's Court Road, London W8 6EJ (T 0171-938 3366); *South American Experience*, 47 Causton Street, Pimlico, London SW1P 4AT (T 0171-976 5511); *Last Frontiers*, Swan House, High Street, Long Crendon, Buckinghamshire, HP18 9AF (T 01844 208405); *Passage to South America*, Fovant Mews, 12 Noyna Road, London SW17 7PH (T 0181-767 8989); *STA Travel*, Priory House, 6 Wrights Lane, London W8 6TA (T 0171-938 4711); *Cox & Kings Travel*, St James Court, 45 Buckingham Gate, London (T 0171-873 5001); *Hayes*

& Jarvis, 152 King Street, London W6 0QU (T 0181 222 7844); *Austral Tours*, 120 Wilton Road, London SW1V 1JZ (T 0171-233 5384).

In the USA: *Ladatco Tours*, 2220 Coral Way, Miami, Florida 33156 (T USA (305) 854-8422).

The very busy seasons are 7 Dec-15 Jan and 10 July-10 Sept. If you intend travelling during those times, book as far ahead as possible. Between Feb-May and Sept-Nov special offers may be available.

3. Other fares fall into three groups, and are all on scheduled services:

Excursion (return) fares with restricted validity eg 5-90 days. Carriers are introducing flexibility into these tickets, permitting a change of dates on payment of a fee.

Yearly fares: these may be bought on a one-way or return basis. Some airlines require a specified return date, changeable upon payment of a fee. To leave the return completely open is possible for an extra fee. You must fix the route (some of the cheapest flexible fares now have 6 months validity).

Student (or Under 26) fares (Do not assume that student tickets are the cheapest; though they are often very flexible, they are usually more expensive than A or B above.) Some airlines are flexible on the age limit, others strict. One way and returns available, or 'Open Jaws' (see below). **NB** If you foresee returning home at a busy time (eg Christmas, Aug), a booking is advisable on any type of open-return ticket.

4. For people intending to travel a linear route and return from a different point from that which they entered, there are 'Open Jaws' fares, which are available on student, yearly, or excursion fares.

5. Many of these fares require a change of plane at an intermediate point, and a stopover may be permitted, or even obligatory, depending on schedules. Simply because a flight stops at a given airport does not mean you can break your journey there – the airline must have traffic rights to pick up or set down passengers between points A and B before it will be permitted. This is where dealing with a specialized agency (like Journey Latin America!) will really pay dividends. On multi-stop itineraries, the specialized agencies can often save clients hundreds of pounds.

6. Although it's a little more complicated, it's possible to sell tickets in London for travel originating in Latin America at substantially cheaper fares than those available locally. This is useful for the traveller who doesn't know where he will end up, or who plans to travel for more than a year. Because of high local taxes a one-way ticket from Latin America is more expensive than a one-way in the other direction, so it's always best to buy a return. Taxes are calculated as a percentage of the full IATA fare; on a discounted fare the tax can therefore make up as much as 30-50% of the price.

7. Travellers starting their journey in continental Europe may try: Uniclam-Voyages, 63 rue Monsieur-le Prince, 75006 Paris, for charters. The Swiss company, Balair (owned by Swissair) has regular charter flights to South America. For cheap flights in Switzerland, Globetrotter Travel Service, Renweg, 8001 Zürich, has been recommended. Also try Nouvelles Frontières, Paris, T (1) 41-41-58-58; Hajo Siewer Jet Tours, Martinstr 39, 57462 Olpe, Germany, T (02761) 924120. The German magazine *Reisefieber* is useful.

8. If you buy discounted air tickets *always* check the reservation with the airline concerned to make sure the flight still exists. Also remember the IATA airlines' schedules change in Mar and Oct each year, so if you're going to be away a long time it's best to leave return flight coupons open.

In addition, check whether you are entitled to any refund or re-issued ticket if you lose, or have stolen, a discounted air ticket. Some airlines require the repurchase of a ticket before you can apply for a refund, which will not be given until after the validity of the original ticket has expired. The Iberia group and Air France, for example, operate this costly system. Travel insurance in some cases covers lost tickets.

9. Note that some South American carriers change departure times of short-haul or domestic flights at short notice and, in some instances, schedules shown in the computers of transatlantic carriers differ from those actually flown by smaller, local carriers. If you book, and reconfirm, both your transatlantic and onward sectors through your transatlantic carrier you may find that your travel plans have been based on out-of-date information. The surest solution is to reconfirm your outward flight in an office of the onward carrier itself.

OVERLAND FROM NEIGHBOURING COUNTRIES

By land: roads connect Santiago with Mendoza, and Osorno and Puerto Montt with Bariloche, in Argentina. Less good road connections N and S of Santiago are described in the main text. The main route connecting northern Chile with Bolivia (Arica-La Paz) is paved. Other routes are poor. Note that any of the passes across the Andes to Argentina can be blocked by snow from April onwards. Chile and Peru are linked by a road between Arica and Tacna.

Four international **railways** link Chile with its neighbours. There are two railways to Bolivia: between Arica and La Paz (448 km), and from Antofagasta via Calama to La Paz; and one to Peru: Arica-Tacna. Between Chile and Argentina there is only one line now in operation, between Antofagasta and Salta, in the Argentine NW. There is no international passenger service on this line.

BY SEA

Enquiries regarding passages should be made through agencies in your own country, or through John Alton of Strand Cruise and Travel

Centre, Charing Cross Shopping Concourse, The Strand, London WC2N 4HZ, T 0171-836 6363, F 0171-497 0078. In Switzerland, contact Wagner Frachtschiffreisen, Stadlerstrasse 48, CH-8404 Winterthur, T (052) 242 14 42, F 242 14 87. In the USA, contact Freighter World Cruises, 180 South Lake Ave, Pasadena, CA 91101, T (818) 449-3106, or Traveltips Cruise and Freighter Travel Association, 163-07 Depot Road, PO Box 188, Flushing, NY 11358, T (800) 872-8584. The *Nordwoge* Shipping Company carries 7 passengers on a 70-day round trip: Felixstowe, Bilbao, Panama Canal, Buenaventura, Guayaquil, Callao, Arica (or Iquique), San Antonio, Valparaíso, Talcahuano, Antofagasta, Guayaquil, Buenaventura, Panama Canal, Bilbao, various N European ports, Felixstowe, £5,300 pp. Chilean Line's *Laja* and *Lircay*, New Orleans, Houston, Tampico, Cristóbal, Panama Canal, Guayaquil, Callao, Antofagasta, San Antonio, Arica, Callao, Buenaventura, Panama Canal, Cristóbal, New Orleans, 48-day round trip, US$4,800-5,280 pp.

CUSTOMS

● **Duty free allowance**

500 cigarettes, 100 cigars, 500 grams of tobacco, 3 bottles of liquor, camera, and all articles of personal use. Fruit, vegetables, meat, flowers and milk products may not be imported. It has been reported that bringing a video recorder into Chile involves a great deal of paperwork.

NB There are internal customs checks for all travellers going S on leaving the First Region (ie for duty-free goods from the Zofri free zone in Iquique).

ON ARRIVAL

● **Clothing**

Warm sunny days and cool nights are usual during most of the year except in the far S where the climate is like that of Scotland. Ordinary European medium-weight clothing can be worn during the winter (June to mid-Sept). Light clothing is best for summer (Dec to Mar), but men do not wear white tropical suits.

Chileans are very fashion-conscious. How you dress is mostly how people will judge you. Dress well though conservatively: practical travel clothing makes you stick out as a foreigner. Buying clothing locally can help you to look less like a tourist. A medium weight shawl with some wool content is recommended for women: it can double as pillow, light blanket, bathrobe or sunscreen as required. For men, a smart jacket can be very useful.

● **Courtesy**

Remember that politeness – even a little ceremoniousness – is much appreciated. In this connection professional or business cards are useful. Men should always remove any headgear and say "con permiso" when entering offices, and be prepared to shake hands; always say "Buenos días" (until midday) or "Buenas tardes" and wait for a reply before proceeding further. Always remember that the traveller from abroad has enjoyed greater advantages in life than most Latin American minor officials, and should be friendly and courteous in consequence. Never be impatient; do not criticize situations in public: the officials may know more English than you think and they can certainly interpret gestures and facial expressions. Politeness can be a liability, however, in some situations; most Latin Americans are disorderly queuers. In commercial transactions (buying a meal, goods in a shop, etc) politeness should be accompanied by firmness, and always ask the price first.

Politeness should also be extended to street traders; saying "No, gracias" with a smile is better than an arrogant dismissal. Whether you give money to beggars is a personal matter, but your decision should be influenced by whether a person is begging out of need or trying to cash in on the tourist trail. In the former case, local people giving may provide an indication. Giving money to children is a separate issue, upon which most agree: don't do it. There are occasions where giving food in a restaurant may be appropriate, but first inform yourself of local practice.

● **Entry tax**

A US$20 entry tax is charged on all US citizens, valid until expiry of passport.

● **Hours of business**

Banks: 0900-1400, but closed on Sat. Government offices: 1000-1230 (the public is admitted for a few hrs only). Business houses: 0830-1230, 1400-1800 (Mon to Fri). Shops (Santiago): 1030-1930, but 0930-1330 Sat.

● **Law enforcement**

Officers are Carabineros (brown military uniforms), who handle all tasks except immigration. Investigaciones, in civilian dress, are the detective police who deal with everything except traffic. Policia Internacional, a division of

Investigaciones, handle immigration.

In Chile, you should never offer an official a bribe.

● **Official time**

GMT minus 4 hrs; minus 3 hrs in summer. Clocks change from mid-Sept or Oct to early March.

● **Safety**

Chile is generally a safe country to visit, although like all major cities, Santiago and Valparaíso do have a crime problem in the centre. Keep all documents secure; hide your main cash supply in different places or under your clothes: extra pockets sewn inside shirts and trousers, pockets closed with a zip or safety pin, moneybelts (best worn below the waist rather than outside or at it or around the neck), neck or leg pouches, a thin chain for attaching a purse to your bag or under your clothes and elasticated support bandages for keeping money and cheques above the elbow or below the knee have been repeatedly recommended (the last by John Hatt in *The Tropical Traveller*). Keep cameras in bags (preferably with a chain or wire in the strap to defeat the slasher) or briefcases; take spare spectacles (eyeglasses); don't wear wrist-watches or jewellery. If you wear a shoulder-bag in a market, carry it in front of you. A backpack should be lockable at its base.

Be wary of 'plainclothes policemen'; insist on seeing identification and on going to the police station by main roads. Do not hand over your identification (or money – which he should not need to see anyway) until you are at the station. On no account take them directly back to your lodgings. Be even more suspicious if he seeks confirmation of his status from a passer-by. If someone tries to bribe you, insist on a receipt. If attacked, remember your assailants may well be armed, and try not to resist.

It is best, if you can trust your hotel, to leave any valuables you don't need in safe-deposit there, when sightseeing locally. Always keep an inventory of what you have deposited. If you lose valuables, always report to the police and note details of the report – for insurance purposes.

● **Shopping**

There is an excellent variety of handicrafts: woodwork, pottery, copperware, leatherwork, Indian woven goods inc rugs and ponchos in the S. VAT is 18%.

● **Tipping**

10% in restaurants and a few pesos in bars and soda fountains. Railway and airport porters: US$0.10 a piece of luggage. Cloakroom attendants and cinema usherettes: US$0.05. Taxi-drivers are not tipped.

● **Travelling alone**

The following hints have mainly been supplied by women, but most apply to any single traveller. When you set out, err on the side of caution until your instincts have adjusted to the customs of a new culture. If, as a single woman, you can befriend a local woman, you will learn much more about the country you are visiting. Unless actively avoiding foreigners like yourself, don't go too far from the beaten track; there is a very definite 'gringo trail' which you can join, or follow, if seeking company. This can be helpful when looking for safe accommodation, especially if arriving after dark (which is best avoided). Remember that for a single woman a taxi at night can be as dangerous as wandering around on her own. At borders dress as smartly as possible. Travelling by train is a good way to meet locals, but buses are much easier for a person alone; on major routes your seat is often reserved and your luggage can usually be locked in the hold. It is easier for men to take the friendliness of locals at face value; women may be subject to much unwanted attention. To help minimize this, do not wear suggestive clothing and, advises Alex Rossi of Jawa Timur, Indonesia, do not flirt. By wearing a wedding ring, carrying a photograph of your 'husband' and 'children', and saying that your "husband" is close at hand, you may dissuade an aspiring suitor. If politeness fails, do not feel bad about showing offence and departing. When accepting a social invitation, make sure that someone knows the address and the time you left. Ask if you can bring a friend (even if you do not intend to do so). A good rule is always to act with confidence, as though you know where you are going, even if you do not. Someone who looks lost is more likely to attract unwanted attention.

● **Voltage**

220 volts AC, 50 cycles.

● **Weights & measures**

The **metric** system is obligatory but the quintal of 46 kilos (101.4 lb) is used.

● **What to take**

Everybody has his/her own list, but those most often mentioned include air cushions for slatted seats, inflatable travel pillow for neck support, strong shoes (and remember that footwear over 9 1/2 English size, or 42 European size, is difficult to obtain), a small first-aid kit and handbook, fully waterproof top clothing, waterproof treatment for leather footwear, wax earplugs (which are almost impossible to find outside large cities) and airline-type eye mask to help you sleep in noisy and poorly curtained hotel rooms, sandals (rubber-thong Japanese-type or other – can be worn in showers to avoid athlete's foot), a polyethylene sheet 2 x 1 metres to cover possibly infested beds and shelter your luggage, polyethylene bags of varying sizes (up to heavy duty rubbish bag size) with ties, a toilet bag you can tie round your waist, if you use an electric shaver, take a rechargeable type, a sheet sleeping-bag and pillow-case, a 1 1/2-2m piece of 100% cotton can be used as a towel, a bedsheet, beach towel, makeshift curtain and wrap; a straw hat which can be rolled or flattened and reconstituted after 15 mins soaking in water, a clothes line, a nailbrush (useful for scrubbing dirt off clothes as well as off oneself), a vacuum flask, a water bottle, a small dual-voltage immersion heater, a small dual-voltage (or battery-driven) electric fan, a light nylon waterproof shopping bag, a universal bath- and basin-plug of the flanged type that will fit any waste-pipe (or improvise one from a sheet of thick rubber), string, velcro, electrical insulating tape, large penknife preferably with tin and bottle openers, scissors and corkscrew – the famous Swiss Army range has been repeatedly recommended (for knife sharpening, go to a butcher's shop), alarm clock or watch, candle, torch (flashlight) – especially one that will clip on to a pocket or belt, pocket mirror, pocket calculator, an adaptor and flex to enable you to take power from an electric-light socket (the Edison screw type is the most commonly used). Remember not to throw away spent batteries containing mercury or cadmium; take them home to be disposed of, or recycled properly.

Useful medicaments are given at the end of the 'Health' section (page 424); to these might be added some lip salve with sun protection, and pre-moistened wipes (such as 'Wet Ones'). Always carry toilet paper. Dental floss can be used for backpack repairs, in addition to its original purpose. **Never** carry firearms. Their possession could land you in serious trouble.

A note for **contact lens wearers**: lens solution can be difficult to find, especially outside major cities. Ask for it in a chemist/pharmacy, rather than an optician's.

ON DEPARTURE

● **Airport & other taxes**
7,500 pesos, or US$18.25 for international flights; US$8 for domestic flights. There is a tourist tax on single air fares of 2%, and 1% on return fares beginning or ending in Chile; also a sales tax of 5% on all transport within Chile.

WHERE TO STAY

● **Hotels**
On hotel bills service charges are usually 10%, and VAT on bills is 18%. Prices increase in January. **If you pay in dollars cash or TCs, you do not have to pay VAT**. Dollar rates posted in hotels should not include VAT; peso rates should by law. Whether or not the 18% is added to bills in hotel restaurants that are signed and charged to the hotel bill depends on the policy of the establishment. When booking-in make certain whether meals are included in the price or only breakfast or nothing at all, and don't rely on the posted sheet in the bedroom for any prices. It is often worth asking for a discount, especially out of season. Particularly in North and Central Chile breakfast is likely to be coffee and bread or toast. In more popular tourist destinations, especially in the S, large numbers of families offer accommodation: these are usually advertised by a sign in the window; people often meet buses to offer accommodation. If you are looking for a motel, ask for a *motel turístico*; most motels are short stay.

Cockroaches These are ubiquitous and unpleasant, but not dangerous. Take some insecticide powder if staying in cheap hotels; Baygon (Bayer) has been recommended. Stuff toilet paper in any holes in walls that you may suspect of being parts of cockroach runs.

Toilets Many hotels, restaurants and bars have inadequate water supplies. **Almost without exception used toilet paper should not be flushed down the pan, but placed in the receptacle provided**. This applies even in quite expensive hotels. Failing to observe this custom will block the pan or drain, a considerable health risk. If you are concerned about the hygiene of the facility, put paper on the seat.

● **Camping**
Camping is easy but no longer cheap at official sites. A common practice is to charge US$10 for up to 5 people, with no reductions for fewer

Hotel prices

Our hotel price ranges, including taxes and service charges but without meals unless stated, are as follows:

L1	Over US$200	**L2**	US$151-200	**L3**	US$101-150
A1	US$81-100	**A2**	US$61-80	**A3**	US$46-60
B	US$31-45	**C**	US$21-30	**D**	US$12-20
E	US$7-11	**F**	US$4-6	**G**	Up to US$3

NB Prices are for double rooms, except in **F** and **G** ranges where the price is almost always per person.

Other abbreviations used in the book (apart from pp = per person; a/c = air conditioned; rec = recommended; T = telephone; TCs = travellers' cheques; s/n = "sin número", no street number; p = piso – floor) should be self-explanatory.

than 5. 'Camping Gaz International' stoves are rec, since green replaceable cylinders are available in Santiago (white gas – *benzina blanca* – is available in hardware shops; for good value try the *Sodimac* chain of DIY stores). Copec run a network of 33 'Rutacentros' along Ruta 5 which have showers, cafeterias and offer free camping. Free camping is also available at many filling stations.

● **Youth hostels**

There are youth hostels throughout Chile; average cost about US$5-8 pp. Although some hostels are open only from Jan to the end of Feb, many operate all year round. The IYHA card is usually readily accepted. In summer they are usually crowded and noisy, with only floor space available. Chilean YHA card costs US$4. An additional stamp costing US$4 enables you to use the card in Argentina, Uruguay and Brazil. IYHA card costs US$15. These can be obtained from the Asociación Chilena de Albergues Turísticos Juveniles, Providencia 2594, oficina 420-421, Providencia, Santiago, T 233-3226; together with a useful guidebook of all Youth Hostels in Chile, *Guía Turística de los Albergues Juveniles*. In summer there are makeshift hostels in many Chilean towns, usually in the main schools.

FOOD AND DRINK

FOOD

For information on Chilean cuisine, see the Introductory Article, page 62.

Make sure whether vegetables are included in the price for the main dish; menus often don't make this clear. Always best, if being economical, to stick to fixed-price *table d'hôte* meals or try the local markets.

Lunch is about 1300 and dinner not before 2030. *Onces* (Elevenses) is tea taken at 1700, often accompanied by a snack. The cocktail hour starts at 1900. Waiters are known as *garzón* – never as *mozo*. Good, cheap meals can usually be found in Centros Españoles or Casinos de Bomberos. By law restaurants have to serve a cheaper set meal at lunchtime; it is called *colación* and may not be included on the menu.

Vegetarians should be able to list all the foods they cannot eat; saying "Soy vegetariano/a" (I'm a vegetarian) or "no como carne" (I don't eat meat) is often not enough.

DRINK

Coffee is generally instant except in expresso bars including popular chains of cafés such as *Café Haiti*, *Café Brasil* and *Dino*, found in major cities. Elsewhere specify *café-café*, *expresso*. The soluble tea should be avoided, but teabags are widely available. If you order '*café*, or *té, con leche*', it will come with all milk; to have just a little milk in either, you must specify that. After a meal, instead of coffee, try an *agüita* – hot water in which herbs such as mint, or aromatics such as lemon peel, have been steeped. There is a wide variety, available in sachets, and they are very refreshing.

The local wines are very good; the best are from the central areas. See the Introductory Article, page 65. The bottled wines are graded, in increasing excellence, as *gran vino*, *vino especial* and *vino reservado*. Champagne-style wines are also cheap and acceptable. A small deposit, US$0.30, is charged on most wine bottles. Beer is quite good and cheap (about US$0.75, plus US$0.75 deposit in shops); the draught lager known as Schop is good; also try Cristal Pilsener or Royal Guard in the central regions and Escudo and Polar in the S. Malta, a brown ale, is rec for those wanting a British-type beer.

Good gin is made in Chile. Reasonably good brandy, *anis* and crème de menthe are all bottled in Chile. *Manzanilla* is a local liqueur, made from *licor de oro* (like Galliano); *crema de cacao*, especially Mitjans, has been rec. Two popular drinks are *vaina*, a mixture of sherry, egg and sugar and *cola de mono*, a mixture of *aguardiente*, coffee, milk and vanilla served very cold at Christmas. *Chicha* is any form of alcoholic drink made from fruit; *chicha cocida* is 3-day-old fermented grape juice boiled to reduce its volume and then bottled with a tablespoonful of honey. Cider (*chicha de manzana*) is popular in the S. *Chicha fresca* is plain apple juice. *Mote con huesillo*, made from wheat hominy and dried peaches, is very refreshing in summer.

GETTING AROUND

AIR TRANSPORT

Most flights of LanChile, Ladeco and National, between Santiago and major towns and cities, are given in the text. A new airline, Alta, flies Beechcraft 1900-C planes the length of the country, linking smaller cities. Try to sit on the left flying S, on the right flying N to get the best views of the Andes.

LanChile and Ladeco offer a 21-day 'Visit Chile' ticket; 5 prices: US$300, valid for Santiago and northern Chile, or Santiago and southern Chile; US$550 for all mainland Chile; Pacific 1, US$812, Santiago-Easter Island-Santiago; Pacific 2, US$1,080, valid for a trip to Easter Island and either northern Chile, or southern Chile; Pacific 3, US$1,290 for all mainland Chile and Easter Island. It must be purchased abroad in conjunction with an international ticket and reservations made well ahead since many flights are fully booked in advance. Rerouting charge US$30. Booked destinations can be left out so it is worth including as many destinations as possible. The airpass is not interchangeable between airlines. It is also possible for the route Santiago-Antofagasta-Arica-Santiago to take a coupon ticket which allows greater flexibility. **NB** Book well in advance (several months) for flights to Easter Island in Jan-February. Check with the airlines for matrimonial, student and other discounts. Both LanChile and Ladeco sell out-price tickets (up to 50% off) either as part of special promotions or to stand-by

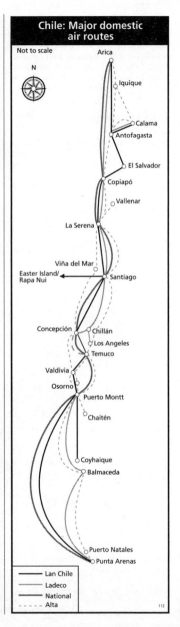

Chile: Major domestic air routes

Not to scale

N

Arica
Iquique
Calama
Antofagasta
El Salvador
Copiapó
Vallenar
La Serena
Viña del Mar
Easter Island/ Rapa Nui
Santiago
Concepción
Chillán
Los Angeles
Temuco
Valdivia
Osorno
Puerto Montt
Chaitén
Coyhaique
Balmaceda
Puerto Natales
Punta Arenas

—— Lan Chile
—— Ladeco
—— National
- - - - Alta

112

passengers (though the availability of standby fares is often denied). Note that with some fares it is as cheap to fly long distance as take a *salón cama* bus, especially with National, whose fares are usually considerably lower than LanChile or Ladeco. **NB** You have to confirm domestic flights at least 24 hrs before departure.

LAND TRANSPORT

● Train

There are 4,470 km of line, of which most are state owned. Most of the privately owned 2,130 km of line are in the desert N, where the northern terminal is Iquique. The main gauge on the Valparaíso and southern lines is 5 ft 6 in (1.676m). Passenger services in the S go as far as Puerto Montt. Passenger services N of the Valparaíso area have ceased except for the international routes to La Paz. The Ferrocarriles

del Estado publish an annual *Guía Turística*, available in various languages from the larger stations.

Trains in Chile are moderately priced, and not as slow as in other Andean countries, but dining car food is expensive. Student discounts are given on *económico* and *salón* fares, but not on sleepers. There is a railway information office at O'Higgins 853 (at end of arcade), Santiago, for all lines except the Antofagasta-Bolivia (Ahumada 11, Oficina 602, T 698-5536). English spoken.

● Road

About one-half of the 79,593 km of roads can be used the year round, though a large proportion of them is unimproved and about 11,145 km are paved. The region round the capital and the Central Valley are the best served.

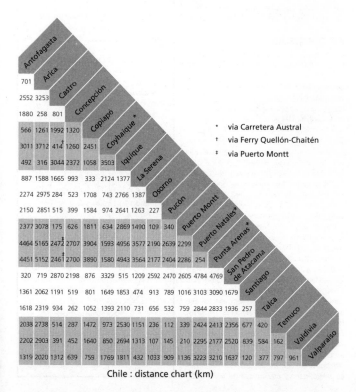

* via Carretera Austral
† via Ferry Quellón-Chaitén
‡ via Puerto Montt

Chile : distance chart (km)

The Pan-American (Longitudinal) Highway, Ruta 5, from Arica through Santiago to Puerto Montt and recently extended by the Carretera Austral beyond Cochrane to within 30 km of its terminus, is vital to the Chilean economy and is paved to Puerto Montt.

● **Bus**

Buses are frequent and on the whole good. Apart from holiday times, there is little problem getting a seat on a long-distance bus. *Salón-cama* services run between main cities (TurBus and Tramaca highly rec). Generally avoid back seats near toilet due to smell and disruption of passing passengers. *Salón-cama* means 25 seats, *semi-cama* means 34 and *Salón-ejecutivo* means 44 seats. Stops are infrequent. Prices are highest between Dec-Mar and fares from Santiago double during the Independence celebrations in September. Since there is lots of competition between bus companies, fares may be bargained lower, particularly just before departure. Students and holders of IYHA cards may get discounts, amount varies, but not usually in high season. Most bus companies will carry bicycles, but may ask for payment (on TurBus payment is mandatory).

● **Motoring**

Documents Always carry your passport and driving licence. According to the Chilean Ley de Tránsito, foreign drivers need only have their national driver's licence, but in the N especially, the carabineros will only accept an international driver's licence. To avoid problems, obtain one before leaving home. Car drivers also require a *Relaciones de pasajeros* document, available at borders, and must present the original registration document of their vehicle, as must motor cyclists. In the case of a car registered in someone else's name, carry a notarized letter of authorization. Car drivers should have all their papers in order and to hand since there are frequent checks, but fewer in the S. Carabineros are strict about speed limits: Turistel maps mark police posts, make sure you are not speeding when you pass them.

According to the RAC in the UK there are three recognized documents for taking a vehicle into South America: a *carnet de passages* issued by the Fedération Internationale de l'Automobile (FIA – Paris), a *carnet de passages* issued by the Alliance Internationale de Tourisme (AIT-Geneva), and the *Libreta de Pasos por Aduana* issued by the Federación Interamericana de Touring y Automóvil Clubs (FITAC).

Officially, any one of these three is required for Chile, but in practice, none is asked for. The *libreta*, a 10-page book of three-part passes for customs, should be available from any South American automobile club member of FITAC; cost seems to be US$200, half refundable. The *carnet de passages* is issued only in the country where the vehicle is registered (in the UK it costs £65 for 25 pages, £55 for 10 pages, valid 12 months, either bank indemnity or insurance indemnity, half of the premium refundable value of the vehicle and countries to be visited required), available from the RAC or the AA. In the USA the AAA seems not to issue the *carnet*, although the HQ in Washington DC may give advice. It is available from the Canadian Automobile Association (1775 Courtwood Crescent, Ottawa, K2C 3JZ, T 613-226-7631, F 613-225-7383) for Canadian and US citizens, cost C$450; full details obtainable from the CAA.

Insurance for the vehicle is obligatory and can be bought at borders. It is getting increasingly difficult to insure against accident, damage or theft in the country of origin. It is very expensive to insure against accident and theft, especially as you should take into account the value of the car increased by duties calculated in real (ie non devaluing) terms. If the car is stolen or written off you will be required to pay very high import duty on its value. Get the legally required minimum cover, not expensive, as soon as you can, because if you should be involved in an accident and are uninsured, your car could be confiscated. If anyone is hurt, do not pick them up (you may become liable). Seek assistance from the nearest police station or hospital if you are able to do so.

Information and maps Members of foreign motoring organizations may join the Automóvil Club de Chile, Av Vitacura 8620, Santiago, T 212-5702, F 229-5295 (US$58/3months) and obtain discounts at hotels. Road maps may be obtained from the Santiago headquarters, or other regional offices. You will find several individual maps provide much greater detail than the Club's road atlas. The *Turistel* Guides (see **Further reading**) are very useful for roads and town plans, but note that not all distances are exact and that the description 'ripio' (gravel) usually requires high clearance; 'buen ripio' should be OK for ordinary cars. The **Further reading** section, in **Rounding up**, gives more details of maps and guide books.

Fuel Gasoline (sold in litres) costs the equivalent of US$2.40 a gallon; it becomes more expensive the further N and further S you go. Unleaded fuel, 93 octane, is available at many service stations, but less frequently outside Santiago and not in the Atacama region. Unleaded 95 and 97 octane are less common. Diesel fuel is widely available. Service stations are frequently reluctant to accept credit cards. Often when they advertise that they accept credit cards, they refuse to do so: always ask beforehand. When driving in the S (on the Carretera Austral particularly), and in the desert N, always top up your fuel tank and carry spare petrol/gasoline. Car hire companies may not have fuel cans. These are obtainable from some supermarkets but not from service stations. The standard of facilities in service stations is generally good.

Preparation Preparing your own car for the journey is largely a matter of common sense: obviously any part that is not in first class condition should be replaced. It's well worth installing extra heavy-duty shock-absorbers (such as Spax or Koni) before starting out, because a long trip on rough roads in a heavily laden car will give heavy wear. Tyres need to be hard-wearing (avoid steel belt). Fit tubes on 'tubeless' tyres, since air plugs for tubeless tyres are hard to find, and if you bend the rim on a pothole, the tyre will not hold air. Take spare tubes, and an extra spare tyre. For car and motorcycle tyres try Serranos 32, Santiago, reported to be the best stock in South America. Also take spare plugs, fanbelts, radiator hoses and headlamp bulbs; even though local equivalents can easily be found in cities, it is wise to take spares for those occasions late at night or in remote areas when you might need them. You can also change the fanbelt after a stretch of long, hot driving to prevent wear (eg after 15,000 km/10,000 miles). If your vehicle has more than one fanbelt, always replace them all at the same time (make sure you have the necessary tools if doing it yourself). If your car has sophisticated electrics, spare 'black boxes' for the ignition and fuel injection are advisable, plus a spare voltage regulator or the appropriate diodes for the alternator, and elements for the fuel, air and oil filters if these are not a common type. (Some drivers take a spare alternator of the correct amperage, especially if the regulator is incorporated into the alternator.) Dirty fuel is a frequent problem, so be prepared to change filters more often than you would at home: in a diesel car you will need to check the sediment bowl often, too. An extra in-line fuel filter is a good idea if feasible (although harder to find, metal canister type is preferable to plastic), and for travel on dusty roads an oil bath air filter is best for a diesel car. It is wise to carry a spade, jumper cables, tow rope and an air pump. Fit tow hooks to both sides of the vehicle frame. A 12 volt neon light for camping and repairs will be invaluable. Spare fuel containers should be steel and not plastic, and a siphon pipe is essential for those places where fuel is sold out of the drum. Take a 10 litre water container for self and vehicle. In Santiago car parts available from many shops on C 10 de Julio.

Security Apart from the mechanical aspects, spare no ingenuity in making your car secure. Use heavy chain and padlocks to chain doors shut, fit security catches on windows, remove interior window winders (so that a hand reaching in from a forced vent cannot open the window). All these will help, but none is foolproof. Anything on the outside – wing mirrors, spot lamps, motifs etc – is likely to be stolen too. So are wheels if not secured by locking nuts. Try never to leave the car unattended except in a locked garage or guarded parking space. Remove all belongings and leave the empty glove compartment open when the car is unattended. Also lock the clutch or accelerator to the steering wheel with a heavy, obvious chain or lock. Street children will generally protect your car fiercely in exchange for a tip. Be sure to note down key numbers and carry spares of the most important ones (but don't keep all spares inside the vehicle).

Driving at night is not recommended; be especially careful on major roads into and out of cities in the early evening because people tend to cross the highway without warning.

● **Car hire**
Many agencies, both local and international, operate in Chile. Vehicles may be rented by the day, the week or the month, with or without unlimited mileage. Rates quoted do not normally include insurance or 18% VAT. Make sure you know what the insurance covers, in particular third-party insurance. Often this is only likely to cover small bumps and scratches. Ask about extra cover for a further premium. If you are in a major accident and your insurance is inadequate, your stay in Chile may well be prolonged beyond its intended end. A small car, with unlimited mileage costs about US$500 a week in high season, a pick-up much

more. In some areas rates are much lower off-season. (At peak holiday times, eg Independence cele)rations, car hire is very difficult.) Shop around, there is much competition. Note that the Automóvil Club de Chile has a car hire agency (with discounts for members or affiliates) and that the office may not be at the same place as the Club's regional delegation. **NB** If intending to leave the country in a hired car, you must obtain an authorization from the hire company, otherwise you will be turned back at the frontier. When leaving Chile this is exchanged for a quadruple form, one part of which is surrendered at each border control. (If you plan to leave more than once you will need to photocopy the authorization.)

● **Taxis**

Taxis have meters, but agree beforehand on fares for long journeys out of city centres or special excursions. A 50% surcharge is applied after 2100 and on Sun. Taxi drivers rarely know the location of any streets away from the centre. There is no need to tip unless some extra service, like the carrying of luggage, is given.

● **Motorcycling**

People are generally very amicable to motorcyclists and you can make many friends by returning friendship to those who show an interest in you.

The Machine It should be off road capable: a good choice would be the BMW R80/100/GS for its rugged and simple design and reliable shaft drive, but a Kawasaki KLR 650s, Honda Transalp/Dominator, or the ubiquitous Yamaha XT600 Tenere would also be suitable. A road bike can go most places an off road bike can go at the cost of greater effort.

Preparations Fit heavy duty front fork springs and the best quality rebuildable shock absorber you can afford (Ohlins, White Power). Fit lockable luggage such as Krausers (reinforced luggage frames) or make some detachable aluminium panniers. Fit a tank bag and tank panniers for better weight distribution. A large capacity fuel tank (Acerbis), +300 mile/480 km range is essential if going off the beaten track. A washable air filter is a good idea (K&N), also fuel filters, fueltap rubber seals and smaller jets for high altitude Andean motoring. A good set of trails-type tyres as well as a high mudguard are useful. Get to know the bike before you go, ask the dealers in your country what goes wrong with it and arrange a link whereby you

can get parts flown out to you. If riding a chain driven bike, a fully enclosed chaincase is useful. A hefty bash plate/sump guard is invaluable.

Spares Reduce service intervals by half if driving in severe conditions. A spare rear tyre is useful but you can buy modern tyres (see under **Motoring** above). Take oil filters, fork and shock seals, tubes, a good manual, spare cables (taped into position), a plug cap and spare plug lead. A spare electronic ignition is a good idea, try and buy a second-hand one and make arrangements to have parts sent out to you. A first class tool kit is a must and if riding a bike with a chain then a spare set of sprockets and an 'o' ring chain should be carried. Spare brake and clutch levers should also be taken as these break easily in a fall. Parts are few and far between, but mechanics are skilled at making do and can usually repair things. Castrol oil can be bought everywhere and relied upon.

Take a puncture repair kit and tyre levers. Find out about any weak spots on the bike and improve them. Get the book for international dealer coverage from your manufacturer, but don't rely on it. They frequently have few or no parts for modern, large machinery.

For motorcyclists the following shops in Santiago have been rec: *Calvin y Calvin*, Av Las Condes 8038, T 224-3434, run by Winston Calvin, friendly, helpful, speaks English, knows about necessary paperwork for buying bikes, Honda and Yamaha parts and service; *Solo Moto*, Vitacura 2760, T 2311178, English spoken, service and parts for Honda and Yamaha; *Moto Service*, Vitacura 2715, new and second-hand Honda and Yamaha dealer; *Guillermo de Freitas Rojas* (Willy), C Félix Mendelson, 4740-Santiago, T 521-1853, excellent BMW mechanic; *Miebacc*, Doble Almeda 1040, Nunoa, T 2237533, for BMW parts and service. Mechanics, etc outside Santiago are given in the text.

Clothes and equipment A tough waterproof jacket, comfortable strong boots, gloves and a helmet with which you can use glass goggles (Halycon) which will not scratch and wear out like a plastic visor. The best quality tent and camping gear that you can afford and a petrol stove which runs on bike fuel is helpful.

Security Try not to leave a fully laden bike on its own. An Abus D or chain will keep the bike secure. A cheap alarm gives you peace of mind if you leave the bike outside a hotel at night. Most hotels will allow you to bring the bike inside. Look for hotels that have a courtyard or more secure parking and never leave luggage on the bike overnight or whilst unattended.

Documents Passport, International Driving Licence, bike registration document are necessary. Riders fare much better with a *carnet de passages* than without it.

● **Cycling**
At first glance a bicycle may not appear to be the most obvious vehicle for a major journey, but given ample time and reasonable energy it most certainly is the best. It can be ridden, carried by almost every form of transport from an aeroplane to a canoe, and can even be lifted across one's shoulders over short distances. Cyclists can be the envy of travellers using more orthodox transport, since they can travel at their own pace, explore more remote regions and meet people who are not normally in contact with tourists.

Choosing a bicycle The choice of bicycle depends on the type and length of expedition being undertaken and on the terrain and road surfaces likely to be encountered. Unless you are planning a journey almost exclusively on paved roads – when a high quality touring bike such as a Dawes Super Galaxy would probably suffice – a mountain bike is strongly recommended. The good quality ones (and the cast iron rule is **never** to skimp on quality) are incredibly tough and rugged, with low gear ratios for difficult terrain, wide tyres with plenty of tread for good road-holding, cantilever brakes, and a low centre of gravity for improved stability. Although touring bikes, and to a lesser extent mountain bikes, and spares are available in the larger cities, remember that most indigenous manufactured goods are shoddy and rarely last. Buy everything you possibly can before you leave home.

Bicycle equipment A small but comprehensive tool kit (to include chain rivet and crank removers, a spoke key and possibly a block remover), a puncture repair kit with plenty of extra patches and glue, a set of brake blocks, brake and gear cables and all types of nuts and bolts, at least 12 spokes (best taped to the chain stay), a light oil for the chain (eg Finish-Line Teflon Dry-Lube), tube of waterproof grease, a pump secured by a pump lock, a Blackburn parking block (a most invaluable accessory, cheap and virtually weightless), a cyclometer, a loud bell, and a secure lock and chain. *Richard's Bicycle Book* makes useful reading for even the most mechanically minded.

Luggage and equipment Strong and waterproof front and back panniers are a must. When packed these are likely to be heavy and should be carried on the strongest racks available. Poor quality racks have ruined many a journey for they take incredible strain on unpaved roads. A top bag cum rucksack (eg Carradice) makes a good addition for use on and off the bike. A Cannondale front bag is good for maps, camera, compass, altimeter, notebook and small tape-recorder. (Other rec panniers are Ortlieb – front and back – which is waterpoof and almost 'sandproof', Mac-Pac, Madden and Karimoor.) 'Gaffa' tape is excellent for protecting vulnerable parts of panniers and for carrying out all manner of repairs.

All equipment and clothes should be packed in plastic bags to give extra protection against dust and rain. (Also protect all documents, etc carried close to the body from sweat.) Always take the minimum clothing. It's better to buy extra items en route when you find you need them. Generally it is best to carry several layers of thin light clothes than fewer heavy, bulky ones. Always keep one set of dry clothes, including long trousers, to put on at the end of the day. The incredibly light, strong, waterproof and wind resistant goretex jacket and overtrousers are invaluable. Training shoes can be used for both cycling and walking.

Useful tips Wind, not hills is the enemy of the cyclist. Try to make the best use of the times of day when there is little; mornings tend to be best but there is no steadfast rule. Take care to avoid dehydration, by drinking regularly. In hot, dry areas with limited supplies of water, be sure to carry an ample supply. For food, carry the staples (sugar, salt, dried milk, tea, coffee, porridge oats, raisins, dried soups, etc) and supplement these with whatever local foods can be found in the markets. Give your bicycle a thorough daily check for loose nuts or bolts or bearings. See that all parts run smoothly. A good bike should last 2,000 miles, 3,200 km or more but be sure to keep it as clean as possible – an old toothbrush is good for this – and to oil it lightly from time to time. Remember that thieves are attracted to towns and cities, so when sight-seeing, try to leave your bicycle with someone such as a café owner or a priest. Country people tend to be more honest and are usually friendly and very inquisitive. However, don't take unnecessary risks; always see that your bicycle is secure (most hotels will allow bikes to be kept in rooms). In more remote regions dogs can be vicious; carry a stick or some small stones to frighten them off. Traffic on main roads can be a nightmare; it is usually far more rewarding to keep to the smaller roads or to paths if they exist. Most towns have a bicycle shop of some description, but it is best to do your own repairs and adjustments whenever possible.

The Expedition Advisory Centre, administered by the Royal Geographical Society, 1, Kensington Gore, London SW7 2AR has published a useful monograph entitled *Bicycle Expeditions*, by Paul Vickers. Published in Mar 1990, it is available direct from the Centre, price £6.50 (postage extra if outside the UK). (In the UK there is also the Cyclist's Touring Club, CTC, Cotterell House, 69 Meadrow, Godalming, Surrey, GU7 3HS, T 01483-417217, e-mail cycling@ctc.org.uk, for touring, and technical information.)

Most cyclists agree that the main danger comes from other traffic. A rearview mirror has been frequently recommended to forewarn you of vehicles which are too close behind. You also need to watch out for oncoming, overtaking vehicles, unstable loads on trucks, protruding loads etc. Make yourself conspicuous by wearing bright clothing and a helmet.

● **Hitchhiking**

Hitchhiking is easy and safe, but in some regions traffic is sparse.

BOAT

Shipping information is given in the text under Santiago and all the relevant southern ports. Local newspapers are useful for all transport schedules.

COMMUNICATIONS

● **Language**

The local pronunciation of Spanish, very quick and lilting, with final syllables cut off, can present difficulties to the foreigner.

● **Newspapers**

Santiago daily papers *El Mercurio, La Nación* (state-owned), *La Epoca* (liberal/left), *La Segunda, La Tercera* and *La Quarta. Las Ultimas Noticias. The Latest Daily News* is an English language paper, published daily except Mon, in Santiago, with international news and tourism details. Also in English, *The News Review* is published on Wed and Sat (which includes the *Guardian Weekly*) – Casilla 151/9, Santiago, T 236-1423/24, F 235-9891; *Condor*, weekly in German.

Weekly magazines: *Hoy, Qué Pasa, Ercilla*. Monthly: *Rutas* (official organ, Automobile Association).

● **Postal services**

Airmail takes 3-4 days from the UK. Seamail takes 8-12 weeks. There is a daily airmail service to Europe with connections to the UK. Poste restante only holds mail for 30 days, then returns it to sender. Lista de Correo in Santiago, Central Post Office, is good and efficiently organized. Rates: letters to Europe/North America US$1.20, aerogrammes US$0.75. To register a letter costs US$0.75. Surface mail rates for parcels to Europe: less than 1 kg US$14; 1-3 kg US$18; 10 kg US$30.

● **Radio**

World Band Radio South America has more local and community radio stations than practically anywhere else in the world; a shortwave (world band) radio offers a practical means to brush up on the language, sample popular culture and absorb some of the richly varied regional music. International broadcasters such as the BBC World Service, the Voice of America, Boston (Mass)-based Monitor Radio International (operated by *Christian Science Monitor*) and the Quito-based Evangelical station, HCJB, keep the traveller abreast of news and events, in both English and Spanish.

Compact or miniature portables are recommended, with digital tuning and a full range of shortwave bands, as well as FM, long and medium wave. Detailed advice on radio models (£150 for a decent one) and wavelengths can be found in the annual publication, *Passport to World Band Radio* (Box 300, Penn's Park, PA 18943, USA). Details of local stations is listed in *World TV and Radio Handbook* (WTRH), PO Box 9027, 1006 AA Amsterdam, The Netherlands, US$19.95. Both of these, free wavelength guides and selected radio sets are available from the BBC World Service Bookshop, Bush House Arcade, Bush House, Strand, London WC2B 4PH, UK, T 0171-257 2576.

● **Telephone services**

National and international calls have been opened up for competition. In May 1996 there were eight main companies (*portadores* carriers) offering competing rates (widely advertised). Callers choose companies by dialling an access code before the city code. Access codes: Entel 123; CTC Mundo 188, CNT (Telefónica del Sur – in Regions X and XI) 121: VTR 120; Chilesat 171; Bell South Chile 181; Iusatel Chile

155 (under new ownership, Jan 1997); Transam Comunicaciones 113. For international calls you dial the company code, then 0, then the country code. International calls are cheap. Ask which carrier has the best links with the country you wish to call (eg for making collect calls); for instance CTC is good for phoning Germany.

Telephone boxes can be used to make local and long-distance calls, for making collect calls and receiving calls. Although it is possible to make international calls from these phones, in practice it may be easier to go to a company office. Telephone boxes have been programmed to direct calls via one carrier: to make a local call, simply dial the number you require and pay the rate charged by the carrier who owns the booth, US$0.20-0.30/minute. To make an inter-urban call, dial '0' plus the area code (DDD) and the number; if you wish to select a carrier, dial its code, then the area code (leaving out '0'), then the number. The area codes given in the text include '0'; omit this if selecting a carrier. To make an international call from a carrier's booth without choosing a different company, dial '00' before the country code. Yellow phones accept only 50 peso coins. Blue phones accept pre-paid phone cards costing 5,000 pesos (tarjeta telefónica); available from kiosks. On phone cards, only the time of the call is charged rather than the normal 3 min minimum. There are special phones for long-distance domestic calls which accept credit cards (Mastercard and Visa). Entel has strategically-placed, self-dialling phones, which are white. Users press a button and are instantly connected with the operator from their own country.

To send a fax abroad costs US$4-5, depend-ing on the company. There is also a charge for receiving a fax. VTR also operate telex services. Amex Card holders can often use telex facilities at Amex offices free of charge.

● **Television**
TV channels include TVUC (Universidad Católica) on Channel 13, the leading station; TVN (government operated) on Channel 7; Megavisión (private) on Channel 9 and La Red (private) on Channel 4.

SPORTS

Sernatur will give all the necessary information about sport. Adventure sports are listed at the beginning of the book.

Horse racing is popular and meetings are held every Sun and on certain feast days at Viña del Mar, Santiago and Concepción throughout the year; horse riding and rodeo are also popular. Other popular sports are football and basketball. Viña del Mar has a cricket ground; on Sat there are polo matches at Santiago.

HOLIDAYS AND FESTIVALS

1 Jan	New Year's Day
Easter	Holy Week (2 days)
1 May	Labour Day
21 May	Navy Day
15 Aug	Assumption
18, 19 Sept	Independence Days
12 Oct	Discovery of America
1 Nov	All Saints Day
8 Dec	Immaculate Conception
25 Dec	Christmas Day.

Rounding up

ACKNOWLEDGEMENTS

Charlie Nurse would like to thank the following for their assistance and hospitality in Chile during research visits for this Handbook in Jan 1996, Aug 1996 and Jan 1997 and on earlier research visits for the *South American Handbook* (in chronological order): Don Santiago and Doña Maria Castillo, San Bernardo; Doña Alicia Castillo, Blanca Solar and Enrique García, Antofagasta; Juan and Ivania Solar, Chuquicamata; Ernesto Cienfuegos, Hostal Licahue, Contulmo; Carlos Grady, Hospedaje Esmeralda By The Sea, Chonchi; Adrian Turner, Travellers', Puerto Montt; Werner and Cecilia Ruf-Chaura, Casa Cecilia, Puerto Natales; Helen Fell, Arka Patagonia, Punta Arenas; Arturo Aliaga Mancilla, Turismo Comapa, Punta Arenas.

Special thanks for encouragment, hospitality and help are also due to Manuel and Ximena Fernández and their sons, Antonio, Jano and Robin, and to their relatives, Sra Leontina vda de Standen and Alicia in Santiago and Don Luis Pineda and family in Puente Alto. Support and assistance were also generously given by Chilean friends in Britain, notably Leonardo and Patricia Castillo and Jim and Mini Infield; Nelson González patiently explained some of the secrets of Rodeo.

We are also grateful to the staff of Sernatur especially in Santiago, Concepción, Arica and Punta Arenas, as well as to Sr Angel Lazo and the staff of Conaf in Santiago.

Thanks are also due to the following for specialist contributions, Peter Pollard for Geology and Climate sections; Nigel Dunstone for Flora and Fauna; Huw Clough for Archaeology and Prehistory; Valerie Fraser for Fine Art and Sculpture; Nigel Gallop for Music and Dance; Jaime Baez for Food; Simon Harvey and Mark Duffy for Adventure Tourism; Josselyn van der Pol and Leandro Yáñez Sarmiento for Skiing; Robert and Caroline Ely for Yachting and Sailing; Sarah Cameron for the Economics sections; Barbara Knapton on the Parque Nacional Lauca; Bob Headland on Torres del Paine and Antarctica and Kim Crosbie on the Falkland Islands/Islas Malvinas.

Ben Box wrote the literature sections and was, as usual, a constant source of support, encouragement and ideas; without his efforts in the final stages, the end product would have been far inferior.

We are most grateful to Elaine Vassiliou, Representative of the Falkland Islands Government London office, for her help.

Final thanks must also go to the travellers who contributed to the 1997 edition of the *South American Handbook*.

FURTHER READING

MAPS AND GUIDE BOOKS

A rec guide book is *Turistel*, published annually in three parts, *Norte*, *Centro*, and *Sur*, sponsored by the CTC telephone company, with information and a wealth of maps covering the whole country and neighbouring tourist centres in Argentina (eg Mendoza, San Martín de los Andes, Bariloche), in Spanish only. Each volume costs between US$11-15, depending where you buy it, but buying the whole set is better value; they can be found in CTC offices, bookshops, but best of all in the news stands in the centre of Santiago. Turistel also publishes a *Mapa rutero* annually, US$4 from news stands and a guide to camping US$9. The publisher is Impresora y Comercial Publiguías SA.

Geophysical and topographical maps (US$11) are available from **Instituto Geográfico Militar**, at the main office Dieciocho 369, T 698-7278, open 0900-1800 Mon-Fri, closed in Jan/February. In 1991 the Instituto Geográfico published a *Guía Caminera*, with roads and city plans, for US$8.75 (available only at IGM offices, not 100% accurate). The Biblioteca Nacional, Moneda 650, has an excellent collection of maps which can be photocopied, particularly useful for climbing.

Conaf (see under **Flora and fauna** and Santiago, **Tourist offices**) publishes a series of illustrated booklets in Spanish/English on Chilean trees, shrubs and flowers, rec, as well as **Juventud, Turismo y Naturaleza**, which lists National Parks, their facilities and the flora and fauna of each. Bird-lovers will appreciate *Guía de Campo de Las Aves de Chile*, by B Araya and G Millie.

A recommended series of general maps is that published by *International Travel Maps* (ITM), 345 West Broadway, Vancouver BC, V5Y 1P8, Canada, T (604) 879-3621, F (604) 879-4521, compiled with historical notes, by the late Kevin Healey.

OTHER SUGGESTIONS

Chile's recent history is examined in S Collier and W F Slater, *A History of Chile 1808-1994* (Cambridge University Press, 1996)

while M H Spooner's *Soldiers In A Narrow Land* (University of California Press, 1994) is a readable account of the Pinochet dictatorship by a North American journalist resident in the country at the time. Among travellers, Bruce Chatwin's *In Patagonia* (Pan 1977) is a classic for those visiting the far S, though Chatwin is heavily criticized by John Pilkington in *An Englishman In Patagonia* (Century 1991). Rosie Swale in *Back to Cape Horn* (Glasgow: Fontana, 1988) describes her epic horse ride the length of Chile; Sara Wheeler recounts her journey through Chile in *Travels in a Thin Country* (London: Little, Brown and Co, 1994).

Jan Read's *The Wines of Chile* (Mitchell Beazley, 1994) is a gazeteer of the vineyards and wineries, ideal for the discerning specialist. *Patagonia*, by Claudio Almarza V (Punta Arenas: GeoPatagonia) is a book of photographs, with text, on the region.

Further reading on activities and adventure tourism is given at the end of the **Adventure tourism** section. The **Literature** and **Arts and crafts** sections also contain many other suggestions for further reading. The latter mentions information on the Mapuche; more can be found, within the entire American Indian context, in *Return of the Indian: Conquest and Revival in the Americas*, by Phillip Wearne (London: Cassell/Latin America Bureau, 1996).

The South American Explorer, the journal of the *South American Explorers Club*, regularly publishes articles on Chile (126 Indian Creek Rd, Ithaca, New York 14850, USA). Issues 22 (Aug 1989) and 31 (May 1992) both had features on Easter Island. Other titles on Easter Island will be found in that chapter.

Useful addresses

Argentina
Tagle 2762, Buenos Aires,
T 54(1)8027020, F 54(1)8045927

Australia
Monaro Cres Act 2603, PO Box 69, Canberra, T 61(6)2862430, F 61(6)2861289

Austria
Lugeck 1/3/9, Vienna 1010,
T 43(1)5129208, F 43-1-5129208

Belgium
40 Rue Montoyer, 1040 Brussels,
T 32(2)2801620, F 32(2)2801481

Brazil
Ses-Avda de las Naciones, Lote 11,
Brasília, T 55(61)2265545,
F 55(61)2255478

Canada
151 Slater St, Suite 605, Ottawa, Ontario
K1P 5H3, T 1(613)2352313,
F 1(613)2351176, echile@globalx.net

Colombia
Calle 100 Nro 11 B-44, Apartado Aereo
90061, Santa Fe de Bogotá,
T 57(1)2147990, F 57(1)6193863

Costa Rica
Del Automercado Los Yoses, 50 Mts Este
y 225 Mts Norte, A Postal 10102, T 506-
2241702, F 506-2537016

Denmark
Kastelsvej 15, Iii 2100, Copenhagen,
T 45-31385834, F 45-31384201,
chiledk@inet.uni-c.dk

Ecuador
Juan Pablo Sanz 3617 y Amazonas, 4°
Piso, Edificio Xerox, Quito,
T 593(2)249403, F 593(2)444470

El Salvador
Pas Bellavista 121, Entre 9A Calle Pnte y
9A Calle Pnte Bis, Colonia, T 503-
237132, F 503-793647

Finland
Erottajankatu 11 - 0130 Helsinki,
T 358(0)611699, F 358(0)611377

France
2 Avenue de la Motte Picouet, 75007
Paris, T 33(1)45518490, F 33(1)44185961

Germany
Kronprinzen Strasse 20, 53173 Bonn,
T 49(228)955840, F 49(228)9558440

Guatemala
14 Calle 15-21, Zona 13, Casilla 643, Ciudad de Guatemala, T 502(2)348273,
F 502(2)348276

Honduras
Ed Cia de Seguros Inter Piso 6 BL, Mazan
Colonia Los Castaòos, Tegucigalpa, T 504-
313703, F 504-328853

Indonesia
Bina Mulia I Bldg 7th Flr, Jl HR Rasuna
Said, Kav 10, Kuningan, Jakarta,
T 62(21)5201131, F 62(21)5201955

Israel
Wingate 205, Herzlya Pituah, Tel Aviv,
T (09)506944, F 5662121

Italy
Via PO No 23, 00198 Rome,
T 39(6)8841435, F 39(6)8841452

Japan
Nihon Seimei Akabanebashi Bldg 8F, 3-1-
14 Shiba, Minato-ku, Tokyo 105,
T 81(3)34527561, F 81(3)37694156

Malaysia
Peti 27 Wisma Selangor Dredging West

Block 8 Piso, 142-C Jalan Ampang,
T 60(3)2616203, F 60(3)2622219

Mexico
Montes Urales 460, 1 er Piso, Colonia
Lomas Chapultepec, CP 11000 Mexico,
T 52(5)5200361, F 52(5)5202357

Netherlands
Mauritskade 51, Casilla 2514, The
Hague, T 31(70)3639884,
F 31(70)3616227

New Zealand
1-3 Willeston St, Willis Corroon House
7th Flr, PO Box 3861, Wellington,
T 64(4)4725180, F 64(4)4725324,
embchile@ihug.co.nz

Nicaragua
Edif Julia 2 do Piso Carretera Sur AP
4541, Telcor Central, Managua,
T 505(2)660302, F 505(2)660181

Norway
Meltzers Gate 5, 0257 Oslo, T 47-
22448955, F 47-22442421

Panama
Edif Banco De Boston, Piso 11, Elvira
Mendez y Via España, Panama, T 507-
2694915, F 507-2635530

Paraguay
Guido Spano 1687 C/Juan B Motta, Asun-
cion, T 595(21)660344, F 595(21)662755

Peru
Avda Javier Prado Oeste 790, San Isidro,
Lima, T 51(1)2212084, F 51(1)2212085

Portugal
Avda Miguel Bombarda 5-1 1000, Lis-
bon, T 351(1)528054, F 351(1)3150909

Singapore
105 Cecil St 14-01/02, The Octagon
Building, Singapore 106, T 65-2238577,
F 65-2250677

South Africa
5 Flr, Campus Centre (Volkskas Bank
Bldg), Burnett & Hilda St, Pretoria,
T 27(12)3421511, F 27(12)3421658

Spain
Lagasca 88, 6 Piso, Madrid 28001,
T 34(1)4319160, F 34(1)5775560

Switzerland
Eigerplatz 5, 12 Piso, 3007 Berne,

T 41(31)3710745, F 41(31)3720025

Thailand
15 Sukhumvit Soi 61, Prakanong, Bang-
kok 10110, T 66(2)3914858,
F 66(2)3918380

UK
12 Devonshire St, London, W1N 2DS,
T 44(71)5806392, F 44(71)4365204

Uruguay
Calle Andes 1365, Piso 1 y 2, Montevideo, T 598(2)982223, F 598(2)921649

USA
1732 Massachusetts Ave NW, Washington DC 20036, T 1(202)7851746,
F 1(202)8875579

Venezuela
Paseo Enrique Erazo, Edif Torre la Noria,
Urbaniz las Mercedes, Caracas,
T 58(2)9935770, F 58(2)920614

TOURIST INFORMATION

The addresses of all Sernatur offices are
given in the text. The head office is at Av
Providencia 1550, Casilla 14082, Santiago,
T 236-1416. Those seeking information before leaving home are advised to contact
the Commercial Department of the nearest
Embassy of Chile, called Pro Chile (eg London, 12 Devonshire Street, London W1N
2DS, T 0171-580 6392, F 0171-255 1848).
The Tourism Promotion Corporation of
Chile is at Antonio Bellet 77, Oficina 602,
Providencia, Santiago, T 235-0105, F 236-
2166. In the Netherlands, the office is at
Siemenwei 63, 4464 BX, Goes, T (31) 113
270 096, F 113 613 610, e-mail ad-
dewit@pi.net.

On the Internet, there are a great many
sites about Chile which surfers may wish to
explore, but note that you may have to
weed out the sites related to chile peppers.
Two sites of general interest on Latin America are The Latin American Travel Advisor
http://www.amerispan.com/latc, the home
page for *The Latin American Travel Advisor*,
published in Quito (PO Box 17-17-908, F
593-2-562-566), and *El Planeta Platica: Eco
Travels in Latin America*, edited by Ron
Mader, http://www.txinfinet.com/mader/
ecotravel/schools/schools.html.

418

SPECIALIST TOUR COMPANIES

South American Experience
47 Causton Street, Pimlico, London SW1P 4AT, T 0171 976 5511, F 0171 976 6908. Apart from booking flights and accommodation, also offer tailor-made trips.

Passage to South America
Fovant Mews, 12 Noyna Road, London SW17 7PH, T 0181-767 8989. Wide range of tailor-made packages throughout the region including the lost kingdom of the Incas.

Journey Latin America
14-16 Devonshire Road, Chiswick, London W4 2HD, T 0181-747 3108. Long established company running escorted tours throughout the region. They also offer a wide range of flight options.

Hayes & Jarvis
152 King Street, London W6 0QU, T 0181 222 7844. Long established operator. Offers tailor-made itineries as well as packages.

Ladatco Tours
2220 Coral Way, Miami, Florida 33145, USA, T USA (305) 854-8422, F (USA) (305)

285-0504. Run 'themed' explorer tours based around the Incas, mysticism etc.

Austral Tours
120 Wilton Road, London SW1V 1JZ, T 0171-233 5384, F 0171-233 5385.

Last Frontiers
Swan House, High Street, Long Crendon, Buckinghamshire, HP18 9AF, T 01844 208405.

South American Explorers Club
126 Indian Creek Rd, Ithaca, New York 14850, USA, T USA (607) 277-0488, F USA (607) 277 6122.

Trailfinders
48 Earl's Court Road, London W8 6EJ, T 0171-938 3366.

STA Travel
Priory House, 6 Wrights Lane, London W8 6TA, T 0171-938 4711.

Cox & Kings Travel
St James Court, 45 Buckingham Gate, London, T 0171-873 5001.

Useful words and phrases

NO AMOUNT of dictionaries, phrase books or word lists will provide the same enjoyment as being able to communicate directly with the people of the country you are visiting. Learning Spanish is an important part of the preparation for any trip to Chile and you are encouraged to make an effort to grasp the basics before you go. As you travel you will pick up more of the language and the more you know, the more you will benefit from your stay. The following section is designed to be a simple point of departure.

General pronunciation

The stress in a Spanish word conforms to one of three rules: 1) if the word ends in a vowel, or in **n** or **s**, the accent falls on the penultimate syllable (*ventana, ventanas*); 2) if the word ends in a consonant other than **n** or **s**, the accent falls on the last syllable (*hablar*); 3) if the word is to be stressed on a syllable contrary to either of the above rules, the acute accent on the relevant vowel indicates where the stress is to be placed (*pantalón, metáfora*). Note that adverbs such as *cuando*, 'when', take an accent when used interrogatively: *¿cuándo?*, 'when?'

Vowels

a   not quite as short as in English 'cat'

e   as in English 'pay', but shorter in a syllable ending in a consonant

i   as in English 'seek'

o   as in English 'shop', but more like 'pope' when the vowel ends a syllable

u   as in English 'food'; after 'q' and in 'gue', 'gui', **u** is unpronounced; in 'güe' and 'güi' it is pronounced

y   when a vowel, pronounced like 'i'; when a semiconsonant or consonant, it is pronounced like English 'yes'

ai, ay   as in English 'ride'

ei, ey   as in English 'they'

oi, oy   as in English 'toy'

Unless listed below **consonants** can be pronounced in Spanish as they are in English.

b, v   their sound is interchangeable and is a cross between the English 'b' and 'v', except at the beginning of a word or after 'm' or 'n' when it is like English 'b'

c   like English 'k', except before 'e' or 'i' when it is as the 's' in English 'sip'

g   before 'e' and 'i' it is the same as **j**

h   when on its own, never pronounced

j   as the 'ch' in the Scottish 'loch'

ll   as the 'g' in English 'beige'; sometimes

as the 'lli' in 'million'

ñ as the 'ni' in English 'onion'

rr trilled much more strongly than in English

x depending on its location, pronounced as in English 'fox', or 'sip', or like 'gs'

z as the 's' in English 'sip'

GREETINGS, COURTESIES
hello
  hola
good morning
  buenos días
good afternoon/evening/night
  buenas tardes/noches
goodbye
  adiós/chao
see you later
  hasta luego
how are you?
  ¿cómo está?/¿cómo estás?
pleased to meet you
  mucho gusto/encantado/encantada
please
  por favor
thank you (very much)
  (muchas) gracias
yes
  sí
no
  no
excuse me/I beg your pardon
  permiso
I do not understand
  no entiendo
please speak slowly
  hable despacio por favor
what is your name
  ¿cómo se llama?
Go away!
  ¡Váyase!

BASIC QUESTIONS
where is_?
  ¿dónde está_?
how much does it cost?
  ¿cuánto cuesta?
how much is it?
  ¿cuánto es?
when?
  ¿cuándo?

when does the bus leave?
  ¿a qué hora sale el autobus?
    – arrive?
    – llega –
why?
  ¿por qué?
what for?
  ¿para qué?
what time is it?
  ¿qué hora es?
how do I get to_?
  ¿cómo llegar a_?
is this the way to the church?
  ¿la iglesia está por aquí?

BASICS
bathroom/toilet
  el baño
police (policeman)
  la policía (el policía)
hotel
  el hotel (la pensión,el residencial, el alojamiento)
restaurant
  el restaurante
post office
  el correo
telephone office
  el centro de llamadas
supermarket
  el supermercado
bank
  el banco
exchange house
  la casa de cambio
exchange rate
  la tasa de cambio
notes/coins
  los billetes/las monedas
travellers' cheques
  los travelers/los cheques de viajero
cash
  el efectivo
breakfast
  el desayuno
lunch
  el almuerzo
dinner/supper
  la cena
meal
  la comida
drink
  la bebida

mineral water
el agua mineral
soft fizzy drink
la gaseosa/cola
beer
la cerveza
without sugar
sin azúcar
without meat
sin carne

Getting around
on the left/right
a la izquierda/derecha
straight on
derecho
second street on the left
la segunda calle a la izquierda
to walk
caminar
bus station
la terminal (terrestre)
train station
la estación (de tren/ferrocarril)
bus
el bus/el autobus/ la flota/el colectivo/ el micro etc
train
el tren
airport
el aeropuerto
aeroplane/airplane
el avión
first/second class
primera/segunda clase
ticket
el boleto
ticket office
la taquilla
bus stop
la parada

ACCOMMODATION

room
el cuarto/la habitación
single/double
sencillo/doble
with two beds
con dos camas
with private bathroom
con baño
hot/cold water
agua caliente/fría

noisy
ruidoso
to make up/clean
limpiar
sheets
las sábanas
blankets
las mantas
pillows
las almohadas
clean/dirty towels
toallas limpias/sucias
toilet paper
el papel higiénico
Chemist
farmacia
(for) pain
(para) dolor
stomach
el estómago
head
la cabeza
fever/sweat
la fiebre/el sudor
diarrhoea
la diarrea
blood
la sangre
altitude sickness
el soroche
doctor
el médico
condoms
los preservativos
contraceptive (pill)
anticonceptivo (la píldora anticonceptiva)
period/towels
la regla/las toallas
contact lenses
las lentes de contacto
aspirin
la aspirina

TIME
at one o'clock
a la una
at half past two/ two thirty
a las dos y media
at a quarter to three
a cuarto para las tres
or a las tres menos quince
it's one o'clock
es la una

it's seven o'clock
son las siete
it's twenty past six/
six twenty
son las seis y veinte
it's five to nine
son cinco para las nueve/
son las nueve menos cinco
in ten minutes
en diez minutos
five hours
cinco horas
does it take long?
¿tarda mucho?
Monday lunes
Tuesday martes
Wednesday miercoles
Thursday jueves
Friday viernes
Saturday sábado
Sunday domingo
January enero
February febrero
March marzo
April abril
May mayo
June junio
July julio
August agosto
September septiembre
October octubre
November noviembre
December diciembre

NUMBERS

one uno/una
two dos
three tres
four cuatro
five cinco
six seis
seven siete
eight ocho
nine nueve
ten diez
eleven once
twelve doce
thirteen trece
fourteen catorce
fifteen quince

sixteen dieciseis
seventeen diecisiete
eighteen dieciocho
nineteen diecinueve
twenty veinte
twenty one, two veintiuno, veintidos etc
thirty treinta
forty cuarenta
fifty cincuenta
sixty sesenta
seventy setenta
eighty ochenta
ninety noventa
hundred cien or ciento
thousand mil

KEY VERBS

To Go
ir
I go voy; you go (familiar singular) vas; he, she, it goes, you (unfamiliar singular) go va; we go vamos; they, you (plural) go van.

To Have (possess)
tener
tengo; tienes; tiene; tenemos; tienen (also used as To Be, as in 'I am hungry' tengo hambre)
(**NB** haber also means to have, but is used with other verbs, as in 'he has gone' ha ido. he; has; ha; hemos; han.
Hay means 'there is'; perhaps more common is No hay meaning 'there isn't any')

To Be (in a permanent state)
ser
soy (profesor – I am a teacher); eres; es; somos; son
To Be (positional or temporary state)
estar
estoy (en Londres – I am in London); estás; está (contenta – she is happy); estamos; están.

This section has been compiled on the basis of glossaries compiled by André de Mendonça and David Gilmour of South American Experience, London, and the Latin American Travel Advisor, No 9, March 1996.

Health in Latin America

WITH the following advice and precautions you should keep as healthy as you do at home. Most visitors return home having experienced no problems at all apart from some travellers' diarrhoea. In Latin America the health risks, especially in the lowland tropical areas, are different from those encountered in Europe or the USA. It also depends on where and how you travel. There are clear health differences between the countries of Latin America and in risks for the business traveller, who stays in international class hotels in large cities, the backpacker trekking from country to country and the tourist who heads for the beach. There is huge variation in climate, vegetation and wildlife from the deserts of Chile to the rain forests of Amazonia and from the icy remoteness of Andean peaks, to the teeming capital cities. There are no hard and fast rules to follow; you will often have to make your own judgment on the healthiness or otherwise of your surroundings. There are English (or other foreign language) speaking doctors in most major cities who have particular experience in dealing with locally-occurring diseases. Your Embassy representative will often be able to give you the name of local reputable doctors and most of the better hotels have a doctor on standby. If you do fall ill and cannot find a recommended doctor, try the Outpatient Department of a hospital – private hospitals are usually less crowded and offer a more acceptable standard of care to foreigners.

BEFORE TRAVELLING

Take out medical insurance. Make sure it covers all eventualities especially evacuation to your home country by a medically equipped plane, if necessary. You should have a dental check up, obtain a spare glasses prescription, a spare oral contraceptive prescription (or enought pills to last) and, if you suffer from a chronic illness (such as diabetes, high blood pressure, ear or sinus troubles, cardio-pulmonary disease or nervous disorder) arrange for a check up with your doctor, who can at the same time provide you with a letter explaining the details of your disability in English and if possible Spanish and/or Portuguese. Check the current practice in countries you are visiting for malaria prophylaxis (prevention). If you are on regular medication, make sure you have enough to cover the period of your travel.

Children

More preparation is probably necessary for babies and children than for an adult and perhaps a little more care should be taken when travelling to remote areas where health services are primitive. This is because children can be become more rapidly ill than adults (on the other hand they often recover more quickly). Diarrhoea and vomiting are the most common problems, so take the usual precautions, but more intensively. Breastfeeding is best and most convenient for babies, but powdered milk is generally available and so are baby foods in most countries. Papaya, bananas and avocados are all nutritious and can be cleanly prepared. The treatment of diarrhoea is the same as for adults, except that it should start earlier and be continued with more persistence. Children get dehydrated very quickly in hot countries and can become drowsy and uncooperative unless cajoled to drink water or juice plus salts. Upper respiratory infections, such as colds, catarrh and middle ear infections are also common and if your child suffers from these normally take some antibiotics against the possibility. Outer ear infections after swimming are also common and antibiotic eardrops will help. Wet wipes are always useful and sometimes difficult to find in South America as, in some places are disposable nappies.

MEDICINES AND WHAT TO TAKE

There is very little control on the sale of drugs and medicines in South America. You can buy any and every drug in pharmacies without a prescription. Be wary of this because pharmacists can be poorly trained and might sell you drugs that are unsuitable, dangerous or old. Many drugs and medicines are manufactured under licence from American or European companies, so the trade names may be familiar to you. This means you do not have to carry a whole chest of medicines with you, but remember that the shelf life of some items, especially vaccines and antibiotics, is markedly reduced in hot conditions. Buy your supplies at the better outlets where there are refrigerators, even though they are more expensive and check the expiry date of all preparations you buy. Immigration officials occasionally confiscate scheduled drugs (Lomotil is an example) if they are not accompanied by a doctor's prescription.

Self-medication may be forced on you by circumstances so the following text contains the names of drugs and medicines which you may find useful in an emergency or in out-of-the-way places. You may like to take some of the following items with you from home:

Sunglasses
ones designed for intense sunlight

Earplugs
for sleeping on aeroplanes and in noisy hotels

Suntan cream
with a high protection factor

Insect repellent
containing DET for preference

Mosquito net
lightweight, permethrin-impregnated for choice

Tablets
for travel sickness

Tampons
can be expensive in some countries in Latin America

Condoms

Contraceptives

Water sterilising tablets

Antimalarial tablets

Anti-infective ointment eg Cetrimide

Dusting powder for feet etc
containing fungicide

Antacid tablets
for indigestion

Sachets of rehydration salts
plus anti-diarrhoea preparations

Painkillers
such as Paracetamol or Aspirin

Antibiotics
for diarrhoea etc

First Aid kit
Small pack containing a few sterile syringes and needles and disposable gloves. The risk of catching hepatitis etc from a dirty needle used for injection is now negligible in Latin America, but some may be reassured by carrying their own supplies – available from camping shops and airport shops.

Vaccination and immunisation

Smallpox vaccination is no longer required anywhere in the world. Neither is cholera vaccination recognized as necessary for international travel by the World Health Organisation – it is not very effective either. Nevertheless, some immigration officials are demanding proof of vaccination against cholera in Latin America and in some countries outside Latin America, following the outbreak of the disease which originated in Peru in 1990-91 and subsequently affected most surrounding countries. Although very unlikely to affect visitors to Latin America, the cholera epidemic continues making its greatest impact in poor areas where water supplies are polluted and food hygiene practices are insanitary.

Vaccination against the following diseases are recommended:

Yellow Fever

This is a live vaccination not to be given to children under 9 months of age or persons allergic to eggs. Immunity lasts for 10 years, an International Certificate of Yellow Fever Vaccination will be given and should be kept because it is sometimes asked for. Yellow fever is very rare in Latin America, but the vaccination is practically without side effects and almost totally protective.

Typhoid

A disease spread by the insanitary preparation of food. A number of new vaccines against this condition are now available; the older TAB and monovalent typhoid vaccines are being phased out. The newer, eg Typhim Vi, cause less side effects, but are more expensive. For those who do not like injections, there are now oral vaccines.

Poliomyelitis

Despite its decline in the world this remains a serious disease if caught and is easy to protect against. There are live oral vaccines and in some countries injected vaccines. Whichever one you choose it is a good idea to have booster every 3-5 years if visiting developing countries regularly.

Tetanus

One dose should be given with a booster at 6 weeks and another at 6 months and 10 yearly boosters thereafter are recommended. Children should already be prop-

Water purification

There are a number of ways of purifying water in order to make it safe to drink. Dirty water should first be strained through a filter bag (camping shops) and then boiled or treated. Bringing water to a rolling boil at sea level is sufficient to make the water safe for drinking, but at higher altitudes you have to boil the water for longer to ensure that all the microbes are killed.

There are sterilising methods that can be used and there are proprietary preparations containing chlorine (eg Puritabs) or iodine (eg Pota Aqua) compounds. Chlorine compounds generally do not kill protozoa (eg giardia).

There are a number of water filters now on the market available in personal and expedition size. They work either on mechanical or chemical principles, or may do both. Make sure you take the spare parts or spare chemicals with you and do not believe *everything* the manufacturers say.

erly protected against diphtheria, poliomyelitis and pertussis (whooping cough), measles and HIB all of which can be more serious infections in Latin America than at home. Measles, mumps and rubella vaccine is also given to children throughout the world, but those teenage girls who have not had rubella (german measles) should be tested and vaccinated. Hepatitis B vaccination for babies is now routine in some countries. Consult your doctor for advice on tuberculosis inoculation: the disease is still widespread in Latin America.

Infectious Hepatitis

Is less of a problem for travellers than it used to be because of the development of two extremely effective vaccines against the A and B form of the disease. It remains common, however, in Latin America. A combined hepatitis A & B vaccine is now licensed and will be available in 1997 – one jab covers both diseases.

Other vaccinations:

Might be considered in the case of epidemics eg meningitis. There is an effective vaccination against rabies which should be considered by all travellers, especially those going through remote areas or if there is a particular occupational risk, eg for zoologists or veterinarians.

FURTHER INFORMATION

Further information on health risks abroad, vaccinations etc may be available from a local travel clinic. If you wish to take specific drugs with you such as antibiotics these are best prescribed by your own doctor. Beware, however, that not all doctors can be experts on the health problems of remote countries. More detailed or more up-to-date information than local doctors can provide are available from various sources. In the UK there are hospital departments specialising in tropical diseases in London, Liverpool, Birmingham and Glasgow and the Malaria Reference Laboratory at the London School of Hygiene and Tropical Medicine provides free advice about malaria, T 0891 600350. In the USA the Public Health Services can give such information and information is available centrally from the Centre for Disease Control (CDC) in Atlanta, T (404) 3324559.

There are additional computerized databases which can be assessed for destination-specific up-to-the-minute information. In the UK there is MASTA (Medical Advisory Service to Travellers Abroad), T 0171 631 4408, F 0171 436 5389, Tx 8953473 and Travax (Glasgow, T 0141 946 7120, ext 247). Other information on medical problems overseas can be obtained from the book by Dawood, Richard (Editor) (1992) *Travellers' Health: How to stay healthy abroad*, Oxford University Press 1992, £7.99. We strongly recommend this revised and updated edition, especially to the intrepid traveller heading for the more out of the way places. General advice is also available in the UK in *Health Information for Overseas Travel* published by the Department of Health and available from HMSO, and *International Travel and Health* published by WHO, Geneva.

STAYING HEALTHY

INTESTINAL UPSETS

The thought of catching a stomach bug worries visitors to Latin America but there have been great improvements in food hygiene and most such infections are preventable. Travellers' diarrhoea and vomiting is due, most of the time, to food poisoning, usually passed on by the insanitary habits of food handlers. As a general rule the cleaner your surroundings and the smarter the restaurant, the less likely you are to suffer.

Foods to avoid: uncooked, undercooked, partially cooked or reheated meat, fish, eggs, raw vegetables and salads, especially when they have been left out exposed to flies. Stick to fresh food that has been cooked from raw just before eating and make sure you peel fruit yourself. Wash and dry your hands before eating – disposable wet-wipe tissues are useful for this.

Shellfish eaten raw are risky and at certain times of the year some fish and shellfish concentrate toxins from their environment and cause various kinds of food poisoning. The local authorities notify the public not to eat these foods. Do not ignore the warning. **Heat treated milk** (UHT) pasteurized or sterilized is becoming more available in Latin America as is pasteurized cheese. On the whole matured or processed cheeses are safer than the fresh varieties and fresh unpasteurized milk from whatever animal can be a source of food poisoning germs, tuberculosis and brucellosis. This applies equally to icecream, yoghurt and cheese made from unpasteurized milk, so avoid these homemade products – the factory made ones are probably safer.

Tap water is rarely safe outside the major cities, especially in the rainy season. Stream water, if you are in the countryside, is often contaminated by communities living surprisingly high in the mountains. Filtered or bottled water is usually available and safe, although you must make sure that somebody is not filling bottles from the tap and hammering on a new crown cap. If your hotel has a central hot water supply this water is safe to drink after cooling. Ice for drinks should be made from boiled water, but rarely is so stand your glass on the ice cubes, rather than putting them in the drink. The better hotels have water purifying systems.

TRAVELLERS' DIARRHOEA

This is usually caused by eating food which has been contaminated by food poisoning germs. Drinking water is rarely the culprit. Sea water or river water is more likely to be contaminated by sewage and so swimming in such dilute effluent can also be a cause.

Infection with various organisms can give rise to travellers' diarrhoea. They may be viruses, bacteria, eg Escherichia coli (probably the most common cause worldwide), protozoal (such as amoebas and giardia), salmonella and cholera. The diarrhoea may come on suddenly or rather slowly. It may or may not be accompanied by vomiting or by severe abdominal pain and the passage of blood or mucus when it is called dysentery.

How do you know which type you have caught and how to treat it?

If you can time the onset of the diarrhoea to the minute ('acute') then it is probably due to a virus or a bacterium and/or the onset of dysentery. The treatment in addition to rehydration is Ciprofloxacin 500 mg every 12 hrs; the drug is now widely avail-

able and there are many similar ones.

If the diarrhoea comes on slowly or intermittently ('sub-acute') then it is more likely to be protozoal, ie caused by an amoeba or giardia. Antibiotics such a Ciprofloxacin will have little effect. These cases are best treated by a doctor as is any outbreak of diarrhoea continuing for more than 3 days. Sometimes blood is passed in ameobic dysentery and for this you should certainly seek medical help. If this is not available then the best treatment is probably Tinidazole (Fasigyn) 1 tablet four times a day for 3 days. If there are severe stomach cramps, the following drugs may help but are not very useful in the management of acute diarrhoea: Loperamide (Imodium) and Diphenoxylate with Atropine (Lomotil) They should not be given to children.

Any kind of diarrhoea, whether or not accompanied by vomiting, responds well to the replacement of water and salts, taken as frequent small sips, of some kind of rehydration solution. There are proprietary preparations consisting of sachets of powder which you dissolve in boiled water or you can make your own by adding half a teaspoonful of salt (3.5 gms) and 4 tablespoonsful of sugar (40 gms) to a litre of boiled water.

Thus the lynch pins of treatment for diarrhoea are rest, fluid and salt replacement, antibiotics such as Ciprofloxacin for the bacterial types and special diagnostic tests and medical treatment for the amoeba and giardia infections. Salmonella infections and cholera, although rare, can be devastating diseases and it would be wise to get to a hospital as soon as possible if these were suspected.

Fasting, peculiar diets and the consumption of large quantities of yoghurt have not been found useful in calming travellers' diarrhoea or in rehabilitating inflamed bowels. Oral rehydration has on the other hand, especially in children, been a life saving technique and should always be practised, whatever other treatment you use. As there is some evidence that alcohol and milk might prolong diarrhoea they should be avoided during and immediately after an attack.

Diarrhoea occurring day after day for

long periods of time (chronic diarrhoea) is notoriously resistent to amateur attempts at treatment and again warrants proper diagnostic tests (most towns with reasonable sized hospitals have laboratories for stool samples). There are ways of preventing travellers' diarrhoea for short periods of time by taking antibiotics, but this is not a foolproof technique and should not be used other than in exceptional circumstances. Doxycycline is possibly the best drug. Some preventatives such as Enterovioform can have serious side effects if taken for long periods.

Paradoxically **constipation** is also common, probably induced by dietary change, inadequate fluid intake in hot places and long bus journeys. Simple laxatives are useful in the short-term and bulky foods such as maize, beans and plenty of fruit are also useful.

HIGH ALTITUDE

Spending time at high altitude in South America, especially in the tropics, is usually a pleasure – it is not so hot, there are no insects and the air is clear and spring like. Travelling to high altitudes, however, can cause medical problems, all of which can be prevented if care is taken.

On reaching heights above about 3,000m, heart pounding and shortness of breath, especially on exertion are a normal response to the lack of oxygen in the air. A condition called acute mountain sickness (*Soroche* in South America) can also affect visitors. It is more likely to affect those who ascend rapidly, eg by plane and those who over-exert themselves (teenagers for example). Soroche takes a few hours or days to come on and presents with a bad headache, extreme tiredness, sometimes dizziness, loss of appetite and frequently nausea and vomiting. Insomnia is common and is often associated with a suffocating feeling when lying in bed. Keen observers may note their breathing tends to wax and wane at night and their face tends to be puffy in the mornings – this is all part of the syndrome. Anyone can get this condition and past experience is not always a good guide: the author, having spent years in Peru travelling constantly between sea level and very high

altitude never suffered symptoms, then was severely affected whilst climbing Kilimanjaro in Tanzania.

The treatment of acute mountain sickness is simple – rest, painkillers, (preferably not aspirin based) for the headache and anti sickness pills for vomiting. Oxygen is actually not much help, except at very high altitude. Various local panaceas – Coramina glucosada, Effortil, Micoren are popular in Latin America and mate de coca (an infusion of coca leaves widely available and perfectly legal) will alleviate some of the symptoms.

To **prevent** the condition: on arrival at places over 3,000m have a few hours rest in a chair and avoid alcohol, cigarettes and heavy food. If the symptoms are severe and prolonged, it is best to descend to a lower altitude and to reascend slowly or in stages. If this is impossible because of shortage of time or if you are going so high that acute mountain sickness is very likely, then the drug Acetazolamide (Diamox) can be used as a preventative and continued during the ascent. There is good evidence of the value of this drug in the prevention of soroche, but some people do experience peculiar side effects. The usual dose is 500 mg of the slow release preparation each night, starting the night before ascending above 3,000m.

Watch out for **sunburn** at high altitude. The ultraviolet rays are extremely powerful. The air is also excessively dry at high altitude and you might find that your skin dries out and the inside of your nose becomes crusted. Use a moisturiser for the skin and some vaseline wiped into the nostrils. Some people find contact lenses irritate because of the dry air. It is unwise to ascend to high altitude if you are pregnant, especially in the first 3 months, or if you have a history of heart, lung or blood disease, including sickle cell.

A more unusual condition can affect mountaineers who ascend rapidly to high altitude – **acute pulmonary oedema**. Residents at altitude sometimes experience this when returning to the mountains from time spent at the coast. This condition is often preceded by acute mountain sickness and comes on quite rapidly with severe breathlessness, noisy breathing, cough, blueness of the lips and frothing at the mouth. Anybody who develops this must be brought down as soon as possible, given oxygen and taken to hospital.

A rapid descent from high places will make sinus problems and middle ear infections worse and might make your teeth ache. Lastly, don't fly to altitude within 24 hrs of SCUBA diving. You might suffer from 'the bends'.

HEAT AND COLD

Full acclimatisation to high temperatures takes about 2 weeks. During this period it is normal to feel a bit apathetic, especially if the relative humidity is high. Drink plenty of water (up to 15 litres a day are required when working physically hard in the tropics), use salt on your food and avoid extreme exertion. Tepid showers are more cooling than hot or cold ones. Large hats do not cool you down, but do prevent sunburn. Remember that, especially in the highlands, there can be a large and sudden drop in temperature between sun and shade and between night and day, so dress accordingly. Warm jackets or woollens are essential after dark at high altitude. Loose cotton is still the best material when the weather is hot.

INSECTS

These are mostly more of a nuisance than a serious hazard and if you try, you can prevent yourself entirely from being bitten. Some, such as mosquitos are, of course, carriers of potentially serious diseases, so it is sensible to avoid being bitten as much as possible. Sleep off the ground and use a mosquito net or some kind of insecticide. Preparations containing Pyrethrum or synthetic pyrethroids are safe. They are available as aerosols or pumps and the best way to use these is to spray the room thoroughly in all areas (follow the instructions rather than the insects) and then shut the door for a while, re-entering when the smell has dispersed. Mosquito coils release insecticide as they burn slowly. They are widely available and useful out of doors. Tablets of insecticide which are placed on a heated mat plugged into a wall socket are probably the most effective. They fill the room with insecticidal fumes in the same way as aerosols or coils.

You can also use insect repellents, most of which are effective against a wide range of pests. The most common and effective is diethyl metatoluamide (DET). DET liquid is best for arms and face (care around eyes and with spectacles – DET dissolves plastic). Aerosol spray is good for clothes and ankles and liquid DET can be dissolved in water and used to impregnate cotton clothes and mosquito nets. Some repellents now contain DET and Permethrin, insecticide. Impregnated wrist and ankle bands can also be useful.

If you are bitten or stung, itching may be relieved by cool baths, antihistamine tablets (care with alcohol or driving) or mild corticosteroid creams, eg. hydrocortisone (great care: never use if any hint of infection). Careful scratching of all your bites once a day can be surprisingly effective. Calamine lotion and cream have limited effectiveness and antihistamine creams are not recommended – they can cause allergies themselves.

Bites which become infected should be treated with a local antiseptic or antibiotic cream such as Cetrimide, as should any infected sores or scratches.

When living rough, skin infestations with body lice (crabs) and scabies are easy to pick up. Use whatever local commercial preparation is recommended for lice and scabies.

Crotamiton cream (Eurax) alleviates itching and also kills a number of skin parasites. Malathion lotion 5% (Prioderm) kills lice effectively, but avoid the use of the toxic agricultural preparation of Malathion, more often used to commit suicide.

TICKS

They attach themselves usually to the lower parts of the body often after walking in areas where cattle have grazed. They take a while to attach themselves strongly, but swell up as they start to suck blood. The important thing is to remove them gently, so that they do not leave their head parts in your skin because this can cause a nasty allergic reaction some days later. Do not use petrol, vaseline, lighted cigarettes etc to remove the tick, but, with a pair of tweezers remove the beast gently by gripping it at the attached (head) end and rock it out in very much the same way that a tooth is extracted. Certain tropical flies which lay their eggs under the skin of sheep and cattle also occasionally do the same thing to humans with the unpleasant result that a maggot grows under the skin and pops up as a boil or pimple. The best way to remove these is to cover the boil with oil, vaseline or nail varnish so as to stop the maggot breathing, then to squeeze it out gently the next day.

SUNBURN

The burning power of the tropical sun, especially at high altitude, is phenomenal.

Always wear a wide brimmed hat and use some form of suncream lotion on untanned skin. Normal temperate zone suntan lotions (protection factor up to 7) are not much good; you need to use the types designed specifically for the tropics or for mountaineers or skiers with protection factors up to 15 or above. These are often not available in Latin America. Glare from the sun can cause conjunctivitis, so wear sunglasses especially on tropical beaches, where high protection factor sunscreen should also be used.

PRICKLY HEAT

A very common intensely itchy rash is avoided by frequent washing and by wearing loose clothing. Cured by allowing skin to dry off through use of powder and spending two nights in an airconditioned hotel!

ATHLETES FOOT

This and other fungal skin infections are best treated with Tolnaftate or Clotrimazole.

OTHER RISKS AND MORE SERIOUS DISEASES

Remember that rabies is endemic throughout Latin America, so avoid dogs that are behaving strangely and cover your toes at night from the vampire bats, which also carry the disease. If you are bitten by a domestic or wild animal, do not leave things to chance: scrub the wound with soap and water and/or disinfectant, try to have the animal captured (within limits) or at least determine its ownership, where possible, and seek medical assistance at once. The course of treatment depends on whether you have already been satisfactorily vaccinated against rabies. If you have (this is worthwile if you are spending lengths of time in developing countries) then some further doses of vaccine are all that is required. Human diploid vaccine is the best, but expensive: other, older kinds of vaccine, such as that derived from duck embryos may be the only types available. These are effective, much cheaper and interchangeable generally with the human derived types. If not already vaccinated then anti rabies serum (immunoglobulin) may be required in addition. It is important to finish the course of treatment whether the animal survives or not.

AIDS

In South America AIDS is increasing but is not wholly confined to the well known high risk sections of the population, ie homosexual men, intravenous drug abusers and children of infected mothers. Heterosexual transmission is now the dominant mode and so the main risk to travellers is from casual sex. The same precautions should be taken as with any sexually transmitted disease. The Aids virus (HIV) can be passed by unsterilized needles which have been previously used to inject an HIV positive patient, but the risk of this is negligible. It would, however, be sensible to check that needles have been properly sterilized or disposable needles have been used. If you wish to take your own disposable needles, be prepared to explain what they are for. The risk of receiving a blood transfusion with blood infected with the HIV virus is greater than from dirty needles because of the amount of fluid exchanged. Supplies of blood for transfusion should now be screened for HIV in all reputable hospitals, so again the risk is very small indeed. Catching the AIDS virus does not always produce an illness in itself (although it may do). The only way to be sure if you feel you have been put at risk is to have a blood test for HIV antibodies on your return to a place where there are reliable laboratory facilities. The test does not become positive for some weeks.

MALARIA

In South America malaria is theoretically confined to coastal and jungle zones, but is now on the increase again. Mosquitos do not thrive above 2,500m, so you are safe at altitude. There are different varieties of malaria, some resistant to the normal drugs. Make local enquiries if you intend to visit possibly infected zones and use a prophylactic regime. Start taking the tablets a few days before exposure and continue to take them for 6 weeks after leaving the malarial zone. Remember to give the drugs to babies and children also. Opinion varies on the precise drugs and dosage to be used for protection. All the drugs may have some side effects and it is important to balance the risk of catching the disease against the albeit rare side effects. The increasing complexity of the subject is such that as the malarial parasite becomes immune to the new generation of drugs it has made concentration on the physical prevention from being bitten by mosquitos more important. This involves the use of long sleeved shirts or blouses and long trousers, repellants and nets. Clothes are now available impregnated with the insecticide Permethrin or Deltamethrin or it is possible to impregnate the clothes yourself. Wide meshed nets impregnated with Permethrin are also available, are lighter to carry and less claustrophobic to sleep in.

Prophylaxis and treatment

If your itinerary takes you into a malarial area, seek expert advice before you go on a suitable prophylactic regime. This is especially true for pregnant women who are particularly prone to catch malaria. You can still catch the disease even when sticking to a proper regime, although it is unlikely. If you do develop symptoms (high fever, shivering, headache, sometimes diarrhoea), seek medical advice immediately. If this is not possible and there is a great likelihood of malaria, the treatment is:

Chloroquine, a single dose of 4 tablets (600 mg) followed by 2 tablets (300 mg) in 6 hrs and 300 mg each day following.

Falciparum type of malaria or type in doubt: take local advice. Various combinations of drugs are being used such as Quinine, Tetracycline or Halofantrine. If falciparum type malaria is definitely diagnosed, it is wise to get to a good hospital as treatment can be complex and the illness very serious.

INFECTIOUS HEPATITIS (JAUNDICE)

The main symptoms are pains in the stomach, lack of appetite, lassitude and yellowness of the eyes and skin. Medically speaking there are two main types. The less serious, but more common is Hepatitis A for which the best protection os the careful preparation of food, the avoidance of contaminated drinking water and scrupulous attention to toilet hygiene. The other, more serious, version is Hepatitis B which is acquired usually as a sexually transmitted disease or by blood transfusions. It can less commonly be transmitted by injections with unclean needles and possibly by insect bites. The symptoms are the same as for Hepatitis A. The incubation period is much longer (up to 6 months compared with 6 weeks) and there are more likely to be complications.

Hepatitis A can be protected against with gamma globulin. It should be obtained from a reputable source and is certainly useful for travellers who intende to live rough. You should have a shot before leaving and have it repeated every 6 months. The dose of gamma globulin depends on the concentration of the particular preparation used, so the manufacturer's advice should be taken. The injection should be given as close as possible to your departure and as the dose depends on the likely time you are to spend in potentially affected areas, the manufacturer's instructions should be followed. Gamma globulin has really been superceded now by a proper vaccination against Hepatitis A (Havrix) which gives immunity lasting up to 10 years. After that boosters are required. Havrix monodose is now widely available as is Junior Havrix. The vaccination has negligible side effects and is extremely effective. Gamma globulin injections can be a bit painful, but it is much cheaper than Havrix and may be more available in some places.

Hepatitis B can be effectively prevented by a specific vaccine (Engerix) – 3 shots over 6 months before travelling. If you have had jaundice in the past it would be worthwhile having a blood test to see if you are immune to either of these two types, because this might avoid the necessity and costs of vaccination or gamma globulin. There are other kinds of viral hepatitis (C, E etc) which are fairly similar to A and B, but vaccines are not available as yet.

TYPHUS

Can still occur carried by ticks. There is usually a reaction at the site of the bite and a fever. Seek medical advice.

INTESTINAL WORMS

These are common and the more serious ones such as hookworm can be contracted from walking barefoot on infested earth or beaches.

Various other tropical diseases can be caught in jungle areas, usually transmitted by biting insects. They are often related to African diseases and were probably introduced by the slave labour trade. Onchocerciasis (river blindness) carried by black flies is found in parts of Mexico and Venezuela. Leishmaniasis (Espundia) is carried by sandflies and causes a sore that will not heal or a severe nasal infection. Wearing long trousers and a long sleeved shirt in infected areas protects against these flies. DET is also effective. Epidemics of meningitis occur from time-to-time. Be careful about swimming in piranha or caribe infested rivers. It is a good idea not to swim naked: the Candiru fish can follow urine currents and become lodged in body orifices. Swimwear offers some protection.

LEPTOSPIROSIS

Various forms of leptospirosis occur throughout Latin America, transmitted by a bacterium which is excreted in rodent urine. Fresh water and moist soil harbour the organisms which enter the body through cuts and scratches. If you suffer from any form of prolonged fever consult a doctor.

SNAKE BITE

This is a very rare event indeed for travellers. If you are unlucky (or careless) enough to be bitten by a venomous snake, spider, scorpion or sea creature, try to identify the creature, but do not put yourself in further danger. Snake bites in particular are very frightening, but in fact rarely poisonous – even venomous snakes bite without injecting venom. What you might expect if bitten are: fright, swelling, pain and bruising around the bite and soreness of the regional lymph glands, perhaps nausea, vomiting and a fever. Signs of serious poisoning would be the following symptoms: numbness and tingling of the face, muscular spasms, convulsions, shortness of breath and bleeding. Victims should be got to a hospital or a doctor without delay. Commercial snake bite and scorpion kits are available, but usually only useful for the specific type of snake or scorpion for which they are designed. Most serum has to be given intravenously so it is not much good equipping yourself with it unless you are used to making injections into veins. It is best to rely on local practice in these cases, because the particular creatures will be known about locally and appropriate treatment can be given.

Treatment of snake bite Reassure and comfort the victim frequently. Immobilize the limb by a bandage or a splint or by getting the person to lie still. Do not slash the bite area and try to suck out the poison because this sort of heroism does more harm than good. If you know how to use a tourniquet in these circumstances, you will not need this advice. If you are not experienced do not apply a tourniquet.

Precautions

Avoid walking in snake territory in bare feet or sandals – wear proper shoes or boots. If you encounter a snake stay put until it slithers away, and do not investigate a wounded snake. Spiders and scorpions may be found in the more basic hotels, especially in the Andean countries. If stung, stay rest and take plenty of fluids and call a doctor. The best precaution is to keep beds away from the walls and look inside your shoes and under the toilet seat every morning. Certain tropical sea fish when trodden upon inject venom into bathers' feet. This can be exceptionally painful. Wear plastic shoes when you go bathing if such creatures are reported. The pain can be relieved by immersing the foot in extremely hot water for as long as the pain persists.

DENGUE FEVER

This is increasing worldwide including in South and Central American countries and the Caribbean. It can be completely prevented by avoiding mosquito bites in the same way as malaria. No vaccine is available. Dengue is an unpleasant and painful disease, presenting with a high temperature and body pains, but at least visitors are spared the more serious forms (haemorrhagic types) which are more of a problem for local people who have been exposed to the disease more than once. There is no specific treatment for dengue – just pain killers and rest.

CHAGAS' DISEASE (SOUTH AMERICAN TRYPANOSOMIASIS)

This is a chronic disease, very rarely caught by travellers and difficult to treat. It is transmitted by the simultaneous biting and excreting of the Reduvid bug, also known as the Vinchuca or Barbeiro. Somewhat resembling a small cockroach, this nocturnal bug lives in poor adobe houses with dirt floors often frequented by opossums. If you cannot avoid such accommodation, sleep off the floor with a candle lit, use a mosquito net, keep as much of your skin covered as possible, use DET repellent or a spray insecticide. If you are bitten overnight (the bites are painless) do not scratch them, but wash thoroughly with soap and water.

DANGEROUS ANIMALS

Apart from mosquitos the most dangerous animals are men, be they bandits or behind steering wheels. Think carefully about violent confrontations and wear a seat belt if you are lucky enough to have one available to you.

WHEN YOU RETURN HOME

Remember to take your antimalarial tablets for 6 weeks after leaving the malarial area. If you have had attacks of diarrhoea it is worth having a stool specimen tested in case you have picked up amoebas. If you have been living rough, blood tests may be worthwhile to detect worms and other parasites. If you have been exposed to bilharzia (*schistosomiasis*) by swimming in lakes etc, check by means of a blood test when you get home, but leave it for 6 weeks because the test is slow to become positive. Report any untowards symptoms to your doctor and tell the doctor exactly where you have been and, if you know, what the likelihood of disease is to which you were exposed.

The above information has been compiled for us by Dr David Snashall, who is presently Senior Lecturer in Occupational Health at the United Medical Schools of Guy's and St Thomas' Hospitals in London and Chief Medical Adviser to the British Foreign and Commonwealth Office. He has travelled extensively in Central and South America, worked in Peru and in East Africa and keeps in close touch with developments in preventative and tropical medicine.

Travelling with children

People contemplating overland travel in South America with children should remember that a lot of time can be spent waiting for buses, trains, and especially for aeroplanes. On bus journeys, if the children are good at amusing themselves, or can readily sleep while travelling, the problems can be considerably lessened. If your child is of an early reading age, take reading material with you as it is difficult, and expensive to find. A bag of, say 30 pieces, of Duplo or Lego etc can keep young children occupied for hours. Travel on trains, while not as fast or at times as comfortable as buses, allows more scope for moving about. Some trains provide tables between seats, so that games can be played. Beware of doors left open for ventilation especially if air-conditioning is not working.

Food

Food can be a problem if the children are not adaptable. It is easier to take biscuits, drinks, bread etc on longer trips than to rely on meal stops where the food may not be to taste. Avocados are safe, easy to eat and nutritious; they can be fed to babies as young as 6 months and most older children like them. A small immersion heater and jug for making hot drinks is invaluable, but remember that electric current varies. Try and get a dual-voltage one (110v and 220v).

Fares

On all long-distance buses you pay for each seat, and there are no half-fares if the children occupy a seat each. For shorter trips it is cheaper, if less comfortable, to seat small children on your knee. Often there are spare seats which children can occupy after tickets have been collected. In city and local excursion buses, small children generally do not pay a fare, but are not entitled to a seat when paying customers are standing. On sightseeing tours you should *always* bargain for a family rate – often children can go free. (In trains, reductions for children are general, but not universal.)

All civil airlines charge half for children under 12. Note that a child travelling free on a long excursion is not always covered by the operator's travel insurance; it is advisable to pay a small premium to arrange cover.

Hotels

In all hotels, try to negotiate family rates. If charges are per person, always insist that two children will occupy one bed only, therefore counting as one tariff. If rates are per bed, the same applies. In either case you can almost always get a reduced rate at cheaper hotels. Occasionally when travelling with a child you will be refused a room in a hotel that is 'unsuitable'. (In restaurants, you can normally buy children's helpings, or divide one full-size helping between two children.)

Travel with children can bring you into closer contact with Latin American families and, generally, presents no special problems – in fact the path is often smoother for family groups. Officials tend to be more amenable where children are concerned and they are pleased if your child knows a little Spanish. Moreover, even thieves and pickpockets seem to have some of the traditional respect for families, and may leave you alone because of it!

Tinted boxes

Illustrations

Index

444

Advertisers

Maps

Map Symbols

Administration

International Border
State / Province Border
Cease Fire Line

Neighbouring country
Neighbouring state

State Capitals ☐
Other Towns ○

Roads and travel

Main Roads
(National Highways)
Other Roads
Jeepable Roads, Tracks
Railways with station

Water features

River   *Amazon*
Lakes, Reservoirs, Tanks
Seasonal Marshlands
Sand Banks, Beaches
Ocean
Waterfall
Ferry

Topographical features

Contours (approx),
Rock Outcrops
Mountains
Mountain Pass
Gorge
Escarpment
Palm trees

Cities and towns

Built Up Areas
One Way Street
National Parks, Gardens, Stadiums

Fortified Walls
Airport ⊗
Banks ⑤
Bus Stations (named in key) 🚍 🚍¹ 🚍²
Hospitals ⊕
Market Ⓜ
Police station Ⓟ
Post Office ✉
Telegraphic Office ✆
Tourist Office ⓘ

Key Numbers ❶ ❷ ❸ ❹ ❺

Bridges
Cathedral, church ✝
Guided routes ....

National parks, trekking areas

National Parks and
Bird Sanctuaries ◆
Hide ⌂
Camp site ⍙
Refuge ⌂
Motorable track - - - - -
Walking track ....

Other symbols

Archaeological Sites ⁖
Places of Interest ○
Viewing point ✹

Footprint Handbooks

All of us at Footprint Handbooks hope you have enjoyed reading and travelling with this Handbook, one of the first published in the new Footprint series. Many of you will be familiar with us as Trade & Travel, a name that has served us well for years. For you and for those who have only just discovered the Handbooks, we thought it would be interesting to chronicle the story of our development from the early 1920's.

It all started 75 years ago in 1921, with the publication of the Anglo-South American Handbook. In 1924 the South American Handbook was created. This has been published each year for the last 73 years and is the longest running guidebook in the English language, immortalised by Graham Greene as "the best travel guide in existence".

One of the key strengths of the South American Handbook over the years, has been the extraordinary contact we have had with our readers through their hundreds of letters to us in Bath. From these letters we learnt that you wanted more Handbooks of the same quality to other parts of the world.

In 1989 my brother Patrick and I set about developing a series modelled on the South American Handbook. Our aim was to create the ultimate practical guidebook series for all travellers, providing expert knowledge of far flung places, explaining culture, places and people in a balanced, lively and clear way. The whole idea hinged, of course, on finding writers who were in tune with our thinking. Serendipity stepped in at exactly the right moment: we were able to bring together a talented group of people who know the countries we cover inside out and whose enthusiasm for travelling in them needed to be communicated.

The series started to grow. We felt that the time was right to look again at the identity that had brought us all this way. After much searching we commissioned London designers Newell & Sorrell to look at all the issues. Their solution was a new identity for the Handbooks representing the books in all their aspects, looking after all the good things already achieved and taking us into the new millennium.

The result is Footprint Handbooks: a new name and mark, simple yet assertive, bold, stylish and instantly recognisable. The images we use conjure up the essence of real travel and communicate the qualities of the Handbooks in a straightforward and evocative way.

For us here in Bath, it has been an exciting exercise working through this dramatic change. Already the 'new us' fits like our favourite travelling clothes and we cannot wait to get more and more Footprint Handbooks onto the book shelves and out onto the road.

James Dawson

The Footprint list

Andalucía Handbook
Cambodia Handbook
Caribbean Islands Handbook
Chile Handbook
East Africa Handbook
Ecuador Handbook
  with the Galápagos
Egypt Handbook
India Handbook
Indonesia Handbook
Laos Handbook
Malaysia & Singapore Handbook
Mexico & Central America
  Handbook
Morocco Handbook
  with Mauritania
Myanmar (Burma) Handbook
Namibia Handbook
Pakistan Handbook
Peru Handbook
South Africa Handbook
South American Handbook
Sri Lanka Handbook
Thailand Handbook
Tibet Handbook
Tunisia Handbook with Libya
Vietnam Handbook
Zimbabwe & Malawi Handbook
  with Moçambique

New in Autumn 1997
Israel Handbook
Nepal Handbook

In the pipeline
Argentina Handbook
Brazil Handbook
Colombia Handbook
Cuba Handbook
Venezuela Handbook

Footprint T-shirt

The Footprint T-shirt is available in 100% cotton in various colours.

Mail Order

Footprint Handbooks are available worldwide in good bookstores. They can also be ordered directly from us in Bath (see below for address). Please contact us if you have difficulty finding a title.

The Footprint Handbook website will be coming to keep you up to date with all the latest news from us. For the most up-to-date information and to join our mailing list please contact us at:

Footprint Handbooks
6 Riverside Court
Lower Bristol Road
Bath BA2 3DZ, England
T +44(0)1225 469141
F +44(0)1225 469461
E Mail handbooks@footprint.cix.co.uk